Readings on the Development of Children

Readings
on the
Development
of
Children

_____

EDITED BY

Mary Gauvain
University of California, Riverside

Michael Cole
University of California, San Diego

SCIENTIFIC
AMERICAN
BOOKS

An imprint of W. H. Freeman and Company

Library of Congress Cataloging-in-Publication Data

Readings on the development of children / [edited by] Mary Gauvain,
Michael Cole
p.   cm.
ISBN 0-7167-2480-4 (hard)— ISBN 0-7167-2492-8 (soft)
1. Developmental psychology. 2. Child psychology. 3. Child
development. I. Gauvain, Mary, 1952- . II. Cole, Michael, 1938- .
BF713.R43 1993   93-10142
155.4—dc20   CIP

Printed in the United States of America

Scientific American Books is an imprint of W. H. Freeman and Company
41 Madison Avenue, New York, NY 10010
20 Beaumont Street, Oxford OX1 2NQ, England

2 3 4 5 6 7 8 9 0 VB 9 9 8 7 6 5 4 3

Contents

Preface

Human development is a series of changes produced by the interaction of biological, social, and cultural factors over the lifespan that begins with conception. Developmental psychologists strive to explain this process of change by observing children, conducting experiments, and devising theories.

Students approach the subject of human development with a rich background based on their own experience of growing up as well as their observations of people of all ages. This background is a valuable resource when attempting to understand the scientific approaches to the study of human development encountered in textbooks. However, it has been our experience as instructors that textbooks alone, despite their great value as organized overviews of the field, often leave students puzzled about the process by which developmental psychologists construct their theories, collect their data, and draw conclusions. Textbooks, by their very nature, cannot devote sufficient space to the in-depth discussion of concepts or studies that form the basis of developmental theory.

The entries included in this book of readings have been selected with this problem in mind. Our intention has been to provide students with primary source material that introduces them to a broad range of scientific thinking about human development in all its diversity. We do not shy away from exposing students to classical contributions to the field simply because they do not carry an up-to-the-minute publication date; after all, physicists do not hesitate to teach about Newton's laws of motion although they were formulated several hundred years ago. On the other hand, human development is a rapidly developing discipline, so the bulk of our selections—especially research reports and literature reviews—were first published in the past few years.

The inspiration for this reader came from *The Development of Children,* Second Edition, by Michael Cole and Sheila R. Cole. Although typical of introductory texts in many ways, *The Development of Children* is unusual in the balanced emphasis it places on the biological, social, and cultural factors that make up development. We have not, however, specifically keyed these readings to any one textbook. Instead we have selected articles that provide a representative sample of the wide range of approaches to the study of human development.

The theoretical articles provide students direct access to important and provocative statements by acknowledged leaders in the field. For example, we pair selections by Jean Piaget and Lev Vygotsky discussing the relationship between learning and development. Each article was chosen for its power to capture the essence of each theorist's ideas in a brief, but compelling manner. The articles focusing on research were selected to provoke thought and discussion about the ways researchers collect evidence on the process of development and how they interpret and draw conclusions from their data. We have taken special care to include articles about the development of children from many cultures in order to avoid the misrepresentation of middle-class Euro-Americans as the criterion against which the development of all children is measured.

All the articles were selected with the undergraduate reader in mind. Because most of our selections were originally written for a professional audience, the text sometimes contains concepts which at first may be difficult to grasp. To alleviate this problem, we have provided brief introductory notes that should help orient the reader to the article's main points. Finally, we would like to express our appreciation to the many colleagues who provided valuable feedback to us in the course of developing this reader.

Introduction

1

The Child Yesterday, Today, and Tomorrow

DAVID ELKIND

In this essay, David Elkind reviews prominent images of the child from the distant and recent past. He argues that current characterizations of childhood, although they draw on scientific evidence, actually reflect more general beliefs current in society at large. When bolstered by the authority of science, they may lead to extreme views that actually have harmful effects on children. By tracing the ways that later generations of developmental psychologists react to (and often against) the overstatements of previous generations, Elkind illustrates that science can most usefully be considered a dialogue—a search for truth—rather than a set of recipes for generating facts and theories. His essay also serves as a poignant reminder that, across history, children themselves have not always benefitted from the changing images of childhood.

The child is a gift of nature, the image of the child is man's creation. It is the image of the child, rather than nature's gift, that determines educational practice in any historical epoch. And the image of the child, man's creation, is as often wrong as it is correct. Wrong images are more powerful and more easily grasped than true ones. In the present as in the past, our task as educators of young children is not simply to be true to nature's gift, but also to fight against the false images that, in any age, threaten the healthy education of young children.

IMAGES OF THE PAST

The image of the child in antiquity was that of young citizen who had to be educated by the laws and culture of society. The children of Babylon went to

Reprinted with permission from *Young Children*, May, 1987, 6–11. Copyright 1987 by the National Association for the Education of Young Children.

This article is, with a few minor changes, the address Dr. Elkind gave at NAEYC's November 1986 Annual Conference at the Opening General Session, Washington Hilton Hotel. David Elkind is NAEYC's President.

school at age 6 and even poor children learned to read and write except that their books were bricks and their writing tools a reed and damp clay. Children in ancient Greece played with go-carts and dolls, and at the age of 7 boys went to school. In ancient Rome, women had a more equal place and both boys and girls went to school where the discipline was strict and where they learned to write with a stylus and wax tablet.

During the Middle Ages, children fared less well and the prevailing image of the child was that of chattel, or piece of property consistent with the ideology of serfdom. The medieval castle was no place for a child, built as it was for defense rather than for comfort. The children of serfs worked and lived with the animals. Discipline was strict and punishment harsh. In England, there was a brief, golden era for children during the reign of Good Queen Bess. And during this era, the faithful nanny begins to appear in folklore and literature.

Toward the end of the 17th Century, the struggle between Cavaliers and Puritans was reflected in their quite dissimilar images of children. The Cavaliers held a mixed image of the child as part nuisance, part plaything. In contrast, the Puritans constructed an image of the child as one tainted with original sin. "Your child," wrote James Janeway, "is never too young to go to hell."

In this country the images of children changed with our rapidly changing society. In colonial times children were seen as financial assets who could help work the farm or be apprenticed out of the home at an early age. The children of slaves were an extreme example of this, but they were not the only children who labored from dawn to dark. With the industrial revolution, children, especially the children of immigrants and the poor, came to be seen as cheap factory workers until the cruelty of child labor was made public. The ensuing social reform movement transformed the image of the child from one of cheap factory labor to one of apprentice to factory work. Instead of being sent to the factory, children were sent to school to prepare them to work in factories. School bells, like factory whistles, signaled the beginning and the end of the school day. And children, like their parents, carried lunch pails to be opened at the noon whistle.

As we see, there have been many different images of children, some of which were more beneficial to child health, welfare, and education than others. And there have always been those who, at any given point in history, have been critical of the image of the child current at that time. Often this criticism took the form of an attack on parents and upon parenting, but in fact it was an attack upon the then "accepted"

image of the child. A review of these attacks upon the images of the child that were raised in earlier times is instructive. It tells us that the image of the child at any point in history never goes unchallenged and that the challengers in the past, as today, often come from the ranks of early childhood educators.

The criticism of prevailing images of the child has a long history. For his ideal Republic, Plato wanted children to be raised by professional child caretakers, and St. Augustine proclaimed, "Give me other mothers and I will give you other worlds." Rousseau's opening statement in *Emile* to the effect that everything is good as it comes from the hand of the Maker and deteriorates in the hands of man, is an indictment of the image of the child as a young savage who had to be socialized.

Pestalozzi and Froebel did not criticize parents directly, but did believe that parents needed to be given a truer image of the child that would result in more healthy childrearing practices. Parent education was an important component of early childhood education practiced by Pestalozzi and Froebel. Pestalozzi's book, *How Gertrude Teaches Her Children,* which is subtitled *An Attempt To Help Mothers Teach Their Own Children,* reflects this emphasis upon training parents. The same theme was repeated in Froebel's *The Education of Man* and in his *Songs for Mothers and Nursery Songs.*

Their successor Maria Montessori never criticized parents either, but she had less faith in parent education than her predecessors. Like Plato she wanted children reared by professionals, not by parents. For her, childrearing was too important a task to be left to untrained parents whose image of the child gave too little credit to their budding intellectual powers.

In the past, the prevailing image of the child that dictated childrearing and education was determined by a complex of social, economic, and cultural factors that may have had little or nothing to do with the natural child. And since early times, there have been critics of the prevailing conception of the child. These critics fought to replace the false image of the child with a truer one that would provide for a healthier, happier, and more productive child life.

IMAGES OF THE PRESENT

Historically, predominant images of the child were derived from the prevailing political, social, or religious ethos. What is remarkable about modern images of the child is that they are, or are said to be, scientific in origin. Unfortunately, their scientific origin has not rendered them any more valid than those that had social, political, or religious derivations. In some ways, the scientific origin of some of the contemporary images of the child makes them even more difficult to combat than previous images. I want now to usurp the role of critic and review and comment upon three modern images of the child that have contributed to what I call miseducation, namely putting children at risk for no purpose.

The Sensual Child

The advent of Freudian psychology gave rise to the image of the sensual child. In this view, the child was "polymorphous perverse" in the sense of having the whole gamut of sexual instincts and proclivities that were once reserved to adults. In Freudian terms, children whose sexual instincts were unduly repressed were destined to become neurotic. The childrearing and educational implications of this image of the sensual child were straightforward. Children had to be allowed to express themselves, and play was   the natural medium of self-expression. With adequate self-expression at home and at school, children would develop healthy personalities and their intelligence would take care of itself.

Like so many images of the child, this idea contains a partial truth. Freud made it clear that a certain amount of repression was healthy, indeed necessary, for people to live in a society. It was *excessive* repression, not repression, that produced neuroses. But that point was sometimes lost on those who fought for expression at all costs.

The Malleable Child

Another image of the child that has dominated contemporary thought has come from the anthropologists who were concerned with the conflict between generations. The leading writers of this genre were Kingsley Davis, Ruth Benedict, and Margaret Mead. Although they differed in detail, they were all making the same point, namely, when it comes to adapting to social change, children are plastic and adaptable whereas adults are rigid and unadaptable. Children, they argued, are better suited to social change than are adults.

Davis, for example, argued that adults are locked into the orientation they received as children and this makes it difficult, if not impossible, for them to appreciate the changed circumstances of their offspring, hence the generational conflict. Benedict said that adults are independent and children are dependent, and that it was the adult's inability to deal with the child's growing independence that was the cause of the generational conflict. And Margaret Mead argued

that in a rapidly changing culture, children, who are free of ingrained habits of thought, are much better able to adapt to new and changing technologies than adults.

This image of child malleability in contrast to adult rigidity is sometimes misinterpreted. Anthropologists are talking about change in the overall society, *not* about changes within the immediate family. When a family moves, the children have more trouble with the change than adults. And, while divorce may be hard on adults, it is certainly much harder on children. Children thrive on consistency, stability, and security, while it is adults who seek new experience and adventure. Children adapt less easily to change within the family than adults do, but the reverse image fostered by a misapplication of social scientists' ideas about change in society persists and contributes to miseducation.

The introduction of computers into early childhood education, and the teaching of programming to young children, is a direct offshoot of this malleability conception. It is simply a fact of technological development that as technology develops it requires more, rather than less, intellectual maturity. A child can use a shovel but not a power shovel; a child can use a hand saw or hand drill, but not a power saw or power drill; a child can ride a horse, but cannot drive an automobile and certainly cannot fly an airplane. The more advanced the technology, the more advanced the intelligence required to use it. Modern warfare is another example. Modern weapons require college graduates if they are to be used properly. The modern army has no place for a Sergeant York trained with a hunting rifle. And even when a technology is easy to use, such as television, it can still be dangerous to young children.

Yet the idea that children should be programming and running computers persists despite the fact that the complexity and technological sophistication of computers is far beyond what a young child can really comprehend and master. To be used by young children, computers have to be converted into teaching machines presenting programmed learning. And programmed learning is simply boring. Exposing young children to computers in this way runs the risk that they will get turned off to computers before they have a chance to see what they can really do. It is a good example of miseducation, of putting children at risk for no purpose.

In the same way, I am often asked about programs to inform young children about the threats of nuclear war. Presumably, children have to be exposed to this idea at an early age so they will be better prepared for a nuclear holocaust when it comes. Even if one accepts this shaky premise, it has to be recognized that the concept of nuclear war is completely foreign to young children, who do not even have a conception of biological death, much less of millions of people and the power of nuclear weapons to destroy them. Recent suggestions that young children be taught about AIDS also stem from this wrongheaded image of child malleability.

To be sure, children are fresh learners to the extent that they are not handicapped by previous ideas and concepts. But this does not mean that they are ready to learn everything and anything—far from it. Their openness to learning is limited and we need to recognize these limitations. There is a time and a place for everything and early childhood education is not the time nor the place to teach children computer programming, the threat of nuclear war, or for that matter, the dangers of AIDS.

The Competent Infant

Perhaps the most pervasive and most pernicious contemporary image of the child is one that has been promoted by psychologists writing in the 60s. Responding to the Civil Rights Movement, to the War on Poverty, and to the inadequacies of the educational system, many writers gave voice to a vision of childhood that would undo these wrongs and undo them at an early age. All these wrongs, it was said, could be righted if we only got to children early enough. The result was a new image of infants and young children as having much more capacity to learn academic skills than children, regardless of background, actually have. It is true that all young children have intellectual abilities and that their thinking should be encouraged but within the context of their psychological stage of development. This 60s image of the child as consumer of skills has come to haunt us in the 80s.

In his book *The Process of Education*, Jerome Bruner voiced his now famous hypothesis that you can "teach any child, any subject matter at any age in an intellectually responsible way." Bruner was really speaking to curriculum writers and probably did not fully appreciate the extent to which his hypothesis would be accepted, not as a hypothesis, but rather as a fact by the public at large. And it has also become the motto of entrepreneurs hawking flash cards to parents with the proclamation that you can teach a young child "anything."

But is it true? It is only true if you either redefine the child or redefine the subject matter. The curriculum writers of the 60s, academicians such as Max Beberman at the University of Illinois or Robert Karplus at Berkeley knew their subject matter but not young children. The curricula they designed in effect redefined the competence of children without recourse to children's actual abilities or limitations. For example, variable base arithmetic was said to be easier for children to learn than base ten arithmetic. But even parents had trouble with variable base arithmetic! It was also claimed that children would learn math better if it were introduced as a language. Instead of answering what is the sum of 2 + 2, children were asked to "Make this sentence true."

The error here came from confusing what is simple to an expert in a subject with what is simple for the novice. Simplicity is the end result of learning a skill or a discipline, not its starting point. Reading is simple once you know how, but is far from simple when you first start out. Understanding multiple base arithmetic may be simple once you know base ten, but not if you don't. Understanding the relation of language to mathematics is simple if you have a firm grasp of language and mathematics, but not if you don't. We have to always be aware of the danger of assuming that the end point for us as adults should be the starting point for children.

The other side of Bruner's hypothesis requires redefining the subject matter. When an infant who responds to flash cards is said to be "reading" or doing "math," these subject matters have been drastically redefined. Suppose, for example, that I tell you that I can balance 100 pounds on my finger. You would not believe me. But suppose I take out a 3×5 card and write *100 pounds* on it. Now I put the card on my finger, and voilà, I am holding 100 pounds on my finger. Claiming to teach infants to read and do math is the same; it is a sleight-of-hand trick accomplished by redefining what is usually meant by reading and by math.

Yet people are taken in by this trickery and really believe that they are teaching their children these subjects. And this trickery has another negative fallout effect. Redefining the subject matter makes it much easier to acquire. Parents then believe that their child who is "reading" flash cards at age 2 is a budding genius. But they will be disappointed in the end. Unfortunately, making a task easier does not make children brighter.

Another contribution to the image of the competent infant came from educational psychologist Benjamin Bloom who argued from statistical summaries of IQ data that 4 year-olds had attained half of their intellectual ability and that it was incumbent upon us to impose formal learning on young children because otherwise we might lose out on this period of phenomenal mental growth. This idea that you must teach as much as possible to young children because their minds are growing so rapidly has become part of the contemporary folk wisdom and is deeply ingrained in our contemporary image of the child.

But is it true? Bloom was talking about mental test data, not about mental growth. Because infants and young children are not good test takers, their intelligence test performance is not a good index of their later test performance. By the age of 4, however, the child is sufficiently verbal and has sufficient ability to concentrate attention, and her or his test performance is a better index of true ability. From the test score a child attains at the age of 4 you can predict with some 50% accuracy what that child's test score will be at age 17. And that is all that a child attaining half of her or his mental ability at age 4 means.

It does not mean that at age 4 the child has half of all the knowledge, skills, and values she or he will ever have. It does not mean that if a child attains an IQ of 100 at age 4 she or he will attain an IQ score of 200 at age 17. It does not mean that a child at age 4 is a better learner than she or he will be at age 17. Even if we grant that mental growth is rapid during the early years of life, it does not follow as dawn follows the night, that this calls for formal, teacher-directed learning. During periods of rapid mental growth, children seek out the stimuli to nourish themselves mentally. We serve them best by providing an environment rich in materials to observe, explore, manipulate, talk, write, and think about. You do not prune during the growing season.

Still a third writer who has contributed to the contemporary image of the competent infants is J. McV. Hunt. In his book *Intelligence and Experience* he surveyed a great deal of evidence and concluded that intelligence was malleable and not fixed, the view he attributed to professionals of the time. But no reputable psychologist ever claimed that intelligence was fixed. In 1954, in a chapter of the *Handbook of Child Psychology*, Florence Goodenough made it clear that all the evidence supported the view that the environmental factors accounted for between 20 and 40% of an individual's IQ.

Up until the 60s, however, psychologists were mainly concerned with middle-class children who, presumably, had maximized their environmental potential. It was only when attention was turned to low-income children who had less than optimal environmental input that the significance of environmental input became a matter of concern. Consider the following analogy. Suppose you place a group of undernourished children on a full calorie, well-balanced diet. Surely such children will make significant gains in both height and weight, but similar gains will not be made by children who are already on a full calorie, well-balanced diet. The potential benefits of an improved program are always relative to the quality of the previous environment.

This idea of intellectual malleability has become common currency among parents who are being told that with the proper program of stimulation they can have a "brighter child" or that they can raise their child's IQ. Yet there is no evidence that children growing up in an environment where they are talked to, played with, and read to, and which is rich in things to look at, listen to, and explore, will derive additional benefit from prescribed exercises and symbolic materials. If anything, most middle-class children today are over- rather than understimulated.

The last contributor to the image of the competent child is not a psychologist but a historian. In his book *Centuries of Childhood*, Phillip Aries argues that childhood is a social invention and that there was no such conception in the Middle Ages when children were depicted and treated much as adults. The implication is that for the last couple of hundred years we have been coddling children and infantalizing them and ignoring their true competence and abilities. This thesis fit in neatly with the other ideas about infant competence and gave it a historical dimension.

More recent historians of childhood, like Pollack, have shown Aries was wrong. Even in the times Aries was writing, diaries of parents show quite clearly that adults appreciated that children were different from adults and had to be treated differently. Sir Francis Bacon, writing in the 16th Century, even talked about the value of "allowances" and the negative effects of not giving a child a sufficient allowance, and suggested that "The proof is best when men keep their authority towards their children, but not their purse."

These four ideas, then, that a child can be taught any subject at any age, that children have half their intellectual ability at age 4 when mental growth is more rapid, that the IQ is malleable, and that childhood is an invention, all emerged in the 1960s to form a new image of child competence. Although this new image may have corrected a previous image that played down child competence, it went to the other extreme. Ideas meant to improve the conditions of low-income children have been taken over by middle-class parents and have become the rationale for much of the miseducation of young children today.

As in the past, we have not only to assert the values of child-centered early childhood education, but we must also struggle to reveal the concepts of early childhood malleability and competence for what they are, namely distortions of how young children really grow and learn.

IMAGES OF THE FUTURE

Given the brief history I have just outlined, it seems reasonable to predict that the false images of children today will be replaced by equally false images tomorrow. I have no crystal ball, only a belief that history is prologue and that the image of the child at any point in history always fills the predominant parent needs and defenses of that developmental epoch. We have to ask then what the needs of future parents will be and how these will be reflected in a new image of the child.

Our society is already a service and information society with more than 70% of our population in these occupations. I believe that we will eventually get high quality child care for all those youngsters who need it and that those who care for infants and young children will have positions of respect and will be paid well. We may even have parent professionals to care for and rear other people's children. This will not happen immediately and without a great deal of hard work and pain, but I do believe we will get there.

What then? What new image will emerge when the image of the malleable competent child has run its course? What sort of image of the child will be most in keeping with the needs of tomorrow's parents? If present trends continue, it appears that parents will spend less time than ever parenting. Once parents no longer feel guilty or uncomfortable about this, the need for the image of child intellectual competence will diminish. In its place will emerge a new image of child social sophistication and self-sufficiency. In an information and service society these are the requisite

skills. We already see hints of this in the current emphasis upon social cognition. Psychologists are eager to point out that Piaget was wrong and that infants and young children are much more socially skilled than we gave them credit for being.

And while it may be true that children are more socially proficient and self-sufficient than we may have recognized, they will not be as socially proficient as the image of social sophistication will have us believe. And the cycle will once again repeat itself, the next generation of early childhood educators will have to challenge the new image of the child as, to use the computer term that may well become the catchword of this new image, *an expert system* with respect to social interaction. The next generation will once again have to reassert the values of sound early childhood education.

Our task as early childhood educators then is never ending. Each generation presents a new challenge and a new battle. And it is a battle that we can never really win, because each new generation is prone to the same mistakes. Yet if we do not fight it is a battle we can most assuredly lose. For those of us in early childhood education it is a battle well worth fighting and, even if we fall before our time, we can take comfort in the knowledge that there will always be others, sufficiently committed to the well-being of young children, to carry on the fight.

Bibliography

Aries, P. (1962). *Centuries of childhood*. New York: Knopf.

Benedict, R. (1938). Continuities and discontinuities in cultural conditioning. *Psychiatry, 1,* 161–167.

Bloom, B. (1964). *Stability and change in human behavior.* New York: Wiley.

Bruner, J. (1962). *The process of education*. Cambridge, MA: Harvard University Press.

Davis, K. (1940). The sociology of parent-youth conflict. *American Sociological Review, 5,* 523–525.

Freud, S. (1905). *Three essays on sexuality.* New York: Basic.

Hunt, J. McV. (1961). *Intelligence and experience*. New York: Ronald.

Mead, M. (1970). *Culture and commitment*. New York: Natural History Press/Doubleday.

Pollack, L. (1983). *Forgotten children*. Cambridge: Cambridge University Press.

2

Darwin and the Beginnings of Child Psychology

WILLIAM KESSEN

T he work of Charles Darwin had a formative influence on the emergence of developmental psychology. Among Darwin's contributions was the simple yet profound idea that change is a natural part of living systems. By pointing to change as a natural and required feature of life, Darwin cast the analysis of development as central to understanding life forms. Although Darwin is best known for his theories of biological evolution, he also wrote about child development in the form of a baby biography describing his own observations of his firstborn son's early infancy. In the following article, William Kessen discusses Darwin's role in the development of child psychology as a scientific discipline and presents a passage from Darwin's baby biography. This passage illustrates how careful observation can advance our understanding of child development; it also illustrates how subjectively based inferences may obscure objective interpretation.

There is enough cruelty, enough poverty, and enough theology left in the world for us to imagine the life of a child bereft of the medical and social reforms of the last century or two. It is far harder to imagine what scholars thought of children before the publication and slow assimilation of *The Origin of Species* (1859). Our notion of the child—in fact, of all psychology—was changed so dramatically by Darwin's work that the remainder of this history will become an account of extended variations on the naturalist's basic themes.

There are several ways in which Darwin's speculations directed the history of child psychology. In the first place, the notion of species evolution gave a mechanism in full scientific dress for the notions of perfectibility that the ideologues of the eighteenth century had proposed on grounds less certain. To be sure, the struggle for survival was a grim affair that did not fit well with the conception of man as rational and free, but clearly the result of the ugly contest was the development of a truly superior being. Perhaps the loss of biological uniqueness was painful but in return Darwin provided a rationale for boundless expectations for man. Just as animal life had grown in a natural way from protozoan to rational being, so society had grown from its primitive savagery to Victorian sensibility and might yet grow more. In the hands of the practical social Darwinians, chief among them the members of the Establishment who had thus far survived the struggle, this doctrine did not always lead to greater interest in the protection of the child, but it became an article of faith in the Western community that evolution, developing and developed by science and industry, would bring society to its natural fulfillment.

But Darwin's proposals had more direct effects on the study of man. The notion that the phylogenetic progression had its homologues in the development of man in society (an idea of Rousseau's, too) found expression in the sociology of Sumner and his students. It took the study of primitive cultures from the hands of literate tourists and made it into anthropology. The Darwinian proposals did more than build a base for the comparative study of societies; Darwin looked the other way, toward the signs of man in animal life, and it was this innovation that assured him the enmity of theologians and influenced so strongly the formation of empirical psychology. With the chapter comparing "the mental powers of man and the lower animals" in *Descent of Man*,* Darwin invented the discipline of comparative psychology, and the course of its development is clear and unbroken through Romanes and Lloyd Morgan to Thorndike and Watson to contemporary investigators of animal behavior. There are ironies in the genealogical record; Darwin put psychology into the animal and made the comparative study of mind a wholesome and permitted occupation but, by modifications of greater or less scope, the study of animal behavior shifted until, in mid-twentieth century, the questions about mind that intrigued Darwin were abandoned but the systematic study of the animal was kept.

The contribution of the evolutionary revolution to psychology did not end with the creation of com-

parative psychology. In at least three other ways, widely varying in their later historical development, the Darwinian principles influenced psychology and the study of the child. At the most general level, so well assimilated into the definition of psychological problems that we forget its origins, lies the model of a struggle for existence among competing responses of the organism. Learning is an expression of the war among conflicting tendencies of the animal or person and the strongest of them survive. Taine saw this point clearly.

> . . . So, in the struggle for life, in which all our images are constantly engaged, the one furnished at the outset with most force, retains in each conflict, by the very law of repetition which gives it being, the capacity of treading down its adversaries; this is why it revives, incessantly at first, then frequently, until at last the laws of progressive decay, and the continual accession of new impressions, take away its preponderance, and its competitors, finding a clear field, are able to develop in their turn.**

And, in a footnote to the passage, Taine writes, "The theory of the great English naturalist is nowhere more precisely applicable than in psychology." Henceforth, it will be difficult to see association as the passionless building of connections.

The irreducible contribution of Darwin to the study of children was, however, in his assignment of scientific value to childhood. Species develop, societies develop, man develops. From the publication of *The Origin of Species* to the end of the nineteenth century, there was a riot of parallel-drawing between animal and child, between primitive man and child, between early human history and child. The developing human being was seen as a natural museum of human phylogeny and history; by careful observation of the infant and child, one could see the descent of man. Enthusiasts found parallels of remarkable scope and the child-as-prototype movement reached its peak with the publication in 1901 of *The Child: A Study in the Evolution of Man* by Alexander Francis Chamberlain. Chamberlain discusses, with more restraint than some of his contemporaries showed, the place of the child in evolutionary theory and summarizes part of his conclusions in these words.

---

*C. Darwin, *The Descent of Man and Selection in Relation to Sex*. (New ed.), New York: Appleton, 1897. The first edition was published in two volumes in 1871.
** H. Taine, *On Intelligence* (Translated by T. D. Haye), 2 vol., New York: Holt, 1889. Vol. I, p. 81. The first French edition was published in 1869.

The "ages of man," the epochs noticeable in the origin and growth in the individual of somatic characteristics, anatomical and physiological peculiarities; "critical periods," physical and intellectual; epochal development of the senses, of language, etc.; periodicity and epochism in the growth of the sense of self, of character, of emotiveness, of psychic activities in general and in particular, of sociality, of religiosity, or morality, of the various artistic activities, etc., furnish a multitude of facts, many of which, seemingly, cannot receive their interpretation except upon the theory that they represent things once important, useful, necessary to, or characteristic of, the race-ancestry of the individual, in whom they are repeated more or less completely.*

Nothing much is left of this radical notion now. The functionalist revisions in biology and psychology cleared away almost all the defenders of what was held to be a teleological view of man and his workings; the late nineteenth-century notion of parallels between animal and man remains in the academic literature only as a half joking reference to the phrase "Ontogeny recapitulates phylogeny." But, as we shall see later, the idea of animal-child parallels has been subtly transmuted to remain one of the central postulates of child study.

Putting aside later refinements of the doctrine of developmental recapitulation, however, there is good reason for noting the enthusiasm of turn-of-the-century commentators for the assignment of remarkable animal and cultural analogues to the behavior of children. It was a fact in the history of child study, a fact as secure and as highly respected by contemporary true believers as was Hall's questionnaire method and today's Rorschach. But, more than that, the search for phylogenetic and society shades in the child marked the beginning of a science of child behavior. Man was not to be understood by the analysis of his adult functions, an analysis that was rational in conception and closely linked to logic; rather, man was to be understood by a study of his origins—in nature and in the child. When did consciousness dawn? What were the beginnings of morality? How could we know the world of the infant? Questions like these which, in form of more or less sophistication, were to dominate child psychology for many years, derive their sense from a genetic view of man. The Rousseauan child is put on a firm biological pedestal. He is neither made at birth nor understandable in his adult guise alone; man develops, grows, and becomes through the course of his first years, and it is the particular and special function of the child psychologist to record the visible changes. Darwin gave us the child as a legitimate source of scientific information about the nature of man. He also legitimized the baby journal.

As several commentators have noted, Rousseau was never more in error than when he predicted no imitators of his *Confessions*. In Brett's words, "The sentimental romance became the medium of self-expression, and the example set by Rousseau gradually became the basis of a new literature."** And a new psychology! The introspective analysis of sensation and emotion by eighteenth- and early nineteenth-century gentlemen prepared the ground for Fechner's quantification and for Wundt's systematization. That development is not part of our story, but diaries and notebooks also led to an innovation of great significance to child study—the baby biography. First used at length by Dieterich Tiedemann† the procedure of keeping a day-book of infant behavior (almost invariably, the behavior of the investigator's first child) became usual in the nineteenth century. Taine used his observations of children in his book *On Intelligence* (1869), and it was the publication of some notes on language acquisition by Taine that led Darwin to the preparation of the paper which follows here. Drawing on observations of his first-born, William Erasmus (Doddy), in 1840 and 1841, Darwin shows in brief compass the attraction and the problems of the baby biographer. No one can know as well as the attentive parent the subtle and cumulative changes that take place in the world of the child and in his behavior but, on the other hand, no one can distort as convincingly as a loving parent. Darwin, like almost every baby biographer after him, not only saw children, he also

---

*A. F. Chamberlain, *The Child: A Study in the Evolution of Man*, London: Walter Scott, 1901, p. 446.

**G. S. Brett, *A History of Psychology*, 3 vol., London: George Allen, 1912–1921, Vol. II, p. 321.

†Apparently, no full English translation of Tiedemann's *Record of an Infant's Life* (1787) exists, for all its popularity as a citation in secondary sources. Soldan's transition of Perez' commentary on Michelant's French translation of the original German [F. L. Soldan, *Tiedemann's Record of Infant-Life. An English version of the French translation and commentary by Bernard Perez*. Syracuse: Bardeen, 1890] does not permit any general statement about Tiedemann's techniques or principles.

saw a living expression of his theoretical position. The evolutionist is clearly at work in this charming little account, and there are two details that are particularly illuminating of Darwin's attitude and his psychology. One is the ascription to the child of specific affect (the "violent passion" of anger, for example), an ascription which we will find imitated for many years. The other is Darwin's perplexed and obviously parental proposition that the tendency to throw objects is inherited—in boys.

* * *

A BIOGRAPHICAL SKETCH OF AN INFANT BY CHARLES ROBERT DARWIN (1809–1882)*

M. Taine's very interesting account of the mental development of an infant, translated in the last number of MIND, has led me to look over a diary which I kept thirty-seven years ago with respect to one of my own infants. I had excellent opportunities for close observation, and wrote down at once whatever was observed. My chief object was expression, and my notes were used in my book on this subject; but as I attended to some other points, my observations may possibly possess some little interest in comparison with those by M. Taine, and with others which hereafter no doubt will be made. I feel sure, from what I have seen with my own infants, that the period of development of the several faculties will be found to differ considerably in different infants.

During the first seven days various reflex actions, namely sneezing, hickuping, yawning, stretching, and of course sucking and screaming, were well performed by my infant. On the seventh day, I touched the naked sole of his foot with a bit of paper, and he jerked it away, curling at the same time his toes, like a much older child when tickled. The perfection of these reflex movements shows that the extreme imperfection of the voluntary ones is not due to the state of the muscles or of the coordinating centres, but to that of the seat of the will. At this time, though so early, it seemed clear to me that a warm soft hand applied to his face excited a wish to suck. This must be considered as a reflex or an instinctive action, for it is impossible to believe that experience and association with the touch of his mother's breast could so soon have come into play. During the first fortnight he often started on hearing any sudden sound, and blinked his eyes. The same fact was observed with some of my other infants within the first fortnight. Once, when he was 66 days old, I happened to sneeze, and he started violently, frowned, looked frightened, and cried rather badly: for an hour afterwards he was in a state which would be called nervous in an older person, for every slight noise made him start. A few days before this same date, he first started at an object suddenly seen; but for a long time afterwards sounds made him start and wink his eyes much more frequently than did sight; thus when 114 days old, I shook a paste-board box with comfits in it near his face and he started, whilst the same box when empty or any other object shaken as near or much nearer to his face produced no effect. We may infer from these several facts that the winking of the eyes, which manifestly serves to protect them, had not been acquired through experience. Although so sensitive to sound in a general way, he was not able even when 124 days old easily to recognise whence a sound proceeded, so as to direct his eyes to the source.

With respect to vision,—his eyes were fixed on a candle as early as the 9th day, and up to the 45th day nothing else seemed thus to fix them; but on the 49th day his attention was attracted by a bright-coloured tassel, as was shown by his eyes becoming fixed and the movements of his arms ceasing. It was surprising how slowly he acquired the power of following with his eyes an object if swinging at all rapidly; for he could not do this well when seven and a half months old. At the age of 32 days he perceived his mother's bosom when three or four inches from it, as was shown by the protrusion of his lips and his eyes becoming fixed; but I much doubt whether this had any connection with vision; he certainly had not touched the bosom. Whether he was guided through smell or the sensation of warmth or through association with the position in which he was held, I do not at all know.

The movements of his limbs and body were for a long time vague and purposeless, and usually performed in a jerking manner; but there was one exception to this rule, namely that from a very early period, certainly long before he was 40 days old, he could move his hands to his own mouth. When 77 days old, he took the sucking bottle (with which he was partly fed) in his right hand, whether he was held on the left

*C. Darwin, A biographical sketch of an infant, *Mind, 11,* 1877, 286–294.

or right arm of his nurse, and he would not take it in his left hand until a week later although I tried to make him do so; so that the right hand was a week in advance of the left. Yet this infant afterwards proved to be left-handed, the tendency being no doubt inherited—his grandfather, mother, and a brother having been or being left-handed. When between 80 and 90 days old, he drew all sorts of objects into his mouth, and in two or three weeks' time could do this with some skill; but he often first touched his nose with the object and then dragged it down into his mouth. After grasping my finger and drawing it to his mouth, his own hand prevented him from sucking it; but on the 114th day, after acting in this manner, he slipped his own hand down so that he could get the end of my finger into his mouth. This action was repeated several times, and evidently was not a chance but a rational one. The intentional movements of the hands and arms were thus much in advance of those of the body and legs; though the purposeless movements of the latter were from a very early period usually alternate as in the act of walking. When four months old, he often looked intently at his own hands and other objects close to him, and in doing so the eyes were turned much inwards, so that he often squinted frightfully. In a fortnight after this time (*i.e.* 132 days old) I observed that if an object was brought as near to his face as his own hands were, he tried to seize it, but often failed; and he did not try to do so in regard to more distant objects. I think there can be little doubt that the convergence of his eyes gave him the clue and excited him to move his arms. Although this infant thus began to use his hands at an early period, he showed no special aptitude in this respect, for when he was 2 years and 4 months old, he held pencils, pens, and other objects far less neatly and efficiently than did his sister who was then only 14 months old, and who showed great inherent aptitude in handling anything.

ANGER It was difficult to decide at how early an age anger was felt; on his eighth day he frowned and wrinkled the skin round his eyes before a crying fit, but this may have been due to pain or distress, and not to anger. When about ten weeks old, he was given some rather cold milk and he kept a slight frown on his forehead all the time that he was sucking, so that he looked like a grown-up person made cross from being compelled to do something which he did not like. When nearly four months old, and perhaps much earlier, there could be no doubt, from the manner in which the blood gushed into his whole face and scalp, that he easily got into a violent passion. A small cause sufficed; thus, when a little over seven months old, he screamed with rage because a lemon slipped

away and he could not seize it with his hands. When eleven months old, if a wrong plaything was given him, he would push it away and beat it; I presume that the beating was an instinctive sign of anger, like the snapping of the jaws by a young crocodile just out of the egg, and not that he imagined he could hurt the plaything. When two years and three months old, he became a great adept at throwing books or sticks, &c., at anyone who offended him; and so it was with some of my other sons. On the other hand, I could never see a trace of such aptitude in my infant daughters; and this makes me think that a tendency to throw objects is inherited by boys.

FEAR This feeling probably is one of the earliest which is experienced by infants, as shown by their starting at any sudden sound when only a few weeks old, followed by crying. Before the present one was 4½ months old I had been accustomed to make close to him many strange and loud noises, which were all taken as excellent jokes, but at this period I one day made a loud snoring noise which I had never done before; he instantly looked grave and then burst out crying. Two or three days afterwards, I made through forgetfulness the same noise with the same result. About the same time (*viz.* on the 137th day) I approached with my back towards him and then stood motionless: he looked very grave and much surprised, and would soon have cried, had I not turned round; then his face instantly relaxed into a smile. It is well known how intensely older children suffer from vague and undefined fears, as from the dark, or in passing an obscure corner in a large hall, &c. I may give as an instance that I took the child in question, when 2¼ years old, to the Zoological Gardens, and he enjoyed looking at all the animals which were like those that he knew, such as deer, antelopes, &c., and all the birds, even the ostriches, but was much alarmed at the various larger animals in cages. He often said afterwards that he wished to go again, but not to see "beasts in houses"; and we could in no manner account for this fear. May we not suspect that the vague but very real fears of children, which are quite independent of experience, are the inherited effects of real dangers and abject superstitions during ancient savage times? It is quite conformable with what we know of the transmission of formerly well-developed characters, that they should appear at an early period of life, and afterwards disappear.

PLEASURABLE SENSATIONS It may be presumed that infants feel pleasure while sucking, and the expression of their swimming eyes seems to show that this is the case. This infant smiled when 45 days, a second infant when 46 days old; and these were true smiles, indicative of pleasure, for their eyes brightened and eyelids slightly closed. The smiles arose chiefly when looking at their mother, and were therefore probably of mental origin; but this infant often smiled then, and for some time afterwards, from some inward pleasurable feeling, for nothing was happening which could have in any way excited or amused him. When 110 days old he was exceedingly amused by a pinafore being thrown over his face and then suddenly withdrawn; and so he was when I suddenly uncovered my own face and approached his. He then uttered a little noise which was an incipient laugh. Here surprise was the chief cause of the amusement, as is the case to a large extent with the wit of grown-up persons. I believe that for three or four weeks before the time when he was amused by a face being suddenly uncovered, he received a little pinch on his nose and cheeks as a good joke. I was at first surprised at humour being appreciated by an infant only a little above three months old, but we should remember how very early puppies and kittens begin to play. When four months old, he showed in an unmistakable manner that he liked to hear the pianoforte played; so that here apparently was the earliest sign of an aesthetic feeling, unless the attraction of bright colours, which was exhibited much earlier, may be so considered.

AFFECTION This probably arose very early in life, if we may judge by his smiling at those who had charge of him when under two months old; though I had no distinct evidence of his distinguishing and recognising anyone, until he was nearly four months old. When nearly five months old, he plainly showed his wish to go to his nurse. But he did not spontaneously exhibit affection by overt acts until a little above a year old, namely, by kissing several times his nurse who had been absent for a short time. With respect to the allied feeling of sympathy, this was clearly shown at 6 months and 11 days by his melancholy face, with the corners of his mouth well depressed, when his nurse pretended to cry. Jealousy was plainly exhibited when I fondled a large doll, and when I weighed his infant sister, he being then 15½ months old. Seeing how strong a feeling jealousy is in dogs, it would probably be exhibited by infants at an earlier age than that just specified, if they were tried in a fitting manner.

ASSOCIATION OF IDEAS, REASON, &C. The first action which exhibited, as far as I observed, a kind of practical reasoning, has already been noticed, namely, the slipping his hand down my finger so as to get the end of it into his mouth; and this happened on the 114th day. When four and a half months old, he repeatedly smiled at my image and his own in a mirror, and no doubt mistook them for real objects; but he

showed sense in being evidently surprised at my voice coming from behind him. Like all infants he much enjoyed thus looking at himself, and in less than two months perfectly understood that it was an image; for if I made quite silently any odd grimace, he would suddenly turn round to look at me. He was, however, puzzled at the age of seven months, when being out of doors he saw me on the inside of a large plate-glass window, and seemed in doubt whether or not it was an image. Another of my infants, a little girl, when exactly a year old, was not nearly so acute, and seemed quite perplexed at the image of a person in a mirror approaching her from behind. The higher apes which I tried with a small looking-glass behaved differently; they placed their hands behind the glass, and in doing so showed their sense, but far from taking pleasure in looking at themselves they got angry and would look no more.

When five months old, associated ideas arising independently of any instruction became fixed in his mind; thus as soon as his hat and cloak were put on, he was very cross if he was not immediately taken out of doors. When exactly seven months old, he made the great step of associating his nurse with her name, so that if I called it out he would look round for her. Another infant used to amuse himself by shaking his head laterally: we praised and imitated him, saying "Shake your head"; and when he was seven months old, he would sometimes do so on being told without any other guide. During the next four months the former infant associated many things and actions with words; thus when asked for a kiss he would protrude his lips and keep still,—would shake his head and say in a scolding voice "Ah" to the coal-box or a little spilt water, &c., which he had been taught to consider as dirty. I may add that when a few days under nine months old he associated his own name with his image in the looking-glass, and when called by name would turn towards the glass even when at some distance from it. When a few days over nine months, he learnt spontaneously that a hand or other object causing a shadow to fall on the wall in front of him was to be looked for behind. Whilst under a year old, it was sufficient to repeat two or three times at intervals any short sentence to fix firmly in his mind some associated idea. In the infant described by M. Taine, the age at which ideas readily became associated seems to have been considerably later, unless indeed the earlier cases were overlooked. The facility with which associated ideas due to instruction and others spontaneously arising were acquired, seemed to me by far the most strongly marked of all the distinctions between the mind of an infant and that of the cleverest full-grown dog that I have ever known. What a contrast does the mind of an infant present to that of the pike, described by Professor Möbius, who during three whole months dashed and stunned himself against a glass partition which separated him from some minnows; and when, after at last learning that he could not attack them with impunity, he was placed in the aquarium with these same minnows, then in a persistent and senseless manner he would not attack them!

Curiosity, as M. Taine remarks, is displayed at an early age by infants, and is highly important in the development of their minds; but I made no special observation on this head. Imitation likewise comes into play. When our infant was only four months old I thought that he tried to imitate sounds; but I may have deceived myself, for I was not thoroughly convinced that he did so until he was ten months old. At the age of 11½ months he could readily imitate all sorts of actions, such as shaking his head and saying "Ah" to any dirty object, or by carefully and slowly putting his forefinger in the middle of the palm of his other hand, to the childish rhyme of "Pat it and pat it and mark it with T." It was amusing to behold his pleased expression after successfully performing any such accomplishment.

I do not know whether it is worth mentioning, as showing something about the strength of memory in a young child, that this one when 3 years and 23 days old on being shown an engraving of his grandfather, whom he had not seen for exactly six months, instantly recognised him and mentioned a whole string of events which had occurred whilst visiting him, and which certainly had never been mentioned in the interval.

MORAL SENSE The first sign of moral sense was noticed at the age of nearly 13 months: I said "Doddy (his nickname) won't give poor papa a kiss,—naughty Doddy." These words, without doubt, made him feel slightly uncomfortable; and at last when I had returned to my chair, he protruded his lips as a sign that he was ready to kiss me; and he then shook his hand in an angry manner until I came and received his kiss. Nearly the same little scene recurred in a few days, and the reconciliation seemed to give him so much satisfaction, that several times afterwards he pretended to be angry and slapped me, and then insisted on giving me a kiss. So that here we have a touch of the dramatic art, which is so strongly pronounced in most young children. About this time it became easy to work on his feelings and make him do whatever was wanted. When 2 years and 3 months old, he gave his last bit of gingerbread to his little sister, and then cried out with high self-approbation "Oh kind Doddy, kind Doddy." Two months later, he became extremely sensitive to ridicule, and was so suspicious

that he often thought people who were laughing and talking together were laughing at him. A little later (2 years and 7½ months old) I met him coming out of the dining room with his eyes unnaturally bright, and an odd unnatural or affected manner, so that I went into the room to see who was there, and found that he had been taking pounded sugar, which he had been told not to do. As he had never been in any way punished, his odd manner certainly was not due to fear, and I suppose it was pleasurable excitement struggling with conscience. A fortnight afterwards, I met him coming out of the same room, and he was eyeing his pinafore which he had carefully rolled up; and again his manner was so odd that I determined to see what was within his pinafore, notwithstanding that he said there was nothing and repeatedly commanded me to "go away," and I found it stained with pickle-juice; so that here was carefully planned deceit. As this child was educated solely by working on his good feelings, he soon became as truthful, open, and tender, as anyone could desire.

UNCONSCIOUSNESS, SHYNESS No one can have attended to very young children without being struck at the unabashed manner in which they fixedly stare without blinking their eyes at a new face; an old person can look in this manner only at an animal or inanimate object. This, I believe, is the result of young children not thinking in the least about themselves, and therefore not being in the least shy, though they are sometimes afraid of strangers. I saw the first symptom of shyness in my child when nearly two years and three months old: this was shown towards myself, after an absence of ten days from home, chiefly by his eyes being kept slightly averted from mine; but he soon came and sat on my knee and kissed me, and all trace of shyness disappeared.

MEANS OF COMMUNICATION The noise of crying or rather of squalling, as no tears are shed for a long time, is of course uttered in an instinctive manner, but serves to show that there is suffering. After a time the sound differs according to the cause, such as hunger or pain. This was noticed when this infant was eleven weeks old, and I believe at an earlier age in another infant. Moreover, he appeared soon to learn to begin crying voluntarily, or to wrinkle his face in the manner proper to the occasion, so as to show that he wanted something. When 46 days old he first made little noises without any meaning to please himself, and these soon became varied. An incipient laugh was observed on the 113th day, but much earlier in another infant. At this date I thought, as already remarked, that he began to try to imitate sounds, as he certainly did at a considerably later period. When five and a half months old, he uttered an articulate sound "da" but without any meaning attached to it. When a little over a year old, he used gestures to explain his wishes; to give a simple instance, he picked up a bit of paper and giving it to me pointed to the fire, as he had often seen and liked to see paper burnt. At exactly the age of a year, he made the great step of inventing a word for food, namely, *mum,* but what led him to it I did not discover. And now instead of beginning to cry when he was hungry, he used this word in a demonstrative manner or as a verb, implying "Give me food." This word therefore corresponds with *ham* as used by M. Taine's infant at the later age of 14 months. But he also used *mum* as a substantive of wide signification; thus he called sugar *shu-mum,* and a little later after he had learned the word "black," he called liquorice *black-shu-mum,*—black-sugar food.

I was particularly struck with the fact that when asking for food by the word *mum* he gave to it (I will copy the words written down at the time) "a most strongly marked interrogatory sound at the end." He also gave to "Ah," which he chiefly used at first when recognising any person or his own image in a mirror, an exclamatory sound, such as we employ when surprised. I remark in my notes that the use of these intonations seemed to have arisen instinctively, and I regret that more observations were not made on this subject. I record, however, in my notes that at a rather later period, when between 18 and 21 months old, he modulated his voice in refusing peremptorily to do anything by a defiant whine, so as to express "That I won't"; and again his humph of assent expressed "Yes, to be sure." M. Taine also insists strongly on the highly expressive tones of the sounds made by his infant before she had learnt to speak. The interrogatory sound which my child gave to the word *mum* when asking for food is especially curious; for if anyone will use a single word or a short sentence in this manner, he will find that the musical pitch of his voice rises considerably at the close. I did not then see that this fact bears on the view which I have elsewhere maintained that before man used articulate language, he uttered notes in a true musical scale as does the anthropoid ape Hylobates.

Finally, the wants of an infant are at first made intelligible by instinctive cries, which after a time are modified in part unconsciously, and in part, as I believe, voluntarily as a means of communication,—by the unconscious expression of the features,—by gestures and in a marked manner by different intonations,—lastly by words of a general nature invented by himself, then of a more precise nature imitated from those which he hears; and these latter are acquired at a wonderfully quick rate. An infant understands to a certain extent, and as I believe at a very early period, the meaning or feelings of those who tend him, by the expression of their features. There can hardly be a doubt about this with respect to smiling; and it seemed to me that the infant whose biography I have here given understood a compassionate expression at a little over five months old. When 6 months and 11 days old he certainly showed sympathy with his nurse on her pretending to cry. When pleased after performing some new accomplishment, being then almost a year old, he evidently studied the expression of those around him. It was probably due to differences of expression and not merely of the form of the features that certain faces clearly pleased him much more than others, even at so early an age as a little over six months. Before he was a year old, he understood intonations and gestures, as well as several words and short sentences. He understood one word, namely, his nurse's name, exactly five months before he invented his first word *mum;* and this is what might have been expected, as we know that the lower animals easily learn to understand spoken words.

3

Perspectives on Children's Development from Cultural Psychology

BARBARA ROGOFF AND GILDA MORELLI

Over the last several decades, many psychologists have come increasingly to recognize the importance of cultural context in children's development. One important trend has been the gradual shift away from laboratory-based research that relies on manipulation and control of isolated variables toward studies of behaviors as they occur in children's everyday lives in the cultural communities in which they grow. However, understanding the importance of cultural context in development cannot result from methodological changes alone. Theoretical and conceptual changes are also required. In the following article Barbara Rogoff and Gilda Morelli discuss a contextual approach to development that focuses on the complex interaction between children's development and the cultural system in which their growth occurs.

This article summarizes how cultural research can inform mainstream psychology. It focuses on an organizing theme that has been explored in research in non-Western groups: the role of specific cultural practices in organizing human endeavors. This perspective has influenced the direction of mainstream research, encouraging the advancement of our ideas of the domain-specific nature of psychological processes, and their relation to sociocultural practices. The article provides a brief

Reprinted with permission from the authors and *American Psychologist, 44*, 1989, 343–348. Copyright 1989 by the American Psychological Association.

We thank Ana Estrada for her comments on this essay. Correspondence concerning this article should be addressed to Barbara Rogoff, Department of Psychology, University of Utah, Salt Lake City, UT 84112.

description of Vygotsky's theoretical approach, a perspective comfortable for many working within this tradition. Finally, a discussion of research on children in cultural groups in the United States suggests that the cultural perspective can be useful in advancing research on issues involving American children with different cultural backgrounds.

Attention to the cultural context of child development has yielded important insights into the opportunities and constraints provided by the society in which children mature. Research with children of different cultures provides a broader perspective on human development than is available when considering human behavior in a single cultural group.

The purpose of this article is to indicate how cultural research can inform mainstream psychology. We discuss one organizing theme that has been explored in research in non-Western groups, the role of specific cultural practices in organizing all human endeavors. This perspective has influenced the direction of mainstream research, encouraging the advancement of our ideas of the domain-specific nature of psychological processes, and their relation to sociocultural practices. We provide a brief description of Vygotsky's theoretical approach, a perspective comfortable for many working within this tradition. Finally, we suggest that the cultural perspective can be useful in advancing research on issues involving American children varying in cultural background.

LESSONS LEARNED FROM CROSS-CULTURAL STUDIES OF DEVELOPMENT

Investigations of the role of culture in development have taken advantage of the impressive variations in the human condition, which occur around the world, to advance understanding of human adaptation. Reviews and discussion of cross-cultural developmental research appear in Bornstein (1980); Dasen (1977); Field, Sostek, Vietze, and Leiderman (1981); Laboratory of Comparative Human Cognition (1979, 1983); Leiderman, Tulkin, and Rosenfeld (1977); LeVine (in press); Munroe and Munroe (1975); Munroe, Munroe, and Whiting (1981); Rogoff, Gauvain, and Ellis (1984); Rogoff and Mistry (1985); Schieffelin and Ochs (1986); Serpell (1976); Super and Harkness (1980); Triandis and Heron (1981); Wagner and Stevenson (1982); Werner (1979); and Whiting and Edwards (1988).

Cross-cultural studies have focused especially on children in nontechnological (non-Western) societies

because these children contrast in important ways with children from the United States and other Western nations. This first section thus describes lessons learned from cross-cultural studies involving children around the world; psychological research on minorities in the United States has followed a somewhat different course, described later.

Perspectives Offered by Cross-cultural Research

An important function of cross-cultural research has been to allow investigators to look closely at the impact of their own belief systems (folk psychology) on scientific theories and research paradigms. When subjects and researchers are from the same population, interpretations of development may be constrained by implicit cultural assumptions. With subjects sharing researchers' belief systems, psychologists are less aware of their own assumptions regarding the world of childhood, the involvement of others in child development, and the physical and institutional circumstances in which development is embedded. Working with people from a quite different background can make one aware of aspects of human activity that are not noticeable until they are missing or differently arranged, as with the fish who reputedly is unaware of water until removed from it. Viewing the contrasts in life's arrangements in different cultures has enabled psychologists to examine very basic assumptions regarding developmental goals, the skills that are learned, and the contexts of development.

Cross-cultural research also allows psychologists to use cultural variation as a natural laboratory to attempt to disentangle variables that are difficult to tease apart in the United States and to study conditions that are rare in the United States. For example, one can examine how gender differences manifest themselves in differing cultural circumstances (Whiting & Edwards, 1988). Cross-cultural studies have examined the extent to which advances in intellectual skills are related to schooling versus children's age, a comparison that cannot be made in a country with compulsory schooling (Laboratory of Comparative Human Cognition, 1979; Rogoff, 1981). Other research examines conditions that are seen as normal in other cultures but carry connotations of being problematic in the United States. For example, studies have been made of gender roles in polygynous societies in which fathers are absent from the household because they have several wives (Munroe & Munroe, 1975), and of child care and infant psychological development in societies in which nonmaternal care (care by other adults or by child nurses) is valued and expected (Fox, 1977; Tronick, Morelli, & Winn, 1987; Zaslow, 1980).

Another function of cross-cultural studies is to examine the generality of theories of development that have been based on Western children. Examples include investigations of the universality of the stages of development proposed by Piaget, the family role relations emphasized by Freud, and patterns of mother-infant interaction taken to index security of attachment (Bretherton & Waters, 1985; Dasen, 1977; Dasen & Heron, 1981; Greenfield, 1976; Malinowski, 1927; Price-Williams, 1980). In such research, modifications to the assumptions of generality have often been suggested by cross-cultural findings. For example, findings that the highest stage of Piaget's theory, formal operations, seldom can be seen in non-Western cultures prompted Piaget to modify his theory in 1972 to suggest that the formal operational stage may not be universal but rather a product of an individual's expertise in a specific domain.

Research in a variety of cultures has also provided evidence of impressive regularities across cultures in developmental phenomena. For instance, there is marked similarity across cultures in the sequence and timing of sensorimotor milestones in infant development, smiling, and separation distress (Gewirtz, 1965; Goldberg, 1972; Konner, 1972; Super, 1981; Werner, 1988) and in the order of stages in language acquisition (Bowerman, 1981; Slobin, 1973).

An Emphasis on Understanding the Context of Development

An important contribution resulting from cultural challenges to researchers' assumptions is the conceptual restructuring emphasizing that human functioning cannot be separated from the contexts of their activities. Although there are other sources of contextual theorizing in the field of psychology, an important impetus has been the consistent findings that behavior and development vary according to cultural context.

Developmental researchers who have worked in other cultures have become convinced that human functioning cannot be separated from the cultural and more immediate context in which children develop. They observed that skills and behavior that did not appear in laboratory situations appeared in the same individuals in everyday situations. A subject whose logical reasoning or memory in a laboratory task seemed rudimentary could skillfully persuade the researcher or remind the researcher of promises outside the laboratory, or might be very skilled in a complex everyday task such as navigation or weaving

(Cole, 1975; Cole, Hood, & McDermott, 1978; Gladwin, 1970; Laboratory of Comparative Human Cognition, 1979; Rogoff, 1981; Scribner, 1976). Such informal observations called into question the widespread assumption that individuals' skills and behaviors have a generality extending across contexts.

Systematic studies noted the close relation between the skills or behavior exhibited by an individual and the contexts of elicitation and practice (Lave, 1977; Saxe, 1988). Children's nurturance and aggression varied as a function of the age and gender of the people with whom they interacted (Wenger, 1983; Whiting & Whiting, 1975). Perceptual modeling skills of Zambian and English children varied as a function of the cultural familiarity of the specific modeling activity (Serpell, 1979). Literacy provides practice with specific cognitive activities, leading to advances in particular skills rather than conferring general cognitive ability (Scribner & Cole, 1981). Such results point to the importance of considering the contexts in which people practice skills and behaviors, as well as those in which we as researchers observe them.

Many of the cognitive activities examined in developmental research, such as memory, perception, logical reasoning, and classification, have been found in cross-cultural studies to relate to children's experience of schooling (Lave, 1977; Rogoff, 1981; Sharp, Cole, & Lave, 1979). The extensive studies of the relation between school and cognitive skills call attention to a context of learning that is easily overlooked as an influence on cognitive development in the United States, where school is ubiquitous in the lives of children.

Remembering or classifying lists of unrelated objects may be unusual activities outside of literate or school-related activities (Goody, 1977; Rogoff & Waddell, 1982). The taxonomic categories seen as most appropriate in literate situations may not be valued in other circumstances, as is illustrated by Glick's (1975) report of Kpelle subjects' treatment of a classification problem. They sorted the 20 objects into functional groups (e.g., knife with orange, potato with hoe) rather than into categorical groups that the researcher considered more appropriate. When questioned, they often volunteered that that was the way a wise man would do things. "When an exasperated experimenter asked finally, 'How would a fool do it,' he was given back sorts of the type that were initially expected—four neat piles with food in one, tools in another, and so on" (p. 636).

People who have more schooling, such as older children and Western peoples, may excel on many kinds of cognitive tests because not only the skills but also the social situations of testing resemble the activities specifically practiced in school. In contrast with everyday life, where people classify and remember things in order to accomplish a functional goal, in schools and tests they perform in order to satisfy an adult's request to do so (Skeen, Rogoff, & Ellis, 1983; Super, Harkness, & Baldwin, 1977). Individuals with experience in school are likely to have more experience carrying out cognitive processes at the request of an adult without having a clear practical goal (Cazden & John, 1971; Rogoff & Mistry, in press).

Similar emphasis on contexts of development has come from other domains of cross-cultural research. In the area of infant sensorimotor development, Super (1981) and Kilbride (1980) have argued that the controversy over precocious development in African infants is best resolved by considering the practices of the cultural system in which the babies develop. African infants routinely surpass American infants in their rate of learning to sit and to walk, but not in learning to crawl or to climb stairs. African parents provide experiences for their babies that are apparently intended to teach sitting and walking—propping young infants in a sitting position supported by rolled blankets in a hole in the ground, exercising the newborn's walking reflex, and bouncing babies on their feet. But crawling is discouraged, and stairclimbing skills may be limited by the absence of access to stairs. Infant sensorimotor tests assess an aggregate of skills varying in rate of development according to the opportunity or encouragement to practice them.

Even infant sleep patterns vary as a function of culturally determined sleeping arrangements (Super, 1981). In the United States, the common developmental milestone of sleeping for eight uninterrupted hours by age four to five months is regarded as a sign of neurological maturity. In many other cultures, however, the infant sleeps with the mother and is allowed to nurse on demand with minimal disturbance of adult sleep. In such an arrangement, there is less parental motivation to enforce "sleeping through the night," and Super reported that babies continue to wake about every four hours during the night to feed, which is about the frequency of feeding during the day. Thus, it appears that this developmental milestone, in addition to its biological basis, is a function of the context in which it develops.

Cross-cultural studies demonstrating that individuals' behavior and skills are closely tied to specific activities have contributed to examination of important questions regarding the generality of the development of skills and behaviors, the structure of the ecology of development, and how to conceptualize the sociocultural context of practice of skills and behavior. These issues have recently pervaded the study of developmental psychology, with some large measure of influence from research on culture.

Conceptualizing the Sociocultural Context

Many researchers in the field of culture and development have found themselves comfortable with Vygotsky's theory, which focuses on the sociocultural context of development. Vygotsky's theory, developed in the 1930s in the Soviet Union, has gradually become more accessible to English-speaking researchers, with a rapid upsurge of interest following the publication of *Mind in Society* in 1978 (see also Laboratory of Comparative Human Cognition, 1983; Rogoff, 1982; Scribner & Cole, 1981; Wertsch, 1985a, 1985b). Although Vygotsky's theory focuses on cognitive development, it is gaining interest with researchers in emotional and social development as well, perhaps due to its integration of cognitive and social processes, as well as its emphasis on socialization (see, for example, Newson & Newson, 1975).

Vygotsky's theory offers a picture of human development that stresses how development is inseparable from human social and cultural activities. This contrasts with the image of the solitary little scientist provided by Piaget's theory. Vygotsky focused on how the development of higher mental processes such as voluntary memory and attention, classification, and reasoning involve learning to use inventions of society (such as language, mathematical systems, and memory devices) and how children are aided in development by guidance provided by people who are already skilled in these tools. Central to Vygotsky's theory is a stress on both the institutional and the interpersonal levels of social context.

THE INSTITUTIONAL LEVEL Cultural history provides organizations and tools useful to cognitive activity (through institutions such as school and inventions such as the calculator or literacy) along with practices that facilitate socially appropriate solutions to problems (e.g., norms for the arrangement of grocery shelves to aid shoppers in locating or remembering what they need; common mnemonic devices). Particular forms of activity are practiced in societal institutions such as schools and political systems.

For example, Kohlberg's hierarchy of moral development can be tied to the political system of a society, with the bureaucratic systems' perspective (Stage Four) appropriate for people whose political frame of reference is a large industrialized society, but inappropriate for people in small traditional tribal societies: "The two types of social systems are very different (though of course both are valid working types of systems), and thus everyday social life in them calls forth different modes of moral problem solving whose adequacy must be judged relative to their particular contexts" (Edwards, 1981, p. 274). The political institutions of a society may channel individual moral reasoning by providing standards for the resolution of moral problems.

The cultural institution of Western schooling provides norms and strategies for performance that are considered advanced in cognitive tests. Goodnow (1976) has suggested that differences between cultural groups may be ascribed largely to the interpretation of what problem is being solved in the task and to different values regarding "proper" methods of solution (e.g., speed, reaching a solution with a minimum of moves or redundancy, physically handling materials versus mental shuffling). The cultural tools and techniques used in school involve specific conventions and genres, such as conventions for representing depth in two-dimensional pictures and story problem genres (similar to logical syllogisms) in which one must rely only on information given in the problem to reach the answer. Cross-cultural studies indicate that nonschooled subjects are unfamiliar with such conventions and genres. For example, they are uncomfortable having to answer questions for which they cannot verify the premises (Cole, Gay, Glick, & Sharp, 1971; Scribner, 1977).

THE INTERPERSONAL LEVEL In Vygotsky's theory (1978), children develop skills in higher mental processes through the immediate social interactional context of activity, as social interaction helps structure individual activity. Information regarding tools and practices is transmitted through children's interaction with more experienced members of society during development, and patterns of interpersonal relations are organized by institutional conventions and the availability of cultural tools. For example, social aspects of experimental and observational situations relate to cultural practices. The relation between experimenter and subject may be rapidly grasped by Western children familiar with testing in school, but it may be highly discrepant from familiar adult–child interactions for non-Western children and young Western children. In some cultural settings, it is unusual for an adult who already knows an answer to request information from a child who may only partially know the subject matter, and it may be inappropriate for children to show off knowledge (Cazden & John, 1971; Irvine, 1978; Rogoff, Gauvain, & Ellis, 1984).

Similarly, in observational situations such as mother–child interaction, culturally varying agendas for public behavior may influence what people do in the presence of an observer (Zaslow & Rogoff, 1981). "It seems likely that one influence of the observer on parents is to produce a heightened frequency of behavior that the participants judge to be more socially desirable and inhibit behavior considered socially undesirable" (Pedersen, 1980, p. 181). Graves and Glick (1978) found that exchanges between middle-class mothers and their toddlers varied as a function of whether mothers thought that they were being videotaped. Mothers spoke more, used indirect directives more often, and spent more time in joint interactive focus with their children when they thought they were being observed. Clearly, peoples' interpretation of the goals of a task and cultural rules guiding social behavior influence the display of public behavior. Values regarding interpersonal relations may be inseparable from the activities observed for research purposes.

In addition to the cultural structuring of social interaction that has importance for research into human development, social interaction provides an essential context for development itself. Vygotsky stressed that interpersonal situations are important for guiding children in their development of the skills and behaviors considered important in their culture. Working within the "zone of proximal development," adults guide children in carrying out activities that are beyond the children's individual skills, and this joint problem solving provides children with information appropriate to stretch their individual skills. Cole (1981) argues that the zone of proximal development is "where culture and cognition create each other." Thus Vygotsky's conceptualization of how individual efforts are embedded in the interpersonal and institutional contexts of culture is proving useful for understanding the relation between culture and the individual.

RESEARCH ON CULTURE INVOLVING MINORITIES IN THE UNITED STATES

Historically, research on minorities in the United States has followed a different course than the cross-cultural investigations discussed earlier. For many years, researchers were intent on comparing the behavior and skills of minority children with mainstream children without taking into consideration the cultural contexts in which minority and mainstream children develop. This approach involved "deficit model" assumptions that mainstream skills and upbringing are normal and that variations observed with minorities are aberrations that produce deficits; intervention programs were designed to provide minority children with experiences to make up for their assumed deficits (Cole & Bruner, 1971; Hilliard & Vaughn-Scott, 1982; Howard & Scott, 1981; Ogbu, 1982).

The deficit model previously used in research on minority children contrasts sharply with the assumptions of the cross-cultural approach, which attempts to avoid ethnocentric evaluation of one group's practices and beliefs as being superior without considering their origins and functions from the perspective of the reality of that cultural group. With research in their own country, however, researchers have had more difficulty avoiding the assumption that the majority practices are proper (Ogbu, 1982). Variations have been assumed to account for the generally lower social status of the minority group members. It is only recently, and largely through the efforts of researchers with minority backgrounds, that deficit assumptions have been questioned in research on minority children.

The working model that appears to predominate in current minority research is one in which the positive features of cultural variation are emphasized. Although this is a valuable shift, we feel that research on minorities must move beyond reiterating the value of cultural diversity and begin more seriously to examine the source and functioning of the diversity represented in the United States to increase our understanding of the processes underlying development in cultural context.

Not only is the diversity of cultural backgrounds in our nation a resource for the creativity and future of the nation, it is also a resource for scholars studying how children develop. To make good use of this information, cultural research with minorities needs to focus on examining the processes and functioning of the cultural context of development. This requires "unpackaging" culture or minority status (Whiting, 1976) so as to disentangle the workings of the social context of development. This has become a central effort of cross-cultural research on non-Western populations.

Pioneering researchers of minorities are also beginning to look at the contexts in which children from different cultures develop, and these efforts provide a basis for a greater understanding of how culture channels development. (Examples include Brown & Reeve, 1985; Cazden, John, & Hymes, 1975; Chisholm, 1983; Erickson & Mohatt, 1982; Laboratory of Comparative Human Cognition, 1986; Ogbu, 1982.) It is notable that some of the most interesting efforts involve combining approaches from anthropology and education with those of psychology (see also recent issues of *Anthropology and Education Quarterly*).

The potential from research on cultural groups around the world as well as down the street lies in its challenge to our systems of assumptions and in the creative efforts of scholars to synthesize knowledge from observations of differing contexts of human development. Such challenge and synthesis is fruitful in the efforts to achieve a deeper and broader understanding of human nature and nurture.

References

Bornstein, M. H. (1980). Cross-cultural developmental psychology. In M. H. Bornstein (Ed.), *Comparative methods in psychology* (pp. 231–281). Hillsdale, NJ: Erlbaum.

Bowerman, M. (1981). Language development. In H. C. Triandis & A. Heron (Eds.), *Handbook of cross-cultural psychology* (Vol. 4, pp. 93–185). Boston: Allyn & Bacon.

Bretherton, I., & Waters E. (Eds.). (1985). Growing points of attachment theory and research. *Monographs of the Society for Research in Child Development, 50*(1–2, Serial No. 209).

Brown, A. L., & Reeve, R. A. (1985). *Bandwidths of competence: The role of supportive contexts in learning and development* (Tech. Rep. No. 336). Champaign: University of Illinois at Urbana–Champaign, Center for the Study of Reading.

Cazden, C. B., John, V. P., & Hymes, D. (Eds.). (1975). *Functions of language in the classroom*. New York: Teachers College Press.

Cazden, C. B., & John, V. P. (1971). Learning in American Indian children. In M. L. Wax, S. Diamond, & F. O. Gearing (Eds.), *Anthropological perspectives in education* (pp. 252–272). New York: Basic Books.

Chisholm, J. S. (1983). *Navajo infancy: An ethological study of child development*. Hawthorne, NY: Aldine.

Cole, M. (1975). An ethnographic psychology of cognition. In R. W. Brislin, S. Bochner, & W. J. Lonner (Eds.), *Cross-cultural perspectives on learning* (pp. 157–175). New York: Wiley.

Cole, M. (1981, September). *The zone of proximal development: Where culture and cognition create each other* (Report No. 106). San Diego: University of California, Center for Human Information Processing.

Cole, M., & Bruner, J. S. (1971). Cultural differences and inferences about psychological processes. *American Psychologist, 26*, 867–876.

Cole, M., Gay, J., Glick, J. A., & Sharp, D. W. (1971). *The cultural context of learning and thinking*. New York: Basic Books.

Cole, M., Hood, L., & McDermott, R. P. (1978). Concepts

of ecological validity: Their differing implications for comparative cognitive research. *The Quarterly Newsletter of the Institute for Comparative Human Development, 2,* 34–37.

Dasen, P. R. (Ed.). (1977). *Piagetian psychology: Cross-cultural contributions.* New York: Gardner Press.

Dasen, P. R., & Heron, A. (1981). Cross-cultural tests of Piaget's theory. In H. C. Triandis & A. Heron (Eds.), *Handbook of cross-cultural psychology* (Vol. 4, pp. 295–341). Boston: Allyn & Bacon.

Edwards, C. P. (1981). The comparative study of the development of moral judgment and reasoning. In R. H. Munroe, R. L. Munroe, & B. B. Whiting (Eds.), *Handbook of cross-cultural human development* (pp. 501–528). New York: Garland.

Erickson, F., & Mohatt, G. (1982). Cultural organization of participation structures in two classrooms of Indian students. In G. Spindler (Ed.), *Doing the ethnography of schooling* (pp.132–174). New York: Holt, Rinehart & Winston.

Field, T. M., Sostek, A. M., Vietze, P., & Leiderman, P. H. (Eds.). (1981). *Culture and early interactions.* Hillsdale, NJ: Erlbaum.

Fox, N. A. (1977). Attachment of kibbutz infants to mother and metapelet. *Child Development, 48,* 1228–1239.

Gewirtz. J. L. (1965). The course of infant smiling in four child-rearing environments in Israel. In B. M. Foss (Ed.), *Determinants of infant behavior* (Vol. 3, pp. 205–248). London, England: Methuen.

Gladwin, T. (1970). *East is a big bird.* Cambridge, MA: Belknap Press.

Glick, J. (1975). Cognitive development in cross-cultural perspective. In F. Horowitz (Ed.), *Review of child development research* (Vol. 4, pp. 595–654). Chicago: University of Chicago Press.

Goldberg, S. (1972). Infant care and growth in urban Zambia. *Human Development, 15,* 77–89.

Goodnow, J. J. (1976). The nature of intelligent behavior. Questions raised by cross-cultural studies. In L. B. Resnick (Ed.), *The nature of intelligence* (pp. 169–188). Hillsdale, NJ: Erlbaum.

Goody, J. (1977). *The domestication of the savage mind.* Cambridge, England: Cambridge University Press.

Graves, Z. R., & Glick, J. (1978). The effect of context on mother–child interaction. *The Quarterly Newsletter of the Institute for Comparative Human Development, 2,* 41–46.

Greenfield, P. M. (1976). Cross-cultural research and Piagetian theory: Paradox and progress. In K. R Riegel & J. A. Meacham (Eds.), *The developing individual in a changing world* (Vol. 1, pp. 322–345). Chicago: Aldine.

Hilliard, A. G., III, & Vaughn-Scott, M. (1982). The quest for the "minority" child. In S. G. Moore & C. R. Cooper (Eds.), *The young child: Reviews of research* (Vol. 3, pp. 175–189). Washington, DC: National Association for the Education of Young Children.

Howard, A., & Scott, R. A. (1981). The study of minority groups in complex societies. In R. H. Munroe, R. L. Munroe, & B. B. Whiting (Eds.), *Handbook of cross-cultural human development* (pp. 113–152). New York: Garland.

Irvine, J. T (1978). Wolof "magical thinking": Culture and conservation revisited. *Journal of Cross-Cultural Psychology, 9,* 300–310.

Kilbride, P. L. (1980). Sensorimotor behavior of Baganda and Samia infants. *Journal of Cross-Cultural Psychology, 11,* 131–152.

Konner, M. (1972). Aspects of the developmental ethology of a foraging people. In N. Blurton-Jones (Ed.), *Ethological studies of child behavior* (pp. 285–328). Cambridge, England: Cambridge University Press.

Laboratory of Comparative Human Cognition. (1979). Cross-cultural psychology's challenges to our ideas of children and development. *American Psychologist, 34,* 827–833.

Laboratory of Comparative Human Cognition. (1983). Culture and cognitive development. In W. Kessen (Ed.), *Handbook of Child Psychology: Vol. 1. History, theory, and methods* (pp. 294–356). New York: Wiley.

Laboratory of Comparative Human Cognition. (1986). Contributions of cross-cultural research to educational practice. *American Psychologist, 41,* 1049–1058.

Lave, J. (1977). Tailor-made experiments and evaluating the intellectual consequences of apprenticeship training. *The Quarterly Newsletter of the Institute for Comparative Human Development, 1,* 1–3.

Leiderman, P. H., Tulkin, S. R., & Rosenfeld, A. (Eds.). (1977). *Culture and infancy.* New York: Academic Press.

LeVine, R. A. (in press). Environments in child development: An anthropological perspective. In W. Damon (Ed.), *Child development today and tomorrow.* San Francisco: Jossey-Bass.

Malinowski, B. (1927). *The father in primitive psychology.* New York: Norton.

Munroe, R. L., & Munroe, R. H. (1975). *Cross-cultural human development.* Monterey, CA: Brooks/Cole.

Munroe, R. H., Munroe, R. L., & Whiting, B. B. (Eds.). (1981). *Handbook of cross-cultural human development.* New York: Garland.

Newson, J., & Newson, E. (1975). Intersubjectivity and the transmission of culture: On the social origins of symbolic functioning. *Bulletin of the British Psychological Society, 28,* 437–446.

Ogbu, J. U. (1982). Socialization: A cultural ecological approach. In K. M. Borman (Ed.), *The social life of children in a changing society* (pp. 253–267). Hillsdale, NJ: Erlbaum.

Pedersen, R A. (1980). *The father–infant relationship: Observational studies in the family setting.* New York: Praeger.

Piaget, J. (1972). Intellectual evolution from adolescence to adulthood. *Human Development, 15,* 1–12.

Price-Williams, D. R. (1980). Anthropological approaches to

cognition and their relevance to psychology. In H. C. Triandis & W. Lonner (Eds.), *Handbook of cross-cultural psychology* (Vol. 3, pp. 155–184). Boston: Allyn & Bacon.

Rogoff, B. (1981). Schooling and the development of cognitive skills. In H. C. Triandis & A. Heron (Eds.), *Handbook of cross-cultural psychology* (Vol. 4, pp. 233–294). Boston: Allyn & Bacon.

Rogoff, B. (1982). Integrating context and cognitive development. In M. E. Lamb & A. L. Brown (Eds.), *Advances in developmental psychology* (Vol. 2, pp. 125–170). Hillsdale, NJ: Erlbaum.

Rogoff, B., Gauvain, M., & Ellis, S. (1984). Development viewed in its cultural context. In M. H. Bornstein & M. E. Lamb (Eds.), *Developmental Psychology* (pp. 533–571). Hillsdale, NJ: Erlbaum.

Rogoff, B., & Mistry, J. J. (1985). Memory development in cultural context. In M. Pressley & C. Brainerd (Eds.), *Progress in cognitive development* (pp. 117–142). New York: Springer-Verlag.

Rogoff, B., & Mistry, J. J. (in press). The social and motivational context of children's memory skills. In R. Fivish & J. Hudson (Eds.), *What young children remember and why.* Cambridge, England: Cambridge University Press.

Rogoff, B., & Waddell, K. J. (1982). Memory for information organized in a scene by children from two cultures. *Child Development, 53,* 1224–1228.

Saxe, G. B. (1988). *Mathematics in and out of school.* Unpublished manuscript, University of California at Los Angeles.

Schieffelin, B. B., & Ochs, E. (Eds.). (1986). *Language socialization across cultures.* Cambridge, England: Cambridge University Press.

Scribner, S. (1976). Situating the experiment in cross-cultural research. In K. F. Riegel & J. A. Meacham (Eds.), *The developing individual in a changing world* (Vol. 1, pp. 310–321). Chicago: Aldine.

Scribner, S. (1977). Modes of thinking and ways of speaking: Culture and logic reconsidered. In P. N. Johnson-Laird & P. C. Wason (Eds.), *Thinking* (pp. 483–500). Cambridge, England: Cambridge University Press.

Scribner, S., & Cole, M. (1981). *The psychology of literacy.* Cambridge, MA: Harvard University Press.

Serpell, R. (1976). *Culture's influence on behavior.* London, England: Methuen.

Serpell, R. (1979). How specific are perceptual skills? A cross-cultural study of pattern reproduction. *British Journal of Psychology, 70,* 365–380.

Sharp, D., Cole, M., & Lave, C. (1979). Education and cognitive development: The evidence from experimental research. *Monographs of the Society for Research in Child Development, 44*(1–2, Serial No. 178).

Skeen, J., Rogoff, B., & Ellis, S. (1983). Categorization by children and adults in communication contexts. *International Journal of Behavioral Development, 6,* 213–220.

Slobin, D. I. (1973). Cognitive prerequisites for the development of grammar. In C. A. Ferguson & D. I. Slobin (Eds.),

Studies of child language development (pp. 175–200). New York: Holt, Rinehart & Winston.

Super, C. M. (1981). Behavioral development in infancy. In R. H. Munroe, R. L. Munroe, & B. B. Whiting (Eds.), *Handbook of cross-cultural human development* (pp. 181–270). New York: Garland.

Super, C. M., & Harkness, S. (Eds.), (1980). *Anthropological perspectives on child development.* San Francisco: Jossey-Bass.

Super, C. M., Harkness, S., & Baldwin, L. M. (1977). Category behavior in natural ecologies and in cognitive tests. *The Quarterly Newsletter of the Institute for Comparative Human Development, 1,* 4–7.

Triandis, H. C., & Heron, A. (Eds.). (1981). *Handbook of cross-cultural psychology* (Vol. 4). Boston: Allyn & Bacon.

Tronick, E. Z., Morelli, G. A., & Winn, S. (1987). Multiple caretaking of Efe (pygmy) infants. *American Anthropologist, 89*(1), 96–106.

Vygotsky, L. S. (1978). *Mind in society.* Cambridge, MA: Harvard University Press.

Wagner, D. A., & Stevenson, H. W. (Eds.). (1982). *Cultural perspectives on child development.* San Francisco: Freeman.

Wenger, M. (1983). *Gender role socialization in East Africa: Social interactions between 2-to-3-year olds and older children, a social ecological perspective.* Unpublished doctoral dissertation, Harvard University, Cambridge, MA.

Werner, E. E. (1979). *Cross-Cultural child development.* Monterey, CA: Brooks/Cole.

Werner, E. E. (1988). A cross-cultural perspective on infancy. *Journal of Cross-Cultural Psychology, 19*(1), 96–113.

Wertsch, J. V. (Ed.). (1985a). *Culture, communication, and cognition: Vygotskian perspectives.* Cambridge, England: Cambridge University Press.

Wertsch, J. V. (1985b). *Vygotsky and the social formation of mind.* Cambridge, MA: Harvard University Press.

Whiting, B. B. (1976). The problem of the packaged variable. In K. F. Riegel & J. A. Meacham (Eds.), *The developing individual in a changing world.* Chicago: Aldine.

Whiting, B. B., & Edwards, C. P. (1988). *Children of different worlds.* Cambridge, MA: Harvard University Press.

Whiting, B. B., & Whiting, J. W. M. (1975). *Children of six cultures: A psycho-cultural analysis.* Cambridge, MA: Harvard University Press.

Zaslow, M. (1980). Relationships among peers in kibbutz toddler groups. *Child Psychiatry and Human Development, 10,* 178–189.

Zaslow, M., & Rogoff, B. (1981). The cross-cultural study of early interaction: Implications from research in culture and cognition. In T. Field, A. Sostek, P. Vietze, & H. Leiderman (Eds.), *Culture and early interactions* (pp. 237–256). Hillsdale, NJ: Erlbaum.

4

Development and Learning

JEAN PIAGET

This selection and the following paper were written by two of the most influential developmental psychologists of the twentieth century, Jean Piaget and Lev Vygotsky. Although written at different times and for different forums, these papers are united in their attention to the relationship between two key psychological processes: learning and development.

Both Piaget and Vygotsky considered learning and development to be important and distinct psychological processes. However, they differed in how they viewed the relationship between these processes as well as the role that each played in organizing and guiding development. Piaget believed that development precedes learning while Vygotsky believed that learning precedes development. While exploring their different approaches, consider the types of educational orintervention programs that might be designed from each of these views. Such programs will differ in many aspects, including the role other people play in promoting growth.

In his opening remarks Piaget makes a distinction between development and learning—development being a spontaneous process tied to embryogenesis, learning being provoked by external situations. He proceeds to discuss the concept of an operation as an interiorized action linked to other operations in a structure. Four stages of development are enumerated—sensori-motor, pre-operational, concrete operations, and formal operations. Factors explaining the development of one structure of operations from *another are discussed—maturation, experience, social transmission, and equilibration. Equilibration is defended as the most fundamental factor. Commenting on the inadequacy of the stimulus-response approach to understanding learning, Piaget presents evidence negating the effectiveness of external reinforcement in hastening the development of operational structures. These operational structures can be learned only if one bases the learning on simpler, more elementary structures—only if there is a*

This article was reprinted with permission from R. E. Ripple (ed. with V. N. Rockcastle) from
Piaget Rediscovered, 1964 and 1972, 7–20.

natural relationship and development of structures. The learning of these structures is held to follow the same basic laws as does their natural development, i.e., learning is subordinated to development. Piaget concludes that the fundamental relation involved in development and learning is assimilation, not association.

My dear colleagues, I am very concerned about what to say to you, because I don't know if I shall accomplish the end that has been assigned to me. But I've been told that the important thing is not what you say, but the discussion which follows, and the answers to questions you are asked. So this morning I shall simply give a general introduction of a few ideas which seem to me to be important for the subject of this conference.

First I would like to make clear the difference between two problems: the problem of *development* in general, and the problem of *learning*. I think these problems are very different, although some people do not make this distinction.

The development of knowledge is a spontaneous process, tied to the whole process of embryogenesis. Embryogenesis concerns the development of the body, but it concerns as well the development of the nervous system, and the development of mental functions. In the case of the development of knowledge in children, embryogenesis ends only in adulthood. It is a total developmental process which we must re-situate in its general biological and psychological context. In other words, development is a process which concerns the totality of the structures of knowledge.

Learning presents the opposite case. In general, learning is provoked by situations—provoked by a psychological experimenter; or by a teacher, with respect to some didactic point; or by an external situation. It is provoked, in general, as opposed to spontaneous. In addition, it is a limited process—limited to a single problem, or to a single structure.

So I think that development explains learning, and this opinion is contrary to the widely held opinion that development is a sum of discrete learning experiences. For some psychologists development is reduced to a series of specific learned items, and development is thus the sum, the cumulation of this series of specific items. I think this is an atomistic view which deforms the real state of things. In reality, development is the essential process and each element of learning occurs as a function of total development, rather than being an element which explains development. I shall begin, then, with a first part dealing with development, and I shall talk about learning in the second part.

To understand the development of knowledge, we must start with an idea which seems central to me—the idea of an *operation*. Knowledge is not a copy of reality. To know an object, to know an event, is not simply to look at it and make a mental copy, or image, of it. To know an object is to act on it. To know is to modify, to transform the object, and to understand the process of this transformation, and as a consequence to understand the way the object is constructed. An operation is thus the essence of knowledge; it is an interiorised action which modifies the object of knowledge. For instance, an operation would consist of joining objects in a class, to construct a classification. Or an operation would consist of ordering, or putting things in a series. Or an operation would consist of counting, or of measuring. In other words, it is a set of actions modifying the object, and enabling the knower to get at the structures of the transformation.

An operation is an interiorised action. But in addition, it is a reversible action; that is, it can take place in both directions, for instance, adding or subtracting, joining or separating. So it is a particular type of action which makes up logical structures.

Above all, an operation is never isolated. It is always linked to other operations, and as a result it is always a part of a total structure. For instance, a logical class does not exist in isolation; what exists is the total structure of classification. An asymmetrical relation does not exist in isolation. Seriation is the natural, basic operational structure. A number does not exist in isolation. What exists is the series of numbers, which constitute a structure, an exceedingly rich structure whose various properties have been revealed by mathematicians.

These operational structures are what seem to me to constitute the basis of knowledge, the natural psychological reality, in terms of which we must understand the development of knowledge. And the central problem of development is to understand the formation, elaboration, organization, and functioning of these structures.

I should like to review the stages of development of these structures, not in any detail, but simply as a reminder. I shall distinguish four main stages. The first is a sensory-motor, pre-verbal stage, lasting approximately the first 18 months of life. During this stage is developed the practical knowledge which constitutes the substructure of later representational knowledge. An example is the construction of the schema of the permanent object. For an infant, during the first months, an object has no permanence. When it disappears from the perceptual field it no longer exists. No attempt is made to find it again. Later, the infant will try to find it, and he will find it by localizing it spatially. Consequently, along with the construction of the permanent object there comes the construction of practical, or sensory-motor, space. There is similarly the construction of temporal succession, and of elementary sensory-motor causality. In other words, there is a series of structures which are indispensable for the structures of later representational thought.

In a second stage, we have pre-operational representation—the beginnings of language, of the symbolic function, and therefore of thought, or representation. But at the level of representational thought, there must now be a reconstruction of all that was developed on the sensory-motor level. That is, the sensory-motor actions are not immediately translated into operations. In fact, during all this second period of pre-operational representations, there are as yet no operations as I defined this term a moment ago. Specifically, there is as yet no conservation which is the psychological criterion of the presence of reversible operations. For example, if we pour liquid from one glass to another of a different shape, the pre-operational child will think there is more in one than in the other. In the absence of operational reversibility, there is no conservation of quantity.

In a third stage the first operations appear, but I call these concrete operations because they operate on objects, and not yet on verbally expressed hypotheses. For example, there are the operations of classification, ordering, the construction of the idea of number, spatial and temporal operations, and all the fundamental operations of elementary logic of classes and relations, of elementary mathematics, of elementary geometry and even of elementary physics.

Finally, in the fourth stage, these operations are surpassed as the child reaches the level of what I call formal or hypothetic-deductive operations; that is, he can now reason on hypotheses, and not only on objects. He constructs new operations, operations of propositional logic, and not simply the operations of classes, relations, and numbers. He attains new structures which are on the one hand combinatorial, corresponding to what mathematicians call lattices; on the other hand, more complicated group structures. At the level of concrete operations, the operations apply within an immediate neighborhood: for instance, classification by successive inclusions. At the level of the combinatorial, however, the groups are much more mobile. These, then, are the four stages which we identify, whose formation we shall now attempt to explain.

What factors can be called upon to explain the development from one set of structures to another? It seems to me that there are four main factors: first of all, *maturation,* in the sense of Gesell, since this development is a continuation of the embryogenesis; second, the role of *experience* of the effects of the physical environment on the structures of intelligence; third, *social transmission* in the broad sense (linguistic transmission, education, etc.); and fourth, a factor which is too often neglected but one which seems to me fundamental and even the principal factor. I shall call this the factor of *equilibration* or if you prefer it, of self-regulation.

Let us start with the first factor, maturation. One might think that these stages are simply a reflection of an interior maturation of the nervous system, following the hypotheses of Gesell, for example. Well, maturation certainly does play an indispensable role and must not be ignored. It certainly takes part in every transformation that takes place during a child's development. However, this first factor is insufficient in itself. First of all, we know practically nothing about the maturation of the nervous system beyond the first months of the child's existence. We know a little bit about it during the first two years but we know very little following this time. But above all, maturation doesn't explain everything, because the average ages at which these stages appear (the average chronological ages) vary a great deal from one society to another. The ordering of these stages is constant and has been found in all the societies studied. It has been found in various countries where psychologists in universities have redone the experiments but it has also been found in African peoples for example, in the children of the Bushmen, and in Iran, both in the villages and in the cities. However, although the order of succession is constant, the chronological ages of these stages vary a great deal. For instance, the ages which we have found in Geneva are not necessarily the ages which you would find in the United States. In Iran, furthermore, in the city of Teheran, they found approximately the same ages as we found in Geneva, but there is a systematic delay of two years in the children in the country. Canadian psychologists who redid our experiments, Monique Laurendeau and Father Adrien Pinard, found once again about the same ages in Montreal. But when they redid the experiments in Martinique, they found a delay of four years in all the experiments and this in spite of the fact that the children in Martinique go to a school set up according to the French system and the French curriculum and attain at the end of this elementary school a certificate of higher primary education. There is then a delay of four years, that is, there are the same stages, but systematically delayed. So you see that these age variations show that maturation does not explain everything.

I shall go on now to the role played by experience. Experience of objects, of physical reality, is obviously a basic factor in the development of cognitive structures. But once again this factor does not explain everything. I can give two reasons for this. The first reason is that some of the concepts which appear at the beginning of the stage of concrete operations are such that I cannot see how they could be drawn from experience. As an example, let us take the conservation of the substance in the case of changing the shape of a ball of plasticene. We give this ball of plasticene to a child who changes its shape into a sausage form and we ask him if there is the same amount of matter, that is, the same amount of substance as there was before. We also ask him if it now has the same weight and thirdly if it now has the same volume. The volume is measured by the displacement of water when we put the ball or the sausage into a glass of water. The findings, which have been the same every time this experiment has been done, show us that first of all there is conservation of the amount of substance. At about eight years old a child will say, "There is the same amount of plasticene." Only later does the child assert that the weight is conserved and still later that the volume is conserved. So I would ask you where the idea of the conservation of substance can come from. What is a constant and invariant substance when it doesn't yet have a constant weight or a constant volume? Through perception you can get at the weight of the ball or the volume of the ball but perception cannot give you an idea of the amount of substance. No experiment, no experience, can show the child that there is the same amount of substance. He can weigh the ball and that would lead to the conservation of weight. He can immerse it in water and that would lead to the conservation of volume. But the notion of substance is attained before either weight or volume. This conservation of substance is simply a logical necessity. The child now understands that when there is a transformation something must be conserved because by reversing the transformation you can come back to the point of departure and once again have the ball. He knows that something is conserved but he doesn't know what. It is not yet the weight, it is not yet the volume; it is simply a logical form—a logical necessity. There, it seems to me, is an example of a progress in knowledge, a logical necessity for something to be conserved even though no experience can have led to this notion.

My second objection to the sufficiency of experience as an explanatory factor is that this notion of experience is a very equivocal one. There are, in fact, two kinds of experience which are psychologically very different and this difference is very important from the pedagogical point of view. It is because of the pedagogical importance that I emphasize this distinction. First of all, there is what I shall call physical experience, and secondly, what I shall call logical-mathematical experience.

Physical experience consists of acting upon objects and drawing some knowledge about the objects by abstraction from the objects. For example, to discover that this pipe is heavier than this watch, the child will weigh them both and find the difference in the objects themselves. This is experience in the usual sense of the term—in the sense used by empiricists. But there is a second type of experience which I shall call logical-mathematical experience where the knowledge is not drawn from the objects, but it is drawn by the actions effected upon the objects. This is not the same thing. When one acts upon objects, the objects are indeed there, but there is also the set of actions which modify the objects.

I shall give you an example of this type of experience. It is a nice example because we have verified it many times in small children under seven years of age, but it is also an example which one of my mathematician friends has related to me about his own childhood, and he dates his mathematical career from this experience. When he was four or five years old—I don't know exactly how old, but a small child—he was seated on the ground in his garden and he was counting pebbles. Now to count these pebbles he put them in a row and he counted them one, two, three, up to ten. Then he finished counting them and started to count them in the other direction. He began by the end and once again he found ten. He found this marvelous that there were ten in one direction and ten in the other direction. So he put them in a circle and counted them that way and found ten once again. Then he counted them in the other direction and found ten once more. So he put them in some other direction and found ten once more. So he put them in some other arrangement and kept counting them and kept finding ten. There was the discovery that he made.

Now what indeed did he discover? He did not discover a property of pebbles; he discovered a property of the action of ordering. The pebbles had no order. It was his action which introduced a linear order or a cyclical order, or any kind of an order. He discovered that the sum was independent of the order. The order was the action which he introduced among the pebbles. For the sum the same principle applied. The pebbles had no sum; they were simply in a pile. To make a sum, action was necessary—the operation of putting together and counting. He found that the sum was independent of the order, in other words, that the action of putting together is independent of the action of ordering. He discovered a property of actions and not a property of pebbles. You may say that it is in the nature of pebbles to let this be done to them and this is true. But it could have been drops of water, and drops of water would not have let this be done to them because two drops of water and two drops of water do not make four drops of water as you know very well. Drops of water then would not let this be done to them, we agree to that.

So it is not the physical property of pebbles which the experience uncovered. It is the properties of the actions carried out on the pebbles and this is quite another form of experience. It is the point of departure of mathematical deduction. The subsequent deduction will consist of interiorizing these actions and then of combining them without needing any pebbles. The mathematician no longer needs his pebbles. He can combine his operations simply with symbols and the point of departure of this mathematical deduction is logical-mathematical experience and this is not at all experience in the sense of the empiricists. It is the beginning of the coordination of actions, but this coordination of actions before the stage of operations needs to be supported by concrete material. Later, this coordination of actions leads to the logical-mathematical structures. I believe that logic is not a derivative of language. The source of logic is much more profound. It is the total coordination of actions, actions of joining things together, or ordering things, etc. This is what logical-mathematical experience is. It is an experience of the actions of the subject, and not an experience of objects themselves. It is an experience which is necessary before there can be operations. Once the operations have been attained this experience is no longer needed and the coordinations of actions can take place by themselves in the form of deduction and construction for abstract structures.

The third factor is social transmission—linguistic transmission or educational transmission. This factor, once again, is fundamental. I do not deny the role of any one of these factors; they all play a part. But this factor is insufficient because the child can receive valuable information via language or via education directed by an adult only if he is in a state where he can understand this information. That is, to receive the information he must have a structure which enables him to assimilate this information. This is why you cannot teach higher mathematics to a five-year-old. He does not yet have structures which enable him to understand.

I shall take a much simpler example, an example of linguistic transmission. As my very first work in the realm of child psychology, I spent a long time studying the relation between a part and a whole in concrete experience and in language. For example, I used Burt's test employing the sentence, "Some of my flowers are buttercups." The child knows that all buttercups are yellow, so there are three possible conclusions: the whole bouquet is yellow, or part of the bouquet is yellow, or none of the flowers in the bouquet is yellow. I found that up until nine years of age (and this was in Paris, so the children certainly did

understand the French language) they replied, "The whole bouquet is yellow or some of my flowers are yellow." Both of those mean the same thing. They did not understand the expression, "some *of* my flowers." They did not understand this *of* as a partitive genitive, as the inclusion of some flowers in my flowers. They understood some of my flowers to be my several flowers as if the several flowers and the flowers were confused as one and the same class. So there you have children who until nine years of age heard every day a linguistic structure which implied the inclusion of a sub-class in a class and yet did not understand this structure. It is only when they themselves are in firm possession of this logical structure, when they have constructed it for themselves according to the developmental laws which we shall discuss, that they succeed in understanding correctly the linguistic expression.

I come now to the fourth factor which is added to the three preceding ones but which seems to me to be the fundamental one. This is what I call the factor of equilibration. Since there are already three factors, they must somehow be equilibrated among themselves. That is one reason for bringing in the factor of equilibration. There is a second reason, however, which seems to me to be fundamental. It is that in the act of knowing, the subject is active, and consequently, faced with an external disturbance, he will react in order to compensate and consequently he will tend towards equilibrium. Equilibrium, defined by active compensation, leads to reversibility. Operational reversibility is a model of an equilibrated system where a transformation in one direction is compensated by a transformation in the other direction. Equilibration, as I understand it, is thus an active process. It's a process of self-regulation. I think that this self-regulation is a fundamental factor in development. I use this term in the sense in which it is used in cybernetics, that is, in the sense of processes with feedback and with feedforward, of processes which regulate themselves by a progressive compensation of systems. This process of equilibration takes the form of a succession of levels of equilibrium, of levels which have a certain probability which I shall call a sequential probability, that is, the probabilities are not established a priori. There is a sequence of levels. It is not possible to reach the second level unless equilibrium has been reached at the first level, and the equilibrium of the third level only becomes possible when the equilibrium of the second level has been reached, and so forth. That is, each level is determined as the most probable given that the preceding level has been reached. It is not the most probable at the beginning, but it is the most probable once the preceding level has been reached.

As an example, let us take the development of the idea of conservation in the transformation of the ball of plasticene into the sausage shape. Here you can discern four levels. The most probable at the beginning is for the child to think of only one dimension. Suppose that there is a probability of 0.8, for instance, that the child will focus on the length, and that the width has a probability of 0.2. This would mean that of ten children, eight will focus on the length alone without paying any attention to the width, and two will focus on the width without paying any attention to the length. They will focus only on one dimension or the other. Since the two dimensions are independent at this stage, focusing on both at once would have a probability of only 0.16. That is less than either one of the two. In other words, the most probable in the beginning is to focus only on one dimension and in fact the child will say, "It's longer, so there's more in the sausage." Once he has reached this first level, if you continue to elongate the sausage, there comes a moment when he will say, "No, now it's too thin, so there's less." Now he is thinking about the width, but he forgets the length, so you have come to a second level which becomes the most probable after the first level, but which is not the most probable at the point of departure. Once he has focused on the width, he will come back sooner or later to focus on the length. Here you will have a third level where he will oscillate between width and length and where he will discover that the two are related. When you elongate you make it more thin, and when you make it shorter, you make it thicker. He discovers that the two are solidly related and in discovering this relationship, he will start to think in terms of the transformation and not only in terms of the final configuration. Now he will say that when it gets longer it gets thinner, so it's the same thing. There is more of it in length but less of it in width. When you make it shorter it gets thicker; there's less in length and more in width, so there is compensation—compensation which defines equilibrium in the sense in which I defined it a moment ago. Consequently, you have operations and conservation. In other words, in the course of these developments you will always find a process of self-regulation which I call equilibration and which seems to me the fundamental factor in the acquisition of logical-mathematical knowledge.

I shall go on now to the second part of my lecture, that is, to deal with the topic of learning. Classically, learning is based on the stimulus-response schema. I think the stimulus-response schema, while I won't say it is false, is in any case entirely incapable of explaining cognitive learning. Why? Because when you think of a stimulus-response schema, you think usually that first of all there is a stimulus and then a response is set off by this stimulus. For my part, I am convinced that the response was there first, if I can express myself in this way. A stimulus is a stimulus only to the extent that it is significant and it becomes significant only to the extent that there is a structure which permits its assimilation, a structure which can integrate this stimulus but which at the same time sets off the response. In other words, I would propose that the stimulus-response schema be written in the circular form—in the form of a schema or of a structure which is not simply one way. I would propose that above all, between the stimulus and the response there is the organism, the organism and its structures. The stimulus is really a stimulus only when it is assimilated into a structure and it is this structure which sets off the response. Consequently, it is not an exaggeration to say that the response is there first, or if you wish at the beginning there is the structure. Of course we would want to understand how this structure comes to be. I tried to do this earlier by presenting a model of equilibration or self-regulation. Once there is a structure, the stimulus will set off a response, but only by the intermediary of this structure.

I should like to present some facts. We have facts in great number. I shall choose only one or two and I shall choose some facts which our colleague, Smedslund, has gathered. (Smedslund is currently at the Harvard Center for Cognitive Studies.) Smedslund arrived in Geneva a few years ago convinced (he had published this in one of his papers) that the development of the ideas of conservation could be indefinitely accelerated through learning of a stimulus-response type. I invited Smedslund to come to spend a year in Geneva to show us this, to show us that he could accelerate the development of operational conservation. I shall relate only one of his experiments.

During the year that he spent in Geneva he chose to work on the conservation of weight. The conservation of weight is, in fact, easy to study since there is a possible external reinforcement, that is, simply weighing the ball and the sausage on a balance. Then you can study the child's reactions to these external results. Smedslund studied the conservation of weight on the one hand, and on the other hand, he studied the transitivity of weights, that is, the transitivity of equalities if A = B and B = C, then A = C, or the transitivity of the equalities if A is less than B, and B is less than C, then A is less than C.

As far as conservation is concerned, Smedslund succeeded very easily with five- and six-year-old children in getting them to generalize that weight is conserved when the ball is transformed into a different shape. The child sees the ball transformed into a sausage or into little pieces or into a pancake or into any other form, he weighs it, and he sees that it is always the same thing. He will affirm it will be the same thing, no matter what you do to it; it will come out to be the same weight. Thus Smedslund very easily achieved the conservation of weight by this sort of external reinforcement.

In contrast to this, however, the same method did not succeed in teaching transitivity. The children resisted the notion of transitivity. A child would predict correctly in certain cases but he would make his prediction as a possibility or a probability and not as a certainty. There was never this generalized certainty in the case of transitivity.

So there is the first example, which seems to me very instructive, because in this problem in the conservation of weight there are two aspects. There is the physical aspect and there is the logical-mathematical aspect. Note that Smedslund started his study by establishing that there was a correlation between conservation and transitivity. He began by making a statistical study on the relationships between the spontaneous responses to the questions about conservation and the spontaneous responses to the questions about transitivity, and he found a very significant correlation. But in the learning experiment, he obtained a learning of conservation and not of transitivity. Consequently, he was successful in obtaining learning of what I called earlier physical experience (this is not surprising; it is simply a question of noting facts about objects) but he was not successful in obtaining a learning in the construction of the logical structure. This doesn't surprise me either, since the logical structure is not the result of physical experience. It cannot be obtained by external reinforcement. The logical structure is reached only through internal equilibration, by self-regulation, and the external reinforcement of seeing the balance did not suffice to establish this logical structure of transitivity.

I could give many other comparable examples, but it seems to me useless to insist upon these negative examples. Now I should like to show that learning is possible in the case of these logical-mathematical structures, but on one condition—that is, that the structure which you want to teach to the subjects can be supported by simpler, more elementary, logical-mathematical structures. I shall give you an example. It is the example of the conservation of number in the case of one-to-one correspondence. If you give a child seven blue tokens and ask him to put down as many red tokens, there is a pre-operational stage where he will put one red one opposite each blue one. But when you spread out the red ones, making them into a longer row, he will say to you, "Now, there are more red ones than there are blue ones."

Now how can we accelerate, if you want to accelerate, the acquisition of this conservation of num-

ber? Well, you can imagine an analogous structure but in a simpler, more elementary, situation. For example, with Mlle. Inhelder, we have been studying recently the notion of one-to-one correspondence by giving the child two glasses of the same shape and a big pile of beads. The child puts a bead into one glass with one hand and at the same time a bead into the other glass with the other hand. Time after time he repeats this action, a bead into one glass with one hand and at the same time a bead into the other glass with the other hand and he sees that there is always the same amount on each side. Then you hide one of the glasses. You cover it up. He no longer sees this glass but he continues to put one bead into it while putting at the same time one bead into the other glass which he can see. Then you ask him whether the equality has been conserved, whether there is still the same amount in one glass as in the other. Now you will find that very small children, about four years old, don't want to make a prediction. They will say, "So far, it has been the same amount, but now I don't know. I can't see anymore, so I don't know." They do not want to generalize. But the generalization is made from the age of about five and one-half years.

This is in contrast to the case of the red and blue tokens with one row spread out, where it isn't until seven or eight years of age that children will say there are the same number in the two rows. As one example of this generalization, I recall a little boy of five years and nine months who had been adding the beads to the glasses for a little while. Then we asked him whether, if he continued to do this all day and all night and all the next day, there would always be the same amount in the two glasses. The little boy gave this admirable reply, "Once you know, you know for always." In other words, this was recursive reasoning. So here the child does acquire the structure in this specific case. The number is a synthesis of class inclusion and ordering. This synthesis is being favored by the child's own actions. You have set up a situation where there is an iteration of one same action which continues and which is therefore ordered while at the same time being inclusive. You have, so to speak, a localized synthesis of inclusion and ordering which facilitates the construction of the idea of number in this specific case, and there you can find, in effect, an influence of this experience on the other experience. However, this influence is not immediate. We study the generalization from this recursive situation to the other situation where the tokens are laid on the table in rows, and it is not an immediate generalization but it is made possible through intermediaries. In other words, you can find some learning of this structure if you base the learning on simpler structures.

In this same area of the development of numerical

structures, the psychologist Joachim Wohlwill, who spent a year at our Institute at Geneva, has also shown that this acquisition can be accelerated through introducing additive operations, which is what we introduced also in the experiment which I just described. Wohlwill introduced them in a different way but he too was able to obtain a certain learning effect. In other words, learning is possible if you base the more complex structure on simpler structures, that is, when there is a natural relationship and development of structures and not simply an external reinforcement.

Now I would like to take a few minutes to conclude what I was saying. My first conclusion is that learning of structures seems to obey the same laws as the natural development of these structures. In other words, learning is subordinated to development and not vice-versa as I said in the introduction. No doubt you will object that some investigators have succeeded in teaching operational structures. But, when I am faced with these facts, I always have three questions which I want to have answered before I am convinced.

The first question is, "Is this learning lasting? What remains two weeks or a month later?" If a structure develops spontaneously, once it has reached a state of equilibrium, it is lasting, it will continue throughout the child's entire life. When you achieve the learning by external reinforcement, is the result lasting or not and what are the conditions necessary for it to be lasting?

The second question is, "How much generalization is possible?" What makes learning interesting is the possibility of transfer of a generalization. When you have brought about some learning, you can always ask whether this is an isolated piece in the midst of the child's mental life, or if it is really a dynamic structure which can lead to generalizations.

Then there is the third question, "In the case of each learning experience what was the operational level of the subject before the experience and what more complex structures has this learning succeeded in achieving?" In other words, we must look at each specific learning experience from the point of view of the spontaneous operations which were present at the outset and the operational level which has been achieved after the learning experience.

My second conclusion is that the fundamental relation involved in all development and all learning is not the relation of association. In the stimulus-response schema, the relation between the response and the stimulus is understood to be one of association. In contrast to this, I think that the fundamental relation is one of assimilation. Assimilation is not the same as association. I shall define assimilation as the integra-

tion of any sort of reality into a structure, and it is this assimilation which seems to me fundamental in learning, and which seems to me the fundamental relation from the point of view of pedagogical or didactic applications. All of my remarks today represent the child and the learning subject as active. An operation is an activity. Learning is possible only when there is active assimilation. It is this activity on the part of the subject which seems to me underplayed in the stimulus-response schema. The presentation which I propose puts the emphasis on the idea of self-regulation, on assimilation. All the emphasis is placed on the activity of the subject himself, and I think that without this activity there is no possible didactic or pedagogy which significantly transforms the subject.

Finally, and this will be my last concluding remark, I would like to comment on an excellent publication by the psychologist Berlyne. Berlyne spent a year with us in Geneva during which he intended to translate our results on the development of operations into stimulus-response language, specifically into Hull's learning theory. Berlyne published in our series of studies of genetic epistemology a very good article on this comparison between the results of Geneva and Hull's theory. In the same volume, I published a commentary on Berlyne's results. Now the essence of Berlyne's results is this: our findings can very well be translated into Hullian language, but only on condition that two modifications are introduced. Berlyne himself found these modifications quite considerable, but they seemed to him to concern more the conceptualization than the Hullian theory itself. I'm not so sure about that. The two modifications are these. First of all, Berlyne wants to distinguish two sorts of responses in the S-R schema. First, responses in the ordinary, classical sense, which I shall call "copy responses," and secondly, what Berlyne called "transformation responses." Transformation responses consist of transforming one response of the first type into another response of the first type. These transformation responses are what I call operations, and you can see right away that this is a rather serious modification of Hull's conceptualization because here you are introducing an element of transformation and thus of assimilation and no longer the simple association of stimulus-response theory.

The second modification which Berlyne introduces into the stimulus-response language is the introduction of what he calls internal reinforcements. What are these internal reinforcements? They are what I call equilibration or self-regulation. The internal reinforcements are what enable the subject to eliminate contradictions, incompatibilities, and conflicts. All development is composed of momentary conflicts and incompatibilities which must be overcome to reach a higher level of equilibrium. Berlyne calls this elimination of incompatibilities internal reinforcements.

So you see that it is indeed a stimulus-response theory, if you will, but first you add operations and then you add equilibration. That's all we want!

Editor's note: A brief question and answer period followed Professor Piaget's presentation. The first question related to the fact that the eight-year-old child acquires conservation of substance prior to conservation of weight and volume. The question asked if this didn't contradict the order of emergence of the pre-operational and operational stages. Piaget's response follows:

The conservation of weight and the conservation of volume are not due only to experience. There is also involved a logical framework which is characterized by reversibility and the system of compensations. I am only saying that in the case of weight and volume, weight corresponds to a perception. There is an empirical contact. The same is true of volume. But in the case of substance, I don't see how there can be any perception of substance independent of weight or volume. The strange thing is that this notion of substance comes before the two other notions. Note that in the history of thought, we have the same thing. The first Greek physicists, the pre-socratic philosophers, discovered conservation of substance independently of any experience. I do not believe this is contradictory with the theory of operations. This conservation of substance is simply the affirmation that something must be conserved. The children don't know specifically what is conserved. They know that since the sausage can become a ball again there must be something which is conserved, and saying "substance" is simply a way of translating this logical necessity for conservation. But this logical necessity results directly from the discovery of operations. I do not think that this is contradictory with the theory of development.

Editor's note: The second question was whether or not the development of stages in children's thinking could be accelerated by practice, training, and exercise in perception and memory. Piaget's response follows:

I am not very sure that exercise of perception and memory would be sufficient. I think that we must distinguish within the cognitive function two very different aspects which I shall call the figurative aspect and the operative aspect. The figurative aspect deals with static configurations. In physical reality there are states, and in addition to these there are transformations which lead from one state to another. In cognitive functioning one has the figurative aspects—for example, perception, imitation, mental imagery, etc.

Secondly, there is the operative aspect, including operations and the actions which lead from one state to another. In children of the higher stages and in adults, the figurative aspects are subordinated to the operative aspects. Any given state is understood to be the result of some transformation and the point of departure for another transformation. But the pre-operational child does not understand transformations. He does not have the operations necessary to understand them so he puts all the emphasis on the static quality of the states. It is because of this, for example, that in the conservation experiments he simply compares the initial state and the final state without being concerned with the transformation.

In exercising perception and memory, I feel that you will reinforce the figurative aspect without touching the operative aspect. Consequently, I'm not sure that this will accelerate the development of cognitive structures. What needs to be reinforced is the operative aspect—not the analysis of states, but the understanding of transformations.

5

Interaction Between Learning and Development

LEV S. VYGOTSKY

Editor's Note: Please see the introduction to the previous article on Piaget for editorial comments on this related paper.

The problems encountered in the psychological analysis of teaching cannot be correctly resolved or even formulated without addressing the relation between learning and development in school-age children. Yet it is the most unclear of all the basic issues on which the application of child development theories to educational processes depends. Needless to say, the lack of theoretical clarity does not mean that the issue is removed altogether from current research efforts into learning; not one study can avoid this central theoretical issue. But the relation between learning and development remains methodologically unclear because concrete research studies have embodied theoretically vague, critically unevaluated, and sometimes internally contradictory postulates, premises, and peculiar solutions to the problem of this fundamental relationship; and these, of course, result in a variety of errors.

Essentially, all current conceptions of the relation between development and learning in children can be reduced to three major theoretical positions.

The first centers on the assumption that processes of child development are independent of learning. Learning is considered a purely external process that is not actively involved in development. It merely utilizes the achievements of development rather than providing an impetus for modifying its course.

In experimental investigations of the development of thinking in school children, it has been assumed that processes such as deduction and understanding, evolution of notions about the world, interpretation of physical causality, and mastery of logical forms of thought and abstract logic all occur by themselves, without any influence from school learning. An example of such a theory is Piaget's extremely complex and interesting theoretical principles, which also shape the experimental methodology he employs. The questions Piaget uses in the course of his "clinical

This article is reprinted with permission of Harvard University Press, from L. S. Vygotsky, 1978, *Mind in Society*. Cambridge, MA: Harvard University Press, 79–91.

conversations" with children clearly illustrate his approach. When a five-year-old is asked "why doesn't the sun fall?" it is assumed that the child has neither a ready answer for such a question nor the general capabilities for generating one. The point of asking questions that are so far beyond the reach of the child's intellectual skills is to eliminate the influence of previous experience and knowledge. The experimenter seeks to obtain the tendencies of children's thinking in "pure" form entirely independent of learning.[1]

Similarly, the classics of psychological literature, such as the works by Binet and others, assume that development is always a prerequisite for learning and that if a child's mental functions (intellectual operations) have not matured to the extent that he is capable of learning a particular subject, then no instruction will prove useful. They especially feared premature instruction, the teaching of a subject before the child was ready for it. All effort was concentrated on finding the lower threshold of learning ability, the age at which a particular kind of learning first becomes possible.

Because this approach is based on the premise that learning trails behind development, that development always outruns learning, it precludes the notion that learning may play a role in the course of the development or maturation of those functions activated in the course of learning. Development or maturation is viewed as a precondition of learning but never the result of it. To summarize this position: learning forms a superstructure over development, leaving the latter essentially unaltered.

The second major theoretical position is that learning is development. This identity is the essence of a group of theories that are quite diverse in origin.

One such theory is based on the concept of reflex, an essentially old notion that has been extensively revived recently. Whether reading, writing, or arithmetic is being considered, development is viewed as the mastery of conditioned reflexes; that is, the process of learning is completely and inseparably blended with the process of development. This notion was elaborated by James, who reduced the learning process to habit formation and identified the learning process with development.

Reflex theories have at least one thing in common with theories such as Piaget's: in both, development is conceived of as the elaboration and substitution of innate responses. As James expressed it, "Education, in short, cannot be better described than by calling it the organization of acquired habits of conduct and tendencies to behavior."[2] Development itself is reduced primarily to the accumulation of all possible responses. Any acquired response is considered either a more complex form of or a substitute for the innate response.

But despite the similarity between the first and second theoretical positions, there is a major difference in their assumptions about the temporal relationship between learning and developmental processes. Theorists who hold the first view assert that developmental cycles precede learning cycles; maturation precedes learning and instruction must lag behind mental growth. For the second group of theorists, both processes occur simultaneously; learning and development coincide at all points in the same way that two identical geometrical figures coincide when superimposed.

The third theoretical position on the relation between learning and development attempts to overcome the extremes of the other two by simply combining them. A clear example of this approach is Koffka's theory, in which development is based on two inherently different but related processes, each of which influences the other.[3] On the one hand is maturation, which depends directly on the development of the nervous system; on the other hand is learning, which itself is also a developmental process.

Three aspects of this theory are new. First, as we already noted, is the combination of two seemingly opposite viewpoints, each of which has been encountered separately in the history of science. The very fact that these two viewpoints can be combined into one theory indicates that they are not opposing and mutually exclusive but have something essential in common. Also new is the idea that the two processes that make up development are mutually dependent and interactive. Of course, the nature of the interaction is left virtually unexplored in Koffka's work, which is limited solely to very general remarks regarding the relation between these two processes. It is clear that for Koffka the process of maturation prepares and makes possible a specific process of learning. The learning process then stimulates and pushes forward the maturation process. The third and most important new aspect of this theory is the expanded role it ascribes to learning in child development. This emphasis leads us directly to an old pedagogical problem, that of formal discipline and the problem of transfer.

Pedagogical movements that have emphasized formal discipline and urged the teaching of classical languages, ancient civilizations, and mathematics have assumed that regardless of the irrelevance of these particular subjects for daily living, they were of the greatest value for the pupil's mental development. A variety of studies have called into question the soundness of this idea. It has been shown that learning in one area has very little influence on overall development. For example, reflex theorists Woodworth and Thorndike found that adults who, after special exercises, had achieved considerable success in determining the length of short lines, had made virtually no progress in their ability to determine the length of long lines. These same adults were successfully trained to estimate the size of a given two-dimensional figure, but this training did not make them successful in estimating the size of a series of other two-dimensional figures of various sizes and shapes.

According to Thorndike, theoreticians in psychology and education believe that every particular response acquisition directly enhances overall ability in equal measure.[4] Teachers believed and acted on the basis of the theory that the mind is a complex of abilities—powers of observation, attention, memory, thinking, and so forth—and that any improvement in any specific ability results in a general improvement in all abilities. According to this theory, if the student increased the attention he paid to Latin grammar, he would increase his abilities to focus attention on any task. The words "accuracy," "quick-wittedness," "ability to reason," "memory," "power of observation," "attention," "concentration," and so forth are said to denote actual fundamental capabilities that vary in accordance with the material with which they operate; these basic abilities are substantially modified by studying particular subjects, and they retain these modifications when they turn to other areas. Therefore, if someone learns to do any single thing well, he will also be able to do other entirely unrelated things well as a result of some secret connection. It is assumed that mental capabilities function independently of the material with which they operate, and that the development of one ability entails the development of others.

Thorndike himself opposed this point of view. Through a variety of studies he showed that particular forms of activity, such as spelling, are dependent on the mastery of specific skills and material necessary for the performance of that particular task. The development of one particular capability seldom means the development of others. Thorndike argued that specialization of abilities is even greater than superficial observation may indicate. For example, if, out of a hundred individuals we choose ten who display the ability to detect spelling errors or to measure lengths, it is unlikely that these ten will display better abilities regarding, for example, the estimation of the weight of objects. In the same way, speed and accuracy in adding numbers are entirely unrelated to speed and accuracy in being able to think up antonyms.

This research shows that the mind is not a complex network of general capabilities such as observation, attention, memory, judgment, and so forth, but a set of specific capabilities, each of which is, to some extent, independent of the others and is developed independently. Learning is more than the acquisition of the ability to think; it is the acquisition of many specialized abilities for thinking about a variety of things. Learning does not alter our overall ability to focus attention but rather develops various abilities to focus attention on a variety of things. According to this view, special training affects overall development only when its elements, material, and processes are similar across specific domains; habit governs us. This leads to the conclusion that because each activity depends on the material with which it operates, the development of consciousness is the development of a set of particular, independent capabilities or of a set of particular habits. Improvement of one function of consciousness or one aspect of its activity can affect the development of another only to the extent that there are elements common to both functions or activities.

Developmental theorists such as Koffka and the Gestalt School—who hold to the third theoretical position outlined earlier—oppose Thorndike's point of view. They assert that the influence of learning is never specific. From their study of structural principles, they argue that the learning process can never be reduced simply to the formation of skills but embodies an intellectual order that makes it possible to transfer general principles discovered in solving one task to a variety of other tasks. From this point of view, the child, while learning a particular operation, acquires the ability to create structures of a certain type, regardless of the diverse materials with which she is working and regardless of the particular elements involved. Thus, Koffka does not conceive of learning as limited to a process of habit and skill acquisition. The relationship he posits between learning and development is not that of an identity but of a more complex relationship. According to Thorndike, learning and development coincide at all points, but for Koffka, development is always a larger set than learning. Schematically, the relationship between the two processes could be depicted by two concentric circles, the smaller symbolizing the learning process and the larger the developmental process evoked by learning.

Once a child has learned to perform an operation, he thus assimilates some structural principle whose sphere of application is other than just the operations of the type on whose basis the principle was assimilated. Consequently, in making one step in learning, a child makes two steps in development, that is, learning and development do not coincide. This concept is the essential aspect of the third group of theories we have discussed.

ZONE OF PROXIMAL DEVELOPMENT: A NEW APPROACH

Although we reject all three theoretical positions discussed above, analyzing them leads us to a more adequate view of the relation between learning and development. The question to be framed in arriving at a solution to this problem is complex. It consists of two separate issues: first, the general relation between learning and development; and second, the specific features of this relationship when children reach school age.

That children's learning begins long before they attend school is the starting point of this discussion. Any learning a child encounters in school always has a previous history. For example, children begin to study arithmetic in school, but long beforehand they have had some experience with quantity—they have had to deal with operations of division, addition, subtraction, and determination of size. Consequently, children have their own preschool arithmetic, which only myopic psychologists could ignore.

It goes without saying that learning as it occurs in the preschool years differs markedly from school learning, which is concerned with the assimilation of the fundamentals of scientific knowledge. But even when, in the period of her first questions, a child assimilates the names of objects in her environment, she is learning. Indeed, can it be doubted that children learn speech from adults; or that, through asking questions and giving answers, children acquire a variety of information; or that, through imitating adults and through being instructed about how to act, children develop an entire repository of skills? Learning and development are interrelated from the child's very first day of life.

Koffka, attempting to clarify the laws of child learning and their relation to mental development, concentrates his attention on the simplest learning processes, those that occur in the preschool years. His error is that, while seeing a similarity between preschool and school learning, he fails to discern the difference—he does not see the specifically new elements that school learning introduces. He and others assume that the difference between preschool and school learning consists of non-systematic learning in one case and systematic learning in the other. But "systematicness" is not the only issue; there is also the fact that school learning introduces something fundamentally new into the child's development. In order to elaborate the dimensions of school learning, we will describe a new and exceptionally important concept without which the issue cannot be resolved: the zone of proximal development.

A well known and empirically established fact is that learning should be matched in some manner with the child's developmental level. For example, it has been established that the teaching of reading, writing, and arithmetic should be initiated at a specific age level. Only recently, however, has attention been directed to the fact that we cannot limit ourselves merely to determining developmental levels if we wish to discover the actual relations of the developmental process to learning capabilities. We must determine at least two developmental levels.

The first level can be called the *actual developmental level*, that is, the level of development of a child's mental functions that has been established as a result of certain already completed developmental cycles. When we determine a child's mental age by using tests, we are almost always dealing with the actual developmental level. In studies of children's mental development it is generally assumed that only those things that children can do on their own are indicative of mental abilities. We give children a battery of tests or a variety of tasks of varying degrees of difficulty, and we judge the extent of their mental development on the basis of how they solve them and at what level of difficulty. On the other hand, if we offer leading questions or show how the problem is to be solved and the child then solves it, or if the teacher initiates the solution and the child completes it or solves it in collaboration with other children—in short, if the child barely misses an independent solution of the problem—the solution is not regarded as indicative of his mental development. This "truth" was familiar and reinforced by common sense. Over a decade even the profoundest thinkers never questioned the assumption; they never entertained the notion that what children can do with the assistance of others might be in some sense even more indicative of their mental development than what they can do alone.

Let us take a simple example. Suppose I investigate two children upon entrance into school, both of whom are ten years old chronologically and eight years old in terms of mental development. Can I say that they are the same age mentally? Of course. What does this mean? It means that they can independently deal with tasks up to the degree of difficulty that has been standardized for the eight-year-old level. If I stop at this point, people would imagine that the subsequent course of mental development and of school learning for these children will be the same, because it depends on their intellect. Of course, there may be other factors, for example, if one child was sick for half a year while the other was never absent from school; but generally speaking, the fate of these children should be the same. Now imagine that I do not terminate my study at this point, but only begin it. These children seem to be capable of handling problems up to an eight-year-old's level, but not beyond that. Suppose that I show them various ways of dealing with the problem. Different experimenters might employ different modes of demonstration in different cases: some might run through an entire demonstration and ask the children to repeat it, others might initiate the solution and ask the child to finish it, or offer leading questions. In short, in some way or another I propose that the children solve the problem with my assistance. Under these circumstances it turns out that the first child can deal with problems up to a twelve-year-old's level, the second up to a nine-year-old's. Now, are these children mentally the same?

When it was first shown that the capability of children with equal levels of mental development to learn under a teacher's guidance varied to a high degree, it became apparent that those children were not mentally the same age and that the subsequent course of their learning would obviously be different. This difference between twelve and eight, or between nine and eight, is what we call *the zone of proximal development. It is the distance between the actual developmental level as determined by independent problem solving and the level of potential development as determined through problem solving under adult guidance or in collaboration with more capable peers.*

If we naively ask what the actual developmental level is, or, to put it more simply, what more independent problem solving reveals, the most common answer would be that a child's actual developmental level defines functions that have already matured, that is, the end products of development. If a child can do such-and-such independently, it means that the functions for such-and-such have matured in her. What, then, is defined by the zone of proximal development, as determined through problems that children cannot solve independently but only with assistance? The zone of proximal development defines those functions that have not yet matured but are in the process of maturation, functions that will mature tomorrow but are currently in an embryonic state. These functions could be termed the "buds" or "flowers" of development rather than the "fruits" of development. The actual developmental level characterizes mental development retrospectively, while the zone of proximal development characterizes mental development prospectively.

The zone of proximal development furnishes psychologists and educators with a tool through which the internal course of development can be understood. By using this method we can take account of not only the cycles and maturation processes that have already been completed but also those processes that are currently in a state of formation, that are just beginning to mature and develop. Thus, the zone of proximal development permits us to delineate the child's immediate future and his dynamic developmental state, allowing not only for what already has been achieved developmentally but also for what is in the course of maturing. The two children in our example displayed the same mental age from the viewpoint of developmental cycles already completed, but the developmental dynamics of the two were entirely different. The state of a child's mental development can be determined only by clarifying its two levels: the actual developmental level and the zone of proximal development.

I will discuss one study of preschool children to demonstrate that what is in the zone of proximal development today will be the actual developmental level tomorrow—that is, what a child can do with assistance today she will be able to do by herself tomorrow.

The American researcher Dorothea McCarthy showed that among children between the ages of three and five there are two groups of functions: those the children already possess, and those they can perform under guidance, in groups, and in collaboration with one another but which they have not mastered independently. McCarthy's study demonstrated that this second group of functions is at the actual developmental level of five-to-seven-year-olds. What her subjects could do only under guidance, in collaboration, and in groups at the age of three-to-five years they could do independently when they reached the age of five-to-seven years.[5] Thus, if we were to determine only mental age—that is, only functions that have matured—we would have but a summary of completed development while if we determine the maturing functions, we can predict what will happen to these children between five and seven, provided the same developmental conditions are maintained. The zone of proximal development can become a powerful concept in developmental research, one that can markedly enhance the effectiveness and utility of the application of diagnostics of mental development to educational problems.

A full understanding of the concept of the zone of proximal development must result in reevaluation of the role of imitation in learning. An unshakable tenet of classical psychology is that only the independent activity of children, not their imitative activity, indicates their level of mental development. This view is expressed in all current testing systems. In evaluating mental development, consideration is given to only those solutions to test problems which the child reaches without the assistance of others, without demonstrations, and without leading questions. Imitation and learning are thought of as purely mechanical processes. But recently psychologists have shown that a person can imitate only that which is within her developmental level. For example, if a child is having difficulty with a problem in arithmetic and the teacher solves it on the blackboard, the child may grasp the solution in an instant. But if the teacher were to solve a problem in higher mathematics, the child would not be able to understand the solution no matter how many times she imitated it.

Animal psychologists, and in particular Köhler, have dealt with this question of imitation quite well.[6] Köhler's experiments sought to determine whether primates are capable of graphic thought. The principal question was whether primates solved problems independently or whether they merely imitated solutions they had seen performed earlier, for example, watching other animals or humans use sticks and other tools and then imitating them. Köhler's special experiments, designed to determine what primates could imitate, reveal that primates can use imitation to solve only those problems that are of the same degree of difficulty as those they can solve alone. However, Köhler failed to take account of an important fact, namely, that primates cannot be taught (in the human sense of the word) through imitation, nor can their intellect be developed, because they have no zone of proximal development. A primate can learn a great deal through training by using its mechanical and mental skills, but it cannot be made more intelligent, that is, it cannot be taught to solve a variety of more advanced problems independently. For this reason animals are incapable of learning in the human sense of the term; *human learning presupposes a specific social nature and a process by which children grow into the intellectual life of those around them.*

Children can imitate a variety of actions that go well beyond the limits of their own capabilities. Using imitation, children are capable of doing much more in collective activity or under the guidance of adults. This fact, which seems to be of little significance in itself, is of fundamental importance in that it demands a radical alteration of the entire doctrine concerning the relation between learning and development in children. One direct consequence is a change in conclusions that may be drawn from diagnostic tests of development.

Formerly, it was believed that by using tests, we determine the mental development level with which education should reckon and whose limits it should not exceed. This procedure oriented learning toward yesterday's development, toward developmental stages already completed. The error of this view was discovered earlier in practice than in theory. It is demonstrated most clearly in the teaching of mentally retarded children. Studies have established that mentally retarded children are not very capable of abstract thinking. From this the pedagogy of the special school drew the seemingly correct conclusion that all

teaching of such children should be based on the use of concrete, look-and-do methods. And yet a considerable amount of experience with this method resulted in profound disillusionment. It turned out that a teaching system based solely on concreteness—one that eliminated from teaching everything associated with abstract thinking—not only failed to help retarded children overcome their innate handicaps but also reinforced their handicaps by accustoming children exclusively to concrete thinking and thus suppressing the rudiments of any abstract thought that such children still have. Precisely because retarded children, when left to themselves, will never achieve well-elaborated forms of abstract thought, the school should make every effort to push them in that direction and to develop in them what is intrinsically lacking in their own development. In the current practices of special schools for retarded children, we can observe a beneficial shift away from this concept of concreteness, one that restores look-and-do methods to their proper role. Concreteness is now seen as necessary and unavoidable only as a stepping stone for developing abstract thinking—as a means, not as an end in itself.

Similarly, in normal children, learning which is oriented toward developmental levels that have already been reached is ineffective from the viewpoint of a child's overall development. It does not aim for a new stage of the developmental process but rather lags behind this process. Thus, the notion of a zone of proximal development enables us to propound a new formula, namely that the only "good learning" is that which is in advance of development.

The acquisition of language can provide a paradigm for the entire problem of the relation between learning and development. Language arises initially as a means of communication between the child and the people in his environment. Only subsequently, upon conversion to internal speech, does it come to organize the child's thought, that is, become an internal mental function. Piaget and others have shown that reasoning occurs in a children's group as an argument intended to prove one's own point of view before it occurs as an internal activity whose distinctive feature is that the child begins to perceive and check the basis of his thoughts. Such observa-tions prompted Piaget to conclude that communication produces the need for checking and confirming thoughts, a process that is characteristic of adult thought.[7] In the same way that internal speech and reflective thought arise from the interactions between the child and persons in her environment, these interactions provide the source of development of a child's voluntary behavior. Piaget has shown that cooperation provides the basis for the development of a child's moral judgment. Earlier research established that a child first becomes able to subordinate her behavior to rules in group play and only later does voluntary self-regulation of behavior arise as an internal function.

These individual examples illustrate a general developmental law for the higher mental functions that we feel can be applied in its entirety to children's learning processes. We propose that an essential feature of learning is that it creates the zone of proximal development; that is, learning awakens a variety of internal developmental processes that are able to operate only when the child is interacting with peo-ple in his environment and in cooperation with his peers. Once these processes are internalized, they become part of the child's independent developmental achievement.

From this point of view, learning is not development; however, properly organized learning results in mental development and sets in motion a variety of developmental processes that would be impossible apart from learning. Thus, learning is a necessary and universal aspect of the process of developing culturally organized, specifically human, psychological functions.

To summarize, the most essential feature of our hypothesis is the notion that developmental processes do not coincide with learning processes. Rather, the developmental process lags behind the learning process; this sequence then results in zones of proximal development. Our analysis alters the traditional view that at the moment a child assimilates the meaning of a word, or masters an operation such as addition or written language, her developmental processes are basically completed. In fact, they have only just begun at that moment. The major consequence of analyzing the educational process in this manner is to show that the initial mastery of, for example, the four arithmetic operations provides the basis for the subsequent development of a variety of highly complex internal processes in children's thinking.

Our hypothesis establishes the unity but not the identity of learning processes and internal developmental processes. It presupposes that the one is converted into the other. Therefore, it becomes an important concern of psychological research to show how external knowledge and abilities in children become internalized.

Any investigation explores some sphere of reality. An aim of the psychological analysis of development is to describe the internal relations of the intellectual processes awakened by school learning. In this respect, such analysis will be directed inward and is analogous to the use of x-rays. If successful, it should reveal to the teacher how developmental processes stimulated by the course of school learning are carried through inside the head of each individual child. The revelation of this internal, subterranean developmental network of school subjects is a task of primary importance for psychological and educational analysis.

A second essential feature of our hypothesis is the notion that, although learning is directly related to the course of child development, the two are never accomplished in equal measure or in parallel. Development in children never follows school learning the way a shadow follows the object that casts it. In actuality, there are highly complex dynamic relations between developmental and learning processes that cannot be encompassed by an unchanging hypothetical formulation.

Each school subject has its own specific relation to the course of child development, a relation that varies as the child goes from one stage to another. This leads us directly to a reexamination of the problem of formal discipline, that is, to the significance of each particular subject from the viewpoint of overall mental development. Clearly, the problem cannot be solved by using any one formula; extensive and highly diverse concrete research based on the concept of the zone of proximal development is necessary to resolve the issue.

Notes

1. J. Piaget, *The Language and Thought of the Child* (New York: Meridian Books, 1955).

2. William James, *Talks to Teachers* (New York: Norton, 1958), pp. 36–37.

3. Koffka, *The Growth of the Mind* (London: Routledge and Kegan Paul, 1924).

4. E. L. Thorndike, *The Psychology of Learning* (New York: Teachers College Press, 1914).

5. Dorothea McCarthy, *The Language Development of the Pre-school Child* (Minneapolis: University of Minnesota Press, 1930).

6. W. Köhler, *The Mentality of Apes* (New York: Harcourt, Brace, 1925).

7. Piaget, *Language and Thought.*

PART I

In the Beginning

6

On Heroes and Fools in Science

STEPHEN JAY GOULD

Science is often thought of as the accumulation of facts that reflect fixed universal processes that transcend historical periods. Scientific ideas and interpretations, however, like other methods of understanding, often reflect the times, values, and procedures that exist when the scientist works. In the following essay, Stephen Jay Gould discusses changing views on one of the key questions about development: How do biological forms arise? He documents how the early theory that later forms are contained in earlier ones (preformationism) gave way to the current theory that new forms arise in the process of change itself (epigenesis). Gould cautions us to resist the idea that earlier theories were necessarily foolish. In particular, he points out that the kernel of truth in preformationist ideas has been reaffirmed by modern research on the genetic code. For Gould, these past efforts should be understood within the terms of the epoch that helped produce them and also be valued for what they can teach us in our own time.

As a romantic teen-ager, I believed that my future life as a scientist would be justified if I could discover a single new fact and add a brick to the bright temple of human knowledge. The conviction was noble enough; the metaphor was simply silly. Yet that metaphor still governs the attitude of many scientists toward their subject.

In the conventional model of scientific "progress," we begin in superstitious ignorance and move toward final truth by the successive accumulation of facts. In this smug perspective, the history of science contains little more than anecdotal interest—for it can only chronicle past errors and credit the bricklayers for discerning glimpses of final truth. It is as transparent as an old-fashioned melodrama: truth (as we perceive it today) is the only arbiter and the world of past scientists is divided into good guys who were right and bad guys who were wrong.

Historians of science have utterly discredited this model during the past decade. Science is not a heartless pursuit of objective information. It is a creative human activity, its geniuses acting more as artists than as information processors. Changes in theory are not simply the derivative results of new discoveries but the work of creative imagination influenced by contemporary social and political forces. We should not judge the past through anachronistic spectacles of our own convictions—designating as heroes the scientists whom we judge to be right by criteria that had nothing to do with their own concerns. We are simply foolish if we call Anaximander (sixth century B.C.) an evolutionist because, in advocating a primary role for water among the four elements, he held that life first inhabited the sea; yet most textbooks so credit him.

In this essay, I will take the most notorious of textbook baddies and try to display their theory as both reasonable in its time and enlightening in our own. Our villains are the eighteenth century "preformationists," adherents to an outmoded embryology. According to the textbooks, preformationists believed that a perfect miniature homunculus inhabited the human egg (or sperm), and that embryological development involved nothing more than its increase in size. The absurdity of this claim, the texts continue, is enhanced by its necessary corollary of *emboîtement* or encasement—for if Eve's ovum contained a homunculus, then the ovum of that homunculus contained a tinier homunculus, and so on into the inconceivable—a fully formed human smaller than an electron. The preformationists must have been blind, antiempirical dogmatists supporting an *a priori* doctrine of immutability against clear evidence of the senses—for one only has to open a chicken's egg in order to watch an embryo develop from simplicity to complexity. Indeed, their leading spokesman, Charles Bonnet, had proclaimed that "preformationism is the greatest triumph of reason over the senses." The heroes of our textbooks, on the other hand, were the "epigeneticists"; they spent their time looking at eggs rather than inventing fantasies. They proved by observation that the complexity of adult form developed gradually in the embryo. By the mid-nineteenth century, they had triumphed. One more victory for unsullied observation over prejudice and dogma.

In reality, the story is not so simple. The preformationists were as careful and accurate in their empirical observations as the epigeneticist. Moreover, if heroes we must have, that honor might as well fall to the preformationists who upheld, against the epigeneticists, a view of science quite congenial with our own.

The imagination of a few peripheral figures must not be taken as the belief of an entire school. The great preformationists—Malpighi, Bonnet, and von Haller—all knew perfectly well that the chick embryo seemed to begin as a simple tube and become more and more complex as organs differentiated within the egg. They had studied and drawn the embryology of the chick in a series of astute observations that matched anything achieved by contemporary epigeneticists.

Preformationists and epigeneticists did not disagree about their observations; but, whereas epigeneticists were prepared to take those observations literally, the preformationists insisted on probing "behind appearance." They claimed that the visual manifestations of development were deceptive. The early embryo is so tiny, so gelatinous, and so transparent that the preformed structures could not be discerned by the crude microscopes then available. Bonnet wrote in 1762: "Do not mark the time when organized beings begin to exist by the time when they begin to become visible; and do not constrain nature by the strict limits of our senses and instruments." Moreover, the preformationists never believed that preformed structures were organized into a perfect miniature homunculus in the egg itself. The rudiments existed in the egg to be sure, but in relative positions and proportions bearing little relationship to adult morphology. Again, Bonnet in 1762: "While the chick is still a germ, all its parts have forms, proportions and positions which differ greatly from those that they will attain during development. If we were able to see the germ enlarged, as it is when small, it would be impossible for us to recognize it as a chick. All the parts of the germ do not develop at the same time and uniformly."

But how did the preformationists explain the *reductio ad absurdum* of encasement—the encapsulation of our entire history in the ovaries of Eve? Very simply—this concept was not absurd in an eighteenth-century context.

First of all, scientists believed that the world had existed—and would endure—for only a few thousand years. One had, therefore, to encapsulate only a limited number of generations, not the potential products of several million years on a twentieth-century geological time chart.

Secondly, the eighteenth century had no cell theory to set a lower boundary to organic size. It now seems absurd to postulate a fully formed homunculus smaller than the minimum size of a single cell. But an eighteenth-century scientist had no reason to postulate a lower limit to size. In fact, it was widely believed that Leeuwenhoek's animalcules, the single-celled microscopic creatures that had so aroused the imagination of Europe, had complete sets of miniature organs. Thus Bonnet, supporting the corpuscular theory (that light is made of discrete particles), rhapsodized about the inconceivable tininess of the several million globules of light that penetrate all at once into the supposed eyes of animalcules. "Nature works as small as it wishes. We know not at all the lower boundary of the division of matter, but we see that it has been prodigiously divided. From the elephant to the mite, from the whale to the animalcule 27 million times smaller than the mite, from the globe of the sun to the globule of light, what an inconceivable multitude of intermediate degrees!"

Why did the preformationists feel such a need to penetrate behind appearances? Why would they not accept the direct evidence of their senses? Consider the alternatives. Either the parts are present from the first or the fertilized egg is utterly formless. If the egg is formless, then some external force must unerringly impose a design upon matter only potentially capable of producing it. But what kind of a force could this be? And must there be a different force for each species of animal? How can we learn about it, test it, perceive it, touch it, or understand it? How could it represent any more than an insubstantial appeal to a mysterious and mystical vitalism?

Preformationism represented the best of Newtonian science. It was designed to save a general attitude, which we would recognize today as "scientific," from a vitalism that the evidence of raw sensation implied. If the egg were truly unorganized, homogeneous material without preformed parts, then how could it yield such wondrous complexity without a mysterious directing force? It does so, and can do so, only because the structure (not merely the raw material) needed to build this complexity already resides in the egg. In this light, Bonnet's statement about the triumph of reason over the senses seems itself more reasonable.

Finally, who can say that our current understanding of embryology marks the triumph of epigenesis? Most great debates are resolved at Aristotle's golden mean, and this is no exception. From our perspective today, the epigeneticists were right; organs differentiate sequentially from simpler rudiments during embryological development; there are no preformed parts. But the preformationists were also right in insisting that complexity cannot arise from formless raw material—that there must be something within the egg to regulate its development. All we can say (as if it mattered) is that they incorrectly identified this "something" as preformed parts, where we now understand it as encoded instructions built of DNA. But what else could we expect from eighteenth-century scientists, who knew nothing of the player piano, not to mention the computer program? The idea of a coded program was not part of their intellectual equipment.

And, come to think of it, what could be more fantastic than the claim that an egg contains thousands of instructions, written on molecules that tell the cell to turn on and off the production of certain substances that regulate the speed of chemical processes? The notion of preformed parts sounds far less contrived to me. The only thing going for coded instructions is that they seem to be there.

7

Developmental Theories for the 1990s: Development and Individual Differences

SANDRA SCARR

A primary goal of psychology as a scientific discipline is to understand individual variation; developmental psychology, a particular branch of this discipline, focuses on the processes of growth and change. In order to learn about these processes, psychologists collect data from large groups of people and use statistics in the hope of discovering typical, or normative, psychological patterns by averaging across individuals. Although this approach seems sensible, it tends to obscure individual patterns. Individual patterns of growth are unique in many ways and are, therefore, not represented by "typical development." In this article Sandra Scarr discusses the strengths and weaknesses of normative and individual-differences approaches to development by examining genetic and environmental contributions to growth. She argues that an evolutionary perspective may increase our understanding of both typical and individual patterns of development. An important point emphasized by Scarr is that the relationship between genetic and environmental contributions in development is not simple. Individuals contribute to the environments in which their development occurs, and thus the psychological character of these situations is influenced by inherited characteristics.

Reprinted with permission from *Child Development*, *63*, 1992, 1–19. Copyright 1992 by the Society for Research in Child Development.

Presidential address to the biennial meetings of the Society for Research in Child Development, April 20, 1991, Seattle, WA. Requests for the paper may be sent to Sandra Scarr, Department of Psychology, Gilmer Hall, University of Virginia, Charlottesville, VA 22903. My thanks to Anne Ricciuti, with whom I have coauthored a chapter from which some of this address is taken (Scarr & Ricciuti, in press). For the past 20 years, Richard A. Weinberg has been my collaborator and friend. It is impossible to thank him enough for all of the synergy that we have found in our research, writing, and mutual understandings.

Understanding both typical human development and individual differences within the same theoretical framework has been difficult because the two orientations arise from different philosophical traditions. It is argued that an evolutionary perspective can unite the study of both species-typical development and individual variation. Research on determinants of development from many perspectives can be understood within an evolutionary framework in which organism and environment combine to produce development. Species-normal genes and environments and individual variations in genes and environments both affect personality, social, and intellectual development. These domains are used as examples to integrate theories of normal development and individual differences. Within the usual samples of European, North American, and developed Asian countries, the results of family and twin studies show that environments within the normal species range are crucial to normal development. Given a wide range of environmental opportunities and emotional supports, however, most children in these societies grow up to be individually different based on their individual genotypes. Understanding the ways in which genes and environments work together helps developmentalists to identify children in need of intervention and to tailor interventions to their particular needs.

Not long ago, most developmentalists believed the major purpose of their research was to discover eternal laws about human development—laws that could apply to all of the people all of the time. *Nomothetic* laws about human development focus on universal sequences and their contexts. At the same time, a smaller group of developmentalists focused its research on individual variation in development and on *idiographic* developmental patterns—patterns that are unique to individuals.[1]

The history of the two orientations to research can be traced to what Cronbach (1957) called "the two disciplines of scientific psychology." Psychology's two scientific disciplines have their parallel in Ernst Mayr's contrast of typological and population approaches in biology. The study of the typical human is philosophically Platonic: Although individual differences within species are observed, they are considered merely unimportant variations on the ideal type. Understanding the "true" nature of development means to abstract typical patterns and to ignore

variations. Population theories have their roots in Darwin and evolutionary theory. Variation within species is what exists and must be understood. Developmental patterns are unique to individuals; the causes of these differences are central to developmental research.

I propose that it is possible now to incorporate both typical development and individual variations on typical patterns in new theories that describe and explain human development as both typically human and uniquely so. The first requirement of any scientific theory is that it account for observations to which nearly everyone can agree, the second that its explanatory principles do not violate assumptions of causality held by most scientists (e. g., temporal order of events), and the third that the theory must be scientifically persuasive to one's peers (Scarr, 1985). It is only on the last that I fear my theory may fail.

I argue that most developmental theories today are unnecessarily limited in the observations they subsume and that they seldom address issues of causality in development and individual variations with the same concepts. The underlying question that has motivated my research for 25 years is, "How do organisms and environments combine to produce human development and the many variations on that theme?" I hope to persuade you that developmental theories can and should address this question.

Observations and Inferences

First, some common observations to subsume. Both parents and psychologists observe pervasive correlations between characteristics of parents, the environments they provide, and their children's outcomes. Both parents and psychologists make causal attributions on the basis of those correlations: They believe that differences in parental behaviors and environments cause differences in children's outcomes. The construction of causal inferences from the web of parent–child correlations is fraught with logical and scientific problems (Scarr, 1985).

Ever since Bell's (1968) seminal paper on children's effect on their own environments, as well as the reverse effect, numerous studies have shown that, indeed, children do have an effect on the behavior of their caregivers (e.g., Bell & Harper, 1977; Breitmayer & Ricciuti, 1988; Lytton, 1980; McCartney, in press). Using a variety of research designs and outcome measures, these studies all have demonstrated that, rather than being passive recipients of care, in-

---
[1] Unless they are identical twins.

fants and children are active, influential partners in their interactions with the people around them. The notion that parental behaviors cause all observed differences among children is thus called into question.

European psychologists have for the last decade investigated the participation of young people in their own development (e.g., Magnusson, Stattin, & Allen, 1985; Silbereisen & Noack, 1988). Action theory incorporates the idea that people influence in important ways the course of their development through choices across time. The theory presented here is consonant with this line of theory and inquiry.

It is proposed here that each child constructs a reality from the opportunities afforded by the rearing environment, and that the constructed reality does have considerable influence on variations among children and differences in their adult outcomes.

CONSTRUCTING EXPERIENCES FROM ENVIRONMENTS

The idea that people make their own environments (Scarr & McCartney, 1983) runs counter to the mainstream of developmental psychology. A large base of literature examining the relations between familial, parental, and child characteristics has found that these characteristics are, indeed, related to each other. Developmental psychologists most often interpret these findings as evidence that the rearing conditions that parents provide for their children make differences in the children's life chances and eventual adult statuses—both socioeconomic achievements and mental health. Thus, although some developmentalists have suggested that children may affect their environments as well as vice versa (Bell, 1968), the theory that children actually construct their own environments challenges the basic tenets of much of mainstream developmental psychology.

The idea that children create their own experiences from the environments they encounter also challenges parents' beliefs about their impact on their children's development. After all, most parents invest tremendous efforts in rearing their children—efforts that involve emotional, personal, and financial sacrifices for the parents. If parents can be given accurate information about how much influence they might or might not have on their children's development, it might help alleviate needless sacrifices and emotional turmoil on their part.

How people make the transitions from age to age and stage to stage in life is the most fascinating longitudinal study in all of behavioral science. Accurate information about the extent to which differences between families contribute to differences between children is particularly important for the design and implementation of timely and effective intervention programs for at-risk children and families. Thus, although the theory that children construct their own environments challenges widely held ideas about families and children, it is important to consider and evaluate it, given available data.

Causal assumptions about the direction of effects between parental behavior and children's outcomes have been called into question even more strongly by research over the past 20 years in the field of developmental behavior genetics. Behavioral genetic methods are used to investigate the sources of individual variation in a population (Plomin, 1986). The focus is on what makes individuals different from one another, not on the causes of the particular mean value of a trait in a population. By studying family members with varying degrees of relatedness, estimates can be obtained of the proportion of observed variation in a population that is due to genetic variation. This estimate is referred to as heritability, and is limited to the particular population under study.

Behavior genetic research has shown that, for a wide variety of traits, including measures of intelligence, specific cognitive abilities, personality, and psychopathology in North American and European populations, the heritability of such traits is between .40 and .70. Of the remaining reliable variance, there is more variation *within* families than *between* families (Plomin & Daniels, 1987). Being reared in one family, rather than another, within the range of families sampled makes few differences in children's personality and intellectual development. These data suggest that environments most parents provide for their children have few *differential effects* on the offspring. Most families provide sufficiently supportive environments that children's individual genetic differences develop.

Means and Variances

The statement that parents have few differential effects on children does not mean that not having parents is just as good as having parents. It may not matter much that children have *different* parents, but it does matter that they have parent(s) or some supportive, affectionate person who is willing to be parent-like. This is essentially the distinction between examining sources of variation between individuals and examining mean values in the population. The methods best suited to the former are not necessarily also appropriate for the latter.

The distinction between causes of mean or average values and causes of variation around mean values can be confusing to both psychologists and parents. For some characteristics, there is very little individual variation around the mean, but for other characteristics, there is a broad distribution of results, for which a mean and a variance can be described. For some human characteristics there is no normal variation at one level of analysis, for example, having bilateral limbs, two eyes, and a cerebral cortex. Every normal member of the species has these characteristics. At another level of analysis, however, all of these species-typical characteristics show variation (e.g., limb length, eye shape, brain size). The structural genes that cause the development of species-typical characteristics may have no normal variants; but there may be regulatory genes that influence the developmental patterns and the eventual amount or type of each characteristic a given individual has. There is no necessary association between the structural causes of species-typical characteristics and the regulatory causes of variation. Research on variation has no necessary implications for the causes of the average value of the population (but see Turkheimer, in press). Thus, a good developmental theory must have concepts of both variant and invariant species patterns.

This distinction is particularly important to remember when considering analyses of heritability, as pointed out by Arthur Jensen (1989): "Hence, the results of any heritability analysis are necessarily limited to statements concerning variation around the overall *mean* of the group in which the analysis is performed, and it affords no information whatsoever about the factors responsible for the particular value of the group mean" (p. 241). Similarly, as McGuffin and Gottesman (1985) emphasize, heritability estimates have no meaning for a given individual. Such

estimates simply tell us the proportion of variance in some trait that is due to genetic and environmental variation in that particular population. They cannot tell us what percent of individual A's limb length is due to which influences.

To see the effects of having no parents (or parent surrogates), one would have to return to the orphanages of long ago (or study those in use today in the Soviet Union), or see children trapped in crack houses of inner cities in the United States, locked in basements and attics by vengeful, crazy relatives (see Clarke & Clarke, 1976). Really deprived, abusive, and neglectful environments do not support normal development for any child. Having no parental figures or being reared in terribly deprived circumstances have clear detrimental effects on a child's development, regardless of the child's genetic background (Dumaret & Stewart, 1985). The important point here is that *variations* among environments that support normal human development are not very important as determinants of *variations* in children's outcomes.

Common and Uncommon Assumptions

The prevailing belief among both psychologists and parents is that variations in normal environments, particularly those provided by their families, (1) shape children's development and (2) determine their adult futures. The commonly accepted model is one in which parental characteristics (phenotypes, Pp) determine the child's environment (Ec), which in turn

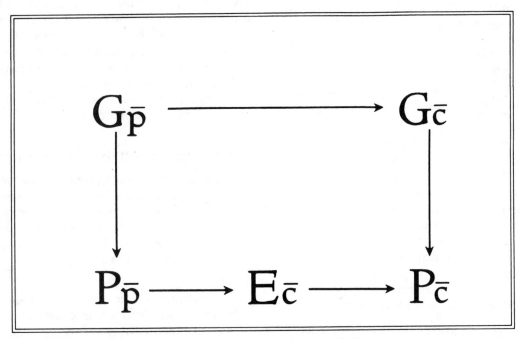

FIGURE 1 A model of parent–child genetic and environmental effects.

determines the child's behavioral outcomes (Pc). A more complete version of this model is shown in Figure 1. Here the transmission of genes from parents to child is recognized, and the role of genes in determining (in part) phenotypes is included in the model. In this model, the parents still determine the child's environment, which affects the child's behavioral development.

It also commonly is assumed that parental characteristics and home environments are arbitrarily or even randomly associated with individual children's characteristics (Bandura, 1982). Parents are, in this sense, "the luck of the draw." The structure of experience is assumed to be given in the environment, which acts to provide stimuli that impinge and shape children, regardless of who they are. The uncorrelated nature of people's characteristics and their environments is challenged by constructivist views of how people determine their own experiences. In fact, several lines of research in cognitive, clinical, and social psychology have been based on theories about individual differences in experience and on the idea that, not only do individuals' responses to environments differ, but people construct their own experiences. Some brief examples follow.

1. In cognitive psychology, Bower has pursued the idea that people construct their own experiences and personal histories (Bower, 1987). Faced with the same brief story, different individuals remembered and recalled different versions of the story.

2. Clinical psychology has found that people differ in their emotional responses to situations; for example, Eysenck (1982, 1983) compared psychopaths and normals in their emotional reactivity to punishment and reward; Wexler, Schwartz, Warrenburg, Servis, and Taratzis (1986) examined stress reactions that shape their behaviors in those situations.

3. Social psychology has presented evidence that personal characteristics affect how others respond to the stimulus person (Langlois & Roggman, 1990). Physical attractiveness may be in the eye of the beholder, but there is a great deal of cultural consensus in judgments about what constitutes physical attractiveness. People judged to be physically attractive by others are more likely to be asked for dates, more likely to be hired for jobs, and once hired more likely to be promoted than others judged to be less physically attractive (Berscheid & Walster, 1974).

4. In personality psychology, Henry Murray (Kluckhohn, Murray, & Schneider, 1953) pursued for many years the idea that each person constructs a personal myth, which gives coherence to his or her life, just as larger cultural myths give coherence to a society. Personality characteristics that are moderately heritable (30% to 50%) have been shown to influence how people react across time and situations. Sociable and outgoing people experience social interactions with strangers differently from shy, fearful people (Eysenck, 1983; Kagan, Reznick, & Gibbons, 1989). Optimistic, internally directed older adults cope much better with aging than others who are less optimistic and feel less in control of their lives. A twin study of older adults shows these life-outlook characteristics, like all personality variables, to be moderately heritable (Pedersen, Gatz, Plomin, & Nesselroade, 1989).

5. The new field of cultural psychology is actually predicated on the assumption that no sociocultural environment exists apart from the meaning that human participants give it (Shweder, 1990). Nothing real "just is"; realities are the product of the way things get represented, embedded, implemented, and reacted to.

Although cultural psychology uses non-Platonic, philosophical constructivism to explore ethnic differences in personality, intelligence, and social behavior, the same ontological and epistemological principles apply to individual differences within cultures (Scarr, 1985). Different people, at different developmental stages, interpret and act upon their environments in different ways that create different experiences for each person. In this view, human experience is the construction of reality, not a property of a physical world that imparts the same experience to everyone who encounters it.

Thus, there are contradictory theories in psychology about how people are influenced by their environments and how they construct their own experiences from those environments.

The Average Expectable Environment

A resolution of the seeming contradictions in theories about how families affect their children can be found in the concept of the "average expectable environment" (Hartmann, 1958). Based on evolutionary theory, there are three components that describe normal organisms in normal environments (LeVine, 1987).

1. *Preadaptation.* Infants and children are preadapted by their human species genetic inheritance to respond to a specific *range* of environmental opportunities for stimulation and knowledge acquisition.

2. *Variation.* Within the genetically specified range of normal environments, a variety of environmental patterns of stimulation can act to promote normal human developmental patterns. Wide variations in environments within this normal range present "functionally equivalent" opportunities for people to construct their own experiences (Scarr & Weinberg, 1983).

3. *Limits.* Environments that fall outside of the species-normal range will not promote normal developmental patterns. Contemporary examples are violent, abusive, and neglectful families.

Thus, normal development does occur in a wide variety of human environments, but not in those lacking "average expectable" conditions under which the species has evolved. For infants, species-normal environments include protective, parenting adults and a surrounding social group to which the child will be socialized. For older children, a normal environment includes a supportive family, peers with whom to learn the rules of being young, and plentiful opportunities to learn how to be a normal adult who can work and love. The exact details and specifications of the socialization patterns are not crucial to normal development (although they are crucial to understanding the meaning people give to their experiences), but having a rearing environment that falls within the limits of normal environments *is* crucial to normal development.

Although I argue that genotype-environment correlations are more pervasive and important than gene-environment interactions, there are in the human literature a few examples of how different genotypes respond to the "same" rearing environment. A striking example of genotype-environment interaction has been reported by Gottesman and Bertelsen (1989) in their follow-up study of offspring of identical and fraternal twins discordant for schizophrenia. They found that the risk for schizophrenia in the offspring of schizophrenic fraternal twins was 17.4% and for the offspring of their normal co-twins was 2.1%. However, the risk for the offspring of schizophrenic identical twins was 16.8% and for those of their normal co-twins was 17.4%. Gottesman and Bertelsen concluded that "discordance in identical twins may primarily be explained by the capacity of a schizophrenic genotype or diathesis to be unexpressed unless it is released by some kinds of environmental, including nonfamilial, stressors" (p. 867).

Thus, it is clear from research in many areas of psychology, most notably cultural psychology, and from the investigation of organism-environment interaction that the "environment" does not necessarily have the same meaning for all individuals.

Models of Genes and Environments

Another source of confusion in theories of how humans develop is the nature of the phenotype (observ-

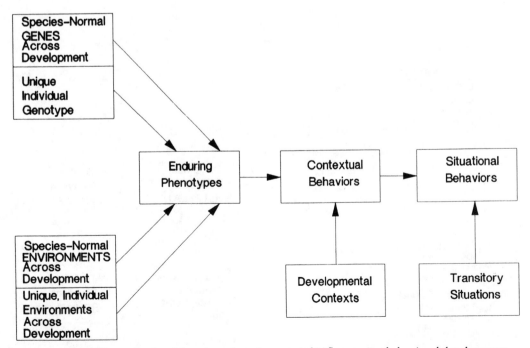

FIGURE 2 Different levels of genetic and environmental influences on behavioral development.

able characteristics) that is the outcome to be predicted. Some behaviors are indices of enduring personality and intellectual characteristics of the person, traits that show considerable stability across many situations and years. Other behaviors are temporally less stable but consistent responses to contemporary contexts in which development is occurring. Still more transitory behaviors are situation-specific. Figure 2 shows a model of how development can be construed at different levels of behavioral analysis from enduring traits to situational behaviors.

The path model, shown in Figure 2, invokes causality. Having a genotype within the species-normal range is necessary for normal development, as is having a species-normal environment, an average predictable rearing environment. In addition to a "normal" environment that supports development in a normal range, the developing person also has an individual environment selected, evoked, and constructed by the person. The person also has a unique genotype composed of normal alleles in loci that have normal variants in the population. Normal genes, normal environments, and individually different genes and environments combine to produce the development of enduring behavioral phenotypes, such as personality, interests, and intelligence.

The model posits that how people behave in various contexts depends on enduring phenotypes and on environmental contexts. Situational or transitory behaviors are further influenced by transitory situations and by contextual behaviors that are relevant to the situation.

The first example of the model does not show all of the possible causal paths, as does the next example. The example chosen is temperament and social development (see Figure 3). In this model of peer relations and peer behaviors, species-normal genes and species-normal social rearing environments are correlated because normal organisms evoke different rearing than abnormal ones. Unique genes combine with unique individual environments to produce individually variable, enduring phenotypes (measurable traits, such as sociability). Enduring traits are hypothesized to combine with developmental contexts (long-range contexts, such as home and school) to produce contextual behaviors, such as relationships with peers. Finally, relationships with peers are predicted to combine with situations to produce specific, situational behaviors, such as how a child behaves at a school party.

Genes may predict contextual and situational behaviors directly through paths other than the measured personality trait (here, sociability), such as impulsiveness, emotionality, and so forth. The model permits direct as well as indirect or mediated pathways to development and behavior.

Which of these kinds of personal traits or behaviors is to be explained will have great influence on the level of genetic and environmental characteristics one should choose to include in the prediction. Much of the 20-year debate about situation-specific behaviors versus enduring personality traits was mired in the confusion between relatively stable traits and situationally determined behaviors. Discussions of genetic and environmental variability in "behavior"

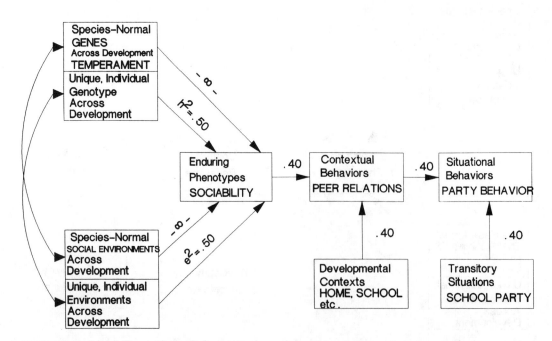

FIGURE 3 Sociability and peer behaviors.

risk the same misunderstandings unless the level of behavior is defined.

I decided to combine information in our field, some of which I will present in the next section of the paper, to speculate about what the solution of this model might yield. Figure 3 shows the path coefficients. Note first that the species-normal environment and genes have infinite coefficients (set at zero in the model), because it is assumed that the data are based only on genetically normal people who developed in average expectable environments. If one were comparing development of abnormal with that of normal genotypes, or development in very deprived with that in normal environments, these coefficients could have values.

Based on a considerable amount of data from families and twins, the heritability (h^2; path from unique genotype to enduring phenotype) is about .50. Unique environments explain about half of the reliable variance in personality, so that e^2 is also predicted to be .50. I will not try to defend any of the values in this model; I will only say that the numbers fit my reading of the developmental literature. There is much to argue about here! To evoke even more controversy, let me show my estimates for intelligence, school achievement, and a grade on a math test (Figure 4).

Of greater importance is the idea that one can understand both typical development of normal genotypes in average expectable environments, and individual development of unique persons in unique environments, as they develop enduring characteristics and display contextually consistent behaviors and situationally specific behaviors. The next step is to explain how unique individuals make their own experiences.

A TRIARCHIC THEORY OF EXPERIENCE

How might individuals create their own experiences? In earlier publications (McCartney, in press; Scarr, 1985; Scarr & McCartney, 1983; Scarr & Weinberg, 1983), we have proposed that people make their own environments in three ways: First, children's genes necessarily are correlated with their environments because parents provide both, so that their experiences are constructed from opportunities that are correlated positively with their personal characteristics; second, people evoke from others responses that are correlated with their own characteristics; and third, people actively select environments that are correlated with their interests, talents, and personality characteristics.

Although the proposed theory is based on the idea that, given the same "objective" environment, individuals will react differently, Scarr (1989) has argued that *genotype–environment correlations,* rather than gene-environment interactions, predominate in the construction of experiences. Many environmental opportunities are taken in by some individuals and not by others, depending on the individuals' characteristics. This selective use of environmental opportunities is better thought of as genotype–environment correlation than as genotype-environment interaction.

The theory of genotype → environment effects has three propositions:

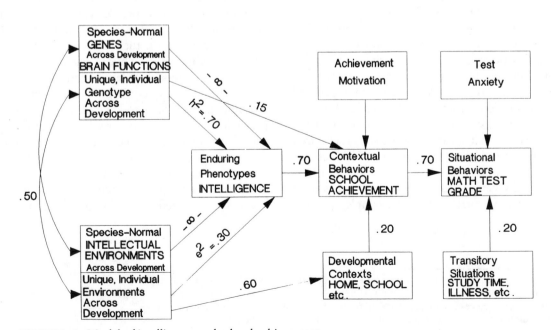

FIGURE 4   Model of intelligence and school achievement.

1. There are three kinds of genotype → environment effects, as described above: passive, evocative, and active.

2. The balance of genotype → environment effects changes from passive to active with development, as children move out from the family to make their own choices of interests and activities.

3. Genetic differences become more important across development, as people actively make their own environments.

The theory of genotype → environment effects holds that *genotypes drive experiences.* Following Hayes (1962), we proposed that the state of development and the individual characteristics of people shape the experiences they gather from exposures to their environments. In this model, parental genes determine their phenotypes, the child's genes determine his or her phenotype, and the child's environment is merely a reflection of the characteristics of both parents and child. Here differences among children's common home environments, *within the normal species range,* have no effect on differences among children's outcomes. The obvious challenge posed by this model is the proposition that differences among normal environments are a product of parental and child characteristics and not a causal path in the determination of differences among children's behavioral phenotypes.

General Theory

People are both individually different and developmentally different in the ways they encode and experience their environments. Experiences the person constructs from exposures to various environments are uniquely correlated to that person's perceptions, cognition, emotions, and more enduring characteristics of intelligence, interests, and personality. In this theory there are three ways by which genotypes and environments become correlated (Plomin, DeFries, & Loehlin, 1977). First, one must take into account the fact that most biological parents provide their children with both genes and home environments. The fact that parents provide both genes and environments means that the child's genes and environments necessarily will be positively correlated. For example, parents

who read well and who like to read will be likely to subscribe to magazines and papers, buy and borrow books, take books from the local library, and read to the child. Parents who have reading problems are less likely to expose themselves to this world of literacy, so that their children are more likely to be reared in a less literate environment. Those same children are also more likely to have reading problems themselves and to prefer nonreading activities. Thus, the reading abilities of parents are likely to be correlated with the reading abilities of their children and with the environments parents provide for their children—a positive genotype-environments effect.

Second, each person at each developmental stage *evokes* from others responses that reinforce positively or negatively that person's behaviors. Evocative effects have profound effects on a person's self-image and self-esteem throughout the lifespan. Smiling, cheerful infants who evoke positive social interactions from parents and other adults (Wachs & Gruen, 1982) seem likely to form positive impressions of the social world and its attractions. Infants who are fussy, irritable, and who experience negative or neutral interactions with their caregivers and others would seem less likely to form the impression that social interactions are a source of positive reinforcement. Toddler siblings evoke individually tailored but different verbal exchanges with their mothers at the same chronological ages (McCartney, in press). School-age children from disadvantaged families who are more intelligent and more "spunky" (Garmezy, Masten, & Tellegen, 1994) are more likely to be given positive attention and encouragement by teachers than less intelligent or less "spunky" children. Third, each person makes choices about what environments to experience. Past infancy, people who are in a varied environment[2] choose what to attend to and what to ignore. Depending on their personal interests, talents, and personality, people choose pursuits, whether educational, occupational, or leisure activities.

The idea that people sort themselves into environments according to their interests, talents, and personality has a long history in industrial/organizational psychology. People choose occupational environments that correlate with their personal preferences for social interaction or solitary work, for independent or supervised work, for salesmanship or social service. Preferences for one kind of work en-

---

[2]The entire theory depends on people having a varied environment from which to choose and construct experiences. The theory does not apply, therefore, to people with few choices or few opportunities for experiences that match their genotypes. This caveat applies particularly to children reared in very disadvantaged circumstances and to adults with little or no choice about occupations and leisure activities.

vironment or another are correlated with other aspects of personality (Grotevant, Scarr, & Weinberg, 1977; Holland, 1973). Differences in preferences for work environments turn out to be just as heritable as other aspects of personality (Bouchard, Scarr, & Weinberg, 1991). Thus, differences in choices among various kinds of environments have been shown to be, in part, functions of the personal characteristics of the individual.

A test of the notion of gene-environment correlation can be seen in a study of reading (Hayes et al., 1989). Pervasive differences in reading choices and amount of reading were found by age, gender, and ability levels—all of which are consistent with the theory that people choose and make their own environments.

> These measurements on popular children's books showed: (*a*) the most able British children read approximately 50 percent more than their less able peers (within that four week period), and (*b*) the average text grows more demanding (lexically) and longer in the older age cohorts. . . . The most able children not only read more books than their peers, those books were slightly more difficult. When this one month language experience is multiplied across years, the highest ability students must have accumulated a huge advantage over their less able peers. They encounted many more uncommon terms and non-mundane topics from their reading. *Even if these most able children were no more efficient* in extracting, integrating and retrieving information from what they read than their less able peers, they would still have the much richer language experience from their book reading. If it can be shown that they are also more efficient, their advantage over their peers would be still greater. (p. 13)

The genotype → environment effects theory predicts that developmental differences are *very important*, pervasive, and large, based on *the same* principles as individual differences. For many behaviors, developmental changes based on genotype and environmental changes (genes are turned on; environments are perceived and experienced differently) will be much larger than individual variations at any one age. All of these is in accord with the theory of developmental and individual differences in the selection and construction of experience.

Families as Environments

The idea of correlated personal and environmental characteristics has been ignored and even opposed in developmental psychology (e.g., Rheingold & Cook,

1975). Most attention has been focused on differences among families in the opportunities they provide for their children. Beginning with family differences in social class, however measured, it has been assumed that observations of ubiquitous correlations between family education, occupational status, and income and children's intellectual and other outcomes *were caused* by differences *among families' environments* (Scarr, 1985). Clearly, there are family differences; it is not clear that most of those differences are environmental. In fact, among families in the mainstream of Western European and North American societies, differences in family environments seem to have little effect on intellectual and personality outcomes of their children.

This point is worth pondering. How can it be that different parents have few differential effects on the intellectual or personality development of their children? For parents who care, it is impossible to believe that this could be the case. This is not to say that parents may not have effects on children's self-esteem, motivation, ambitiousness, and other important characteristics. It is to say that parental *differences* in rearing styles, social class, and income have small effects on the measurable *differences* in intelligence, interests, and personality among their children.

The Data

Family resemblances have been reported for intelligence and personality measures for relatives who vary in genetic and environmental relatedness. Table 1 summarizes much of the data on IQ test score similarities of late adolescent and adult relatives who are genetically identical, of those related by half of their genes, and of genetically unrelated individuals.

Let us focus on genetically identical pairs reared together and apart and on adopted pairs of siblings reared together since infancy. These are the most startling findings. Identical (MZ) twins reared together score as much alike (r = .86) on IQ tests as the same person tested twice (r = .87). MZ twins reared in different families are slightly less similar (r = .76). The remarkable studies of MZ twins reared in different families challenge many cherished beliefs in developmental psychology (but fit very nicely in the genotype → environment theory). The fact that these twins, in four studies, are nearly as similar intellectually (Bouchard et al., 1990) as identicals reared together, and are just as similar in personality (Tellegen et al., 1988), raises critical questions about what observed family differences really mean for development. Table 2 shows the IQ correlations for MZ twins reared apart in four studies.

By contrast, genetically unrelated siblings, reared from infancy to adulthood in the same family, do not

TABLE 1

IQ and Degrees of Relatedness: Similarities of Genetically Related and Unrelated Persons Who Live Together and Apart

Relationship	Correlation	No. of Pairs
Genetically identical:		
Identical twins together	.86	1,300
Identical twins apart	.76	137
Same person tested twice	.87	456
Genetically related by half of the genes:		
Fraternal twins together	.55	8,600
Biological sisters and brothers	.47	35,000
Parents and children together	.40	4,400
Parents and children apart	.31	345
Genetically unrelated:		
Adopted children together	.00	200
Unrelated persons apart	.00	15,000

Source: Adapted from Plomin and DeFries (1980).
Note: Based on data from Scarr and Weiberg (1978) and Teasdale and Owen (1985) on older adolescents who are comparable in age to other samples of this table. Younger adopted children resemble each other to a greater degree, with correlations around .24, according to samples of 800 pairs.

resemble each other at all in IQ. This result, based on two initial studies (Scarr & Weinberg, 1978; Teasdale & Owen, 1985), has been exactly replicated in two additional studies of late adolescents and young adults (Horn, Loehlin, & Willerman, 1982; Kent, 1985). Studies of younger adopted siblings show that they do have some intellectual resemblance ($r = .24$), about half that of biological siblings ($r = .47$). A major reason for the greater resemblance of younger adoptees is that families have greater effects on their younger than older children, as will be explained in later sections. Another reason for greater resemblance of younger than older adoptees is selective placement, as shown in Table 3.

In this sample (Scarr & Weinberg, 1976, 1977), 75% of the 101 adoptive families also had their own biological offspring. Thus, one can examine the resemblances of biological and adoptive relatives, living together and apart. Correlations of parents and their biological children range from .33 to .43, whether the (natural) parents have never seen the children since birth or whether the parents (adoptive parents, but the biological parents of these children) have reared them to the average age of 7 years.

These are intellectual resemblances between adoptive parents and their adopted child ($r = .21$ and $r = .27$), but this similarity must be modified by the intellectual resemblances between the natural parents of the adopted child and the biological offspring of the adoptive parents ($r = .15$ and $r = .19$). There is absolutely no environmental or genetic reason to think that birth parents of adopted children should bear any resemblance to biological children of the families who adopted their children, except for selective placement by adoption agencies.

Social workers are likely to try to match their expectations for children's intellectual development to the adoptive families' educational levels. Thus, by being more likely to place an illegitimate child of two university students with a college-educated family and to place a child of two high school dropouts with a working-class family, adoption agencies can create a

TABLE 2

Sample Sizes and Intraclass Correlations for All IQ Measures and Weighted Averages for Five Studies of MZA Twins

Study and Test Used (Primary/Secondary/Tertiary)	N for Each Test	Primary Test	Secondary Test	Tertiary Test	Mean of Multiple Test
Newman et al. (1938) (Stanford-Binet/Otis)	19/19	.68	.74	...	.71
Juel-Nielsen (1965) (Wechsler-Bellevue/Raven)	12/12	.64	.73	...	.69
Shields (1962) (Mill-Hill/Dominoes)	38/37	.74	.76	...	.75
Bouchard et al. (1990) (WAIS/Raven-Mill-Hill/First Principal Component)	50/45/44	.69	.78	.78	.75
Weighted average	119/113/112	.70	.76	.78	.74

TABLE 3

**Comparisons of Biological and Unrelated Parent–Child IQ Correlations
in 101 Transracial Adoptive Families**

	N (pairs)	r
Parents–unrelated children:		
Adoptive mother—adopted child	174	.21 (.23)[a]
Natural mother—own child of adoptive family[b]	217	.15
Adoptive father—adopted child	170	.27 (.15)[a]
Natural father—own child of adoptive family[b]	86	.19
Parents—biological children:		
Adoptive mother—own child	141	.34
Natural mother—adopted child[b]	135	.33
Adoptive father—own child	142	.39
Natural father—adopted child[b]	46	.43

Source: Scarr & Weinberg research.
[a] Early adopted only (N = 111).
[b] Educational level, not IQ scores.

correlation between the child's probable abilities and the adoptive home environment. The matching characteristics that social workers select are educational levels of natural parents with educational, occupational, and income characteristics of adoptive families (Scarr & Weinberg, 1977, 1978, 1983).

The implication of the unexpected resemblance between birth parents and biological children in the family who adopted their children is that the resemblance of adoptive parents and adopted children must be corrected for selective placement (.21–.15 and .27–.19), which reduces adoptive family correlations to small effects (.06 and .08), even in early childhood.

From our adolescent adoption study (Scarr & Weinberg, 1978), the prediction of biological offspring IQ test scores from the average of the parents' IQ scores is remarkable (r = .68), as shown in Figure 5. By contrast, the prediction of adopted children's IQ test scores from adoptive parents' scores is minimal (r = .13), as shown in Figure 6.

The theory of genotype → environment effects can explain the slight resemblances among adopted relatives and the great resemblances between MZ twins reared together and apart. If genes drive experience, then the degree to which relatives have similar experiences will depend upon their degree of genetic resemblance. Identical twins, whose genetic correlation is 1.00, evoke similar responses from others, and they make similar choices in their en-

vironments. They respond cognitively and emotionally in similar ways, and they construe their experiences in similar ways. By contrast, adopted children, who are genetically unrelated, have uncorrelated experiences even within the same household, school, and neighborhood environments. This part of the theory explains the family data from behavior genetic studies more satisfactorily than any other model.

Developmental Patterns

Longitudinal studies of twins, most notably the Louisville, Kentucky, study headed for many years by the late Ronald S. Wilson, have contributed to our understanding of the role of genetic variability in regulating developmental patterns. Wilson (1983) reported on mental development tests administered on nine occasions to infants and young children from 3 months to 6 years. Overall results were that MZ twins scored very similarly (correlations in the mid-80s throughout early childhood) and DZ twins less similarly (correlations declining from the mid-70s in infancy to the low 60s over the preschool years). But the longitudinal pattern of mental development was also strikingly similar for MZ co-twins, as shown in Figure 7. Although each pair had a different pattern of spurts and lags in mental growth, the similarity between co-twins was very high within each pair. The four pairs presented by Wilson were representative of

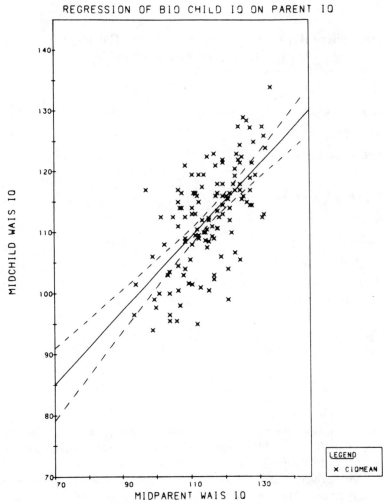

FIGURE 5 Scatterplot of the regression of midchild IQ scores on mid-parent IQ scores in biologically-related families.

the several hundreds of twin pairs studied over 20 years. Figure 7 also shows the typical patterns of mental developmental resemblance for DZ twins. Because they are siblings with about half of their genes in common, their developmental patterns are similar but not as parallel to one another as those of MZ twins.

Environments within the Family

The same body of behavioral genetic literature that illustrates the importance of genetic variation also highlights the importance of environmental variation (Scarr & Grajek, 1982). As Plomin (1990) indicated, "the majority of the variance for most behaviors is due to non-genetic factors, the environment" (p. 117). However, one of the most striking findings of the behavior genetic literature is that, for a variety of traits, most of the environmental variance is contributed by *nonshared* environmental influences (Scarr & Grajek, 1982). Nonshared environmental influences are those that are not shared by members of a family; that is, they act to make family members different from one another. As Plomin and Thompson (1987) highlight, this finding "implies that the unit of environmental transmission is not the family, but rather micro-environments within families" (p. 20). I would add that micro-environments are largely the construction of individual family members in the ways they evoke responses from others, actively select or ignore opportunities, and construct their own experiences.

Siblings adopted in infancy do not resemble each other in any measured talents, interests, or personality. Yet, they have grown up in the same home with the same parents, schools, neighborhoods, and overall family circumstances. According to normal developmental science, differences in parental child-rearing techniques, interactional patterns, educational levels, occupational statuses, and income, among many other family variables, should cause siblings to

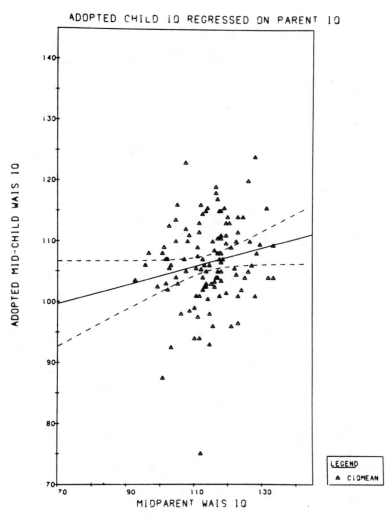

FIGURE 6 Scatterplot of the regression of midchild IQ scores on midparent IQ scores in adoptive families.

resemble each other, *if common family and larger contexts have common influences* on siblings, regardless of their genetic relationship. The data do not support normal developmental theory and challenge us to rethink how the environment can be construed in such different ways by different family members, even if they are biologically related and especially when they are not genetically related.

Good Enough Parents

Ordinary differences between families have little effect on children's development, unless the family is outside of a normal, developmental range. Good enough, ordinary parents probably have the same effects on their children's development as culturally defined super-parents (Rowe, in press). This comforting idea gives parents a lot more freedom to care for their children in ways they find comfortable for them, and it gives them more freedom from guilt when they

deviate (within the normal range) from culturally prescribed norms about parenting. As Richard Weinberg and I said (Scarr & Weinberg, 1978), children's outcomes do not depend on whether parents take children to the ball game or to a museum so much as they depend on genetic transmission, on plentiful opportunities, and on having a good enough environment that supports children's development to become themselves.

The idea of good enough parents is a constructive step toward recognizing that parents do not have the power to make their children into whatever they want, or in John Watson's (1928) terms, to ruin them in so many ways. Fortunately, evolution has not left development of the human species, nor any other, at the easy mercy of variations in their environments. We are robust and able to adapt to wide-ranging circumstances—a lesson that seems lost on some ethnocentric developmentalists. If we were so vulnerable as to be led off the normal developmental track by

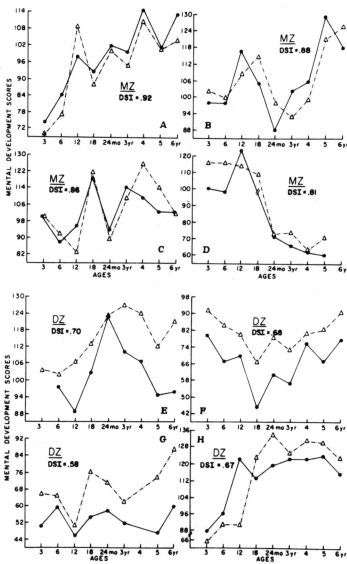

FIGURE 7 Trends in mental development during early childhood for four MZ and four DZ pairs (Wilson, 1983). DSI is the developmental synchronies index, a measure of how closely the curves of the co-twins correlate.

slight variations in our parenting, we should not long have survived.

The flip side of this message is that it is not easy to intervene deliberately in children's lives to change their development, unless their environments are outside the normal species range. We know how to rescue children from extremely bad circumstances and to return them to normal developmental pathways by providing rearing environments within a normal range. But for children whose development is on a predictable but undesirable trajectory and whose parents are providing a supportive environment, interventions have only temporary and limited effects (Clarke & Clarke, 1989). Should we be surprised?

Feeding a well-nourished but short child more and more will not give him the stature of a basketball player. Feeding a below-average intellect more and more information will not make her brilliant. Exposing a shy child to socially demanding events will not make him feel less shy. The child with a below-average intellect and the shy child may gain some specific skills and helpful knowledge of how to behave in specific situations, but their enduring intellectual and personality characteristics will not be fundamentally changed.

Developmentalists can have more respect for individual differences among parents in the ways they rear their children. And we need to take our own textbook advice and actually believe that correlations are not causes. The associations between a child's characteristics, those of the parents, and the rearing environment they provide are neither accidental nor a likely source of fruitful intervention, unless the child's opportunities for normal development are quite limited. Developmental research of the past 25 years supports the idea that normal genes and normal environments promote species-typical development and that, given a wide range of opportunities, individuals make their own environments, based on their own heritable characteristics.

References

Baltes, P. B., Featherman, D. L., & Lerner, R. M. (Eds.). (1987). *Life-span development and behavior* (Vol. 8). Hillsdale, NJ: Erlbaum.

Bandura, A. (1982). The psychology of chance encounters and life paths. *American Psychologist, 37,* 747–755.

Bell, R. Q. (1968). A reinterpretation of the direction of effects in studies of socialization. *Psychological Review, 75,* 81–95.

Bell, R., & Harper, L. (1977). *Child effects on adults.* Lincoln: University of Nebraska Press.

Bersheid, E., & Walster, E. (1974). Physical attractiveness. In L. Berkowitz (Ed.), *Advances in experimental social psychology* (pp. 157–215). New York: Academic Press.

Bouchard, T. et al. (1990). Sources of human psychological differences: The Minnesota study of twins reared apart. *Science, 250,* 223–228.

Bouchard, T., Scarr, S., & Weinberg, R. (1991). *Vocational interests among relatives of varying genetic relatedness.* Unpublished manuscript.

Bower, G. H. (1987). Commentary on mood and memory. *Behavior Research and Therapy, 25,* 443–455.

Breitmayer, B. J., & Ricciuti, H. N. (1988). The effect of neonatal temperament on caregiver behavior in the newborn nursery. *Infant Mental Health Journal, 9,* 158–172.

Clarke, A. M., & Clarke, A. D. B. (1976). *Early experience: Myth and evidence.* New York: Free Press.

Clarke, A. M., & Clarke, A. D. B. (1989). The later cognitive effects of early intervention. *Intelligence, 13,* 289–297.

Clarke-Stewart, A. (1989). Infant day care: Maligned or malignant? *American Psychologist, 44,* 266–273.

Cooper, R. M., & Zubek, J. P. (1958). Effects of enriched and restricted early environments on the learning ability of bright and dull rats. *Canadian Journal of Psychology, 12,* 159–164.

Cronbach, L. J. (1957). Two disciplines of scientific psychology. *American Psychologist, 12,* 671–684.

Dumaret, A., & Stewart, J. (1985). IQ, scholastic performance and behavior of sibs raised in contrasting environments. *Journal of Child Psychology and Psychiatry and Allied Disciplines, 26,* 553–580.

Eysenck, H. J. (1982). Why do conditional responses show incrementation, while unconditional responses show habituation? *Behavioral Psychotherapy, 10,* 217–220.

Eysenck, H. J. (1983). Human learning and individual differences: The genetic dimension. *Educational Psychology, 3,* 169–188.

Garmezy, N., Masten, A., & Tellegen, A. (1984). The study of stress and competence in children: A building block for developmental psychopathology. *Child Development, 55,* 97–111.

Gottesman, I. I., & Bertelsen, A. (1989). Confirming unexpressed genotypes for schizophrenia. *Archives of General Psychiatry, 46,* 867–872.

Grotevant, H. D., Scarr, S., & Weinberg, R. A. (1977). Patterns of interest similarity in adoptive and biological families. *Journal of Personality and Social Psychology, 35,* 667–676.

Hartmann, H. (1958). *Ego psychology and the problem of adaptation.* New York: International Universities Press.

Hayes, D., Whitehead, F., Wellings, A., Thompson, W., Marschlke, C., & Moran, M. (1989). *How strongly do genes drive children's choice of experiences?* (pp. 16–17). (Technical Report Ser. 89–13, Cornell University, November 1989).

Hayes, K. J. (1962). Genes, drives, and intellect. *Psychological Reports, 10,* 299–342.

Holland, J. L. (1973). *Making vocational choices: A theory of careers.* Englewood Cliffs, NJ: Prentice-Hall.

Horn, J. M., Loehlin, J. C., & Willerman, L. (1982). Aspects of the inheritance of intellectual abilities. *Behavior Genetics, 12,* 479–516.

Jensen, A. R. (1989). Review: Raising IQ without increasing "g"? *Developmental Review, 9,* 234–258.

Juel-Nielsen, N. (1965). Individual and environment: A psychiatric-psychological investigation of MZ twins reared apart. *Acta Psychiatrica Scandinavia (Suppl.), 183.* Copenhagen: Munksgaard.

Kagan, J., Reznick, J. S., & Gibbons, J. (1989). Inhibited and uninhibited types of children. *Child Development, 60,* 838–845.

Kent, J. (1985). *Genetic and environmental contributions to cognitive abilities as assessed by a telephone test battery. Unpublished doctoral dissertation,* University of Colorado, Boulder.

Kluckhohn, C., Murray, H. A., & Schneider, D. M. (Eds.). (1953). *Personality in nature, society, and culture* (2d ed.). New York: Knopf.

Langlois, J. H., & Roggman, L. A. (1990). Attractive faces are only average. *Psychological Science, 1,* 115–121.

LeVine, R. A. (1987). *Beyond the "average expectable environment"of psychoanalysis: Cultural differences in mother–infant interaction.* Paper presented at American Anthropological Association Meeting, Chicago.

Lytton, H. (1980). *Parent–child interaction.* New York: Plenum.

Magnusson, D., Stattin, H., & Allen, V. L. (1985). Differential maturation among girls and its relation to social adjustment: A longitudinal perspective. In D. L. Featherman & R. M. Lerner (Eds.), *Life-span development and behavior* (Vol. 7, pp. 123–132). New York: Academic Press.

McCartney, K. (in press). Mothers' language with first- and second-born children: A within-family study. In K. Pillemer & K. McCartney (Eds.), *Parent–child relations across the life span.*

McGuffin, P., & Gottesman, I. I. (1985). Genetic influences on normal and abnormal development. In M. Rutter & L. Hersov (Eds.), *Child and adolescent psychiatry* (pp. 17–33). Oxford: Blackwell Scientific.

Newman, H. H., Freeman, F. N., & Holzinger, K. J. (1938). *Twins: A study of heredity and environment.* Chicago: University of Chicago Press.

Pedersen, N. L., Gatz, M., Plomin, R., & Nesselroade, J. R. (1989). Individual differences in locus of control during the second half of the life span for identical and fraternal twins reared apart and reared together. *Journal of Gerontology, 44,* 100–105.

Plomin, R. (1986). *Development, genetics, and psychology.* Hillsdale, NJ: Erlbaum.

Plomin, R. (1990). *Nature and nurture.* Pacific Grove, CA: Brooks/Cole.

Plomin, R., & Daniels, D. (1987). Why are children in the same family so different from one another? *Behavioral and Brain Sciences, 10,* 1–60.

Plomin, R., & DeFries, J. C. (1980). Genetics and intelligence: Recent data. *Intelligence, 4,* 15–24.

Plomin, R., DeFries, J. C., & Loehlin, J. C. (1977). Genotype-environment interaction and correlation in the analysis of human behavior. *Psychological Bulletin, 84,* 309–322.

Plomin, R., & Thompson, R. (1987). Life-span developmental behavioral genetics. In P. B. Baltes, D. L. Featherman, & R. M. Lerner (Eds.), *Life-span development and behavior* (Vol. 8, pp. 111–123). Hillsdale, NJ: Erlbaum.

Rheingold, H. L., & Cook, K. V. (1975). The contents of boys' and girls' rooms as an index of parents' behavior. *Child Development, 46,* 459–463.

Rowe, D. C. (in press). As the twig is bent? The myth of child-rearing influences on personality development. *Journal of Counseling and Development.*

Scarr, S. (1985). Constructing psychology: Making facts and fables for our times. *American Psychologist, 40,* 499–512.

Scarr, S. (1989). How genotypes and environments combine: Development and individual differences. In G. Downey, A. Caspi, & N. Bolger (Eds.), *Interacting systems in human development* (pp. 217–244). New York: Cambridge University Press.

Scarr, S., & Grajek, S. (1982). Similarities and differences among siblings. In M. Lamb & B. Sutton-Smith (Eds.), *Sibling relationships* (pp. 357–381). Hillsdale, NJ: Erlbaum.

Scarr, S., & McCartney, K. (1983). How people make their own environments: A theory of genotype → environment effects. *Child Development, 54,* 424–435.

Scarr, S., & Ricciuti, A. (in press). What effects *do* parents have on their children? In L. Okagaki & R. J. Sternberg (Eds.), *Directors of development: Influences on the development of children's thinking.* Hillsdale, NJ: Erlbaum.

Scarr, S., & Weinberg, R. A. (1976). IQ test performance of black children adopted by white families. *American Psychologist, 31,* 726–739.

Scarr, S., & Weinberg, R. A. (1977). Intellectual similarities within families of both adopted and biological children. *Intelligence, 1,* 170–191.

Scarr, S., & Weinberg, R. A. (1978). The influence of "family background" on intellectual attainment. *American Sociological Review, 43,* 674–692.

Scarr, S., & Weinberg, R. A. (1983). The Minnesota adoption studies: Genetic differences and malleability. *Child Development, 54,* 260–267.

Shields, J. (1962). *Monozygotic twins brought up together and apart.* London: Oxford University Press.

Shweder, R. A. (1990). Cultural psychology—what is it? In J. W. Stigler, R. A. Shweder, & G. Herdt (Eds.), *Cultural psychology* (pp. 1–43). New York: Cambridge University Press.

Silbereisen, R. K., & Noack, P. (1988). On the constructive role of problem behavior in adolescence. In G. Downey, A. Caspi, & N. Bolger (Eds.), *Interacting systems in human development* (pp. 152–180). New York: Cambridge University Press.

Teasdale, T., & Owen, K. (1985). Heredity and familial environment in intelligence and educational level—a sibling study. *Nature, 309,* 620–622.

Tellegen, A., Lykken, D. T., Bouchard, T. J., Jr., Wilcox, K. J., Seal, N. L., & Rich, S. (1988). Personality similarity in twins reared apart and together. *Journal of Personality and Social Psychology, 54,* 1031–1039.

Turkheimer, E. (in press). Individual and group differences in adoption studies of IQ. *Psychological Bulletin.*

Wachs, T. D. & Gruen, G. (1982). *Early experience and human development.* New York: Plenum.

Watson, J. B. (1928). *Psychological care of infant and child.* New York: W. W. Norton.

Wexler, B. E., Schwartz, C., Warrenburg, S., Servis, M., & Tarlatzis, I. (1986). Effects of emotion on perceptual asymmetry: Interactions with personality. *Neuropsychologia, 24,* 699–710.

Wilson, R. A. (1983). The Louisville Twin Study: Developmental synchronies in behavior. *Child Development, 54,* 298–316.

8

Neonatal Behavior Among Urban Zambians and Americans

T. BERRY BRAZELTON, BARBARA KOSLOWSKI, AND EDWARD TRONICK

Psychologists can assess the contributions of biological and experiential factors in human development by comparing behaviors and abilities across individuals reared in very different cultural settings. In the research described below, T. Berry Brazelton, Barbara Koslowski, and Edward Tronick compared the ability of newborns in Zambia and the United States to regulate their emotional states and their responsiveness to the environment over their first ten days of life. They found differences in the rate that these skills developed over this brief period between these two populations. But more interesting than the identification of these differences is how such differences developed. Brazelton and colleagues offer a thought-provoking hypothesis as to how genetic and nongenetic inheritance may be coordinated with child-rearing practices to produce particular patterns of human growth.

Geber's classic report of infant development in Africa (Geber and Dean, 1959) suggested that African babies are developmentally more advanced in their first year than are their Western European counterparts. Her tests reported precocity in motor development between the two groups, but did not document sensory or cognitive differences.

Studies of other cultures (Ainsworth, 1967; Brazelton et al., 1969; Freedman and Freedman, 1969; Goldberg, 1971; Schaffer, 1960) have supported Geber's finding that developmental differences can be found early in a child's life—indeed, as early as the neonatal period. Several of these studies also suggested that infants in different cultural groups showed

Reprinted with permission from *Journal of Child Psychiatry, 15,* 1976, 97–107. Copyright 1976 by Pergamon Press Ltd.

This research was supported in part by a grant from the National Early Childhood Research Council, Inc. (Edcom), Princeton, N.J., and was presented at the Biennial Meeting of the Society for Research in Child Development, Minneapolis, Minn., in 1971.

Reprints may be requested from Dr. Brazelton, 23 Hawthorn Street, Cambridge, Mass. 02138.

differences in behavior at birth that might influence the outcome of their subsequent development.

We wondered whether these observations might be relevant to observed Zambian-American differences in early childhood. Would these groups of infants differ during the neonatal period? Would these differences lie in interactive and perceptual abilities as well as in motor development?

PROCEDURE

Ten Zambian and 10 American infants were seen on days 1, 5, and 10 after birth. All mothers were reported to have had normal pregnancies terminated at 40 weeks, and no bleeding or infection was noted.

The U.S. babies were delivered via "natural childbirth": no anesthesia was administered to the mothers, and no more than one injection of Nisentil (a mild muscle relaxant, 30 mgm.) was given during the period of labor 6 hours prior to delivery. No other medication was administered. All the infants were firstborn and came from middle-class families. They were normal at birth. Apgars were above 8-9-9 at 1, 5, and 15 minutes (Apgar, 1953). Neurological and pediatric examinations were consistently normal. We evaluated all babies for neurological adequacy on the scale taught one of us (ET) by Prechtl (Prechtl and Beintema, 1964). In addition, we evaluated each baby with the Brazelton (1973) Neonatal Behavioral Assessment at 1, 5, and 10 days.

This Neonatal Behavioral Assessment Scale is a psychological scale for the newborn human infant. It assesses his reflexive and motor behavior, as well as his general physical state as he recovers from labor and delivery. It allows for an assessment of the infant's capabilities along dimensions that we think are relevant to his developing social relationships. It reconceptualizes Prechtl's use of state[1] in such an assessment. State is no longer regarded as a static error variable, but serves to set a dynamic pattern which reflects the wholeness of the infant. Specifically, the examination tracks the pattern of state change over the course of the examination, its lability, and its directionality in response to external and internal

stimuli. Thus, the variability of state becomes a dimension of assessment, pointing to the infant's initial abilities for self-organization.

An assessment of the infant's ability for self-organization is contained in the items which measure his capacity for self-quieting after exposure to aversive stimuli. This is contrasted to the infant's use of external stimuli to help him quiet after such stimulation. The latter item contains a graded series of examiner-administered procedures—talking to him, placing one's hand on his belly, rocking and holding him—maneuvers which are designed to calm the infant. The assessment results in an evaluation of how control is achieved by the infant. The infant's responsiveness to animate stimulation (voice and face, holding and cuddling, etc.) as well as to inanimate stimulation (rattle, bell, red ball, pinprick, temperature change, etc.) are quantified. Other items assess neuroreflexive adequacy and the vigor and attentional excitement exhibited by the infant throughout the exam. In all of this test, there is an attempt to elicit the infant's *best* performance in response to different kinds of stimulation.

The Zambian mothers were given no medication before or during delivery. These mothers had had several pregnancies in rapid succession at about 12- to 13-month intervals, among these several spontaneous abortions. But they all had more than three children living at home. There was historical evidence of low protein intake both before and during pregnancy, coupled with a high incidence of gastrointestinal infection in the mother during pregnancy. The resulting intrauterine conditions of a depleted uterus, low protein, and increased infections were a reflection of the conditions of recent urbanization as well as of a breakdown in traditional practices (Goldberg, 1970).

The Zambian mothers we saw had recently moved to the urbanized slums of Lusaka because of the disruption of the economy in the country under an economic plan that stressed industrialization. In the country, the maternal grandmother dictated her daughter's diet and saw to it that protein was a daily requirement. In the urbanized group, the husband took over this prerogative. He set up a series of myths which we heard from our subjects: "If you eat fish,

---

[1] "State" or "state of consciousness" is one of the most important variables in any observation period of neonatal behavior. Reactions to stimuli must be interpreted within the context of the present state of consciousness. We used a schema of six states (two sleep, three awake, and one intermediate state). State depends on physiological variables such as hunger, degree of hydration, time within the sleep-wake cycle. But each observable reaction is governed by the state within which it is perceived. The infant's state patterns and his use of state to govern his physiological and psychological reactions may be uniquely individual and may be the most important framework for observing all of his reactions.

your baby will drown. If you eat meat, your baby will bleed to death. If you eat eggs, your baby will be born bald." The breakdown in dietary protection of pregnant women occurs in the city, where jobs and money are scarce and protein is expensive, and the family cannot afford to spend the little money they have on high-protein foods which might not satisfy hunger. The other powerful change in the urbanized groups around Lusaka had to do with birth control practices centered around pregnancy. In the country, a family is made up of several women and one man. A sexual relationship is maintained with a wife who is not pregnant and not nursing. This practice fosters a kind of birth control and recovery of the uterus in the postnatal period before subsequent pregnancy. In Lusaka, given the economic conditions, this pattern is impossible. A family is made up of a male and one female, and she suffers from the effects of rapidly repeated pregnancies.

All of the infants of the group examined lived in the semirural urbanized slum area which surrounds the city of Lusaka. Dwellings ranged from huts to small brick cottages. All families were reported to be recently (one generation) urbanized, and few had the advantage of extended families nearby (Goldberg, 1970, 1971).

Our study consisted of three examinations on days 1, 5, and 10 after birth for each infant. We all shared the examinations of the Zambians, although one (ET) was responsible for most of the examinations of U.S. controls. Interscorer reliability on the Brazelton scale had been tested in the United States and was retested in Africa, for we feared that we were becoming biased by our experience there. Repeated reliability tests were .85 or more on all items and between each pair of observers. The infants were scored on the 24 items listed in Table 1 as well as on 18 neurological items adapted from Prechtl and Beintema's (1964) neurological exam.

The first examination of the American infants was done in the hospital nurseries of the Boston Hospital for Women and Cambridge City Hospital, and on the Zambian infants in the University Hospital of Lusaka. On the first day the examination was administered two hours after feeding. The examinations on days 5 and 10 were carried out in the homes. An attempt was made to control conditions, e.g., to have the baby fed and comfortable; to include the mother, but exclude the other members of the family; and to standardize light, temperature, and noise as much as possible. This was difficult in the home examinations.

TABLE 1
Behavioral Measures in Neonatal Scale

Vigor	General tonus
Lability of states	Self-quieting activity
Tremulousness	Habituation to light in eyes
Amount of startling	Motor maturity
Amount of mouthing	Pulled-to-sit response
Hand to mouth activity	Passive movements
Motor activity	Following with eyes
Rapidity of buildup	Cuddliness
Defensive movements to cloth on face	Alertness
Tempo of activity at peak	Social interest in *E*
Irritability	Reactions to sound
Consolability	Reactivity to stimulation

An estimate of the infants' pediatric, neurological, and nutritional status[2] was made in each case, and two infants were excluded because of possibly abnormal reactions. None of the babies in either group was found to be abnormal on any examination, including neurological evaluations. All babies in each group were being breastfed.

RESULTS

In the Zambian group, observations in the neonatal nursery on day 1 demonstrated pediatric evidence of intrauterine depletion in each of these infants. The average birth weight was 6 pounds, and the length was an average of 19 1/2 inches. The infants' skin was dry and scaly; their faces were wrinkled. The stumps of their umbilical cords were somewhat dried and yellow at birth. In short, the infants demonstrated the signs of dysmaturity which indicate recent depletion of nutrients in utero (Clifford, 1954). Their weight and size suggested placental dysfunction, and suggested that the infants had been affected by their mothers' inadequate protein diet and their stressed uteri with placentae inadequate to feed them—especially in the period just prior to birth. On this first

---

[2]Pediatric and nutritional assessments for evidences of prematurity and dysmaturity according to Dubowitz et al. (1970) and Clifford (1954).

examination, the Zambian infants' muscle tone was very poor. Little resistance was evidenced to passive extension or flexion of their limbs. Head control on being pulled to sit was extremely poor. And, lastly, when held, the Zambian infants made no active attempt to mold or adjust themselves to being held. They were essentially limp and unresponsive in the motor sphere.

The American infants were not depleted. They averaged 7.6 pounds, 20¼ inches in length, and showed no clinical evidence of dysmaturity or prematurity. They were active and responsive on the first day in all spheres of behavior.

On days 5 and 10 the Zambian infants were no longer clinically dehydrated. Because the mothers were multiparous and had nursed infants before, their milk came in rapidly, and nursing was uniformly successful. By day 5, the Zambian infants were filled out, dry skin was peeling away, and their eyes and mouths were moist. Their skin and subcutaneous tissue were normal again. Their energy level had considerably increased, as was reflected in their performance (see Table 2).

The performance of the two groups of infants on the Brazelton scale was compared item by item for each day of the examination with the Mann-Whitney U Test. The most striking differences were found on the 1st-day (6 items) and 10th-day (8 items) examinations, with only 2 items differentiating the two groups on the 5th-day examination.

Before describing these differences, we wish to note a certain stability and lack of change discernible in the United States babies. The scores of the American infants in this sample stayed within an average range on all three days. This is in contrast to results obtained in other groups of American infants who typically score below the average on day 1 and who recover by day 5 (Brazelton, 1970). These latter groups were obtained from mothers who were medicated during delivery and whose infants demonstrated a resulting depression in all behavior. Note that the infants in the present sample were delivered with a minimal use of drugs, and by "natural" childbirth.

On the day 1 examination, there were 6 items on which the two groups of infants were significantly different. The Zambian infants scored lower on following with eyes (p < .05), motor activity (p < .02), tempo at height (p < .10), irritability (p < .05), rapidity of buildup (p < .10), and cuddliness (p < .10). On the day 5 examination, only 2 items differentiated the groups, with Americans scoring lower on rapidity of buildup (p < .10) and on alertness (p < .10).

The 10th-day examination comparisons found 8 items which distinguished the two groups. The Zambian infants scored lower on reactivity to stimulation (p < .07), defensive movements (p < .05), motor ac-

TABLE 2

Mean Scores for Zambians and for Americans on Day 1, 5, and 10 for All Measures that Distinguished between Groups on at Least One Day[a]

Measures	Day 1		Day 5		Day 10	
	Zamb.	Amer.	Zamb.	Amer.	Zamb.	Amer.
Motor activity	3.00	4.90	5.89	5.50	4.60	5.90
Tempo at height	3.20	5.77	5.90	5.50	4.40	6.44
Rapidity of buildup	3.22	4.80	5.62	4.50	3.50	5.50
Irritability	2.50	4.40	4.40	4.70	3.80	5.00
Consolability	6.60	5.56	5.00	4.63	6.12	4.75
Social interest	4.20	4.29	6.20	5.22	6.70	4.33
Alertness	3.40	4.20	6.30	5.11	7.40	4.80
Follow with eyes	2.40	4.16	4.60	4.70	4.67	5.11
Reactivity to stimulation	3.35	4.38	5.30	4.71	6.14	4.67
Defensive movements	3.20	4.38	5.11	5.50	4.90	6.11
Cuddliness	3.30	4.40	5.22	5.60	6.30	5.12

[a]Scores in italics indicate that the difference between them was significant.

tivity (p < .05), rapidity of buildup (p < .05), and tempo at height (p < .02). The Zambians scored higher on consolability (p < .06), social interest (p < .02), and alertness (p < .02). By day 10, also, muscle tone was better than average, in contrast to day 1. No longer were the Zambians limp. Their head control was good; passive resistance of limbs to flexion and extension normal; and they actively responded upon being held (scores on cuddliness were above average). Reference to Table 2 emphasizes again that it is the Zambian group which is changing, not the American group.

To summarize: the Americans remained approximately within the average range on all three days. On day 1, the Zambians scored lower than the Americans on items that seemed to reflect reactivity. By day 10, however, although (or maybe, because) the Zambians were still scoring low on items which measured motor reactivity, they were scoring higher on items which measured social attentiveness.

DISCUSSION

One of the questions we had been interested in was whether behavioral differences existed between cultural groups during the neonatal period. This question was certainly answered in the affirmative.

The most striking feature of the results is the difference in the pattern of increase in the scores of the Zambian and American infants. On the day 1 examination the Zambian infants scored low relative to the American infants and to their own later performance on behaviors related to activity and to alertness. They were not very irritable and did not invest much energy in being upset (as indicated by their scores on irritability, tempo, and rapidity of buildup). They also lacked energy for relating to the social and inanimate environment (as demonstrated by poor responses to being cuddled and to visual stimulation).

By the 10th day, there had been a dramatic change. They were alert, controlled in motor activities, and oriented toward their social environment. Their high scores on alertness and social interest were coupled with a high degree of consolability and low scores on overreactiveness—motor activity, rapidity of buildup, and tempo at height of disturbance. Their scores in defensive reactions and reactivity to inanimate stimulation seemed to indicate that their energy was directed toward and invested in the social environment. In contrast, the American infants' scores remained stable throughout the first 10 days.

Interesting though these differences may be, the real question is: what accounts for them?

We suggest that these differences are compatible with a view of some so-called "cultural" differences as resulting from a combination of the effects of genetic and nongenetic inheritance, operating in conjunction with certain child-rearing practices.

We start with the nongenetic inherited factors. We know that nongenetic inheritance certainly plays a role in determining the characteristics of children under some circumstances. The effects of changes in nongenetic inheritance are exemplified in a number of situations: Down's syndrome (which results from chromosomal changes that are highly correlated with mother's age); changes in the infant that result either from drugs ingested by the mother in early pregnancy or from hormonal imbalance during pregnancy (Baker, 1960; Brazelton, 1970; Money et al., 1968). Additionally, there are the nongenetic but inherited effects of protein malnutrition (Schaffer, 1960; Zamenhof et al., 1968); of infections suffered by the mother during pregnancy (Klein et al., 1971); and of depletion of the uterus, a depletion that results from a series of pregnancies following so closely upon one another that there is no opportunity for the uterus to recover. We know that the last three factors affect the infant's gain in body weight and growth in length in the uterus. Might they not also be responsible for behavioral differences between the neonates of different cultures?

The differences between Zambians and Americans on day 1 were differences in behavior that are usually associated with sheer physical energy. That the lack of energy was, in fact, the primary cause of the Zambian infants' low scores is made more credible by what we know of these infants' physical state. We could see that they were dehydrated. We also knew that their mothers had had low protein intake during pregnancy as well as a series of closely spaced pregnancies. These facts made it clear that the day 1 differences could easily reflect the effects of a stressed intrauterine environment. This environment was inherited, but nongenetic, and its effects were dramatic. Once their mothers began to nurse them, thereby both rehydrating them and providing them with needed nutrients, the Zambian infants became much more reactive.

An additional and complementary argument is also possible. Behavioral differences after birth are rapidly affected by factors other than inheritance. They are quickly molded by social factors, especially by such divergent child-rearing practices as these two groups were exposed to.

The change in behavior that was evident by day 10 was of a different quality from the changes that took place between days 1 and 5. First, the change involved more than simple recovery from a poor physiological environment. The behaviors that improved from day 1 to day 5 were behaviors that seemed to require a certain level of physical energy: the behaviors that changed from day 5 to day 10 were those commonly seen as requiring a certain level of social interest.

The changes from day 1 to day 5 seemed to be primarily attributable to the rehydration and nutrition that resulted from nutrients. We thought that the changes from day 5 to day 10 resulted primarily from certain child-rearing practices, and that these were of the sort that facilitate the development of muscle tone, alertness, and social responsivity.

The kind of motoric stimulation that the infants received seemed to put a premium on developing muscle tone. When asked to rouse their babies, the Zambian mothers picked them up under the arms and tossed them up and down in the air. All cries were first responded to with nursing. However, if this did not quiet the infant, the mother resorted to vigorous activity and bouncing. Goldberg (1971) has noted that from as early as 24 hours after delivery, the Zambian mother secures her infant to her body with a *dashica*, a long piece of cloth, in such a way that the infant essentially rides on the mother's hip. In this position, the infant's body has no support from the armpits up. Since his head is not supported, the infant must maintain a strong shoulder girdle response to keep his head steady. The mother places the infant in her *dashica* either by holding him by the arm or by holding his trunk under the arm and then swinging him over her shoulder. In short, this active handling of the infant seems to encourage the development of muscle tone.

But in addition to favoring the development of muscle tone, carrying the infant in a *dashica* seems to encourage alertness as well (Korner, 1970). In this position, an infant is able to see more than he would in other positions. Long periods of being carried also provide more opportunities for the infant to be tactually stimulated. This tactile stimulation by another person encourages social responsiveness on the part of the infant, but other practices also seem to facilitate social responsivity. Breast feeding is frequent and in response to any indication from the infant that he is either hungry or fussy. There is little attempt to make him wait (Goldberg, 1970, 1971).

When the infants are not being carried about, they are left uncovered on a bed in a family room where everyone, including siblings and visitors, can admire, play with, and hold the tiny infant. At night, the infant is swaddled loosely next to his mother in the same bed.

Since at birth the Zambian infants were very limp and quite unresponsive, one might wonder at their mothers's willingness to provide the infants with vigorous, stimulating experiences. We concluded that the mothers' practices were based on their expectancies

of how their infants would develop. Assuming that the infants in our sample were not atypical of the population, one can infer that the Zambian mothers in our sample had seen other Zambian infants recover shortly after birth. One can also infer that these mothers thus had reason to expect that their infants, too, would recover in the same way. Individually, each mother's expectations were probably also reinforced by the dramatic change in muscle tone and responsivity that took place in her infant from day 1 to day 5, which she could easily have interpreted as evidence that her infant would continue to show improvement.

These expectations were based both on the Zambian mother's observation of her own and other infants' recovery from their state on day 1. The infants' ability to recover must reflect genetic capacities to respond to these practices. Such rapid recovery seems to point to inherited potential which is not incapacitated by conditions of intrauterine deprivation.

Contrast the Zambian caretaker practices with those of our American mothers. The American infants' behavior reflected very different inherited (genetic and nongenetic) potential at birth. In addition, they remained in the hospital environment for a minimum of 4 days. Five of the babies roomed in with their mothers after 48 hours, and it is presumed that their cries were responded to with nursing or handling by their mothers. The 5 infants who were kept in the nursery were fed every 4 hours, day and night, on hospital schedules. The rooming-in mothers were urged to feed the babies on a similar schedule, and because of their inexperience and the delay in getting breast milk (4 to 5 days in a primiparous mother), it is obvious that there was less feeding and handling than there was among Zambian mothers. When these American mothers went home, they followed the cultural emphasis in the United States on quieting the infant and protecting him from external stimulation. There is no care practice that even approximates the Zambian mother's almost constant contact with her infant. From our observation of them in their homes, it was quite obvious that these American mothers provided a very different early environment for their infants. The unchanging behavior over the 10 days reflects a different inheritance as well as the relatively nonstimulating environment to which the babies were exposed in this period.

SUMMARY

The abilities of an infant and the changes in those abilities reflect inherited factors—both genetic and nongenetic—cultural practices and expectations. An understanding of the recovery of the Zambian infants and the pattern of performance of the American infants reflects all three. The Zambian infants recovered rapidly from an intrauterine (inherited) environment which had been physiologically inadequate. Their rapid recovery reflected the infants' genetic abilities as well as the supportive child-rearing practices and the cultural expectations for early precocious development. The American infants reflected an adequate intrauterine environment with their more unchanging behavioral patterns. The protective, relatively nonstimulating child-rearing practices were suited to genetic capabilities as well as to cultural expectations of a "prolonged" and protected infancy.

References

AINSWORTH, M. D. S. (1967), *Infancy in Uganda: Infant Care and the Growth of Love.* Baltimore: Johns Hopkins Press.

APGAR. V. (1953), A proposal for a new method of evaluation of the newborn infant. *Curr. Res. Anesth. Analges.,* 32:260–283.

BAKER. J. B. E. (1960), The effects of drugs on the fetus. *Pharmacol. Rev.,* 12:37–90.

BRAZELTON, T. B. (1970), Effect of prenatal drugs on the behavior of the neonate. *Amer. J. Psychiat.* 126:1261–1266.

——— (1973), *Neonatal Behavioral Assessment Scale.* London: Heinemann.

———, KOSLOWSKI, B., & MAIN, M. (1973), Origins of reciprocity: mother and infant interaction. In: *Origins of Behavior,* Vol. I, ed. M. Lewis & L. Rosenblum. New York: Wiley, pp. 49–76.

———, ROBEY, J. S., & COLLIER, G. A. (1969), Infant development in the Zinacanteco Indians of Southern Mexico. *Pediatrics,* 44:274–290.

CLIFFORD, S. H. (1954), Postmaturity with placental dysfunction: clinical syndrome and pathologic findings. *J. Pediat.,* 44:1–13.

DUBOWITZ, L. M. S., DUBOWITZ, V., & GOLDBERG, C. (1970), Clinical assessment of gestational age in the newborn infant. *J. Pediat.,* 77:1–10.

FREEDMAN, D. G. & FREEDMAN, N. (1969), Behavioral differences between Chinese-American and American newborns. *Nature,* 224:1227.

GEBER. M. & DEAN, R. F. A. (1959), The state of development of newborn African children. *Lancet,* 1: 1216.

GOLDBERG, S. A. (1970), Infant care in Zambia: Measuring maternal behavior. HDRU Reports No. 13, Lusaka, Zambia.

——— (1971), Infant care and growth in urban Zambia. Presented at the meetings of the Society for Research in Child Development, Minneapolis, Minn., April 4.

KLEIN, R. E., HABICHT, J. P., & YARBROUGH, C. (1971), Effect of protein-calorie malnutrition on mental development. Incap (Institute of Nutrition of Central America, Panama) publication no. I-571, Guatemala, CA.

KORNER, A. (1970), Visual alertness in neonates: individual differences and their correlates. *Percept. Mot. Skills,* 31:499–509.

MONEY, J., EHRHARDT, A. A., & MASICA, D. N. (1968), Fetal feminization induced by androgen insensitivity in the Testicular Feminizing Syndrome. *Johns Hopkins Med. J.,* 123:105–114.

PRECHTL, H. & BEINTEMA, O. (1964), *The Neurological Examination of the Full Term Newborn Infant.* London: Heinemann.

SCHAFFER, A. J. (1960), *Diseases of the Newborn.* Philadelphia: Saunders, p. 628.

ZAMENHOF, S., VAN MARTHENS, E., & MARGOLIS, F. L. (1968), DNA and protein in neonatal brain: alteration by maternal dietary restriction. *Science,* 160:322–323.

9

Of Human Bonding: Newborns Prefer Their Mothers' Voices

ANTHONY J. DECASPER AND WILLIAM P. FIFER

Over the past two decades there has been a huge increase in developmental research describing infant capabilities. This increase is due in part to technical innovations that allow researchers to study infant behavior during the early days and months of life. But it also reflects a shift in psychologists' conception of infancy. Whereas infants were once seen as having few inherent capabilities, they are now considered capable living systems with an innate competence to interact with the world around them. The following article describes one of these early capabilities: the neonate's ability to discriminate sounds—in particular human voices. The adaptive benefits of this ability are immense and its presence in newborns attests to the complex biological preparedness of the human infant—a preparedness that helps even very young babies play an active role in their own development.

By sucking on a nonnutritive nipple in different ways, a newborn human could produce either its mother's voice or the voice of another female. Infants learned how to produce the mother's voice and produced it more often than the other voice. The neonate's preference for the maternal voice suggests *that the period shortly after birth may be important for initiating infant bonding to the mother.*

Human responsiveness to sound begins in the third trimester of life and by birth reaches sophisticated levels (1), especially with respect to speech (2). Early

Reprinted with permission from the authors and *Science*, 208, 1980, 1174-1176. Copyright 1980 by the American Association for the Advancement of Science.

auditory competency probably subserves a variety of developmental functions such as language acquisition (*1, 3*) and mother-infant bonding (*4, 5*). Mother-infant bonding would best be served by (and may even require) the ability of a newborn to discriminate its mother's voice from that of other females. However, evidence for differential sensitivity to or discrimination of the maternal voice is available only for older infants for whom the bonding process is well advanced (*6*). Therefore, the role of maternal voice discrimination in formation of the mother-infant bond is unclear. If the newborn's sensitivities to speech subserves bonding, discrimination of and preference for the maternal voice should be evident near birth. We now report that a newborn infant younger than 3 days of age can not only discriminate its mother's voice but also will work to produce her voice in preference to the voice of another female.

The subjects were ten Caucasian neonates (five male and five female) (*7*). Shortly after delivery we tape-recorded the voices of mothers of infants selected for testing as they read Dr. Seuss's *To Think That I Saw It On Mulberry Street*. Recordings were edited to provide 25 minutes of uninterrupted prose, and testing of whether infants would differentially produce their mothers' voices began within 24 hours of recording. Sessions began by coaxing the infant to a state of quiet alertness (*8*). The infant was then placed supine in its basinette, earphones were secured over its ears, and a nonnutritive nipple was placed in its mouth. An assistant held the nipple loosely in place; she was unaware of the experimental condition of the individual infant and could neither hear the tapes nor be seen by the infant. The nipple was connected, by way of a pressure transducer, to the solid-state programming and recording equipment. The infants were then allowed 2 minutes to adjust to the situation. Sucking activity was recorded during the next 5 minutes, but voices were never presented. This baseline period was used to determine the median interburst interval (IBI) or time elapsing between the end of one burst of sucking and the beginning of the next (*9*). A burst was defined as a series of individual sucks separated from one another by less than 2 seconds. Testing with the voices began after the baseline had been established.

For five randomly selected infants, sucking burst terminating IBI's equal to or greater than the baseline median (*t*) produced only his or her mother's voice (IBI $\geq t$), and bursts terminating intervals less than the median produced only the voice of another infant's mother (*10*). Thus, only one of the voices was presented, stereophonically, with the first suck of a burst and remained on until the burst ended, that is, until 2 seconds elapsed without a suck. For the other five

infants, the conditions were reversed. Testing lasted 20 minutes.

A preference for the maternal voice was indicated if the infant produced it more often than the nonmaternal voice. However, unequal frequencies not indicative of preference for the maternal voice per se could result either because short (or long) IBI's were easier to produce or because the acoustic qualities of a particular voice, such as pitch or intensity, rendered it a more effective form of feedback. The effects of response requirements and voice characteristics were controlled (i) by requiring half the infants to respond after short IBI's to produce the mother's voice and half to respond after long ones and (ii) by having each maternal voice also serve as the nonmaternal voice for another infant.

Preference for the mother's voice was shown by the increase in the proportion of IBI's capable of producing her voice; the median IBI's shifted from their baseline values in a direction that produced the maternal voice more than half the time. Eight of the ten medians were shifted in a direction of the maternal voice (mean = 1.90 seconds, a 34 percent increase) (sign test, $P = .02$), one shifted in the direction that produced the nonmaternal voice more often, and one median did not change from its baseline value (Figure 1).

If these infants were working to gain access to their mother's voice, reversing the response requirements should result in a reversal of their IBI'S. Four infants, two from each condition, who produced their mother's voice more often in session 1 were able to complete a second session 24 hours later, in which the response requirements were reversed (*11*). Differential feedback in session 2 began immediately after the 2-minute adjustment period. The criterion time remained equal to the baseline median of the first session. For all four infants, the median IBI's shifted toward the new criterion values and away from those which previously produced the maternal voice. The average magnitude of the difference between the medians of the first and reversal sessions was 1.95 seconds.

Apparently the infant learned to gain access to the mother's voice. Since specific temporal properties of sucking were required to produce the maternal voice, we sought evidence for the acquisition of temporally differentiated responding. Temporal discrimination within each condition was ascertained by constructing the function for IBI per opportunity: IBI's were collected into classes equal to one-fifth the baseline median, and the frequency of each class was divided by the total frequency of classes having equal and larger values (*12*). When IBI's less than the baseline median were required, the likelihood of terminating interburst intervals was highest for classes

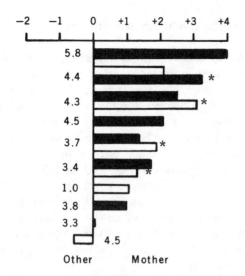

FIGURE 1 For each subject, signed difference scores between the median IBI's without vocal feedback (baseline) and with differential vocal feedback (session 1). Differences of the four reversal sessions (*) are based on medians with differential feedback in sessions 1 and 2. Positive values indicate a preference for the maternal voice and negative values a preference for the nonmaternal voice. Filled bars indicate that the mother's voice followed IBI's of less than the baseline median; open bars indicate that her voice followed intervals equal to or greater than the median. Median IBI's of the baseline (in seconds) are shown opposite the bars.

less than the median (Figure 2), whereas when longer intervals were required, the probability of terminating an IBI was maximal for intervals slightly longer than the median. Feedback from the maternal voice effectively differentiated the temporal character of responding that produced it: the probability of terminating IBI's was highest when termination resulted in the maternal voice.

Repeating the experiment with 16 female neonates and a different discrimination procedure confirmed their preference for the maternal voice (*13*). The discriminative stimuli were a 400-Hz tone of 4 seconds duration (tone) and a 4-second period of silence (no tone). Each IBI contained an alternating sequence of tone-no-tone periods, and each stimulus was equally likely to begin a sequence. For eight infants, a sucking burst initiated during a tone period turned off the tone and produced the Dr. Seuss story read by the infant's mother, whereas sucking bursts during a no-tone period produced the nonmaternal voice. The elicited voice remained until the sucking burst ended, at which time the tone-no-tone alternation began anew. The discriminative stimuli were reversed for the other eight neonates. Testing with the

voices began immediately after the 2-minute adjustment period and lasted 20 minutes. Each maternal voice also served as a nonmaternal voice.

During the first third of the testing session, the infants were as likely to suck during a stimulus period correlated with the maternal voice as during one correlated with the nonmaternal voice (Table 1). However, in the last third of the session the infants sucked during stimulus periods associated with their mother's voice approximately 24 percent more often than during those associated with the nonmaternal voice, a significant increase [$F(1, 14) = 8.97$, $P < .01$]. Thus, at the beginning of testing there was no indication of stimulus discrimination or voice preference. By the end of the 20-minute session, feedback from the maternal voice produced clear evidence of an auditory discrimination; the probability of sucking during tone and no-tone periods was greater when sucking produced the maternal voice.

The infants in these studies lived in a group nursery; their general care and night feedings were handled by a number of female nursery personnel. They were fed in their mothers' rooms by their mothers at 9:30 a.m. and at 1:30, 5:00, and 8:30 p.m. At most, they had 12 hours of postnatal contact with their mothers before testing. Similarly reared infants prefer the human voice to other acoustically complex stimuli (*14*). But, as our data show, newborns reared in group nurseries that allow minimal maternal contact can also discriminate between their mothers and other speakers and, moreover, will work to produce their mothers' voices in preference to those of other

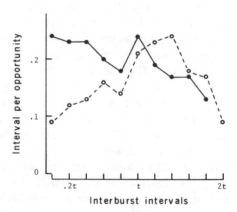

FIGURE 2 Interburst interval per opportunity when the maternal voice followed intervals less than the baseline median (solid line) and intervals equal to or greater than the median (dashed line). The IBI's are represented on the abscissa by the lower bound of interval classes equal to one-fifth the baseline median (*t*).

TABLE 1

Mean ($\overline{X}$) and Standard Deviation (S.D.) of the Relative Frequency of Sucking During a Stimulus Associated with the Maternal Voice Divided by the Relative Frequency of Sucking During a Stimulus Associated with the Nonmaternal Voice

Stimulus associated with maternal voice	First third		Last third	
	$\overline{X}$	S.D.	$\overline{X}$	S.D.
Tone	0.97	.33	1.26	.33
No tone	1.04	.31	1.22	.19
Combined	1.00[a]	.32	1.24	.27

[a] A ratio of 1.0 indicates no preference.

females. This, within the first 3 days of postnatal development, newborns prefer the human voice, discriminate between speakers, and demonstrate a preference for their mothers' voices with only limited maternal exposure.

The neonate's capacity to rapidly acquire a stimulus discrimination that controls behavior (15) could provide the means by which limited postnatal experience with the mother results in preference for her voice. The early preference demonstrated here is possible because newborns have auditory competencies adequate for discriminating individual speakers: they are sensitive to rhythmicity (16), intonation (17), frequency variation (1, 13), and phonetic components of speech (18). Their general sensory competency may enable other maternal cues, such as her odor (19) and the manner in which she handles her infant (20), to serve as supporting bases for discrimination and vocal preference. Prenatal (intrauterine) auditory experience may also be a factor. Although the significance and nature of intrauterine auditory experience in humans is not known, perceptual preferences and proximity-seeking responses of some infrahuman infants are profoundly affected by auditory experience before birth (21).

References and Notes

1. R. B. Eisenberg, *Auditory Competence in Early Life: The Roots of Communicative Behavior* (University Park Press, Baltimore, 1976.)

2. P. D. Eimas, in *Infant Perception: From Sensation to Cognition*, L. B. Cohen and P. Salapatek, Eds. (Academic Press, New York, 1975), vol. 2., p. 193.

3. B. Friedlander, *Merrill-Palmer Q., 16*, 7 (1970).

4. R. Bell, in *The Effect of the Infant on Its Caregiver*, M. Lewis and L. A. Rosenblum, Eds. (Wiley, New York, 1974). p. 1; T. B. Brazelton, E. Tronick, L. Abramson, H. Als, S. Wise, *Ciba Found. Symp., 33*, 137 (1975).

5. M. H. Klaus and J. H. Kennel, *Maternal Infant Bonding* (Mosby, St. Louis, 1976); P. DeChateau, *Birth Family J., 41*, 10 (1977).

6. M. Miles and E. Melvish, *Nature (London) 252*, 123 (1974); J. Mehler, J. Bertoncini, M. Baurière, D. Jassik-Gershenfeld, *Perception, 7*, 491 (1978).

7. The infants were randomly selected from those meeting the following criteria: (i) gestation, full term; (ii) delivery, uncomplicated; (iii) birth weight, between 2500 and 3850 grams; and (iv) APGAR score, at least eight at 1 and 5 minutes after birth. If circumsized, males were not observed until at least 12 hours afterward. Informed written consent was obtained from the mother, and she was invited to observe the testing procedure. Testing sessions began between 2.5 and 3.5 hours after the 6 a.m. or 12 p.m. feeding. All infants were bottle-fed.

8. P. H. Wolff, *Psychol. Issues, 5*, 1 (1966). The infants were held in front of the experimenter's face, spoken to, and then presented with the nonnutritive nipple. Infants failing to fixate visually on the experimenter's face or to suck on the nipple were returned to the nursery. Once begun, a session was terminated only if the infant cried or stopped sucking for two consecutive minutes. The initial sessions of two infants were terminated because they cried for 2 minutes. Their data are not reported. Thus, the results are based on 10 of 12 infants meeting the behavioral criteria for entering and remaining in the study.

9. With quiet and alert newborns, nonnutritive sucking typically occurs as bursts of individual sucks, each separated by a second or so, while the bursts themselves are separated by several seconds or more. Interburst intervals tend to be unimodally distributed with modal values differing among infants. [K. Kaye, in *Studies in Mother-Infant Interaction*, H. R. Schaffer, Ed. (Academic Press, New York, 1977)]. A suck was said to occur when the negative pressure exerted on the nipple reached 20 mm-Hg. This value is almost always exceeded during nonnutritive sucking by healthy infants, but is virtually never produced by nonsucking mouth movement.

10. The tape reels revolved continuously, and one or the other of the voices was electronically switched to the earphones when the response threshold was met. Because the thresholds were detected electronically, voice onset occurred at the moment the negative pressure reached 20 mm-Hg.

11. Two infants were not tested a second time, because we could not gain access to the testing room, which served as an auxiliary nursery and as an isolation room. The sessions of two infants who cried were terminated. Two other infants were tested a second time, but in their first session one had shown no preference and the other had shown only a slight preference for the nonmaternal voice. Their performance may have been affected by inconsistent feedback. Because their peak sucking pressures were near the threshold of the apparatus, very similar sucks would sometimes produce feedback and sometimes not, and sometimes feedback would be terminated in the midst of a sucking burst. Consequently, second session performances of these two infants, which were much like their initial performances, were uninterpretable.

12. D. Anger, *J. Exp. Psychol., 52,* 145 (1956).

13. Three other infants began testing with the voices, but their sessions were terminated because they cried. Their data are not included. This study is part of a doctoral thesis submitted by W.P.F.

14. E. Butterfield and G. Siperstein, in *Oral Sensation and Perception: The Mouth of the Infant,* J. Bosma, Ed. (Thomas, Springfield, Ill., 1972).

15. E. R. Siqueland and L. P. Lipsitt, *J. Exp. Child. Psychol. 3,* 356 (1966); R. E. Kron, in *Recent Advances in Biological Psychiatry,* J. Wortis, Ed. (Plenum, New York, 1967), p. 295.

16. W. S. Condon and L. W. Sander, *Science, 183,* 99 (1974).

17. R. B. Eisenberg, D. B. Cousins, N. Rupp, *J. Aud. Res., 7,* 245 (1966); P. A. Morse, *J. Exp. Child. Psychol., 14,* 477 (1972).

18. E. C. Butterfield and G. F. Cairns, in *Language Perspectives: Acquisition, Retardation and Intervention,* R. L. Schiefelbusch and L. L. Lloyd, Eds. (University Park Press, Baltimore, 1974), p. 75; A. J. DeCasper, E. C. Butterfield, G. F. Cairns, paper presented at the fourth biennial conference on Human Development, Nashville. April 1976.

19. A. MacFarlane, *Ciba Found. Symp., 33,* 103 (1975).

20. P. Burns, L. W. Sander, G. Stechler, H. Julia. *J. Am. Acad. Child Psychiatry, 11,* 427 (1972), E. B. Thoman, A. F. Korner, L. Bearon-Williams, *Child Dev., 48,* 563 (1977).

21. G. Gottlieb, *Development of Species Identification in Birds: An Inquiry into the Prenatal Determinants of Perception* (Univ. of Chicago Press, Chicago, 1971); E. H. Hess. *Imprinting* (Van Nostrand-Reinhold, New York, 1973).

22. Supported by Research Council grant 920. We thank the infants, their mothers, and the staff of Moses Cane Hospital, where this work was performed, and A. Carstens for helping conduct the research.

PART II

Infancy

10

Early Rule Structure:
The Case of "Peekaboo"

JEROME S. BRUNER AND V. SHERWOOD

Humans are social animals who create and participate in social activities that are highly governed by rules. From the beginning of life infants engage in many social activities that connect them in meaningful ways to other people, especially their primary caregivers. Some of these activities are quite structured, some less so. However, all these activities are united in their reliance on the emerging skills and capabilities of infants as they become coordinated with their "partners in development." A common activity involving adults and young children is peekaboo, a game that joins the infant's emerging skills of responsiveness, anticipation, and object knowledge with an adult who helps to coordinate the infant's skills with the rule structure of the game. In the following article, Bruner and Sherwood describe this social synchronization and suggest that development occurs through participation in such activities.

Peekaboo surely must rank as one of the most universal forms of play between adults and infants. It is rich indeed in the mechanisms it exhibits. For in point of fact, the game depends upon the infant's capacity to integrate a surprisingly wide range of phenomena. For one, the very playing of the game depends upon the child having some degree of mastery of object permanence, the capacity to recognize the continued existence of an object when it is out of sight (e.g. Piaget, 1954). Charlesworth (1966) has shown, moreover, that the successful playing of the game is dependent in some measure on the child being able to keep track of the location in which a face has disappeared, the child showing more persistent effects when the reappearance of a face varied unexpectedly with respect to its prior position. Greenfield (1970) has also indicated that the initial effect of the game depends upon the presence not only of the reappearing face, but also of an accompanying vocalization by the mother, although with repetition the role of vocalization declined. She also found that the voice was increasingly important the less familiar the setting in which the game was played. It is quite plain, then, that complex expectancies are built up in the infant in the course of playing the game, and that these expectancies are characterized by considerable spatio-temporal structuring.

Another way of saying the same thing is to note that the child very soon becomes sensitive to the 'rules of the game' as he plays it. That is to say, he expects disappearance and reappearance to be in a certain place, at a certain time, accompanied by certain vocalizations, in certain general settings. The bulk of the studies reported in the literature suggest that these 'conventions', though they may rest upon certain preadapted readinesses to respond to disappearance and reappearance, are soon converted into rules for defining the pattern of play. If this were the case, one would expect that not only would the child have learned procedures, but would have learned them in a way that is characteristic of rule learning—i.e. in a general form, with assignable roles, with permissible substitutions of moves, etc.

The present study is concerned specifically with the conversion of peekaboo procedures into rule structures and, without intending to minimize the importance of preadapted patterns of response in making the game possible, we shall concentrate upon this aspect of the matter.

The study is based upon an intensive investigation of six infants over a period of 10 months, from seven to 17 months of age. The infants and their mothers were seen once a fortnight at our laboratory for an hour, and among the instructions given to the mothers was one asking them to show us the games that they and their infants most enjoyed playing. Our observations of peekaboo are all based upon behaviour spontaneously produced by the mothers in play, all but one of them including peekaboo in the play they exhibited. All sessions were videotaped and analysis was carried out on the video records. Partly for convenience of reporting and partly because each pair developed somewhat different procedures, we shall concentrate on a single mother-infant dyad over the 10-month period. The corpus of such play for this dyad consisted of 22 episodes of peekaboo, the first at 10 months, the last at 15 months. Peekaboo starts earlier than our initial age and goes on later, but the sample of games over the five-month period suffices to illustrate the points we wish to make. Though the other infant-mother dyads show some differences

from the one we are reporting, they are in no sense different in pattern.

OBSERVATIONS

The first thing to be noted in the one mother–daughter (Diane) dyad on which we shall concentrate is that all instances of the game are quite notably constrained with respect to their limits. That is to say, the game always starts after the two players have made an explicit contact. This is the opening move, but it should be noted immediately that here, as in other features of the game, variation prevails. In most instances, initial contact is by face-to-face mutual looking. Where this does not occur, the mother may use either vocalization to contact the child or make the hiding 'instrument' conspicuous. The following table gives the frequencies of opening moves.

Face-to-face contact	16 (of 21 episodes in which orientation could be ascertained)
Vocalization	9 (of 22)
Highlighting of instrument	3 (of 22)

Typically, vocalization and face-to-face contact go together, with seven out of nine episodes of vocalization being accompanied by face-to-face contact. Interestingly enough, the mother will sometimes use a chance event as a 'starter' as when, inadvertently, her smock hides the child's face and the mother uses this as a start for a round of peekaboo. Also, there is what might best be called the 'opportunistic start', in which the mother when drying the child's hair after a bath 'lightens' the occasion by turning the drying with towel into an episode of peekaboo—a pattern also used by mothers to divert a fretting baby.

As Garvey (in press) has put it, social games can be described in terms of (a) the nature of the format, (b) the turns of each player and (c) the rounds in which the turns are sequenced. In the peekaboo situation, the initial round is a mutual attention-focusing episode that seems invariant although its form, as we have seen, may vary from one instance of the peekaboo format to the next.

The second round of peekaboo is the actual act of hiding and its accompaniments. Note first that there are four alternatives possible: mother can be hidden, or child, and the act of hiding can be initiated by the mother or the infant. The four alternatives and their frequencies are as follows.

M initiated, M hidden	8
C initiated, C hidden	2
M initiated, C hidden	11
C initiated, M hidden	0
[Ambiguous	1]

We may note that whilst there are at most three instances of the child initiating the hiding act, and all of these came at 15 months, they indicate that the child is by no means always a passive participant. We shall have more to say of this later in discussing role reversal. One of the striking features of what is hidden is that it is about equally distributed between the mother's face being masked and the child's—one of the forms of variation that the mother uses in order to keep uncertainty operative within the game. The child seems readily to accept this variation in the format and, indeed, seems to take a certain delight in it.

What is very notable is that there is virtually complete openness with regard to the instrument and mode used for hiding. The game when first observed was carried out exclusively with a nappy and hiding was controlled by the mother, and this occurred six times, hiding herself four times and the child twice. Thereafter, the distribution of the remaining episodes was five times nappy, five times clothing, three times a towel, two times a chair, and once with the child averting her head. In short, the nature of the hiding instrument and the masking act might almost be called optional in contrast to certain obligatory features, such as the requirement of initial contact.

During the period of hiding, and we shall discuss the limits on its length below, there is a further ancillary feature of the game—a mode of sustaining contact during hiding. This occurs both on the mother's side and on the child's. In 16 of the 22 episodes, mother uses either the rising intonation pattern of the typical Where question ('Where's Diane?' or 'Where's baby?' or 'Where's mummy?') or employs an extended 'Ahhhh', sometimes with a rising intonation pattern. In one sense, this act on the part of the mother can be thought of as helping the child sustain attention and bridging any uncertainty concerning the mother's 'conservation' behind the hiding instrument. The child's responses during hiding seem, on the other hand, to be expressions of excitement or anticipation, though they help the mother control her own output of bridging vocalizations to keep the child at an appropriate activation level. There are 13 in 19 episodes

involving a hiding cloth where the child actively seeks to remove the hiding mask from the mother's or her own face. It is to these initiatives that the mother often responds with vocalization as if to control the child's activation. This part of the game is characteristically 'non-rule bound' and seems to be an instance, rather, of the mother providing a scaffold for the child.

We come now to a crucial round in the game: uncovering and reappearance. Note first a point already made—hiding time is very constrained: 19 of the 22 episodes range between two and seven seconds, with only one being above seven (at 10 months) and two at one second. It is only at 15 months, when the child consistently controls reappearance, that there is a fairly homogeneous and rapid hiding time: five episodes in a row ranging from one to two seconds. But note that at this age the child has virtually given up 'static' peekaboo for an ambulatory version, so that variation is now in format rather than in timing. The five uniformly fast episodes were all with a nappy—an old and familiar game that is much less exciting for the child than the ambulatory game we shall describe below. One of these episodes, a one-second instance, was completely controlled by the child, and between two was an instance where the child demanded the game vocatively after she had failed to cover her own face successfully. We believe that the constraint on time of hiding is a reflection of the appreciation of the child's limited attention span by both members of the pair—the mother reacting to signs of the child's impatience, the child responding directly to his own.

The actual act of uncovering is open to considerable variation. We find instances where it is controlled by the child, others where the mother controls uncovering. Occasionally, the mother, by drawing near and vocalizing, provokes the child into removing the mask from her face, as if to stimulate more control from the infant. Indeed, one even encounters partial, 'tempting' uncovering by the mother to provoke the child into completion, where the mother exposes a corner of her eye. In terms of control of unmasking, we note that before 12 months, nine of 12 of the episodes of unmasking are controlled by the mother. From 12 on, none are, and six in 10 are controlled by the child alone—a phenomenon seen only once before this age.

Following uncovering, there is again a rather standard ritual: remaking contact. In the 19 episodes where we were able to determine it 14 uncoverings were accompanied by face-to-face contact immediately or shortly after. In all instances of uncovering but one, mother sought to establish such conduct, though in four she failed to do so. Moreover, in 16 of

22 episodes, mother vocalized upon uncovering, usually with a 'Boo' or a 'Hello' or an 'Ahhh'. Obviously, there is considerable release of tension at this point, since laughter accompanies the above 15 times for the child (and indeed 12 for the mother, always in accompaniment with the child).

At 15 months, the child invents and controls a new variation of the game, as already noted. It consists of her moving behind a chair, out of sight of her mother, then reappearing and saying 'Boo'. She has now become the agent in the play, mother being recipient of her action. The format has been revised by the child and the prior role of agent and recipient reversed. This variation in agency has, of course, appeared before in the more static form of the game involving a hiding instrument. But it is important to note that the child has now extended the rules under her own control to a new, but formally identical format—again involving initial face-to-face contact, hiding and reappearing by self-initiated movement, and reestablishing contact. From there on out, peekaboo is a game embedded in self-directed movement by the child that produces disappearance and reappearance. The child has not only learned to conform to the rules of the static game as initiated by mother and by child, but also to use the rules for the initiation of a variant of the old format. At this point, the range of possible games incorporating the basic rules of peekaboo becomes almost limitless, and what provides unity is the agreement of mother and infant to maintain a skeleton rule structure with new instruments for hiding and new settings in which to play. We can say that at this point the child is no longer performance-bound, but rather has achieved a proper 'competence' for generating new versions of an old game.

But we must turn now to the question of what brought the child to a full realization of the 'syntax' of the game of peekaboo so that he can henceforth be fully 'generative' in his disappearance-reappearance play. Before we do so, however, we must examine briefly three of the other children on whom we have sufficient data for analysis.

In the case of Lynn and her mother, the pattern is much the same as described, save for the fact that she begins to take over the active role of initiator of the game and controller of the mask as early as 10 months. She too, at 10 months, begins to use a stationary object, a chair, as a hiding mask behind which she moves, looking through the legs to effect reappearance. But she is still quite confused about it, and when mother says 'Boo' to herald her reappearance hides again rather than remaking contact. But she is on the way towards mastering the ambulatory variant.

Where Nan is concerned, the game is rather more sophisticated in an important respect. She and her mother share control. For example, at 11 months Nan lifts her petticoat over her face and leaves it in place until her mother says 'Boo' and then lowers it. This joint feature is a very consistent aspect of their games, but it must be regarded as a variant, for instances occur without joint control as well. Their turn-taking is also much more precisely segmented. For example, Nan raises her petticoat over her face, then lowers it after a few seconds, and waits for mother to say 'Boo' before showing any reaction herself—then usually responding to the mother's vocalizations with laughter. There is, in this instance, a separation between unmasking and vocalization, with a further timing element between the two.

Sandy and his mother are instances of a failure to develop workable rules because of excessive variation and some misreading by the mother. But the failure is instructive. Too often, the mother starts the game without having enlisted Sandy's attention. In other instances, when Sandy is having difficulty in hiding his own face behind a cloth, the mother takes the cloth (and the initiative) away from him and tries to do the masking herself. Interestingly, the game does not develop, and in its place there emerges a game in which Sandy crawls away from mother, she in pursuit, with excitement being exhibited by both when she catches him. He never serves as agent in this game. They are an instructive failure, and the disappearance of the game is reminiscent of the failures reported by Nelson (1973) that occur when mother attempts to correct the child's linguistic usage or insists upon an interpretation of the child's utterance that does not accord with his own. Under the circumstances, the lexical items in question disappear from the child's lexicon, just as peekaboo disappears from the game repertory of this pair.

DISCUSSION

When peekaboo first appears, our mothers often report, it is an extension or variation of a looming game in which the mother approaches the child from a distance of a meter or so, looms towards him almost to face-to-face contact, accompanying the close approach with a 'Boo' or a rising intonation. We know from the work of Bower (1971), Ball and Tronick (1971) and White (1963) that such looming produces considerable excitement and, indeed, when the loom is directly towards the face, a real or incipient avoidance response. The play may start by substituting disappearance of the face at a close point at which excitement has already been aroused. But this is not necessary. The only point one would wish to make is that, at the start, peekaboo involves an arousal of responses that are either innate or fairly close to innate. For even without the link to the looming game, disappearance and reappearance are 'manipulations' of object permanence, which is itself either innate or maturing through very early experience along the lines indicated by Piaget (1954). At least one can say unambiguously that, at the outset, peekaboo is not a game in the sense of it being governed by rules and conventions that are, in any respect, arbitrary. It is, rather, an exploitation by the mother of very strong, preadapted response tendencies in the infant, an exploitation that is rewarded by the child's responsiveness and pleasure.

William James (1890) comments in the *Principles* that an instinct is a response that only occurs once, thereafter being modified by experience. And surely one could say the same for the interaction involved in peekaboo. For once it has occurred, there rapidly develops a set of reciprocal anticipations in mother and child that begin to modify it and, more importantly, to conventionalize it. At the outset, this conventionalization is fostered by a quite standard or routine set of capers on the part of the mother—as we have noted, the early version involves a very limited range of hiding instruments, masking acts, vocalizations and time variations. At the outset, it is also very important for mother to keep the child's activation level at an appropriate intensity, and one is struck by the skill of mothers in knowing how to keep the child in an anticipatory mood, neither too sure of outcome nor too upset by a wide range of possibilities.

But what is most striking thereafter is precisely the systematic introduction of variations constrained by set rules. The basic rules are:

Initial contact

Disappearance

Reappearance

Reestablished contact

Within this rule context, there can be variations in degree and kind of vocalization for initial contact, in kind of mask, in who controls the mask, in whose face is masked, in who uncovers, in the form of vocalization upon uncovering, in the relation between uncovering and vocalization, and in the timing of the constituent elements (though this last is strikingly constrained by a capacity variable). What the child appears to be learning is not only the basic rules of the game, but the range of variation that is possible within the rule set. It is this emphasis upon patterned variation within a constraining rule set that seems crucial to the mastery of competence and generativeness. The process appears much as in concept attainment, in which the child learns the regularity of a concept by learning the variants in terms of which it expresses itself. What is different in peekaboo is that the child is not only learning such variants, but obviously getting great pleasure from the process and seeking it out.

It is hard to imagine any function for peekaboo aside from practice in the learning of rules in converting 'gut play' into play with conventions. But there may be one additional function. As Garvey (in press) has noted, one of the objectives of play in general is to give the child opportunity to explore the boundary between the 'real' and the 'make-believe'. We have never in our sample of peekaboo games seen a child exhibit the sort of separation pattern noted by Ainsworth (1964) when mother *really* leaves the scene. Mothers often report, moreover, that they frequently start their career of playing peekaboo by hiding their own faces rather than the infant's for fear of his being upset. Eight of the nine mothers asked about this point reported behaving in this way (Scaife, 1974). This suggests a sensitivity on the part of mothers to where the line may be between 'real' and 'make-believe' for the child. This function doubtless dwindles in time. Yet the game continues in its formal pattern, sustained in its attractiveness by being incorporated into new formats involving newly emergent behaviours (such as crawling or walking). An old pattern seems, then, to provide a framework for the pleasurable expression of new behaviour and allows the new behaviour to be quickly incorporated into a highly skilled, rule-governed pattern.

References

Ainsworth, M. D. S. (1964). Patterns of attachment behaviour shown by the infant in interaction with his mother. *Merrill-Palmer Quarterly, 10,* 51.

Ball, W., and Tronick, E. (1971). 'Infant responses to impending collision: optical and real', *Science, 171,* 818.

Bower, T. G. R. (1971). 'The object in the world of the infant', *Scientific American, 225,* 30.

Charlesworth, W. R. (1966). 'Persistence of orienting, and attending behaviour in infants as a function of stimulus-locus uncertainty', *Child Development, 37,* 473.

Garvey, C. (In press). 'Some properties of social play', *Merrill-Palmer Quarterly*.

Greenfield, P. M. (1970). 'Playing peekaboo with a four-month-old: a study of the role of speech and nonspeech sounds in the formation of a visual schema', Unpublished manuscript.

James, W. (1890). *The Principles of Psychology*, New York, Henry Holt.

Nelson, K. (1973). 'Structure and strategy in learning to talk', *Monographs of The Society for Research in Child Development, 38*, 1.

Piaget, J. (1954). *The Construction of Reality in the Child*, New York, Basic Books.

Scaife, M. (1974). Personal communication, Department of Experimental Psychology, Oxford University, Oxford.

White, B. L. (1963). 'Plasticity in perceptual development during the first six months of life', Paper presented to the American Association for the Advancement of Science, Cleveland, Ohio, 30 December.

11

A New Perspective on Cognitive Development in Infancy

JEAN M. MANDLER

A recent major accomplishment in developmental psychology has been better understanding of cognitive development in infancy. For many years developmentalists followed Piaget's belief that infants are not capable of true thoughts. According to Piaget, infants go through an extended period during which they build up sensorimotor schemes of objects and relations between them. True thinking arises only when symbols are used to stand for the schemes; infants would therefore be unable to remember experiences or objects from the past, anticipate or imagine what may happen in the future, or make causal connections between events they experience. In the following article Jean M. Mandler reviews a large body of research investigating early perceptual and conceptual development. Taken together, the studies she reviews suggest that young infants are capable of conceptual thought and that they act upon their thinking far earlier than was previously believed.

Over the past decade something of a revolution has been taking place in our understanding of cognitive development during infancy. For many years one theory dominated the field—that of the Swiss psychologist Jean Piaget. Piaget's views on infancy were so widely known and respected that to many psychologists at least one aspect of development seemed certain: human infants go through a protracted period during which they cannot yet think. They can learn to recognize things and to smile at them, to crawl and to manipulate objects, but they do not yet have concepts or ideas. This period, which Piaget called the sensorimotor stage of development, was said to last until one-and-a-half to two years of

Reprinted with permission from the author and *American Scientist*, 78, 1990, 236–243. Copyright 1990 by Sigma Xi Science Research Society.

Preparation of this article was supported by an NSF grant. Address: Department of Cognitive Science D-015, University of California, San Diego, La Jolla, CA 92093.

age. Only near the end of this stage do infants learn how to represent the world in a symbolic, conceptual manner, and thus advance from infancy into early childhood.

Piaget formulated this view of infancy primarily by observing the development of his own three children—few laboratory techniques were available at the time. More recently, experimental methods have been devised to study infants, and a large body of research has been accumulating. Much of the new work suggests that the theory of a sensorimotor stage of development will have to be substantially modified or perhaps even abandoned. The present article provides a brief overview of Piaget's theory of sensorimotor development, a summary of recent data that are difficult to reconcile with that theory, and an outline of an alternative view of early mental development.

In Piaget's (1951, 1952, 1954) theory, the first stage of development is said to consist of sensorimotor (perceptual and motor) functioning in an organism that has not yet acquired a representational (conceptual) capacity. The only knowledge infants have is what things look and sound like and how to move themselves around and manipulate objects. This kind of sensorimotor knowledge is often termed procedural or implicit knowledge, and is contrasted with explicit, factual (conceptual) knowledge (e.g., Cohen and Squire 1980; Schacter 1987; Mandler 1988). Factual knowledge is the kind of knowledge one can think about or recall; it is usually considered to be symbolic and propositional. Some factual information may be stored in the form of images, but these are also symbolic, in the sense that they are constructed from both propositional and spatial knowledge. Sensorimotor knowledge, on the other hand, is subsymbolic knowledge; it is knowing *how* to recognize something or use a motor skill, but it does not require explicitly knowing *that* something is the case. It is the kind of knowledge we build into robots in order to make them recognize and manipulate objects in their environment, and it is also the kind of knowledge we ascribe to lower organisms, which function quite well without the ability to conceptualize facts. It is the kind of knowledge that tends to remain undisturbed in amnesic patients, even when their memory for facts and their personal past is severely impaired.

In the case of babies, the restriction of functioning to sensorimotor processing implies that they can neither think about absent objects nor recall the past. According to Piaget, they lack the capacity even to form an image of things they have seen before; a fortiori, they have no capacity to imagine what will happen tomorrow. Thus, the absence of a symbolic capacity does not mean just that infants cannot understand language or reason; it means that they cannot remember what they did this morning or imagine their mother if she is not present. It is, in short, a most un-Proustian life, not thought about, only lived (Mandler 1983).

According to Piaget, to be able to think about the world requires first that perceptual-motor schemas of objects and relations among them be formed. Then, symbols must be created to stand for these schemas. Several aspects of Piaget's formulation account for the slow course of both these developments. First, on the basis of his observations Piaget assumed that the sensory modalities are unconnected at birth, each delivering separate types of information. Thus, he thought that one of the major tasks of the first half of the sensorimotor stage is to construct schemas integrating the information from initially disconnected sights, sounds, and touches. Until this integration is accomplished, stable sensorimotor schemas of three-dimensional, solid, sound-producing, textured objects cannot be formed and hence cannot be thought about.

In addition, babies must learn about the causal interrelatedness of objects and the fact that objects continue to exist when not being perceived. Piaget thought that these notions were among the major accomplishments of the second half of the sensorimotor stage. He suggested that they derive from manual activity—for example, repeated covering and uncovering, poking, pushing, and dropping objects while observing the results. Handling objects leads to understanding them; it allows the integration of perceptual and motor information that gives objects substantiality, permanence, and unique identities separate from the self. Since motor control over the hands is slow to develop, to the extent that conceptual understanding requires physical interaction with objects, it is necessarily a late development. Much of the first year of life, then, is spent accomplishing the coordination of the various sources of perceptual and motor information required to form the sensorimotor object schemas that will then be available to be conceptualized.

According to Piaget, the development of the symbolic function is itself a protracted process. In addition to constructing sensorimotor schemas of objects and relations, which form the basic content or meaning of what is to be thought about, symbols to refer to these meanings must be formed. Piaget assumed that the latter development has its precursors in the expectancies involved in conditioning. For example, the sight of a bottle can serve as a signal that milk will follow, and babies soon learn to make anticipatory sucking movements. This process, essentially the same as that involved in Pavlovian conditioning, does not imply a symbolic function; there is no indication that the baby can use such signals to represent bottles in their absence.

All the anticipatory behavior that Piaget observed throughout the first 18 months was accounted for in similar terms. Signs of anticipation of future events became more wide-ranging and complex but did not seem to require the use of images or other symbols to represent what was about to happen. Rather, Piaget assumed that an established sensorimotor schema set up a kind of imageless expectation of the next event, followed by recognition when the event took place. He used strict criteria for the presence of imagery—for example, verbal recall of the past (which implies the ability to represent absent events to oneself) or rapid problem-solving without trial and error. Neither of these can be ascribed merely to running off a practiced sensorimotor schema, but they require instead some representation of information not perceptually present.

Piaget did not observe recall or covert problem-solving until the end of the sensorimotor period. One might think that the fact that infants begin to acquire language during the latter part of the first year would be difficult to reconcile with a lack of symbolic capacity. However, Piaget characterized early words as imitative schemas, no different in kind from other motor schemas displayed in the presence of familiar situations.

Imitation, in fact, plays an important role in this account, because it provides the source of the development of imagery. Piaget assumed that images are not formed merely from looking at or hearing something, but arise only when what is being perceived is also analyzed. The attempt to imitate the actions of others provides the stimulus for such analysis to take place. Although infants begin to imitate early, it was not until near the end of the first year or beyond that Piaget found his children able to imitate novel actions or actions involving parts of their bodies they could not see themselves, such as blinking or sticking out their tongues. He took this difficulty as evidence that they could not form an image of something complex or unobserved until detailed analysis of it had taken place; it is presumably during this analysis that imagery is constructed. Piaget's study of imitation suggested that such analysis, and therefore the formation of imagery, was a late development in infancy. To complete the process of symbol formation, then, the anticipatory mechanisms of sensorimotor schemas become speeded up and appear as images of what will occur, thus allowing genuine representation. Finally, by some mechanism left unspecified, these newly created images can be used to represent the world independent of ongoing sensorimotor activity.

All these developments—constructing sensorimotor schemas, establishing a coherent world of objects and events suitable to form the content of ideas, learning to imitate and to form images that can be used to stand for things—are completed in the second half of the second year, and result in the child's at last being able to develop a conceptual system of ideas. Images can now be used to recall the past and to imagine the future, and even perceptually present objects can begin to be interpreted conceptually as well as by means of motor interactions with them. With the onset of thought, an infant is well on the way to becoming fully human.

This theory of the sensorimotor foundations of thought has come under attack from two sources. One is experimental work suggesting that a stable and differentiated perceptual world is established much earlier in infancy than Piaget realized. The other is recent work suggesting that recall and other forms of symbolic activity (presumably mediated by imagery) occur by at least the second half of the first year. I will discuss each of these findings in turn.

PERCEPTUAL DEVELOPMENT

The notion that the senses are unconnected at birth and that they become integrated only through experience is an old idea that was popularized by William James's (1890) description of the perceptual world of the infant as a "blooming, buzzing confusion." Recent work, however, suggests that either the senses are interrelated at birth or the learning involved in their integration is extremely rapid. There is evidence for integration of auditory and visual information as well as of vision and touch in the first months of life. What follows is a small sample of the research findings.

From birth, infants turn their heads to look at the source of a sound (Wertheimer 1961; Mendelson and Haith 1976). This does not mean that they have any particular expectations of what they will see when they hear a given sound, but it does indicate a mechanism that would enable rapid learning. By four months, if one presents two films of complex events not seen before and accompanied by a single sound track, infants prefer to look at the film that matches the sound (Spelke 1979). Perhaps even more surprising, when infants are presented with two films, each showing only a speaker's face, they will choose the correct film, even when the synchrony between both films and the soundtrack is identical (Kuhl and Meltzoff 1988). In addition, one-month-olds can recognize visually presented objects that they have only felt in their mouths (Figure 1; Meltzoff and Borton 1979; Walker-Andrews and Gibson 1986). Such data suggest either that the output of each sensory transducer consists in part of the same amodal pattern of information or that some central processing of two similar patterns of information is accomplished. In either case, the data strongly support the view that there is more order and coherence in early perceptual experience than Piaget or James realized.

In addition to sensory coordination, a good deal of information about the nature of objects is provided by the visual system alone, information to which young infants have been shown to be sensitive. For example, it used to be thought that infants have difficulty separating objects from a background, but it appears that such confusion is a rare event, not the norm. Infants may not "see" that a cup is separable from a saucer without picking it up, but in general they do not have difficulty determining the boundaries of objects. They use information from motion to parse objects from the perceptual surround long before they are able to manipulate them manually. At an age as young as three months, they can use the relative motion of objects against both stationary and moving backgrounds to determine the objects' boundaries (Figure 2; Kellman and Spelke 1983; Spelke 1988). Even stationary objects are seen as separate if they are spatially separated, whether in a plane or in depth. Infants also use motion to determine object identity, treating an object that moves behind a screen and then reappears as one object rather than two (Spelke and Kestenbaum 1986).

Other work by Spelke and by Baillargeon (Baillargeon et al. 1985; Baillargeon 1987a; Spelke 1988) shows that infants as young as four months expect objects to be substantial, in the sense that the objects cannot move through other objects nor other objects through them (Figure 3), and permanent, in the sense that the objects are assumed to continue to exist when hidden. Finally, there is evidence that by six months

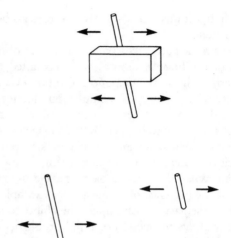

FIGURE 2 Infants as young as three months can use the perception of relative movement to determine object boundaries. They are habituated to the display shown at the top, which represents a rod moving back and forth behind a block of wood. Then they are tested with the two displays on the bottom: the rod moving as it did before, but with no block in front, or the two pieces of the rod that were visible behind the block, also moving as they did before. Infants tend to continue to habituate to the whole moving rod—that is —they cease to look at it, indicating that it is familiar to them. They prefer to look at the broken rod, indicating that they consider it something new. If the same experiment is done with a stationary rod behind a block, infants exhibit no preference when presented with a whole stationary rod or a broken stationary rod. (After Kellman and Spelke 1983.)

infants perceive causal relations among moving objects (Leslie 1988) in a fashion that seems to be qualitatively the same as that of adults (Michotte 1963).

From this extensive research program, we can conclude that objects are seen as bounded, unitary, solid, and separate from the background, perhaps from birth but certainly by three to four months of age. Such young infants obviously still have a great deal to learn about objects, but the world must appear both stable and orderly to them, and thus capable of being conceptualized.

CONCEPTUAL DEVELOPMENT

It is easier to study what infants see than what they are thinking about. Nevertheless, there are a few ways

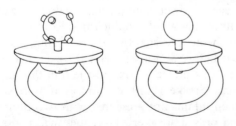

FIGURE 1 The old idea that the senses are unconnected at birth and are gradually integrated through experience is contradicted by an experiment using bumpy and smooth pacifiers to study the visual recognition of an object that has been experienced only tactilely. A one-month-old infant is habituated to one of the two kinds of pacifiers in its mouth without being allowed to see it. The pacifier is then removed, and the infant is shown both kinds of pacifiers. Infants look longer at the nipple they felt in their mouth. (After Meltzoff and Borton 1979.)

to assess whether or not infants are thinking. One way is to look for symbolic activity, such as using a gesture to refer to something else. Piaget (1952) himself called attention to a phenomenon he called motor recognition. For example, he observed his six-month-old daughter make a gesture on catching sight of a familiar toy in a new location. She was accustomed to kicking at the toy in her crib, and when she saw it across the room she made a brief, abbreviated kicking motion. Piaget did not consider this true symbolic activity, because it was a motor movement, not a purely mental act; nevertheless, he suggested that his daughter was referring to, or classifying, the toy by means of her action. In a similar vein, infants whose parents use sign language have been observed to begin to use conventional signs at around six to seven months (Prinz and Prinz 1979; Bonvillian et al. 1983; see Mandler 1988 for discussion).

Another type of evidence of conceptual functioning is recall of absent objects or events. Indeed, Piaget accepted recall as irrefutable evidence of conceptual representation, since there is no way to account for recreating information that is not perceptually present by means of sensorimotor schemas alone; imagery or other symbolic means of representation must be involved. Typically we associate recall with verbal recreation of the past, and this, as Piaget observed, is not usually found until 18 months or older. But recall need not be verbal—and indeed is usually not when we think about past events—so that in principle it is possible in preverbal infants.

One needs to see a baby do something like find a hidden object after a delay or imitate a previously observed event. Until recently, only diary studies provided evidence of recall in the second half of the first year—for example, finding an object hidden in an unfamiliar location after a 24-hour delay (Ashmead and Perlmutter 1980). Now, however, similar phenomena are beginning to be demonstrated in the laboratory. Meltzoff (1988) showed that nine-month-olds could imitate actions that they had seen performed 24 hours earlier. Each action consisted of an unusual gesture with a novel object—for example, pushing a recessed button in a box (which produced a beeping sound)—and the infants were limited to watching the experimenter carry it out; thus, when they later imitated the action, they could not be merely running off a practiced motor schema in response to seeing the object again. Control subjects, who had been shown the objects but not the actions performed on them, made the correct responses much less frequently. We have replicated this phenomenon with 11-month-olds (McDonough and Mandler 1989).

Because of the difficulties that young infants have manipulating objects, it is not obvious that this tech-

nique can be used with infants younger than about eight months. One suspects, however, that if nine-month-olds can recall several novel events after a 24-hour delay, somewhat younger infants can probably recall similar events after shorter delays.

There is a small amount of data from a procedure that does not require a motor response and that, although using quite short delays, suggests recall-like processes. Baillargeon's experiments on object permanence, mentioned earlier, use a technique that requires infants to remember that an object is hidden behind a screen. For example, she has shown that infants are surprised when a screen appears to move backward through an object they have just seen hidden behind it (see Figure 3). In her experiments with

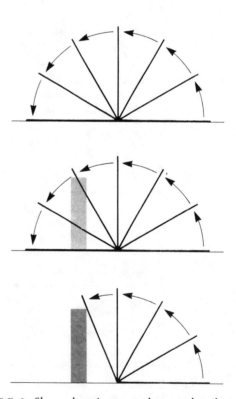

FIGURE 3 Shown here is a procedure used to demonstrate four- and five-month-olds' memory for the location of a hidden object. At the top is a screen moving through a 180° rotation, to which infants viewing from the right are habituated by repetition. Following habituation, a box is placed behind the screen, and the infants see two test events: an impossible (*middle*) and a possible event (*bottom*). In the impossible event, the screen continues to rotate 180°, moving "magically" through the hidden box (which the experimenter has surreptitiously removed). In the possible event, the screen rotates only to the point where it would hit the box. The infants' surprise at the impossible event demonstrates that they remember an object they cannot see. (After Baillargeon 1987a.)

four- and five-month-olds, the infants had to remember for only about 8 to 12 seconds that there was an object behind the screen (Baillargeon et al. 1985; Baillargeon 1987a). However, in more recent work with eight-month-olds, Baillargeon and her colleagues have been successful with a delay of 70 seconds (Figure 4; Baillargeon et al. 1989). This kind of perfor-

mance seems to require a representational capacity not attributable to sensorimotor schemas. Not only is an absent object being represented, but the information is rather precise—for example, Baillargeon (1987b) found that infants remembered not only that an object was hidden but where it was located and how tall it was.

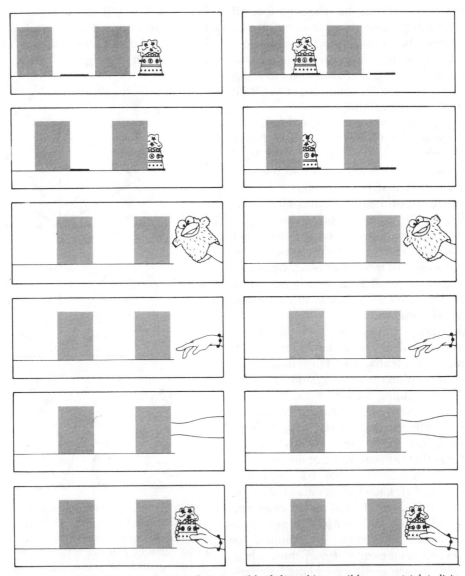

FIGURE 4 Another procedure involving possible (*left*) and impossible events (*right*) elicits meaningful responses from eight-month-old infants after a delay of 70 seconds. Moving from top to bottom, an object is hidden respectively behind the right or left of two screens; puppets and hand tiptoes are used to keep infants attentive during the delay period; the experimenter reaches behind the right screen and brings the hidden object into view from behind it. (The object was placed there surreptitiously as part of the impossible event.) Surprise at the impossible event indicates memory of the place where the object was hidden. The apparent recall suggests a kind of conceptual functioning that goes beyond the sensorimotor functioning described by Piaget. (After Baillargeon et al. 1989.)

WHERE DO CONCEPTS COME FROM?

The data described above indicate that the theory of an exclusively sensorimotor stage of development, in which babies cannot yet represent the world conceptually, is in need of considerable revision. There does not appear to be a protracted period during which infants have no conception of objects or events and cannot represent them in their absence. A great deal of information is available to and used by infants from an early age, even before they have developed the motor coordination enabling manual exploration that Piaget thought was crucial to conceptual development.

Indeed, a good deal of evidence suggests that we have tended to confuse infants' motor incompetence with conceptual incompetence. Piaget was particularly influenced in his theorizing by the difficulties that children as old as a year have finding a hidden object, especially when it is hidden in more than one location a number of times in succession. The phenomena he demonstrated have been replicated many times, but it now appears that much of the difficulty infants have on such situations is due not to a lack of understanding of object permanence but to other factors. For example, repeatedly hiding an object in different locations can be confusing and leads to perseverative responding to the same place (see Diamond 1985; Mandler 1988, in press).

If a conceptual system of knowledge has begun to be formed by at least six months and perhaps earlier, where does it come from? Piaget's theory of a transformation of well-developed action schemas into conceptual thought cannot account for conceptual knowledge occurring before the action schemas themselves have developed. On the other hand, perceptual schemas about objects and events develop early. What is needed, then, is some mechanism for transforming these schemas into concepts, or ideas, about what is being perceived, preferably a mechanism that can operate as soon as perceptual schemas are formed.

Little has been written about this problem. One approach is to assume that even young infants are capable of redescribing perceptual information in a conceptual format. I have suggested a mechanism that might accomplish this (Mandler 1988): perceptual analysis, a process by which one perception is actively compared to another and similarities or differences between them are noted. (Such analysis, like other sorts of concept formation, requires some kind of vocabulary; this aspect, still little understood, is discussed below.) The simplest case of perceptual analysis occurs when two simultaneously presented objects are compared, or a single object is compared to an already established representation (i.e., one

notes similarities or differences between what one is looking at and what one recalls about it). It is the process by which we discover that sugar bowls have two handles and teacups only one, or that a friend wears glasses. Unless we have engaged in this kind of analysis (or someone has told us), the information will not be accessible for us to think about. Much of the time, of course, we do not make such comparisons, which is why we often can recall few details of even recent experiences.

Although it is analytic, perceptual analysis consists primarily of simplification. Our perceptual system regularly processes vast amounts of information that never become accessible to thought. For example, we make use of a great deal of complex information every time we recognize a face: proportions, contours, subtle shading, relationships among various facial features, and so on. Yet little of this information is available to our thought processes. Few people are aware of the proportions of the human face—it is not something they have ever conceptualized. Even fewer know how they determine whether a face is male or female (this categorization depends on subtle differences in proportions). For the most part we do not even have words to describe the nuances that our perceptual apparatus uses instantly and effortlessly to make such a perceptual categorization.

For us to be able to think about such matters, the information must be reduced and simplified into a conceptual format. One way this redescription is done is via language; someone (perhaps an artist who has already carried out the relevant analytic process) conceptualizes aspects of a face for us. The other way is to look at a face and analyze it ourselves, such as noting that the ears are at the same level as the eyes. The analysis is often couched in linguistic form, but it need not be. Images can be used, but these, in spite of having spatial properties, have a major conceptual component (e.g., Kosslyn 1983).

An infant, of course, does not have the benefit of language, the means by which older people acquire much of their factual knowledge. So if infants are to transform perceptual schemas into thoughts, they must be able to analyze the perceptual information they receive. The perceptual system itself cannot decide that only animate creatures move by themselves or that containers must have bottoms if they are to hold things, and so forth. These are facts visually observed, but they are highly simplified versions of the information available to be conceptualized.

The notion of perceptual analysis is similar to the process that Piaget theorized as being responsible for the creation of images. He thought that this kind of analysis does not even begin until around eight or nine months and does not result in imagery until later still. However, he had no evidence that image formation is such a late-developing process, and his own description of his children's imitative performance as early as three or four months strongly suggests that the process of perceptual analysis had begun. For example, he observed imitation of clapping hands at that time, a performance that would seem to require a good deal of analysis, considering the difference between what infants see and what they must do. In many places in his account of early imitation, Piaget noted that the infants watched him carefully, studying both their own and his actions. Other developmental psychologists have commented on the same phenomenon. For example, Werner and Kaplan (1963) noted that infants begin "contemplating" objects at between three and five months. Ruff (1986) has documented intense examination of objects at six months (the earliest age she studied).

To investigate contemplation or analysis of objects experimentally is not easy. A possible measure is the number of times an infant looks back and forth between two objects that are presented simultaneously. Janowsky (1985), for example, showed that this measure increased significantly between four and eight months. At four months infants tend to look first at one object and then the other; at eight months they switch back and forth between the two a good many times. Fox and his colleagues (1979) have reported a similar phenomenon. Interestingly, Janowsky found that the differences in looking back and forth are not associated with differences in total looking time, the rate at which infants habituate to objects (cease to look at them), or accuracy of recognition. So the looking back and forth must serve some other function. I would suggest that it is a comparison process, by which one object is being contrasted with the other.

A VOCABULARY FOR CONCEPTS

Assuming that perceptual analysis can lead to concept formation, it is still necessary to formulate the vocabulary in which the resulting concepts are couched. But here we face one of the major stumbling blocks in psychological theory: the problem of specifying conceptual primitives (see Smith and Medin 1981). Perhaps because of its difficulty, it has been largely ignored by developmental psychologists, in spite of the fact that any theory of conceptual development must resolve the issue of what the earliest concepts are like, no matter when they may first be formed. Leslie (1988) has offered an analysis of the primitives involved in early causal concepts, and people working on language acquisition have speculated about sem-

antic primitives. For example, Slobin (1985) points out that children must already have concepts of objects and events, as well as relational notions about them, in order for language to be acquired. Since language comprehension begins at around nine to ten months (and perhaps earlier for sign language), some kind of conceptual system must be well established by that time. But we have almost no information as to its character.

Help may come from recent studies by cognitive linguists (e.g., Fauconnier 1985; Johnson 1987; Lakoff 1987). Although the primary goal of these theorists is to understand how language works, their analyses of the root concepts expressed in language may be of use in our search for babies' earliest concepts. For example, Lakoff and Johnson have proposed that image schemas—notions derived from spatial structure, such as trajectory, up-down, container, part-whole, end-of-path, and link—form the foundation of the conceptualizing capacity. These authors suggest that image schemas are derived from preconceptual perceptual structures, forming the core of many of our concepts of objects and events and of their metaphorical extensions to abstract realms. They demonstrate in great detail how many of our most complex concepts are grounded in such primitive notions. I would characterize image schemas as simplified redescriptions of sensorimotor schemas, noting that they seem to be reasonably within the capacity of infant conceptualization.

The potential usefulness of image schemas as conceptual primitives can be illustrated by the example of the container schema. According to Johnson and Lakoff, the structural elements of this image schema are "interior," "boundary," and "exterior." It has a bodily basis likely to be appreciated by quite young infants, and a perceptual basis that seems to require minimal redescription of the object schemas described earlier. It also has a simple binary logic—either in or not-in; if A is in B and B is in C, then A is in C—that may or may not be the sensorimotor basis of the Boolean logic of classes, as Lakoff suggests, but is certainly a characteristic of concepts as opposed to percepts. (The conceptual system tends to reduce the continuous information delivered by the perceptual system to a small number of discrete values.)

The use of such an image schema might be responsible for the better performance nine-month-old infants show on hiding tasks when a container is used rather than cloths or screens (Freeman et al. 1980). Current work by Baillargeon (pers. com.) suggests that at approximately the same age infants are surprised when containers without bottoms appear to hold things. Of course, these are only fragments of the kind of information needed to document the development of the idea of a container, but they indicate how we might go about tracking the early establishment of simple concepts.

A more complex concept may also be acquired relatively early in infancy is that of animacy. Consider some possible sources for such a concept. We know that infants differentiate biological from nonbiological motion as early as three months (Figure 5; Bertenthal et al. 1987). This perceptual differentiation, although an excellent source of information, does not constitute a concept by itself; it is an accomplishment similar to categorizing male and female faces, which infants have learned to do by six months (Fagan and Singer 1979). As discussed earlier, such perceptual categorization is not accessible for purposes of conceptual thought unless it has been redescribed in conceptual terms. An infant needs to conceptualize some differences between categories of moving objects, such as noting that one type starts up on its own and (sometimes) responds to the infant's signals, whereas the other type does not. An image schema of a notion such as beginning-of-path could be used to redescribe the perceptual information involved in initiation of motion. A link schema (whose elements are two entities and some kind of path between them) could be used to describe the observation of responsivity to self. From such simple foundations might arise a primitive concept of animal, a concept that we have reason to believe is present in some form by at least the end of the first year of life (Golinkoff and Halperin 1983; Mandler and Bauer 1988).

These are some examples of how a conceptual system might emerge from a combination of perceptual input and some relatively simple redescriptions of that input. I have suggested that a mechanism of perceptual analysis could enable such redescription, with the terms of the redescription being derived from spatial structure. The mechanism would not require an extended period of exclusively sensorimotor func-

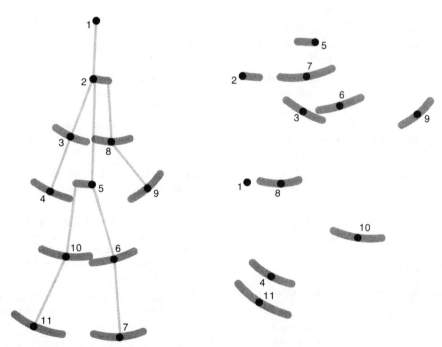

FIGURE 5 An equally subtle ability is involved in this demonstration of three-month-olds' responses to biological as opposed to nonbiological motion. The infants watch videotapes of computer-generated displays. On the left is a display of 11 point-lights moving as if attached to the head and major joints of a person walking. The motion vectors drawn through each point represent the perceived motions of the display; the lines connecting points, like the numbers and vectors, are not visible to the infants. The display on the right is identical to the normal walker except that the relative locations of the point-lights are scrambled. Correspondingly numbered points in the two displays undergo identical motions. Infants show greater interest in the scrambled display, indicating that they consider it novel. (After Bertenthal et al. 1987.)

tioning but would allow conceptualization of the world to begin early in infancy. The data I have summarized indicate that babies do indeed begin to think earlier than we thought. Therefore, it seems safe to assume that they either are born with or acquire early in life the capacity to form concepts, rather than to assume that conceptual functioning can occur only as an outcome of a lengthy sensorimotor stage.

References

Ashmead, D. H., and M. Perlmutter. 1980. Infant memory in everyday life. In *New Directions for Child Development: Children's Memory*, vol. 10, ed. M. Perlmutter, pp. 1–16. Jossey-Bass.

Baillargeon, R. 1987a. Object permanence in 3.5- and 4.5-month-old infants. *Devel. Psychol.* 23:655–64.

———. 1987b. Young infants' reasoning about the physical and spatial properties of a hidden object. *Cognitive Devel.* 2:179–200.

Baillargeon, R., J. De Vos, and M. Graber. 1989. Location memory in 8-month-old infants in a nonsearch AB task: Further evidence. *Cognitive Devel.* 4:345–67.

Baillargeon, R., E. S. Spelke, and S. Wasserman. 1985. Object permanence in five-month-old infants. *Cognition* 20:191–208.

Bertenthal, B. I., D. R. Proffitt, S. J. Kramer, and N. B. Spetner. 1987. Infants' encoding of kinetic displays varying in relative coherence. *Devel. Psychol.* 23:171–78.

Bonvillian, J. D., M. D. Orlansky, and L. L. Novack. 1983. Developmental milestones: Sign language and motor development. *Child Devel.* 54:1435–45.

Cohen, N. J., and L. R. Squire. 1980. Preserved learning and retention of pattern-analyzing skills in amnesia: Dissociation of knowing how and knowing that. *Science* 210:207–10.

Diamond, A. 1985. The development of the ability to use recall to guide action, as indicated by infants' performance on AB. *Child Devel.* 56:868–83.

Fagan, J. F., III, and L. T. Singer. 1979. The role of simple feature differences in infant recognition of faces. *Infant Behav. Devel.* 2:39–46.

Fauconnier, G. 1985. *Mental Spaces*. MIT Press.

Fox, N., J. Kagan, and S. Weiskopf. 1979. The growth of memory during infancy. *Genetic Psychol. Mono.* 99:91–130.

Freeman, N. H., S. Lloyd, and C. G. Sinha. 1980. Infant search tasks reveal early concepts of containment and canonical usage of objects. *Cognition* 8:243–62.

Golinkoff, R. M., and M. S. Halperin. 1983. The concept of animal: One infant's view. *Infant Behav. Devel.* 6:229–33.

James, W. 1890. *The Principles of Psychology*. Holt.

Janowsky, J. S. 1985. Cognitive development and reorganization after early brain injury. Ph.D. diss., Cornell Univ.

Johnson, M. 1987. *The Body in the Mind: The Bodily Basis of Meaning, Imagination, and Reason*. Univ. of Chicago Press.

Kellman, P. J., and E. S. Spelke. 1983. Perception of partly occluded objects in infancy. *Cognitive Psychol.* 15:483–524.

Kosslyn, S. M. 1983. *Ghosts in the Mind's Machine: Creating and Using Images in the Brain*. Norton.

Kuhl, P. K., and A. N. Meltzoff. 1988. Speech as an intermodal object of perception. In *Perceptual Development in Infancy: The Minnesota Symposia on Child Psychology*, vol. 20, ed. A. Yonas, pp. 235–66. Erlbaum.

Lakoff, G. 1987. *Women, Fire, and Dangerous Things: What Categories Reveal about the Mind*. Univ. of Chicago Press.

Leslie, A. 1988. The necessity of illusion: Perception and thought in infancy. In *Thought without Language*, ed. L. Weiskrantz, pp. 185–210. Clarendon Press.

Mandler, J. M. 1983. Representation. In *Cognitive Development*, ed. J. H. Flavell and E. M. Markman, pp. 420–94. Vol. 3 of *Manual of Child Psychology*, ed. P. Mussen. Wiley.

———. 1988. How to build a baby: On the development of an accessible representational system. *Cognitive Devel.* 3:113–36.

———. In press. Recall of events by preverbal children. In *The Development and Neural Bases of Higher Cognitive Functions*, ed. A. Diamond. New York Academy of Sciences Press.

Mandler, J. M., and P. J. Bauer. 1988. The cradle of categorization: Is the basic level basic? *Cognitive Devel.* 3:247–64.

McDonough, L., and J. M. Mandler. 1989. Immediate and deferred imitation with 11-month-olds: A comparison between familiar and novel actions. Poster presented at meeting of the Society for Research in Child Development, Kansas City.

Meltzoff, A. N. 1988. Infant imitation and memory: Nine-month-olds in immediate and deferred tests. *Child Devel.* 59:217–25.

Meltzoff, A. N., and R. W. Borton. 1979. Intermodal matching by human neonates. *Nature* 282:403–04.

Mendelson, M. J., and M. M. Haith. 1976. The relation between audition and vision in the newborn. *Monographs of the Society for Research in Child Development*, no. 41, serial no. 167.

Michotte, A. 1963. *The Perception of Causality*. Methuen.

Piaget, J. 1951. *Play, Dreams and Imitation in Childhood*, trans. C. Gattegno and F. M. Hodgson. Norton.

———. 1952. *The Origins of Intelligence in Children*, trans. M. Cook. International Universities Press.

———. 1954. *The Construction of Reality in the Child*, trans. M. Cook. Basic Books.

Prinz, P. M., and E. A. Prinz. 1979. Simultaneous acquisition of ASL and spoken English (in a hearing child of a deaf mother and hearing father). Phase 1: Early lexical development. *Sign Lang. Stud.* 25:283–96.

Ruff, H. A. 1986. Components of attention during infants' manipulative exploration. *Child Devel.* 57:105–14.

Schacter, D. L. 1987. Implicit memory: History and current status. J. *Exper. Psychol.: Learning, Memory, Cognition* 13:501–18.

Slobin, D. I. 1985. Crosslinguistic evidence for the language-making capacity. In *The Cross-linguistic Study of Language Acquisition*, vol. 2, ed. D. I. Slobin, pp. 1157–1256. Erlbaum.

Smith, E. E., and D. L. Medin. 1981. *Categories and Concepts.* Harvard Univ. Press.

Spelke, E. S. 1979. Perceiving bimodally specified events in infancy. *Devel. Psychol.* 15: 626–36.

———. 1988. The origins of physical knowledge. In *Thought without Language,* ed. L. Weiskrantz, pp. 168–84. Clarendon Press.

Spelke, E. S., and R. Kestenbaum. 1986. Les origines du concept d'objet. *Psychologie Française* 31:67–72.

Walker-Andrews, A. S., and E. J. Gibson. 1986. What develops in bimodal perception? In *Advances in Infancy Research,* vol. 4, ed. L. P. Lipsitt and C. Rovee-Collier, pp. 171–81. Ablex.

Werner, H., and B. Kaplan. 1963. *Symbol Formation.* Wiley.

Wertheimer, M. 1961. Psychomotor coordination of auditory and visual space at birth. *Science* 134:1692.

12

Treadmill-Elicited Stepping in Seven-Month-Old Infants

ESTHER THELEN

Most human behaviors rely on a complex coordination of several actions or processes. An interesting question for developmentalists is when and how the various components of a complex behavior first appear. Consider walking. What types of movements are required for bipedal locomotion? What types of experiences or contextual supports facilitate the development of these movements? And how do new forms of movements grow out of old ones? Thelen's innovative approach to these questions, illustrated in the following article, suggests that new behaviors emerge from the confluence of biological, social, and contextual factors interacting as elements of a single, dynamically changing system.

When infants begin to walk independently, their step patterns, while not fully mature, are different in kinematic details from those of newborn stepping and supine kicking. Six 7-month-old infants, who performed little or no stepping movements, were supported over a small, motorized treadmill. All showed immediate alternating stepping. These movements were more similar to adult-like steps than newborn steps. The implications of eliciting a more mature pattern by the treadmill are discussed. Although infants normally perform few steps at this age, the underlying mechanism has not "disappeared."

The development of upright locomotion has been one of the most well-studied early motor skills (e.g., Bernstein, 1967; Forssberg, 1985; McGraw, 1940; Shirley, 1931; Statham & Murray, 1971; Sutherland, Olshen, Cooper, & Woo, 1980). The ontogeny of

Reprinted with permission from *Child Development*, 57, 1986, 1498–1506. Copyright 1986 by the Society for Research in Child Development.

I thank Karl Skala, David Niles, Deborah Cooke, and Tim Grove for their excellent help in conducting this study and for many stimulating discussions. This work was supported by NSF BNS 8200434 and NICHID RCDA HD-00492. Address correspondence to: Department of Psychology, Indiana University, Bloomington, IN 47405.

locomotion is particularly intriguing because it is a classic example of so-called U-shaped behavioral development (Strauss, 1982), that is, the early appearance of the behavior as newborn stepping, its apparent regression at about 2 months of age, and its subsequent reappearance in the last months of the first year.

The prevailing accounts of locomotor development invoke essentially hierarchical explanations. In these views, increasing skill is a function of a maturing executive function. This executive may be the motor cortex (McGraw, 1940), a set of cognitive plans or representations (Zelazo, 1983), or a motor program presumed to be in the spinal cord (Forssberg, 1985). Such explanations have not been successful, however, in accounting for the disappearance and reappearance of stepping or in delineating the relation between the earlier and later forms of the behavior (Thelen, 1984).

An alternative to such hierarchical perspective is that locomotor skill, like other skills, is not driven solely by an executive function but is emergent from the confluence and interaction of many developing components (Thelen, in press; Thelen & Fogel, in press; Thelen, Kelso, & Fogel, in press). In this view, new skills are a product not only of cognitive or central instructions, but also of perceptual, affective, attentional, motivational, postural, and anatomic elements interacting within a particular context. The developmental course of these essential components may not be either synchronous or linear. Thus, at any point in time, one component may facilitate, mask, or inhibit performance. In particular, one or more components may be identified as *rate-limiting*. That is, while other components are "ready" and at an appropriate maturational status for the particular skill, the behavior will not appear until the final elements are sufficiently developed and the context affords the expression of the behavior.

For example, it seems likely that the ability to generate alternating, steplike patterning in the legs is available at, and even before, birth (Heriza, 1985; Thelen, Bradshaw, & Ward, 1981; Thelen & Fisher, 1982, 1983). The expression of that ability, however, depends on the interaction of the pattern-generating neural substrate with other developing systems, including anatomic, postural, and biomechanical factors. For example, Thelen and Fisher (1982) suggested that the well-known newborn stepping response "disappeared" at about 2 months not because of changes in the central processes generating the motor patterns, but due to parallel developmental changes in body size and composition that masked stepping performance.

Similarly, the onset of independent locomotion may not depend on a cortical or cognitive "switch" but on the gradual acquisition of the necessary component skills and skeleto-muscular apparatus (Thelen, 1984). Many of these component skills appear to be in place long before actual independent locomotion. I have suggested previously that a combination of postural control and strength are the rate-limiting elements. For infants to walk alone, they must develop the ability to support the body in the upright position, and most important, to remain balanced on one leg while the other leg is stretched back and then lifted off the ground. Once balance and strength are sufficient, they combine with the existing abilities—step pattern generation, motivation, perceptual processes, and voluntary control—to allow a new configuration—independent locomotion—to emerge.

In this report, I provide support for this systems approach by demonstrating that the ability to generate mature-like step configurations is in place long before actual independent locomotion, but that the performance of these movements is likely constrained by the infant's inability to provide postural support and stability to stretch the legs backward. To do this, I substitute for this mechanical stretch of the legs backward by placing essentially nonstepping 7-month-old infants on a small, motorized treadmill. The experiment uses a within-subject design to compare the rate, laterality, intralimb and interlimb coordination, and step-phase durations for four conditions: supine kicking, stepping with no treadmill, and stepping at two treadmill speeds. If walking patterns indeed emerge as a result of the biomechanical context, more adult locomotor patterns would be expected with the treadmill than in the two conditions (supine and no-treadmill baseline) where this context is not provided.

METHOD

SUBJECTS Subjects were six 7-month-old (range 6.75–7.75) normal infants, three girls and three boys. The subjects were recruited by telephone from published birth announcements. None were walking, cruising, or standing independently at the time of testing.

PROCEDURE The procedure consisted of videotaped recording of kick and step movements while infants were in the supine and upright position both on a stationary and moving treadmill. The videotapes were scanned frame by frame to provide data on frequency, laterality, and duration of movements. The angular displacements of hip, knee, and ankle joints were determined by digitizing the marked joints.

The subjects' legs were bared and their joints were marked with 3-mm white tape squares affixed to small strips of black tape. Markers were placed over the lateral surfaces of the hip, knee, and ankle joints, and the fifth metatarsal head. The videocamera was positioned to record a lateral view of the infants' right legs.

The treadmill was constructed with a 25.4 × 91.4-cm moving belt over a wooden platform and was driven by a variable-speed motor. Each infant was tested at two treadmill speeds, *slow*, .10 m/sec, and *fast*, .19 m/sec.

Each experimental session included five 2-min conditions, separated by only sufficient time to change the infant's position or adjust the treadmill speed. In the first condition, *supine*, infants were placed on their backs on a padded table to record spontaneous leg kicks. In the *baseline 1* condition, the infant was held under the arms facing the experimenter. The experimenter allowed the infants to bear an apparently comfortable amount of weight on their feet, but the treadmill remained stationary. In the treadmill conditions, *slow and fast*, the treadmill was allowed to run at the set speeds in a direction counter to forward locomotion. Again, the experimenter supported the infants but allowed them to bear weight as they would. For the final condition, *baseline 2*, the treadmill was turned off, as in the earlier no-treadmill condition, with the support and handling conditions similar. Every effort was made to equate the amount of support and position of the infant among the conditions.

DATA CODING Movements were analyzed from the videotapes by three separate coding methods. First, two independent coders viewed each tape in real time and scored each right and left kick or step on an event recorder. Three measures were obtained from this record: kick/step rate, degree of alternation of movements, and laterality of movements. Interobserver reliability for all three measures was better than .95 (Pearson's *r*).

Second, the interjoint coordination and movement kinematics were coded by digitizing the marked hip, knee, and ankle joints of the right leg from the videotapes frame by frame (frame rate, 60 Hz) using a sonic digitizing pad. Joint angles were calculated according to trigometric formulas. Resulting angles were filtered for high-frequency noise using a numerical filter (Winter, 1979) based on a Fourier analysis for dominant frequencies performed on each coded sample (see Thelen & Fisher, 1983, for procedural details). Because frame-by-frame digitizing is very tedious, we sampled kick and step movements for analysis by choosing the first consecutive steps or kicks on the tape where all markers were visible after a 10-sec adjustment period. For the treadmill con-

ditions, we coded three continuous steps and two interstep (stance) intervals for an average of 7 sec of movement in the slow and 5.8 sec in the fast treadmill conditions. Because stepping in the baseline conditions was rare, the average movement time coded was 1.5 sec and included 1–2-step cycles. We were able to code two to three supine kicks from each infant, for an average of 3.33 sec of movement. All digitizing was done by a single, experienced coder, who had reached high levels of reliability on previous studies (see Thelen, Skala, & Kelso, in press).

The final movement coding was to determine the duration of swing and stance phases in the two treadmill conditions. For this analysis, the entire treadmill session was scanned frame by frame for times of onset of each phase in each leg, as described in Thelen et al. (1981). *Swing* phase was defined as beginning when all of the foot left the supporting surface and terminating when any portion of the foot touched the surface. *Stance* phase was when the foot was in contact with the surface, whether or not weight was born on the leg.

Previously recorded and coded steps from an adult female subject are presented for purposes of comparison. The subject was instructed to walk normally and to "march" to simulate early infant stepping.

RESULTS

RATE, INTERLIMB COORDINATION, AND LATERALITY
One infant performed no kicks in the supine condition and two infants performed no steps in the first baseline condition, but each of the six infants showed frequent, alternating steps as soon as the treadmill began to move (Table 1). Repeated-measures ANOVA showed a significant effect of condition on kick/step rate, $F(4,20) = 7.23$, $p < .002$. Planned comparisons showed that the supine and both treadmill conditions were significantly different from the baseline conditions, $F(1,5) = 174$, $p < .001$, that baseline 1 was different from baseline 2, $F(1,5) = 10.0$, $p < .03$, and that the slow treadmill rate was different from the fast treadmill rate, $F(2,5) = 11.1$, $p < .02$. Thus, movements in both legs decreased to a minimum when infants were held upright, but dramatically increased on the moving treadmill. An increase of treadmill speed resulted in an increase of steps. The second no-treadmill condition saw a significant reduction in stepping, although rates were higher than in the first baseline in all but one infant.

Because several infants did not perform kicks and steps in the supine and baseline 1 conditions, ANOVAs for percentage alternations and laterality preference were done only using the two treadmill and baseline 2 conditions as the repeated measures.

TABLE 1

Effect of Posture and Treadmill Condition on Rate,
Alternation, and Laterality of Movements

	Condition				
	Supine	Baseline 1	Slow	Fast	Baseline 2
Rate (mean steps/kicks/min)	22.9	6.3	35.7	46.8	15.5
Mean percentage of alternating movements	47.4	40.6	84.4	85.4	36.5
Mean percentage of right leg movements	46.6	55.3	49.4	46.9	45.1

The treadmill significantly increased the percentage of right-left alternating movements (percentage of movements that followed a movement on the opposite leg). Overall ANOVA for alternation percentage was highly significant, $F(2,20) = 60.7$, $p < .001$, with both treadmill conditions different from the baseline ($p < .001$), but not different from each other. No differences were found in laterality (percentage of right leg movements) as a function of condition. Although there were no differences in the overall lateral preference as a result of the treadmill, all of the individual infants showed more asymmetrical movements in the baseline conditions.

Subjectively, infants did not appear to voluntarily initiate movements. None looked surprised when the treadmill was turned on or glanced at their legs, and several continued to suck on fingers and toys during treadmill stepping.

INTERJOINT COORDINATION Figure 1 provides an illustration of the angular joint excursions of one male infant in four conditions (this infant did not step in baseline 1). Note that the three joints can work in close temporal or spatial synchrony or be more complexly phased. A similarly coded single adult normal step and a "march" step are provided for comparison in Figure 2. The pairwise correlations of the angular displacements of the hip, knee, and ankle joints provide a quantitative measure of such synchrony of movement. In the adult march step, the three joints flexed and extended together and the joint correlations were very high (see Table 2). In contrast, in

TABLE 2

Pairwise Correlations of Joint Angles as a Function of
Posture and Treadmill Conditions

	Condition				
	Supine	Baseline 1	Slow	Fast	Baseline 2
Hip-knee (mean)	.45	.61	.16	.30	.59
Hip-ankle (mean)	.56	.42	.29	.12	.42
Knee-ankle (mean)	.59	.73	.22	.14	.31
	Adult ($N = 1$)				
	"March"				Step
Hip-knee	.99				−.09
Hip-ankle	.98				.59
Knee-ankle	.96				-.78

Note: Means computed on *z* conversions of *r*.

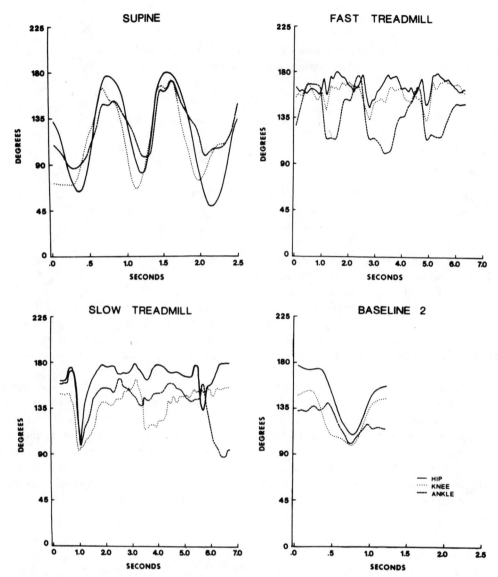

FIGURE 1   Joint angle excursions of a 7-month-old male infant during spontaneous supine kicking and stepping on a non-moving treadmill and a treadmill moving at two speeds. This infant performed no steps in the baseline 1 condition. Smaller joint angles indicate a flexion of the joint, larger angles an extension. Note the smooth and nearly synchronous excursions of hip, knee, and ankle in the supine and baseline conditions and the more elaborated and complex phasings with the treadmill.

mature locomotion, the joints were not strictly in phase. In the infants, the effect of the treadmill was to reduce the correlations of the movements, that is, to make the steps less synchronous and more adult-like. The effect was especially potent in the hip-knee correlation. Repeated-measures ANOVAs on fast and slow treadmill conditions and baseline 2 showed a significant effect for the hip-knee correlations, $F(2,10) = 10.6$, $p < .01$, with all conditions significantly different from one another. Correlations in the other joint pairs did not reach statistical signifi-

cance in this small sample, but four of the six infants had lower correlations in both treadmill conditions than in the baseline 2, and the fifth infant had lower correlations in baseline 1 but not baseline 2 in the hip-knee.

SWING/STANCE PHASE DURATIONS   When adults change the speed of their locomotion, most of the adjustment is made in the stance phase, which shortens as walking speed increases; there is much less change in the swing-phase duration. Similarly,

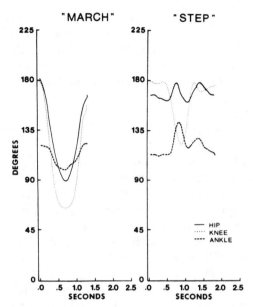

FIGURE 2   Joint angle excursions of an adult subject during a normal slow step and after being instructed to "march."

treadmill-stepping infants respond to velocity changes in the treadmill largely by shortening the time when the stance foot contacts the surface, although the swing phase is shortened somewhat (Table 3). A 2×2 ANOVA (repeated measures) showed a significant effect of treadmill speed on phase duration, $F(1,5) = 40.1$, $p < .01$, a significant difference between swing and stance phase, $F(1,5) = 435.4$, $p < .001$, and a significant interaction, $F(1,5) = 86.7$, $p < .001$. When phase times are regressed against the total duration of

TABLE 3

Effect of Treadmill Speed on Step-phase Duration and Regression Coefficients of Phase Duration on Cycle Time

	Treadmill Speed	
	Fast	Slow
Phase duration (sec):		
Swing	.644	.600
Stance	1.884	1.376
Regression *R*:		
Swing vs. step	.32	.48
Stance vs. step	.69	.73

the step cycle (stance plus swing) for each individual step, Table 3 also shows that variations in step cycle time (the reciprocal of rate) are largely in the stance phase; as cycle time increases, so does stance phase. The regression of swing time on cycle time is not as high. In this analysis, there was no significant effect of treadmill speed on the regression coefficients, but a significant effect of the phase, $F(1,5) = 13.7$, $p < .02$, and no interaction.

DISCUSSION

When 7-month-old infants were placed on a moving treadmill they performed immediate alternating stepping movements with many characteristics of more mature walking. Infants in the upright, no-treadmill condition showed few or no steps, and those movements that were performed had elements of the simple patterning of the newborn step. Likewise, when the infants were placed supine, their spontaneous pattern of movements was more like the kicks and steps of young infants than the complex coordination of mature locomotion.

Specifically, in both kicks and steps, the angular joint rotations of very young infants are tightly synchronized, with the hip, knee, and ankle moving together in time and space. (This topography can be simulated by asking an adult to "march.") Although by 7 months of age this pattern is considerably less stereotyped than at 1 month (Thelen, 1985), the joint excursions are still highly correlated, especially when compared to the phasing of mature locomotion. Nonetheless, a more adultlike phasing, especially in the coordination between the hip and knee, emerged when infants were placed on the treadmill. When the treadmill stretched the stance leg backward, the swing was initiated, as in adult movement, first with a flexion at the knee. In addition, supine and no-treadmill leg movements were often asymmetrical, with fluctuating and unstable interlimb coordination (Thelen, Ridley-Johnson, & Fisher, 1983). Treadmill steps were regularly alternating. Infants increased their step rate on the treadmill as the treadmill speed was increased, and their adjustments in the step phases were similar to speed compensations in adult humans (and many other animals). Speed compensations involved proportionally more adjustment in the stance or support phase than in the swing phase. Although experience on the treadmill facilitated stepping in the second, no-treadmill condition, the topography and symmetry of the steps in the second baseline were similar to first baseline and supine configurations.

The crucial questions raised by these results are, first, how does the treadmill elicit more mature patterning at an age when these topographies are not normally seen or practiced, and second, what is the relation between these experimental manipulations and the actual developmental processes that lead to independent locomotion?

Treadmills have been used extensively in animal studies to elicit locomotion in various experimental preparations that would not walk unassisted. For example, when trained on a treadmill and given adequate postural support, deafferented, decerebrate, and even spinalized cats will "walk" (for recent reviews of this extensive literature, see Grillner, 1980, 1985).

In both experimental animals and the infants in the present study, the treadmill appears to elicit stepping by mechanically stretching the legs backward. Pearson and Duysens (1976) have suggested that two reflex responses may be involved in initiating the swing phase of stepping, the crucial transition in lifting one leg off the ground. One reflex may be triggered by receptors in the hip joint signaling that the joint is stretched (see Grillner & Rossignol, 1978; Shik & Orlovsky, 1976). Pearson and Duysens postulated that a more important reflex may be elicited by the unloading of the ankle extensor muscles at the end of stance. In normal locomotion, the stance leg bears the weight at the initiation of stance, but as the leg is stretched backward and the center of gravity propelled forward, the leg becomes increasingly unloaded. Thus, one possibility is that by providing the necessary stance-leg stretch, the treadmill elicits stepping initiation in 7-month-old infants by either hip extension or ankle-unloading reflexes.

A second alternative can also be considered. In normal independent locomotion, much of the force driving the swing leg upward and forward is derived not so much from active muscle contractions at the initiation of swing but by passive and inertial forces built into the stance leg as it is stretched backward. After the period of double support, "the muscles all but turn off and allow the leg to swing through like a jointed pendulum" (McMahon, 1984, p. 198). McMahon has, in fact, modeled walking like a ballistic projectile that moves entirely under the action of gravity once the swing has begun. Thus, it is possible that by mechanically stretching the support legs, the treadmill motor is supplying part of the passive energy needed to overcome gravity and swing the leg forward (Pearce et al., 1983). This boost may be especially important for infants, who appear to have difficulty in lifting their legs when upright after the first month or two (Thelen & Fisher, 1983; Thelen, Fisher, & Ridley-Johnson, 1984).

The increase of stepping seen in the second, no-treadmill condition after experience on the treadmill

is intriguing. Since the coordinative pattern reverts back to a more immature pattern, it seems unlikely that this experience "taught" the infant an adult-like step. A more likely explanation is a general tonic excitation of the pattern-generating mechanism, which results in increased ability to lift the legs in the primitive step, just as tonic arousal facilitated stepping in the newborn period (Thelen, Fisher, Ridley-Johnson, & Griffin, 1982).

Although these 7-month-old infants performed few or no steps without the treadmill assist, in the succeeding months they will acquire the ability to stand alone, step while supported, and finally step independently. What do these infants acquire in those months that was mimicked by the treadmill? Whether the treadmill works by stretching the hip, unloading the ankle, or providing a power boost, the crucial element appears to be the simultaneous stretching of the support leg and shifting the weight forward as the swing leg is lowered to the surface, and the subsequent shifting of the weight to the opposite leg. Several factors are essential to these skills. Clearly the infant must have the ability to maintain balance during these intricate changes of the center of gravity. Woollacott (in press) recently reported directionally specific postural responses to balance perturbations in the trunk muscles of even 5-month-old infants, the youngest tested in the sitting position. Infants aged 11–14 months tested while standing had leg and neck muscle responses consistent with the adult patterns, although adult-like integration of postural sensory input develops only gradually during the first years of life (Shumway-Cook & Woollacott, 1985).

While it is important to maintain balance when upright, it may be equally essential to acquire the strength necessary to support the body weight on a single leg while the opposite leg is airborne. This stability is gained primarily through the extensor muscles of the knee and ankle, which become active just prior to the foot striking the ground. These muscles provide stability in the support leg primarily by exerting a decelerating force on these joints (Sutherland, Cooper, & Daniel, 1980; Sutherland, Olshen, Cooper, & Woo, 1980). These authors attach particular significance to the ankle plantar-flexor (toe-pointing) muscles in the maturity of gait patterns as both preventing the drop of the center of mass of the body and making it possible for the body to be extended forward beyond the point of support. As strength and control in these muscles increases over the first few years, walking becomes more mature in cadence, step length, walking velocity, duration of single-limb support, and degree of outward rotation. Sutherland, Olshen, Cooper, and Woo (1980) claim that these parameters, which reflect dimensions of stability and balance rather than patterns of coordination, are what differentiate immature from mature gait. In a detailed examination of new walkers at onset of independent locomotion and at 2 weeks, and 1 and 3 months after onset, Clark and Phillips (1985) also found differences in the new walkers suggesting deficiencies in maintaining balance. Importantly, many of these differences disappeared when new walkers were supported.

Just as the refinements of locomotion seem to emerge with stability and balance in the second year, I suggest that the treadmill, by providing a supportive dynamic context, elicits a complex pattern from an underlying more general pattern-generating substrate, that is, that the characteristic morphology of locomotor movements arises as much from the constraints and opportunities of the moving segments and their gravitational and inertial properties as from specific and iconic instructions from the nervous system. The treadmill works because it provides mechanically the stance leg stretch that infants can

provide for themselves when they have the strength and balance. Thus, the pattern generation need not undergo involution, inhibition, or dramatic remodeling but may remain as a general substrate whose details are emergent from the entire dynamic context of the infant.

These results have several developmental implications. The first is the importance of a multisystems perspective for understanding developmental milestones. Cortical maturation alone is insufficient to explain the onset of walking, just as single causes may not suffice for other developmental phenomena. Second is the emphasis on context for eliciting task-specific actions and determining the topography of the motor output. This may include social as well as physical context, as parents commonly provide support for new walkers and for other emergent skills (Thelen & Fogel, in press). Finally, I suggest that by considering this dynamic flexibility of behavior, apparent discontinuities in ontogenesis may be better understood.

References

Bernstein, N.(1967). *Coordination and regulation of movements*. New York: Pergamon.

Clark, J. E., & Phillips, S. J. (1985). *The organization of early upright locomotion*. Paper presented at the biennial meeting of the Society for Research in Child Development, Toronto.

Forssberg, H. (1985). Ontogeny of human locomotor control: I. Infant stepping, supported locomotion, and transition to independent locomotion. *Experimental Brain Research, 57,* 480–493.

Grillner, S. (1980). Control of locomotion in bipeds, tetrapods, and fish. In V. B. Brooks (Ed.), *Handbook of physiology: Vol. 3. Motor control* (pp. 1179–1236). Bethesda, MD: American Physiological Society.

Grillner, S. (1985). Neurobiological bases of rhythmic motor acts in vertebrates. *Science, 228,* 143–149.

Grillner, S., & Rossignol, S. (1978). On the initiation of the swing phase of locomotion in chronic spinal cats. *Brain Research, 146,* 269–277.

Heriza, C. (1985). *The organization of spontaneous leg movements in premature infants*. Paper presented at biennial meeting of the Society for Research in Child Development, Toronto.

McGraw, M. B. (1940). Neuromuscular development of the human infant as exemplified in the achievement of erect locomotion. *Journal of Pediatrics, 17,* 747–771.

McMahon, T. A. (1984). *Muscles, reflexes, and locomotion*. Princeton, NJ: Princeton University Press.

Pearce, M. E., Cunningham, D. A., Donner, A. P., Rechnitzer, P. A., Fullerton, G. M., & Howard, J. H. (1983). Energy cost of treadmill and floor walking at self-selected paces. *European Journal of Applied Physiology, 52,* 115–119.

Pearson, K. G., & Duysens, J. (1976). Function of segmental reflexes in the control of stepping in cockroaches and cats. In R. M. Herman, S. Grillner, P. S. G. Stein, & D. G. Stuart (Eds.), *Neural control of locomotion* (pp. 519–537). New York: Plenum.

Shik, M. L., & Orlovsky, G. N. (1976). Neurophysiology of locomotor automatism. *Physiological Reviews, 56,*465–501.

Shirley, M. M. (1931). *The first two years: A study of twenty-five babies: Vol. 1. Postural and locomotor development*. Minneapolis: University of Minnesota Press.

Shumway-Cook, A., & Woollacott, M. H. (1985). The growth of stability: Postural control from a developmental perspective. *Journal of Motor Behavior, 17,* 131–147.

Statham, L., & Murray, M. P. (1971). Early walking patterns of normal children. *Clinical Orthopaedics, 79,* 8–24.

Strauss, S. (1982). *U-shaped behavioral growth*. New York: Academic Press.

Sutherland, D. H., Cooper, L., & Daniel, D. (1980). The role of the ankle plantar flexors in normal walking. *Journal of Bone and Joint Surgery, 62,* 354–363.

Sutherland, D. H., Olshen, R., Cooper, L., & Woo, S. L.-Y. (1980). The development of mature gait. *Journal of Bone and Joint Surgery, 62,* 336–353.

Thelen, E. (1984). Learning to walk: Ecological demands and phylogenetic constraints. In L. P. Lipsitt (Ed.), *Advances in infancy research* (Vol. 3, pp. 213–250). Norwood, NJ: Ablex.

Thelen, E. (1985). Developmental origins of motor coordination: Leg movements in human infants. *Developmental Psychobiology, 18,* 1–22.

Thelen, E. (in press). Development of coordinated movement: Implications for early human development. In H. T. A. Whiting & M. G. Wade (Eds.), *Motor skills acquisition.* Dordecht (Netherlands): Martinus Nijhoff.

Thelen, E., Bradshaw, G., & Ward, J. A. (1981). Spontaneous kicking in month-old infants: Manifestations of a human central locomotor program. *Behavioral and Neural Biology, 32,* 45–53.

Thelen, E., & Fisher, D. M. (1982). Newborn stepping: An explanation for a "disappearing reflex." *Developmental Psychology, 18,* 760–775.

Thelen, E., & Fisher, D. M. (1983). The organization of spontaneous leg movements in newborn infants. *Journal of Motor Behavior, 15,* 353–377.

Thelen, E., Fisher, D. M., & Ridley-Johnson, R. (1984). The relationship between physical growth and a newborn reflex. *Infant Behavior and Development, 7,* 479–493.

Thelen, E., Fisher, D. M., Ridley-Johnson, R., & Griffin, N. (1982). The effects of body build and arousal on newborn stepping. *Developmental Psychology, 15,* 447–453.

Thelen, E., & Fogel, A. (in press). Toward an action-based theory of infant development. In J. Lockman & N. Hazen (Eds.), *Action in social context.* New York: Plenum.

Thelen, E., Kelso, J. A. S., & Fogel, A. (in press). Self-organizing systems and infant motor development. *Developmental Review.*

Thelen, E., Ridley-Johnson, R., & Fisher, D. M. (1983). Shifting patterns of bilateral coordination and lateral dominance in the leg movements of young infants. *Developmental Psychobiology, 16,* 29–46.

Thelen, E., Skala, K, & Kelso, J. A. S. (in press). The dynamic nature of early coordination: Evidence from bilateral leg movements in young infants. *Developmental Psychology.*

Winter, D. A. (1979). *Biomechanics of human movement.* New York: Wiley.

Woollacott, M. H. (in press). Children's development of posture and balance control: Changes in motor coordination and sensory integration. In D. Gould & M. Weiss (Eds.), *Advances in pediatric sport sciences: Behavioral issues.* Champaign, IL: Human Kinetics Publishers.

Zelazo, P. R. (1983). The development of walking: New findings and old assumptions. *Journal of Motor Behavior, 15,* 99–137.

13

Patterns of Attachment in Two- and Three-Year-Olds in Normal Families and Families with Parental Depression

MARIAN RADKE-YARROW, E. MARK CUMMINGS, LEON KUCZYNSKI, AND MICHAEL CHAPMAN

A unique and universal characteristic of the human species is the lengthy period of dependence required early in life. The theory of attachment considers the relationship between young children and their primary caregivers as critical for organizing and supporting early socioemotional development. In the following article a team of developmental psychologists used an experimental procedure known as the Strange Situation to explore attachment between depressed mothers and their children, illustrating the intricate connection between social processes and individual development. Since depression interferes with the normal flow of interaction, mothers and children in these dyads may be at risk for developing an unhealthy attachment relationship. Depressed mothers may also model modes of response that lead to long-term individual effects in children.

Reprinted with permission from *Child Development, 56,* 1985, 884–893. Copyright 1985 by the Society for Research in Child Development.

This work was supported by the National Institute of Mental Health, Bethesda, MD, and by the John D. and Catherine T. MacArthur Foundation, Research Network Award on the Transition from Infancy to Early Childhood, Chicago, IL. We wish to acknowledge the assistance of Judy Stillwell, Barbara Hollenbeck, Jonita Conners, Christine Kirby, Anne Mayfield, Wendy Rozario, and Rita Dettmers in the many phases of the research process. Requests for reprints should be sent to Marian Radke-Yarrow, Laboratory of Developmental Psychology, National Institute of Mental Health, Bldg. 15K, 9000 Rockville Pike, Bethesda, MD 20205.

Patterns of attachment were examined in normal and depressed mothers. Mother's diagnosis (bipolar, major unipolar, or minor depression, or no psychiatric disorder), self-reported current mood states, and affective behavior in interaction with the child were considered. A modified version of Ainsworth and Wittig's Strange Situation was used to assess attachment. Insecure (A, C, and A/C patterns) attachments were more common among children of mothers with a major depression (bipolar or unipolar) than among children of mothers with minor depression or among children of normal mothers. Insecure attachment was more frequent in children of mothers with bipolar depression than in children of mothers with unipolar depression. A/C attachments were associated with histories of most severe depression in the mother. In families in which mothers were depressed, depression in the father did not increase the likelihood of anxious attachment between mother and child. However, if mothers with a major affective disorder were without a husband in the household, risk of an insecure mother-child attachment was significantly increased. The mothers' expressed emotions (positive vs. negative) in interaction with their children in situations other than the Strange Situation, and independent of diagnosis, predicted patterns of attachment: mothers of insecurely attached children expressed more negative and less positive emotion. Mothers' self-reports of moods on the days they were observed were unrelated to attachment. Results are discussed in terms of the transmission of social and emotional disorders in relation to mothers' affective functioning.

Depression is known to aggregate in families, to be transmitted from one generation to the next. Significantly higher frequencies of psychopathology have been reported among children of parents with affective disorders than among children of normal parents, with a variety of mechanisms proposed as explanations (see reviews by Akisal & McKinney, 1975; Beardslee, Bemporad, Keller, & Klerman, 1983; Cytryn, McKnew, Zahn-Waxler, & Gershon, in press; Rutter & Garmezy, 1983). The likelihood of a genetic predisposition has been emphasized; and particularly for manic-depression, there is considerable evidence for biologically or genetically based transmission (see review by Meyersberg & Post, 1979). Although few investigators would rule out influences of environmental factors, such influences have not been extensively studied. Moreover, when the environment has been considered, both the conceptualizations and the methods used to assess its qualities have been inadequate. These deficiencies impose serious limitations

on what is known about the role of environment and the interaction of genetic and environmental factors in the development of the offspring of depressed parents.

The depressed parent *is* the primary environment of the young child. The conditions of care and rearing that the parent provides must, of necessity, reflect the symptomatic behaviors of depression, the impairments that constitute the illness (emotional unavailability, sad affect, hopelessness, irritability, confusion, etc.). Although depressive illness does not present a homogeneous pattern of behaviors in every parent, the behaviors and mental status of the depressed person are all potentially interfering with the functions and responsibilities of a caregiver and with the development of a good affective relationship with the child. The present study focuses on the quality of the affective bond that forms between mother and child under such conditions.

The quality of attachment between mother and child has been associated with the young child's adaptive and maladaptive behaviors in an impressively consistent succession of studies. Insecurely attached children, compared with those securely attached, have been found to be less competent in their relationships with peers and adults, more fearful of strangers, more prone to behavior problems, including social withdrawal and anxiety, and more dependent on adults (Arend, Gove, & Sroufe, 1979; Erickson, Sroufe, & Egeland, in press; LaFreniere & Sroufe, in press; Lieberman, 1977; Londerville & Main, 1981; Matas, Arend, & Sroufe, 1978; Pastor, 1981; Sroufe, Fox, & Pancake, 1983; Waters, Wippman, & Sroufe, 1979).

The literature on attachment identifies certain characteristics of mothering that are associated with the infant's secure attachment. These include the mother's responsivity, her emotional availability, and warm and accepting attitude toward the child (Ainsworth, Blehar, Waters, & Wall, 1978; Belsky, Rovine, & Taylor, 1984; Blehar, Lieberman, & Ainsworth, 1976; Londerville & Main, 1981; Main, Tomasini, & Tolan, in press; Stayton & Ainsworth, 1973; Tracy & Ainsworth, 1981). However, knowledge of the rearing environment at a level of detail and directness that allows examination of the processes through which a secure or insecure relationship develops and is maintained is very incomplete. This is particularly the case with regard to our understanding of the role of affective aspects of the environment in which the child is reared.

In the present study we have used parents' diagnoses of affective disorders (depression and manic-depression) and parental reports and expressions of their emotions and moods as indices of the affective quality of the child's rearing environment. How do attachment patterns in families with parental depression differ from patterns in normal families?

Research findings and theory support an expectation of increased attachment disturbances in the depressed families. A recent study of toddler-age offspring of manic-depressive parents shows attachment disturbances and early behavior problems (Gaensbauer, Harmon, Cytryn, & McKnew, 1984; Zahn-Waxler, Cummings, & McKnew, 1984; Yarrow, 1984). Bowlby (1969, 1973), Bretherton (in press), and Main, Kaplan, and Cassidy (in press) have hypothesized that early insecure attachment relationships result in children developing a fundamental view or working model of themselves as unlovable, and of others as rejecting and unresponsive. Some findings supportive of these expectations have been reported by Main and her colleagues (Cassidy & Main, 1983; Main, Kaplan, & Cassidy, in press). Moreover, since the depressed parent is likely to be self-deprecating, it is quite possible that such views are conveyed to the child and extend to perceptions of the child.

If disturbed attachment patterns are characteristic of the offspring of affectively ill parents, a number of important research questions follow: (*a*) Within depressed and normal families, what are the parental behaviors that promote or interfere with the development of a secure attachment relationship? (*b*) Are the links between attachment patterns and child's (outcome) behavioral characteristics in the clinical population similar to the links found in nonclinical populations, or is the developmental course of the offspring of depressed parents more preprogrammed for maladaptive affective, cognitive, and social characteristics (i.e., more independent of environmental variables) than is the case for children of normal parents? (*c*) How may discordances (secure attachment and poor psychosocial development, or the obverse case) be explained?[1]

METHOD

Sample

The sample consists of 99 children: 14 offspring of bipolar depressive (manic-depressive) mothers, 42 of mothers with major unipolar depression, 12 of mothers with minor depression, and 31 of mothers with no history of affective disturbance.

Families (normal and depressed) were recruited by advertising for participants in a study of child rearing and development in healthy families and families in which the mother is depressed. Of the mothers who responded to announcements, approximately two-thirds wished to participate after learning more about the study. All volunteers were given a standard psychiatric interview, the Schedule for Affective Disorders and Schizophrenia (SADS) (Spitzer & Endicott, 1977). On the basis of the interview, families were selected who met specific diagnostic criteria, as well as criteria of SES, race, age, and sex of children. For a family to be selected for the normal group, both parents had to be present and had to be without a history of affective disorder. In families in which the mother had a diagnosis of depression, father's psychiatric status varied. Fathers could be with or without a diagnosis of depression; however, schizophrenic, alcoholic, and antisocial personalities were excluded. In eight families with major maternal depression, there was no father in the household. Of the families given psychiatric interviews, about half were screened out by us because they did not meet diagnostic requirements, or because their cell within the design was complete. Table 1 provides more information on the characteristics of the sample.

Families differed in terms of the percent of the child's lifetime in which the mother had episodes of depression. For bipolar mothers, the mean percent of the child's lifetime was 39.8 (range, 0%–100%); for mothers with unipolar depression, the mean percent was range, 61.6 (range, 0%–100%); and for mothers with minor depression, the mean percent was 13.7 (range, 0%–47%). (0 indicates mother's depression occurred before the child was born.)

Each mother who received a psychiatric diagnosis was rated on the severity of psychopathology on the Global Assessment Scale (GAS) (Spitzer, Gibbon, & Endicott, 1978). The mother is rated on her poorest functioning during the child's lifetime, on a continuous scale of 0 (needing continuous care and supervision) to 100 (superior functioning). The mean score for bipolar mothers was 47.6 (range, 15–65), for mothers with unipolar depression, 54.2 (range, 30–70), and for mothers with minor depression, 76.3 (range, 60–79). Mothers whose depression occurred before the child was born and could be rated for poorest functioning in their own lifetime ($N = 6$) had a mean rating of 43.7 (range, 1–65). Normal mothers

---

[1] Data addressing these questions are being gathered in an ongoing study involving observations of parental and child behaviors at two periods in the child's life—at 2–3 years and at 5–6 years. The data reported here are from the first phase of this study.

TABLE 1

Comparisons of Diagnostic Groups on
Age, Sex, and Race

Demographic Characteristics	Diagnostic Group		Major Affective Disorder	
	Normal (N = 31)	Minor Depression (N = 12)	Unipolar Depression (N = 42)	Bipolar Depression (N = 14)
Age[a] (months)	31.9	31.4	30.4	36.0
Sex:				
Boys	13	7(1)[b]	24(4)[b] (2)[c]	3(2)[b]
Girls	18	5(2)[b]	18(3)[b] (3)[c]	11(4)[b] (3)[c]
Race:				
White	24	12(3)[b]	34(6)[b] (1)[c]	12(6)[b] (3)[c]
Black	7	0	8(0)[b] (4)[c]	2(0)[b]
Hollingshead SES[d]	52.9	47.6	46.1	51.1

[a] Ranges in age are 25–39 months, 25–34 months, 16–44 months, and 30–47 months for the diagnostic groups, respectively.

[b] Number of families in which the father had a diagnosis of major depression.

[c] Number of families in which the father was not present.

[d] Ranges in SES in each of the groups, from low to high status, are 17–66, 34–64, 11–64.5, and 33.5–64, respectively.

are not given ratings. Treatments that mothers had received for affective illness were as follows: Seven had been hospitalized (three in the lifetime of their child), 25 were on drug treatment at some time (four currently), and 51 had sought professional help (19 were currently seeing a mental health professional).

PROCEDURE

The Strange Situation, developed by Ainsworth and Wittig (1969), was used in the present study to assess quality of attachment. The families came to the laboratory, an informal homelike apartment, for a series of half-days over a period of several weeks. Their behavior was observed (videotaped) over a variety of conditions constructed to approximate a range of natural rearing situations and demands. The Strange Situation was introduced in their first visit to the apartment. The procedure involves eight brief episodes in which the child's reactions to two separations from and reunions with the mother and to the presence of a stranger are observed. The sequence of episodes according to the individuals present is: (1) mother, child, and experimenter; (2) mother and child; (3) stranger, mother, and child; (4) stranger and child (separation from the mother); (5) mother and child (reunion with the mother); (6) child alone (separation from the mother); (7) stranger and child; and (8) mother and child (reunion with the mother). The traditional version of the Strange Situation was followed with two exceptions: (a) episode 3 was allowed to continue for 7 minutes instead of the usual 3, and the mother and also the stranger were asked to approach the child in a series of graded steps; (b) when the mother returned in episode 8, she brought with her a small case of toys, rather than returning empty-handed. The modifications were adaptations consistent with objectives of the larger study, in which (a) the child's capacities in familiar and unfamiliar interpersonal situations, and (b) the child's approach to a novel nonpersonal situation, were of interest.

Mother's current moods and emotions were assessed by self-report. An inventory of mood ratings, the Profile of Mood States (McNair, Lorr, & Droppleman, 1971), was filled out by the mother at the time of arrival for each laboratory visit.

Finally, the mothers' expressed affect was coded "live" during the Strange Situation and during subsequent half-day observations of mother-child interaction. The predominant emotions expressed were recorded on a minute-to-minute basis. Approximately

6 hours of the mother's affective behavior in the presence of her child was rated ($\overline{X}$ = 356.7 min, SD = 3.8).

Measures

ASSESSMENT OF THE QUALITY OF ATTACHMENT
Ratings were made of interactive behaviors, including contact maintaining and proximity seeking, avoidance, resistance, search, and distance interaction. Two coders were given intensive training by one of the investigators, with whom reliability checks were also done. The mean Pearson product-moment reliability coefficient for ratings of interactive behaviors in the Strange Situation was .86 (range, .66–1.00) based on 50 Strange Situations coded by two independent observers. The percentage of interobserver agreement for classification of the quality of attachment was 96%. Coders of the attachment relationship did not take part in other aspects of the study and were blind to family diagnoses.

Quality of attachment was classified based on criteria outlined in Ainsworth et al. (1978). Consistent with the work of others, judgments of quality of attachment heavily emphasized responses to the two reunions with the mother. On the basis of studies of age changes in attachment behavior (Maccoby & Feldman, 1972; Marvin, 1972, 1977), we expected our 2–3-year-olds to show less proximity seeking and contact maintaining, but comparable levels of avoidance and resistance vis-à-vis the 12–18-month-olds on which this system was based. Accordingly, to obtain distributions of classifications as close to Ainsworth's as possible, avoidance and resistance were stressed in classification decisions. Children were classified as securely attached (B); insecurely attached, either insecure-ambivalent (C) or insecure-avoidant (A); or (3) insecurely attached, manifesting both ambivalence and avoidance (A/C).

The first three categories closely follow from Ainsworth et al. Secure children respond promptly to the mother on reunion, either by seeking proximity or physical contact with her, or by greeting her across a distance. Insecure-avoidant children ignore or avoid the mother on reunion. Insecure-ambivalent children resist contact with the mother on reunion, but may alternate this with proximity seeking. The fourth category (A/C), is not reported by Ainsworth et al., but is similar, although not identical, to Crittenden's A/C (1983) classification and Main and Weston's (1981) Unclassified category. These children showed moderate to high avoidance and moderate to high resistance during reunion, which served as the basis for classification, and most also displayed one or more of the following: "Affectless or sad with signs of

depression," "Odd or atypical body posture or movement," and "Moderate to high proximity seeking." These responses were reported by those making attachment classifications, and by independent observers carefully reviewing the A/C tapes. Finally, one child of a mother diagnosed for current major depression could not be classified because his mother, responding to his protests, could not leave in either separation episode.

Analyses were conducted to determine the extent to which differences within the sample in age, sex, SES, and race might influence the interpretation of findings. The only age difference in interactive behaviors in the present study was a decline with age in contact-maintaining behavior during the two reunions with the mother: in episodes 5, $r(89) = -.25$, $p < .05$, and episode 8, $r(89) = -.50$, $p < .01$. There were no differences as a function of age in classifications (B, A, C, or A/C) of the quality of attachment. This is consistent with the findings from other research on age changes in attachment; children seldom show evidence of entering into qualitatively different forms of attachment relationships before 3 years of age (Marvin & Greenberg, 1982). Quality of attachment did not vary as a function of Hollingshead SES, whether calculated on a continuum or as a function of categories of status structure. Within the five categories of SES status structure, disregarding diagnostic classifications, there was insecure attachment in four of the 10 families in the lowest two categories, in 16 of the 40 families in the middle two categories, and in 23 of the 48 families in the highest categories. Other studies have also failed to find differences in patterns of attachment as a function of social class (Schneider-Rosen & Cicchetti, 1984; Vaughn, Egeland, Sroufe, & Waters, 1979). Boys and girls and blacks and whites also did not differ significantly in the distribution of classifications of attachment. Subjects were collapsed across age, sex, race, and SES in further analyses.

MOTHERS' SELF-REPORT OF MOODS ON THE POMS Six mood scales from mothers' responses on the POMS were: (1) agreeable–hostile, (2) elated–depressed, (3) energetic–tired, (4) clear-headed–confused, (5) composed–anxious, and (6) confident–unsure. Scores were derived for each scale for each of 3 days in the laboratory apartment.

MOTHERS' EXPRESSED EMOTIONS OBSERVED IN ACTIONS AND REACTIONS IN THE APARTMENT
Mothers' affects were scored, on a minute-by-minute basis, as cheerful–happy, tender–loving, tense-anxious, irritable–angry, sad–tearful, neutral–posi-

tive, or neutral–negative. The mean interobserver reliability, using the Kappa statistic (Bartko & Carpenter, 1976), which corrects for chance agreement, was .78. Because coders were not blind to mothers' diagnoses, a subset of sessions ($N = 21$) was coded from the videotapes by a coder who was blind to mothers' diagnoses. There was a high level of agreement; the mean intercoder reliability was Kappa = .79. Scores were derived for each of the affect categories by summing the number of minutes in which the emotion was observed, dividing by the total number of minutes of observation. Overall scores for any type of positive and any type of negative affect were also derived.

RESULTS

Maternal Depression and Quality of Attachment

Distributions of attachment patterns by diagnostic groups are shown in Table 2. Insecure attachments were relatively infrequent in both the normal and minor depression groups (25%–30% of cases), and are comparable to rates reported in other studies of normal populations among younger children (e.g., Ainsworth et al., 1978; Waters, 1978). By contrast, insecure attachments were relatively frequent in families with major affective disorders (55% of cases), particularly among children of bipolar mothers (79%). Compared by means of tests of proportions (Hays, 1963), the difference between children of nor-

mal mothers and children of mothers with minor depression in incidence of insecure attachments was not significant, $z < 1$. There was a greater incidence of insecure attachments in families with major affective disorders than in normal families, $z = 2.33$, $p < .05$, or in families with minor depression, $z = 1.89$, $p < .10$ (all reported p values are two-tailed). Within the major affective disorders groups, insecure attachment was more frequent among children of bipolar mothers an among children of mothers with unipolar depression, $z = 2.08$, $p < .05$.

In 18 of the two-parent families with maternal depression, the father, too, had a diagnosis of depression. Forty-two percent of children in this group were insecurely attached, and 50% of the children within the depression group in which only the mother was depressed were insecurely attached, $z < 1$. Thus, whether mother only or both mother and father were depressed made no difference in the number of children with insecure attachments to mother. However, father's absence or presence did make a difference in the security of attachment to the mother. Because the number of families in which fathers were absent was small ($N < 10$), groups were compared by means of Fisher Exact Tests (Siegel, 1956). In the eight families (six girls and two boys) with major maternal depression and no father present, anxious attachment characterized seven of the children, a proportion higher than in families with major depression in which both parents were present, Fisher Exact Test, $p < .06$.

As noted earlier, a subgroup of children were classified as A/C. This classification occurred significantly more often among children of mothers with

TABLE 2

Maternal Diagnostic Status and Quality of Attachment Relationship

| | | Attachment (%) | | | |
| | | Secure | Insecure | | |
Diagnostic Group	N	B	A	C	A/C
Normal	31	71 (22)[a]	29 (9)	0	0
Minor depression	12	75 (9)	17 (2)	8(1)	0
Major affective disorder	55	45(25)	31 (18)	4(2)	20 (10)
Unipolar depression[b]	41	53 (22)	27 (11)	2(1)	17 (7)
Bipolar	14	21 (3)	43 (7)	7(1)	29 (3)

[a] Number of children receiving the classification.
[b] One child could not be classified, because his mother, responding to his extreme protests, would not leave in either separation episode.

major affective disorders, Fisher Exact Test, $p < .01$. In fact, this pattern was observed only in children of mothers with a major affective disorder. Also, a disproportionate number of A/C's ($N = 4$) were in the single-parent major depression group.

In further analyses of attachment and mother's depression, the percent of the child's lifetime in which the mother was ill, the severity (GAS) of her worst depressive episode, and her history of treatment for affective illness (number of forms of treatments received from among hospitalization, drug therapy, and psychotherapy) were considered. Analyses of variance with one between-subjects factor (attachment group) were performed for these indices: For the percent of the child's lifetime in which the mother was depressed, $F(2,91) = 8.96$, $p < .001$; for the severity of the mother's worst depressive episode, $F(2,56) = 4.68$, $p < .05$; and for the index of treatment history, $F(2,91) = 6.00$, $p < .005$. These relationships are shown in Table 3. Post-hoc Tukey tests were conducted to compare groups. Mothers of A/C children compared with mothers of children with B classifications or with A or C classifications had histories indicative of significantly more serious depression (all comparisons, $p < .05$). Mothers of B classification children and mothers of children with traditional insecure classifications (A or C) did not differ.

Next we examined the extent to which variables pertaining to mothers' depression contributed nonredundantly to prediction of attachment classification. For this analysis, three groups were distinguished: B, A or C, and A/C. The multiple correlation between attachment classification and maternal depression variables was $R = .38$, thus accounting for 15% of the variance in attachment classification. Stepwise multiple regression analyses indicated that mother's diagnosis was the best predictor, and the severity of her worst depressive episode was the second best predictor. Adding whether the father was absent into the analysis increased R to .47 and R^2 to 22%.

Mothers' Current Affect and Quality of Attachment

To examine relations between mother's current emotions (disregarding diagnosis) and child's security of attachment, one-way analyses of variance with attachment group as the between-subjects factor were conducted for mother's self-assessed moods and for her expressed affect in interaction. There were no significant findings involving mothers' self-assessed moods. However, mothers' expressed emotions in interaction with their children during half-days in the apartment differentiated groups. Composite scores of positive and negative emotions showed that mothers of securely attached children expressed positive affect more often, and negative affect less often, than mothers of insecurely attached children (positive affect appeared in 80% and 69% of the minutes and negative affect in 18% and 31% of the minutes, respectively), F's$(1,80) \geq 4.02$, p's $< .05$. There were no significant differences between groups in expression of specific emotions.

Mothers' expressions of emotions and their diagnoses independently predicted attachment classification: Correlations between the percent of minutes rated positive or negative in affect and mother's diagnoses were nonsignificant. Multiple regression analyses indicated that mothers' general affective tone added significantly (5%) to the variance accounted for in attachment classification.

DISCUSSION

That affective illness of the mother may interfere with her ability to relate to her child in ways that promote a secure attachment is documented in these data. Depression decreased the likelihood of secure attachment between mother and child, at least as this is reflected in the child's responses to the mother in reunions after separation in the Strange Situation. Also, A/C patterns appear in children of mothers with major depression. The similarities with Crittenden's (1983) and Main and Weston's (1981) "unclassifi-

TABLE 3

Mothers' Affective Functioning in the Child's Lifetime and Quality of Attachment Relationship

| | Attachment | | |
| | Secure | Insecure | |
Index	B	A or C	A/C
Percent of the child's lifetime mother is ill	26.5	25.9	79.7
Severity of mother's illness[a]	58.3	58.2	44.5
Treatment history[b]	.65	.73	1.60

[a] GAS scores varied from 0 (needing continuous care and supervision) to 100 (superior functioning); normal mothers are not given ratings.
[b] Number of forms of treatment received: hospitalization, drug therapy, psychotherapy; maximum score equals 3.

able" patterns observed among younger children are of interest. Crittenden's A/C's showed moderate to high avoidance and resistance, and most also showed some stereotypic or maladaptive behaviors, including "huddling on the floor," which might be interpreted as sadness. Main and Weston's "U's" showed extreme avoidance and distress, behaved "oddly" during the Strange Situation, and were affectless with signs of depression. Another interesting parallel is that Crittenden's A/C's and those in the present study were found only among children of mothers with psychopathology: In Crittenden's study mothers were highly abusing, while our mothers were severely depressed. Mothers of Main and Weston's U's were unscreened for maternal psychopathology, so it is unclear whether psychopathology was a factor. These studies suggest that Ainsworth's classification system may not describe the entire range of patterns of attachment, and that important new patterns maybe found in atypical samples. Another implication is that there is more than a dichotomy between security and insecurity; it may be necessary to distinguish between secure, insecure, and very insecure (A/C) patterns, or introduce more divisions along a dimension of anxiety (Crittenden, in press; Main, Kaplan, & Cassidy, in press). External validation is required, however, before any firm conclusions about the significance of new patterns can be drawn. The search for very insecure patterns may be complicated by the fact that they may vary as a function of the mothers' particular psychopathology or the age of the child.

The children of unipolar and bipolar depressed mothers had different patterns of attachment. Although children of mothers with major unipolar depression were more likely to be insecurely attached than children of mothers with no history of affective disturbance (47% vs. 29%), the difference in incidence of insecure attachment is not as great as with bipolar depression. Children of mothers with bipolar depression were more than twice as likely to be insecurely attached as children of normal mothers. This greater vulnerability in the bipolar families is consistent with existing evidence of a strong genetic component determining offspring development, as well as with an environmental interpretation that takes into account the difficulties posed not only by the severity of symptoms but also by the contrasting extremes and alternations in behavior in bipolar parents.

We know from the responses of depressed mothers on the SADS interview that their children had been exposed to episodes of maternal sad affect, hopelessness and helplessness, irritability, confusions, and, in bipolar depression, to these episodes alternating with periods of euphoria and grandiosity. It would be desirable to know the effects on the child of

each of these patterns of behavior. We have suggestive evidence on the importance of various elements within these patterns. There is indication that, regardless of diagnosis, mothers' negative affective expression in interaction is associated with insecure attachment. Amount of exposure to disturbed affect was also associated with increased probability of a poor mother-child relationship. The significant relation between severity of disturbance and attachment classification suggests that mother's own ability to cope or to function well despite her disorder is one factor to be considered.

One can speculate concerning the effect of other depression-related behaviors. Consistent and positively responsive mothering has been repeatedly shown to be beneficial to the child in the literature of child development. To some degree, major depression precludes consistency of mothering, since depression is episodic (both unipolar and bipolar). Depressed mothers are likely, therefore, to be experienced by their children as unpredictable or inconsistent. Since confusion and preoccupations with self are conditions of depression, young children of depressed mothers are also likely to find their mothers unresponsive as well as physically and emotionally unavailable.

The hopeless and self-deprecating outlook of the parent who is severely depressed raises questions concerning another kind of possible impact on the child: How is this dimension of depression conveyed to the child, and with what effects? The research of Cummings, Zahn-Waxler, and Radke-Yarrow (1981), Klinnert, Campos, Sorce, Emde, and Svejda (1983), Radke-Yarrow and Zahn-Waxler (1984), and others has documented very young children's keen awareness of affective signals in others (in facial expressions, body language, and speech), whether or not the affect is directed to the child. What are the consequences of the exaggerated as well as the flat affect of depressed mothers for the cognitive and social-emotional aspects of the child's relationship with her? An important next step is to observe each of these aspects of maternal affect in interaction with the child in order to assess the child's responses to these encounters on a day-to-day basis.

We have been discussing the present findings as group differences between normal and depressed mothers. Not all mother-child pairs conform to the group difference. Normal mothers and mothers with a diagnosis of minor depression did not differ in frequencies of secure attachment (roughly three-fourths of the pairs were securely attached). The drop in the secure attachments to 53% in unipolar depression and 21% in bipolar depression, although impressive, still leaves "discordant" cases. Conditions outside the mother's illness-based behavior are surely contributory to the mother-child relationship. The attachment relationship, we assume, has contributions from the child. Since the present study provides information primarily on the mother component, the child's characteristics and coping mechanisms are unknowns.

One might assume that the father's relationship with the mother, his relationship with the child, and specifically his functioning when the mother is ill would be important. Although the present study has limited information concerning the father's role, the significance of father absence in increasing the frequency of insecure attachments throws some light on these questions. It suggests an interpretation in terms of the availability of an alternative attachment figure when the mother is ill. Bowlby (1969) has suggested that the effect of physical separation on attachment relationships depends in part on the physical availability of acceptable alternative figures during separation. In the case of maternal depression, when the mother may be emotionally unavailable, an available alternative paternal attachment figure appears to be important. In a related vein, the social supports available to the mother have been shown to be important in the quality of attachment relationship with the mother (Crockenberg, 1981). Social supports from father or others are likely to be important for depressed mothers in determining their ability to cope with their depression and with their role as parent.

However, the findings suggest that whether the father has psychopathology may not be a critical factor in the social support provided by the father.

The father's illness was anticipated to be a factor influencing the child's relationship with the mother. It might be expected to influence the mother-child bond by virtue of its effects on both the mother's and child's well-being, as well as by its possible genetic contribution to the child's makeup. The expected effect of father's illness was not observed. It is possible that father's illness affected the child in other ways, which our data did not explore.

Research on the specific qualities of the rearing environment created for the child by parental pathology and on the conditions that moderate or modify the pathogenic aspects of parental rearing has a number of implications. If there are identifiably different rearing conditions associated with secure and insecure attachment in depressed families and with correspondingly good and poor child development, then there are implications for interpretations of epidemiological data. Questions could be raised as to the soundness of giving depressed parents specific probability statements about the likelihood of pathology in their children. Also, such data on rearing would provide instructive bases for interventions that would enhance the chances for adaptive development in the offspring of depressed parents.

References

Ainsworth, M. D. S., Blehar, M. C., Waters, E., & Wall, S. (1978). *Patterns of attachment: A psychological study of the strange situation*. Hillsdale, NJ: Erlbaum.

Ainsworth, M. D. S., & Wittig, B. A. (1969). Attachment and exploratory behavior of one-year-olds in a Strange Situation. In B. M. Foss (Ed.), *Determinants of infant behavior* (Vol. 4, pp. 111–136). London: Methuen.

Akisal, H., & McKinney, W. (1975). Overview of recent research in depression: Integration of ten conceptual models into a comprehensive clinical frame. *Archives of General Psychiatry, 32*, 285–305.

Arend, R., Gove, F. L, & Sroufe, L. A. (1979). Continuity of individual adaptation from infancy to kindergarten: A predictive study of egoresiliency and curiosity in preschoolers. *Child Development, 50*, 950–959.

Bartko, J. J., & Carpenter, W. T. (1976). On the methods and theory of reliability. *Journal of Nervous and Mental Disease*, 1976, *163*, 307–317.

Beardslee, W., Bemporad J., Keller, M., & Klerman G.

(1983). Children of parents with major affective disorder: A review. *American Journal of Psychiatry, 140*(7), 825–832.

Belsky, J., Rovine, M., & Taylor, D. (1984). The Pennsylvania Infant and Family Development Project: III. The origins of individual differences in infant-mother attachment: Maternal and infant contributions. *Child Development, 55*, 718–728.

Blehar, M. C., Lieberman, A. F., & Ainsworth, M. D. S. (1976). Early face-to-face interaction and its relation to later infant-mother attachment. *Child Development, 48*, 182–194.

Bowlby, J. (1969). *Attachment and loss: Vol. 1. Attachment*. London: Hogarth.

Bowlby, J. (1973). *Attachment and loss: Vol. 2. Separation: Anxiety and anger*. New York: Basic.

Bretherton, I. (in press). Attachment theory: Retrospect and prospect. In I. Bretherton & E. Waters (Eds.), Growing points in attachment theory and research. *Monographs of the Society for Research in Child Development*.

Cassidy, J., & Main, M. (1983, March). *Secure attachment in infancy as a precursor of the ability to tolerate a brief laboratory separation at six years.* Paper presented at the Second World Congress of Infant Psychiatry, Cannes, France.

Crittenden, P. M. (1983, April). *Maltreated infants: Vulnerability and resilience.* Paper presented at the meeting of the Society for Research in Child Development, Detroit.

Crittenden, P. M. (in press). Social networks, quality of child-rearing, and child development. *Child Development.*

Crockenberg, S. B. (1981). Infant irritability, mother responsiveness, and social support influences on the security of infant-mother attachment. *Child Development, 52,* 857–865.

Cummings, E. M., Zahn-Waxler, C., & Radke-Yarrow, M. (1981). Young children's responses to expressions of anger and affection by others in the family. *Child Development, 52,* 1274–1282.

Cytryn, L., McKnew, D. H., Zahn-Waxler, C., & Gershon, E. S. (in press). Developmental issues in risk research: The offspring of affectively ill parents. In M. Rutter, C. E. Izard, & P. B. Read (Eds.), *Depression in children: Developmental perspectives.* New York: Guilford.

Erickson, M. F., Sroufe, L., & Egeland, B. (in press). The relationship between quality of attachment and behavior problems in preschool in a high risk sample. In I. Bretherton & E. Waters (Eds.), Growing points in attachment theory and research. *Monographs of the Society for Research in Child Development.*

Gaensbauer, T. J., Harmon, R. J., Cytryn, L., & McKnew, D. H. (1984). Social and affective development in children with a manic-depressive parent. *American Journal of Psychiatry, 141,* 223–229.

Hays, W. L (1963). *Statistics.* New York: Holt, Rinehart & Winston.

Klinnert, M., Campos, J., Sorce, J., Emde, R., & Svejda, M. (1983). Emotions as behavior regulators: Social referencing in infancy. In R. Plutchek & H. Kellerman (Eds.), *Emotions in early development: Vol. 2. The emotions.* New York: Academic Press.

LaFreniere, P., & Sroufe, L. A. (in press). Profiles of peer competence in the preschool: Interrelations among measures, influence of social ecology, and relation to attachment history. *Developmental Psychology.*

Lieberman, A. F. (1977). Preschoolers' competence with a peer: Influence of attachment and social experience. *Child Development, 48,* 1277–1287.

Londerville, S., & Main, M. (1981). Security of attachment, compliance, and maternal training methods in the second year of life. *Developmental Psychology, 17,* 289–299.

Maccoby, E., & Feldman, S. (1972). Mother-attachment and stranger-reactions in the third year of life. *Monographs of the Society for Research in Child Development, 37*(1, Serial No. 146).

Main, M., Kaplan, N., & Cassidy, J. (in press). Security in infancy, childhood, and adulthood: A move to the level of representation. In I. Bretherton & E. Waters (Eds.), Growing points in attachment theory and research. *Monographs of the Society for Research in Child Development.*

Main, J., Tomasini L., & Tolan, W. (in press). Differences among mothers of infants judged to differ in security. *Infant Behavior and Development.*

Main, M., & Weston, D. R. (1981). The quality of the toddlers' relationship to mother and father: Related to conflict behavior and the readiness to establish new relationships. *Child Development, 52,*932–940.

Marvin, R. S. (1972). *Attachment and cooperative behavior in two-, three-, and four-year olds.* Unpublished doctoral dissertation, University of Chicago.

Marvin, R. S. (1977). An ethological-cognitive model for the attenuation of mother-child attachment behavior. In T. M. Alloway & L. Kramer (Eds.), *Advances in the study of communication and affect: Vol. 3. The development of social attachments* (pp. 25–29). New York: Plenum.

Marvin, R. S., & Greenberg, M. T. (1982). Preschoolers' changing conceptions of their mothers: A social-cognitive study of mother-child attachment. In D. Forbes & M. T. Greenberg (Eds.), *New directions in child development: Vol. 14. Developing plans for behavior* (pp. 47–60). San Francisco: Jossey-Bass.

Matas, L., Arend, R. E., & Sroufe, L. A. (1978). Continuity of adaptation in the second year: The relationship between quality of attachment and later competence. *Child Development, 49,* 547–556.

McNair, D. M., Lorr, M., & Droppleman, L. F. (1971). *POMS—Profile of mood states.* San Diego, CA: Educational and Industrial Testing Service.

Meyersberg, M. A., & Post, R. M. (1979). An holistic developmental view of neural and psychological processes: A neurobiological-psychoanalytic integration. *British Journal of Psychiatry, 135,* 139–155.

Pastor, D. L. (1981). The quality of mother-infant attachment and its relationship to toddlers' initial sociability with peers. *Developmental Psychology, 17,* 326–335.

Radke-Yarrow, M., & Zahn-Waxler, C. (1984). Roots, motives, and patternings in children's prosocial behavior. In E. Staub, D. Bar-Tal, J. Karylowski, & J. Reykowski (Eds.), *The development and maintenance of prosocial behavior. International perspectives on positive morality.* New York: Plenum.

Rutter, M., & Garmezy, N. (1983). Developmental psychopathology. In E. M. Hetherington (Ed.), P. H. Mussen (Series Ed.), *Handbook of child psychology: Vol. 4. Socialization, personality, and social development* (pp. 775–911). New York: Wiley.

Schneider-Rosen, K., & Cicchetti, D. (1984). The relationships between affect and cognition in maltreated infants: Quality of attachment and the development of self recognition. *Child Development, 55,* 648–658.

Siegel, S. (1956). *Nonparametric statistics.* New York: McGraw Hill.

Spitzer, R. L., & Endicott, J. (1977). *The schedule for affective disorders and schizophrenia: Lifetime version.* New York: New York State Psychiatric Institute, Biometrics Research.

Spitzer, R. L., Gibbon, M., & Endicott, J. (1978). *Global as-*

sessment scale. New York: New York State Psychiatric Institute, Biometrics Research.

Sroufe, L. A., Fox, N. E., & Pancake, V. R. (1983). Attachment and dependency in developmental perspective. *Child Development, 54,* 1615–1627.

Stayton, D. J., & Ainsworth, M. D. S. (1973). Individual differences in infant responses to brief everyday separations as related to other infant and maternal behavior. *Developmental Psychology, 9,* 226–235.

Tracy, R., & Ainsworth, M. D. S. (1981). Maternal affectionate behavior and infant-mother attachment patterns. *Child Development, 52,* 1341–1343.

Vaughn, B., Egeland, B., Sroufe, L. A., & Waters, E. (1979).

Individual differences in infant-mother attachment at twelve and eighteen months: Stability and change in families under stress. *Child Development, 50,* 971–975.

Waters, E. (1978). The reliability and stability of individual differences in infant-mother attachment. *Child Development, 49,* 483–494.

Waters, E., Wippman, J., & Sroufe, L. A. (1979). Attachment, positive affect, and competence in the peer group: Two studies in construct validation. *Child Development, 50,* 821–829.

Zahn-Waxler, C., Cummings, E. M., McKnew, D. H., & Radke-Yarrow, M. (1984). Affective arousal and social interactions in young children of manic-depressive parents. *Child Development, 55,* 112–122.

14

Children of the Garden Island

EMMY E. WERNER

Does exposure to problematic and stressful experiences in early life lead to, as is often assumed, the development of an unhealthy personality? Are some individuals more resilient than others to developmental difficulties such as birth complications or poverty? The best technique available in developmental psychology for addressing this issue is the longitudinal research design: the same individuals are observed over time to determine if and how their early experiences are related to their later development. A classic longitudinal investigation of the long term effects of early developmental difficulties was conducted on the Hawaiian island of Kauai by Werner and colleagues. This study took place over a thirty-year period and involved a group of approximately 700 individuals. The research team found a number of children who, despite experiential barriers to healthy development, were resistant to these barriers and developed into healthy adults. Resilient children such as these challenge the traditional assumption that there is a simple and direct link between early experiences and later development.

In 1955, 698 infants on the Hawaiian island of Kauai became participants in a 30-year study that has shown how some individuals triumph over physical disadvantages and deprived childhoods.

Kauai, the Garden Island, lies at the northwest end of the Hawaiian chain, 100 miles and a half-hour flight from Honolulu. Its 555 square miles encompass mountains, cliffs, canyons, rain forests and sandy beaches washed by pounding surf. The first Polynesians who crossed the Pacific to settle there in the eighth century were charmed by its beauty, as were the generations of sojourners who visited there after Captain James Cook "discovered" the island in 1778.

The 45,000 inhabitants of Kauai are for the most part descendants of immigrants from Southeast Asia and Europe who came to the island to work on the sugar plantations with the hope of finding a better life for their children. Thanks to the islanders' unique spirit of cooperation, my colleagues Jessie M. Bierman and Fern E. French of the University of California at Berkeley, Ruth S. Smith, a clinical psychologist on Kauai, and I have been able to carry out a longitudinal study on Kauai that has lasted for more than three decades. The study has had two principal goals: to assess the long-term consequences of prenatal and perinatal stress and to document the effects of adverse early rearing conditions on children's physical, cognitive and psychosocial development.

The Kauai Longitudinal Study began at a time when the systematic examination of the development of children exposed to biological and psychosocial risk factors was still a bit of a rarity. Investigators attempted to reconstruct the events that led to physical or psychological problems by studying the history of individuals in whom such problems had already surfaced. This retrospective approach can create the impression that the outcome is inevitable, since it takes into account only the "casualties," not the "survivors." We hoped to avoid that impression by monitoring the development of all the children born in a given period in an entire community.

We began our study in 1954 with an assessment of the reproductive histories of all the women in the community. Altogether 2,203 pregnancies were reported by the women of Kauai in 1954, 1955 and 1956; there were 240 fetal deaths and 1,963 live births. We chose to study the cohort of 698 infants born on Kauai in 1955, and we followed the development of these individuals at one, two, 10, 18 and 31 or 32 years of age. The majority of the individuals in the birth cohort—422 in all—were born without complications, following uneventful pregnancies, and grew up in supportive environments.

But as our study progressed we began to take a special interest in certain "high risk" children who, in spite of exposure to reproductive stress, discordant and impoverished home lives and uneducated, alcoholic or mentally disturbed parents, went on to develop healthy personalities, stable careers and strong interpersonal relations. We decided to try to identify the protective factors that contributed to the resilience of these children.

Finding a community that is willing or able to cooperate in such an effort is not an easy task. We chose Kauai for a number of reasons, not the least of which was the receptivity of the island population to our endeavors. Coverage by medical, public-health, educational and social services on the island was comparable to what one would find in communities of similar size on the U.S. mainland at that time. Furthermore, our study would take into account a variety of cultural influences on childbearing and child rearing, since the population of Kauai includes individuals of Japanese, Philipino, Portuguese, Chinese, Korean and northern European as well as of Hawaiian descent.

We also thought the population's low mobility would make it easier to keep track of the study's par-

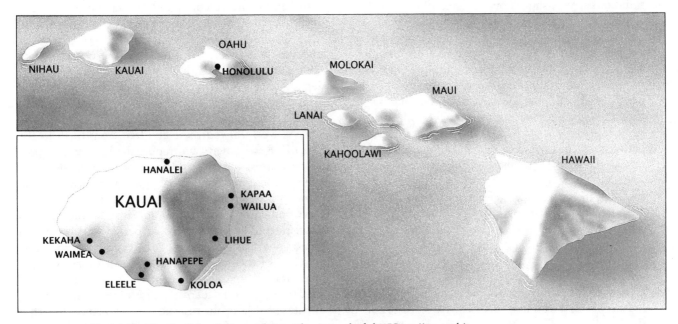

FIGURE 1   Kauai, the Garden Island, lies at the northwest end of the Hawaiian archipelago. The towns that participated in the Kauai Longitudinal Study are shown in the inset. Lihue is the county seat; it is about 100 miles from Honolulu, the capital of Hawaii.

ticipants and their families. The promise of a stable sample proved to be justified. At the time of the two-year follow-up, 96 percent of the living children were still on Kauai and available for study. We were able to find 90 percent of the children who were still alive for the 10-year follow-up, and for the 18-year follow-up we found 88 percent of the cohort.

In order to elicit the cooperation of the island's residents, we needed to get to know them and to introduce our study as well. In doing so we relied on the skills of a number of dedicated professionals from the University of California's Berkeley and Davis campuses, from the University of Hawaii and from the island of Kauai itself. At the beginning of the study five nurses and one social worker, all residents of Kauai, took a census of all households on the island, listing the occupants of each dwelling and recording demographic information, including a reproductive history of all women 12 years old or older. The interviewers asked the women if they were pregnant; if a woman was not, a card with a postage-free envelope was left with the request that she mail it to the Kauai Department of Health as soon as she thought she was pregnant.

Local physicians were asked to submit a monthly list of the women who were coming to them for prenatal care. Community organizers spoke to women's groups, church gatherings, the county medical society and community leaders. The visits by the census takers were backed up with letters, and milk cartons were delivered with a printed message urging mothers to cooperate. We advertised in newspapers, organized radio talks, gave slide shows and distributed posters.

Public-health nurses interviewed the pregnant women who joined our study in each trimester of pregnancy, noting any exposure to physical or emotional trauma. Physicians monitored any complications during the prenatal period, labor, delivery and the neonatal period. Nurses and social workers interviewed the mothers in the postpartum period and when the children were one and 10 years old; the interactions between parents and offspring in the home were also observed. Pediatricians and psychologists independently examined the children at two and 10 years of age, assessing their physical, intellectual and social development and noting any handicaps or behavior problems. Teachers evaluated the children's academic progress and their behavior in the classroom.

From the outset of the study we recorded information about the material, intellectual and emotional aspects of the family environment, including stressful life events that resulted in discord or disruption of the family unit. With the parents' permission we also were given access to the records of public-health, educational and social-service agencies and to the files of

the local police and the family court. My collaborators and I also administered a wide range of aptitude, achievement and personality tests in the elementary grades and in high school. Last but not least, we gained the perspectives of the young people themselves by interviewing them at the age of 18 and then again when they were in their early 30's.

Of the 698 children in the 1955 cohort, 69 were exposed to moderate prenatal or perinatal stress, that is, complications during pregnancy, labor or delivery. About 3 percent of the cohort—23 individuals in all—suffered severe prenatal or perinatal stress; only 14 infants in this group lived to the age of two. Indeed, nine of the 12 children in our study who died before reaching two years of age had suffered severe perinatal complications.

Some of the surviving children became "casualties" of a kind in the next two decades of life. One out of every six children (116 children in all) had physical or intellectual handicaps of perinatal or neonatal origin that were diagnosed between birth and the age of two and that required long-term specialized medical, educational or custodial care. About one out of every five children (142 in all) developed serious learning or behavior problems in the first decade of life that required more than six months of remedial work. By the time the children were 10 years old, twice as many children needed some form of mental-health service or remedial education (usually for problems associated with reading) as were in need of medical care.

By the age of 18, 15 percent of the young people had delinquency records and 10 percent had mental health problems requiring either in- or outpatient care. There was some overlap among these groups. By the time they were 10, all 25 of the children with long-term mental-health problems had learning problems as well. Of the 70 children who had mental health problems at 18, 15 also had a record of repeated delinquencies.

As we followed these children from birth to the age of 18 we noted two trends: the impact of reproductive stress diminished with time, and the developmental outcome of virtually every biological risk condition was dependent on the quality of the rearing environment. We did find some correlation between moderate to severe degrees of perinatal trauma and major physical handicaps of the central nervous system and of the musculo-skeletal and sensory systems; perinatal trauma was also correlated with mental retardation, serious learning disabilities and chronic mental-health problems such as schizophrenia that arose in late adolescence and young adulthood.

But overall rearing conditions were more powerful determinants of outcome than perinatal trauma.

The better the quality of the home environment was, the more competence the children displayed. This could already be seen when the children were just two years old: toddlers who had experienced severe perinatal stress but lived in middle-class homes or in stable family settings did nearly as well on developmental tests of sensory-motor and verbal skills as toddlers who had experienced no such stress.

Prenatal and perinatal complications were consistently related to impairment of physical and psychological development at the ages of 10 and 18 only when they were combined with chronic poverty, family discord, parental mental illness or other persistently poor rearing conditions. Children who were raised in middle-class homes, in a stable family environment and by a mother who had finished high school showed few if any lasting effects of reproductive stress later in their lives.

How many children could count on such a favorable environment? A sizable minority could not. We designated 201 individuals—30 percent of the surviving children in this study population—as being high-risk children because they had experienced moderate to severe perinatal stress, grew up in chronic poverty, were reared by parents with no more than eight grades of formal education or lived in a family environment troubled by discord, divorce, parental alcoholism or mental illness. We termed the children "vulnerable" if they encountered four or more such risk factors before their second birthday. And indeed, two-thirds of these children (129 in all) did develop serious learning or behavior problems by the age of 10 or had delinquency records, mental-health problems or pregnancies by the time they were 18.

Yet one out of three of these high-risk children—72 individuals altogether—grew into competent young adults who loved well, worked well and played well. None developed serious learning or behavior problems in childhood or adolescence. As far as we could tell from interviews and from their record in the community, they succeeded in school, managed home and social life well and set realistic educational and vocational goals and expectations for themselves when they finished high school. By the end of their second decade of life they had developed into competent, confident and caring people who expressed a strong desire to take advantage of whatever opportunity came their way to improve themselves.

They were children such as Michael, a boy for whom the odds on paper did not seem very promising. The son of teen-age parents, Michael was born prematurely, weighing four pounds five ounces. He spent his first three weeks of life in a hospital, separated from his mother. Immediately after his birth his father was sent with the U.S. Army to Southeast Asia, where he remained for two years. By the time Michael was eight years old he had three siblings and his parents were divorced. His mother had deserted the family and had no further contact with her children. His father raised Michael and his siblings with the help of their aging grandparents.

Then there was Mary, born after 20 hours of labor to an overweight mother who had experienced several miscarriages before that pregnancy. Her father was an unskilled farm laborer with four years of formal education. Between Mary's fifth and 10th birthdays her mother was hospitalized several times for repeated bouts of mental illness, after having inflicted both physical and emotional abuse on her daughter.

Surprisingly, by the age of 18 both Michael and Mary were individuals with high self-esteem and sound values who cared about others and were liked by their peers. They were successful in school and looked forward to the future. We looked back at the lives of these two youngsters and the 70 other resilient individuals who had triumphed over their circumstances and compared their behavioral characteristics and the features of their environment with those of the other high-risk youths who developed serious and persistent problems in childhood and adolescence.

We identified a number of protective factors in the families, outside the family circle and within the resilient children themselves that enabled them to resist stress. Some sources of resilience seem to be constitutional: resilient children such as Mary and Michael tend to have characteristics of temperament that elicit positive responses from family members and strangers alike. We noted these same qualities in adulthood. They include a fairly high activity level, a low degree of excitability and distress and a high degree of sociability. Even as infants the resilient individuals were described by their parents as "active," "affectionate," "cuddly," "easygoing" and "even tempered." They had no eating or sleeping habits that were distressing to those who took care of them.

The pediatricians and psychologists who examined the resilient children at 20 months noted their alertness and responsiveness, their vigorous play and their tendency to seek out novel experiences and to ask for help when they needed it. When they entered elementary school, their classroom teachers observed their ability to concentrate on their assignments and noted their problem-solving and reading skills. Although they were not particularly gifted, these children used whatever talents they had effectively. Usually they had a special hobby they could share with a friend. These interests were not narrowly sex-

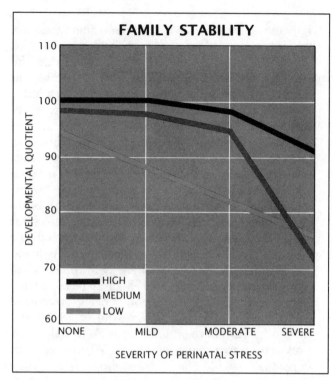

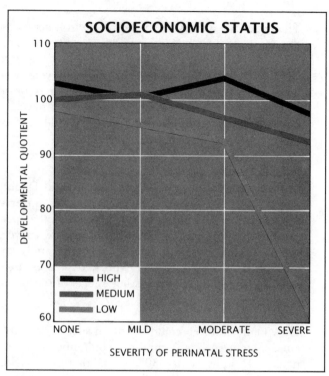

FIGURE 2 Influence of environmental factors such as family stability (*left*) or socio-economic status (*right*) appears in infancy. The "developmental quotients" derived from tests given at 20 months show that the rearing environment can buffer or worsen the stress of perinatal complications. Children who had suffered severe perinatal stress but lived in stable, middle-class families scored as well as or better than children in poor, unstable households who had not experienced such stress.

typed; we found that girls and boys alike excelled at such activities as fishing, swimming, horseback riding and hula dancing.

We could also identify environmental factors that contributed to these children's ability to withstand stress. The resilient youngsters tended to come from families having four or fewer children, with a space of two years or more between themselves and the next sibling. In spite of poverty, family discord or parental mental illness, they had the opportunity to establish a close bond with at least one caretaker from whom they received positive attention during the first years of life.

The nurturing might come from substitute parents within the family (such as grandparents, older siblings, aunts or uncles) or from the ranks of regular baby-sitters. As the resilient children grew older they seemed to be particularly adept at recruiting such surrogate parents when a biological parent was unavailable (as in the case of an absent father) or incapacitated (as in the case of a mentally ill mother who was frequently hospitalized).

Maternal employment and the need to take care of younger siblings apparently contributed to the pronounced autonomy and sense of responsibility noted among the resilient girls, particularly in households where the father had died or was permanently absent because of desertion or divorce. Resilient boys, on the other hand, were often firstborn sons who did not have to share their parents' attention with many additional children in the household. They also had some male in the family who could serve as a role model (if not the father, then a grandfather or an uncle). Structure and rules in the household and assigned chores were part of the daily routine for these boys during childhood and adolescence.

Resilient children also seemed to find a great deal of emotional support outside their immediate family. They tended to be well liked by their classmates and had at least one close friend, and usually several. They relied on an informal network of neighbors, peers and elders for counsel and support in times of crisis and transition. They seem to have made school a home away from home, a refuge from a disordered household. When we interviewed them at 18, many resilient youths mentioned a favorite teacher who had become a role model, friend and confidant and was particularly supportive at times when their own family was beset by discord or threatened with dissolution.

For others, emotional support came from a church group, a youth leader in the YMCA or YWCA or a favorite minister. Participation in extracurricular activities—such as 4-H, the school band or a cheerleading team which allowed them to be part of a cooperative enterprise—was also an important source of emotional support for those children who succeeded against the odds.

With the help of these support networks, the resilient children developed a sense of meaning in their lives and a belief that they could control their fate. Their experience in effectively coping with and mastering stressful life events built an attitude of hopefulness that contrasted starkly with the feelings of helplessness and futility that were expressed by their troubled peers.

In 1985, 12 years after the 1955 birth cohort had finished high school, we embarked on a search for the members of our study group. We managed to find 545 individuals—80 percent of the cohort—through parents or other relatives, friends, former classmates, local telephone books, city directories and circuit-court, voter-registration and motor-vehicle registration records and marriage certificates filed with the State Department of Health in Honolulu. Most of the young men and women still lived on Kauai, but 10 percent had moved to other islands and 10 percent lived on the mainland; 2 percent had gone abroad.

We found 62 of the 72 young people we had characterized as "resilient" at the age of 18. They had finished high school at the height of the energy crisis and joined the work force during the worst U.S. recession since the Great Depression. Yet these 30-year-old men and women seemed to be handling the demands of adulthood well. Three out of four (46 individuals) had received some college education and were satisfied with their performance in school. All but four worked full time, and three out of four said they were satisfied with their jobs.

Indeed, compared with their low-risk peers from the same cohort, a significantly higher proportion of high-risk resilient individuals described themselves as being happy with their current life circumstances (44 percent versus 10 percent). The resilient men and women did, however, report a significantly higher number of health problems than their peers in low-risk comparison groups (46 percent versus 15 percent). The men's problems seemed to be brought on by stress: back problems, dizziness and fainting spells, weight gain and ulcers. Women's health problems were largely related to pregnancy and childbirth.

And although 82 percent of the women were married, only 48 percent of the men were. Those who were married had strong commitments to intimacy and sharing with their partners and children. Personal competence and determination support from a spouse or mate and a strong religious faith were the shared qualities that we found characterized resilient children as adults.

We were also pleasantly surprised to find that many high-risk children who had problems in their teens were able to rebound in their twenties and early thirties. We were able to contact 26 (90 percent) of the teen-age mothers, 56 (80 percent) of the individuals with mental-health problems and 74 (75 percent) of the former delinquents who were still alive at the age of 30.

Almost all the teen-age mothers we interviewed were better off in their early thirties than they had been at 18. About 60 percent (16 individuals) had gone on to additional schooling and about 90 percent (24 individuals) were employed. Of the delinquent youths, three-fourths (56 individuals) managed to avoid arrest on reaching adulthood. Only a minority (12 individuals) of the troubled youths were still in need of mental-health services in their early thirties. Among the critical turning points in the lives of these individuals were entry into military service, marriage, parenthood and active participation in a church group. In adulthood, as in their youth, most of these individuals relied on informal rather than formal sources of support: kith and kin rather than mental-health professionals and social-service agencies.

Our findings appear to provide a more hopeful perspective than can be had from reading the extensive literature on "problem" children that come to the attention of therapists, special educators and social-service agencies. Risk factors and stressful environments do not inevitably lead to poor adaptation. It seems clear that, at each stage in an individual's development from birth to maturity, there is a shifting balance between stressful events that heighten vulnerability and protective factors that enhance resilience.

As long as the balance between stressful life events and protective factors is favorable, successful adaptation is possible. When stressful events outweigh the protective factors, however, even the most resilient child can have problems. It may be possible to shift the balance from vulnerability to resilience through intervention, either by decreasing exposure to risk factors or stressful events or by increasing the number of protective factors and sources of support that are available.

It seems clear from our identification of risk and protective factors that some of the most critical determinants of outcome are present when a child is very young. And it is obvious that there are large individual differences among high-risk children in their responses to both negative and positive circumstances in their caregiving environment. The very fact of individual variation among children who live in adverse conditions suggests the need for greater assistance to some than to others.

If early intervention cannot be extended to every child at risk, priorities must be established for choosing who should receive help. Early-intervention programs need to focus on infants and young children who appear most vulnerable because they lack—permanently or temporarily—some of the essential social bonds that appear to buffer stress. Such children may be survivors of neonatal intensive care, hospitalized children who are separated from their families for extended periods of time, the young offspring of addicted or mentally ill parents, infants and toddlers whose mothers work full time and do not have access to stable child care, the babies of single or teen-age parents who have no other adult in the household and migrant and refugee children without permanent roots in a community.

Assessment and diagnosis, the initial steps in any early intervention, need to focus not only on the risk factors in the lives of the children but also on the protective factors. These include competencies and informal sources of support that already exist and that can be utilized to enlarge a young child's communication and problem-solving skills and to enhance his or her self-esteem. Our research on resilient children has shown that other people in a child's life—grandparents, older siblings, day-care providers or teachers—can play a supportive role if a parent is incapacitated or unavailable. In many situations it might make better sense and be less costly as well to strengthen such available informal ties to kin and community than it would to introduce additional layers of bureaucracy into delivery of services.

Finally, in order for any intervention program to be effective, a young child needs enough consistent nurturing to trust in its availability. The resilient children in our study had at least one person in their lives who accepted them unconditionally, regardless of temperamental idiosyncracies or physical or mental handicaps. All children can be helped to become more resilient if adults in their lives encourage their independence, teach them appropriate communication and self-help skills and model as well as reward acts of helpfulness and caring.

Thanks to the efforts of many people, several community-action and educational programs for high-risk children have been established on Kauai since our study began. Partly as a result of our findings, the legislature of the State of Hawaii has funded special mental-health teams to provide services for troubled children and youths. In addition the State Health Department established the Kauai Children's Services, a coordinated effort to provide services related to child development, disabilities, mental retardation and rehabilitation in a single facility.

The evaluation of such intervention programs can in turn illuminate the process by which a chain of protective factors is forged that affords vulnerable children an escape from adversity. The life stories of the resilient individuals on the Garden Island have taught us that competence, confidence and caring can flourish even under adverse circumstances if young children encounter people in their lives who provide them with a secure basis for the development of trust, autonomy and initiative.

Further Reading

KAUAI'S CHILDREN COME OF AGE. Emmy E. Werner and Ruth S. Smith. The University of Hawaii Press, 1977.

VULNERABLE BUT INVINCIBLE: A LONGITUDINAL STUDY OF RESILIENT CHILDREN AND YOUTH. Emmy E. Werner and Ruth S. Smith. McGraw-Hill Book Company, 1982.

LONGITUDINAL STUDIES IN CHILD PSYCHOLOGY AND PSYCHIATRY: PRACTICAL LESSONS FROM RESEARCH EXPERIENCE. Edited by A. R. Nichol. John Wiley & Sons, Inc., 1985.

HIGH RISK CHILDREN IN YOUNG ADULTHOOD: A LONGITUDINAL STUDY FROM BIRTH TO 32 YEARS. Emmy E. Werner in *American Journal of Orthopsychiatry*, Vol. 59, No. 1, pages 72–81; January, 1989.

15

Infant Day Care: Maligned or Malignant?

K. ALISON CLARKE-STEWART

The effect of day care on child development is one of the most critical and divisive issues confronting specialists and parents in the United States today. Over the past twenty years women have entered the labor force in great numbers, with the majority of these women having young children in need of supervision and care while their mothers are at work. In general, research findings suggest that quality care for children over 1 year of age does not interfere with the development of healthy parent-child relations and may even increase the development of social skills. (Note that this statement specifies *quality* care; psychologists agree that poor care does not promote healthy development.) However, this issue is more complicated when one considers out-of-home care for infants under 1 year of age. The first year of life is widely believed to be critical for establishing socioemotional ties to primary caregivers. What effects might early and repeated separations of the parent and infant have on the development of this early social relationship? In the following paper K. Alison Clarke-Stewart reviews research on this issue, focusing on how infant day care may affect the development of emotional security and adjustment.

Today, the mothers of half the infants in the United States work outside the home. This concerns psychologists and parents because of the possible detrimental effects on these infants of separations from mother and experience in day care. Available data suggest that infants whose mothers work full time are somewhat more likely as one-year-olds to avoid their mothers after a brief separation and later to be less compliant with their mothers and more aggressive with their peers. The argument that these behaviors indicate that infants in day care are at risk for emotional insecurity and social maladjustment is

Reprinted with permission from the author and *American Psychologist, 44,* 1989, 266–273. Copyright 1989 by the American Psychological Association.

Correspondence concerning this article should be addressed to K. Alison Clarke-Stewart, Program in Social Ecology, University of California, Irvine, CA 92717.

evaluated in light of current research results. It is concluded that other interpretations of the data are more plausible and that further research on the factors moderating and mediating the effects of infant day care is needed.

One of the most striking social changes in this country over the past decade has been the dramatic increase in the number of mothers going back to work within the first few months after their babies are born. What was rare in the 1960s and unusual in the 1970s is now common. Half of the infants in the United States today have employed mothers, twice the proportion that there were in 1970. Mothers of young infants are the fastest growing segment of the labor market (U.S. Bureau of the Census, 1986).

Not surprisingly, this social change has been greeted by concerned questions. What are the effects on these infants of repeated separations from their mothers? What will be the long-term outcomes for these children of spending so many hours with paid professionals instead of with their loving parents? What will happen to society when these children themselves become parents? These are important questions, but when they have been put to developmental psychologists, the answers have been inconsistent. The results of studies addressed to the issue of short- and long-term effects of infant day care have been unclear enough to allow varied interpretations. Thus, some (e.g., Barglow, Vaughn, & Molitor, 1987; Belsky, 1988a), interpreting the available data, have claimed that full-time maternal employment puts infants at risk for developing emotional insecurities and becoming socially maladjusted. Others (e.g., Clarke-Stewart, 1988; Phillips, McCartney, Scarr, & Howes, 1987), evaluating the same studies, have concluded that there is insufficient evidence to support this claim. What is the empirical evidence concerning the effects of infant day care, and how has the controversy over interpreting this evidence arisen? Is day care truly bad for babies, or has it been undeservedly maligned?

OUTCOMES OF INFANT DAY CARE

Does Day Care Result in Emotional Insecurity?

The major source of controversy has been the research assessing infants' relationships with their mothers. The infant–mother relationship has been central in theories of development from Freud onward and has been shown to be an important index of infants' overall emotional well-being. It is also a likely candidate for disturbance when infants are separated from their mothers for 8 to 10 hours a day. Although research consistently has shown that infants of working mothers do form attachments to their mothers and prefer their mothers to their substitute caregivers (Clarke-Stewart & Fein, 1983), the question is whether the *quality* of their attachments is as good, as emotionally secure, as the attachments of infants who are being raised exclusively by their parents.

As a first step in answering this question, one can tabulate data from all studies that have included the current standard assessment of children's attachment to their mothers, Ainsworth's Strange Situation (Ainsworth, Blehar, Waters, & Wall, 1978)—studies by Ainslie and Anderson (1984); Barglow et al. (1987); Beckwith (1987); Belsky and Rovine (1988); Benn (1986); Burchinal and Bryant (1988); Chase-Lansdale and Owen (1987); Easterbrooks and Goldberg (1985); Easterbrooks and Harmon (1987); Goossens (1987); Jacobson and Wille (1984); Lipsitt and LaGasse (1987); Owen and Cox (1988); Owen, Easterbrooks, Chase-Lansdale, and Goldberg (1984); Rodning (1987); Thompson, Lamb, and Estes (1982); and Vaughn, Gove, and Egeland (1980). Tabulation of these data shows that infants whose mothers are employed full time, compared with infants whose mothers do not work or who work part time, are disproportionately likely to be classified as insecurely attached. Of the infants of full-time working mothers, 36% have been classified as insecure; of the infants of nonemployed or part-time working mothers, only 29% have been so classified.[1] Although differences in individual studies often are not statistically significant, this overall difference, with a sample size of 1,247, certainly is ($X^2 = 6.21$, $p < .01$).

There is no disagreement that this difference exists and that it merits examination. The question is: What does the difference mean? Does it mean, as Barglow et al. (1987) and Belsky (1988a) have suggested, that infants of working mothers are at risk for emotional insecurity because they interpret their mothers' absence as rejection, or because repeated separations have disturbed their emerging attachment relationship, making them doubt their mothers' availability and responsiveness and leading them to develop a coping style that masks this anger? These interpretations, extrapolated from knowledge of the

---

[1] A copy of a table giving further details of these studies is available upon request from the author.

correlates of insecure attachment in children raised exclusively by their parents, may be correct. However, at present, they are highly speculative. They are not based on data, and indeed alternative explanations have some empirical support.

At the heart of the problem is the fact that the observed difference between infants of working and nonworking mothers is based on behavior observed in a single assessment procedure. Although having a common assessment method is invaluable for combining subjects from different studies, having only one assessment method raises problems. The Strange Situation has turned out in past research to be a reliable and useful measure of the mother–infant relationship and a predictor of later behavior problems in home-reared children (Ainsworth et al., 1978). But it is important to validate the behavior patterns observed in the Strange Situation for infants whose mothers work using other—ecologically valid—assessment procedures.

This is important, for one thing, because the Strange Situation may not be psychologically equivalent for infants of working and nonworking mothers. The validity of the Strange Situation procedure depends on creating a situation in which infants feel moderately stressed and therefore display proximity-seeking behavior to the object of their attachment. The Strange Situation may not be equally stressful for the infants of working and nonworking mothers. Consider the features that make up the Strange Situation—the infant plays with someone else's toys in a room that is not his or her own; the infant is left by his or her mother with a woman who is a stranger; the infant plays with and is comforted by that woman in the mother's absence; the mother returns to pick the infant up. Although at least some infants of nonworking mothers undoubtedly have had experiences like these before their assessment in the Strange Situation, infants of working mothers are more likely to have had them regularly and routinely and, therefore, to be more accustomed to them.

Any of these elements of familiarity could affect infants' behavior in the Strange Situation. Although strong evidence that infants whose mothers work find the Strange Situation less stressful has not yet been collected, there are hints that this may be the case.

Researchers have found that in the Strange Situation infants who have been in day care, compared with infants who have not, are less wary initially (they are less likely to resist contact with the stranger and less likely to seek proximity and contact with the mother [Hock, 1980]), are less disturbed by the mother's absence (they are less likely to search for the mother and more likely to play comfortably with the toys after the mother has left the room [Doyle & Somers, 1978; Jacobson & Wille, 1984[2]]), and are less likely to seek proximity and contact with the mother on her return (Goossens, 1987).

Clearly, we need to assess infants' attachment using procedures that are not biased by differential familiarity and potentially differential stressfulness. Several recent attempts to do this by using a Q-sort assessment technique in which mothers, teachers, or observers rate infants' attachment behavior in daily situations have not revealed differences between infants of working and nonworking mothers (Belsky, 1988b; Howes, Rodning, Galluzzo, & Myers, in press; Strayer, Moss, & Blicharski, in press; Weinraub, Jaeger, & Hoffman, in press). But, of course, these studies do not settle the issue. It may be that with a larger data set of Q-sort ratings differences between infants of working and nonworking mothers would be revealed; in Belsky's data, for example, the Q-sort results, although not significant, were in the same direction as the Strange Situation results.[3] More research using more clinically sensitive assessments is needed.

A second issue of importance for interpreting the observed difference in attachment between the infants of working and nonworking mothers is the question of how large the difference is. The difference may be statistically significant, but in practical terms how significant is it? Is it large enough to conclude that infants are in danger if their mothers work? There are several ways of presenting the differences observed between infants of working and nonworking mothers in the studies using the Strange Situation. The most extremely negative way (in terms of the dangers for infants) is to select only the low-risk subjects from the data set and to use the small percentage of insecure at-home infants as the base, saying that for the "average" infant there is a 39% increased risk of an

---

[2]Although Jacobson and Wille's (1984) curvilinear regression analysis suggests that infants with 20 hr or more of extrafamilial care per week are less likely to play comfortably in the Strange Situation than infants with 4 to 19 hr of extrafamilial care per week, inspection of Figure 1 in the article demonstrates that this is based on 4 infants who did not play during the episode alone with the stranger; 4 of the 13 infants with 20 hr or more of day care played comfortably during more than 40% of the episode.

[3]Although they were not significantly different, the Q-sort results in the Belsky (1988b) study increased the level of significant difference in a composite measure of security.

insecure attachment when the mother works full time (11% ÷ 28%). Less extreme would be the parallel statement, based on the entire data set, that for a "wide range" of infants there is a 24% increased risk of insecurity when the mother works (7% ÷ 29%). These same data could be used to make a statement that reduces the apparent difference substantially, however, by using as the base the percentage of secure children in maternal care. Then the statement would be that the probability that an infant will be securely attached is only 10% less if the mother works (7% ÷ 71%). Finally, the most positive statement of the differences would be the statement that for infants from high-risk families there is a 19% lower likelihood that an infant will be insecure if the mother works (9% ÷ 47%). Thus, one can pick one's statement to emphasize or minimize the extent of the difference.

Moving beyond this semantic sleight of tongue, in an effort to evaluate the risk of insecure attachment for infants of working mothers, one might use the strategy of comparing the distribution of attachment categories for the infants of working mothers in this data set with a broader sampling of studies, including those in other countries. As it turns out, the observed distribution of insecure infants of working mothers in the United States (22% type As and 14% type Cs) is virtually identical to the global distribution reported by van IJzendoorn and Kroonenberg (1988)[4] for studies around the world (21% type As and 14% type Cs). This seems to suggest that the observed likelihood of insecurity in infants of working mothers, even if it is somewhat elevated (more or less depending on the sample and the form of the statement one chooses) is within the normal population range.

Yet another way of looking at how different the infants of working and nonworking mothers are is to examine the size of the mean difference between the groups on the scale of insecure (avoidant) attachment behavior. When this is done for the combined samples from the studies reporting these data (Barglow et al., 1987; Belsky & Rovine, 1988; Schwartz, 1983), the average avoidance score for infants of working mothers is 5.0 ($n = 129$; SD = 2.9),[5] and for the infants of nonworking or part-time working mothers it is 3.8 ($n = 198$; SD = 2.0). This difference of about 1 point on a 7-point scale, similarly, suggests that although day-care infants are more avoidant of their mothers they are not extremely so.

A third issue in interpreting the difference between infants of working and nonworking mothers in the Strange Situation concerns the meaning of attachment itself. In theory, an attachment is a relationship; it is not a global personality trait. If the children of working mothers are more insecure with them, this does not necessarily mean that these children are emotionally insecure in general. Before labeling the infants of working mothers emotionally insecure, we need to assess their emotional health in a range of situations and with a variety of partners. On other measures of security, self-confidence, and emotional adjustment, children who were in day care as infants have been observed to do as well as children who were not (Andersson, 1987; Golden et al., 1978; Ramey, Dorval, & Baker-Ward, 1983; Rubenstein, Howes, & Boyle, 1981; Vandell & Corasaniti, 1988).[6] In the one study in which children who had been in infant day care[7] were rated as more anxious by their teachers (McCartney, Scarr, Phillips, Grajek, & Schwarz, 1982), these children were still well within the normal range and, in fact, were rated by their parents as less anxious. As further evidence that day-care infants are not emotionally disturbed in general, it might also be noted that the infants of working mothers who were coded as insecure in the Strange Situation have been found to perform better than the infants of nonworking mothers on a variety of other tasks (Strayer & Moss, 1987; Vaughn, Deane, & Waters, 1985).[8] Taken together, these findings seem

---

[4]Unfortunately, Van IJzendoorn and Kroonenberg did not report separate distributions for working and nonworking mothers, so this global estimate (based on 1,990 subjects) does include a small number of infants whose mothers worked.

[5]These standard deviations are based on Barglow, Vaughn, and Molitor's (1987) and Schwartz's (1983) studies; Belsky and Rovine (1988) did not report their standard deviations.

[6]As will be discussed later, some of these studies included other measures (e.g., aggression) on which day-care children did more poorly; here, the focus is specifically on evidence of children's emotional insecurity.

[7]In McCartney, Scarr, Phillips, Grajek, and Schwarz's (1982) study, there was a negative association between teacher ratings of children's anxiety and the age at which the children entered day care (3–24 months).

[8]Infants of working mothers did consistently, if not always significantly, better in problem-solving interactions with mothers in Strayer and Moss's (1987) study and on the Bayley Scale of Mental Development and in behavioral assessments of task persistence and the quality of mother–infant interaction in Vaughn, Deane, and Waters's (1985) study.

to suggest that day-care infants are not more anxious, insecure, or emotionally disturbed overall.

The final and perhaps most significant difficulty in interpreting the data showing that infants of working mothers are more likely to be insecurely attached to their mothers is the problem of self-selection. Mothers who work (and their infants) differ in many ways from those who do not (e.g., Hock, Christman, & Hock, 1980; McBride & Belsky, 1985). These differences may lead to the disproportionate number of children classified as insecure among the infants of working mothers.

In sum, there are a number of major obstacles to our interpretation of the observed difference in attachment between infants of working and nonworking mothers. At the present time, in my view, it is not appropriate to interpret the difference as suggesting that these children are emotionally insecure.

Does Day Care Result in Social Maladjustment?

One reason that psychologists have interpreted the difference in infants' attachments as reflecting emotional insecurity is that they have put this difference together with another provocative finding. In a number of studies, children who spent their first year in day care later were observed to be more aggressive with their peers and less compliant with their parents (Barton & Schwarz, 1981; Haskins, 1985; McCartney et al., 1982; Rubenstein & Howes, 1983; Schwarz, Strickland, & Krolick, 1974; Vandell & Corasaniti, 1988; Vaughn et al., 1985). Unfortunately, it is impossible to combine data from these studies as was done for attachment to get an overall estimate of the likelihood of aggression and noncompliance among children who were in infant day care because no common measure of these behaviors was used in these studies. One can only point out that although these studies do provide strong evidence of greater aggression and noncompliance in day-care children, no such evidence has been obtained in other studies using similar measures (Braun & Caldwell, 1973; Golden et al., 1978; Gottfried, Gottfried, & Bathhurst, 1988; Howes, 1988; Kagan, Kearsley, & Zelazo, 1978), or in the same studies using other measures (McCartney et al., 1982, aggression to peers; Rubenstein & Howes, 1983, behavior problems; Vaughn et al., 1985, compliance and aggression to mother) or assessing the children at later ages (McCartney et al., 1982; Schwarz et al., 1974).

Even accepting the possibility that a meta-analysis would reveal a trend for children who had been in day care as infants to be more aggressive and less compliant, however, one might question whether these behaviors should themselves be interpreted as evidence of maladjustment. It is possible that the pattern of aggression and noncompliance observed in these studies to some extent reflects greater independence rather than disturbed behavior. One notes that children who had been in day care as infants in these and other studies did as well as or better than children who had not on measures of advanced development—sociability, social competence, language, persistence, achievement, self-confidence, and problem solving (Andersson, 1987; Golden et al., 1978; Haskins, 1985; Lay & Meyer, 1972; Macrae & Herbert-Jackson, 1976; McCartney et al., 1982; Ramey et al., 1983; Rubenstein & Howes, 1983; Rubenstein et al, 1981; Schwartz, 1983; Schwarz, Krolick, & Strickland, 1973; Strayer & Moss, 1987). Another argument against viewing children who were in infant day care as maladjusted is the argument that this same pattern of negative behavior and advanced development appears in children who start full-time day care after infancy, as toddlers or preschoolers (Clarke-Stewart & Fein, 1983).

What this pattern of behavior may suggest, then, is not that children who have been in day care beginning in infancy or later are socially maladjusted, but that they think for themselves and that they want their own way. They are not willing to comply with adults' arbitrary rules. In one study (Siegal & Storey, 1985), for example, preschoolers who had been in day care thought that moral transgressions (like hitting or stealing) were worse than social transgressions (like not putting toys away), but children who were just starting day care thought that it was just as bad to break the social rules. Children who have spent time in day care, then, may be more demanding and independent, more disobedient and aggressive, more bossy and bratty than children who stay at home because they want their own way and do not have the skills to achieve it smoothly, rather than because they are maladjusted. To find out whether maladjustment is a consequence of infant day care, what is called for, again, are more clinically sensitive assessments.

Does Day Care Result in Intellectual Precocity?

The third finding in the literature on infant day care is that children who have been in infant day care are, on the average, advanced in their intellectual development. Quite consistently, researchers have found that when children are given intelligence tests any time between 18 months and 5 years, those who had been in day care as infants score higher than those who had not (Clarke-Stewart & Fein, 1983).

What does this difference in intellectual functioning mean? Is day care giving infants an intellectual head start, increasing their level of intelligence, or pushing them too fast? Longitudinal studies of children suggest that the difference is a temporary acceleration of children's intellectual development, not a permanent enhancement of abilities. As home-care children enter day care, preschool, kindergarten, or elementary school, they too make intellectual gains and quickly catch up to the children with early day-care experience (Clarke-Stewart & Fein, 1983). Infancy does not appear to be a critical period for accelerating intellectual development. There is also no evidence that infant day care pushes infants too fast; when homecare children catch up, they do not surpass day-care children. In brief, day care does appear to give infants an intellectual head start—but a short-lived one.

MODERATORS AND MEDIATORS OF INFANT DAY-CARE EFFECTS

Not all the children who are in day care as infants are insecurely attached, aggressive, noncompliant, or intellectually advanced. There are individual differences in development for infants in day care just as there are for infants at home. What factors contribute to these developmental outcomes in day-care children and tip the balance to produce group differences between day-care and home-care infants?

Mediators of Emotional Insecurity

DAY-CARE FACTORS It has been suggested that the emotional security of individual infants in day care may be related to the type, stability, or quality of day care experienced by the infants. To date, however, very limited support for this suggestion has been found. Insecure attachments have been observed in a wide range of day-care programs—in sitter care (Barglow et al., 1987; Schwartz, 1983) as well as centers (Belsky & Rovine, 1988), and in stable arrangements (Barglow et al., 1987) as well as unstable ones (Vaughn et al., 1985). Deliberate efforts to link insecure attachment to the quality of day care generally have not been successful (Belsky & Rovine, 1988; Benn, 1986; Burchinal & Bryant, 1986; Howes et al., in press; Thompson, Lamb, & Estes, 1982), although in one of these studies (Howes et al.) insecurity of attachment to mother was more likely for children in centers with poor adult–child ratios. Perhaps it is not surprising that the quality of day care is not closely related to the development of infants' attachments to

their mothers. Poor day care might affect the attachment relationship because it would affect the child's general emotional well-being, but it does not follow that good day care would enhance the infant–mother relationship or ensure its security.

CHILD FACTORS It is somewhat more likely that moderating factors would be found in the characteristics of the children themselves. It has been suggested (Belsky, 1988a), for example, that boys whose mothers work are more likely to develop insecure attachments than are girls. In a meta-analysis of studies of attachment in day-care children, however, the child's sex did not turn out to be a significant moderator of day-care effects (McCartney & Phillips, 1988). It has also been suggested that the child's constitutional vulnerability might moderate the effects of day care. So far, only data from one study (Belsky & Rovine, 1988) are available to examine this issue. This study did reveal that among infants of working mothers those who were insecurely attached had more difficult temperaments. More interesting though, was the finding in this study that it was not the objective assessment of infants' behavior that was linked to insecure attachment, but rather mothers' perceptions of their infants' temperaments—suggesting that mothers' perceptions, attitudes, and actions may be more important than child characteristics for determining who is vulnerable and who is at risk.

FAMILY FACTORS There are several kinds of working mothers who might promote their children's insecure attachments. One kind undoubtedly is the mother whose rejection of contact with the infant has been linked to insecurity in home-reared children. Perhaps there is even an increased likelihood of this kind of rejection among working mothers. This could occur through self-selection: Mothers who like babies stay home; mothers who don't, go to work. In a study by Hock, Morgan, and Hock (1985), for example, mothers who intended to stay home when their babies were born but who ended up going to work in the baby's first year did so after experiencing a decline in their positive attitude toward motherhood and expressed a strong aversion to infant fussiness. It could also occur through the increased stress of handling two full-time jobs, work and motherhood, which would lead to more rejection of every additional burden, including the baby. Other mothers might foster insecure attachments in their infants because of their lack of availability, not only because they are away all day at work, but because they have to do chores and tasks that compete with the infant when they *are* together. Yet other mothers might be psychologically inaccessible. Many working mothers feel overworked and tired; they feel life is hard; they are rushed and harried. It is not unreasonable that these mothers would be less accessible to their infants. The reason their infants might be insecurely attached, in other words, is not that 40 hours of day care is hard on infants but that 40 hours of work is hard on mothers. Yet another kind of mother whose infant might be insecurely attached is the insensitive mother, whose insensitivity could be increased by spending less time with the infant and so knowing the infant's needs and signals less well. Finally, employed mothers might value and deliberately encourage their infants' independence more than nonworking mothers, and so their infants would not appear to be as securely attached.

What then is the empirical evidence that working mothers' attitudes and behavior are sources of infants' insecure development? Unfortunately there have been only a few studies in which links between working mothers' behavior and their infants' development have been explored. Farber and Egeland (1982) found that working mothers whose infants were insecure expressed less desire for motherhood even before their infants were born. Benn (1986) and Belsky and Rovine (1988) observed that working mothers whose infants were insecure were less competent, sensitive, integrated, empathic, and happily married. In Owen and Cox's (1988) study, mothers who had to work long hours (more than 40 hours a week) were more dissatisfied and anxious, anxious[9] mothers were less sensitive, animated, and reciprocal in their interactions with their infants; and their infants were more likely to develop insecure attachments. These studies suggest that there are links between mothers' behavior and attitudes and infants' development in families with working mothers, just as there are in families with nonworking mothers. We need more research to identify and clarify these links.

Mediators of Sociability and Aggressiveness

DAY-CARE FACTORS The positive side of the social behavior pattern observed in day-care children—advanced sociability, social competence, and self-confidence—has been associated with characteristics of day care in a straightforward and reasonable way. Children who are most socially competent are found in day-care programs in which they interact with a variety of peers, including some who are older and more socially skilled, under the close supervision and guidance of caregivers who are educated, responsive, nurturant, and positive, who offer children choices and suggestions and encourage their activities (Clarke-Stewart, 1987; Golden et al., 1978; Hamilton & Gordon, 1978; Rubenstein & Howes, 1979).

More surprising is the fact that the dark side of children's social behavior—aggression and noncompliance—also has been linked to participation in such "good" programs (Haskins, 1985; McCartney et al., 1982; Schwarz et al., 1974). The responsive style of teaching in such programs, which contrasts with the more authoritarian style of mothers (Clarke-Stewart, 1984; Hess, Price, Dickson, & Conroy, 1981; Rubenstein & Howes, 1979), could easily be seen as permitting or even promoting children's assertiveness, noncompliance, and even aggression. It is a style fostered by training in child development and an academic orientation. Teachers with child development training and an academic orientation are more likely to have attitudes and behaviors that encourage children's independence, not their obedience (Arnett, 1987; Berk 1985; Howes, 1983), that foster social and cognitive knowledge, but neglect social skills (Clarke-Stewart, 1984; Finkelstein, 1982).

Of course increased noncompliance and aggression are not just the province of good day care. Low social competence and aggression have also been observed in children who are in poor day care, that is, day-care settings in which children spend most of their time playing with peers rather than interacting with the caregiver because there are too many children for the caregiver to give close attention to everyone and because the caregiver has no training in child development (Clarke-Stewart, 1987; Howes, 1988; Phillips, McCartney, & Scarr, 1987; Vandell & Corasaniti, 1988; Vaughn et al., 1985). This is especially true if the poor-quality day care begins in infancy and continues through the preschool years (Howes, 1988). In good or poor day-care programs, it seems, children do not learn to follow social rules or to resolve social conflicts without resorting to aggression unless special efforts are made by their caregivers. If children are given direct training in social skills, however, they are more socially competent and less likely to exhibit aggression (e.g., Finkelstein, 1982; Iannotti, 1978; Orlick, 1981; Smith, Leinbach, Stewart, & Blackwell, 1983).

---

[9] Actually in this study (Owen & Cox, 1988) the mothers who worked long hours were more anxious even before they began work (though not before the baby was born), suggesting that self-selection or anticipation of work conditions might be involved.

CHILD FACTORS Although there is some suggestion that boys may be more susceptible to day-care influences on negative social behavior and girls to day-care influences on positive social behavior (e.g., Vandell & Corasaniti, 1988), sex differences are not always found, and the data are still insufficient to make strong claims that sex—or other child characteristics—acts as moderator of day-care effects on social adjustment or behavior.

FAMILY FACTORS The data are also insufficient to determine whether parents moderate the effects of day care on their children's social behavior. The pattern of obnoxious behavior and advanced social competence we have described has been observed in both rich and poor families, although more of the latter have been studied. There is only the slightest hint that the effect on negative behavior may be stronger for children in lower class families (e.g., Vandell & Corasaniti, 1988); we have no reason to make strong claims that families moderate these day-care effects. More likely, families reinforce their children's experiences in day care. Children in high-quality day-care programs, for instance, have been found to have parallel experiences at home: Their mothers are more nurturant and responsive and less restrictive and authoritarian than other mothers (e.g., Edwards, Logue, Loehr, & Roth, 1987; Howes & Stewart, 1987).

Mediators of Intellectual Gains

DAY-CARE FACTORS Many attempts have been made to identify aspects of day care that predict intellectual gains in toddlers and preschool children. There have been fewer attempts to identify qualities of infant care that predict later intellectual levels. Golden et al. (1978) did observe that more stimulating, positive, and affectionate care was related to infants' language development, and other researchers (Burchinal, Lee, & Ramey, 1986; McCartney, Scarr, Phillips, & Grajek, 1985) report that children who had been in cognitively oriented model programs as infants did better than children in community day-care programs. The problem is that measurable differences in children's IQs do not show up until past infancy, and by then infants who were in high-quality infant care have also received high-quality toddler and preschool care, confounding the quality of infant care with the quality of later care (which we know also contributes to intellectual gains). We need research in which the quality of later experience is controlled, before we can establish the qualities of infant care that are linked to intellectual gains.

CHILD FACTORS Once again, the literature contains only hints about whether individual differences between infants moderate the effects of day care on intellectual development. Perhaps most interesting is Ramey, MacPhee, and Yeates's (1982) finding that easy infants gained more on IQ tests if they were in a day-care center than if they were at home, whereas difficult infants did better at home. This makes intuitive sense, but requires further study.

FAMILY FACTORS Day-care-linked IQ gains have been observed for infants from a range of socioeconomic levels; the size of the gain has not been found to be systematically related to socioeconomic status (Fowler & Khan, 1974; Kagan et al., 1978). Thus, there is no evidence that families moderate day-care effects on children's intellectual development, but do parents contribute to the IQ gains observed in day-care infants? Parents of children in good day care have been observed to be less authoritarian and more stimulating and playful than parents of children who are not in these day-care programs (Edwards et al., 1987; Garber & Heber, 1980; Ramey et al., 1983; Rubenstein et al., 1981). One might question, therefore, whether parents are mediating the apparent day-care effect on children's intellectual development. Because samples in the studies showing this difference between parents include subjects who were randomly assigned to day care as well as subjects who chose the better programs themselves, and because the changes in parents' behavior seem to be at least to some extent responses to changes in children's behavior rather than initiated by the parents, it seems more likely that parents are augmenting the day-care effect than that they are causing it.

CONCLUSION

As should be clear from even this brief review, we have much to learn about the effects of day care on infants' development. We know that there is a somewhat elevated likelihood that infants in day care will avoid their mothers after a brief separation and that children who were in day care as infants are more likely to disobey their mothers and bully their peers. We also know that infants and children in day care gain knowledge and self-confidence from their experience. We know less of whether these patterns have any short- or long-term benefits or disadvantages for individuals or society and of the factors that moderate and mediate these effects. The consequences of infant day care need continued monitoring by patient, painstaking researchers, who carry out longitudinal studies of infants' development in the context of their family characteristics and their early and later experiences in day care. In the meantime, infant day care policy must proceed from reality. Maternal employment is a reality. The issue today, therefore, is not whether infants should be in day care but how to make their experiences there and at home supportive of their development and of their parents' peace of mind.

References

Ainslie, R. D., & Anderson, C. W. (1984). Day care children's relationships to their mothers and caregivers: An inquiry into the conditions for the development of attachment. In R. C. Ainslie (Ed.), *The child and the day care setting* (pp. 98–132). New York: Praeger.

Ainsworth, M. D. S., Blehar, M., Waters, E., & Wall, S. (1978). *Patterns of attachment: Observations in the Strange Situation and at home.* Hillsdale, NJ: Erlbaum.

Andersson, B. -E. (1987, April). *The importance of public day-care for preschool children's later development.* Paper presented at the biennial meetings of the Society for Research in Child Development, Baltimore.

Arnett, J. (1987, April). *Training for caregivers in day care centers.* Paper presented at the biennial meetings of the Society for Research in Child Development, Baltimore.

Barglow, P., Vaughn, B. E., & Molitor, N. (1987). Effects of maternal absence due to employment on the quality of infant–mother attachment in a low-risk sample. *Child Development, 58,* 945–954.

Barton, M., & Schwarz, J. (1981, August). *Day care in the middle class: Effects in elementary school.* Paper presented at the annual meeting of the American Psychological Association, Los Angeles.

Bayley, N. (1969). *The Bayley Scales of Mental Development.* New York: Psychological Corporation.

Beckwith, L. (1987). [Longitudinal study at UCLA of high-risk preterm infants). Work in progress.

Belsky, J. (1988a). [Unpublished data]. Data from Belsky & Rovine's (1988) study.

Belsky, J. (1988b). The "effects" of infant day care reconsidered. *Early Childhood Research Quarterly, 3,* 235–272.

Belsky, J., & Rovine, M. (1988). Nonmaternal care in the first year of life and infant–parent attachment security. *Child Development, 59,* 157–167.

Benn, R. K. (1986). Factors promoting secure attachment relationships between employed mothers and their sons. *Child Development, 57,* 1224–1231.

Berk, L. (1985). Relationship of educational attainment, child oriented attitudes, job satisfaction, and career commitment to caregiver behavior toward children. *Child Care Quarterly, 14,* 103–129.

Braun, S. J., & Caldwell, B. T (1973). Emotional adjustment of children in day care who enrolled prior to or after the age of three. *Early Child Development and Care, 2,* 13–21.

Burchinal, M., & Bryant, D. M. (1986, August). *Does day care affect infant–mother attachment level?* Paper presented at the annual meeting of the American Psychological Association, Washington, DC.

Burchinal, M., & Bryant, D. M. (1988). [Longitudinal study at the Frank Porter Graham Center, University of North Carolina, of a mixed SES sample]. Work in progress.

Burchinal, M., Lee, M. W., & Ramey, C. T (1986, August). *Day-care effects on preschool intellectual development in poverty children.* Paper presented at the annual meeting of the American Psychological Association, Washington, DC.

Chase-Lansdale, P. L., & Owen, M. T (1987). Maternal employment in a family context: Effects on infant–mother and infant–father attachments. *Child Development, 58,* 1505–1512.

Clarke-Stewart, K. A. (1984). Day care: A new context for research and development. In M. Perlmutter (Ed.), *Parent–child interaction and parent–child relations in child development. The Minnesota Symposia on Child Psychology* (Vol. 17, pp. 61–100). Hillsdale, NJ: Erlbaum.

Clarke-Stewart, K. A. (1987). Predicting child development from day-care forms and features: The Chicago study. In D. A. Phillips (Ed.), *Quality in child care: What does research tell us? Research Monographs of the National Association for the Education of Young Children* (Vol. 1, pp. 21–42). Washington, DC: National Association for the Education of Young Children.

Clarke-Stewart, K. A. (1988). "The 'effects' of infant day care reconsidered" reconsidered: Risks for parents, children, and researchers. *Early Childhood Research Quarterly, 3,* 293–318.

Clarke-Stewart, K. A., & Fein, G. G. (1983). Early childhood programs. In P. H. Mussen (Ed.), *Handbook of child psychology: Vol. 2. Infancy and developmental psychobiology* (pp. 917–1000). New York: Wiley.

Doyle, A., & Somers, K. (1978). The effects of group and family day care on infant attachment behaviors. *Canadian Journal of Behavioral Science, 10,* 38–45.

Easterbrooks, M. A., & Goldberg, W. (1985). Effects of early maternal employment on toddlers, mothers, and fathers. *Developmental Psychology, 21,* 774–783.

Easterbrooks, M. A., & Harmon, R. J. (1987). [Longitudinal study at the University of Colorado of preterm and full-term infants from middle-class, two-parent families]. Work in progress.

Edwards, C. P., Logue, M. E., Loehr, S. R., & Roth, S. B. (1987). The effects of day care participation on parent–infant interaction at home. *American Journal of Orthopsychiatry, 57,* 116–119.

Farber, E. A., & Egeland, B. (1982). Developmental consequences of out-of-home care for infants in a low-income population. In E. F Zigler & E. W. Gordon (Eds.), *Day care: Scientific and social policy issues* (pp. 102–125). Boston: Auburn House.

Finkelstein, N. W. (1982). Aggression: Is it stimulated by day care? *Young Children, 37,* 3–12.

Fowler, W., & Khan, N. (1974). *The later effects of infant group care: A follow-up study.* Toronto: Ontario Institute for Studies in Education.

Garber, H., & Heber, R. (1980, April). *Modification of predicted cognitive development in high-risk children through early intervention.* Paper presented at the annual meeting of the American Educational Research Association, Boston.

Golden, M., Rosenbluth, L., Grossi, M. T., Policare, H. J., Freeman, H., Jr., & Brownlee, E. M. (1978). *The New York City Infant Day Care Study.* New York: Medical and Health Research Association of New York City.

Goossens, F A. (1987). Maternal employment and day care: Effects on attachment. In L. W. C. Tavecchio & M. H. van IJzendoorn (Eds.), *Attachment in social networks* (pp. 135–183). Amsterdam: North-Holland.

Gottfried, A. E., Gottfried, A. W., & Bathurst, K. (1988). Maternal employment, family environment and children's development: Infancy through the school years. In A. E. Gottfried, & A. W Gottfried (Eds.), *Maternal employment and children's development: Longitudinal research.* New York: Plenum.

Hamilton, V. J., & Gordon, D. A. (1978). Teacher–child interactions in preschool and task persistence. *American Educational Research Journal, 15,* 459–466.

Haskins, R. (1985). Public school aggression among children with varying day-care experience. *Child Development, 56,* 689–703.

Hess, R. D., Price, G. G., Dickson, W. P., & Conroy, M. (1981). Different roles for mothers and teachers: Contrasting styles of child care. In S. Kilmer (Ed.), *Advances in early education and day care* (Vol. 2, pp. 1–28). Greenwich, CT: JAI Press.

Hock, E. (1980). Working and nonworking mothers and their infants: A comparative study of maternal caregiving characteristics and infant social behavior. *Merrill Palmer Quarterly, 26,* 79–102.

Hock, E., Christman, K., & Hock, M. (1980). Factors associated with decisions about return to work in mothers of infants. *Developmental Psychology, 16,* 535–536.

Hock, E., Morgan, K. C., & Hock, M. D. (1985). Employment decisions made by mothers of infants. *Psychology of Women Quarterly, 9,* 383–402.

Howes, C. (1983). Caregiver behavior in center and family day care. *Journal of Applied Developmental Psychology, 4,* 99–107.

Howes, C. (1988, April). *Can the age of entry and quality of infant care predict behaviors in kindergarten?* Paper presented at the International Conference on Infancy Studies, Washington, DC.

Howes, C., Rodning, C., Galluzzo, D. C., & Myers, L. (in press). Attachment and child care: Relationships with mother and caregiver. *Early Childhood Research Quarterly*

Howes, C., & Stewart, P. (1987). Child's play with adults, toys, and peers: An examination of family and child-care influences. *Developmental Psychology, 23,* 423–430.

Iannotti, R. J. (1978). Effect of role-taking experiences on role taking, empathy, altruism, and aggression. *Developmental Psychology, 14,* 119–124.

Jacobson, J. L., & Wille, D. E. (1984). Influence of attachment and separation experience on separation distress at 18 months. *Developmental Psychology, 20,* 477–484.

Kagan, J., Kearsley, R. B., & Zelazo, P. R. (1978). *Infancy: Its place in human development.* Cambridge, MA: Harvard University Press.

Lay, M. Z., & Meyer, W. J. (1972). *Effects of early day care experience on subsequent observed program behaviors* (Final report to the Office of Education, Subcontract 70-007). Syracuse, NY: Syracuse University.

Lipsitt, L., & LaGasse, L. (1987). [Longitudinal study at Brown University of normal full-term infants]. Work in progress.

Macrae, J. W., & Herbert-Jackson, E. (1976). Are behavioral effects of infant day care program specific? *Developmental Psychology, 12,* 269–270.

McBride, S. L., & Belsky, J. (1985, April). *Maternal work plans, actual employment and infant temperament.* Paper presented at the biennial meetings of the Society for Research in Child Development, Toronto.

McCartney, K., & Phillips, D. (1988). *Motherhood and child care.* In B. Birns & D. Hayes (Eds.), *Different faces of motherhood.* New York: Plenum.

McCartney, K., Scarr, S., Phillips, D., & Grajek, S. (1985). Day care as intervention: comparisons of varying quality programs. *Journal of Applied Developmental Psychology, 6,* 247–260.

McCartney, K., Scarr, S., Phillips, D., Grajek, S., & Schwarz, J. C. (1982). Environmental differences among day care centers and their effects on children's development. In E. F. Zigler & E. W. Gordon (Eds.), *Day care: Scientific and social policy issues* (pp. 126–151). Boston: Auburn House.

Orlick, T. D. (1981). Positive socialization via cooperative games. *Developmental Psychology, 17,* 426–429.

Owen, M., & Cox, M. (1988). Maternal employment and the transition to parenthood. In A. E. Gottfried & A. W. Gottfried (Eds.), *Maternal employment and children's development: Longitudinal research.* New York: Plenum.

Owen, M. T, Easterbrooks, M. A., Chase-Lansdale, L., & Goldberg, W. A. (1984). The relation between maternal employment status and the stability of attachments to mother and to father. *Child Development, 55,* 1894–1901.

Phillips, D. A., McCartney, K., & Scarr, S. (1987). Child-care quality and children's social development. *Developmental Psychology, 23,* 537–543.

Phillips, D. A., McCartney, K., Scarr, S., & Howes, C. (1987). Selective review of infant day care research: A cause for concern. *Zero to Three, 7*(3), 18–21.

Ramey, C. T, Dorval, B., & Baker-Ward, L. (1983). Group day care and socially disadvantaged families: Effects on the child and the family. In S. Kilmer (Ed.), *Advances in early education and day care* (Vol. 3, pp. 69–106). Greenwich, CT: JAI Press.

Ramey, C. T, MacPhee, D., & Yeates, K. O. (1982). Preventing developmental retardation: A general systems model. In L. Bond & J. Joffe (Eds.), *Facilitating infant and early childhood development* (pp. 343–401). Hanover, NH: University Press of New England.

Rodning, C. (1987). [Longitudinal study at UCLA of infants in middle-class, two-parent families]. Work in progress.

Rubenstein, J. L., & Howes, C. (1979). Caregiving and infant behavior in day care and in homes. *Developmental Psychology, 15,* 1–24.

Rubenstein, J. L., & Howes, C. (1983). Social-emotional development of toddlers in day care: The role of peers and of individual differences. In S. Kilmer (Ed.), *Early education and day care* (Vol. 3, pp. 21–45). Greenwich, CT: JAI Press.

Rubenstein, J. L., Howes, C., & Boyle. P. (1981). A two year follow-up of infants in community based infant day care. *Journal of Child Psychology and Psychiatry, 22,* 209–218.

Schwartz, P. (1983). Length of day-care attendance and attachment behavior in eighteen-month-old infants. *Child Development, 54,* 1073–1078.

Schwarz, J. C., Krolick, G., & Strickland, G. (1973). Effects of early day care experience on adjustment to a new environment. *American Journal of Orthopsychiatry, 43,* 340–346.

Schwarz, J. C., Strickland, R. G., & Krolick, G. (1974). Infant day care: Behavioral effects at preschool age. *Developmental Psychology, 10,* 502–506.

Siegal, M., & Storey, R. M. (1985). Day care and children's conceptions of moral and social rules. *Child Development, 56,* 1001–1008.

Smith, C. L., Leinbach, M. D., Stewart, B. J., & Blackwell, J. M. (1983). Affective perspective taking exhortations, and children's presocial behavior. In D. L. Bridgeman (Ed.), *The nature of prosocial development* (pp. 113–137). New York: Academic Press.

Strayer, F. F., & Moss, E. (1987, April). *Social constraints on information exchange during mother–child interaction.* Paper presented at the biennial meeting of the Society for Research in Child Development, Baltimore.

Strayer, F. F., Moss, E., & Blicharski, T. (in press). Biosocial bases of representational activity during early childhood. In L. T. Winegar (Ed.), *Social interaction and the development of children's understanding.* Norwood, NJ: Ablex.

Thompson, R. A., Lamb, M. E., & Estes, D. (1982). Stability of infant–mother attachment and its relationship to changing life circumstances in an unselected middle-class sample. *Child Development, 53,* 144–148.

U.S. Bureau of the Census. (1986). *Estimates of the Population of the U.S. by age, sex, and race, 1980–1985* (Current Population Reports, Series P-25, No. 985). Washington, DC: U.S. Government Printing Office.

Vandell, D. L., & Corasaniti, M. A. (1988). *Variations in early child care: Do they predict subsequent social, emotional, and cognitive differences?* Unpublished manuscript, University of Texas at Dallas.

van IJzendoorn, M. H., & Kroonenberg, P. M. (1988). Cross-cultural patterns of attachment: A meta-analysis of the Strange Situation. *Child Development, 59,* 147–156.

Vaughn, B. E., Deane, K. E., & Waters, E. (1985). The impact of out-of-home care on child–mother attachment quality: Another look at some enduring questions. *Monographs of the Society for Research in Child Development, 50*(1-2, Serial No. 209), 110–135.

Vaughn, B. E., Gove, F. L., & Egeland, B. (1980). The relationship between out-of-home care and the quality of infant–mother attachment in an economically disadvantaged population. *Child Development, 51,* 1203–1214.

Weinraub, M., Jaeger, E., & Hoffman, L. W. (in press). Predicting infant outcomes in families of employed and non-employed mothers. *Early Childhood Research Quarterly.*

PART III

Early Childhood

16

From Communicating to Talking

JEROME S. BRUNER

Language is a uniquely human capability that develops rapidly in the early years of life. What are the roles of our dual heritage as human beings—our biological capabilities and our use of culture to express these capabilities in the development of language? In the following selection, Bruner discusses children's transformation from nontalking communicative companions to talkers in their own right. Bruner argues that culture provides the medium through which this critical transition occurs. Using this framework, he offers a provocative examination of infant capabilities, human action, and social experience, with language and culture as the connecting pieces that give these processes both form and direction.

If we are to consider the transition from prelinguistic communication to language, particularly with a concern for possible continuities, we had better begin by taking as close a look as we can at the so-called "original endowment" of human beings. Might that endowment affect the acquisition and early use of language? I do not mean simply the prelinguistic precursors of grammar or an "innate capacity" for language. The question must be a more general one. What predisposes a living being to use language and be changed by its use? Suppose we grant that there is some innate capacity to master language as a symbolic system, as Noam Chomsky urged, or even to be predisposed toward particular linguistic distinctions, as Derek Bickerton has recently proposed? Why is language used? After all, chimpanzees have some of the same capacities and they don't use them.

The awkward dilemma that plagues questions about the original nature and later growth of human faculties inheres in the unique nature of human competence. For human competence is both biological in origin and cultural in the means by which it finds expression. While the *capacity* for intelligent action has deep biological roots and a discernible evolutionary history, the *exercise* of that capacity depends upon man appropriating to himself modes of acting and thinking that exist not in his genes but in his culture. There is obviously something in "mind" or in "human nature" that mediates between the genes and the culture that makes it possible for the latter to be a prosthetic device for the realization of the former.

When we ask then about the endowment of human beings, the question we put must be twofold. We must ask not only about capacities, but also about how humans are aided in expressing them in the medium of culture. The two questions, of course, are inseparable, since human intellectual capacity necessarily evolved to fit man for using the very prosthetic devices that a culture develops and accumulates for the enablement of its members.

There is some point in studying early human capacities and their development in seemingly cultureless laboratories, as if they were simply expressions of man's biological dispositions and endowment. But we must also bear in mind that the idealization of this endowment depends on the tool kit of the culture, whatever we choose to do in the laboratory. The main trend of the last quarter century has been to look increasingly at the contexts that enable human beings to act as they do; increasingly, we can see the futility of considering human nature as a set of autonomous dispositions.

I can easily outline what seems to me, at least, to be "infant endowment" in the so-called cognitive sphere. But to do so relevantly I must focus on those aspects that fit and perhaps even compel human beings to operate in the culture. For I think that it is the requirement of *using* culture as a necessary form of coping that forces man to master language. Language is the means for interpreting and regulating the culture. The interpreting and negotiating start the moment the infant enters the human scene. It is at this stage of interpretation and negotiation that language acquisition is acted out. So I shall look at "endowment" from the point of view of how it equips the infant to come on stage in order to acquire the means for taking his place in culture.

INITIAL COGNITIVE ENDOWMENT

Let me begin with some more or less "firm" conclusions about perception, skill, and problem solving in the prelinguistic infant and consider how they might conceivably predispose the child to acquire "culture" through language.

The first of these conclusions is that much of the cognitive processing going on in infancy appears to operate in support of goal-directed activity. From the start, the human infant is *active* in seeking out regularities in the world about him. The child is active in a uniquely human way, converting experience into species-typical means-end structures. Let me begin with the unlikely example of nonnutritive sucking.

The human infant, like mammals generally, is equipped with a variety of biological processes that ensure initial feeding, initial attachment to a caretaker, initial sensory contact with the world—all quite well buffered to prevent the infant from overreacting. Nonnutritive sucking, an example of one of these buffering mechanisms, has the effect of relaxing large muscle groups, stilling movements of the gut, reducing the number of eye movements in response to excessively patterned visual fields, and in general assuring the maintenance of a moderate level of arousal in the face of even a demanding environment. That much is probably "hard-wired."

But such sucking soon comes under the child's own control. Infants as young as five to six weeks are quite capable, we found, of sucking on a pacifier nipple in order to bring a visual display from blur into focus—increasing their rate of sucking well above baseline when the picture's focus is made contingent on speed of sucking. Sucking and looking, moreover, are coordinated to assure a good view. When babies suck to produce clarity, they suck as they look, and when they stop they soon learn to look away. The same infants, when their sucking in a later session produces blur, suck while looking away from the blurred picture their sucking is producing and desist from sucking while looking at the picture. (We should note, by the way, that infants do not like blurred pictures.)

The Czech pediatrician Hanus Papousek has reported the same capacity for coordination of action in another domain, head turning. He taught six-to-ten-week-old babies to turn their heads to the right (or the left) in order to activate an attractive set of flashing lights. The infants soon learned the required response and, indeed, could even be taught to turn twice to each side for the desired lights. With mastery, their reactions became quite economical: They turned just enough to bring on the lights. But more interesting still, as the experiment progressed and the light display became familiar, they looked at it only briefly, just enough of a glance to confirm that the lights had gone on as expected (following which there was often a smile) and would then begin visually exploring other features of the situation. Successful prediction seems finally to have been the rewarding feature of the situation. With habituation, performance deteriorated—prediction was no longer interesting.

The point is not that infants are cleverer than was suspected before. Rather, it is that their behavior from early on is guided by active means-end readiness and by search. To put it another way, more in keeping with our general point, the infant from the start is tuned to the coordinative requirements of action. He seems able to appreciate, so to speak, the structure of action and particularly the manner in which means and ends must be combined in achieving satisfactory outcomes—even such arbitrary means as sucking to produce changes in the visual world. He seems, moreover, to be sensitive to the requirements of prediction and, if Papoušek's interpretation of the "smile of predictive pleasure" is to be taken seriously, to get active pleasure from successful prediction. Anyone who has bothered to ponder the pleasure infants derive from achieving repetitive, surefire prediction will appreciate this point.

To say that infants are also "social" is to be banal. They are geared to respond to the human voice, to the human face, to human action and gesture. Their means-end readiness is easily and quickly brought into coordination with the actions of their caretakers. The pioneering work of Daniel Stern and Berry Brazelton and their colleagues underlines how early and readily activated infants are by the adults with whom they interact and how quickly their means-end structuring encompasses the actions of another. The infant's principal "tool" for achieving his ends is another familiar human being. In this respect, human infants seem more socially interactive than any of the Great Apes, perhaps to the same degree that Great Apes are more socially interactive than Old or New World Monkeys, and this may be a function of their prolonged and uniquely dependent form of immaturity, as I have argued elsewhere.

Infants are, in a word, tuned to enter the world of human action. Obvious though the point may seem, we shall see that it has enormous consequences for the matter at hand. This leads directly to the second conclusion about infant "endowment."

It is obvious that an enormous amount of the activity of the child during the first year and a half of life is extraordinarily social and communicative. Social interaction appears to be both self-propelled and self-rewarding. Many students of infant behavior, like Tom Bower, have found that a social response to the infant is the most powerful reinforcer one can use in ordinary learning experiments. And withholding social response to the child's initiatives is one of the most disruptive things one can do to an infant—e.g., an unresponding face will soon produce tears. Even in the opening weeks of life the infant has the capacity to imitate facial and manual gestures (as Andrew Meltzoff has shown); they respond with distress if their mothers are masked during feeding; and, they show a sensitivity to expression in the mother by turn taking in vocalization when their level of arousal is moderate and by simultaneous expression when it is high.

While the child's attachment to the mother (or caretaker) is initially assured by a variety of innate response patterns, there very quickly develops a reciprocity that the infant comes to anticipate and count on. For example, if during play the mother assumes a sober immobile face, the infant shows fewer smiles and turns his head away from the mother more frequently than when the mother responds socially, as Edward Tronick and his colleagues have shown. The existence of such reciprocity—buttressed by the mother's increasing capacity to differentiate an infant's "reasons" for crying as well as by the infant's capacity to anticipate these consistencies— soon creates a form of mutual attention, a harmony or "intersubjectivity," whose importance we shall take up later.

In any case, a pattern of inborn initial social responses in the infant, elicited by a wide variety of effective signs from the mother—her heartbeat, the visual configuration of her face and particularly her eyes, her characteristic smell, the sound and rhythms of her voice—is soon converted into a very complex joint anticipatory system that converts initial biological attachment between mother and child into something more subtle and more sensitive to individual idiosyncrasies and to forms of cultural practice.

The third conclusion is that much of early infant action takes place in constrained, familiar situations and shows a surprisingly high degree of order and "systematicity." Children spend most of their time doing a very limited number of things. Long periods are spent in reaching and taking, banging and looking, etc. Within any one of these restricted domains, there is striking "systematicity." Object play provides an example. A single act (like banging) is applied successively to a wide range of objects. Everything on which the child can get his hands is banged. Or the child tries out on a single object all the motor routines of which he or she is capable—grasping the object, banging it, throwing it to the floor, putting it in the mouth, putting it on top of the head, running it through the entire repertory.

Nobody has done better than Jean Piaget in characterizing this systematicity. The older view that pictured the infant as "random" in his actions and saw growth as consisting of becoming "coordinated" can no longer stand up to the evidence. Given the limits of the child's range of action, what occurs within that range is just as orderly and systematic as is adult behavior. There may be differences of opinion concerning the "rules" that govern this orderly behavior, but there can be no quarrel about its systematicity. Whether one adopts a Piagetian view of the matter or one more tuned to other theories, like Heinz Werner's, is, in light of the more general issues, quite irrelevant.

It is not the least surprising, in light of this conclusion, that infants enter the world of language and of culture with a readiness to find or invent systematic ways of dealing with social requirements and linguistic forms. The child reacts "culturally" with characteristic hypotheses about what is required and enters language with a readiness for order. We shall, of course, have much more to say about this later.

There are two important implications that follow from this. The first is obvious, though I do not recall ever having encountered the point. It is that from the start, the child becomes readily attuned to "making a lot out of a little" by combination. He typically works on varying a small set of elements to create a larger range of possibilities. Observations of early play behavior and of the infant's communicative efforts certainly confirm this "push" to generativeness, to combinatorial and variational efforts. Indeed, Ruth Weir's classic study of the child's spontaneous speech while alone in his crib after bedtime speaks volumes on this combinatorial readiness, as does Melissa Bowerman's on children's spontaneous speech errors.

The second implication is more social. The acquisition of prelinguistic and linguistic communication takes place, in the main, in the highly constrained settings to which we are referring. The child and his caretaker readily combine elements in these situations to extract meanings, assign interpretations, and infer intentions. A decade ago there was considerable debate among developmental linguists on whether in writing "grammars" of child speech one should use a method of "rich interpretation"—taking into account not only the child's actual speech but also the ongoing actions and other elements of the context in which speech was occurring. Today we take it for granted that one must do so. For it is precisely the combining of all elements in constrained situations (speech and nonspeech alike) that provides the road to communicative effectiveness. It is for this reason that I shall place such heavy emphasis on the role of "formats" in the child's entry into language.

A fourth conclusion about the nature of infant cognitive endowment is that its systematic character is surprisingly abstract. Infants during their first year appear to have rules for dealing with space, time, and even causation. A moving object that is transformed in appearance while it is moving behind a screen produces surprise when it reappears in a new guise. Objects that seem to be propelled in ways that *we* see as unnatural (e.g., without being touched by an approaching object) also produce surprise reactions in a three-month-old as well. Objects explored by touch alone are later recognized by vision alone. The infant's perceptual world, far from being a blooming, buzzing confusion, is rather orderly and organized by what seem like highly abstract rules.

Again, it was Piaget who most compellingly brought this "abstractness" to our attention in describing the logical structure of the child's search for invariance in his world—the search for what remains unchanged under the changing surface of appearance. And again, it is not important whether the "logic" that he attributed to this systematic action is correct or not. What is plain is that, whether Piagetian logical rules characterize early "operational behavior" or whether it can be better described by some more general logical system, we know that cognitively and communicatively there is from the start a capacity to "follow" abstract rules.

It is *not* the case that language, when it is encountered and then used, is the first instance of abstract rule following. It is not, for example, in language alone that the child makes such distinctions as those between specific and nonspecific, between states and processes, between "punctual" acts and recurrent ones, between causative and noncausative actions. These abstract distinctions, picked up with amazing speed in language acquisition, have analogues in the child's way of ordering his world of experience. Language will serve to specify, amplify, and expand distinctions that the child has already about the world. But these abstract distinctions are already present, even without language.

These four cognitive "endowments"—means-end readiness, transactionality, systematicity, and abstractness—provide foundation processes that aid the child's language acquisition. None of them "generates" language, for language involves a set of phonological, syntactic, semantic, and illocutionary rules and maxims that constitute a problem space of their own. But linguistic or communicative hypotheses depend upon these capacities as enabling conditions. Language does not "grow out of" prior protophonological, protosyntactic, protosemantic, or protopragmatic knowledge. It requires a unique sensitivity to a patterned sound system, to grammatical constraints, to referential requirements, to communicative intentions, etc. Such sensitivity grows in the process of fulfilling certain general, nonlinguistic functions—predicting the environment, interacting transactionally, getting to goals with the aid of another, and the like. These functions are first fulfilled primitively if abstractly by prelinguistic communicative means. Such primitive procedures, I will argue, must reach requisite levels of functioning before *any* Language Acquisition Device (whether innate or acquired) can begin to generate "linguistic hypotheses."

ENTRY INTO LANGUAGE

We can turn now to the development of language per se. Learning a native language is an accomplishment within the grasp of any toddler, yet discovering how children do it has eluded generations of philosophers and linguists. Saint Augustine believed it was simple. Allegedly recollecting his own childhood, he said, "When they named any thing, and as they spoke turned towards it, I saw and remembered that they called what one would point out by the name they uttered.... And thus by constantly hearing words, as they occurred in various sentences, I collected gradually for what they stood; and having broken in my mouth to these signs, I thereby gave utterance to my will." But a look at children as they actually acquire language shows Saint Augustine to be far, far off target. Alas, he had a powerful effect both on his followers and on those who set out to refute him.

Developmental linguistics is now going through rough times that can be traced back to Saint Augustine as well as to the reactions against him. Let me recount a little history. Saint Augustine's view, perhaps because there was so little systematic research on language acquisition to refute it, prevailed for a long time. It was even put into modern dress. Its most recent "new look" was in the form of behavorist "learning theory." In this view's terms, nothing particularly linguistic needed to be said about language. Language, like any other behavior, could be "explained" as just another set of responses. Its principles and its research paradigms were not derived from the phenomena of language but from "general behavior." Learning tasks, for example, were chosen to construct theories of learning so as to ensure that the learner had no predispositions toward or knowledge of the material to be learned. All was as if *ab initio*, transfer of response from one stimulus to another was assured by the similarity between stimuli. Language learning was assumed to be much like, say, nonsense syllable learning, except that it might be aided by imitation, the learner imitating the performance of the "model" and then being reinforced for correct performance. Its emphasis was on "words" rather than on grammar. Consequently, it missed out almost entirely in dealing with the combinatorial and generative effect of having a syntax that made possible the routine construction of sentences never before heard and that did not exist in adult speech to be imitated. A good example is the Pivot-Open class, P(0), construction of infant speech in which a common word or phrase is combined productively with other words as in *all-gone mummy, all-gone apple,* and even *all-gone bye-bye* (when mother and aunt finally end a prolonged farewell).

It is one of the mysteries of Kuhnian scientific paradigms that this empiricist approach to language acquisition persisted in psychology (if not in philosophy, where it was overturned by Frege and Witt-genstein) from its first enunciation by Saint Augustine to its most recent one in B. F. Skinner's *Verbal Behavior.* It would be fair to say that the persistence of the mindless behavioristic version of Augustinianism finally led to a readiness, even a reckless readiness, to be rid of it. For it was not only an inadequate account, but one that damped inquiry by its domination of "common sense." It set the stage for the Chomskyan revolution.

It was to Noam Chomsky's credit that he boldly proclaimed the old enterprise bankrupt. In its place he offered a challenging, if counterintuitive hypothesis based on nativism. He proposed that the acquisition of the *structure* of language depended upon a Language Acquisition Device (LAD) that had as its base a universal grammar or a "linguistic deep structure" that humans know innately and without learning. LAD was programmed to recognize in the surface structure of any natural language encountered its deep structure or universal grammar by virtue of the kinship between innate universal grammar and the grammar of any and all natural languages. LAD abstracted the grammatical realization rules of the local language and thus enabled the aspirant speaker potentially to generate all the well-formed utterances possible in the language and none that were ill-formed. The universal grammatical categories that programmed LAD were in the innate structure of the mind. No prior nonlinguistic knowledge of the world was necessary, and no privileged communication with another speaker was required. Syntax was independent of knowledge of the world, of semantic meaning, and of communicative function. All the child needed was exposure to language, however fragmentary and uncontextualized his samples of it might be. Or more correctly, the acquisition of syntax could be conceived of as progressing with the assistance of whatever *minimum* world knowledge or privileged communication proved necessary. The only constraints on rate of linguistic development were psychological limitations on *performance:* the child's limited but growing attention and memory span, etc. Linguistic competence was there from the start, ready to express itself when performance constraints were extended by the growth of requisite skills.

It was an extreme view. But in a stroke it freed a generation of psycholinguists from the dogma of association-cum-imitation-cum-reinforcement. It turned attention to the problem of rule learning, even if it concentrated only on syntactic rules. By declaring learning theory dead as an explanation of language acquisition (one of the more premature obituaries of our times), it opened the way for a new account.

George Miller put it well. We now had *two* theories of language acquisition: one of them, empiricist associationism, was impossible; the other, nativism, was miraculous. But the void between the impossible and the miraculous was soon to be filled in, albeit untidily and partially.

To begin with, children in fact had and *needed* to have a working knowledge of the world before they acquired language. Such knowledge gave them semantic targets, so to speak, that "corresponded" in some fashion to the distinctions they acquired in their language. A knowledge of the world, appropriately organized in terms of a system of concepts, might give the child hints as to where distinctions could be expected to occur in the language, might even alert him to the distinctions. There were new efforts to develop a generative semantics out of which syntactical hypotheses could presumably be derived by the child. In an extreme form, generative semantics could argue that the concepts in terms of which the world was organized are the same as those that organize language. But even so, the *linguistic* distinctions still had to be mastered. These were not about the *world* but about morphology or syntax or whatever else characterized the linguistic *code*.

The issue of whether rules of *grammar* can somehow be inferred or generalized from the structure of our knowledge of the world is a very dark one. The strong form of the claim insists that syntax can be derived directly from nonlinguistic categories of knowledge in some way. Perhaps the best claim can be made for a case grammar. It is based on the reasonable claim that the concepts of action are innate and primitive. The aspiring language learner already knows the so called arguments of action: who performed the action, on what object, toward whom, where, by what instrument, and so on. In Charles Fillmore's phrase, "meanings are relativized to scenes," and this involves an "assignment of perspective." Particular phrases impose a perspective on the scene and sentence decisions are perspective decisions. If, for example, the agent of action is perspectively forefronted by some grammatical means such as being inserted as head word, the placement of the nominal that represents agency must be the "deep subject" of the sentence. This leaves many questions unanswered about how the child gets to the point of being able to put together sentences that assign his intended action perspectives to scenes.

The evidence for the semantic account was nonetheless interesting. Roger Brown pointed out, for example, that at the two-word stage of language acquisition more than three-quarters of the child's utterances embody only a half dozen semantic relations that are, at base, case or caselike relations—Agent-Action, Action-Object, Agent-Object, Possession, etc. Do these semantic relations generate the grammar of

the language? Case notions of this kind, Fillmore tells us, "comprise a set of universal, presumably innate, concepts which identify certain types of judgments human beings are capable of making about the events that are going on around them . . . who did it, who it happened to, and what got changed." The basic structures are alleged to be these arguments of action, and different languages go about realizing them in different ways: by function words, by inflectional morphemes as in the case endings of Latin, by syntactic devices like passivization, and so on. Grammatical forms might then be the surface structures of language, depending for their acquisition on a prior understanding of deep semantic, indeed even protosemantic, concepts about action.

Patrica Greenfield then attempted to show that the earliest *one-word* utterances, richly interpreted in context, could also be explained as realizations of caselike concepts. And more recently Katherine Nelson has enriched the argument that children acquire language already equipped with concepts related to action: "The functional core model (FCM) essentially proposed that the child came to language with a store of familiar concepts of people and objects that were organized around the child's experience with these things. Because the child's experience was active, the dynamic aspects would be the most potent part of what the child came to know about the things experienced. It could be expected that the child would organize knowledge around what he could do with things and what they could do. In other words, knowledge of the world would be functionally organized from the child's point of view." To this earlier view she has now added a temporal dimension—the child's mastery of "scripts for event structures," a sequential structure of "causally and temporally linked acts with the actors and objects specified in the most general way." These scripts provide the child with a set of syntagmatic formats that permit him to organize his concepts sequentially into sentencelike forms such as those reported by Roger Brown. The capacity to do this rests upon a basic form of representation that the child uses from the start and gradually elaborates. In effect, it is what guides the formation of utterances beyond the one-word stage.

The role of world knowledge in generating or supporting language acquisition is now undergoing intensive study. But still another element has now been added—the pragmatic. It is the newest incursion into the gap between "impossible" and "miraculous" theories of language acquisition. In this view, the central idea is communicative intent: we communicate with some end in mind, some function to be fulfilled. We request or indicate or promise or threaten. Such functionalism had earlier been a strong thread in linguistics, but had been elbowed aside by a prevailing structuralism that, after Ferdinand de Saussure's monumental work, became the dominant mode.

New developments revived functionalism. The first was in the philosophy of language spearheaded by Ludwig Wittgenstein's use-based theory of meaning, formulated in his *Philosophical Investigations,* and then by the introduction of speech acts in Austin's *How to Do Things with Words.* Austin's argument (as already noted) was that an utterance cannot be analyzed out of the context of its use and its use must include the intention of the speaker and interpretation of that intention by the addressee in the light of communication conventions. A speaker may make a request by many alternative linguistic means, so long as he honors the conventions of his linguistic community. It may take on interrogative construction ("What time is it?"), or it may take the declarative form ("I wonder what time it is").

Roger Brown notes an interesting case with respect to this issue: in the protocols of Adam, he found that Adam's mother used the interrogative in two quite different ways, one as a request for action, the other as a request for information: "Why don't you . . . (e.g., play with your ball now)," and "Why are you playing with your ball?" Although Adam answered informational *why* questions with *Because,* there was no instance of his ever confusing an action and an information-seeking *why* question. He evidently recognized the differing intent of the two forms of utterance quite adequately from the start. He must have been learning speech acts rather than simply the *why* interrogative form.

This raises several questions about acquisition. It puts pragmatics into the middle of things. Is intent being decoded by the child? It would seem so. But linguistics usually defines its domain as "going from sound to sense." But what is "sense?" Do we in fact go from sound to intention, as John Searle proposed? A second question has to do with shared or conventional presuppositions. If children are acquiring notions about how to interpret the intentions encoded in utterances, they must be taking into account not only the structure of the utterance, but also the nature of the conditions that prevail just at the time the utterance is made. Speech acts have at least three kinds of conditions affecting their appropriateness or "felicity": a preparatory condition (laying appropriate ground for the utterance); an essential condition (meeting the logical conditions for performing a speech act, like, for example, being uninformed as a condition for asking for information related to a matter); and sincerity conditions (wishing to have the information that one asks for). They must also meet

affiliative conditions: honoring the affiliation or relation between speaker and hearer, as in requesting rather than demanding when the interlocutor is not under obligation.

Paradoxically, the learning of speech acts may be easier and less mysterious than the learning either of syntax or semantics. For the child's syntactic errors are rarely followed by corrective feedback, and semantic feedback is often lax. But speech acts, on the contrary, get not only immediate feedback but also correction. Not surprising, then, that prelinguistic communicative acts precede lexico-grammatical speech in their appearance. Not surprising, then, that such primitive "speech act" patterns may serve as a kind of matrix in which lexico-grammatical achievements can be substituted for earlier gestural or vocal procedures.

In this view, entry into language is an entry into discourse that requires both members of a dialogue pair to interpret a communication and its intent. Learning a language, then, consists of learning not only the grammar of a particular language but also learning how to realize one's intentions by the appropriate use of that grammar.

The pragmatician's stress on intent requires a far more active role on the part of the adult in aiding the child's language acquisition than that of just being a "model." It requires that the adult be a consenting partner, willing to negotiate with the child. The negotiation has to do, probably, least with syntax, somewhat more with the semantic scope of the child's lexicon, and a very great deal with helping make intentions clear and making their expression fit the conditions and requirements of the "speech community," i.e., the culture.

And the research of the last several years—much of it summarized in Catherine Snow and Charles Ferguson's *Talking to Children*—does indeed indicate that parents play a far more active role in language acquisition than simply modeling the language and providing, so to speak, input for a Language Acquisition Device. The current phrase for it is "fine tuning." Parents speak at the level where their children can comprehend them and move ahead with remarkable sensitivity to their child's progress. The dilemma, as Roger Brown puts it, is how do you teach children to talk by talking baby talk with them at a level that they already understand? And the answer has got to be that the important thing is to keep communicating with them, for by so doing one allows them to learn how to extend the speech that they have into new contexts, how to meet the conditions on speech acts, how to maintain topics across turns, how to know what's worth talking about—how indeed to regulate language use.

So we can now recognize two ways of filling the gap between an impossible empiricist position and a miraculous nativist one. The child must master the conceptual structure of the world that language will map—the social world as well as the physical. He must also master the conventions for making his intentions clear by language.

SUPPORT FOR LANGUAGE ACQUISITION

The development of language, then, involves two people negotiating. Language is not encountered willy-nilly by the child; it is shaped to make communicative interaction effective—fine-tuned. If there is a Language Acquisition Device, the input to it is not a shower of spoken language but a highly interactive affair shaped, as we have already noted, by some sort of an adult Language Acquisition Support System.

After all, it is well known from a generation of research on another "innate" system, sexual behavior, that much experiential priming is necessary before innate sexual responses can be evoked by "appropriate" environmental events. Isolated animals are seriously retarded. By the same token, the recognition and the production of grammatical universals may similarly depend upon prior social and conceptual experience. Continuities between prelinguistic communication and later speech of the kind I alluded to earlier may, moreover, need an "arranged" input of adult speech if the child is to use his growing grasp of conceptual distinctions and communicative functions as guides to language use. I propose that this "arranging" of early speech interaction requires routinized and familiar settings, formats, for the child to comprehend what is going on, given his limited capacity for processing information. These routines constitute what I intend by a Language Acquisition Support System.

There are at least four ways in which such a Language Acquisition Support System helps assure continuity from prelinguistic to linguistic communication. Because there is such concentration on familiar and routine transactional formats, it becomes feasible for the adult partner to highlight those features of the world that are already salient to the child and that have a basic or simple grammatical form. Slobin has suggested, for example, that there are certain prototypical ways in which the child experiences the world: e.g., a "prototypical transitive event" in which "an animate agent is seen willfully . . . to bring about a physical and perceptible change of state or location in a patient by means of direct body contact." Events of this kind, we shall see, are a very frequent feature of mother-child formats, and it is of

no small interest that in a variety of languages, as Slobin notes, they "are encoded in consistent grammatical form by age two." Slobin offers the interesting hypothesis "that [these] prototypical situations are encoded in the most basic grammatical forms available in a language." We shall encounter formats built around games and tasks involving both these prototypical means-end structures and canonical linguistic forms that seem almost designed to aid the child in spotting the referential correspondence between such utterances and such events.

Or to take another example, Bickerton has proposed that children are "bioprogrammed" to notice certain distinctions in real world events and to pick up (or even to invent) corresponding linguistic distinctions in order to communicate about them. His candidates are the distinctions (a) between specific and nonspecific events, (b) between state and process, (c) between "punctual" and continuous events, and (d) between causative and noncausative actions. And insofar as the "fine tuning" of adult interaction with a child concentrates on these distinctions—both in reality and in speech—the child is aided in moving from their conceptual expression to an appreciation of their appropriate linguistic representation. Again, they will be found to be frequent in the formats of the children we shall look at in detail.

A second way in which the adult helps the child through formatting is by encouraging and modeling lexical and phrasal substitutes for familiar gestural and vocal means for effecting various communicative functions. This is a feature of the child's gradual mastery of the request mode.

H. P. Grice takes it as a hallmark of mature language that the speaker not only has an intention to communicate, but that he also has *conventionalized* or "nonnatural" means for expressing his intention. The speaker, in his view, presupposes that his interlocutor will accept his means of communication and will infer his intention from them. The interlocutor presupposes the same thing about the speaker. Grice, concerned with adults, assumes all this to be quite conscious, if implicit.

An infant cannot at the prelinguistic outset be said to be participating in a conscious Gricean cycle when signaling conventionally in his games with his mother. That much selfconsciousness seems unlikely. But what we will find in the following chapters is that the mother acts as if he did. The child in turn soon comes to operate with some junior version of the Gricean cycle, awaiting his mother's "uptake" of his signaling.

In Katherine Nelson's terms, the young child soon acquires a small library of scripts and communicative procedures to go with them. They provide steady frameworks in which he learns effectively, by dint of interpretable feedback, how to make his communicative intentions plain. When he becomes "conscious" enough to be said to be operating in a Gricean cycle is, I think, a silly question.

What is striking is how early the child develops means to signal his focus of attention and his requests for assistance—to signal them by conventionalized means in the limited world of familiar formats. He has obviously picked up the gist of "nonnatural" or conventionalized signaling of his intentions before ever he has mastered the formal elements of lexicogrammatical speech. I think the reader will agree, in reading later chapters, that the functional framing of communication starts the child on his way to language proper. Thirdly, it is characteristic of play formats particularly that they are made of stipulative or constitutive "events" that are created by language and then recreated on demand by language. Later these formats take on the character of "pretend" situations. They are a rich source of opportunity for language learning and language use.

Finally, once the mother and child are launched into routinized formats, various psychological and linguistic processes are brought into play that generalize from one format to another. Naming, for example, appears first in indicating formats and then transfers to requesting formats. Indeed, the very notion of finding linguistic parallels for conceptual distinctions generalizes from one format to another. So too do such "abstract" ideas as segmentation, interchangeable roles, substitutive means—both in action and in speech.

These are the mundane procedures and events that constitute a Language Acquisition Support System, along with the elements of fine tuning that comprise "baby talk" exchanges.

17

Language Acquisition by Deaf Children

RICHARD P. MEIER

The development of the biologically based abilities of speech and language comprehension relies in important ways on the linguistic character of the environment in which these skills develop. Features that compose a rich environment for learning language include the presence of language users and exposure to language from birth. The typical language-learning environment includes auditory linguistic stimulation, but this is not the case for deaf children. The following article on language acquisition among deaf children discusses how language is acquired when several of the critical conditions are absent or arranged differently. Such studies increase our general knowledge of language acquisition because they allow us to gain a better understanding of the conditions upon which it relies.

Contemporary linguists have argued that the ability to learn language is more than an ordinary human skill; it is biologically based. Language is something we are born knowing how to know. Yet the hypothesis that there are biological underpinnings to human linguistic ability does not explain everything. There may indeed be an innate language capacity, a so called universal grammar, but despite the proponents of Esperanto, there is no universal language. Depending on the accidents of birth, a child may end up a native speaker of any one of roughly 4,000 languages. Thus the predisposition to acquire language seems to be remarkably flexible as well as strong.

Given that our innate language capacity does not prescribe a particular language but instead sets the boundaries of the class of possible languages, what precisely is the relation between nature and nurture in language acquisition? What do nature (the innate ability) and nurture (the linguistic environment) each contribute when a child is acquiring a language?

Reprinted with permission from *American Scientist*, 79, 1991, 60–70. Copyright 1991 by Sigma Xi Science Research Society.

This question is easy to ask but very difficult to answer. The obvious experiments would involve manipulating a child's linguistic input. For example, one might expose a child only to an artificial language that violates a hypothesized rule of universal grammar. Could the child acquire such a language? Or one might deprive a child of all linguistic input to see if he or she would develop a language in a linguistic vacuum. Of course, performing such experiments with a human subject is unthinkable.

Similar questions can be answered, however, by studying deaf children, whose linguistic experiences are very different from those of the hearing population. For example, it turns out that a child who has no access to a spoken language will readily acquire a sign language, and that a child deprived of both spoken and signed language sometimes invents his or her own gestural system of communication.

Studies of deaf children make it clear that human linguistic competence is in some sense deeper than the mode of expression. Language can assume either the vocal or the gestural mode as circumstances dictate. In other words, although we are biologically equipped to use language, we are not biologically limited to speech.

EVIDENCE OF INNATENESS

Several lines of evidence support the notion that a child has a biologically based capacity to learn language. At first what is most striking about the world's languages is their diversity, but closer study uncovers many universal elements. All known languages share certain organizational principles. For example, in all languages sentences have a hierarchical structure: words are grouped into phrases, and phrases are combined to form sentences. In no language are the words simply strung together like pearls on a necklace.

Moreover, as Noam Chomsky of the Massachusetts Institute of Technology has observed, it is easy to invent syntactic rules that seem reasonable but that occur in no known language. For example, in no language is an interrogative sentence formed by perfectly inverting the word order of the corresponding declarative sentence. Thus "The linguist from Austin was writing a paper," is never converted into a question having the form, "Paper a writing was Austin from linguist the?" One explanation for these language universals, and for many others that are more subtle, is that they are somehow part of our biological capacity.

A second line of evidence derives from close examination of the linguistic input children receive when they are learning a language. That input appears to be deficient in one key respect. Mature speakers know which sentences are grammatical in

their dialect and which are not, but children are not taught the distinction in any straightforward way. As Roger Brown and Camille Hanlon of Harvard University were the first to show, a child typically is given many examples of grammatical sentences but very little information about grammatical errors.

Children obviously make grammatical errors, but it seems parents seldom correct them. When a child says, "Me want cookie," the parent seldom explains that only the Cookie Monster on "Sesame Street" says it that way. In any case, whether the child obtains the coveted cookie will probably have more to do with the time remaining until dinner than with the grammatical correctness of his or her request. Furthermore, there are many interesting classes of errors that children never make. It may be that children need little explicit instruction in grammar because they are biologically provided with a universal grammar, and that they never make some types of errors because those errors would violate principles of the universal grammar.

A third line of evidence comes from the study of pidgins and creoles, forms of language that arise when groups of people with no common language find themselves in prolonged contact. Such situations arose on the sugar-cane plantations of Hawaii in the 1890s, for example. Pidgins are simplified, limited-purpose languages. Creole languages, in contrast, are complete and fully serviceable languages. Derek Bickerton of the University of Hawaii argues that the creole languages were the creation of the first generation of children born into the polyglot plantation societies. He considers their linguistic input to have been the local pidgin, which provided them with a sizable vocabulary, but with a limited and highly variable syntactic model. The creole they created and continued to speak as adults shows grammatical regularities not present in the pidgin or, for that matter, in any of the other languages spoken in Hawaii. This finding and the remarkable similarity of the syntaxes of the world's creole languages led Bickerton to conclude that the grammars of such languages are the product of what he calls the child's "language bioprogram."

Although each of these areas of research is fascinating, there are many questions they do not answer and that probably cannot be answered by studying hearing children exposed to spoken languages. Research on language acquisition by deaf children can further our understanding of the language capacity we all share.

LINGUISTIC ENVIRONMENTS

The linguistic environment of deaf children often differs in important ways from the typical linguistic environment of early childhood.

The most fundamental property of the typical language-learning environment is that it provides linguistic input that is accessible to the child. The deaf children of hearing parents, however, may not have significant exposure to any language in early childhood. Because of their sensory loss, these children perceive little of their parents' speech. Because in most cases the parents do not sign, the children are also not exposed to a conventional sign language. In the face of this linguistic deprivation, are these children mute?

A second property of the typical language-learning environment is that the input is auditory. Here the best counterexample is provided by the deaf children of deaf parents, who are exposed from birth to a sign language. For these children, linguistic input is visual rather than auditory. Studies of such children can therefore address the question: Does the acquisition of a visual-gestural language proceed in the same way as the acquisition of a spoken language?

A third property of the typical linguistic environment is that the child is exposed to language from birth. The deaf children of hearing parents, however, may not have significant exposure to any language, either signed or spoken, until they are of school age,

or even until they are teens or young adults. This circumstance gives access to another question: If exposure to language is delayed, can the learner still achieve the competence of a native speaker or signer?

A fourth property is that linguistic input is arbitrary rather than iconic. Although there are exceptions, most spoken words do not sound like the things or actions or concepts they represent. Some sign languages, however, have many iconic signs—or at least the signs seem iconic to adults. Do the resemblances between the signs and their referents make it easier for the child to learn to sign?

ABSENCE OF LINGUISTIC STIMULI

More than 90 percent of prelingually deaf children are born to hearing parents. Because of their sensory loss, these children are largely deprived of exposure to a spoken language. Acquiring speech is for them a long, frustrating and difficult endeavor, but many of them have had no alternative but to try. Until recently, the education of the deaf emphasized speech training to the exclusion of sign language. Hearing parents were discouraged from signing to their children and

FIGURE 1 Novel system of gestures was invented by a deaf child, David, raised in the home of hearing parents. In the absence of either spoken language or signed language, David developed his own means of communication, which was documented in studies by Susan Goldin-Meadow and her colleagues at the University of Chicago. Here David produces a fluent, rapidly articulated sequence of three gestures: With a toy in his hand he points to a tray of food *(left drawing)*, makes a bobbing gesture in front of his mouth *(middle)* and finally points to Goldin-Meadow, who was sitting in front of him *(right)*. The meaning of this sentence-like sequence of gestures is "You eat that," but the order of the gestures is "That eat you." Goldin-Meadow observed that David consistently employed this ordering principle, which differs from the usual word order in both English and ASL. In particular, David regularly ordered verb-like gestures after gestures referring to an object that is acted upon. The drawings are based on a videotape made by Goldin-Meadow.

were told that the use of a sign language would impede their child's progress in learning English. Consequently, the deaf children of hearing parents, who were deprived of exposure to spoken language by biology, were deprived of exposure to sign language by society.

Although children in this situation had little exposure to language, they presumably wished to communicate with their parents and others. How did they accomplish this? The answer is that they invented their own gestural systems of communication. Susan Goldin-Meadow and her colleagues at the University of Chicago followed the development of 10 deaf children of hearing parents. The parents had decided to educate their children solely through speech and did not sign to them. When Goldin-Meadow first saw these children, at ages between 13 months and about four years, they had not yet shown significant progress in English.

At an early age, the children produced isolated gestures. These were either pointing gestures or gestures that in some way resembled the object or event to which the child was referring. For example, a gesture meaning "open jar" was a twisting movement of the hand; a gesture for "eat" took the form of a repeated bobbing movement of the fist at the child's mouth.

More impressively, however, the children soon began to combine gestures to form sentences. In such sentences, two or more gestures were concatenated without intervening pauses. The gestures were not produced at random; all of the children showed statistically reliable gesture-order tendencies. A typical ordering was *patient-act,* where *patient* indicates a gesture referring to an object that is acted upon and *act* indicates a verb-like gesture. (Goldin-Meadow avoids the standard terms for parts of speech to avoid imputing to the children a grammatical sophistication she has not yet demonstrated they have.)

The word ordering the children used could not have been borrowed, because it is characteristic neither of English nor of American Sign Language. For example, one child pointed to food, then made a gesture meaning "eat," then pointed to his addressee. This sentence could be transcribed word-for-word as "That eat you," but its meaning is "You eat that." Moreover, the children's word-order tendencies did not seem to have been shaped by any input from their parents. The parents' gesturing was quite limited, and the comparatively few multi-gesture sequences they did produce had no consistent ordering.

These invented gestural systems suggest that certain linguistic properties, including word order and some aspects of vocabulary, are quite resilient in the face of very limited linguistic input. One way to explain this resiliency is to assume that children are biologically prepared to acquire these properties.

THE NATIVE SIGNER

The linguistic environment of deaf children born into deaf families differs from the typical language-learning environment in one crucial respect: the children are exposed to a gestural language, not a spoken one. In the United States and much of Canada, the gestural language is American Sign Language (ASL). Does the acquisition of a sign language differ from that of a spoken language?

A sign language is not merely a transliterated version of a spoken language. ASL, for example, is a complete and well-formed language whose grammar is quite distinct from that of English. It developed naturally within the American deaf community, and it is not mutually intelligible with the sign languages used elsewhere, including those used in other English-speaking countries. (Oliver Sacks's recent book *Seeing Voices: A Journey into the World of the Deaf* offers a good overview of this subject.)

That ASL is a language in its own right and is organized around the same principles as other languages might lead one to expect that it would be acquired like any other. Yet the ubiquity of spoken languages suggests that the mode of linguistic expression is not a matter of total indifference. Although auxiliary sign languages are relatively common among Native Americans and Australian Aborigines, the primary language of every hearing community is a spoken language. Moreover, there is considerable evidence that *Homo sapiens* and speech have co-evolved. For example, evolutionary changes in the position of the larynx and in the structure of the vocal tract enable us to articulate a wider range of sounds than the great apes. These anatomical changes were not without costs—they put us at greater risk of choking—but the advantage they conferred apparently outweighed the costs. Taken together, considerations such as these suggest that children might be slower to acquire signed languages than spoken languages and that the process by which signed languages are acquired might be atypical.

In acquiring a spoken language children pass a series of milestones at relatively predictable ages. Hearing children generally produce their first words at 12 months. They acquire a rudimentary syntax between 18 and 24 months; at this stage they combine words to form simple two-word sentences. English inflectional morphology (such as word endings that mark tense and number) generally emerges between the ages of two and a half and three and a half years.

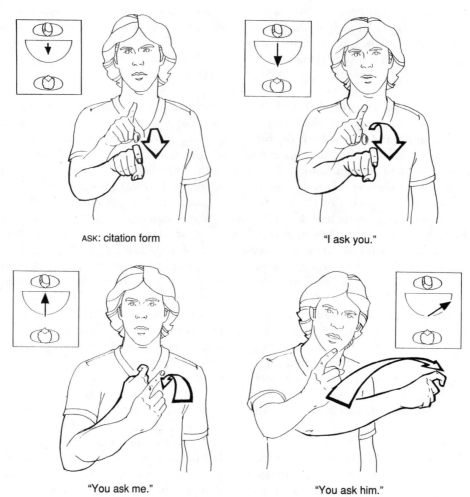

ASK: citation form

"I ask you."

"You ask me."

"You ask him."

FIGURE 2   Sign for ASK in ASL has inflected forms much like those of a verb in a spoken language. Mastery of such morphological complexities is often one of the later milestones of language development. The citation form of ASK—the form that would be listed in a dictionary—is uninflected. The other three forms must agree with both the subject and the object of the sentence. When the sign means "I ask you," the direction of motion is from the signer toward his conversational partner. When the sign means "You ask me," the direction of motion is reversed. ASK can also agree with subjects or objects whose referents are not present, but which can be assigned to an empty location in the space in front of the signer. For example, the sign for "You ask him (or her)" begins close to the conversational partner and ends at an empty location. The drawings are by Frank A. Paul, who was fluent in ASL and worked as an interpreter for the deaf and as an illustrator for the Laboratory for Language and Cognitive Studies at the Salk Institute; Paul died in 1989.

The American linguist Eric H. Lenneberg pointed out that children tend to pass these milestones in the same sequence at roughly the same ages no matter what their linguistic environment (although there is evidence that the timing of the acquisition of morphology varies across languages). He argued that this regularity suggests language acquisition is fundamentally controlled by maturation.

Do signing children pass the same milestones at the same ages? From a review of the literature on the acquisition of ASL, Elissa Newport of the University of Rochester and I concluded that they do. Thus by 12 months, signing children, like speaking children, are at the one-word stage. They produce isolated signs drawn from the vocabulary of the adult language. Between 18 and 24 months, signing children enter the two-word stage. They begin to concatenate signs to form simple sentences. Although the considerable differences between ASL and English make further comparison difficult, it can be said that the children continue to pass comparable milestones at comparable ages. For example, the signer's mastery of ASL rules of verb agreement occurs at roughly the same age as the speaker's mastery of complex verb conjugations.

The two-word stage in the acquisition of English has one particularly interesting feature: Even at the outset, children make few errors in word order. Is this also true for the acquisition of ASL? Before I can answer this question, I must introduce a little of ASL's grammar. In adult ASL, as in English, the canonical word order is subject-verb-object (SVO). For example, in the simple declarative sentence "Mathilda kissed Bob," the postverbal position of "Bob" identifies it as the direct object of the verb "kissed." Consequently, we understand that Bob was the person who was kissed, not the one who did the kissing. Although ASL has the same canonical word order, it allows considerably more freedom in word order than

English does. One reason is that ASL allows the identity of the subject and the object to be conveyed by the verb, by means of a rule of verb agreement. (My use of the term "object" masks a number of syntactic complexities.) Spoken languages with elaborate systems of verb agreement, such as Spanish and Italian, generally also permit considerable freedom in word order.

As English speakers, we have some acquaintance with verb agreement. If a present-tense verb has the suffix -s, we know that the subject of the sentence is in the third-person singular. Thus we say "I kick the football" but "She kicks the football." ASL exploits linguistic devices of this kind more fully. In particular, the verb may agree with both the subject and the object of the sentence. Figure 2 shows four forms of the ASL verb ASK. The citation form, or dictionary-entry form, of this verb is an outward excursion of the hand. When the signer is the subject and his or her addressee is the object, the excursion is longer, and it is directed toward the addressee. When the addressee is the subject and the signer is the object, the direction of motion is reversed. Finally, if the signer wants to

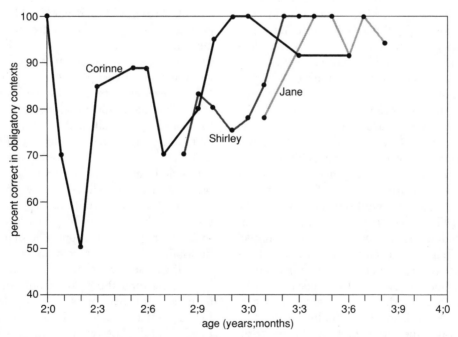

FIGURE 3 Milestones in language acquisition are the same for speaking and for signing children; furthermore, they pass these milestones in the same sequence and at roughly the same times. The progress of three deaf children toward mastery of ASL verb agreement was studied by the author. All three children achieved consistent command of verb agreement in the first half of their third year. Hearing children master English verb agreement at roughly the same age. One child, Corinne, provides an instance of a common learning pattern: near-perfect initial performance followed by deteriorating accuracy and a slower return to mastery. The child's initial performance is thought to be based on rote teaming of a limited number of verbs inflected for agreement.

refer to an absent person, a third, vacant, position can serve as a kind of pronoun. Verbs can then agree with that position.

Bearing in mind the grammatical differences between ASL and English, do deaf children display the same facility in the use of word order as hearing children? It appears that deaf children begin to use word order to indicate the syntactic relations of a verb and its noun arguments early in the two-word stage, even at age two. According to studies done by Robert J. Hoffmeister of Boston University and by Newport and Ashbrook, signing children reliably use SVO order in the two- and three-word stages of language development. Indeed, they may continue to do so even after they have acquired the ASL rule of verb agreement that allows freer ordering. In their reliance on word order, beginning signers resemble beginning English speakers.

In summary, the same sequence of milestones seems to characterize the acquisition of ASL and of spoken language. Nor is there any evidence that language acquisition is delayed in deaf children. Although human beings may have highly evolved mechanisms for the production and processing of speech, those mechanisms are apparently sufficiently flexible that the acquisition of signed languages is not disadvantaged. Helen J. Neville, Albert Schmidt and Marta Kutas, working at the Salk Institute, have uncovered neuropsychological evidence for such plasticity. Their studies of evoked potentials suggest that temporal-lobe regions implicated in auditory processing in the hearing can be reassigned to visual processing in subjects who have been deaf from birth.

So far I have been concerned to show that the sign-language learner is not at a disadvantage. But there is even some evidence that signing children pass the very first milestones of language development *before* their speaking counterparts. The most persuasive evidence has to do with the age at which the child produces his or her first word and the age at which he or she has a small vocabulary. For example, John D. Bonvillian and his colleagues at the University of Virginia have reported that 13 signing children of deaf parents had amassed a 10-sign vocabulary by a mean age of 13.2 months. This is significantly earlier than the 18 English-speaking children studied by Katherine Nelson of the City University of New York, who did not reach the same milestone until a mean age of 15.1 months.

There are a number of plausible, although yet untested, explanations for the apparent precociousness of signing children. It may have a biological basis: The perceptual and motor systems subserving signed language may mature earlier than those required for speech. It is also possible, however, that the young child simply finds manual signs more perspicuous than spoken words, or even that parents (and linguists) are more likely to recognize a child's fumbling attempts at signs than his or her attempts at spoken words. The literature on neurological development provides some support for the first and strongest of these candidate explanations; it turns out that the post-thalamic visual pathways are fully myelinated at an earlier age than the comparable auditory pathways.

It may be that signing children provide a clearer window onto some parts of the language-acquisition process than speaking children do. In particular, the deaf children may begin to sign as soon as they have the linguistic and cognitive maturity to do so. Hearing children, on the other hand, may be delayed by slower development of perceptual or motor abilities needed for the modality of speech.

THE LATE LEARNER

In addition to arguing that the process of language acquisition is maturationally determined, Lenneberg hypothesized that children can gain a native speaker's competence only if they are exposed to linguistic stimuli during a critical period. He argued that this period, whose boundaries are presumably set by neurological development, extends roughly from the age of two (when children begin using two-word combinations) to 13 (the onset of puberty).

In developmental biology the classic example of a critical period is the imprinting of birds. Ducklings, for example, will follow the first moving object, duck or nonduck, to which they are exposed from 9 to 21 hours after hatching. Maturationally determined critical periods also characterize song learning in some birds, such as the white-crowned sparrow. Given the long philosophical tradition in which language is taken as the distinguishing mark of humanity, we might be reluctant to suppose it shares anything with imprinting in birds. But what does the evidence suggest?

Of course, it is more difficult to test Lenneberg's hypothesis than those concerning critical periods in animals. Lenneberg himself marshalled evidence having to do with the acquisition of a second language, the probability of recovery from aphasia, and language acquisition by children with Down's syndrome. For example, the age at first exposure to a second language turns out to be a much better predictor of ultimate proficiency than the number of years of exposure.

The most direct test of Lenneberg's hypothesis is delayed exposure to a first language. In the hearing population, such delays occur rarely and even then

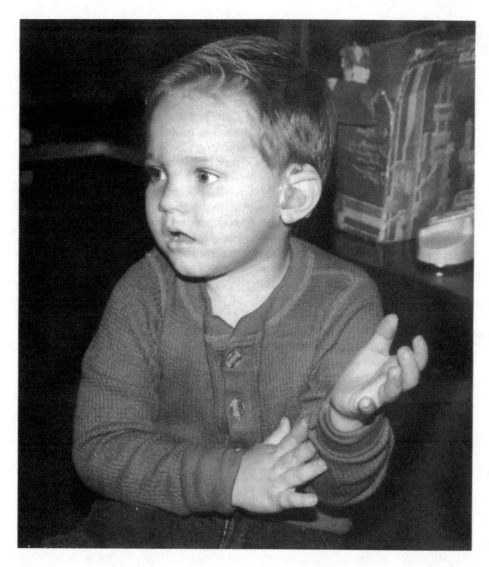

FIGURE 4 ASL sign for TREE is produced by a three-year-old child. The standard form of this sign is shown in the drawing at left. The child's sign differs slightly from the adult form but is still fully intelligible. Such discrepancies are typical of the signing of young children, just as speaking children at the same age have not achieved perfect pronunciation. Note that the child is signing with the left hand; ASL signs are not specifically left- or right-handed. (Photograph by Brian C. Price of the University of Texas at Austin; drawing by Frank A. Paul, from *A Basic Course in American Sign Language*, by Tom Humphries, Carol Padden and Terrence, J. O'Rourke, T. J. Publishers, Inc., 1980.)

they are difficult to interpret. There are interesting historical cases of abandoned children who could not speak when they were found, such as Victor, the wild child of Avignon, but accounts of these cases often reveal more about the history of ideas than about linguistic development.

A more recent case was discussed by Susan Curtiss of the University of California at Los Angeles.

A girl whom Curtiss calls Genie was isolated in a back bedroom of her Los Angeles home by an abusive father. From the age of two until she was thirteen and a half Genie had virtually no exposure to language. At the time of her discovery, she neither spoke nor understood any English. Genie eventually succeeded in acquiring some hallmarks of fluency, such as a sizable vocabulary and command of word order and subordination, but she failed to acquire others, such as inflectional morphology and a command of auxiliary verbs and of the passive voice. Moreover, her speech was phonologically abnormal.

This outcome is certainly consistent with Lenneberg's hypothesis. What prevents us from reaching any firmer conclusions is that Genie's delayed exposure to language was part of a pattern of abuse. She was deprived not only of speech, but also of social, visual and auditory stimulation in general. Moreover, she was physically abused and malnourished.

A stronger test of Lenneberg's hypothesis is afforded by one segment of the deaf population: deaf children born into hearing families. In years past, these children often had little exposure to any language, either spoken or signed, during early childhood. Most of them eventually encountered ASL, but their age at first exposure varied enormously. For many, the first encounter came at age five or six, when they entered a residential school for the deaf. Even there they learned ASL not in the classroom but in the dormitories—from a few schoolmates who were fluent native signers. Other children, who attended strongly oralist day schools, did not encounter ASL until their early twenties.

Newport and Ted Supalla addressed the question of delayed exposure to language in a study of 30 adults who considered ASL to be their primary language. (Their English skills, in contrast, were quite limited.) The subjects all had 30 or more years of exposure to ASL, but the age at which they were initially exposed varied. All of them had attended the same residential school, but some were native signers who were exposed to ASL from birth, some were early learners who first encountered ASL when they enrolled in the residential school at ages between four and six, and others were late learners, whose first encounter occurred after age 12.

Newport and Supalla gave the subjects a battery of tests examining their ability to produce and comprehend various grammatical constructions in ASL. One result is particularly interesting in the light of the other evidence I have discussed. It turned out that a signer's knowledge of ASL word order was unrelated to his or her age of initial exposure; the performance of all three groups was almost error-free. This is consistent with the reliable use of gesture order by the children Goldin-Meadow studied, with the early mastery of basic word order by both beginning speakers and beginning signers, and with Genie's successful acquisition of basic word order.

Another set of tests yielded a very different pattern of results, however. These tests examined the production and comprehension of morphologically complex signs. In English, morphologically complex words are those that have more than one meaningful part. For example, *walked* consists of two morphemes: the verb stem *walk* and the past-tense inflection *-ed*. Similarly, in ASL the inflected form of the verb ASK meaning "You ask me" is made up of three morphemes: the verb stem ASK and the agreement markers for subject and object. Newport and Supalla found that the earlier a signer had been exposed to ASL, the better he or she scored on these tests. Native signers did better than early learners, who in turn did better than late learners.

Newport and Supalla's study provides strong support for the claim that a child can gain native competence in a language only if he or she is exposed to that language during a critical period. These data are particularly significant because signers are the only large population that undergoes delayed exposure to a primary language.

ICONIC LANGUAGE

Only rarely is it possible to infer the meaning of an English word from its sound. The occasional onomatopoeic word, such as *bow-wow* or *meow,* is the exception rather than the rule. More typical is a word such as *give*: nothing about it in any way resembles the action of transferring an object from one person's possession to another's. In fact an arbitrary relation between the form of a word and the form of its referent is so usual that Ferdinand de Saussure, the Swiss linguist whose *Course in General Linguistics* laid the foundations of structuralism, insisted it is a fundamental property of all human language.

Saussure's conclusion rested entirely on the analysis of spoken languages. ASL, by contrast, has many iconic signs. Unlike the English *give,* or for that matter the Spanish *dar* or the French *donner,* the ASL sign GIVE is "motivated." As Figure 6 shows, GIVE closely resembles the act of handing a small object to another person. Many other ASL verbs with inflections that mark subject and object, such as TAKE and GET, also seem impressively pictorial.

At least they seem so to adults acquiring ASL as a second language. But are children acquiring ASL as a first language equally impressed by the iconic aspects of the language? Do the similarities between form and

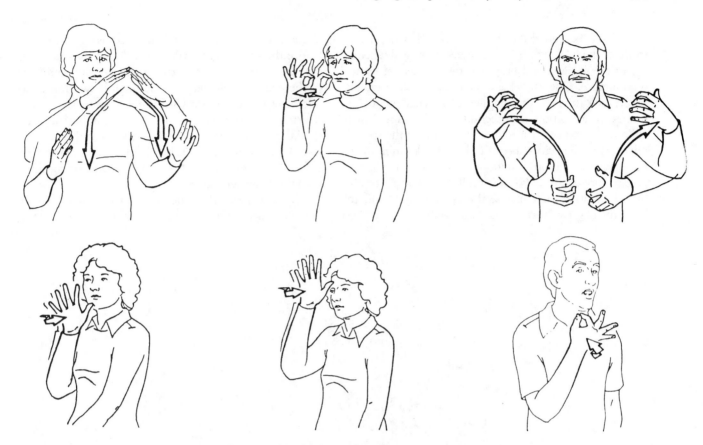

FIGURE 5 Iconic signs in ASL—signs that resemble the things they denote—seem conspicuous to English speakers who learn ASL as a second language in adulthood. Three such signs are shown in the upper row of drawings: HOUSE, CAT and ANGRY. It is tempting to suppose the young language learner uses the resemblance between the sign and its referent to guess at the meaning of the sign. There are several problems with this hypothesis, however. ASL is not consistently iconic. It has many arbitrary signs as well, such as those of the lower row: MOTHER, FATHER and CURIOUS. Moreover, the resemblances are much less apparent in a conversation than they are in drawings of signs, and native signers report being unaware of them. (Drawings by Frank A. Paul, from *A Basic Course in American Sign Language.*)

meaning make it easier for children to acquire an ASL vocabulary? Or are they "expecting" to encounter arbitrary mappings between form and meaning?

This is not a simple question to answer. For one thing, it is difficult to isolate the iconic elements in ASL. ASL has many iconic signs, but it also has many arbitrary ones. Such common signs as MOTHER, FATHER, WHITE, BLACK and AMERICA are essentially unmotivated. In addition, the formation of an ASL sign is never determined solely by resemblance to an object or act; it is also constrained by a complex system of grammatical rules. Finally, even when a sign has an iconic origin, a fluent signer may not experience its iconic content in normal discourse, any more than a native speaker of English is ordinarily aware of a word's etymology—such as the sense of "tongue" in the word "linguistics."

Because iconicity is not a simple phenomenon, it is even conceivable that instead of assisting the language learner, it could place pitfalls in his or her way. For example, a child guided by iconicity might suppose that GIVE could only be used when the verb and the act were very similar. But the sign GIVE can be used to describe the transference of elephants and automobiles as well as of handheld items. Furthermore, the child who attended to iconicity would have to switch strategies when confronted by verbs such as PITY, ASK, HATE and INFORM. These verbs inflect in much the same way as GIVE, but they are not otherwise iconic in form.

I have examined the effect of iconic language in a study of the acquisition of verb agreement by deaf children of deaf parents. I proposed two models of iconic resemblance. One model assumed that children would be attuned to verbs that happen to be enactments, or mimes, of an action. The second model assumed that children would be attuned to verbs that map the spatial relations of the actors. Because these models pin down the somewhat vaporous notion of the iconic, they make precise predictions. For example, according to the model favoring enactments, the child would tend to learn the first two forms of GIVE shown in Figure 6 (the

citation form and the form translated as "I give you") before the third and fourth forms ("You give me" and "He gives her"). The first two forms are simple mimes of the action of giving, whereas the last two forms do not have as straightforward a relation to the action referred to. According to the model emphasizing the spatial relations of actors, the child would learn the last three forms of GIVE before the citation form or before other forms of GIVE that happen not to agree with the agent who gives.

It turned out that the children followed neither model; indeed they seemed quite oblivious to the

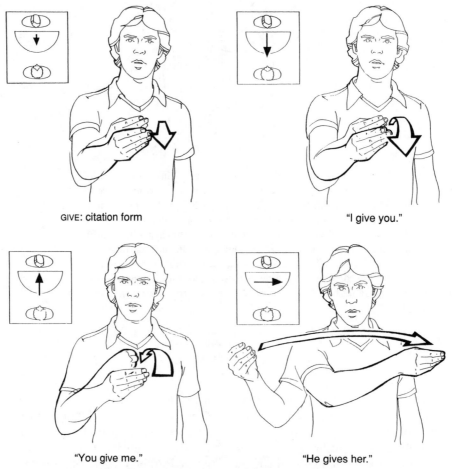

GIVE: citation form

"I give you."

"You give me."

"He gives her."

FIGURE 6 Inflections of the verb GIVE suggest a means of testing the importance of iconic content in ASL. The various forms exhibit different degrees and different forms of iconicity. The citation form and the form translated as "I give you" are iconic in the sense that the gesture is a mime of the action of giving. The forms "You give me" and "He (She) gives her (him)," in contrast, are not accurate mimes of the action they denote. All three inflected forms (but not the citation form) are iconic in a different way: they map the positions of the giver and the recipient in space. If either kind of iconicity aids language acquisition, children ought to learn the iconic forms more quickly and more accurately than the arbitrary forms. The author's studies show no such effect. (Drawings by Frank A. Paul, from *Journal of Memory and Language*, 1987, 26:362–376.)

iconic elements of signs. Three aspects of the study are interesting: the children's progress toward error-free performance, the age at which they achieved error-free performance, and the type of errors they made. I was able to follow one child, Corinne, long enough to capture the acquisition process in detail (see Figure 3). Corinne's use of verb agreement seemed nearly perfect at the age of two, but then deteriorated precipitously. She did not again inflect verbs reliably until 10 months later. This pattern resembles the U-shaped trajectory followed by hearing children learning the rules for morphologically complex forms of words, such as the past tense. At first the children's performance is surprisingly good, apparently because they learn high-frequency words by rote. Later, as they begin to grapple with general rules rather than specific instances, their performance slips. Much the same seems to be true of Corinne. Her early success was largely confined to the use of one verb in a single inflected form. (Parents of two-year-olds will not be surprised to learn that the verb was SAY-NO and the form was second-person object agreement: "I say no to you.")

At what age did the children acquire verb agreement? According to the criterion I chose for the acquisition of a linguistic rule, the children I studied acquired verb agreement at the ages of three years, three years and three months and three years and six months. Under the same criterion, hearing children acquire English verb agreement at ages between two and a half and three and a half. Thus, the acquisition of ASL verb agreement does not seem to be advanced by the iconic properties of many ASL verb forms. Instead the rules for ASL verb agreement seem to be acquired at much the same time as the rules for English verb agreement.

The children in my study showed no tendency to use iconic verb forms—as defined by either of my models—earlier than arbitrary verb forms. And the errors the children made were inconsistent with the notion that they were attending to the iconic properties of the signs. They often erred by omitting verb agreement altogether, and quite frequently the erroneous verb forms were less iconic than the correct forms. As it happens, hearing children also tend to err by omission when they are learning inflectional morphology. For example, a child will say "two shoe" instead of "two shoes." In sign language as in spoken language, it seems grammatical complexity determines which errors children make. Typical errors often yield verb forms that are less iconic than the correct form, but that are grammatically simpler. In

	Acquisition of English: hearing children	Acquisition of ASL: deaf children of deaf parents	Minimal linguistic input: deaf children of hearing parents	Delayed exposure to a spoken language: Genie	Delayed exposure to a sign language: deaf, late learners of ASL
Vocabulary	First word at 12 months	First sign at 12 months (or somewhat earlier)	Gestural vocabulary developed	Successful acquisition of a large vocabulary	Large sign vocabulary
Word Order	Reliable English word order early in two-word period	Reliable ASL sign order early in two-sign period	Reliable gesture-ordering tendencies	Reliable English word order acquired	Age of first exposure has no effect on knowledge of sign order
Morphology	English morphology begins to emerge at roughly 30 months	ASL morphology begins to emerge at roughly 30 months	Some spontaneous morphological development(?)	Very poor control over English morphology	Age of exposure has significant effect on knowledge of ASL morphology

FIGURE 7 Comparison of populations of children with different linguistic experiences demonstrates that some aspects of language are extremely robust, whereas others are more fragile. A large vocabulary and consistent word order are acquired even under the most unpromising conditions. But command of morphologically complex words and signs is affected by the child's linguistic upbringing. Hearing and deaf children attain similar proficiency in similar language-learning environments; it appears not to matter whether the child's first language is a spoken or a signed one.

another study, I asked 10 native-signing children to imitate sentences containing agreeing verbs, and the errors they made also support the claim that it is grammatical complexity that matters.

My studies converge with those of other aspects of ASL. Whether the topic is early vocabulary acquisition, the acquisition of pronouns, or the acquisition of the complex morphology of ASL verbs of motion and location, it seems children are remarkably insensitive to the nonarbitrary properties of ASL signs. Although at first blush ASL sometimes strikes adults as pantomime, children respond as though it were a fully arbitrary language.

CONCLUSION

As we have seen, the linguistic properties of ASL and the demography of the signing community allow us to ask interesting questions about the relation between linguistic input and language development.

The gestural systems invented by the deaf children of hearing parents show that certain linguistic properties emerge even when the child is raised in a virtual language vacuum. This finding suggests that children may come to the task of language acquisition with expectations about how languages are organized, a notion consistent with the assertion that there is an innate, species-specific capacity to acquire language.

On the other hand, we have also seen that children's expectations about language are not so constraining that they find it harder to learn a sign language than to learn a spoken language. The acquisition process itself is relatively independent of modality; acquisition of a language—whether signed or spoken—follows a single maturational schedule.

Finally, we have seen that children are quite insensitive to certain properties of their linguistic input. Adult learners of ASL are charmed by the iconicity of some signs, but children appear to be oblivious to it. It may be that their expectations about language lead them to attend to some aspects of their linguistic input and not to others.

Deaf language learners provide a remarkable opportunity to investigate the child's ability to acquire, and even to create, language. But we must always remember that one reason they do so is that they have so often been denied input from a natural sign language such as ASL.

Bibliography

Bonvillian, J. D., M. D. Orlansky and L. L. Novack. 1983. Developmental milestones: Sign language acquisition and motor development. *Child Development* 54: 1435–1445.

Brown, R. and C. Hanlon. 1970. Derivational complexity and order of acquisition in child speech. In *Cognition and the Development Of Language.*, *ed.* J. R. Hayes, John Wiley and Sons.

Chomsky, N. 1988. *Language and Problems of Knowledge.* The MIT Press.

Curtiss, S. 1977. *Genie: A Psycholinguistic Study of a Modern-Day "Wild Child."* Academic Press.

Feldman, H., S. Goldin-Meadow and L. R. Gleitman. 1978. Beyond Herodotus: The creation of language by linguistically deprived deaf children. In *Action, Symbol, and Gesture: The Emergence of Language,* ed. A. Lock, pp. 351–414. Academic Press.

Goldin-Meadow, S., and C. Mylander. 1983. Gestural communication in deaf children: Noneffect of parental input on language development. *Science* 221:372–374.

Goldin-Meadow, S., and C. Mylander. 1990. Beyond the input given: The child's role in the acquisition of language. *Language* 66:323–355.

Hess, E. H. 1959. Imprinting. *Science 130:*133–141.

Hoffmeister, R. J. 1978. Word order in the acquisition of ASL. Paper presented at the Boston University Conference on Language Development.

Johnson, J. S., and E. L. Newport. 1989. Critical period effects in second language learning: The influence of maturational state on the acquisition of English as a second language. *Cognitive Psychology 21:* 60–99.

Klima, E. S., and U. Bellugi. 1979. The *Signs of Language.* Harvard University Press.

Lane, H. 1984. *When the Mind Hears: A History of the Deaf.* Random House.

Lecours, A. R. 1975. Myelogenetic correlates of the development of speech and language. In *Foundations of Language Development,* ed. E. H. Lenneberg, pp. 121–135. Academic Press.

Lenneberg, E. H. 1967. *Biological Foundations of Language.* John Wiley and Sons.

Lieberman, P. 1984. *The Biology and Evolution of Language.* Harvard University Press.

Marler, P., and P. Mundinger. 1971. Vocal learning in birds. In *The Ontogeny of Vertebrate Behavior,* ed. H. Moltz, pp. 389–450. Academic Press.

Meier, R. P. 1981. Icons and morphemes: Models of the acquisition of verb agreement in ASL. *Papers and Reports on Child Language Development* 20:92–99.

Meier, R. P. 1982. *Icons, Analogues, and Morphemes: The Acquisition of Verb Agreement in American Sign Language.* Dissertation, University of California at San Diego.

Meier, R. P. 1987. Elicited imitation of verb agreement in American Sign Language. *Journal of Memory and Language* 26:362–376.

Meier, R. P., and E. L. Newport. 1990. Out of the hands of babes: On a possible sign advantage in language acquisition. *Language* 66:1–23.

Nelson, K. 1973. *Structure and Strategy in Learning to Talk.* Monographs of the Society for Research in Child Development (serial no. 149), Vol. 38, Nos. 1–2.

Neville, H. J., A. Schmidt and M. Kutas. 1983. Altered visual–evoked potentials in congenitally deaf adults. *Brain Research* 266:127–132.

Newport, E. L. 1990. Maturational constraints on language learning. *Cognitive Science* 14:11—28.

Newport, E. L., and E. Ashbrook. 1977. The emergence of semantic relations in ASL. *Papers and Reports on Child Language Development* 13:16–21.

Newport, E. L., and R. P. Meier. 1985. The acquisition of American Sign Language. In *The Crosslinguistic Study of Language Acquisition*, Vol. 1, ed. D. I. Slobin, pp. 881–938. Lawrence Erlbaum Associates.

Orlansky, M. D., and J. D. Bonvillian. 1984. The role of iconicity in early sign language acquisition. *Journal of Speech and Hearing Disorders* 49:287–292.

Oyama, S. 1976. A sensitive period for the acquisition of a nonnative phonological system. *Journal of Psycholinguistic Research* 5:261–285.

Patkowsky, M. S. 1980. The sensitive period for the acquisition of syntax in a second language. *Language Learning* 30:449–72.

Petitto, L. A. 1987. On the autonomy of language and gesture: Evidence from the acquisition of personal pronouns in American Sign Language. *Cognition* 27:1–52.

Sacks, O. 1989. *Seeing Voices: A Journey into the World of the Deaf.* University of California Press.

Saussure, F. de. 1959. *Course in General Linguistics.* Reprint of third edition (1915). McGraw–Hill.

Supalla, T. 1982. Structure and acquisition of verbs of motion and location in American Sign Language. Dissertation, University of California at San Diego.

Umiker-Sebeok, D. J., and T. A. Sebeok (eds). 1978. *Aboriginal Sign Languages of the Americas and Australia.* Plenum Publishers.

18

Looking for Big Bird: Studies of Memory in Very Young Children

JUDY S. DELOACHE AND ANN L. BROWN

For most of this century, psychological descriptions of the cognitive abilities of pre-school children emphasized their limitations when compared with children a few years older. Preschoolers appeared to have a difficult time thinking logically, planning their course of action, and remembering.

One of the reasons for this rather negative assessment of preschool cognition was the tradition of investigating preschooler's mental abilities on the psychologist's home turf—in a school room or a laboratory setting. In the following study, DeLoache and Brown investigated young children's memory in the familiar settings of their own homes. Furthermore, they made sure that the children were well motivated to remember by using toys to which the children had formed a close attachment. The picture that emerges from this rather simple change in procedure contradicts earlier ideas about young children's memory skills and the best ways of assessing them.

The period between one and three years of age is one of the most fascinating eras in human development: in no other comparable span of time do so many revolutionary changes occur. Cognitive processes undergo an extraordinary degree of reorganization as the child acquires language and makes the transition from sensorimotor to symbolic, representational thought. In spite of the importance of this early period, it has

Reprinted with permission from *The Quarterly Newsletter of the Laboratory of Comparative Human Cognition*, 1, 1979, 53–57. Copyright 1979 by The Laboratory of Comparative Human Cognition.

This research was supported in part by Grants HD 05951 and HD 06864 and Research Career Development Award HD 00111 from the National Institutes of Child Health and Human Development.

been relatively neglected by developmental psychologists until quite recently. One of the main reasons for this neglect has been the fact that young children are notoriously intractable research subjects; it is difficult to enlist their cooperation in the relatively artificial, unfamiliar tasks traditionally favored by psychologists, and even when they do seem to cooperate, their performance tends to be quite low (see, for example, Myers & Perlmutter, 1978). Although most parents recount numerous instances of their toddler remembering personally experienced events over days or even months, we are aware of no memory studies of young children where retention intervals of longer than 30 seconds have been used. It seems reasonable to infer from this discrepancy that the procedures commonly used to study early cognitive development are inadequate.

In this paper we will report an ongoing research project on young children's memory for object location that is aimed at studying the emergence and early refinement of various self-regulatory skills. We have made extensive efforts to avoid artificial experimental formats and to develop naturalistic, meaningful situations. The basic task that we have selected for our current research involves memory for object location (i.e., remembering where something is in space so one can retrieve it later). This is a variant of the delayed response task introduced by Hunter (1917) and used by him to study memory in a variety of species, ranging from rats to his 1-year-old daughter, Thayer. The essential feature of the delayed response problem is that the subject watches while an object is concealed in one of several potential containers. After a specified delay interval, during which the child's attention is typically distracted from the containers, he or she is allowed to find the hidden object.

This general format has been used in several recent studies with children between 1 1/2 and 3 years of age (e.g., Daehler, Bukatko, Benson, & Myers, 1976; Horn & Myers, 1978; Loughlin & Daehler, 1973). In the standard task 2-year-olds, for example, have been found to retrieve the object with no errors on slightly less than 50% of the trials (Daehler et al., 1976; Horn & Myers, 1978). The addition of visual and verbal cues to the spatial cues already present has sometimes increased the level of correct responding, to 66% with labeled pictures (Horn & Myers, 1978) and as high as 69% with containers differing in size (Daehler et al., 1976); but in other studies visual cues have not been helpful (Babska, 1965; Loughlin & Daehler, 1973). Thus, 2-year-old children generally perform above chance (Myers & Ratner, in press) in the standard delayed response task. Getting them to be correct more than half the time, however, requires the addition of carefully engineered cues. Further-

more, we wish to emphasize that in none of the above experiments was the delay interval longer than 25 seconds.

In our research our preliminary goals included devising a task in which we could ask very young children to remember something for more than half a minute. Accordingly, we have attempted to transform the basic delayed response task into a relatively natural situation. It takes the form of a hide-and-seek game that the child plays with a small stuffed animal. Several days before the experiment, each subject is given a toy (Mickey Mouse, Big Bird). Then, following our instructions, the parents teach their child the hide-and-seek game. The children are told that Mickey Mouse is going to hide and that they have to remember where he is hiding so they will be able to find him later. On each trial the child watches while his or her mother (or father) hides the toy in some natural location in their home, with a different location used for each trial. The specific locations obviously depend on the particular home, but include places like behind or under chairs and couches, under pillows, behind curtains, inside desk drawers. A kitchen timer is set for a specified interval and the child is taught to wait for the bell to ring. When it does, the child is allowed to go retrieve the "hiding" toy. The children very readily learn the rules of the hide-and-seek game and show obvious delight and excitement in playing it.

While we hoped that the hide-and-seek task would elicit performance from young children that would more accurately reflect their memorial competence, it was also designed to enable us to study very early forms of self-regulatory skills. These skills are the various processes by which people organize their thoughts and actions (Brown, 1978; Brown & DeLoache, 1978), including activities such as: *planning* ahead, *predicting* the outcome of some action (what will happen if?), *monitoring* ongoing activity (how am I doing?), *checking* on the results of actions (did that work, did it achieve my goal?), *correcting* errors or inadequacies (since what I just did didn't work, what would be a reasonable thing to try now?). These skills are the basic characteristics of efficient thought throughout life, and one of their most important properties is that they are transsituational. They apply to a whole range of problem-solving activities, from artificial experimental settings to everyday life. It is equally important to exercise these skills whether you're reading a textbook or a recipe; whether you're trying to remember who the seventh President of the United States was or where you left your car keys.

What we are referring to here as self-regulatory skills have often been described as a form of metacognition, and they are subsumed under Flavell's (1978) definition of metacognition as "knowledge that takes as its object or regulates any aspect of any cognitive endeavor." However, it is worthwhile noting that this definition comprises two (not necessarily separate) clusters—*knowledge* about cognition and *regulation* of cognition. The first concerns the relatively stable information individuals have about cognitive processes, tasks, strategies, and so forth, in general, as well as the knowledge they have about themselves engaged in those activities and tasks. We would not expect very young children to be capable of this sort of metacognitive activity, i.e., conscious knowledge about cognition. Indeed, Wellman (1977) has demonstrated the very meager extent of such information possessed by 3-year-old children.

It is the second cluster of metacognitive activities included in Flavell's statement, the self-regulatory skills, that we are interested in here. These might be expected to be exhibited by very young children as they attempt to learn or solve problems. However, unlike the activities in the first cluster, whether or not the self-regulatory mechanisms appear depends critically on the nature of the task and the expertise of the child.

One of the prerequisites to observing very early examples of self-regulatory activities is the existence of an appropriate task, one that challenges young children (so that planning, monitoring, and so forth might be helpful), yet that falls within their general competence. Otherwise, even if they have, or are at the point of developing, any rudimentary self-regulatory skills, they may be too overwhelmed by the novelty and difficulty of the task to exercise those skills (Shatz, 1978).

Several features of our hide-and-seek task should increase the likelihood of finding self-regulatory behavior in very young children. The task requires retrieval to be manifested in overt action—finding an object in the environment—rather than the purely internal retrieval of information from memory. In this situation, external cues can be used, and the desired goal state (as well as success or failure in attaining it) is obvious, even to a young child. In addition, the task takes place in the home and with parents, and there is evidence that self-regulation occurs earlier in natural and familiar settings than in artificial, unfamiliar ones (Istomina, 1977). This naturalism of the hide-and-seek task helped us avoid some of the common problems associated with testing children between 1 and 3 years of age. A frequent problem is that one is often not really sure whether the child completely understands the task. The extensive pretraining provided by their parents ensures us that our subjects clearly understand the task before being observed. Also, the children typically enjoy the hide-and-seek game enormously, so they are moti-

vated to participate fully. This is critical, because getting young children to *want* to do whatever it is you want them to do is one of the most difficult aspects of working with them.

We have now completed three studies involving 41 subjects between 18 and 30 months of age.[1] The children participated in a total of four to eight trials of the basic hide-and-seek task for one or two observation days. Except for the first two trials in Study I, the delay intervals were either three or five minutes. (Notice that these are exceptionally long intervals for use with this age group. As stated before, the standard delayed response studies with toddlers have used intervals of less than 30 seconds.)

In all three studies the children's baseline performance was excellent. They went directly (with no errors of any kind) to the hidden toy from 71 to 84% of the trials. For purposes of comparison the subjects in each study were divided into older (25-30 months, mean age = approximately 27 months) and younger (18-24 months, mean age = approximately 20 months) groups. The older children generally did somewhat better (with between 83 and 96% errorless retrievals) than the younger ones (58 to 71% correct).[2]

Although the three- and five-minute intervals we used were much longer than any in the developmental literature, they did not appear to give our subjects much difficulty. In order to examine their performance at much longer intervals, we recruited most of the mothers of subjects in Study I to serve as surrogate experimenters. Each mother made five observations of her own child in the hide-and-seek game—two with 30-minute intervals, two at 60 minutes, and one overnight. They were cautioned to put the toy somewhere the child would not happen upon it by chance. Since the mothers had been given extensive instructions about how to conduct the game with their children, and since we had observed all of them playing with the children, we were fairly confident of their ability to make objective and accurate observations for us. However, as a partial check on their data, one of the regular experimenters was present for one of the 30- or 60-minute observations for each child.

The children did surprisingly well at these longer intervals. They found their toy (with no errors) 88% of the time after a 30-minute wait, and 69% after an hour. After the overnight interval, they scored 77% errorless retrievals. (Several children, after the overnight hiding, retrieved their toy before their parents got up in the morning. One long-suffering mother informed us that her child woke her at 5 A.M. wanting to go downstairs and get Big Bird.) On the occasions we formally observed, the children *always* found their toy, so it seems reasonable to assume that the mothers' reports were not exaggerated.

Most of the children were also given a more complex task on later observation days in Study I. The same basic procedure was followed, except that on each trial three toys were hidden, each one in a different place. After an interval of either three or five minutes, the child was instructed which of the three toys to retrieve (with each serial position during hiding tested equally often). The child was then encouraged to find the other two toys as well. This multiple hiding procedure might be expected to produce a great deal of interference, since each trial involved three different toys hidden in three different locations, and sometimes a location was used more than once over trials. However, performance was again surprisingly good. On 67% of the trials the subjects retrieved the specific toy requested. Overall, they found 70% of the hidden toys, with a mean of 2.1 toys found per trial. These figures were closely replicated in a similar task in Study II.

The data reported so far argue forcefully that if freed from the artificial constraints and demands of standard laboratory tasks, very young children may be willing to demonstrate more of their cognitive competence than they have heretofore done. Given that our young subjects did so well in the standard hide-and-seek task, it seemed reasonable to think that variations in it might elicit some simple forms of the self-regulatory skills in which we are interested. In fact, we believe that in Studies II and III we have evidence showing the appearance of one such skill, intelligent self-correction, during the age period between 18 and 30 months.

A major goal of these two experiments was to examine what can be considered a rudimentary form of metamemory: we wanted to assess how confident our subjects were of their own memory. Only a few studies have examined metamemory in children as young as three. Wellman (1977) investigated 3- to 5-year-olds' knowledge of the effect of various task variables on memory difficulty, and Wellman, Ritter, & Flavell (1975) observed the use of primitive precursors of deliberate memory strategies by 3-year-olds but not 2-year-olds. No form of metamemory has to date been noted for children under three.

An extremely simple form of metamemory would be the assessment of how well or how certainly one knows something. Since our subjects' performance was generally so high, one would expect that they would be quite confident that they remembered correctly, even if they were incapable of verbalizing that confidence. A standard way of assessing certainty in preverbal infants and young children is to present a surprise trial (Charlesworth, 1969; Gelman, 1972),

where the experimenter does something to disconfirm the subject's expectations. The degree of surprise shown is used as an index of how strong the expectation was.

Each subject received two surprise trials on which the toy was hidden as usual, but was surreptitiously moved by the experimenter while the child was out of the room on some pretext. The surprise trials were embedded (as Trials 2 and 5) in a series of six or seven standard hide-and-seek trials (i.e., ones in which the toy was not moved). The surprise trials were administered on a separate day following the standard hide-and-seek testing described earlier.

In Study II two observers independently recorded and coded the subjects' behavior upon looking for and not finding the toy where it had been hidden. To be conservative, we have included only behaviors noted by both observers on the surprise trials. In Study III, the subjects were videotaped while participating in the game in their homes, so data from that study have been scored from the tapes. The figures that follow reflect the combined data from the two studies.

The experimenters' subjective impressions were that the children were very surprised indeed not to find their toy on the surprise trials. Several behaviors indicative of surprise were coded and analyzed (including verbalizations and negative emotional reactions), and they substantiate the experimenters' impressions. In this paper we will discuss in detail one of our surprise measures—the patterns of searching other locations after failing to find the toy in the correct place.

We should first mention that in general, the children almost never searched a location that had not been used previously, either on that day of testing or on a previous day. This was true for both age groups, and for both surprise trials and those trials on which subjects happened to make errors. Thus, the children had some general recollection of the set of hiding locations used.

The older and younger groups displayed different patterns of searching after failing to find their toy on surprise trials. The older children generally behaved in an intelligent fashion, much as an older child or an adult would do. After looking in the correct location and not finding the toy, they usually (on 88% of the surprise trials) searched somewhere else for it, and on the majority of the trials (76%) their searches fell into one or more of the following categories: (1) an adjacent location—if the toy had been hidden under one couch cushion, they might look under the next cushion; (2) a nearby or related location—if the toy had been put in a chair, they might look under or behind the chair; (3) an analogous location—if the toy had been hidden under a pillow at one end of the couch, they might look under the pillow at the other end of the couch; and (4) on the second surprise trial only, they sometimes looked in the place to which the experimenter had moved the toy on the first surprise trial.

The younger children were much less likely to conduct additional searches after failing to find their toy. On slightly over half the surprise trials (54%), they did not look in any other location after searching the correct one. They would often wander around in the middle of the room or stand near their mothers, apparently at a loss for what to do next. Some of the younger subjects returned to the correct location and searched there again, sometimes repeatedly. On only 26% of the surprise trials did the younger children search in the kind of related areas favored by the older subjects. They were just as likely, when they searched somewhere, to go to a place where the toy had been hidden on an earlier trial (especially the immediately preceding one). This tendency to search a prior location is reminiscent of the Stage IV error in object permanence (Harris, 1975) and the perseverative errors frequently observed for toddlers in memory and problem solving tasks (Webb, Massar, & Nadolny, 1972).

The older children's tendency to search additional locations on surprise trials reveals a form of certainty of memory in that they concentrated their searching in areas that were nearby or logically related to the correct location. They looked in places where the toy might reasonably be. They seemed to allow for the possibility that they misremembered some detail ("maybe it's under this cushion instead of that one") or that some fairly plausible event intervened ("maybe the toy fell out of the chair"). One subject verbalized exactly this: he looked in the desk drawer in which his toy had been hidden, said "Did Mickey Mouse fall out?", and then proceeded to search behind the desk. The children were also alert to the possibility that the experimenter was tricking them a second time.

To summarize, both the younger and older children seem certain of their memory for the correct location, but they differ in their ability to re-evaluate the situation after failing to find the toy and in their flexibility in initiating alternative measures. The younger children most often do nothing at all. When they do, they are as likely to simply go to a prior hiding place as to search in a related location. The older children are more flexible and logical in their attempt to deal with the disconfirmation of their expectations. They are able to reflect on the situation and consider where the toy *must* be, given it is not where they remembered. To account for its absence, they appear to consider plausible physical or mental explanations: something happened to the toy, or some detail of their memory must be faulty.

These examples of logical searching on the part of the older children (and a few of the younger ones) represent the exercise of a self-regulatory skill—thoughtful correction of errors. When the children fail to find the toy, they can only assume that they are in error (at least on the first surprise trial). They then try to correct that supposed error by thinking about where the toy is most likely to be. They proceed to conduct the same sort of organized, logical search that an adult might do. If you remembered that you had left your car keys on top of the kitchen counter but then couldn't find them, you would probably look for them behind the cookie jar on the counter and on the floor around the counter.

In conclusion, these very young children performed very competently in our basic hide-and-seek game, which they completely understood and thoroughly enjoyed playing. Even when the game was modified to be presumably more difficult, with multiple hidings and delay intervals extended to as long as an hour, they maintained an excellent level of performance. Furthermore, they showed what is probably the earliest evidence yet observed of self-regulation by the logical search procedures they employed on the surprise trials. The competent and sophisticated behavior of our young subjects suggests that if tasks are made more comprehensible and meaningful to young children, they will be more enthusiastic research participants and provide us with more valid data.

Footnotes

[1]The number of subjects and their mean ages in the three studies were as follows: Study I—17 Subjects, mean age = 23 months (Older = 27 months, Younger = 20 months); Study II—12 Subjects, mean age = 24 months (Older = 27 months, Younger = 22 months); Study III—12 Subjects, mean age = 24 months (Older = 28 months, Younger = 21 months).

[2]The complete data on errorless retrievals in the three studies were as follows: Study I—76% correct overall (Older = 85%, Younger = 67%), Study II—84% correct overall (Older = 96%, Younger = 71%); Study III—71% correct overall (Older = 83%, Younger = 58%).

References

Babska, Z. The formation of the conception of identity of visual characteristics of objects seen successively. In P. H. Mussen (Ed.), European research in cognitive development. *Monographs of the Society for Research in Child Development*, 1965, *30*(2, Serial No. 100), 112–124.

Brown, A. L. Knowing when, where, and how to remember: A problem of metacognition. In R. Glaser (Ed.), *Advances in instructional psychology*. Hillsdale, N.J.: Erlbaum, 1978.

Brown, A. L., & DeLoache, J. S. Skills, plans, and self-regulation. In R. Siegler (Ed.), *Children's thinking: What develops*. Hillsdale, N.J.: Erlbaum, 1978.

Charlesworth, W. R. Surprise and cognitive development. In D. Elkind & J. H. Flavell (Eds.), *Studies in cognitive development: Essays in honor of Jean Piaget*. New York: Oxford University Press, 1969.

Daehler, M., Bukatko, D., Benson, K., & Myers, N. The effects of size and color cues on the delayed response of very young children. *Bulletin of the Psychonomic Society*, 1976, *7*, 65–68.

Flavell, J. H. Metacognitive development. In J. M. Scandura & C. J. Brainerd (Eds.), *Structural-process theories of complex human behavior*. Leyden, The Netherlands: Sijthoff, 1978.

Gelman, R. Logical capacity of very young children: Number invariance rules. *Child Development*, 1972, *43*, 75–90.

Harris, P. L. Development of search and object permanence during infancy. *Psychological Bulletin*, 1975, *82*, 332–344.

Horn, H. A. & Myers, N. A. Memory for location and picture cues at ages two and three. *Child Development*, 1978, *49*, 845–856.

Hunter, W. S. The delayed reaction in a child. *Psychological Review*, 1917, *24*, 74–87.

Istomina, Z. M. The development of voluntary memory in preschool-age children. In M. Cole (Ed.), *Soviet developmental psychology: An anthology*. White Plains, N.Y.: Sharpe, 1977.

Loughlin, K. A., & Daehler, M. A. The effects of distraction and added perceptual cues on the delayed reaction of very young children. *Child Development*, 1973, *44*, 384–388.

Myers, N., & Ratner, H. H. Memory of very young children in delayed response tasks. In J. Sidowski (Ed.), *Cognition, conditioning, and methodology: Contemporary issues in experimental psychology*. Hillsdale, N.J.: Erlbaum, in press.

Myers, N.A., & Perlmutter, M. Memory in the years from two to five. In P.A. Ornstein (Ed.), *Memory development in children*. Hillsdale, N.J.: Erlbaum, 1978.

Shatz, M. The relationship between cognitive processes and the development of communication skills. In B. Keasey (Ed.), *Nebraska Symposium on Motivation*. Lincoln: University of Nebraska Press, 1978.

Webb, R. A., Massar, B., & Nadolny, T. Information and strategy in the young child's search for hidden objects. *Child Development*, 1972, *43*, 91–104.

Wellman, M. Preschoolers' understanding of memory-relevant variables. *Child Development*, 1977, *48*, 1720–1723.

Wellman, H. M., Ritter, R., & Flavell, J. H. Deliberate memory behavior in the delayed reactions of very young children. *Developmental Psychology*, 1975, *11*, 780–787.

19

Emotional Development in the Preschool Child

MICHAEL LEWIS

It has long been believed that infants are born with a small repertoire of basic emotions, such as anger, surprise, disgust, and perhaps fear and sadness. Within a few years, the repertoire of emotions has increased to include disappointment, embarrassment and many others. The study of how the basic repertoire of emotions develops in children is a relatively recent but fast-growing area of study among developmental psychologists. In the following article, Michael Lewis summarizes current themes in the study of socioemotional development, paying particular attention to the role of cognition in the development and organization of emotionality.

This article explores children's emotional development in the first three years of life. The discussion is divided into three parts: (1) the role of emotion in children's lives; (2) the development of emotions over the first three years of life; and (3) individual differences in emotion or emotionality.

ROLE OF EMOTIONS

Darwin viewed emotion as part of the biological apparatus of humans.[1] He saw emotions as a set of action patterns that enable children to behave in specific ways. For example, anger is not only a set of expressions but includes vocal growling and gross motor patterns, which enable the child to try to overcome a frustrating event. Darwin and those after him elaborated a system of scoring facial expression using the neuromusculature of the face.[2-4] This coding system allows developmental investigators to map out emotion.

Although clinicians recognize the importance of children's motor, sensory, and cognitive development, relatively little attention has been paid to children's emotional life. This is surprising because children's emotions play such a central role, both for the parent and the clinician. Consider, for example, a child who looks at an object, decreases his or her activity level, and smiles. On one hand we consider this an accurate marker for central nervous system integrity; that is, the child who is able to attend for long periods is not at risk for subsequent attentional disorders. The same behaviors that index attention also index the emotion of interest. Thus, from a clinical point of view, interest (an emotion) has important implications.

Many other examples of our use of emotions to mark children's ability can be found. Surprise is an emotion that has an important function in assessing development. A child who shows surprise when something unusual occurs has knowledge about the environment. In a series of studies, children as young as 6 months of age were placed in the company of different people.[5,6] We observed that when the infants were placed in the presence of children, the infants smiled and moved toward them. When the infants were placed in the presence of an adult, they showed some wariness (itself an emotion). When the children were placed in the presence of a midget (a small adult) they showed surprise.[6] This emotional response is used as a marker of cognitive ability, as surprise can be interpreted to mean that the infant understands that the midget is an unusual social stimuli. Thus, by 6 months of age the normal infant has already learned something about people.

Emotional behavior as a clinical tool is important. Testing for language acquisition begins with items related to hearing. When testing for hearing loss, children's emotional behavior is assessed. For example, one item in the test asks, "When the infant hears a human voice and sees a human face does it brighten?" This brightening response has to do with changes in emotional expression. The knowledge of children's emotional development aids in the assessment of children's abilities and provides a basis for understanding the normal and dysfunctional development of the young child.

From parents' point of view, the emotional behavior of the child is the first signal parents have to indicate that they are acting appropriately. It is important for the mother to know that the care of a crying child results in the child's smiling. She interprets this signal as an indication that she has solved her child's distress. Careful analysis reveals, therefore, that the emotional life of a child plays a significant role in the ability of adults to determine the child's internal state.

DEVELOPMENT OF EMOTIONS

Emotional differentiation moves from the general to the specific (Figure 1).[7] The first emotions that

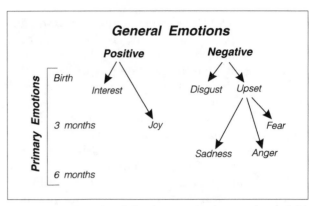

FIGURE 1 Emotional development in the preschool child.

emerge are the most general; they are characterized as positive or negative emotions. This division between a positive and negative emotion soon undergoes differentiation. Joy and interest become differentiated within the positive side, and fear, sadness, anger, and disgust within the negative side. These emotions are called the primary emotions and all emerge within the first 6 months of life.

In terms of the positive emotions, interest appears present at birth. Joy shows a developmental path. Smiling, at least in the first few months of life, is related to a reflex action, in particular the reduction of tension. Smiling as a reflex has less to do with environmental conditions than with simple physiologic changes. At approximately 2 to 3 months of life, smiling as an emotion emerges (joy appears). The smiling response now becomes tied to social events associated with happy situations. For example, at this time children start to smile at facial stimuli, the presence of soothing sounds, and human-like faces. The smiling response becomes further differentiated over the next 6 to 8 months. Smiling becomes increasingly related to external events of a social nature. By 8 months children no longer smile in response to just any social stimulus, the smiles are now restricted to familiar people and events.[8]

Interest is evident at the beginning of life. Children show interest in response to changes in stimulus intensity and complexity. The interest response grows over the first 6 to 8 months of life but, even in the earliest period, interest expressions are tied to autonomic nervous system responses associated with taking in and processing information.[9]

The early negative emotions are also undifferentiated at birth. General upset (characterized by crying and fretting behavior) is the most prevalent, although the disgust emotion appears soon after birth. Disgust is associated with the expelling of noxious tastes and smells and appears early in the child's life, certainly sometime during the first month. This response is quite different from the general upset or distress response, which is related to any uncomfortable or painful stimulus event.

The three negative emotions—sadness, fear, and anger—appear to differentiate themselves from the general upset emotion. Fear occurs early, although it may be seen as a reflex-like response to certain events, such as falling or loud noises.[10] By 6 months, loss of control evokes fear.[11] Sadness also does not appear to emerge before the third or fourth month of life. Sadness occurs to the loss of social interaction. Anger has still another pattern related to specific cognitive abilities. The anger response is evolutionarily programmed as an attempt to overcome an obstacle. Prior to 4 months the child is unable to understand the relationship between the cause of a frustration and the response needed to overcome it. For this reason, prior to 4 months frustration does not produce anger, but general distress. At about 4 months and older, frustration produces anger. For example, a 2-month-old when physically restrained by an experimenter will show general distress. However, by 4 to 6 months when this constraint is applied the child shows anger. In addition to anger, the infant is able to focus attention on the source of frustration. This integration of cognition with emotion to produce anger is only one of the examples of the interface between emotion and cognition.[12]

By the middle of the first year of life, the undifferentiated emotions that existed at birth have become differentiated. By this time *joy* is seen under two conditions: when the child comes in contact with a significant social other, such as the caretaker, mother, father, or other family members; and when the child is able to demonstrate mastery over particular events. *Interest* is observed when the child is confronted with novel events or events that require elaborated attention to be understood. *Fear,* wariness, or suspicion is often observed in situations that involve violation of expectation or being introduced to strange and unusual people. *Sadness* is observed over the loss of the mother or significant other, either if the mother moves away from the child or terminates an interaction. *Anger* emerges in frustrating situations; for example, when the child is unable to reach for something it wishes to obtain. *Disgust* appears early, particularly around noxious tastes and smells.

Secondary emotions emerge after the primary emotions, typically after the first 18 months of life. These emotions are sometimes called *self-conscious emotions,* for their emergence is dependent on the development of a particular important cognitive capacity: self-awareness. Self-awareness or self-consciousness is the human capacity reflected in statements such as "I am," "I am hungry," or "I know you know I am hungry." At about this time the child develops personal pronouns such as "me" or " mine, " and the child seems to know it has a specific location in time and space.[13] We often recognize this cognitive milestone as the "terrible twos." It is at this time that the child demonstrates a "will" of its own; parental directions are ignored and the child follows its own desires rather than parental direction.

This cognitive milestone allows for the development of the self-conscious emotions. This large class of emotions requires a self-system, in particular self-awareness.[14] Consider the emotions of embarrassment, empathy, guilt, shame, and pride. They all require a self-system. Exposure of the self, produced by public attention being drawn to the self, elicits embarrassment.[15] Empathy requires that the young child place itself in the role of the other.[16] However, for emotions such as shame, pride, and guilt to be felt the child must not only be self-aware, but a standard of behavior against which the self can evaluate its own action must be understood. Shame and guilt are elicited when the standard of behavior is not attained; the child evaluates its own behavior and finds it lacking. In the case of pride, the child evaluates itself against the standard and finds that its behavior exceeds the standard. All of these emotions require that the child has a self-system capable of referring to itself, a self-referential concept called *consciousness.*

Figure 2 describes the general developmental model this article presents.[17] In stage 1 the primary emotional states appear. In stage 2, self-consciousness appears. This is the last phase of the self-system, which has been developing during the first two years of life.[18] The appearance and consolidation of this cognitive skill—consciousness—provides the underpinning of all the secondary emotions.

The first class of self-conscious or secondary emotions to appear includes embarrassment, empathy, and perhaps envy; these emerge during the last half of the second year of life. In addition to developing self-consciousness, the child is learning about other aspects of its social world, including how and when to express emotions as well as particular rules of conduct. The development of these standards is a life-long process that begins as the child's cognitive representation of social reality emerges.

Because of this cognitive support, a second class of self-conscious emotions—self-conscious evaluative emotions—becomes possible: emotions such as guilt, shame, and pride. Whereas the first class of self-

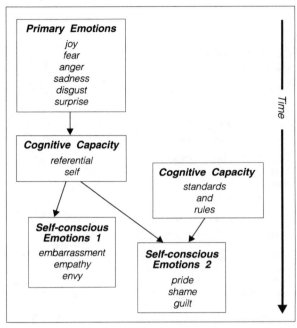

FIGURE 2 Model for the development of emotions.

conscious emotions appears by 18 to 24 months, the self-conscious evaluative emotions appear later because more cognitive capacity is required. This second class of self-conscious emotions emerges sometime after the second half of the third year of life.

The development of these primary and secondary emotions takes place in the first three years of life. The process begins with the undifferentiated emotions of pleasure and pain. Reorganization and differentiation ultimately lead to the complex emotions that are species specific. Their emergence involves the socialization of standards and rules, the cognitive capacities to recognize the nature of environmental stimuli, and the development of self-consciousness. Failure in the emergence of any of these capacities results in distortion of the developmental process. Thus, failures of self-consciousness in autistic children result in their inability to develop the self-conscious evaluative emotions.

INDIVIDUAL DIFFERENCES

The progression of the normal sequence of emotional development is dependent on a complex set of variables. Individual differences in rate of development as well as in intensity of expression are observed by parents and clinicians. Differences in individual rates of emotional development are dependent on the child's cognitive capacities. In terms of anger for example (one of the primary emotions), children who are able to acquire an understanding of the means to achieve a particular goal are more likely to express this emotion earlier than children who have not obtained this cognitive milestone. Likewise children who have not attained a mental age of 15 or 18 months are unlikely to develop self-consciousness.[18]

The rate at which this cognitive capacity is acquired affects all the emotions associated with it. Down's syndrome children who have not attained a mental age of 15 to 18 months do not show self-consciousness and therefore lack self-conscious emotions.[18] Autistic children also show a delay in self-consciousness and, therefore, a delay in secondary emotion development. Individual differences in the parent-child relationship may also affect emotional development.[19, 20] How parents help regulate their child's expressive behavior can lead to differential emotions.

Individual differences in the intensity of emotional expression also have been studied under the general category of temperament, a topic first introduced and made popular by Thomas and Chess[21] and by Carey.[22] Individual differences in temperament appear to be stable over the first few months of life.[23] Temperament relates to three aspects of a child's emotional response to stimulation: (1) level of threshold, (2) ease of dampening the response once it occurs, and (3) patterns of habituation to repeated exposure.[24] Individual differences in temperament are important for both parents and clinicians. Temperament acts on the parent-child interaction.[25] A child with a difficult temperament is most likely to cause parent-child interactive problems, as the parent is unable to soothe the child. Parents of these children are more likely to appear at the pediatrician's office for help. In general, differences in children's emotionality are related to particular features of temperament and are best understood in that context.

CONCLUSION

Emotional development in the young child has received relatively little attention in both the psychological and pediatric literature; in part, because the focus has been on sensory, motor, and cognitive development. Nevertheless, the emotional life of a child is important. A child's emotions are an evolving developmental system progressing from an undifferentiated to a highly differentiated state. This system interacts with other domains of competence and bears upon the child's social life.

References

1. Darwin C: *The Expressions of Emotions in Man and Animals.* Chicago, University of Chicago Press, 1872.

2. Tomkins SS: *Affect, Imagery, Consciousness*, Vol. 2: The Negative Affects. New York, Springer, 1963.

3. Ekman P, Friessen WV: *The Facial Action Coding System (FACS),* Palo Alto, CA. Consulting Psychologists Press, 1978.

4. Izard, CE. *The Face of Emotion.* New York, Appleton, 1971.

5. Lewis M, Brooks J: Self, other, and fear: Infant's reactions to people, in Lewis M, Rosenblum L (eds): *The Origins of Fear: The Origins of Behavior*, ed 2, New York, John Wiley & Sons, 1974.

6. Brooks J, Lewis M: Infants' responses to strangers: Midget, adult and child. *Child Dev* 1976; 47:323–332.

7. Bridges KMB: Emotional development in early infancy. *Child Dev* 1932; 3:324–334.

8. Wolff PH: Observations on early development of smiling, in Foss BM (ed): *Determinants of Infant Behavior.* New York, John Wiley & Sons, 1963, vol. 2.

9. Berk WK, Berg KM: Psychophysiological development in infancy: State, sensory function and attention, in Osofsky JD (ed): *Handbook of Infant Development.* New York, John Wiley & Sons, 1979.

10. Watson JB, Rayner R: Conditioned emotional reactions. *J Exp. Psychol* 1920; 3:1–14.

11. Gunnar MR: Control, warning signals and distress in infancy. *Developmental Psychology* 1980; 16:281–289

12. Stenberg C, Campos J, Emde R: The facial expression of anger in seven-month-old infants. *Child Dev* 1983; 54:178–184.

13. Lewis M: Origins of self knowledge and individual differences in early self recognition, in Greenwald AG, Suls J (eds): *Psychological Perspective on the Self*, ed 3, Hillsdale, NJ, L. Erlbaum Associates, 1986; pp 55–78.

14. Lewis M, Sullivan MW, Stanger C, et al: Self development and self-conscious emotions. *Child Dev* 1989, 60:146–156.

15. Buss AH: *Self Consciousness and Social Anxiety.* San Francisco, W. H. Freeman, 1980.

16. Hoffman ML: Altruistic behavior and the parent-child relationship, *J.Pers Soc Psychol* 1975; 31:937–943(a).

17. Lewis M: Thinking and feeling—The elephant's tail, in Maher CA, Schwebel M, Fagley NS, (eds): *Psychological Perspective on the Self*, ed 3, Hillsdale, NJ, L. Erlbaum Associates, in press.

18. Lewis M, Brooks-Gunn J: *Social Cognition and the Acquisition of Self.* New York, Plenum Press, 1979.

19. Brooks-Gunn J, Lewis M: Affective exchanges between normal and handicapped infants and their mothers, in Field T, Fogel A (eds): *Emotion and Early Interaction.* Hillsdale, NJ, L. Erlbaum Associates, 1982, pp. 161–188.

20. Field T, Fogel A (eds): *Emotion and Interaction: Normal and High Risk Infants.* Hillsdale, NJ, L. Erlbaum Associates, 1976.

21. Thomas A, Chess S: *Temperament and Development.* New York, Bruner-Mazel, 1977.

22. Carey WB: Clinical applications of infant temperament. *J Pediatr* 1972; 81:823–828.

23. Worobey J, Lewis M: Individual differences in the reactivity of young infants. *Dev Psychol*, in press.

24. Lewis M: The development of attention and perception in the infant and young child, in Cruickshank WM, Hallahan DP (eds): *Perceptual and Learning Disabilities in Children*, ed 2, Syracuse, NY, University Press, 1975.

25. Crockenberg SB: Infant irritability, mother responsiveness and social support, influence on the security of infant-mother attachment. *Child Dev* 1981; 52:857–865.

20

Boys and Girls: Superheroes in the Doll Corner

VIVIAN GUSSIN PALEY

Regardless of where a person lives in the world, it matters a great deal in development whether that person is a male or female. Questions about the psychological dimensions of gender have preoccupied psychologists for generations. What is the source of the observed gender-related patterns? Why does gender matter so much in shaping human psychological processes? What features of human cultural life promote or impede the development of patterns of thought, feeling, and behavior associated with maleness and femaleness? One of the best sources of evidence in grappling with this issue is the behavior of young children. By observing young children, especially in the preschool and early school age years when many aspects of culturally stereotypic gender-related behavior emerge, we may gain insight into how gender-related behaviors are developed and maintained. This passage from a book by Vivian Gussin Paley describes an episode from a preschool classroom. This episode captures some of the gender differences that appear in the early years and illustrates the power of naturalistic observation in teaching us about this vital but elusive process of human development.

With the door closed I am more permissive, yet the room is only a little noisier. The boys are noticeably more disruptive for a while—apparently waiting for me to quiet them—before they settle into their usual routines. Unquestionably I have been monitoring their behavior too much; they look my way when it becomes noisy. The girls are more confident that I won't interfere with their play. Several children continue to ask about the closed door:

Reprinted with permission from the author and University of Chicago Press from V. G. Paley, 1984, *Boys and Girls: Superheroes in the Doll Corner*, Chicago: University of Chicago Press, 79–87.

TEACHER: I close it when the room is noisy.

CHARLOTTE: Because of the boys.

TEACHER: Sometimes the girls. Remember when you were running back and forth to the ladder? That was when I first closed the door, so you could finish your police story.

ANDREW: Did you close it for Star Wars?

TEACHER: I'm sure I did.

PAUL: And for shooting?

TEACHER: I still don't like shooting in the classroom.

PAUL: How 'bout if it's quiet like this? P-a-h, p-a-h.

TEACHER: It's better if you do it outside.

JONATHAN: But we can't bring out things.

TEACHER: That's the rule for everyone in the playground. Children run fast outside. If you're holding something and you fall, you could get hurt.

ANDREW: We could hold something in the room because we don't run fast?

Andrew has touched on an inconsistency in my logic. Shooting is always safer indoors and just for the reasons he suggests. As there is less running, the boys have more self-control.

TEDDY: What if you walk? Then could you shoot?

FRANKLIN: Use light sabers. They don't make noise. Wh-sh-sh.

JEREMY: No! Laser beams. That kills you really quietly.

The room is still; the last idea brings a reflective pause. The subject, they think, is running and noise, not images of violence.

TEACHER: It isn't just the noise, you know. Shooting is all about killing people. It looks wrong in a classroom.

Even as I speak, I realize my distinctions are shaky. Is there a difference between "Pretend our parents are dead" and "Pretend I'm killing you"? The children know it is all magical play. The same magic destroys and resurrects, creates an orphan or a mother—the Green Slime. The ability to imagine something is the magic; putting it into action is the play; playing it out is the safe way to discharge the idea.

After the discussion, Andrew turns to Paul:
"Pretend this is bee land."
"No, pretend it's bat land."

"I'm the vampire."
"Pretend there's an explosion."
"Pretend the volcano is exploding."
"Pretend we're vampires and we got melted and we can't breathe."
Exciting images fill their heads during the discussion, and the boys can hardly wait for me to stop talking. They move around each other in a dreamy ballet, shooting at vague targets, murmuring little cries:
"I'm the vampire. You're Batman."
"You're a monster. I'm the Green Slime."
"I'm the Hulk. Pretend I killed you."
"No, you be the Green Slime. Pretend you killed my brother."
Now a chase begins that lasts about thirty seconds. Andrew zigzags between tables and chairs, waving a gun made of interlocking plastic squares. No one watches the boys except Jonathan, who calls out, "Can I play? I'm Luke!" Receiving no answer, he runs after them. "Who's the boss? I'm Luke!"
"We're not playing that. Anyway, you need a weapon."
"Okay. I'll be right back."
Andrew and Paul stop to watch a dice game, periodically taking aim at children crossing the room. "P-ing! Gotcha!" slips out as naturally as the constant appearance of gunshaped objects in their hands.
Few of these boys have toy guns at home. In our community, social pressure weighs heavily against guns. Superhero paraphernalia is purchased but not guns. It is a prohibition, however, that has no effect on play. Even in nursery school, the boys pick up any loose item and shoot. When confronted with the "no-guns" rule, they insist they are holding a walkie-talkie. The euphemism is accepted and the children learn how to negotiate with the teacher. By kindergarten they are masters of guile.
"This isn't a gun," Andrew tells me even before I ask.
"It looks like a gun and sounds like a gun," I say.
"It's an invention."
"What does it do?"
"It X-rays people."
There is a new activity in the room: The children go out into the hall, knock on the door, and re-enter.
"What's going on?" I ask, annoyed. "The door keeps opening and closing."
"I heard a noise in the hall," Paul says.
"I think someone is calling me," Charlotte reports.
"Let's just leave the door open, then," I suggest. It is clear that the children do not like the closed door. Besides, I find that I want to know who is passing by in the hall.

Franklin remembers my reason for closing the door. "Do like you done before. Tell the bad guys to sit down to color."

Franklin's common-sense approach reminds me that there are no short cuts or gimmicks to logical classroom procedure. If Cinderella is acceptable but cops and robbers is not, I should be able to explain why—to myself and to the children.

What are these sensible rules I admire so much, and how does cops and robbers compare with Cinderella when it comes to following them?

The first rule says that a player or group of players may not disturb other players. This rule is hard for the boys, since the whole point of cops and robbers is to intrude and steal something, preferably in the doll corner. However, having watched the girls play strangers and police for three consecutive days, I can no longer accept at face value their complaints against the boys.

The girls could be more accommodating to the robbers were it not for the fact that the girls do not share space and materials—rule 2—as well as the boys. For instance, they do not wish to share any part of the doll corner when they are playing there. They refuse to allow the boys to steal dishes and food or to turn the doll corner into a hideout. Yet, when the girls build a house in the block area, they automatically take all the food, dishes, clothing, and bedding with them and insist that the boys share the blocks. Boys forfeit teacher support because they label their actions as "stealing." Were they to say instead that the girls were not "sharing," the teacher might come to their aid. But, of course, without "stealing," it is not cops and robbers.

A third rule concerns excessive noise and careless running, a problem for both Cinderella and the robber. High heels, crying babies, and runaway pets are as disruptive as the omnipresent bad guy; running is the same whether the runner is Cinderella or Luke Skywalker. Boys do, of course, run more—much more. However, they run more whether or not they are playing cops and robbers. Jonathan gets up and runs around the table every time he gets a king in checkers. I asked him once why he did it and he answered, "That's what you have to do when you get a king."

There is a final rule, applicable only to boys; no grabbing, pushing, punching, or wrestling. They are more likely to break this rule, however, when they line up, walk down the hall, get ready for lunch, or come to the circle—those in-between times when controls are least dependable.

Perhaps, then, instead of steering robbers and superheroes out of the classroom, I ought to help them improve their style. After all, stealing and shooting are stage business, not necessarily more in opposition

to the rules of good play than the selfish behavior of the stepsisters who won't let Cinderella attend the ball.

Teddy is no longer a doll-corner resident; he is now a guest or an intruder there. As a guest, he responds to invitations—usually to be the father. All the boys, even Andrew, will agree to a brief stint as father if they are alone when asked.

The girls understand what turns a guest into an intruder: The magic number is 3. If one boy is summoned into the doll corner, he is likely to cooperate; two, in certain combinations, might still be manageable; three, never. Three boys form a superhero clique and disrupt play. The doll corner is easy to understand, for there is but a single drama to enter, as either protagonist, antagonist, or supporting player.

By contrast, the many unconnected activities in the block area must share the same space and materials, each unit continually readjusting its boundary lines to accommodate the others. A half hour of constructive play in the blocks requires one or more of three conditions: socially mature players, a plot strong enough to make role-playing more important than covetousness, or the presence of leaders with good building skills.

Believing that Franklin would do admirably well in all categories, I urge him to leave the art table and apply his talents to the block area. At both the art table and the wood-bench, he is the model of maturity and aplomb. He performs his self-appointed tasks with such meticulous care that others watch and copy him. His intense concentration on clearly defined goals entices more boys into "work" projects than all my curriculum ideas combined.

Much to our surprise—the children's and the teacher's—Franklin has the opposite effect in the blocks. There he is dictatorial and intolerant; his sense of perfection rules out any notion of group participation. Anything less than total control is an impossible compromise for him to make.

He has this control in art construction and, to some extent, in superhero play, where his detailed knowledge of movie and television scripts usually gives him the final word. In the block area, however, nothing matters so much as a democratic spirit, and Franklin does not yet have this. He ends every session in tears, and block play is in danger of being ruined.

I station myself outside the blocks to see if I can identify the point at which things go wrong. Ordinarily, by the time I arrive on the scene it is too late; everyone is angry and no one can explain what happened.

Jonathan is already building when Franklin runs in, asking, "Can I play?"

"Sure you can," Jonathan replies. "I'm building a house."

"Wait! Don't put it there!" Franklin grabs a block from Jonathan's hand and begins to rearrange the design of the building. "This is the way. Do it like this," he states firmly.

Jonathan tentatively lays a block on its side.

"No! Leave it alone! You're spoiling it!" Franklin yells again. "Just watch me, can't you?" He does not look at Jonathan as he speaks; he concentrates only on the blocks.

Teddy, who has been observing the scene, puts a large arc at one corner of the building. He keeps his eyes on Franklin, testing to see what his friend will do.

"No, Teddy! That ain't the way it has to be!" Franklin removes the arc. "Lemme have that! Just put it away. We don't need it high over there! It don't look nice that way!"

I can no longer remain silent. "Franklin, you're very bossy, You won't let the boys do anything."

He looks surprised. "Yeah they can. I said they can."

"But you grab their blocks the minute they have an idea."

"I'm helping them. They want me to."

"Do you boys want him to?"

Jonathan and Teddy look at each other, but before they can speak, Franklin is crying and pulling Andrew's arm down: "Leave that be, Andrew! It's mine!"

Andrew looks as if he's going to hit Franklin with the block. With me there, all he can do is scream, "He wasn't even using it! He's a stupid pig!"

"I am so using that! It goes right here. I need all those. I was here first. You're spoiling my whole thing." Franklin tearfully runs back and forth to the block shelf, filling his arms with blocks as, one by one, the boys leave.

"Franklin, will you please look around," I say. "Everyone is gone."

"Why?"

"Why? Because you're being very selfish, that's why."

Franklin looks worried. "I ain't selfish. I ain't said they hasta go."

"You're just like the fox in 'The Blue Seed.' Remember that story? He wouldn't let anyone share his house, so the house blew up?"

Franklin nods, squinting to take the measure of his building. "Can I finish my house now?"

The moral of the fox story is of no concern to Franklin. The offending party never sees the connection to his own behavior in a morality tale.

"Franklin, wait. Let me tell you what I mean about the fox," I say, determined to press my point.

"Remember when you were the fox? You had to yell at everyone, 'Get out! You can't live in my house!' That's just what you're doing in the blocks now."

"I ain't doin' that! Soonest I'm done, everyone can come in. First I gotta get it just right."

"But they want to help."

"I said they can help. They wasn't listening."

My approach is useless. He can picture every detail of the ten-story house he plans to erect but nothing of the scene he just had with Jonathan and Teddy. Yet Franklin knows how to listen to dialog and stay in character. When he is the father in the doll corner, he does not act like Darth Vader. Nor does he make the little pig sound like the Big Bad Wolf. Artistic integrity is important to Franklin. What he needs is an objective view of the scene he just played. The analogy of the selfish fox is too abstract and direct criticism too personal. The story-plays come to mind: "Once there was a boy named Franklin. . . . "

The class is seated around the circle. I have asked Jonathan and Teddy to bring a pile of blocks into the center.

"This is a guessing game," I tell everyone. "I'm acting out a true story. You have to guess who I'm pretending to be. You two boys pretend you're building something, and I'm going to keep interrupting."

Self-consciously the boys begin to build a road. I rush over and grab several blocks. "No, not that way! Give it here! Do it this way!" I shout.

The boys are momentarily startled but continue to lay out blocks. I yell at them again: "Stop doing it that way! You're spoiling my road!"

By now everyone is looking at Franklin, who is pounding his thigh and laughing. "That's me! You're pretending you're me! Is that really me?"

"It really is you. I watched you in the blocks. That's the way you sounded. Remember?"

"I do remember! You did that part just right."

When I confronted Franklin earlier in the block area, he denied everything. The moment I make him the star in his own story, he is flattered and attentive. He is not offended and therefore does not need to defend himself. My view of objectivity is the opposite of the children's. They can become objective only when events are seen as make-believe.

"Okay, Franklin, now you come into the circle. I pretended to be you. Now you pretend to be a boy named Franklin who lets people use their own ideas in the blocks. 'Once upon a time there was a boy named Franklin who knew how to play in the blocks.'"

Franklin saunters out, grinning broadly, and starts to build a tower. I motion to Jonathan and Teddy to help him.

"That's good, boys," he says, nodding agreeably.

"You sure got good ideas. Go on, get some more good ideas."

Everyone claps. It is a grand performance, reminiscent of the finale to "The Blue Seed." The fox is gone; long live Virtue!

Lasting changes in behavior are not so easily achieved, of course. But, in kindergarten, appearances are important. Suddenly I recognize the difference between telling a child he must share and saying instead, "Pretend you are a boy who knows how to share." The first method announces that a child has done something wrong. "Pretend" disarms and enchants; it suggests heroic possibilities for making changes, just as in the fairy tales.

21

Birth Order, Age Gap, Gender, and Large Families

JUDY DUNN

Growing up with or without siblings can make a huge difference in one's life. How children spend their time, the relationship they develop with their parents, and the family resources that are available to them across the years are all directly affected by the presence or absence of other children in the family. In the following chapter, excerpted from her book *Sisters and Brothers*, Judy Dunn discusses how such factors as the size of the family, the sequencing of the children's births, and the gender of the children may influence the process of sibling and family relations.

In some families the children constantly fight with and irritate each other; in others they offer each other affectionate support that is moving to see. Compare the following comments by two mothers, each with a three-year-old and a fourteen-month-old:

> He gets into everything of hers. It drives her crazy. They fight such a lot—screaming quarrels. And it's not just screaming—they really go at each other.

> He [the younger sibling] loves being with her and her friends . . . He trails after Laura . . . they play in the sand a lot . . . making pies. She

organizes it and whisks away things that are dangerous and gives him something else. They go upstairs and bounce on the bed. Then he'll lie there while she sings to him and reads books to him. And he'll go off in a trance with his hankie [comfort object]. The important thing is they're becoming games that they'll play together. He'll start something by laughing and running toward some toy, turning round to see if she's following. He'll go upstairs and race into the bedroom and shriek, and she joins him.

What could explain these differences in how the children get along together and in what they feel for each other? Books for parents frequently imply that jealousy and quarrels between siblings are largely the fault of the parents. But it is also often said that a child's birth order, the age difference between her and her siblings, and their sexes all influence how well they get along. How much evidence is there to support these views?

FIRSTBORNS AND LATERBORNS

It certainly seems plausible that firstborn children should feel more hostility toward siblings than is felt by laterborns. The firstborn children are, after all, the ones who have been displaced. As one mother said of her two-year-old's feelings about her younger brother, the secondborn: "She was queen of the world. . . no wonder she minds and seems to resent him." And as a precocious four-year-old put it quite explicitly to his mother on the birth of his brother: "Why have you ruined my life?"

It will not surprise any parent who has more than one child to hear that firstborn children tend to express more ambivalence and hostility about their siblings than vice versa. Both firstborns and laterborns believe that the parents align themselves with the younger siblings rather than with the eldest. This remark by a-five-year-old girl in Helen Koch's study is not an unusual comment from a firstborn child: "Yes, I would like to change places with my baby brother. Then I could yell my head off and my mommy would take care of nobody but me."

Firstborns are less likely to say that they prefer to play with their siblings than with other children. They are seen by both first- and laterborn children as bossier and more dominant than laterborn children, and studies of five- and six-year-olds show that their power tactics in dealing with their siblings tend to differ. Here is a first-born boy describing how he gets his sister to do what he wants: "I told her to get out of my room. And I kept shouting at her and she wouldn't go. And I started hitting her, and she still wouldn't go. So I just picked her up and threw her out."

According to a study of siblings' power tactics by Brian Sutton-Smith, firstborn children attack, use status more, and bribe. Laterborns tend to sulk, pout, plead, cry, and appeal to parents for help. The more polite techniques of explaining, taking turns, and asking are perceived by most children as the strategies only of firstborn girls. Sutton-Smith and his colleagues offer the following interpretation of these differences. The status tactics, bossiness, and dominance of firstborns are typical of the powerful members of any social system—those who are larger and have greater ability; the appeals of laterborn children to their parents for support are typical of the weak members of social groups and are encouraged by the greater indulgence and comfort offered to laterborn children by their parents. The tendency of firstborn girls to explain and give reasons reflects the way in which the girls model themselves on their mother, with whom (it is assumed) they have closer relations than do the secondborn girls. Sutton-Smith's account sounds plausible, but it is probably far too simple, and we simply don't have evidence to support some of the arguments. For instance, there's no good evidence that secondborn girls have a less close relationship with their mothers than firstborn girls.

During their early years, laterborn children are frequently more directly aggressive than their older siblings, according to the interview studies. They may not be any more hostile—but they do express their aggression very directly and physically. Firstborns tend to be more verbally aggressive, criticizing and disparaging their younger brothers and sisters mercilessly. This "childseye" view of firstborns as bossy and dominant is supported by experiments in which siblings are asked to play or carry out tasks together. Seven- and eight-year-old firstborns are in these situations more likely to dominate, to praise, and to teach their siblings than vice versa.

Of course, it is not always the eldest who is the dominating one. When competition or domination comes from a younger sibling it can be particularly devastating for the older sibling. Here are the comments of a Nottingham mother, in the Newsons' study, describing her seven-year-old's reaction to a very bright younger sibling:

> He's not afraid of anything physical—his fears are attached to not being able to understand. He's said once or twice something that rather horrified me: "I don't understand; there must be something the matter with me." This is the business of his relationship with Katherine [aged five-and-a-half]. It's just simply that James is not so intelligent as Katherine, and he's cottoning on to this fact very quickly, and I don't know what to do about it. [Has he been conscious of it for some time?] I think so—since Katherine started going to school and came home with reports of what she'd done, what book they were reading. His initial response was "You couldn't have done"; and she said "We did" and proceeded to show him. He was absolutely devastated.

What is so poignant here is the awareness of both child and mother that this is not a problem that will disappear, but one that will have to be lived with, for a lifetime.

Firstborn children from large families, especially, often have a particular role as disciplinarians, caregivers, and leaders. The study by James Bossard and Eleanor Boll includes many vivid examples of the responsibilities placed on firstborn children. The adults recalling these experiences felt that they had important consequences for their development. These are the recollections of the oldest daughter in a family with nine children:

> For as long as I can remember, I helped with the dishes and then was given the responsibility of other tasks as I grew older. . . There were eleven of us eating every day. Life seemed to be one eternity of dirty dishes after another. . . It was my job to make the chocolate cupcakes for five school lunches that were carried, pack the lunches, and set the table for breakfast. I was in disgrace with my brothers and sisters if I failed to get up in time to make the cakes and I was too poor a baker to make them good enough to be edible the next day. I learned to bake bread and to iron before I was in high school. I have a faint recollection of washing, feeding, and caring for the baby when I was seven years old. I was "mother's little helper" in so many ways for years. Mother certainly needed me. When we went visiting, it was my responsibility to see that the younger children did no damage or did not get hurt. My household tasks gradually increased until I was doing more of it than mother was. Her last baby was born at the beginning of Christmas vacation of my last year in high school, and I was put into complete charge, including mother and the baby. Being the oldest girl in a large family meant that many of my own desires remained unfulfilled.

And here are the comments of the oldest of eight:

> From the time that I was five, I can remember taking care of the children. I used to lie on my mother's bed and push my little brother back and forth in his carriage until he fell asleep. Mother kept on having babies. Many problems beset us. By the time I was in third grade, I was always helping mother while the others played with the neighboring children. This made me old beyond my years, serious, and quite responsible for all that went on in the household. . . Each Saturday, my mother went in to the city six miles away for the groceries and stayed for the day. In the evening she and dad visited

friends and came home at about midnight. From age fifteen to nineteen, I found myself responsible for seeing that the housework was finished, cooking lunch and dinner for the children, and caring for the newest baby. At night, I bathed six children, washed their heads, and tucked them into bed. Saturday nights continued like this until I rebelled. I wanted to have time for dates like other girls had.

In contrast, if we look at siblings in smaller families and take account of individual differences in affection, warmth, aggression, and conflict between siblings, it is surprising how unimportant birth order per se turns out to be. Although power and dominance between siblings are closely related to birth order, these other features of the relationship are *not*. The closeness, intimacy, support, and affection a child feels for his brother or sister is not clearly linked to whether he is a firstborn or laterborn, and it is these features of the sibling relationship that are likely to be of particular importance in the influence of siblings upon one another.

The interview and questionnaire studies of children between the ages of six and twelve suggest that the sex and personality of the firstborn child are more likely to influence the secondborn than vice versa, at least in terms of gender role, interests, and activities. Firstborns, in comparison, are more likely to be influenced by their parents. In families with very young children, laterborn children imitate their older siblings far more than their older siblings imitate them—at least after the first year of life. It is likely, then, that laterborn children model themselves on their older siblings much more than the other way around. But we should not jump to the simple conclusion that whereas laterborns are influenced by their older siblings, firstborns are not influenced by their younger siblings. This is an oversimplification that masks a very complex pattern of mutual influences between siblings and their parents. However, the first child's feelings about the sibling, and his or her behavior toward the sibling in the first years, are of quite special significance as an influence on the way their relationship develops. In one Cambridge study, firstborn children were observed over many months, beginning before the birth of the second child. In families where the first child showed marked affectionate interest in the newborn, the younger child was likely to be particularly friendly to the elder one year later. In these families the firstborns, by their initial interest in the baby sibling, set up a relationship of affection that continued for several years to be very friendly. The differences in the firstborn children's response to the birth were, then, very important in accounting for differences in the relationship which developed between the first two children in the family.

What could explain these differences between firstborn children in their behavior toward the new sibling? One key factor was the nature of the parents' relationship with the first child before and immediately after the sibling's birth. Another was the firstborn's temperament. Children who were anxious, "withdrawing" individuals before the birth usually had little interest in or affection for the new sibling. However, the age gap between the children was *not* related to their interest in the baby. Among the most affectionately interested were some very young children—only eighteen to nineteen months old—and some three- to four-year-olds. And there were no differences between the boys and girls in the sample in how interested they were in the baby sibling.

Follow-up observations of these siblings showed just how important the first child's feelings about the baby were as an influence on their developing relationship. However, it is also likely that differences in the secondborn's behavior toward the first, even in the first eighteen months of life, affect how the older child feels about the second. Michael Lamb studied pairs of siblings when the secondborn was twelve months old, and then again six months later. He found that the behavior of the first children toward their siblings was predicted *better* by the behavior of the secondborn infants at the first visits than it was by the firstborn children's own behavior at those first visits. The more sociable the babies were at the first session, the more sociable their older siblings were toward them at the second visit.

We just do not know, with children older than preschoolers, whether differences in the behavior of the first- and laterborn siblings influence the way in which the relationship between the children develops. This is partly because most studies have looked only at the sex of and age gap between the siblings and not at the individual differences in affection or hostility. It has been assumed that it is the sex of the children and the age gap between them that are of the most significance. But do boys and girls differ in the way they behave toward their siblings?

SEX DIFFERENCES

It's often said that a boy growing up with several sisters will be "feminine" in his interests and a girl with brothers will be a "tomboy." In the 1950s and 1960s several psychologists looked at the relation between the extent to which children and adolescents were "masculine" or "feminine" in their interests, oc-

cupations, and games, and whether they had grown up with brothers or sisters. The results were complicated, and in some ways contradictory. Laterborn children with an older sibling of the same sex did tend to be the most "stereotypically sex typed." A secondborn boy with an older brother was likely to be very "masculine" in his interests, and girls with older sisters were likely to be particularly "feminine" in theirs.

But the picture is not a simple or a consistent one. For instance, some studies suggested that boys with *two* older sisters showed *less* interest in "feminine" games and occupations, and interacted less with girls in the classroom than did boys with brothers. In explaining these results it was argued that whereas some children "identified" with their siblings, imitated them, and modeled their behavior on them, other children reacted against their siblings by developing very different interests and opposing styles.

It is clear that we could "explain" any particular combination of personalities and interests among the brothers and sisters within a family by referring to these two processes of "identification" and its opposite, "deidentification." Certainly we cannot predict with any confidence the personality or behavior of a child simply on the basis of knowing his or her sex and the sex of the other children in the family.

There are no clear or consistent differences between very young boys and girls in the ways that they behave toward their siblings. For instance, it is sometimes assumed that older sisters are more likely to be nurturant—"little mothers"—than older brothers. But in the cross-cultural studies of John and Beatrice Whiting, in which sibling caregiving by both girls and boys was very common, no sex differences were found in the behavior of the older siblings, although the younger siblings asked for help, comfort, and security from older sisters more frequently than from older brothers.

Sisters are sometimes said to be better teachers than brothers. Boys and girls do have rather different teaching styles. Rob Stewart asked a number of children between the ages of four and five to teach their two-year-old siblings how to use a camera. The best teachers were boys with younger brothers, especially those who were relatively advanced in understanding how to take the perspective of another person. In contrast, Victor Cicirelli found that sisters were more effective teachers than brothers: they used a deductive method more than boys, they offered help more often, and their help was more likely to be accepted.

However, children with an older brother appeared to do better when working alone than children with an older sister. Cicirelli suggests that this may be because a child with an older brother is stimulated by the competition and rivalry of an older brother to learn more than from an older sister, but that in a more formal teaching situation the younger child will learn more from an older sister because she expects to give help and the younger expects to receive it.

In contrast to these results from experimental studies, no sex differences in frequency of teaching by older siblings, or in acceptance of teaching by their younger siblings, have yet been found in studies of children at home.

The same contradictions appear when same-sex and different-sex pairs are compared. With very young siblings there is often a greater amount of friendly, helpful interaction and imitation in same-sex pairs. But in Rob Stewart's study, in which sibling pairs were left alone in a laboratory playroom, the older siblings who were *least* likely to comfort and support their younger siblings were brothers in two-boy families. And among older children, aggression and dominance were more often evident in same-sex pairs: mothers of six-year-olds in the Cambridge studies reported more jealousy in same sex pairs, for instance. Yet in Helen Koch's extensive interviews, more six-year-olds with same-sex siblings than with different-sex siblings said that they would prefer to play with their sibling rather than with a friend, and more said that they liked looking after their sibling. It was very rare, among Koch's six-year-olds, for a child who had a same-sex sibling to say that he or she would be happier without the sibling.

Why should there be such contradictory results? The different cultural backgrounds of the families studied, the different ages of the children, differences in the way in which the children were studied—all of these factors could contribute to the inconsistencies. But clearly, sex differences in either younger or older siblings *cannot* be linked in a simple or powerfully predictive way to differences in the way the children relate to one another.

AGE DIFFERENCES

People often hold even stronger views on the importance of the age gap between siblings than on the significance of the sex of siblings. Some parents attribute the intimacy and friendliness of their children to their closeness in age. The close matching of interest and effectiveness as partners in play of children who are only two years apart is held to be of real importance. Other parents believe that their children get along well because there is a large age gap between them. The older child, they argue, does not feel so displaced, and since he's more secure is more friendly toward the younger. Both accounts sound plausible, and we can find evidence to support either point of view. With preschool-aged children, the age

gap does not appear to be nearly as important as physicians and psychiatrists have supposed. The ways in which firstborns react to the arrival of a sibling do differ with age: fifteen-month-olds tend to react by becoming miserable and clinging, whereas three to four-year-olds often become very difficult and demanding. But the age difference does not appear to affect the positive interest in the new baby, or the incidence of marked disturbance, or the quality of the relationship between the two children as they grow up. Play, companionship, and affection are as frequently shown whether the age gap is four years or only eleven months; so too are aggression, hostility, and teasing.

The more "parent-like" behaviors of teaching and caregiving are more frequently shown by the older children in families in which there is a large age gap. But in many studies the larger the age gap between the children, the greater the age of the older child, and it is hardly surprising that with increasing age children are more effective teachers or caregivers.

With children aged six, seven, and eight, the story is rather different. Helen Koch found that if the gap between the children was between two and four years, all the effects she described—modeling, rivalry, competition—were heightened. With a larger age gap the children played less together, but the laterborns accepted teaching from their older siblings more often and more willingly. In general, the age gap between siblings seems to be more important with six- to eight-year-olds than it is with little children, but there are still many inconsistencies in the findings of different studies. For instance, one study compared seven- and eight-year-olds as they played with their siblings in a competitive game, and as they wrapped a very large box together. If the seven- and eight-year-olds had a sibling close in age (with only one to two years between them), they were more aggressive and less likely to be friendly than if the age gap was three to four years. In contrast, Helen Koch found that siblings who were more than two years apart in age had more competitive and stressful relationships. These contradictions show that we clearly should not draw simple conclusions about the significance (or the insignificance) of the age gap between sisters and brothers.

GROWING UP IN A LARGE FAMILY

Until now, I have talked about the relationship between brothers and sisters mostly in terms of *pairs* of siblings. How different is the experience of growing up with lots of brothers and sisters? The focus on two children families reflects both the kind of studies that have been done by psychologists and the typical families of Western Europe and the United States. The study of large families conducted by Bossard and Boll in the 1950s gives a different picture of family life. They interviewed and collected written life histories from over 150 people from families with more than six children. It was a retrospective study, drawing on people's recollections and reflections on their childhood experiences, rather than a direct study of the children themselves. It was also not a formal, systematic study. But the insights it gives us are interesting, and balance the picture of brothers and sisters given by studies of smaller families.

First, for many of the children in those large families there was an important closed world of play with their brothers and sisters: "We rarely had outside company and did not feel the need of it. We had good imaginations and played many games, which were joined in by two dogs and a cat. This life continued for some years, and, as far as we children were concerned, it was the closest thing to heaven." Some children felt that this closed family world limited their ability to relate to others. Most children, however, felt that living in a large family had very important and useful consequences: learning to share, to develop self control, and to show consideration for others were repeatedly mentioned. The following three quotations are typical of the views of people from large families:

> Living in a large family socializes a child to an appreciable extent . . . In general, living and being reared in a large family teaches one that life is not a "bed of roses" and that there are other people in the world all with "equal rights" to the pursuit of happiness in life . . . a child in a large family has brothers and sisters of contemporary age who understand him as a child and in the "give and take" of their everyday life each learns to control emotions, think in terms of "we" and not "me," "to live and let live," to look out for oneself and yet to consider the rights of others, and a host of similar terms all meaning to live as a real human being should and not as an animal.

I think that large family life teaches self-control and self-discipline. When you have three or four or more brothers and sisters who aggravate you in various ways at various times, you soon learn that it is not considered good conduct to grab, shake or strike your brothers and sisters. You learn to control those nasty anti-social acts, or carry their problems to the impartial courts of the law, I don't know. You learn to discipline yourself in many ways, and to govern your conduct along acceptable social ways . . . I think that being part of a large family establishes the desire to belong or to be needed. It makes you like to love and be loved; a large family does not tend to produce cold, aloof, withdrawn people. It teaches respect for private property, and consideration for each other. It produces the desire to help each other or to guide each other.

Yes, I do honestly believe that living in a large family does have its effect on socialization because consideration must be given to each other during the course of living together. A form of unity develops and with it a sense of attachment for each other. Though privacy is at a minimum, or rather impossible, one does gain somewhat of a group spirit which implies thinking through things together and arriving at decisions that are reasonably acceptable to all. I am convinced that a much more charitable consideration for "the other person" is engendered by a person who derives from a large family than one who is a product of a small family.

A second point is that siblings in large families often have special roles as disciplinarians of their younger siblings; this rarely happens in two-child or three-child families. Earlier I quoted the words of one firstborn who had to assume many responsibilities. How do younger siblings feel about the discipline meted out by their older siblings? The quotations show that in many ways sibling discipline can work very well, from the children's point of view. First, the siblings in the study did feel that they understood each other and each other's problems—often better than the parents. Second, they felt that they often had better judgment than the parents as to what should be considered misbehavior. According to them, this meant that discipline imposed by siblings was often more reasonable, and had more meaning, than discipline by parents. Third, and most important, they suggested that sibling discipline was more effective than adult discipline because the disapproval of siblings mattered so much more than the disapproval of adults. And as Bossard and Boll comment: "Siblings know what kinds of discipline are effective. They know that a sound spanking, while it may hurt for the time being, may have far less meaning than not being allowed to go fishing with the others. It may be argued here that children are often very cruel to each other, and this certainly is true. Perhaps the real reason for this is not what adults assume it to be, but because children are realists. They know what matters, and what hurts."

The security provided by siblings was stressed by a surprisingly large number of the people from large families—surprisingly, because according to conventional psychiatric wisdom, security for a child is based on the parent-child (and usually the mother-child) relationship. I have commented on the security that even preschool-aged and infant siblings apparently provide for each other. Here is a parallel emphasis on the security that siblings can provide much later in childhood.

Why should living with a large number of siblings lead to a sense of emotional security? Several reasons were given. One was that within the large family, dependability was highly appreciated, even fostered, in the face of the many hardships with which the family had to cope.

> We did feel a sense of security that must be lacking in small families, because we were required to work together and to the well-being of all of us. This feeling remains—even in our adult years.

> We have the philosophy that if we stick together we can get through any crisis. If we stand alone, it makes a hardship on the family . . . Fear with us was unknown, probably because we never stood completely alone.

> Emotionally there was strength in being a member of a large family. A crisis was met by everyone and to back up an individual there was a whole clan.

It was also stressed that within the group of siblings there was likely to be at least one person with whom a child could pair up, and who would provide support: "We always had at least one other family member to play with. In smaller families, if you are feuding with your only brother or sister, you would be quite lonely. One very seldom feuds with seven or eight other people, though, so in a large family there is always someone left to turn to for consolation and love."

The point that siblings *know* each other so well was believed by many to be the key to the emotional security provided by a large family. According to Bossard and Boll, some informants felt that their own siblings had a better understanding of the problems that younger children faced than did their parents. They not only realized when and why their young siblings felt insecure, but also helped them through such difficult situations.

> My oldest brother took my youngest brother to his first Scout meeting. I took him to his first day at school. When a child is faced with a new experience it must be a great comfort to know that someone is there who has been through it all before.

> Mother spanked my third brother. Sister cried as hard as if she had been spanked and as soon as Mother left the room, she ran to his side, put her arm around him, and said through her tears, "You'll be all right, don't cry."

> Three of us had mumps at the same time. We could console one another as we lay sick in bed.

> The boys down the street and my second brother would get into a fight. The minute my eldest brother and I discovered it we were also in it, beating the other kid up or helping our little brother to hold his own. Surely it is a good feeling for a child to know there are others to help fight his battles, whether he be right or wrong.

For some children in the study, the security of the relationship with the brothers and sisters was closely related to the problem that the children all faced together. Often the children helped each other through the difficulties of coping with an inadequate mother or father, or difficult social circumstances. And some siblings felt that their security together came from the very fact that there was no opportunity for emotional "coddling" of any of them by the parents, with the exception perhaps of the youngest.

The picture of a childhood spent with several brothers and sisters as one of security, strength, and a rich shared world of play is of course only a partial one. Rivalry and competition were described too. Often the large families split into factions and cliques, or shifting alliances against particular children or subgroups of children. But they stressed rivalry less than did individuals from smaller families. It could well be that this was because these informants were recalling their childhood experiences, and tended to remember the better moments rather than the irritations of living with so many siblings. The children who were interviewed while still living at home did in fact stress conflict and rivalry more than the other informants.

We have looked at the issue of why children differ so dramatically in the affection and hostility that they show toward their siblings, and specifically at the question of how the age gap, birth order, and gender of the siblings contribute to these differences. It is clear that if we want to explain the individual differences in how well brothers and sisters get along, and the ways in which they influence one another, we must move away from asking simply: Is it the age gap that matters? Is it the sex of the siblings that is crucial? We must realize first what a complicated equation we are dealing with when we ask what influences the relationship between the children in a family. Not only age and sex, but the personalities of the children, the size of the family, the social circumstances, and especially the children's relations with their parents must be taken into account. A great many factors affect the relationship between siblings. It is hardly surprising that we do not find simple clear connections between a child's position in the family, the sex of his siblings, and the way children get along or the way in which their personalities develop.

However, the studies of birth order and gender do help answer the questions raised by the book's first theme, which concerns the ways in which siblings influence one another's development. The sex and personality of the firstborn are, for instance, more likely to influence the laterborn children in a direct way than vice versa. How a first child feels about his or her sibling appears to influence the way in which their relationship develops from the earliest weeks. Firstborns are more likely to express ambivalence or hostility than laterborns. But the extent of intimacy and affection that a child feels and shows toward a sibling—which is probably of prime importance in *how* he or she influences the sibling—is not simply related to birth order, age gap, or gender.

We still know very little about the way in which the personalities of the individual children affect the quality of the relationship or vice versa. But it is clear that each child's relationship with the parents is closely implicated in many of the differences between siblings.

PART IV

Middle Childhood

22

On Asking Children Bizarre Questions

MARTIN HUGHES AND ROBERT GRIEVE

According to Jean Piaget, mental development occurs in a stage-like fashion in which qualitatively new and more adequate ways of understanding the world replace earlier understanding. His theory rested upon many assumptions, one of which was that each stage of cognitive development represents a structured whole. That is, a child's understanding at each stage is expected to be consistent across domains or problem types. However, researchers have challenged Piaget's ideas of cognitive development, and one of the most interesting challenges pertains to the stage of preoperational thinking. Preschool age children, who Piaget would classify as being in the preoperational stage of thinking, are unable to solve many of the logical problems that Piaget and his followers have posed to them. Piaget said that this is due to their tendency to focus (or center) on only one aspect of a problem and ignore other aspects. Piaget called this problem "centration." In the following article, Martin Hughes and Robert Grieve challenge Piaget's interpretion of this pattern. Basically, they argue that the form of questioning used in Piagetian tasks tells us less about preoperational thinking than about young children's efforts to make sense of what is being asked of them, no matter how bizarre.

When five-and seven-year old children were presented with questions intended to be bizarre (in the sense that their meaning required clarification, or that further information beyond that provided was required for an answer), the children almost invariably gave replies. The older children were more likely to do so by making sense of the questions through characteristics of the elements referred to,

Reprinted with permission from *First Language*, *1*, 1980, 149–160. Copyright 1980 by Alpha Academic, Publishers.

or through rules that might be expected to apply in the situations referred to; the younger children were more likely to make sense of the questions by importing additional context. Older children were also more likely to indicate their uncertainty about the questions by qualifying their responses in some way.

INTRODUCTION

In the study of cognitive and linguistic development it is a commonplace procedure to ask children questions. Yet it is remarkable how little we understand of this interrogative process.

What happens when we ask a child a question? While a full answer to this question is not available, the present paper reports novel information on one aspect of the process. Namely, when presented by an adult with a question, children will locate an answer for the adult's question *even if that question is conceptually ill-formed*.

Usually, of course, when adults ask children questions, these questions are intended to be perspicuous. Their meaning, at least to an adult, is intended to be clear, and the child's answer is frequently used to gauge his cognitive/linguistic understanding. However, it is becoming increasingly clear that the gap between questions as adults present them (intended questions), and questions as children respond to them (received questions), is wider than is often supposed (McGarrigle, Grieve & Hughes 1978).

But how wide is this gap? One way of considering this problem is to present to children questions intended to be bizarre: i.e. unanswerable as they stand. If children demur at attempting to answer such questions, this will indicate that children consider the conceptual well-formedness of what they are asked. But if children do not demur, and attempt to answer bizarre questions, then we will need to reconsider what we think is happening when we present children with questions in studies of their cognitive/linguistic development.

In what follows, we first describe what happens when bizarre questions were presented, in an informal way, to a number of children of different ages. We then describe a study where several bizarre questions were presented in a more systematic way to two groups of children, aged five and seven years.

INFORMAL OBSERVATIONS

If young children are presented with bizarre questions, such as: "One day there were two flies crawling up a wall. Which one got to the top first?", it might be expected that they will be bamboozled, or amused. But when five-year-old children were presented with this question, they replied. And their replies, for example: "The big one", were deadpan. (We owe this observation to G.P.T. Finn.) When we presented a different bizarre question to another child, Sally (6;8), we asked: "Is red wider than yellow?". "Yes", she replied. "Why?". "*Because yellow's thinner than red*". We then presented these two questions to Jenny (5;8). To the "flies" question she replied: "*The one on the left*". That bamboozled us, and we had to ask: "Why?". "*Because he's the biggest*". For the "red wider than yellow" question, she repeated it: "*Is red whiter than yellow?*" "No, not whiter, *wider*. Which is widest, red or yellow?", "*Red*". "Why?". "*Because it's got more colour*". "What about yellow and blue—which is the "widest one?". "*Blue*". "Why?". "*It's darker*".

To the "colour" questions, Jenny's responses seem based on saturation—the more highly saturated member of the pair is judged to be "wider" because it has "more colour", or is "darker", than the other. (And note that the responses do not seem a function of Jenny's initial mishearing of "wider" as "whiter", for then we would expect her choices to have been the opposite.) However responses to bizarre questions involving colour do not invariably involve appeal to their relative saturation. When Alison (6;9) was asked a different bizarre question: "Which is bigger, red or yellow?", she initially looked baffled, then looked round the room and said: "*Yellow*". When asked why, she pointed to two objects in the room and said: "*'Cos that red cushion there is smaller than that yellow curtain there*". A similar response was given by Sarah (5;4), who was asked the "red bigger than yellow" question out of doors, near a colourful boating pond. Again the child searched for and compared two differently sized objects of the specified colours.

When such bizarre questions were presented to Andrew (4;11) he replied to the "flies" question "...Which one got to the top first?" "*The first one*". "Why did he get to the top first?". "*Because he started first, silly*". To the "red wider than yellow" question he replied: "*Red*", but would give no justification other than "*just because*".

Fiona (7;2) gave a different response to the "red wider than yellow" question (the "flies" question was not presented). First she did the same as Jenny, mishearing "wider" as "whiter": "*Which is the whitest?*". "No, not whiter, WIDER. Which is the widest one?". (These "wider" questions were presented to Jenny and Fiona by the same adult, whose pronunciation of "wider" was probably indistinct. Note that both children spontaneously re-iterated the question, presumably to provide an opportunity for the adult to confirm that they had got the question right. It is of course not clear that they misheard the question. Possibly they did hear "wider", but supposed that "whiter" must have been intended, especially in a question involving colours, and where "wider" taken as "wider" is bizarre.) *"Oh, is red "wider" than yellow? What do you mean?"*. "Which is the widest, red or yellow?". *"I don't know what you mean. Do you mean when they are written down, is red or yellow longer on the page?"*.

These informal observations suggest that children do tend to provide answers to bizarre questions. However they justify or implicitly justify their responses in various ways. Sometimes they use linguistic knowledge (e.g., Sally utilizes her knowledge that "thinner" is opposite to "wider"); sometimes they utilize extralinguistic knowledge or knowledge of objects in the environment (big flies travel faster than flies that are not so big; or colours can be distinguished on the basis of their relative saturation; or a yellow object in the immediate environment is identified as being bigger than a red object); and sometimes an aspect of the language leads into an extralinguistic justification (e.g., Andrew's reply to "Which fly got to the top *first*" was "The *first* one" which ". . . started *first*"). Thus these children provide answers to these bizarre questions by importing various sorts of knowledge to the situation. While the oldest child does not conform to this pattern in one sense—she is the only child to make explicit that the meaning of the question is not immediately clear—in another sense she does, for having made explicit the obscurity in the meaning of the question, note how she immediately tries to establish one: "I don't know what you mean. Do you mean. . .".

To consider this phenomenon further, the following study was undertaken, where larger numbers of children were each asked several bizarre questions in less informal circumstances.

EXPERIMENT

Different types of bizarre questions were presented to groups of five- and seven-year-old children, in their usual school setting.

Subjects

A group of eight 5-year-olds (four male, four female; mean age 5;4 years, range 4;11–5;10), and a group of eight 7-year-olds (four male, four female; mean age 7;7 years, range 7;3–7;11) were studied. These children knew the adult experimenter, having worked with him on a different, unrelated experiment a week to ten days previously.

Materials

Four questions, each intended to be bizarre, were prepared: (1) *Is milk bigger than water?; (2) Is red heavier than yellow?; (3) One day there were two flies crawling up a wall. Which fly got to the top first?; (4) One day there were two people standing at a bus-stop. When the bus came along, who got on first?*.

These questions are intended to be bizarre in the sense that they do not permit direct answers. This is so for different reasons. (1) and (2) are intended to involve 'category mistakes', and a reasonable response might be to say: "I don't know what you mean", and request further clarification. The meaning of (3) and (4) on the other hand is perfectly clear, but a reasonable response might be to say: "I don't know", and request further information.

It is of course difficult to be certain that a question intended to be bizarre is received as such. For example, linguistic philosophers suggest it would be a category mistake to predicate time or place of number. But we have all heard both, not only predicated, but bellowed, of number—for example at boating lakes where small craft are rented by the hour: "Come in, Number Four, your time is up". Or, home decorators' manuals may describe certain combinations of colours as being "too heavy"; and we are familiar with red, orange and yellow being described as "warm colours", compared with "cold colours" such as blue and green. Further, (3) and (4) perhaps become more acceptable with slight modifications—e.g., "If several people were standing at a bus stop, when the bus came along which one would we expect to get on first?". The present questions are intended to be bizarre in the sense that they cannot be answered directly. As they stand, they require clarification of their meaning ((1) and (2)), or the provision of additional information ((3) and (4)), before they can be answered.

Procedure

Children were tested individually by the same experimenter. Adult and child sat at a table on which lay some papers, including a sheet on which the adult noted the child's responses, but there were no toys or pictures to be looked at. The adult simply said: "Listen, is milk bigger than water?", or whatever. The questions were always presented in the order: (1), (3), (2), (4). If the child failed to give a response, or said "Don't know", the question was repeated once. If the child gave a response without justifying it (e.g., "Is red heavier than yellow?". *"Yes"*), he was asked "Why?".

RESULTS

We wish to know whether children answered these bizarre questions; how they answered them; whether there were any differences between different types of question; and whether there were any differences between children of different ages. Before summarising on these points, we first describe the responses given.

(1) Is milk bigger than water?

Of the eight younger children, only one child failed to respond (he was the youngest, aged 4;11). Instead he grinned at this, and every other question, saying *"I don't know"*, or *"No idea"*, or *"Don't know, never tried it before"*. (This calls to mind Brendan Behan's story [Behan, 1963] about the new assistant in a Dublin bookshop who was asked if she liked Kipling. "How could I know", she replied, "when I never kippilled".) Of the remaining seven, one said they were the same, and the other six said: *"Yes"*. When asked why, most responses were either in terms of the origins of the liquids (e.g., water comes out of taps, and milk comes out of either cows or bottles), or in terms of their extension (e.g., there is more milk than water when you pour them into bottles). Only one child said that milk was bigger because it was "heavy".

All the older children gave a response. However there were two immediately apparent differences in the responses given. First, the older children were more likely to respond in terms of the characteristics of the liquids themselves—e.g., milk is bigger *"because it's got a colour"*, or *"'cos it's more creamier"*, or because *"milk is heavier"*, or *"because it's more thicker"*.

We will refer to this distinction in terms of the extent to which the children *import context* into their replies. While five of the younger children import context into their replies, talking about where the liquids originate, or what happens when they are poured into containers, only two of the older children do so. Rather than importing additional context, the older children are more likely to remain with the objects referred to in the question, commenting on inherent characteristics such as their colour, texture, or weight.

But the more obvious difference between the younger and older children is that the latter tend to qualify their responses in some way, using phrases such as "I think" (e.g., *"I think milk's bigger than water"*) or, more frequently, by replying with questions, which range from: *"Eh?"*, to *"Milk is heavier, isn't it?"*, or *"Is it because it's more thicker?"* or *"Milk, I think. 'Bigger' did you say?"*. Six of the older children gave what we will call "qualified responses" of this sort, but none of the younger children did so.

(2) Is red heavier than yellow?

Seven 5-year-olds gave replies as did all of the seven-year-olds. An interesting response in the younger group was initially obscure: "Is red heavier than yellow?". *"Yes"*. "Why?". *"Because there's much more red than yellow"*. "Why?". *"Because there's water in it"*. "There's water in what?". *"The paint"*. The explanation becomes clear from another child: *"Yellow is a little. Yellow's got a little plastic box and the red paint's got a big plastic box"*. In school, the children use powdered paint which is mixed with water in plastic containers. So if there is more red than yellow, red *is* heavier! (So much for intentions; and so much for category mistakes.)

Only one of the younger children responded in terms of the characteristics of the colours themselves, rather than the characteristics of the paints which may be mixed using these colours: *"Red's heavier than yellow."* (Why?) *"Yellow's not bright and red is"*. This sort of response was quite common in the older children: red is heavier *"Because it's darker"* (twice), or *"'Cos it's more darker"*, or because *"Red's a darker colour than yellow"* (twice).

So there is again a difference between the groups in the extent to which they import context: the older children tend not to, confining their justifications to a difference between the colours themselves (such as saturation), while the younger children do tend to import additional context, concerned with a situation such as mixing paints from such colours, and referring to attributes such as the size, weight and water content of the containers.

The consistency with which the children responded to this presented colour question in terms of saturation merits further inquiry. Possibly, saturation is a more important characteristic of colours than brightness or hue with young children (R. N. Campbell, personal communication). In the present study, the children's recourse to saturation in response to the presented colour question is certainly very consistent.

There is also a difference in the extent to which the groups qualify their responses, but the distinction is not so marked as in (1). One of the older children says: *"I think red's just as heavy as yellow"*, one says: *"Yes, I think so"*, and one is explicit in his question-as-answer: *"Red . . . Was it 'heavier'?"*.

The reduction in the extent to which the older children qualify their responses may be due to an order effect—recall that question (2) was in fact the third question presented, and the children may be learning that when their replies, initially given in a tentative manner, are accepted by the adult, there is no need to continue to qualify them.

(3) Which fly got to the top first?

All children answered this question, save the youngest child. Four of the 5-year-olds initially said they did not know, but then replied when the question was repeated.

Differences between the groups, in terms of imported context and qualification of response, are not now apparent. One of the younger children imported context, saying that the fly who reached the top first was: *"The first one. 'Cos that was the one leading the other one, taking the other one up"*. One of the older children did likewise, saying: *"The left one"*. (Why?) *"He flew up"*. (And the other one?) *"He crawled up"*.

Otherwise children from both groups replied in terms of the situation described in the question, and responses concerned characteristics of the fly who arrived first: *"The biggest one. Because he got the longest legs"*, or because *"He went more fastest"*, or because he was the one who *"thought of it first"*, or because *"He started first"*, or because he was *"the one that had been drinking milk. . . . Milk makes you stronger"*. (Note that (3) was presented just after (1)). Alternatively, responses concerned the relative location of the two flies; the one who got to the top first was: *"The one nearest the top"*, or the one who was *"nearly at the top"*. Thus appeal was mostly made to the fly's size, length of legs, or strength; to his speed; to his time of departure; or to his place of departure. Importing other factors into the situation was rare.

There was also no qualification of responses, in either group. The "I think it was the big one", or "Was it the big one?" types of response were not observed.

(4) Who got on (the bus) first?

The youngest child remained amused. All other children gave a response. As with (3), there was no qualification of responses.

Two of the younger children imported context, saying that the person who got on first was *"The one who was taking the other one"*, or *"The mummy (taking the child)"*, as did one of the older children, saying that the stronger person got on first because he had been drinking milk, and was stronger than the other one who had been drinking water. (Note this child's use of elements from a previous question, (1). Here, with question (4), the elements do not work well, for we have to conjure up a primaeval struggle at the bus-stop. But they do work well in her answer to the "flies" question (3), where the stronger one got to the top first. This phenomenon—importing as context elements from previous questions—may have occurred elsewhere, though not so clearly. For example,

to what extent do the judgements that red is heavier than yellow because of relative water content in the paints arise from the fact that the children have previously been dealing with water in question (1): where it comes from, how it is used (poured into containers), and so on?).

However there was a difference between the two groups, related to their appeal to a rule which might be expected to hold in the circumstances of the question—namely, rules of queuing. For example, the person who got on first was *"The one there first"*, or *"The one who got there first. The one at the front of the line"*; or this rule was overridden by another concerning good manners: *"The lady"* (Why?) *"Because ladies should go first before men"*. This sort of response was utilized by only two of the younger children, but by five of the older ones. The remainder replied in terms of the person who was *"Nearest the bus"*, or who *"Saw the bus come first"*.

These observations are summarised in Table 1, which shows the number of responses given to the four questions, whether these responses were qualified, and whether context was imported to the situation in the ways indicated above (the maximum entry in any cell is 8).

DISCUSSION

The results are reasonably clear. When presented with questions intended to be bizarre—questions which cannot be answered directly without clarification of meaning (CM questions) or provision of further information (PI questions)—young children almost invariably provide replies. Younger five-year-old children frequently do so by importing additional context to the situation, especially with CM questions, but older seven-year-old children are less likely to do this, tending instead to remain with characteristics of the elements referred to in the questions, or appealing to rules which might be expected to apply in the situation to which the question refers. The other major difference between the groups is that while the older children frequently qualify their responses in some way, indicating uncertainty, the younger children never do so. The result of this paper, that young children answer questions even if these questions are bizarre, confirms the previously mentioned finding of G.P.T. Finn. It is also akin to results detectable in the data of other studies.

For example, in a study of three- and four-year-olds' understanding of prepositions, Wales (1974) presented children with a toy doll and a toy house, and instructed them to: "Put the doll *in/on/at* the house". To estimate whether the children had any

TABLE 1

Responses to Bizarre Questions

Question		Five-year-olds			Seven-year-olds		
		Responses given	Responses qualified	Context imported	Responses given	Responses qualified	Context imported
(1) Milk		7	0	5	8	6	2
(2) Red		7	0	4	8	3	1
	Total	14	0	9	16	9	3
(3) Flies		7	0	1	8	0	1
(4) Bus-stop		7	0	2	8	0	1
	Total	14	0	3	16	0	2
	Totals	28	0	12	32	9	5

response bias, Wales also presented this instruction without any preposition, namely: "Put the doll the house". The great majority of children made a response to this anomalous instruction, failures to respond being very infrequent (4%). It can also be noted that this result is not restricted to children from but one culture, speaking but one language—Wales's study was conducted with Scottish children speaking English, Indian children speaking Tamil, and Bornean children speaking Lun-Bawang. Children also respond to sentences made anomalous, not through deletion of an element as in Wales's study, but through substitution of a nonsense-term for a term in the language. Carey (1978) asked three- and four-year-old children to play a game where they had to give a puppet *more,* or *less,* tea to drink. When she asked the children to give the puppet *tiv* tea to drink, over half the children responded to this anomalous request without comment—some children gave additional tea, some reduced the amount of tea, some stirred the tea, some pretended to drink the tea themselves, and so forth. Children will also respond to questions where the meaning of terms may be to them obscure. In a study of young children's understanding of homonyms (words with the same sound, but different meanings, as in *key* and *quay* Campbell and Bowe (1977) found that three- and four-year-olds would attempt to interpret such homonyms, even though their interpretations might be grotesque in relation to the rest of the context. For example, if the children knew the *key,* but not the *quay,* sense of the

homonym, the term might be interpreted in this way, even if the term's interpretation failed to fit the context. Thus the child might envisage someone visiting the seaside, going for a walk along a key, seeing a rubber boy floating in the water, and so on.

These observations on the data of other studies extend the present result. Young children not only provide answers to questions that are bizarre: they do the same for questions whose terms' intended meaning may be obscure (Campbell and Bowe, 1977), and for questions which are anomalous in various ways (Carey, 1978; Wales, 1974).

Why young children do this is not clear. It may be a characteristic of the exchange of discourse that, other things being equal (e.g., where conversational maxims such as those considered by Grice, 1975, may be supposed to apply), the participants at least try to afford each other's utterances meaning or at least suppose that each other's utterances are intended to have meaning. The task in discourse is thus not so much to *decide whether* the other's utterances have meaning, but to *identify what* his meanings are. This characteristic of human discourse may be fundamental, and can be observed in mothers' communicating with their infants long before the child is capable of understanding language, far less producing it (Bruner, 1974; Trevarthen, 1974).

But if we do not know why children provide answers for bizarre questions, the present paper indicates that this is what children usually do. That they do so, for the sort of bizarre questions presented here, either in terms of the information presented in the question, or by importing additional context into the situation, suggests that the child does assume that the questions are intended to have meaning, and that his task is to identify meaning in what has been said to him.

The observation that children seek to interpret questions that are bizarre seems at first sight an extraordinary finding. Yet we wonder whether it is as extraordinary as it appears. Perhaps making something of whatever information is presented to him, or that information supplemented by imported information, is what the child has to do most, if not all, of the time. Recall that he must be well used to such a task, for when he is younger and still acquiring the language, the meaning of much of what is said to him cannot be immediately transparent. We know that when language is still being acquired, the young child derives meaning not simply from aspects of the language itself, but also from his knowledge of the extralinguistic contexts to which the language refers—his knowledge of objects in the environment, how these customarily are, or should be, related, and so on (Grieve, Hoogenraad and Murray, 1977). We have suggested elsewhere that the young child's early comprehension of language should be viewed as a

process concerned with how, from the child's point of view, such elements of linguistic and extralinguistic context interact (Hoogenraad, Grieve, Baldwin and Campbell, 1978). What the present paper suggests is that later cognitive and linguistic development might well be viewed in a similar light. Thus presenting five- and seven-year-olds with bizarre questions may simply simulate what he has been used to at an earlier age; and his interpretation of these bizarre questions may simply represent the child's practice of a familiar, well-established skill.

Thus the child's propensity to answer questions, even if they are intended to be unanswerable, may not be as startling as might at first be supposed. Nevertheless, the fact that the child will attempt to locate an answer to whatever question he is presented with has significant implications for what we think is happening when we attempt to gauge the young child's cognitive/linguistic abilities by means of the question and answer process.

Psychologists and linguists—and all others who rely on questioning young children—can no longer treat the child as merely a passive recipient of questions and instructions, but must instead start to view the child as someone who is actively trying to make sense of the situation he is in—however bizarre it may seem.

References

Behan, B. *Hold your hour and have another* (Hutchinson, London, 1963)

Bruner, J. S. "From communication to language: a psychological perspective", *Cognition*, 3 (1974), 255–87

Campbell, R.N. and Bowe, T. "Functional asymmetry in early language understanding" in G. Drachman (Ed), *Salzburger Beitrage zur Linguistik III (Salzburg Papers in Linguistics Vol III)* (Tubingen, 1977)

Carey, S. "Less never means more" in R.N. Campbell and P.T. Smith (Eds), *Recent Advances in the Psychology of Language, Vol 1.: Language Development and Mother-Child Interaction* (London, Plenum Press, 1978)

Grice, H. P. "Logic and conversation" in P. Cole and J. Morgan (Eds), *Synta and Semantics, Vol III Speech Acts* (New York, Academic Press, 1975)

Grieve, R., Hoogenraad, R. and Murray, D. "The young

child's use of lexis and syntax in understanding locative instructions", *Cognition*, 5 (1977), 235–50

Hoogenraad, R., Grieve, R., Baldwin, P. and Campbell, R. N. "Comprehension as an interactive process" in R. N. Campbell and P. T. Smith (Eds), *Recent Advances in the Psychology of Language, Vol I: Language Development and Mother-Child Interaction* (London, Plenum Press, 1978)

McGarrigle, T., Grieve, R. and Hughes, M. "Interpreting inclusion: a contribution to the study of the child's cognitive and linguistic development", *Journal of Experimental Child Psychology*, 26 (1978), 528–50

Trevarthen, C. "Conversations with a two-month old", *New Scientist*, 62 (1974), 230–5

Wales, R. J. "Children's sentences make sense of the world" in F. Bresson (Ed), *Les Problèmes Actuels en Psycholinguistique* (Paris, P.U.F., 1974)

23

Mind as a
Cultural Achievement:
Implications for IQ Testing

MICHAEL COLE

Of all the individual differences that distinguish one person from another, none has produced a stormier and more prolonged debate than the elusive quality called intelligence. During the entire twentieth century psychologists have sought ways to measure children's intelligence that would give a valid measure for individual children no matter what their family background or cultural origins, much in the same way that a thermometer measures temperature.

For better or for worse, this goal of creating a "culture free" test has eluded psychologists. In the following article, Michael Cole reviews the logic of how intelligence tests were initially constructed for use in French schools at the turn of the century. He then offers a thought experiment about how a rural African people might go about constructing an analogous test for their cultural circumstances. By taking seriously the way in which intellectual tasks are embedded in particular cultural and historical circumstances, Cole calls into question the entire notion of a culture free test of intelligence.

Reprinted with permission from The National Society for the Study of Education from E. Eisner (ed.), *Learning and Teaching the Ways of Knowing: Eighty-fourth Yearbook of the National Society for the Study of Education*, Chicago:National Society for the Study of Education, 1985, 218–249. Copyright 1985 by The National Society for the Study of Education.

This chapter is an expanded version of an article that appeared in the *Annual Report (1979–1980)* of the Research and Clinical Center for Child Development, Faculty of Education, Hokkaido University, Sapporo, Japan.

For almost as long as there have been IQ tests, there have been psychologists who believe that it is possible to construct "culture free" tests. The desire for such tests springs directly out of the purposes for which tests of general intellectual ability were constructed in the first place: to provide a valid, objective, and socially unbiased measure of individual ability. Our society, founded upon the principle that all men are created equal, has never lived easily with the recognition of enormous *de facto* social inequality. We need a rationale for such inequality and our traditions strongly bias us to seek the causes of inequality, in properties of the individual, not society. At the same time, we realize that social and economic inequality can be the causes of individual intellectual inequalities, as well as their consequences.

What would be more ideal, then, than a psychological test that could measure intellectual potential that is based equally on the experience of people from all cultures. Can't we find universals in human experience and construct a test on this basis? Some psychologists have claimed not only that such tests are possible in principle, but have been applied in practice.[1]

In this chapter I will argue that culture-free intelligence is a contradiction in terms. After working through a "thought experiment" to help clarify the issues, I will turn to some implications for teaching of the view that mental development is always a culturally organized process that can produce great heterogeneity in specific mental skills by the time children reach school. This heterogeneity can cause great difficulties for the classroom teacher. In the final section I will note some promising leads that teachers may use in dealing with culturally organized heterogeneity in their classrooms.

Having made these assertions, I want to provide the evidence upon which they are based. My own personal strategy for thinking about these matters is to think my way back in time into the nineteenth century, when such devices came into existence. I have found it helpful to study the conditions in science and society that allowed some scholars to believe it is possible to assess mind independent of culturally organized experience. To begin, I will review some of that history, emphasizing the logic of the enterprise. I am focusing on an *anthropological* perspective on testing, but it should become clear that anthropology and psychology have always been linked in shaping our understanding of the relation between experience and mind, even when this link is obscured by divergent methods and theories.

The several decades just preceding this century provide a useful starting point from which to trace theories of culture and cognitive development, because it was during this period that both anthropology and psychology took shape as disciplines. Before that time, say the 1860s, there was no distinctive body of methods for the study of the "humane sciences," nor had scholars with different theories been institutionally divided into separate disciplines the way they are today. Obvious differences in technological achievement between peoples living in different parts of the world were common knowledge. Theorizing about sources of these differences had produced rather general acceptance of the notion that it would be possible to study the history of humanity by a study of contemporary peoples at different "levels of progress." E. B. Tylor summarizes, in what he calls "mythic fashion," the general course of culture that most of his fellow scholars would have adhered to:

> We may fancy ourselves looking on Civilization, as in personal figure she traverses the world; we see her lingering or resting by the way, and often deviating into paths that bring her toiling back to where she had passed by long ago; but direct or devious, her path lies forward, and if now and then she tries a few backward steps, her walk soon falls into a helpless stumbling. It is not according to her nature, her feet were not made to plant uncertain steps behind her, for both in her forward view and in her onward gait she is of truly human type.[2]

Tylor's choice of imagery for "Civilization" nicely reveals another basic assumption which he and many of his colleagues made: there is no principled distinction between mind and society. The condition of culture among the various societies of mankind, Tylor tells us, reveals basic information about the laws of human thought. He even adopted the notion of a "mental culture," which he expected to be high or low depending upon the other conditions of culture with which it was associated.

Herbert Spencer, writing at about the same time, shared Tylor's belief in the fusion of mental and cultural phenomena. He also drew a very tight analogy between cultural development on the one hand and mental development on the other.

> During early stages of human progress, the circumstances under which wandering families and small aggregations of families live furnish experiences comparatively limited in their numbers and kinds; and consequently there can be no considerable exercise of faculties which take cognizance of the *general truths* displayed throughout many special truths.[3]

Spencer invites us to consider the most extreme case; suppose that only one experience were repeated over and over again, such that this single event comprised all of the person's experiences. In this case, as Spencer put it, "the power of representation is limited to reproduction of this experience" in the mind. There isn't anything else to think *about*! Next we can imagine that life consists of two experiences, thus allowing at least elementary comparison. Three experiences add to the elementary comparisons, and elementary generalizations that we make on the basis of our limited (three) experiences. We can keep adding experience to our hypothetical culture until we arrive at the rich variety of experiences that characterizes our lives. It follows from this line of reasoning that generalizations, the "general truths" attainable by people, will be more numerous and more powerful the greater one's experience. Since cultures provide experience, and some cultures (Spencer claimed) provide a greater diversity of experience than others, a neat bond between cultural progress and mental progress is cemented.

Although such evolutionary schemes seemed almost transparently obvious in the enthusiasm following publication of Darwin's *Origin of Species,* events toward the close of the nineteenth century proved that there could be a great deal of disagreement about the relation between culture and thought, despite the compelling story constructed by people like Tylor and Spencer. One set of disagreements arose when scholars started to examine more closely the data used to support conclusions about relations between cultures, especially claims for historical or evolutionary sequences. Quite a different set of arguments arose around conflicting claims about mental processes.

The seed of disagreements concerning cultural sequences can be found in Tylor's own work. The main criteria for judging the stage of a culture were the sophistication of industrial arts (including manufacturing techniques for metal tools, agricultural practices) and "the extent of scientific knowledge, the definitions of moral principles, the conditions of religious belief and ceremony, the degree of social and political organization, and so forth.[4] However, in Tylor's words, "If not only knowledge and art, but at the same time moral and political excellence, be taken into consideration" it becomes more difficult to scale societies from lower to higher stages of culture.

This latter theme in Tylor's work was taken up by Franz Boas, who submitted the cultural evolution position to a devastating critique at the close of the nineteenth century. On the basis of his own ethnographic work, Boas concluded that a great deal of the evidence apparently supportive of evolutionary schemes was so deeply flawed that no clear conclu-

sions ranking one culture above another could be accepted.[5] Boas did more than show the flaws in evolutionists' data and arguments concerning *culture*; he also delighted in showing that examples of "primitive mind" produced as part of this argument were based on misunderstandings.

Consider the following example from Boas's classic, *The Mind of Primitive Man,* which repeats evidence used by Spencer to make some generalizations about properties of primitive mind:

> In his description of the natives of the west coast of Vancouver Island, Sproat says, "The native mind, to an educated man, seems generally to be asleep. . . .On his attention being fully aroused, he often shows much quickness in reply and ingenuity in argument. But a short conversation wearies him, particularly if questions are asked that require efforts of thought or memory on his part. The mind of the savage then appears to rock to and fro out of mere weakness."[6]

Spencer's text goes on to cite a number of similar anecdotes corroborating this point. But Boas produces an anecdote of his own.

> I happen to know through personal contact the tribes mentioned by Sproat. The questions put by the traveller seem mostly trifling to the Indian, and he naturally soon tires of a conversation carried on in a foreign language, and one in which he finds nothing to interest him. As a matter of fact, the interest of these natives can easily be raised to a high pitch, and I have often been the one who was wearied out first. Neither does the management of their intricate system of exchange prove mental inertness in matters which concern them. Without mnemonic aids to speak of, they plan the systematic distribution of their property in such a manner as to increase their wealth and social position. These plans require great foresight and constant application.[7]

Thus, Boas tells us that the entire scheme was wrong. Cultures cannot be ranked using evolutionary age as a basis for comparison, and "mind" cannot be seen as rank in developmental age. (Boas also demonstrates the total hopelessness of deducing cultural differences from any differences, real or imagined, in genetic makeup.)

Finally, and very importantly, Boas was a leader in a subtle, but essential change in anthropological thinking about the concept of culture itself. Educated in Germany, Boas had begun his career imbued with the romantic concept of "Kultur," the expression of the highest attainments of human experience, as expressed in the arts, music, literature, and science. This is the conception of culture that allowed Tylor to talk about "the conditions of culture among various societies." Tylor, like Boas as a young man, conceived of culture as something groups and individuals had more or less of. It was a singular noun: one talked of higher or lower *culture,* not more or fewer *cultures.* By the same route that led him to deny the basis for ranking cultures in terms of a hypothetical, evolutionary sequence, Boas arrived at the idea that different societies create different "designs for living," each representing a uniquely adapted fit between their past and their present circumstances in the world. This point of view is central to anthropology, and it clearly has to be taken into account if we want to rank the intellectual achievements (levels of mental development) of people growing up with different cultural experiences. It renders simple more/less comparisons of cultures difficult and restricted, with parallel effects on our inferences about mind.

ENTER PSYCHOLOGY

As we entered the twentieth century, anthropology was still pursuing its goal of reconstructing the history of mankind by studying cultures in different parts of the world. But that goal was now blocked by serious methodological problems (such as those raised by Boas) that needed to be settled before further theoretical progress could be made.

The birth of psychology is usually dated back to 1879, when Wilhelm Wundt officially opened an experimental laboratory in Leipzig. The exact date is not important, because several laboratories opened almost simultaneously in different industrialized countries. But the *reasons* for these laboratory openings are very important indeed.

Boas's critique of developmental theories, whether of mind or culture, produced controversy in both domains of inquiry. Boas earned the enmity of anthropologists who believed his criticisms of their general theories unjust; they sought to rescue the more general theories, criticizing Boas and his students for "historical particularism" (to use Harris's apt phrase). While new competitors for an overall approach to understanding historical links between cultures became a central activity for the new discipline of anthropology, psychologists were people who took up the other half of Boas's critique, problems of specifying mental mechanisms.

The major difficulty facing those who became psychologists was to devise methods for specifying pretty exactly what sorts of activity an individual engages in at those times we want to make claims that some sort of "thinking" is going on. No one could be very precise about what was meant when psychologists referred to a mental process. Competing claims were evaluated by constructing settings to control as exactly as possible the kinds of events a person experienced and to record the kinds of responses these experiences evoked. Since the presumed processes were not observable (they were, as we say, "psychological"), psychologists spent a great deal of time and ingenuity devising ways to pin down what these nonobservable processes might be. The rapidly growing ability to control electricity and to build precision machinery was exploited to the fullest; the early psychology laboratories were marvels of inventions. Their instruments allowed psychologists to present people carefully controlled lights and tones for carefully controlled intervals and to measure precisely the time it took to respond. In their search for ways to make mind observable, they used electrophysiological devices to record internal, organic functioning. The discipline of "psychophysics" advanced appreciably in its quest to relate psychological phenomena of an elementary order (discriminating tones, judging hues). There were even hopes of uncovering a "cognitive algebra" by carefully comparing reaction times to stimuli of various complexities arranged to reveal steps in the thought process.

The activities of the psychologist and the anthropologist soon contrasted very dramatically. The psychologist brought people into the laboratory where behavior could be constrained, stimuli controlled, and mind made visible. The anthropologist wandered the world talking to people, observing their customary behavior, and seeking clues about the factors that made one design for living different from another.

Whereas the anthropologists continued to concentrate on gathering data that would permit firm statements about historical relations between cultures, scholars who came to identify themselves as psychologists concentrated on resolving arguments about thinking such as those illustrated in the passage quoted from Boas. Just as anthropology evolved careful field techniques to disambiguate competing claims about "culture," psychologists developed the laboratory experiment as a way to test competing claims about "mind."

There occurred, in effect, a division of labor in the "humane sciences," a division that was primarily a matter of scientific strategy in the beginning: progress required some concentrated work on specialized subtopics. The overall task remained the same for everyone: how do human beings come to be the way they are?

ENTER TESTING

Despite an increasing gulf between scholars who called themselves psychologists and those who called themselves anthropologists, it was not long before these two areas of inquiry were brought together again. At the end of the nineteenth century, Francis Galton, in England, set out to test hypotheses about mental differences among people, using the newly devised psychological techniques. His concern was not differences between people growing up in different cultures. Rather, he studied people growing up in different families. He sought the inherited sources of variability in mental abilities. Significantly, his tests were theoretically motived; he believed that speed of mental processing was central to intelligence so he created tests of rapid processing of elementary signals. Galton succeeded in finding differences among Englishmen on such tests as simple reaction time to a pure tone, but he did not succeed in relating these "psychological test" differences to human characteristics of greater interest to him such as scientific excellence or musical ability. Galton's tests, based on an oversimplified model of the human mind and the highly controlled procedures adopted from the laboratory appropriate to testing his theory, were not taken up by society. However, in creating an early precursor of existing IQ tests, Galton did begin the development of the statistical techniques that would be necessary to show how test differences correlate with interesting behavioral differences.

The difficulties that Galton encountered in trying to demonstrate that he was testing abilities of general significance were a direct stimulus to the development of that branch of applied mathematics known as statistics, upon which current testing technology relies so heavily. The fact that these difficulties have not been resolved, despite great progress in the technology for evaluating the theory, is a key problem that remains to be dealt with.

Galton did all of his work in England, but other Englishmen, including W. H. R. Rivers, travelled to the Torres Strait northeast of Australia, to see if psychological tests could be used to settle disputes over cultural differences in cognition. Rivers was in some senses an antique. He was both anthropologist and psychologist, which meant that he considered both the evidence of his tests and evidence provided by observation of the people he went to study when he made statements about culture and thought. His conclusions were consistent with Galton's data on in-

dividual differences; natives differed from each other on such simple tasks as their ability to detect a gap in a line, or their recognition of colors. But there were no impressive differences between the natives of the Torres Strait and Englishmen.

It would appear on the basis of this evidence that there are no cultural differences in thinking, at least no differences consistent with what we had been led to believe by Tylor, Spencer, and many others. However, it could be (and was) argued, that the *important* ways in which cultural differences cause mental differences were not even tested by Rivers and his associates. After all, Galton had found no relation between responses to his psychological tests and other presumed indicators of intelligence. Why would anyone, then, expect cultural differences? Perhaps the experiments, limited as they were to *elementary* psychological processes, simply failed to implicate *higher psychological processes* at all. What we needed were tests of higher psychological processes that could be used to compare people from different cultures or different people in the same culture.

This distinction between elementary and higher processes pinpoints a weakness in the basic foundations of experimental psychology, a weakness acknowledged by Wundt, its founder. It is impossible, Wundt believed, to study *higher* psychological functions in experiments because it is impossible to construct appropriately controlled environments of the needed complexity. Wundt believed that scientists should use *ethnological* evidence and folklore if they want to discover the properties of the mind that get constructed on the basis of the elementary processes that he studied in the laboratory.

Wundt's doubts about the experimental method have not been accepted in psychology, but they are very germane to understanding problems with cross-cultural developmental research, as we shall see. These doubts were not accepted because they put psychologists in a very difficult bind. Psychology had been founded on the principle that without carefully controlled environments, it is not legitimate to make statements about how the mind works. But a great many of the questions about how the mind works that interested psychologists and anthropologists alike clearly refer to "higher" psychological processes such as logical reasoning and inference. When Wundt gave up on the idea that such processes could be studied in the laboratory, he was, it seemed, robbing psychology of most of its interesting subject matter. For psychologists, the inability to study higher psychological processes in the laboratory meant that they could not be studied at all. Rejecting this conclusion, many psychologists were attracted to theories claiming that complex processes are compounded of simple ones. The basic task was to understand the elements, before tackling the compound. Relatively simple experimental models thrived, but complex behavior was rarely dealt with.

BINET'S STRATEGY

The major push for research on more complex human problem solving came from a source seemingly outside the scientific community, although respected psychologists were involved. Early in this century, Alfred Binet was asked to deal with a practical, social problem. With the growth of public education in France, there was a growing problem of school failure, or at least severe school underachievement. It seemed not only that some children learned more slowly than others, but that some children, who otherwise appeared perfectly normal, did not seem to benefit much from instruction at all. Binet and his colleagues were asked to see if they could find a way to identify slow-learning children at an early stage in their education. If such identification were possible, special education could be provided them, and the remaining children could be more efficiently taught.

The subsequent history of IQ testing has been described too frequently to bear repetition here, but a sketch of the basic strategy of research is necessary as background to understand just how deeply IQ tests are embedded in cultural experience.

To begin with, early test makers had to decide what to test for. The decision seemed straightforward. They wanted to test people's ability to perform the kinds of tasks that are required by schools. They observed classrooms, looked at textbooks, talked to teachers, and used their intuitions to arrive at some idea of the many different kinds of knowledge and skills that children are eventually expected to master in school.

What Binet and his colleagues found was not easy to describe briefly, as anyone who has looked into a classroom can quickly testify (and all of us have done so, or we would not be reading these words). There was a very obvious need to understand graphic symbols, such as alphabets and number systems. So recognition of these symbols was tested. But mastery of the rudiments of these symbols was not enough. Children were also expected to manipulate these symbols to store and retrieve vast amounts of information, to rearrange this information according to the demands of the moment, and to use the information to solve a great variety of problems that had never arisen before in the experience of the individual pupil. Thus, children's abilities to remember and carry out sequences of movements, to define words, to con-

struct plausible event sequences from jumbled picture sequences, and to recognize the missing element in graphic designs were tested (along with many other components of school-based problems).

It was also obvious that to master more and more esoteric applications of the basic knowledge contained in alpha-numeric writing systems, pupils had to learn to master their own behavior. They had not only to engage in a variety of "mental activities" directed at processing information; they also had to gain control over their own attention, applying it not according to the whim of the moment, but according to the whim of the teacher and the demands of the text.

It was clearly impossible to arrive at a single sample of all the kinds of thinking required by "the" school. Not only was there too much going on in any one classroom to make this feasible; it was equally clear that the school required different abilities from children of different ages. Binet realized that estimates of "basic aptitude" for this range of material would depend upon how much the child had learned about the specific content before he or she arrived at school, but he felt knowing a child's current abilities would be useful to teachers anyway.

In the face of these difficulties, Binet decided to construct a sample of school-like tasks appropriate for each year of education, starting with the elementary grades, and reaching into higher levels of the curriculum. He would have liked to sample so that all essential activities were included in his test and that tasks at one level of difficulty would be stepping stones to tasks at the next higher level. But because no firmly based theory of higher psychological functions existed, Binet had to rely on a combination of his own common sense and a logical analysis of tasks that different classrooms seem to require (for example, you have to be able to remember three random digits before you can remember four; you have to know the alphabet before you can read). He also hit on the handy strategy of letting the children themselves tell him when an item selected for the test was appropriate. Beginning with a large set of possible test questions, Binet hunted for items that half the children at a given age level could solve. An "average" child would then be one who solved problems appropriate to his or her age level. Keeping items that discriminated between children of different ages (as well as items that seemed to sample the activities demanded of kids in their classrooms), he arrived, with help from his colleagues, at the first important prototype of the modern IQ test.

Of course a great deal of work has gone into the construction of tests since Binet's early efforts, but the underlying logic has remained pretty much the same:

sample the kinds of activities demanded by the culture (in the form of the problems it requires that its children master in school) and compare children's performance to see how many of these activities they have mastered. Children who have mastered far less than we would expect given comparable sample of kids their own age are those who will need extra help if they are to reach the level expected by the culture.

This strategy is perfectly reasonable, so long as we stay within the framework that generated the item selection procedures in the first place. However, much to the disapproval of Binet, people found new uses for these tests of school-based knowledge that carried with them the seeds of the current disputes over IQ testing. Although Binet specifically warned against the procedure, his test and tests like it began to be used as *measures* of an overall aptitude for solving problems *in general,* rather than *samples* of problem-solving ability and knowledge *in particular.* Those engaged in such extrapolations acknowledged that in principle it is important to make certain that everyone given the test has an equal opportunity to learn the material that the test demands. But in practice there was no way to guarantee this essential prerequisite for making comparative judgments about basic abilities.

These are important issues in thinking about applications of IQ testing, and they are extensively discussed in the psychological literature. However, it is not until we back up and examine the possible significance of Binet's work in the light of anthropological scholarship that we can see just how limited an enterprise IQ testing was at the beginning, and how restricted it remains today.

A THOUGHT EXPERIMENT IN TEST CONSTRUCTION

A good starting point for this reexamination is to think about what sort of activity Binet would have engaged in if he had been a member of a cultural group vastly different from his own. As a sort of "thought experiment" let us suppose that a "West African" Binet has taken an interest in the kinds of knowledge and skills that a child growing up in his part of the world would need to master as an adult. To make the thought experiment somewhat concrete, I will do my supposing about the tribal groups inhabiting the interior of Liberia, principally the Kpelle people, among whom I have worked and about whom a good deal of relevant information is available.[8]

Following in the footsteps of his French model, our Liberian Binet would want to make a catalogue of the kinds of activities that children are expected to

master by their parents and the village elders. People in rural Liberia make their living by growing rice and other crops, which they supplement with meat and fish when these scarce commodities can be obtained. Rice farming is physically difficult work that demands considerable knowledge and planning for its success, but as practiced by the Kpelle, it is not a technologically sophisticated enterprise. It is carried out using simple tools such as a machete to cut the underbrush; fire to burn the dry brush; vines to tie together fence posts in order to keep out animals, and slingshots to harass.[9] Other aspects of Kpelle material culture are also relatively simple, although in every case the proper use of tools requires a good deal of knowledge about how the tools are supposed to be used. There is division of labor among Kpelle adults (men hunt, women do most of the fishing; men cut the brush on the farms, women plant the seed, children guard the crops), but far more than is true of contemporary America, everyone pretty well knows what there is to know about adult economic activities. There are some specialists (blacksmiths, bonesetters, weavers) whose work is an exception to this generalization, and study of their activities would certainly be important.

Of course, there is more to getting through life as a Kpelle than growing rice or weaving cloth. All descriptions of the social organization of Kpelle life stress that, as in America, knowledge of the social world is essential to adult status. Kpelle people are linked by a complex set of relations that control how much of the resources available to the society actually get to the individual.

Faced with this situation, how should our West African Binet proceed? Should he sample all the kinds of activities valued by adults? This strategy is almost certainly unrealistic. Even allowing for the possibility that aspects of technology make it reasonable to speak of the Kpelle as a "less complex" society than our own, it is very complex indeed. No anthropologist would claim to have achieved a really thorough description of even one such society. Moreover, like Tylor, he would have to admit the possibility that in some respects Kpelle society provides members with more complex tasks than we are likely to face. Since it is unreasonable in Liberia, as it is in the United States, to think that we can come up with a test that samples *all* types of Kpelle adult activities, why not follow Binet's example and sample an important *subset* of those activities? From an anthropological perspective, schools are social institutions for assuring that adult knowledge of highly valued kinds gets transmitted to a society's next generation (it must be transmitted, or there would be no later generations!). While the school is not likely to be a random sample of life's tasks, it is certainly a convenient place to sample activities that adults consider important, activities that are complex enough to make it unlikely that kids would learn what they need to know simply by "hanging around."

So, our Liberian Binet might decide to search for some institutions in his society that correspond roughly with the basic goals of schooling in ours. Not all societies readily manifest such institutions, so that anthropologists are led to speak of "socialization" as the broadest relevant category. Fortunately for discussion, in the case of Liberia, he would undoubtedly discover the existence of institutions called "bush schools" in the Creole vernacular.

There are no detailed accounts of the curriculum of the bush school. The three or four years that youngsters spend are organized by town elders who are leaders in the secret societies that control a variety of esoteric information. This material cannot, on pain of death, be communicated to outsiders.[10] However, we know enough about aspects of bush school activities to continue our hypothetical research; we know that youngsters learn to farm, construct houses, track animals, shoot birds, and carry out a variety of adult economic activities (children live apart from their home villages in something like a scouting camp during their time in bush school). They are also instructed in the important lore of the group. This lore is communicated not only in a variety of ceremonies, but in stories, myths, and riddles. So, let us suppose that our West African Binet decided to use "successful execution of bush school activities" as the abilities he wanted to sample.

Again, like Binet, our researcher would not be able to sample *all* such activities for his test, nor would he want to. He would not, for example, want to sample activities that all children knew how to accomplish *before* they got to school, nor would he want to sample activities considered so universally accessible that everyone mastered them well before the end of schooling. This information would not help him pick out those children who needed extra instruction. Instead, he would seek those activities that discriminated among children, activities that some mastered far earlier than others, and perhaps activities that some mastered only in later life. Once these Binet-like restrictions had been placed upon the activities selected for study, our hypothetical researcher could begin selecting tasks on which he could base test items.

In considering what sort of test would emerge, it is useful first to consider what activities would be excluded as well as those included. Cutting brush or sowing rice seed probably would not be the test; everyone knows how to do that before he or she gets to school. Nor would anyone spend time explicitly

teaching children common vocabulary. However, there would be explicit instruction in such tasks as constructing houses and identifying leaves that are useful in different kinds of medicine. There would also be some mechanism for insuring that the history of the group and its laws and customs were taught to everyone often in the form of stories and dances. Finally, some children would be selected for specialist roles that would require special tests (bonesetter, weaver, midwife, blacksmith, hunter, and so on). These children would receive additional instruction.

Looking at those areas where instruction might be considered important, we can see many candidate activities for testing. We might want to see if children had learned all of the important leaf names for making medicine. Riddles are often important parts of stories and arguments, so we could test to see how many riddles children know and how adept they are at interpreting them. The specialties would be a rich source of test material, especially if we thought that rational testing of ability to perform like adults would improve the quality of our cloth or machetes. In short, it seems possible, in principle, to come up with test items that could perform functions in Kpelle society similar to the way that Binet wanted to use IQ tests.

Could we carry out such a program of research *in practice?* There is no simple answer to this question, but it is useful to consider the obstacles. For some activities such as naming leaves or remembering riddles, it should be relatively easy to make the relevant observations because the Kpelle have already arranged for them: several researchers have described children's games that embody precisely these activities.[11] We could also test people's skills at constructing houses, weaving designs, and forging sturdy hoes. However, from a Kpelle point of view, test of such skills would not be particularly interesting. The real stuff of using one's wits to get along in the world has been excluded.

This point was made very explicitly by a sophisticated Kpelle acquaintance of mine who was versed in the more esoteric aspects of Kpelle secret societies and medicine (or magic, according to American stereotypes). We had been talking about what it means to be intelligent in Kpelle society (the most appropriate term is translated as "clever"). "Can you be a clever farmer?" I asked. "No," came the reply. "You can be a hardworking farmer, or you can be a lucky farmer, but we couldn't say that someone is a clever farmer. Everyone knows how to farm. We use 'clever' when we talk about the way someone gets other people to help him. Some people always win arguments. Some people know how to deal with strangers. Some people know powerful medicine. These are the things we talk about as clever."

In this bit of dialogue we see an emphasis on activities that require social interaction as the arena where intelligence is an appropriate concept. (Among the Kpelle and many other nontechnological groups, display of a good memory for use in discussions is often considered an important component of intelligence.)[12] This usage is quite consistent with Binet's analysis; *it is those activities that differentiate among people* in terms of the way they manipulate information that the Kpelle, like the French, use to mark intelligence.

However, once we reach this point, we face two important difficulties. First, the situations that we have selected for our study of Kpelle intelligence are exceedingly difficult to describe. Second, these contexts are very difficult to arrange. It is not enough to know riddles, everyone knows riddles. What is important about riddles is how they are used to get one's way with other people. Riddles are a resource to be used in a variety of social interactions where people's statuses and rights are at issue.

Consider the first difficulty. Bellman recounts an occasion when an elder member of a secret society told a long story about how he came to be a high ranking shaman.[13] He followed this (presumably autobiographical) story with a long riddle, which was also in story form. A novice such as myself would have no way of figuring out what part of the story was true, and I certainly would not have responded to the riddle as if its interpretation depended upon the autobiographical story; the two monologues appear to be about quite different topics. Bellman succeeds in demonstrating, however, that the riddle is closely linked to the autobiography. Not only are there formal, structural similarities (once one understands the basic categories of the relevant Kpelle belief systems). There is a rhetorical link as well. The autobiographical story actually represents a bit of self-aggrandizement by the person who told it. The man is claiming special knowledge and special power in a covert manner. The riddle reinforces the main point of the story (which raises the teller above his fellow shaman), giving the story "logical" as well as "historical" validity. The fact that listeners are constrained to agree with the riddle also gets them to agree, at least in part, with the message of the autobiographical story.

By almost any account, this man's autobiographical account plus riddle is a clever bit of behavior. It is exactly the kind of thing that our West African Binet ought to be sampling. But, at precisely this point, our cross-cultural thought experiment in IQ testing comes apart. As I have already pointed out, in order to construct a test Binet needed to be able to select a large number of items. But the "item" we have just described (very loosely) is not easily constructable. The participants in this scene were doing social work on each other; the shaman, in

particular, was attempting to establish his preeminence using an account of his past history that would be difficult to check up on, a riddle whose structure was designed to reinforce his account, and his knowledge of his listener's state of knowledge concerning both the shaman's past and Kpelle social structure. This was one item; it was constructed by the subject, not the "tester." It is very difficult for me to imagine how to insure that a test includes one or more items "of this type." Furthermore, because the example's structure and content depend upon the special circumstances surrounding it, how could I insure that I would be able to present the test to the subject since it was the "subject" who did a lot of the presenting in the example I have described?

Here the contrast with Binet's situation is very strong. Like Binet, we have proceeded by figuring out what sorts of activities differentiate people according to some notion of what it means to behave intelligently. Unlike Binet, the activities we need to sample in West Africa to accomplish this goal lead us into domains that are *systematically absent from Binet's tests.* These domains involve interactions among people in which flexibly employed social knowledge is of paramount importance. They are not domains of hypothetical knowledge; rather, they always involve some real operations on the world, operations that require a great deal of care simply to describe. We have no good notion of how to make such activities happen in a manner analogous to the way that teachers make vocabulary tests and multiplication problems happen. Furthermore, even if we solved all these problems, we would have no real theory of the psychological processes that our subject engaged in. Such problems have not been studied by cognitive psychologists.

On both practical and theoretical grounds, then, it appears virtually impossible to come up with a way of testing Kpelle intelligence in a manner really equivalent to what we understand to be intelligence tests in our society. So long as we restrict our attention to Kpelle culture, this conclusion should not cause much consternation. After all, the idea of a West African Binet is rather absurd; Kpelle people have managed to pass on their culture for many years without IQ tests to help them select clever children and give extra assistance to the dull.

SOME IMPLICATIONS FOR THE NOTION OF A CULTURE-FREE TEST

Our characterization of what one has to do to be clever in Kpelle culture and what it would take to sample such cleverness in a test must be discomforting for anyone who imagines that one can construct a culture-free test of intelligence. Imagine, for example, that by some quirk it was our imaginary Liberian Binet who constructed the first IQ test, and that other West African tribal people had refined it. Next, imagine that American children were posed items from the West African test. Even items considered too simple for Kpelle eight-year-olds would cause our children severe problems. Learning the names of leaves, for example, has proven too difficult for more than one American Ph.D.[14] Our children know some riddles, but little use is made of such knowledge in our society except for riddling, which would put them at a severe disadvantage on more "advanced" items.

If our children were forced to take a test constructed by a West African Binet, we might object that these Kpelle-derived items were unfairly biased toward Kpelle culture. If the eventual incomes of our children depended in any way on their ability to interpret Kpelle riddles, we would be outraged. Nor would we be too happy if their incomes depended upon their use of their own riddles as rhetorical devices. At the very minimum, we would want a *culture-free test* if real life outcomes depended upon test performance. However, what kind of test is a West African Binet likely to dream up that we would consider culture-free? It would not involve a set of drawings of geometrically precise figures, because Kpelle, a pre-literate group, do not engage in much graphic representation and they have no technology for drawing straight lines. It would not be recall of lists of nonsense syllables or even lists of words, because there are no corresponding activities in Kpelle adult life. We might try a memory test like recalling all of one's family, but here the Kpelle, who teach their children genealogies, would have a distinct advantage: what is the name of your grandmother's father on your father's side of the family? In fact, if we run down the list of presumably culture-free items that our experiment on Kpelle IQ testing turned up, we would almost certainly find none of the subtests that have been claimed as culture-free tests of intelligence in our society. The reason is very simple; our West African Binet, having scientifically sampled *his* culture, would have come up with items that reflect valued activities and that differentiate people in *his* culture, while Binet and all his successors have come up with items that do the same job in our culture. *They are different kinds of activities.*

The only way to obtain a culture-free test is to construct items that are equally a part of the experience of all cultures. Following the logic of Binet's undertaking, this would require us to sample the valued adult activities in all cultures (or at least two!) and identify activities equivalent in their structure and frequency of occurrence.

I probably do not have to belabor this point further. The simple fact is that we know of no tests that are culture-free, only tests for which we have no good theory of how culture affects performance. Lacking such a theory, we lack any guidelines that would permit us to specify clear connections between cultural experience and performance.

RETURN TO FIRST PRINCIPLES

Our imagined study of cross-cultural test construction makes it clear that tests of ability are inevitably cultural devices. This conclusion must seem dreary and disappointing to people who have been working to construct valid, culture-free tests. But from the perspective of history and logic, it simply confirms the fact, stated so clearly by Franz Boas half a century ago, that "mind, independent of experience, is inconceivable."

The historical experience of anthropologists has led them to consider it axiomatic that the abilities you choose to sample have to be drawn from an analysis of indigenous, culturally organized activities. Because different cultures emphasize different kinds of activities, the valued abilities will differ. From this point of view, a test that is equally valid across cultures would be a test that sampled some domain of activity that occurs in roughly the same form and same frequency in the cultures being compared. While it is possible, in principle, to identify such activities, they may not be of much use for the purposes of ability testing in the tradition of IQ tests. Many psychologists and anthropologists have asserted that some core set of experiences is common to all cultures. Such assertions are at the heart of such major systems as those constructed by Sigmund Freud, Jean Piaget, and Abraham Kardiner, to name just a few important figures who have studied this problem. But it is simultaneously asserted that everyone, irrespective of culture, comes to master those basic activities common to our species. Piaget, whose work is most closely associated with the development of intellectual skills, explicitly assumes that there will be universal acquisition of basic understandings of the physical and social worlds because of universal constraints on behavior common to all cultures. There are no existing data to refute this assumption.

However, both our nineteenth-century anthropological forefathers and twentieth-century scholars such as Piaget readily admit cultural differences *associated with particular domains of activity*. Tylor, Spencer, and other nineteenth-century cultural evolutionists focused on differences traceable to technology. Piaget believes that special institutions and technologies of cultural transmission, such as the modern school, produce culturally determined cultural differences. So long as we restrict ourselves to specifiable domains, it is possible to rank cultures and, consequently, rank the intellectual achievements of individuals from different cultures within those domains. So, for example, we can rank cultures in the sophistication of their means of communication (from oral cultures, to literate cultures, to those possessing electronic media); we can rank cultures in terms of the complexity of dance movements that people are expected to master; we can rank cultures in terms of the degree of urbanization that characterizes the lives of their members, or the degree of rhetorical skill in institutionalized settings that they require.

Any time we engage in such domain-specific comparisons, we can expect cultural differences in the abilities that individual culture users will have developed to achieve the required level of proficiency. Americans will be expected to deal more effectively with graphic symbols than Kpelle or Balinese. But if we chose dance movements as our subject matter, the opposite ordering of culturally linked proficiencies is certain to emerge. In either case, from an anthropological perspective, we would have no illusions that our tests of ability were culture-fair. Why should we? After all, if we choose to compare people in domains where their experience differs, we expect mind to differ as well. That conclusion is certainly a basic legacy of nineteenth-century anthropology.

Sticking to this point of view provides us with a powerful way of understanding the relation between IQ testing and social demands. We can recognize the school as an institutionalized setting designed to provide children with massive practice in activities that are useful and valued in our society. IQ tests sample school activities, and therefore, indirectly, valued social activities, *in our culture*. Insofar as such tests are really used to insure that all children master the required skills, such tests would have to be considered extremely useful. However, insofar as such tests act as screening devices giving access to some people and not to others, without any commitment to insuring that all achieve the level of proficiency required for full participation in the adult life and access to the resources available to adults in our society, their initial purpose has been subverted and must be reexamined. This will be no easy task, since there is little current agreement on the intellectual skills needed for performing in most adult occupations.

IMPLICATIONS FOR TEACHING

Teachers facing the enormous heterogeneity of classrooms in many parts of America may well be tempted to set aside this essay as essentially irrelevant to their classroom practices, whether they agree with my arguments for a culturally conditioned notion of intelligence or not. With respect to classroom organization and curriculum, what follows from the notion that children who may fumble or fail in typical classroom settings shine elsewhere? How can such knowledge be used to advantage?

Perhaps the first thing that needs emphasizing is that a child's skill in a non-classroom setting does *not* imply that poor performance in the classroom is not a problem, either for the child or for the society which uses schooling as a major means of imparting valued social knowledge. The past decade of research on the cognitive consequences of schooling convincingly shows that there are systems of cognitive activity closely correlated with modern schooling that are sharply differentiated from the systems of activity that govern a wide range of activities outside the confines of school.[15] When people who have not experienced schooling are tested using materials and interactional formats characteristic of schooling, they perform poorly. This is a social fact and an important social fact in the lives of the people involved.

While it is true that the activities associated with South Sea navigation,[16] Botswanian story telling,[17] and West African fish mongering[18] each represent highly articulated uses of intelligence, people who excel at these activities must still confront the fact that the domains of activity where these skills are valued are either being stamped out by the economic and political power of schooled, technological societies or they are being encapsulated within lower echelons of them. In the modern world, to be unschooled is to be denied access to the basic contexts where wealth and power are brokered. As Jerome Bruner and I noted more than a decade ago,

> cultural *deprivation* represents a special case of cultural *difference* that arises when an individual is faced with demands to perform in a manner inconsistent with his past (cultural) experience. In the present social context of the United States, the great power of the middle class has rendered differences into deficits because middle-class behavior is the yardstick of success.[19]

I might phrase matters slightly differently now, but I do not think that the significance of that middle-class standard has lessened in the intervening decade. In fact, with respect to a strategy that says that schools must pay increased respect to cultural diversity, the situation has become, if anything, more rigid.

Uniform Treatment Methods

Faced with the enormous heterogeneity of many American schools and the generally poor performance of culturally different peoples, highly structured, bottom-up strategies like the Achievement Goals Program in use in San Diego City Schools have won wide approval. These methods are closely tied to means of measuring time on task and therefore serve as a means of control to insure that all children "get the basics." They emphasize very specific, highly uniform, "correct steps" in mastering the basics. I have grave concerns about these kinds of efforts because I have had too much experience in recent years with children at the bottom 20 percent of my local school system who do not make it through the structure; they seem to do all right in the early grades, but they fail to make the essential transition from "basic" to "higher order" skills in mathematics and reading. Rather than focus on the problems of this highly uniform method of resolving the problem of cultural variation, we have been interested in our research group in ways to take advantage of diversity.

A completely different way of achieving excellence that nonetheless seems to match the urge of the "back to basics" movement and to apply a single method for all children in the classroom at one time is exemplified in demonstrations such as those of Marva Collins and Sylvia Ashton-Warner.[20] These teachers focus uncompromisingly on the highest ideas of western civilization in their teaching. They teach to whole classrooms of diversely prepared students at one time but somehow find a way to involve each child in the excitement, despite very divergent cultural traditions separating children from curriculum. Here the teacher evokes deep involvement from every *individual* child by the exercise of a kind of empathetic skill that makes us call teaching an art, not a science.

As an art, this kind of activity is notorious for its failure to transfer. Marva Collins could not transfer it beyond a single, other teacher working with her at close range; her ideas came apart when the scale of activity was too great for her to control personally. Sylvia Ashton-Warner was *not* able to transfer methods developed in New Zealand among the Maori to Colorado among the privileged.

Master teachers can demonstrate to us what is possible. When the context of teaching is so arranged that the children are truly captivated, there resides a very important achievement. It provides educational science with a goal, however utopian, against which to judge its failures; why can't we make *every* classroom work?

Approaches Emphasizing Diversity

Well, ordinary teachers, among whom I include myself, are not able to weave the kind of magic of a Marva Collins or a Sylvia Warner. But many ordinary teachers do not like to work in the restrictive atmosphere of an AGP school. The problem is to offer a workable, *scientific* alternative. That means an alternative that can approach the same heterogeneity of children's backgrounds as more "uniformitarian" strategies like AGP and succeed. It means an alternative that is transferable because it can be taught in teacher education programs and education schools. It means an alternative that does not cost more, or much more, than the money that is being expended on education now.

No such overall alternative formulation exists, but there has accumulated a set of educational demonstrations that, taken as a group, offers a different, culture-sensitive way to deal with academic diversity in the classroom. Among these culture-sensitive approaches it is possible to see several clusters.

First, there are studies like the Kamehameha Early Education Project (KEEP) and that of Erickson and Mohatt that can establish links between particular modes of pedagogy and the nonschool organization of experience.[21] These efforts are most appropriate in settings where there is a single distinctive cultural tradition shared by most, if not all, of the students.

The Kamehameha Early Education Project was working with Native Hawaiian children who did not succeed with structured, code-emphasis instruction in reading. As they moved into direct teaching of comprehension, they slowly evolved a lesson format that seemed to catch the children up in an active and effective way. An analysis of the successful teaching techniques revealed that the procedures they eventually developed mapped onto an indigenous cultural activity, "talk story."[22] The children had all been present on many occasions of talk story, but they were not old enough themselves to participate in talk story at home. So when they came to school they encountered reading as a variation on an already familiar pattern of instructional interactions.

This program has achieved some of the characteristics I attribute to a scientific alternative. Not only has the program demonstrated success in individual classrooms; it has been taught to new generations of teachers who have used it successfully in new classrooms.

However, many questions remain. Perhaps the correspondence between talk story and the successful KEEP reading procedures is an accident. Perhaps their teaching strategy is simply a good teaching strategy for *any* kids learning to read. The evidence on this question is not in yet, but preliminary results from our own research group suggest that there are elementary school populations for whom the procedure is *not* effective; further pursuit of the reasons why the KEEP program does and does not work will teach more about both reading and Hawaiian culture.

A different kind of demonstration is provided by Erickson and Mohatt from work among the Odawa in Canada. In this case, too, a successful educational strategy was connected to discourse modes prevalent in the children's community.[23] The analysis, based on ethnographic techniques, was specific enough to warrant treatment-specific claims about the effect of the discourse strategy.

The phenomenon that Erickson and Mohatt addressed was the apparent passivity and silence of Native American students in regular classrooms that had been studied by Phillips. Very different modes of classroom discourse feel comfortable to Anglo and Native American children living in the southwestern United States. In particular, it was found that for Native American students

> the notion of a single individual being structurally set apart from all others, in anything other than an observer role, and yet still a part of the group organization, is one that Indian children probably encounter for the first time in school.[24]

Native American children who find themselves with an Anglo teacher encounter a single, powerful person regulating the behavior of many others. They adopt the observer role that they know to be appropriate. Like good observers, they are quiet. They also adhere to the rule that it is not acceptable to single out individuals for praise or censure on a public occasion, and so they also remain silent, or experience difficulty, when singled out to provide an answer to the teacher's questions. The result is what Erickson and Mohatt call the "often reported phenomenon of the 'silent Indian child' in the classroom." Their behavior is inappropriate to the standard mode of instruction in which the teacher acts as a "switchboard operator" who allocates speaking turns, calls on individual children, and expects active participation.

Erickson and Mohatt show that it is possible to construct rules of participation in the classroom that are a functional blend of Anglo school curriculum and Native American discourse styles that make the classroom run much more smoothly. These patterns seemed to be learnable; an Anglo teacher was observed to change his participant structures over the course of the school year in the direction of the Odawa. (These examples demonstrate that culture-sensitive pedagogy can make a difference where it is possible to be explicit about cultural patterns and there is not much cultural heterogeneity in the classroom. In each case, it is important to note that culture-sensitive does *not* mean a focus on the traditional arts, foods, and folklore of a group. Instead culture-sensitive means sensitivity to relatively subtle aspects of interactional etiquettes [that] are likely to go unrecognized by non-Indian teachers.)[25]

Context-Sensitive Approaches

The KEEP and Native American examples are interesting precisely because they map on to identifiable cultural structures that, despite their divergence from the usual pattern of the school, are appropriate for instructional purposes. But many teachers face a situation where it is not a problem of the school having one cultural background and the children one other. Rather, the children are from *many* and varied cultural backgrounds, even if they are from the same general ethnic group. In my own region, for example, there are many Hispanic children from varying countries of origins and years of residence in the U.S., black students of similar heterogeneity, Southeast Asians from several countries, Native Americans, and many more.

What can teachers do in circumstances of extreme student heterogeneity if they are neither master teachers nor cultural experts? There is no single answer to this question, but one of the things that will be very helpful is to have as full a picture of the skills and interests of each individual child when they are *not* in school as possible. Another key element is to construct activity systems that are clearly structured, but where there is room for a good deal of creativity with respect to how each child interacts with the structure.

Activity-centered classrooms with a diversity of learning centers provide one excellent, structural format within which to connect child expertise and interest outside the school with the basic skills required by the school. They also allow a natural way for the classroom to connect with special educational resources in the community (science programs connected with museums such as Berkeley's Lawrence Hall of Science or Toronto's Science Museum, local experts among retired residents, unions, and industries).

Gottfried described the impact on classroom life of visits to the Lawrence Hall of Science, which has an outstanding set of activities for the public.[26] Gottfried studied the way that the visit to Lawrence Hall was taken up in classroom activity. When he spent time in their classrooms with an exhibit that required considerable interaction with various animal species and insects, he found that the materials evoked different patterns of expertise among the participants.

One boy, who was doing poorly in school and of whom the teacher had a rather dim opinion, turned out to be unafraid of crayfish. That alone won him unaccustomed social credits. But it also turned out that he knew more about crayfish than the teacher and more than was provided by the encyclopedia. It turned out he was an *expert* on crayfish. Other children displayed similar kinds of virtuosity, enriching the number of interesting things to be written and worried about. As a result, the teacher learned a lot about the children, and the children displayed prowess that they would not have been known to possess if Gottfried had not disturbed the usual social order. A great deal of basic skills training resulted from the episodes.

No single such activity will captivate everyone, but everyone has some activity that can capture them. The trick is to figure out how to organize experiences out of school and variety in the classroom that will serve as the essential starting point for successful instruction. An activity-centered classroom has the great virtue of allowing parallel activity structures that are only loosely coordinated in time and space. This permits teachers to apply a variety of approaches to a particular area of academic concern, embedding reading (for example) in many contexts. Specific activity structures facilitate connections between the classroom and the outside world, enabling teachers to create occasions for transfer of home-based knowledge into school-based contexts for basic skills.

In our own research we have pursued the special power of computers to create educationally useful activity systems.[27] We have sought to create carefully scripted activity which embeds exercise in the basic skills in ways designed to maximize transfer. Thus, instead of content that replicates the format of pages of printed text, we seek to embed literacy and numeracy activities in activity structures which have some larger goal and are often game-like in their structure. Viewing the computer as a medium for interaction rather than a surrogate teacher leads us to arrange it so that more than one person is usually working at a single console at any one time and that the entire set of operations has a clear socially accepted goal.

In other work on reading we create activity structures that are *group* enterprises, organized around a script with teachers, college students, and children mixed together with respect to roles and expertise.[28] Even children with long histories of educational failure can be caught up in these systems enabling a keener insight into the difficulties and a better chance at remediation.

Culture and Context Specificity

I know of one educational innovation that combines aspects of both types of systems described above. Like the context-specific activity centers, it arranges for education to occur in contexts that can recruit children's out-of-school accomplishments so that both the children and the teacher can succeed at a school task. Like the work in Hawaii and with the Odawa, this case uses cultural understandings that all of the children have in common outside of the classroom and that are not usually used inside the classroom.

Moll and Diaz worked with Hispanic children who had fairly good literacy skills in Spanish, but were failing to learn how to read in English in spite of organized bilingual instruction.[29] When English was being taught in the classroom, the children could not rely on their Spanish skills. The instruction was organized so that a teacher who spoke only English taught them English reading. They worked with a Spanish teacher for other parts of the day, including times when they worked on reading in Spanish at quite a high level—not only complicated comprehension work but even book reports. Yet, when they went to the English class they were faced with what looked like first-grade work. The instructional program was arranged so that until the children could do fairly well in oral English, they would be kept at a beginner level in reading. These children did quite poorly. They did not advance.

The teachers were surprised to see videotapes of the children reading in the two settings: it was hard to believe that children who were so competent at reading in one language were so incompetent at learning to read in another language. No one was happy with this situation.

Moll and Diaz created an intervention that was later picked up by a "real teacher" who had the necessary attributes: she was bilingual, biliterate, and could teach reading. Moll and Diaz had discovered a way to move the children into English reading, and at an advanced grade level. They gave the children English books to read—the very same fourth-grade books that their classmates were reading. The children read the English text, getting a bit of casual help from the teacher, if they asked for any, using either Spanish or English as the medium of communication. Because the teacher and the children could both use Spanish, sometimes the questions and answers were in Spanish. When the children had finished a first reading of the text, the group conversation turned to what it meant. Again, the conversation was in Spanish or in English, whatever seemed most helpful. The children understood the story very well; the problems they had in comprehension were on the same sorts of text and questions that their monolingual English classmates had trouble with.

The children were, very suddenly, reading English at grade level. Granted, in English they could not display their ability as easily. But reading English they were. An "extra" ability of theirs had been the ability to speak Spanish—and they used this ability from home to *read* English. The interesting punch line to this case is that the children changed in another way: once they were allowed to use Spanish to do English reading lessons, they started to use a lot more English. Their lack of ability in speaking English had kept them from reading English in the ordinary instructional program; ironically, Moll and Diaz created a way to "get around" the first problem, only to end up finding an indirect way to solve it!

FINAL COMMENTS

In the decades ahead, we can be certain that the issue of student heterogeneity in our schools is going to be important, even if no one has anything particularly useful to say about it. We do not have to subscribe to the pseudo-scientific aspects of Huxley's *Brave New World* to realize that increased requirements for technical expertise are likely, even when combined with increased technical assistance for gaining expertise, to create a situation where the intellectually rich get richer. There is also no serious doubt that one could

use any of several commercially available culture-fair tests and come up with a statistically significant prediction of who is most likely to become a highly educated, technologically successful, person.

One-sided notions of culture-free testing covertly create a uniform, quantifiable, notion of what intelligence *is*. Although as yet not particularly strong as a scientific and pedagogical tool, a culture-sensitive approach to testing and intelligence seems to provide guidance in the creation of mixed systems of education that will take advantage of the heterogeneity instead of suppressing it. Context-sensitive approaches appear to be especially helpful in dealing with situations of extreme diversity, because they allow the kinds of flexibility that can organize a variety of resources to assist children in benefiting from their educational experiences; they can be shown to work. However, they remain enough of an "art" so that transfer and generalization are still very problematic in many cases. Very often they remain no more than demonstrations, with no scientific framework or bureaucratic structure to engineer their uptake in the educational system.

A decade from now, when the next time rolls around for the National Society for the Study of Education to be thinking of yearbook articles on this topic, it will be interesting to see if the currently successful brands of context- and culture-specific science and pedagogy will have been able to survive, not to say prosper, in a world people are currently fond of calling the "coming information age."

Footnotes

1. For example, see Arthur Jensen, "g: Outmoded Theory or Unconquered Frontier," *Creative Science and Technology* 2, no. 3 (1979): 16–29.

2. Edward B. Tylor, *The Origins of Culture* (New York: Harper and Row, 1958), p. 69.

3. Herbert Spencer, *The Principles of Psychology*, vol. 5 (New York: D. Appleton, 1886), p. 521.

4. Tylor, *The Origins of Culture*, p. 27.

5. Franz Boas, *The Mind of Primitive Man* (New York: Macmillan, 1911).

6. Ibid., pp. 110–11.

7. Ibid., p. 128.

8. See, for example, Beryl L. Bellman, *Village of Curers and Assassins: On the Production of Fala Kpelle Cosmological Categories* (The Hague: Mouton Press, 1975); Michael Cole, John Gay, Joseph A. Glick, and Donald W. Sharp,

The Cultural Context of Learning and Thinking (New York: Basic Books, 1971); James L. Gibbs, "The Kpelle of Liberia," in *Peoples of Africa*, ed. James L. Gibbs (New York: Holt, Rinehart and Winston, 1965).

9. See John Gay, *Red Dust on the Green Leaves* (Thompson, Conn.: Inter-Culture Associates, 1973) for a much better account on this process.

10. See Bellman, *Village of Curers and Assassins*, for the most detailed account of these practices.

11. Cole, Gay, Glick, and Sharp, *The Cultural Context of Learning and Thinking*; David F. Lancy, "Studies of Memory in Culture," *Annals of the New York Academy of Science* 307 (1977): 285–97; Alfred A. Kulah, "The Organization and Learning of Proverbs among the Kpelle of Liberia" (Doctoral dissertation, University of California, Irvine, 1973).

12. See, for example, Ernest F. Dube, "A Cross-cultural Study of the Relationship between 'Intelligence' Level and Story Recall" (Doctoral dissertation, Cornell University, 1977).

13. Beryl L. Bellman, "Ethnohermeneutics: On the Interpretation of Subjective Meaning," in *Language and the Mind,* ed. William C. McCormack and Stephen A. Wurm (The Hague: Mouton and Co., 1978).

14. E. S. Bowen, *Return to Laughter* (New York: Doubleday, 1964).

15. Donald W. Sharp, Michael Cole, and Charles Lave, *Education and Cognitive Development: The Evidence from Experimental Research,* in *Monographs of the Society for Research in Child Development* 44, nos. 1, 2 (1979), Serial No. 178; Harold W. Stevenson, Timothy Parker, Alex Wilkinson, Beatrice Bonnevaux, and Max Gonzales, *Schooling, Environment, and Cognitive Development: A Cross-cultural Study,* in *Monographs of the Society for Research in Child Development* 43, no. 3 (1978), Serial No. 175, pp. 1–92; Barbara Rogoff, "Schooling and the Development of Cognitive Skills," in *Handbook of Cross-cultural Psychology,* ed. Henry C. Triandis and Alistair Heron, vol. 4 (Boston: Allyn and Bacon, 1981).

16. Thomas Gladwin, *East is a Big Bird: Navigation and Logic on Puluwat Atoll* (Cambridge, Mass.: Harvard University Press, 1970); David H. Lewis, "Observations on Route Finding and Spatial Orientation among the Aboriginal Peoples of the Western Desert Region of Central Australia," *Oceania* 46, no. 4 (1976): 249–82.

17. Dube, "A Cross-cultural Study."

18. Naomi Quinn, "Do Mfantse Fish Sellers Estimate Probabilities in Their Heads?" *American Ethnologist* 5 (1978): 206–226.

19. Michael Cole and Jerome S. Bruner, "Cultural Differences and Inferences about Psychological Processes," in *Annual Progress in Child Psychiatry and Child Development,* ed. Stella Chess and Alexander Thomas (New York: Brunner/Mazel, 1972), pp. 47–63.

20. Marva Collins and C. Tamaricus, *Marva Collins' Way* (New York: Houghton-Mifflin, 1982); Sylvia Ashton-Warner, *Spearpoint: "Teacher" in America* (New York: Knopf, 1972).

21. Kathryn H. Au, "Using the Experience-Text-Relationship Method with Minority Children," *Reading Teacher* 32 (March 1979): 677–79; idem, "Participation Structures in a Reading Lesson with Hawaiian Children: Analysis of a Cul-turally Appropriate Instructional Event," *Anthropology and Education Quarterly* 11 (Summer 1980): 91–115; Ron Gallimore and Kathryn H. Au, "The Competence/Incompetence Paradox in the Education of Minority Culture Children," *Quarterly Newsletter of the Laboratory of Comparative Human Cognition* 1 (July 1979): 32–37; G. E. Speidel, Guest Editor, *Educational Perspectives* 20, No. 1 (1981); Frederick Erickson and Gerald Mohatt, "Cultural Organization of Participant Structures in Two Classrooms of Indian Students," in *Doing the Ethnography of Schooling,* ed. George D. Spindler (New York: Holt, Rinehart and Winston, 1980), pp. 132–74.

22. Steven Boggs, *Speaking, Relating, and Learning: A Study of Hawaiian Children at Home and at School,* with the assistance of Karen Watson-Gegeo and Georgia McMillen (Norwood, N.J.: Ablex, forthcoming).

23. Susan Phillips, "Participant Structures and Communicative Competence: Warm Springs Children in Community and Classroom," in *Functions of Language in the Classroom,* ed. Courtney B. Cazden, Vera P. John, and Dell Hymes (New York: Teachers College Press, 1972).

24. Ibid., p. 391.

25. Erickson and Mohatt, "Cultural Organization of Participant Structures," pp. 166–67.

26. Jeffrey Gottfried, "Activity-based Outreach Programs" (Lecture given at the Laboratory of Comparative Human Cognition, University of California, San Diego, n.d.).

27. Laboratory of Comparative Human Cognition, "Culture and Intelligence," in *Handbook of Human Intelligence,* ed. Robert J. Sternberg (New York: Cambridge University Press, 1982), pp. 642–719; James A. Levin and Randall Souviney, eds., "Computers and Literacy": A Time for Tools, special issue of the *Quarterly Newsletter of the Laboratory of Comparative Human Cognition* 5 (July 1983).

28. Peg Griffin, Michael Cole, Stephen Diaz, and Catherine King, "Model Systems for Re-mediating Reading Difficulties," in *Cognition and Instruction,* ed. Robert Glaser (Hillsdale, N.J.: Lawrence Erlbaum Associates, forthcoming).

29. Luis C. Moll and Stephen Diaz, "Bilingual Communication and Reading: The Importance of Spanish in Learning to Read in English" (unpublished manuscript, 1984).

24

How Asian Teachers Polish Each Lesson to Perfection

JAMES W. STIGLER AND HAROLD W. STEVENSON

Much attention has been directed recently to the educational performance of children in the United States relative to that of children in other societies. James W. Stigler and Harold W. Stevenson have examined the practices and goals of schooling in China, Japan, and the United States. Their observations indicate that both the processes and outcomes of schooling in these three societies reflect deeply held cultural values. These values influence the practices and expectations that children encounter in school. These observations suggest that modeling U.S. classrooms after those in other cultures will not necessarily benefit children in the absence of the supporting cultural context from which these practices derive meaning and direction.

Although there is no overall difference in intelligence, the differences in mathematical achievement of American children and their Asian counterparts are staggering.[1]

Let us look first at the results of a study we conducted in 120 classrooms in three cities: Taipei (Taiwan); Sendai (Japan); and the Minneapolis metropolitan area. First and fifth graders from representative schools in these cities were given a test of mathematics that required computation and problem solving. Among the one hundred first graders in the three locations who received the lowest scores, fifty-

Reprinted with permission from the authors and *American Educator*, Spring, 1992, 12–20, 43–47. Copyright 1992 by the American Federation of Teachers. This article is an excerpt from H. S. Stevenson and J. S. Stigler, *The Learning Gap: Why Our Schools Are Failing and What We Can Learn from Japanese and Chinese Education*, New York: Summit Books, 1992.

A thirty-four-minute cassette depicting Japanese and Chinese classroom scenes that illustrate the techniques described in this article is available for $35. Called *The Polished Stones,* it can be ordered from Catherine A. Smith, 300 North Ingalls, 10th floor, University of Michigan, Ann Arbor, Michigan 48109. Checks should be made payable to the university.

eight were American children; among the one hundred lowest-scoring fifth graders, sixty-seven were American children. Among the top one hundred first graders in mathematics, there were only fifteen American children. And only one American child appeared among the top one hundred fifth graders. The highest-scoring American classroom obtained an average score lower than that of the lowest-scoring Japanese classroom and of all but one of the twenty classrooms in Taipei. In whatever way we looked at the data, the poor performance of American children was evident.

These data are startling, but no more so than the results of a study that involved 40 first- and 40 fifth-grade classrooms in the metropolitan area of Chicago—a very representative sample of the city and the suburbs of Cook County—and twenty-two classes in each of these grades in metropolitan Beijing (China). In this study, children were given a battery of mathematics tasks that included diverse problems, such as estimating the distance between a tree and a hidden treasure on a map, deciding who won a race on the basis of data in a graph, trying to explain subtraction to visiting Martians, or calculating the sum of nineteen and forty-five. There was no area in which the American children were competitive with those from China. The Chinese children's superiority appeared in complex tasks involving the application of knowledge as well as in the routines of computation. When fifth graders were asked, for example, how many members of a stamp club with twenty-four members collected only foreign stamps if five-sixths of the members did so, 59 percent of Beijing children, but only 9 percent of the Chicago children produced the correct answer. On a computation test, only 2.2 percent of the Chinese fifth graders scored at or below the mean for their American counterparts. All of the twenty Chicago area schools had average scores on the fifth-grade geometry test that were below those of the Beijing schools. The results from all these tasks paint a bleak picture of American children's competencies in mathematics.[2]

The poor performance of American students compels us to try to understand the reasons why. We have written extensively elsewhere about the cultural differences in attitudes toward learning and toward the importance of effort vs. innate ability and about the substantially greater amounts of time Japanese and Chinese students devote to academic activities in general and to the study of math in particular.[3] Important as these factors are, they do not tell the whole story. For that we have to take a close look inside the classrooms of Japan, China, and the United States to see how mathematics is actually taught in the three cultures.

LESSONS NOT LECTURES

If we were asked briefly to characterize classes in Japan and China, we would say that they consist of coherent lessons that are presented in a thoughtful, relaxed, and nonauthoritarian manner. Teachers frequently rely on students as sources of information. Lessons are oriented toward problem solving rather than rote mastery of facts and procedures and utilize many different types of representational materials. The role assumed by the teacher is that of knowledgeable guide, rather than that of prime dispenser of information and arbiter of what is correct. There is frequent verbal interaction in the classroom as the teacher attempts to stimulate students to produce, explain, and evaluate solutions to problems. These characteristics contradict stereotypes held by most Westerners about Asian teaching practices. Lessons are not rote; they are not filled with drill. Teachers do not spend large amounts of time lecturing but attempt to lead the children in productive interactions and discussions. And the children are not the passive automata depicted in Western descriptions but active participants in the learning process.

We begin by discussing what we mean by the coherence of a lesson. One way to think of a lesson is by using the analog of a story. A good story is highly organized; it has a beginning, a middle, and an end; and it follows a protagonist who meets challenges and resolves problems that arise along the way. Above all, a good story engages the reader's interest in a series of interconnected events, which are best understood in the context of the events that precede and follow it.

Such a concept of a lesson guides the organization of instruction in Asia. The curricula are defined in terms of coherent lessons, each carefully designed to fill a forty- to fifty-minute class period with sustained attention to the development of some concept or skill. Like a good story, the lesson has an introduction, a conclusion, and a consistent theme.

We can illustrate what we are talking about with this account of a fifth-grade Japanese mathematics class:

The teacher walks in carrying a large paper bag full of clinking glass. Entering the classroom with a large paper bag is highly unusual, and by the time she has placed the bag on her desk the students are regarding her with rapt attention. What's in the bag? She begins to pull items out of the bag, placing them, one-by-one, on her desk. She removes a pitcher and a vase. A beer bottle evokes laughter and surprise. She soon has six containers lined up on her desk. The children continue to watch intently, glancing back and forth at each other as they seek to understand the purpose of this display.

The teacher, looking thoughtfully at the containers, poses a question: "I wonder which one would hold the most water?" Hands go up, and the teacher calls on different students to give their guesses: "the pitcher," "the beer bottle," "the teapot." The teacher stands aside and ponders: "Some of you said one thing, others said something different. You don't agree with each other. There must be some way we can find out who is correct. How can we know who is correct?" Interest is high, and the discussion continues.

The students soon agree that to find out how much each container holds they will need to fill the containers with something. How about water? The teacher finds some buckets and sends several children out to fill them with water. When they return, the teacher says: "Now what do we do?" Again there is a discussion, and after several minutes the children decide that they will need to use a smaller container to measure how much water fits into each of the larger containers. They decide on a drinking cup, and one of the students warns that they all have to fill each cup to the same level—otherwise the measure won't be the same for all of the groups.

At this point the teacher divides the class into their groups (*han*) and gives each group one of the containers and a drinking cup. Each group fills its container, counts how many cups of water it holds, and writes the result in a notebook. When all of the groups have completed the task, the teacher calls on the leader of each group to report on the group's findings and notes the results on the blackboard. She has written the names of the containers in a column on the left and a scale from 1 to 6 along the bottom. Pitcher, 4.5 cups; vase, 3 cups; beer bottle, 1. 5 cups; and so on. As each group makes its report the teacher draws a bar representing the amount, in cups, the container holds.

Finally, the teacher returns to the question she posed at the beginning of the lesson: Which container holds the most water? She reviews how they were able to solve the problem and points out that the answer is now contained in the bar graph on the board. She then arranges the containers on the table in order according to how much they hold and writes a rank order on each container, from 1 to 6. She ends the class with a brief review of what they have done. No definitions of ordinate and abscissa, no discus-

sion of how to make a graph preceded the example—these all became obvious in the course of the lesson, and only at the end did the teacher mention the terms that describe the horizontal and vertical axes of the graph they had made.

With one carefully crafted problem, this Japanese teacher has guided her students to discover—and most likely to remember—several important concepts. As this article unfolds, we hope to demonstrate that this example of how well-designed Asian class lessons are is not an isolated one; to the contrary, it is the norm. And as we hope to further demonstrate, excellent class lessons do not come effortlessly or magically. Asian teachers are not born great teachers; they and the lessons they develop require careful nurturing and constant refinement. The practice of teaching in Japan and China is more uniformly perfected than it is in the United States because their systems of education are structured to encourage teaching excellence to develop and flourish. Ours is not. We will take up the question of why and what can be done about this later in the piece. But first, we present a more detailed look at what Asian lessons are like.

COHERENCE BROKEN

Asian lessons almost always begin with a practical problem, such as the example we have just given, or with a word problem written on the blackboard. Asian teachers, to a much greater degree than American teachers, give coherence to their lessons by introducing the lesson with a word problem.

It is not uncommon for the Asian teacher to organize the entire lesson around the solution to this single problem. The teacher leads the children to recognize what is known and what is unknown and directs the students' attention to the critical parts of the problem. Teachers are careful to see that the problem is understood by all of the children, and even mechanics, such as mathematical computation, are presented in the context of solving a problem.

Before ending the lesson, the teacher reviews what has been learned and relates it to the problem she posed at the beginning of the lesson. American teachers are much less likely than Asian teachers to begin and end lessons in this way. For example, we found that fifth-grade teachers in Beijing spent eight times as long at the end of the class period summarizing the lessons as did those in the Chicago metropolitan area.

Now contrast the Japanese math lesson described above with a fifth-grade American mathematics classroom that we recently visited. Immediately after getting the students' attention, the teacher pointed out that today was Tuesday, "band day," and that all students in the band should go to the band room. "Those of you doing the news report today should meet over there in the corner," he continued. He then began the mathematics class with the remaining students by reviewing the solution to a computation problem that had been included in the previous day's homework. After this brief review, the teacher directed the students' attention to the blackboard, where the day's assignment had been written. From this point on, the teacher spent most of the rest of the period walking about the room monitoring the children's work, talking to individual children about questions or errors, and uttering "shushes" whenever the students began talking among themselves.

This example is typical of the American classrooms we have visited, classrooms where students spend more time in transition and less in academic activities, more time working on their own and less being instructed by the teacher; where teachers spend much of their time working with individual students and attending to matters of discipline; and where the shape of a coherent lesson is often hard to discern.

American lessons are often disrupted by irrelevant interruptions. These serve to break the continuity of the lesson and add to children's difficulty in perceiving the lesson as a coherent whole. In our American observations, the teacher interrupted the flow of the lesson with an interlude of irrelevant comments or the class was interrupted by someone else in 20 percent of all first-grade lessons and 47 percent of all fifth-grade lessons. This occurred less than 10 percent of the time at both grade levels in Sendai, Taipei, and Beijing. In fact, no interruptions of either type were recorded during the eighty hours of observation in Beijing fifth-grade classrooms. The mathematics lesson in one of the American classrooms we visited was interrupted every morning by a woman from the cafeteria who polled the children about their lunch plans and collected money from those who planned to eat the hot lunch. Interruptions, as well as inefficient transitions from one activity to another, make it difficult to sustain a coherent lesson throughout the class period.

Coherence is also disrupted when teachers shift frequently from one topic to another. This occurred often in the American classrooms we observed. The teacher might begin with a segment on measurement, then proceed to a segment on simple addition, then to a segment on telling time, and then to a second segment on addition. These segments constitute a math class, but they are hardly a coherent lesson. Such changes in topic were responsible for 21 percent of the changes in segments that we observed in American classrooms but accounted for only 4 percent of the changes in segments in Japanese classrooms.

Teachers frequently capitalize on variety as a means of capturing children's interest. This may explain why American teachers shift topics so frequently within the lesson. Asian teachers also seek variety, but they tend to introduce new activities instead of new topics. Shifts in materials do not necessarily pose a threat to coherence. For example, the coherence of a lesson does not diminish when the teacher shifts from working with numerals to working with concrete objects, if both are used to represent the same subtraction problem. Shifting the topic, on the other hand, introduces variety, but at the risk of destroying the coherence of the lesson.

CLASSROOM ORGANIZATION

Elementary school classrooms are typically organized in one of three ways: the whole class is working as a unit; the class is divided into a number of small groups; or children work individually. In our observations, we noted when the child was receiving instruction or assistance from the teacher and when the student was working on his own. The child was considered to be receiving instruction whenever the teacher was the leader of the activity, whether it involved the whole class, a small group, or only the individual child.

Looking at the classroom in this manner led us to one of our most pronounced findings: Although the number of children in Asian classes is significantly greater than the number in American classes, Asian students received much more instruction from their teachers than American students. In Taiwan, the teacher was the leader of the child's activity 90 percent of the time, as opposed to 74 percent in Japan, and only 46 percent in the United States. No one was leading instruction 9 percent of the time in Taiwan, 26 percent in Japan, and an astonishing 51 percent of the time in the United States (see Figure 1). Even American first graders actually spent more time on their own than they did participating in an activity led by the teacher.

One of the reasons American children received less instruction is that American teachers spent 13 percent of their time in the mathematics classes not working with any students, something that happened only 6 percent of the time in Japan and 9 percent in Taiwan. (As we will see later, American teachers have to steal class time to attend to the multitude of chores involving preparation, assessment, and administration because so little nonteaching time is available for them during the day.)

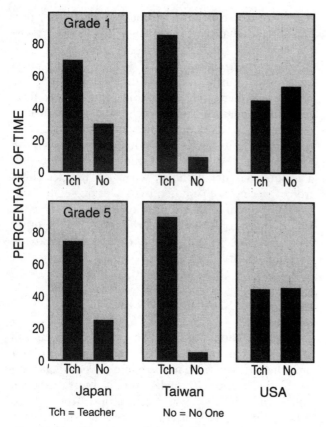

FIGURE 1   Percentage of time students spent in activity led by teacher and by no one.

A much more critical factor in the erosion of instructional time was the amount of time American teachers were involved with individuals or small groups. American children spend 10 percent of their time in small groups and 47 percent of their time working individually. Much of the 87 percent of the time American teachers were working with their students was spent with these individual students or small groups, rather than with the class as a whole. When teachers provide individual instruction, they must leave the rest of the class unattended, so instructional time for all remaining children is reduced.

Children can learn without a teacher. Nevertheless, it seems likely that they could profit from having their teacher as the leader of their activities more than half of the time they are in the classroom. It is the incredibly large amounts of time that American children are left unassisted and the effect that unattended time has on the coherence of the larger lesson that is the problem.

When children must work alone for long periods of time without guidance or reaction from the teacher, they begin to lose focus on the purpose of their activity. Asian teachers not only assign less seatwork

than American teachers, they also use seatwork differently. Chinese and Japanese teachers tend to use short, frequent periods of seatwork, alternating between group discussion of problems and time for children to work problems on their own. Seatwork is thereby embedded into the lesson. After they work individually or in small groups on a problem, Asian students are called upon to present and defend the solutions they came up with. Thus, instruction, practice, and evaluation are tightly interwoven into a coherent whole. In contrast, the average length of seatwork in American fifth-grade classrooms was almost twice as long as it was in Asian classrooms. And, instead of embedding seatwork into the ongoing back and forth of the lesson, American teachers tend to relegate it to one long period at the end of the class, where it becomes little more than a time for repetitious practice. In Chicago, 59 percent of all fifth-grade lessons ended with a period of seatwork, compared with 23 percent in Sendai and 14 percent in Taipei. American teachers often do not discuss the work or its connection to the goal of the lesson, or even evaluate its accuracy. Seatwork was never evaluated or discussed in 48 percent of all American fifth-grade classes we observed, compared to less than 3 percent of Japanese classes and 6 percent of Taiwan classes.

Since Asian students spend so much of their time in whole-group work, we need to say a word about that format. Whole-class instruction in the United States has gotten a somewhat bad reputation. It has become associated with too much teacher talk and too many passive, tuned-out students. But as we will see in more detail as we continue our description of Asian classrooms, whole-class instruction in Japan and China is a very lively, engaging enterprise. Asian teachers do not spend large amounts of time lecturing. They present interesting problems; they pose provocative questions; they probe and guide. The students work hard, generating multiple approaches to a solution, explaining the rationale behind their methods, and making good use of wrong answers.

HANDLING DIVERSITY

The organization of American elementary school classrooms is based on the assumption that whole-group instruction cannot accommodate students' diverse abilities and levels of achievement; thus, large amounts of whole-class time are given up so that the teacher can work individually with students. Asian educators are more comfortable in the belief that all children, with proper effort, can take advantage of a uniform educational experience, and so they are able

HOW WE MADE SURE WE WERE LOOKING AT REPRESENTATIVE SCHOOLS

Frequent reports on television and in books and newspapers purport to depict what happens inside Japanese and Chinese classrooms. These reports usually are based on impressions gathered during brief visits to classrooms—most likely classrooms that the visitor's contacts in Asia have preselected. As a result, it is difficult to gauge the generality of what was seen and reported. Without observing large, representative samples of schools and teachers, it is impossible to characterize the teaching practices of any culture.

The descriptions that we present are based on two large observational studies of first- and fifth-grade classrooms that we conducted in Japan, Taiwan, China, and the United States. In contrast to informal observations, the strength of formal studies such as ours is that the observations are made according to consistent rules about where, when, and what to observe.

In the first study, our observers were in classrooms for a total of over four thousand hours—over a thousand class periods in 20 first- and fifth-grade classrooms in each of three cities: Sendai, Japan; Taipei, Taiwan; and Minneapolis, Minnesota.[1] Our second study took place in two hundred classrooms, forty each in Sendai and Taipei, plus forty in Beijing, China, and eighty in the Chicago metropolitan area of the United States.[2] Care was taken to choose schools that were representative. Our Chicago metropolitan area sample—the urban and suburban areas that make up Cook County—included schools that are predominantly white, black, Hispanic, and ethni-cally mixed; schools that draw from upper, middle, and lower socioeconomic groups; schools that are public and private; and schools that are urban and suburban.

Observers visited each classroom four times over a one- to two-week period, yielding a total of eight hundred hours of observations. The observers, who were residents of each city, wrote down as much as they could about what transpired during each mathematics class. Tape recordings made during the classes assisted the observers in filling in any missing information. These detailed narrative accounts of what transpired in the classrooms yielded even richer information than we obtained in the first study, where the observers followed predefined categories for coding behavior during the course of observations.

After the narrative records had been translated into English, we divided each observation into segments, which we defined as beginning each time there was a change in topic, materials, or activity. For example, a segment began when students put away their textbooks and began working on a worksheet or when the teacher stopped lecturing and asked some of the students to write their solutions to a problem on the blackboard.

Both studies focused on mathematics classes rather than on classes in subjects such as reading, where cultural differences in teaching practices may be more strongly determined by the content of what is being taught. For example, it is likely that the processes of teaching and learning about the multiplication of fractions transcend cultural differences, whereas teaching children how to read Chinese characters may require different approaches from those used to teach children to read an alphabetic language.

References

[1] Stevenson, H. W., Stigler, J. W., Lucker, G. W., Lee, S. Y., Hsu, C. C., & Kitamura, S. (1987). Classroom behavior and achievement of Japanese, Chinese, and American children. In R. Glaser (Ed.), *Advances in instructional psychology*. Hillsdale NJ: Erlbaum.

[2] Stigler, J. W., & Perry, M. (1990). Mathematics learning in Japanese, Chinese, and American classrooms. In Stigler, J. W., Shweder, R. A., & Herdt, G. (Eds.), *Cultural psychology: Essays on comparative human development*. Cambridge, Cambridge University Press. Pp. 328–356.

to focus on providing the same high-quality experience to all students. Our results suggest that American educators need to question their long-held assumption that an individualized learning experience is inherently a higher-quality, more effective experience than is a whole-class learning experience. Although it may be true that an equal amount of time with a teacher may be more effective in a one-on-one situation than in a large-group situation, we must realize that the result of individualized instruction, given realistic financial constraints, is to drastically reduce the amount of teacher instruction every child receives.

Japanese and Chinese teachers recognize individual differences among students, but they handle that diversity in a very different way. First, as we will see in more detail later, they have much greater amounts of nonteaching time than do American teachers, and part of that time is available for working with individual students. They may spend extra time with slower students or ask faster students to assist them, but they focus their lesson on teaching all children regardless of apparent differences in ability or developmental readiness. Before we discuss how they do that in a whole-group setting, we need to first address the question of whether American classrooms are more diverse than Asian ones, thus potentially rendering whole-class instruction more difficult.

Whenever we discuss our research on teaching practices, someone in the audience inevitably reminds us that Japan and China are nations with relatively homogeneous populations while the United States is the melting pot of the world. How could we expect that practices used in Asian societies could possibly be relevant for the American context, where diversity is the rule in race, ethnicity, language, and social class?

What impedes teaching is the uneven preparation of children for the academic tasks that must be accomplished. It is diversity in children's educational backgrounds, not in their social and cultural backgrounds, that poses the greatest problems in teaching. Although the United States is culturally more diverse than Japan or China, we have found no more diversity at the classroom level in the educational level of American than of Asian students. The key factor is that, in the United States, educational and cultural diversity are positively related, leading some persons to the inappropriate conclusion that it is ethnic and cultural diversity, rather than educational diversity, that leads to the difficulties faced by American teachers.

It is true, for example, that there is greater variability in mathematics achievement among American than among Japanese children, but this does not mean that the differences are evident in any particular class-

room. Variability in the United States exists to a large extent across neighborhoods and schools (rather than within them). Within individual classrooms, the variability in levels of academic achievement differs little between the United States and Japan, Taiwan, or China. It is wrong to argue that diversity within classrooms is an American problem. Teachers everywhere must deal with students who vary in their knowledge and motivation.

Tracking does not exist in Asian elementary schools. Children are never separated into different classrooms according to their presumed levels of intellectual ability. This egalitarian philosophy carries over to organization within the classroom. Children are not separated into reading groups according to their ability; there is no division of the class into groups differentiated by the rate at which they proceed through their mathematics books. No children leave the classroom for special classes, such as those designed for children who have been diagnosed as having learning disabilities.

How do teachers in Asian classrooms handle diversity in students' knowledge and skills? For one thing, they typically use a variety of approaches in their teaching, allowing students who may not understand one approach the opportunity to experience other approaches to presenting the material. Periods of recitation are alternated with periods in which children work for short periods on practice problems. Explanations by the teacher are interspersed with periods in which children work with concrete materials or struggle to come up with their own solutions to problems. There is continuous change from one mode of presentation, one type of representation, and one type of teaching method to another.

Asian teaching practices thrive in the face of diversity, and some practices can depend on diversity for their effectiveness. Asking students to suggest alternative solutions to a problem, for example, works best when students have had experience in generating a variety of solutions. Incorrect solutions, which are typically dismissed by the American teacher, become topics for discussion in Asian classrooms, and all students can learn from this discussion. Thus, while American schools attempt to solve the problems of diversity by segregating children into different groups or different classrooms, and by spending large amounts of regular class time working with individual students, Asian teachers believe that the only way they can cope with the problem is by devising teaching techniques that accommodate the different interests and backgrounds of the children in their classrooms.

Asian teachers also exploit the fact that the same instruction can affect different students in different ways, something that may be overlooked by American teachers. In this sense, Asian teachers subscribe to what would be considered in the West to be a "constructivist" view of learning. According to this view, knowledge is regarded as something that must be constructed by the child rather than as a set of facts and skills that can be imparted by the teacher. Because children are engaged in their own construction of knowledge, some of the major tasks for the teacher are to pose provocative questions, to allow adequate time for reflection, and to vary teaching techniques so that they are responsive to differences in students' prior experience. Through such practices, Asian teachers are able to accommodate individual differences in learning, even though instruction is not tailored to each student.

USE OF REAL-WORLD PROBLEMS AND OBJECTS

Elementary school mathematics is often defined in terms of mathematical symbols and their manipulation; for example, children must learn the place-value system of numeration and the operations for manipulating numerals to add, subtract, multiply, and divide. In addition, children must be able to apply these symbols and operations to solving problems. In order to accomplish these goals, teachers rely primarily on two powerful tools for representing mathematics: language and the manipulation of concrete objects. How effectively teachers use these forms of representation plays a critical role in determining how well children will understand mathematics.

One common function of language is in defining terms and stating rules for performing mathematical operations. A second, broader function is the use of language as a means of connecting mathematical operations to the real world and of integrating what children know about mathematics. We find that American elementary school teachers are more prone to use language to define terms and state rules than are Asian teachers, who, in their efforts to make mathematics meaningful, use language to clarify different aspects of mathematics and to intergrate what children know about mathematics with the demands of real-world problems. Here is an example of what we mean by a class in which the teacher defines terms and states rules:

An American teacher announces that the lesson today concerns fractions. Fractions are defined and she names the numerator and denominator. "What do we call this?" she then asks. "And this?" After assuring herself that the children un-

derstand the meaning of the terms, she spends the rest of the lesson teaching them to apply the rules for forming fractions.

Asian teachers tend to reverse the procedure. They focus initially on interpreting and relating a real-world problem to the quantification that is necessary for a mathematical solution and then to define terms and state rules. In the following example, a third-grade teacher in Japan was also teaching a lesson that introduced the notation system for fractions.

The lesson began with the teacher posing the question of how many liters of juice (colored water) were contained in a large beaker. "More than one liter," answered one child. "One and a half liters," answered another. After several children had made guesses, the teacher suggested that they pour the juice into some one-liter beakers and see. Horizontal lines on each beaker divided it into thirds. The juice filled one beaker and part of a second. The teacher pointed out that the water came up to the first line on the second beaker—only one of the three parts was full. The procedure was repeated with a second set of beakers to illustrate the concept of one-half. After stating that there had been one and one-out-of-three liters of juice in the first big beaker and one and one-out-of-two liters in the second, the teacher wrote the fractions on the board. He continued the lesson by asking the children how to represent two parts out of three, two parts out of five, and so forth. Near the end of the period he mentioned the term "fraction" for the first time and attached names to the numerator and the denominator.

He ended the lesson by summarizing how fractions can be used to represent the parts of a whole.

In the second example, the concept of fractions emerged from a meaningful experience; in the first, it was introduced initially as an abstract concept. The terms and operations in the second example flowed naturally from the teacher's questions and discussion; in the first, language was used primarily for defining and summarizing rules. Mathematics ultimately requires abstract representation, but young children understand such representation more readily if it is derived from meaningful experience than if it results from learning definitions and rules.

Asian teachers generally are more likely than American teachers to engage their students, even very young ones, in the discussion of mathematical concepts. The kind of verbal discussion we find in American classrooms is more short-answer in nature, oriented, for example, toward clarifying the correct way to implement a computational procedure.

Teachers ask questions for different reasons in the United States and in Japan. In the United States, the purpose of a question is to get an answer. In Japan, teachers pose questions to stimulate thought. A Japanese teacher considers a question to be a poor one if it elicits an immediate answer, for this indicates that students were not challenged to think. One teacher we interviewed told us of discussions she had with her fellow teachers on how to improve teaching practices. "What do you talk about?" we wondered. "A great deal of time," she reported, "is spent talking about questions we can pose to the class—which wordings work best to get students involved in thinking and discussing the material. One good question can keep a whole class going for a long time; a bad one produces little more than a simple answer."

In one memorable example recorded by our observers, a Japanese first-grade teacher began her class by posing the question to one of her students: "Would you explain the difference between what we learned in yesterday's lesson and what you came across in preparing for today's lesson?" The young student thought for a long time, but then answered the question intelligently, a performance that undoubtedly enhanced his understanding of both lessons.

CONCRETE REPRESENTATIONS

Every elementary school student in Sendai possesses a "Math Set," a box of colorful, well-designed materials for teaching mathematical concepts: tiles, clock, ruler, checkerboard, colored triangles, beads, and many other attractive objects.

In Taipei, every classroom is equipped with a similar, but larger, set of such objects. In Beijing, where there is much less money available for purchasing such materials, teachers improvise with colored paper, wax fruit, plates, and other easily obtained objects. In all cases, these concrete objects are considered to be critically important tools for teaching mathematics, for it is through manipulating these objects that children can form important links between real-world problems and abstract mathematical notations.

American teachers are much less likely than Chinese or Japanese teachers to use concrete objects. At fifth grade, for example, Sendai teachers were nearly twice as likely to use concrete objects as the Chicago area teachers, and Taipei teachers were nearly five times as likely. There was also a subtle, but important, difference in the way Asian and American teachers used concrete objects. Japanese teachers, for example, use the items in the Math Set throughout the elementary school years and introduced small tiles in a high percentage of the lessons we observed in the first grade. American teachers seek variety and may use Popsicle sticks in one lesson, and in another, marbles, Cheerios, M&Ms, checkers, poker chips, or plastic animals. The American view is that objects should be varied in order to maintain children's interest. The Asian view is that using a variety of representational materials may confuse children, and thereby make it more difficult for them to use the objects for the representation and solution of mathematics problems. Having learned to add with tiles makes multiplication easier to understand when the same tiles are used.

Through the skillful use of concrete objects, teachers are able to teach elementary school children to understand and solve problems that are not introduced in American curricula until much later. An example occurred in a fourth-grade mathematics lesson we observed in Japan. The problem the teacher posed is a difficult one for fourth graders, and its solution is generally not taught in the United States until much later. This is the problem:

> There are a total of thirty-eight children in Akira's class. There are six more boys than there are girls. How many boys and how many girls are in the class?

This lesson began with a discussion of the problem and with the children proposing ways to solve it. After the discussion, the teacher handed each child two strips of paper, one six units longer than the other, and told the class that the strips would be used to help them think about the problem. One slip represented the number of girls in the class and the other represented the number of boys. By lining the strips next to each other, the children could see that the degree to which the longer one protruded beyond the shorter one represented 6 boys. The procedure for solving the problem then unfolded as the teacher, through skillful questioning, led the children to the solution: The number of girls was found by taking the total of both strips, subtracting 6 to make the strips of equal length, and then dividing by 2. The number of boys could be found, of course, by adding 6 to the number of girls. With this concrete visual representation of the problem and careful guidance from the teacher, even fourth graders were able to understand the problem and its solution.

STUDENTS CONSTRUCT MULTIPLE SOLUTIONS

A common Western stereotype is that the Asian teacher is an authoritarian purveyor of information, one who expects students to listen and memorize correct answers or correct procedures rather than to construct knowledge themselves. This may or may not be an accurate description of Asian high school teachers,[4] but, as we have seen in previous examples, it does not describe the dozens of elementary school teachers that we have observed.

Chinese and Japanese teachers rely on students to generate ideas and evaluate the correctness of the ideas. The possibility that they will be called upon to state their own solution as well as to evaluate what another student has proposed keeps Asian students alert, but this technique has two other important functions. First, it engages students in the lesson, increasing their motivation by making them feel they are participants in a group process. Second, it conveys a more realistic impression of how knowledge is acquired. Mathematics, for example, is a body of knowledge that has evolved gradually through a process of argument and proof. Learning to argue about mathematical ideas is fundamental to understanding mathematics. Chinese and Japanese children begin learning these skills in the first grade; many American elementary school students are never exposed to them.

We can illustrate the way Asian teachers use students' ideas with the following example. A fifth-grade teacher in Taiwan began her mathematics lesson by calling attention to a six-sided figure she had drawn on the blackboard. She asked the students how they might go about finding the area of the shaded region. "I don't want you to tell me what the actual area is, just tell me the approach you would use to solve the problem. Think of as many different ways as you can of ways you could determine the area that I have drawn in yellow chalk." She allowed the students several minutes to work in small groups and then called upon a child from each group to describe the group's solution. After each proposal, many of which were quite complex, the teacher asked members of the other groups whether the procedure described could yield a correct answer. After several different procedures had been suggested, the teacher moved on to a second problem with a different embedded figure and repeated the process. Neither teacher nor students actually carried out a solution to the problem until all of the alternative solutions had been discussed. The lesson ended with the teacher affirming the importance of coming up with multiple solutions. "After all," she said, "we face many problems every day in the real world. We have to remember that there is not only one way we can solve each problem."

American teachers are less likely to give students opportunities to respond at such length. Although a great deal of interaction appears to occur in American classrooms—with teachers and students posing questions and giving answers—American teachers generally pose questions that are answerable with a yes or no or with a short phrase. They seek a correct answer and continue calling on students until one produces it. "Since we can't subtract 8 from 6," says an American teacher, "we have to ... what?" Hands go up, the teacher calls on a girl who says "Borrow." "Correct," the teacher replies. This kind of interchange does not establish the student as a valid source of information, for the final arbiter of the correctness of the student's opinions is still the teacher. The situation is very different in Asian classrooms, where children are likely to be asked to explain their answers and other children are then called upon to evaluate their correctness.

Clear evidence of these differing beliefs about the roles of students and teachers appears in the observations of how teachers evaluate students' responses. The most frequent form of evaluation used by American teachers was praise, a technique that was rarely used in either Taiwan or Japan. In Japan, evaluation most frequently took the form of a discussion of children's errors.

Praise serves to cut off discussion and to highlight the teacher's role as the authority. It also encourages children to be satisfied with their performance rather than informing them about where they need improvement. Discussing errors, on the other hand, encourages argument and justification and involves students in the exciting quest of assessing the strengths and weaknesses of the various alternative solutions that have been proposed.

Why are American teachers often reluctant to encourage students to participate at greater length during mathematics lessons? One possibility is that they feel insecure about the depth of their own mathematical training. Placing more emphasis on students' explanations necessarily requires teachers to relinquish some control over the direction the lesson will take. This can be a frightening prospect to a teacher who is unprepared to evaluate the validity of novel ideas that students inevitably propose.

USING ERRORS EFFECTIVELY

We have been struck by the different reactions of Asian and American teachers to children's errors. For

Americans, errors tend to be interpreted as an indication of failure in learning the lesson. For Chinese and Japanese, they are an index of what still needs to be learned. These divergent interpretations result in very different reactions to the display of errors—embarrassment on the part of the American children, calm acceptance by Asian children. They also result in differences in the manner in which teachers utilize errors as effective means of instruction.

We visited a fifth-grade classroom in Japan the first day the teacher introduced the problem of adding fractions with unequal denominators. The problem was a simple one: adding one-third and one-half. The children were told to solve the problem and that the class would then review the different solutions.

After everyone appeared to have completed the task, the teacher called on one of the students to give his answer and to explain his solution. "The answer is two-fifths," he stated. Pointing first to the numerators and then to the denominators, he explained: "One plus one is two; three plus two is five. The answer is two-fifths." Without comment, the teacher asked another boy for his solution. "Two point one plus three point one, when changed into a fraction adds up to two-fifths." The children in the classroom looked puzzled. The teacher, unperturbed, asked a third student for her solution. "The answer is five-sixths." The student went on to explain how she had found the common denominator, changed the fractions so that each had this denominator, and then added them.

The teacher returned to the first solution. "How many of you think this solution is correct?" Most agreed that it was not. She used the opportunity to direct the children's attention to reasons why the solution was incorrect. "Which is larger, two-fifths or one-half?" The class agreed that it was one-half. "It is strange, isn't it, that you could add a number to one-half and get a number that is smaller than one-half." She went on to explain how the procedure the child used would result in the odd situation where, when one-half was added to one-half, the answer yielded is one-half. In a similarly careful, interactive manner, she discussed how the second boy had confused fractions with decimals to come up with his surprising answer. Rather than ignoring the incorrect solutions and concentrating her attention on the correct solution, the teacher capitalized on the errors the children made in order to dispel two common misperceptions about fractions.

We have not observed American teachers responding to children's errors so inventively. Perhaps because of the strong influence of behavioristic teaching that conditions should be arranged so that the learner avoids errors and makes only a reinforceable response, American teachers place little emphasis on the constructive use of errors as a teaching technique. It seems likely, however, that learning about what is wrong may hasten children's understanding of why the correct procedures are appropriate.

WHY NOT HERE?

Few who have visited urban classrooms in Asia would disagree that the great majority of Chinese and Japanese teachers are highly skilled professionals. Their dedication is legendary; what is often not appreciated is how thoughtfully and adroitly they guide children through the vast amount of material that they must master during the six years of elementary school. We, of course, witnessed examples of excellent lessons in American classrooms. And there are of course individual differences among Asian teachers. But what has impressed us in our personal observations and in the data from our observational studies is how remarkably well most Asian teachers teach. It is the *widespread* excellence of Asian class lessons, the high level of performance of the *average* teacher, that is so stunning.

The techniques used by Chinese and Japanese teachers are not new to the teaching profession—nor are they foreign or exotic. In fact, they are the types of techniques often recommended by American educators. What the Japanese and Chinese examples demonstrate so compellingly is that when widely implemented, such practices can produce extraordinary outcomes.

Unfortunately, these techniques have not been broadly applied in the United States. Why? One reason, as we have discussed, is the Asian belief that the whole-group lesson, if done well, can be made to work for every child. With that assumption, Asian teachers can focus on the perfection of that lesson. However, even if American educators shared that belief, it would be difficult for them to achieve anything near the broad-based high quality that we observed in Asian classrooms. This is not the fault of American teachers. The fault lies with a system that prepares them inadequately and then exhausts them physically, emotionally, and intellectually while denying them the collegial interaction that every profession relies upon for the growth and refinement of its knowledge base.

The first major obstacle to the widespread development and execution of excellent lessons in America is the fact that American teachers are overworked. It is inconceivable that American teachers, by themselves, would be able to organize lively, vivid, coherent lessons under a regimen that requires that they teach hour after hour every day throughout the school year. Preparing lessons that require the discovery of knowledge and the construction of understanding takes time. Teaching them effectively requires energy. Both are in very short supply for most American teachers.

Being an elementary school teacher in the United States at the end of the twentieth century is extraordinarily difficult, and the demands made by American society exhaust even the most energetic among them. "I'm dancing as fast as I can" one teacher summarized her feelings about her job, "but with all the things that I'm supposed to do, I just can't keep up."

The full realization of how little time American teachers have when they are not directly in charge of children became clear to us during a meeting in Beijing. We were discussing the teachers' workday. When we informed the Chinese teachers that American teachers are responsible for their classes all day long, with only an hour or less outside the classroom each day, they looked incredulous. How could any teacher be expected to do a good job when there is no time outside of class to prepare and correct lessons, work with individual children, consult with other teachers, and attend to all of the matters that arise in a typical day at school! Beijing teachers teach no more than three hours a day, unless the teacher is a homeroom teacher, in which case, the total is four hours. During the first three grades, the teaching assignment includes both reading and mathematics; for the upper three grades of elementary school, teachers specialize in one of these subjects. They spend the rest of their day at school carrying out all of their other responsibilities to their students and to the school. The situation is similar in Japan. According to our estimate, Japanese elementary school teachers are in charge of classes only 60 percent of the time they are at school.

The large amounts of nonteaching time at school are available to Asian teachers because of two factors. The first concerns the number of teachers typically assigned to Asian schools. Although class sizes are considerably larger in Asia, the student-to-teacher ratio within a school does not differ greatly from that in the United States. By having more students in each class and the same number of teachers in the school, all teachers can have fewer teaching hours. Time is freed up for teachers to meet and work together on a daily basis, to prepare lessons for the next day, to work with individual children, and to attend staff meetings.

The second factor increasing the time available to Japanese and Chinese teachers at school is that they spend more hours at school each day than do American teachers. In our study, for example, teachers in Sendai and Taipei spent an average of 9.5 and 9.1 hours per day, respectively, compared to only 7.3 hours for the American teachers. Asian teachers arrive at school early and stay late, which gives them time to meet together and to work with children who need extra help. Most American teachers, in contrast, arrive at school shortly before classes begin and leave not long after they end. This does not mean a shorter work week for American teachers. What it does mean is that they must devote their evenings to working alone on the next day's lessons, further increasing their sense of isolation.

LEARNING FROM EACH OTHER

The second reason Asian classes are so well crafted is that there is a very systematic effort to pass on the accumulated wisdom of teaching practice to each new generation of teachers and to keep perfecting that practice by providing teachers the opportunities to continually learn from each other.

Americans often act as if good teachers are born, not made. We hear this from both teachers and parents. They seem to believe that good teaching happens if the teacher has a knack with children, gets along well with them, and keeps them reasonably attentive and enthusiastic about learning. It is a commonly accepted truism in many colleges of education that teaching is an art and that students cannot be taught how to teach.

Perhaps because of this belief, students emerge from American colleges of education with little training in how to design and teach effective lessons. It is assumed that teachers will discover this for themselves. Courses in teaching methods are designed to serve a different purpose. On the one hand, they present theories of learning and cognitive development. Although the students are able to quote the major tenets of the theorists currently in vogue, the theories remain as broad generalizations that are difficult to apply to the everyday tasks that they will face as classroom teachers. At the opposite extreme, these methods courses provide education students with lists of specific suggestions for activities and materials that are easy to use and that children should enjoy (for example, pieces of breakfast cereal make handy counters for teaching basic number facts). Teachers are faced, therefore, with information that is either too general to be applied readily or so specific that it has only limited usefulness. Because of this, American teachers complain that most of what they know had to be learned by themselves, alone, on the job.

In Asia, graduates of teacher training programs are still considered to be novices who need the guidance and support of their experienced colleagues.

In the United States, training comes to a near halt after the teachers acquire their teaching certificates. American teachers may take additional coursework in the evenings or during summer vacations, or they may attend district or citywide workshops from time to time. But these opportunities are not considered to be an essential part of the American system of teacher training.

In Japan, the system of teacher training is much like an apprenticeship under the guidance of experienced colleagues. The teacher's first year of employment marks the beginning of a lengthy and elaborate training process. By Japanese law, beginning teachers must receive a minimum of twenty days of inservice training during their first year on the job.[5] Supervising the inservice training are master teachers, selected for their teaching ability and their willingness to assist their young colleagues. During one-year leaves of absence from their own classrooms, they observe the beginner in the classroom and offer suggestions for improvement.

In addition to this early tutelage in teaching techniques, Japanese teachers, beginners as well as seasoned teachers, are required to continually perfect their teaching skills through interaction with other teachers. One mechanism is through meetings organized by the vice principal and head teachers of their own school. These experienced professionals assume responsibility for advising and guiding their young colleagues. The head teachers organize meetings to discuss teaching techniques and to devise lesson plans and handouts. These meetings are supplemented by informal districtwide study groups and courses at municipal or prefectural education centers.[6]

A glimpse at what takes place in these study groups is provided in a conversation we recently had with a Japanese teacher. She and her colleagues spend a good deal of their time together working on lesson plans. After they finish a plan, one teacher from the group teaches the lesson to her students while the other teachers look on. Afterward, the group meets again to criticize the teacher's performance and to make suggestions for how the lesson could be improved. In her school, there is an annual "teaching fair." Teachers from other schools are invited to visit the school and observe the lessons being taught. The visitors rate the lessons, and the teacher with the best lesson is declared the winner.

In addition, national television in Japan presents programs that show how master teachers handle particular lessons or concepts. In Taiwan, such demonstrations are available on sets of videotapes that cover the whole curriculum.

Making use of lessons that have been honed over time does not mean that the Asian teacher simply mimics what she sees. As with great actors or musicians, the substance of the curriculum becomes the script or the score; the goal is to perform the role or piece as effectively and creatively as possible. Rather than executing the curriculum as a mere routine, the skilled teacher strives to perfect the presentation of each lesson. She uses the teaching techniques she has learned and imposes her own interpretation on these techniques in a manner that she thinks will interest and motivate her pupils.

Of course, teachers find it easier to share helpful tips and techniques among themselves when they are all teaching the same lesson at about the same time. The fact that Taiwan, Japan, and China each has a national curriculum that provides a common focus is a significant factor in teacher interaction. Not only do we have no national curriculum in the United States, but the curriculum may not be consistent within a city or even within a single school. American textbooks, with a spiral curriculum that repeats topics year after year and with a profusion of material about each topic, force teachers to omit some of each year's material. Even when teachers use the same textbook, their classes differ according to which topics they choose to skip and in the pace with which they proceed through the text. As a result, American teachers have less incentive than Asian teachers to share experiences with each other or to benefit from the successes and failures that others have had in teaching particular lessons.

Adding further to the sense of isolation is the fact that American teachers, unlike other professionals, do not share a common body of knowledge and experience. The courses offered at different universities and colleges vary, and even among their required courses, there is often little common content from college to college. Student teaching, the only other activity in which all budding teachers participate, is a solitary endeavor shared only with the regular classroom teacher and perhaps a few fellow student teachers.

Opportunities for Asian teachers to learn from each other are influenced, in part, by the physical arrangements of the schools. In Japanese and Chinese schools, a large room in each school is designed as a teachers' room, and each teacher is assigned a desk in this room. It is here that they spend their time away from the classroom preparing lessons, correcting students' papers, and discussing teaching techniques. American teachers, isolated in their own classrooms, find it much harder to discuss their work with colleagues. Their desk and teaching materials are in their own classrooms, and the only common space available to teachers is usually a cramped room that often houses supplies and the school's duplicating facilities, along with a few chairs and a coffee machine. Rarely do teachers have enough time in their visits to this room to engage in serious discussions of educational policy or teaching practices.

Critics argue that the problems facing the American teacher are unique and that it is futile to consider what Japanese and Chinese teaching are like in seeking solutions to educational problems in the United States. One of the frequent arguments is that the students in the typical Asian classroom share a common language and culture, are well disciplined and attentive, and are not distracted by family crises and their own personal problems, whereas the typical American teacher is often faced with a diverse, burdened, distracted group of students. To be sure, the conditions encountered by teachers differ greatly among these societies. Week after week, American teachers must cope with children who present them with complex, wrenching personal problems. But much of what gives American classrooms their aura of disarray and disorganization may be traced to how schools are organized and teachers are trained as well as to characteristics of the children.

It is easy to blame teachers for the problems confronting American education, and this is something that the American public is prone to do. The accusation is unfair. We cannot blame teachers when we deprive them of adequate training and yet expect that on their own they will become innovative teachers; when we cast them in the roles of surrogate parents, counselors, and psychotherapists and still expect them to be effective teachers; and when we keep them so busy in the classroom that they have little time or opportunity for professional development once they have joined the ranks of the teaching profession.

Surely the most immediate and pressing task in educating young students is to create a new type of school environment, one where great lessons are a commonplace occurrence. In order to do this, we must ask how we can institute reforms that will make it possible for American teachers to practice their profession under conditions that are as favorable for their own professional development and for the education of children as those that exist in Asia.

Note: The research described in this article has been funded by grants from the National Institute of Mental Health, the National Science Foundation, and the W.T. Grant Foundation. The research is the result of collaboration with a large group of colleagues in China, Japan, Taiwan, and the United States who have worked together for the past decade. We are indebted to each of these colleagues and are especially grateful to Shinying Lee of the University of Michigan who has been a major contributor to the research described in this article.

REFERENCES

[1]The superior academic achievement of Chinese and Japanese children sometimes leads to speculation that they are brighter than American children. This possibility has been supported in a few reports that have received attention in the popular press and in several scientific journals. What has not been reported or widely understood is that, without exception, the studies contending that differences in intelligence are responsible for differences in academic performance have failed to meet acceptable standards of scientific inquiry. In fact, studies that have reported differences in I.Q. scores between Asian and American children have been flawed conceptually and methodologically. Their major defects are nonequivalent tests used in the different locations and noncomparable samples of children.

To determine the cognitive abilities of children in the three cultures, we needed tests that were linguistically comparable and culturally unbiased. These requirements preclude reliance on tests translated from one language to another or the evaluation of children in one country on the basis of norms obtained in another country. We assembled a team with members from each of the three cultures, and they developed ten cognitive tasks falling into traditional "verbal" and "performance" categories.

The test results revealed no evidence of overall differences in the cognitive functioning of American, Chinese, and Japanese children. There was no tendency for children from any of the three cultures to achieve significantly higher average scores on all the tasks. Children in each culture had strengths and weaknesses, but by the fifth grade of elementary school, the most notable feature of children's cognitive performance was the similarity in level and variability of their scores. [Stevenson, H. W., Stigler, J. W., Lee, S. Y., Lucker, G. W., Kitamura, S., & Hsu, C. C. (1985). Cognitive performance and academic achievement of Japanese, Chinese, and American children. *Child Development*, 56, 718–734.]

[2]Stevenson, H. W. (1990). Adapting to school: Children in Beijing and Chicago. *Annual Report*. Stanford CA: Center for Advanced Study in the Behavioral Sciences. Stevenson, H. W., Lee, S., Chen, C., Lummis, M., Stigler, J., Fan, L., & Ge, F. (1990). Mathematics achievement of children in China and the United States. *Child Development*, 61, 1053–1066. Stevenson, H. W., Stigler, J. W., & Lee, S.Y (1986). Mathematics achievement of Chinese, Japanese, and American children. *Science*, 231, 693–699. Stigler,

J. W., Lee, S. Y., & Stevenson, H. W. (1990). *Mathematical knowledge.* Reston, VA: National Council of Teachers of Mathematics.

[3]Stevenson, H. W., Lee, S. Y., Chen C., Stigler, J. W., Hsu, C. C., & Kitamura, S. (1990). Contexts of achievement. *Monographs of the Society for Research in Child Development.* Serial No. 221, 55, Nos. 1–2.

[4]Rohlen, T. P. (1983). *Japan's High Schools.* Berkeley: University of California Press.

[5]Dorfman, C. H. (Ed.) (1987). *Japanese Education Today.* Washington, D.C.: U.S. Department of Education.

[6]Ibid.

25

Cognitive-Motivational Influences on the Task-Related Help-Seeking Behavior of Black Children

SHARON NELSON-LE GALL AND ELAINE JONES

An important part of development is the acquisition of social skills. One such skill is the ability to obtain help from other people, both peers and adults. Psychologists disagree on the merits of help seeking: some see it as creating dependency patterns while others consider it essential for mature functioning. According to Sharon Nelson-Le Gall and Elaine Jones, the benefits of help seeking depend on the context in which this behavior occurs and on individual children's need of support in particular contexts. For example, knowing when and how to obtain help from others in classroom settings may be critical for enabling some children to achieve success in school. Nelson-Le Gall and Jones examine this issue among African American children, focusing on the role of self-evaluation and motivational processes in children's help seeking in the classroom. By examining these processes in a population of children who share ethnicity and academic achievement, the researchers highlight the fact that even in a presumably homogeneous group of children, there is considerable variability in help-seeking behavior and the psychological processes that give rise to it.

Reprinted with permission from *Child Development*, 61, 1990, 581–589. Copyright 1990 by The Society for Research in Child Development.

The authors gratefully acknowledge the cooperation of the students and staff of participating schools. This research was partially supported by a grant to the first author from the Rockefeller Foundation. Requests for reprints should be sent to Sharon Nelson-Le Gall, 829 Learning Research and Development Center, University of Pittsburgh, 3939 O'Hara Street, Pittsburgh, PA 15260.

The present study examined the relation between children's mastery motivation, self-assessment of performance, and task-related help-seeking behavior during task performance. Average-achieving black American children, varying in mastery motivation as measured by subscales of the Harter's Intrinsic-Extrinsic Orientation in the Classroom Scale, performed a multitrial verbal task and were given the opportunity to seek help on each trial after making a tentative response and assessing their performance by rating their confidence in the correctness of the response. A response-contingent payoff system was implemented to encourage children to restrict their help seeking to those instances in which they perceived that they could not make a correct response without assistance. As predicted, children's self-assessments of performance, regardless of their accuracy, appeared to influence help seeking more than the actual performance outcomes. Neither children's self-assessments of performance nor their overall rate of help seeking varied with level of measured mastery motivation. However, the type of help sought varied as expected with mastery motivation. Children characterized by high intrinsic orientations toward independent mastery in academic achievement contexts sought indirect help (i. e., hints) more often than they sought direct help (i. e., answers), whereas children characterized by low intrinsic orientations toward independent mastery showed no preference. These differences in motivational orientation influenced requests for help only when children perceived their initial solutions to be incorrect. These findings are discussed in the context of the analyses of help seeking as an instrumental learning and achievement strategy. The implications of the findings for analyses of black children's achievement styles are highlighted.

Many scholars consider the ability to utilize adults and peers appropriately as resources to cope with difficulties encountered in learning situations to be one of the most important skills children can cultivate (Anderson & Messick, 1974; Nelson-Le Gall, 1981, 1985). In spite of the adaptive role it may play in learning and problem solving, help seeking has more often been examined as dependency behavior in studies of socialization and personality development (e.g., Fischer & Torney, 1976; Sears, Maccoby, & Levin, 1957; Yando, Seitz, & Zigler, 1979). In addition, researchers studying children's achievement motivation (e.g., Winterbottom, 1958) have treated help seeking as being incompatible with self-reliance and achievement, and have tended to consider only the costs of seeking help for the evaluation of independent performance rather than the costs of *not*

seeking help for the acquisition and mastery of skills—outcomes of achievement activity that do not necessarily follow from independent performance of tasks.

The investigation of help-seeking behavior in problem-solving settings is of particular interest in the case of black children from families below the middle socioeconomic strata of American society. The achievement behavior of these children has often been characterized as deviant and/or deficient. As documented by numerous scholars (e.g., Banks, McQuarter, & Hubbard, 1979; Washington, 1982), a common portrayal of these children, by both researchers and educators, is of children who are not intrinsically motivated to learn and who lack the independence, confidence, curiosity, and persistence necessary for problem solving and mastery. Help seeking used instrumentally as a problem-solving strategy, however, requires that the child be active in identifying problems. Furthermore, it requires that the child take and retain responsibility for overcoming obstacles to achievement of goals, and take the initiative to target and make contact with the potential helper. These behaviors would not be expected to be readily forthcoming from a passive, underconfident and uninterested child. Hence, consideration of help seeking as a behavior in its own right, rather than merely as an index of a global personality trait (i.e., dependency), should provide more useful information about the range of these children's achievement behaviors in academic learning and problem-solving settings.

The purpose of the present study was to examine the role of cognitive and motivational influences in black children's use of help seeking as an achievement strategy. One cognitive factor that plays a major role in seeking help is the awareness of the need for help. In conceptualizing help seeking as an intentional act that can be instrumental to learning and achievement (e.g., Ames, 1983; Murphy, 1962; Nelson-Le Gall, 1981) it becomes important that it be the individual who makes the assessment of the need for help (i.e., to decide that his or her own available personal resources are not sufficient to solve a given problem successfully). Determining the need for help entails evaluation of one's performance and knowledge state as well as of the task requirements. The developmental literature on metacognition and learning (see Brown, Bransford, Ferrara, & Campione, 1983, for a review) suggests that the ability to assess one's knowledge state and proficiency in monitoring and evaluating one's performance increase with age across early and middle childhood. Older as opposed to younger children appear to make more complete surveys of what they do and do not know and of what can be inferred from what they do know. If children have some awareness of the extent of their internal resources and are monitoring their task performance well enough to detect difficulties, they are in a relatively good position to utilize help seeking as a strategy to enable themselves to solve encountered problems. Self-assessment of performance, then, can serve as a basis for establishing the perceived necessity of help seeking.

In addition to cognitive factors such as self-assessments of knowledge state and performance, motivational orientations toward learning and performance in achievement settings are thought to influence the use of help seeking as a problem-solving strategy (e.g., Ames, 1983; Nelson-Le Gall, 1985). For example, Nelson-Le Gall (1981, 1985) has noted that help seeking may serve multiple purposes. The child's primary goal in seeking help may be merely task completion, without comprehension of mastery as an objective, or it may be to avoid criticism from an agent of evaluation. Alternatively, help may be sought to increase the child's mastery in current and future learning tasks. These distinctions between goals map onto distinctions made by achievement motivation theorists, who describe individual differences in children's achievement goals and orientations as indicators' of how children will cope with difficulty in learning and problem solving (e.g., Dweck & Elliott, 1983; Harter, 1981). Children whose achievement orientation can be said to be mastery oriented will usually adopt learning goals (Dweck & Elliott, 1983), show more preference for challenging tasks, evidence greater curiosity and interest in problem solving and learning contexts, and stride toward independent mastery in their undertakings to a greater degree than will children who are performance oriented (Harter, 1981). Children who are characterized by mastery orientation in achievement contexts focus their attention on formulating strategies to overcome obstacles to the mastery of tasks. Thus, the mastery-oriented use of help seeking would dictate seeking help that allows children to acquire an understanding and mastery of the problem and its solution that can increase the probability of their solving similar problems in the future for themselves.

In the present study, black children's perceptions of their task performance and their help-seeking behavior under different self-assessments of performance were examined. The child's self-assessment of task performance, measured as confidence in the correctness of responses, was taken as an indicator of the perception of the need for help. Obtaining ratings of confidence in the correctness of responses is a reliable method of ascertaining children's knowledge about

what they do and do not know in a particular domain of performance (Brown, 1978). Self-assessment was expected to be more important than the objective correctness of performance as a determinant of help seeking. Children should be less likely to seek help when they feel their performance has been successful than when they perceive themselves to have performed unsuccessfully.

In addition, individual differences in achievement motivation in terms of mastery motivation (Harter, 1981) were examined for their relation to preferences for different forms of help. When children perceive their task performance as competent, no difference in preferences for different types of help was expected among children with different motivational orientations. It was expected that individual differences in intrinsic orientation to academic learning and mastery would be associated with preferences for different types of help when children perceive their performance as less than competent. Help that is indirect and that enables the help seeker to retain responsibility for achieving the solution to the problem can be seen as instrumental to mastery and skill acquisition. In contrast, direct help that permits the helper to solve the problem without the active involvement of the seeker may be detrimental to the development of mastery and skill, and may even lead to dependency on external resources. In the present study the type of help available by request was varied. Children high in intrinsic motivational orientation were expected to prefer indirect help (i.e., hints) to direct help (i.e., direct answers) to a greater degree than would children low in intrinsic orientation to learning and mastery in academic achievement settings.

Finally, age differences were expected in children's use of help seeking as a problem-solving strategy and in preferences for direct and indirect help (e.g., Nelson-Le Gall, 1987). Around the age of 7 to 9 years, children become increasingly concerned with evaluating their own performance (Dweck & Elliott, 1983). Also at this time children's ability to detect gaps in their knowledge or understanding that can pose the need for help in problem-solving situations increases, although use of this awareness to mediate problem solving may not occur until the end of middle childhood, that is, until 10–12 years of age (Brown et al., 1983). Because they are tentatively more skillful than younger children in filling in gaps in their knowledge by making appropriate inferences from available knowledge (e.g., Swanson, 1985) and because they have had more experience with academic contexts in which getting direct help such as answers to problems may be regarded as copying or cheating, it was expected that older children would request indirect help more often than direct help in comparison to younger children.

METHOD

SUBJECTS Seventy-nine third- and fifth-grade black American children attending local elementary schools participated as subjects in this study. There were 34 third-grade children (10 boys and 24 girls) and 45 fifth-grade children (20 boys and 25 girls) in the sample. Children were from working-class and lower-class backgrounds by school administrator's report. Data on children's academic achievement, as measured by the most recent standardized California Achievement Test (CAT) reading scores in their school records, indicated that participating children were of average achievement (i.e., achievement stanine levels 4–6). Written parental consent was obtained for each child participating in the study.

ASSESSMENT OF MOTIVATIONAL ORIENTATION AND ASSIGNMENT TO GROUPS Two weeks prior to collection of data on their help-seeking behavior, participating children received group administration of a measure of mastery motivation. The motivational subscales of Harter's (1981) Intrinsic versus Extrinsic Orientation in the Classroom Scale were used to measure children's motivational orientation toward learning and mastery. Children's scores on only two of the motivational subscales, namely, the Curiosity/Interest (CI) and the Independent Mastery (IM), were taken. The decision not to include the third motivational subscale (i.e., Preference for Challenge) was based on the fact that the present study was not intended to yield data about children's choice of tasks to perform; rather, the focus was on individual differences in children's preferences for different strategies (i.e., different levels of assistance or no assistance at all) for performing a given task. Table 1 presents the mean Curiosity/Interest and Independent Mastery scores for girls and boys at each grade level. Scores on each of these subscales have a possible range of 1.00 (low intrinsic orientation to academic learning and mastery) to 4.00 (high intrinsic orientation to academic learning and mastery). There were no significant differences between the mean scores of boys and girls on either measure (t's < 1).

Children's scores on the Curiosity/Interest and the Independent Mastery measures were used to create low and high motivational groups at each grade level. Children's scores on each subscale were standardized within grade level. Cutting scores were made on each subscale separately so as not to mask subscale differences in motivational orientation. Children were

TABLE 1

Motivational Orientation Subtest Scores by Grade and Sex

Group and (N)	Curiosity/ Interest (CI)		Independent Mastery (IM)	
	M	SD	M	SD
Grade 3 (34):				
Girls (24)	2.74	.73	2.83	.59
Boys (10)	2.85	.29	2.98	.75
Grade 5 (45):				
Girls (25)	3.05	.50	2.83	.72
Boys (20)	3.01	.69	3.00	.74

divided into four motivational orientation groups based on their standardized scores on each subscale being less than (low) or greater than (high) 0. The number of children in each of the four groups was as follows: low IM/low CI (21), low IM/high CI (17), high IM/low CI (15), and high IM/ high CI (26).

HELP-SEEKING MEASURES AND CONFIDENCE RATINGS With consultation from an educational researcher with expertise in the area of vocabulary skills, vocabulary items were chosen based on their frequency of occurrence in texts and other literature intended for the grade levels of the subjects. A final group of test items of 16 moderately difficult words were selected separately for each grade level. The frequency with which help was sought in the form of either a hint or a direct answer before making a final response across the 16 test items provided measures of children's help-seeking behavior and help preferences. A 7-point certainty rating scale was constructed to assess children's sureness that responses they gave were correct. The rating scale depicted faces of increasing size representing ratings from 1, "very unsure—it's probably wrong" (small, unhappy face) to 7, "very sure, it's correct" (large, happy face).

PROCEDURE Two black female adults, blind to the children's responses on the mastery motivation measure, administered the word task. Individual children were escorted from their classrooms by an experimenter to a quiet room in the school building. Children were told that the experimenter was testing a game designed to teach children the meaning of words and that their participation was needed to help the experimenter choose the best words to include for children their age. Children were also told that their class would receive a gift and that they could help their class earn a nice gift by trying to answer all items correctly that they would be presented in the game. Children were seated at a table and familiarized with the certainty rating scale. Each representation on the rating scale was explained by the experimenter, and then the children answered questions designed to elicit their understanding of how to use the scale to indicate their confidence in the correctness of their responses. For example, children were asked, "How sure are you that your name is [child's name]?" After children demonstrated their understanding of the certainty rating scale, they received instructions for doing the word task.

In the word task, children were presented with 16 words one at a time and asked to identify the meaning by selecting from a list of alternatives that word that most closely matched the target word in meaning. Each target word and the list of alternatives were presented on a separate sheet of paper. Children were told they had two chances to give the correct response for each word. They were instructed to write down a tentative response to each item. For each tentative response, the children marked a face on the rating scale to indicate how sure they were that the response given was correct. After each item, children received the options of giving the tentative response to the experimenter as the final solution, or asking for help with the item and then accepting or rejecting that help and still providing a final solution. The children were always obliged to give the experimenter a final response. The child's initial and final responses were both recorded by the experimenter.

The study manipulated the type of help children received in response to their requests. As part of the orientation to the task, the children were told that the experimenter could not help, but that another child at their grade level who did very well at the task left his or her own answers and also some hints (i.e., target word used in a sentence) to the correct response. The "helper" child was referred to as a boy for male subjects and as a girl for female subjects. Children were told that they could see the answers or hints if they wanted help.

During the orientation to the task, the children learned how to earn the prize tokens that would later be exchanged along with those of their classmates for the class gift. A response contingency reward system was implemented and explained to children to encourage them to seek help only when they perceived it to be absolutely necessary (i.e., when the correct response was unknown). Children earned two prize tokens when they requested no help and gave a correct final response. Children earned one prize token when they requested either an answer or a hint and gave a correct final response. Children did not earn prize tokens for giving an incorrect final response. All children appeared to understand readily the task instructions and the goal of trying to accumulate as many prize tokens as possible to insure a nicer gift for their class.

The children were asked to record their final response for each word on a second slip and to fold and place it in a "solution box" with the other children's responses. The box, however, contained only blank slips of paper. The experimenter also recorded what form of help, if any, was requested. Children were then debriefed, praised for their cooperation, and escorted back to their classrooms.

RESULTS

The goal to construct separate sets of items for younger and older children that would be functionally equivalent in difficulty was met. Overall, third and fifth graders answered the same mean number of items correctly (8.7 vs. 8.9). A mean certainty rating for correct and incorrect items was calculated for each child. These mean ratings were analyzed by a 2 (grade) × 2 (sex) × 4 (motivation group) × 2 (item correctness) analysis of covariance (ANCOVA) with repeated measures on the last factor and achievement stanine as the covariate. The only effect found to be significant in this analysis was the main effect for item correctness. The mean certainty rating for correct items (5.25) was higher than that for incorrect items (4.10), $F(1,71) = 33.14$, $p < .0001$.

SELF-ASSESSMENT AND RATE OF HELP SEEKING
Preliminary examination of the data indicated no significant effects for sex;[1] therefore, data were pooled across this variable for subsequent analyses. Table 2 presents children's help-seeking responses across the 16 items for each of the self-assessment × item cor-

[1] *F* values for main and interaction effects for subject's sex in the ANCOVA tests were <1and/or *p* values were >.10. The actual values for specific effects involving subject's sex in the full factorial ANCOVAs are available from the authors upon request.

TABLE 2

**Mean Help-Seeking Responses across the 16 Items by
Self-Assessment and Item Correctness**

| | Self-Assessment | | | |
| | Correct | | Wrong | |
Item Correctness	M	SD	M	SD
Correct:				
Help	.52	.49	1.38	1.43
No help	6.01	5.03	.90	1.04
Wrong:				
Help	.82	1.19	2.73	2.79
No help	2.28	1.50	1.36	1.06

rectness categories. Children's rate of help seeking was expected to vary both with self-assessment and with item correctness such that help would be sought more frequently when children perceived their responses to be wrong or when responses were actually wrong than when they perceived their responses to be correct or responses were actually correct. However, it was predicted that self-assessments would be a stronger determinant of help seeking than item correctness would be. In order to test these predictions, certainty ratings of 7, 6, and 5 were taken as perceptions that a correct response had been made to the item; ratings of 1, 2, 3, and 4 were taken as perceptions that the response was probably wrong. The proportion of items within each self-assessment category for which help was sought was calculated for each child. Similarly, help-seeking rates were calculated for each item correctness category. Proportions were used since the frequency of responses classified in each of the four categories could vary by subject. These proportions were then subjected to arc sine transformations and the transformed data used in t tests of the planned comparisons. Children were found to seek help more frequently with items they perceived to be wrong ($M = .81$) than with those perceived to be correct ($M = .18$), $t(78) = 10.99$, $p < .0001$; estimated w^2(omega) = .43. Similarly, help was sought more frequently for actual wrong items ($M = .56$) than for actual correct items ($M = .28$), $t(78) = 7.46$, $p < .0001$; estimated $w^2 = .26$. As predicted, self-assessment accounted for more of the variance in rates of help seeking than did item correctness.

MOTIVATIONAL ORIENTATION AND TYPE OF HELP REQUESTED It was predicted that preference for indirect versus direct help as a problem-solving strategy would be a function of children's motivational orientation toward academic learning and mastery. In order to test this prediction, the proportion of answers and hints requested across the 16 items was calculated for each child. Because scores were proportions, arc sine transformations of the data were performed. These transformed data were analyzed in a 2 (grade) × 4 (motivation group) × 2 (self-assessment) × 2 (help type) analysis of covariance in which the last two factors were within-subjects variables and achievement stanine was the covariate. A priori contrasts were conducted to test hypotheses of interest.

There was no significant effect for achievement as a covariate, $F(1,70) = 2.84$, $p = .10$. As reported in the previous section, children sought help more often when they perceived their responses to be wrong than when they perceived their responses to be correct. Significant main effects were found also for grade, $F(1,70) = 8.25$, $p < .005$; and help type, $F(1,71) = 10.52$, $p < .002$. Fifth graders ($M = .10$) sought more help than did third graders ($M = .07$). Also, children overall tended to seek help more often in the form of hints ($M = .11$) than in the form of answers ($M = .05$). As predicted, significant interactions for grade × help type, $F(1,71) = 9.95$, $p < .005$; and for motivation group × self-assessment × help type, $F(3,71) = 3.87$, $p < .02$, were found. Fifth graders showed a clear preference for hints ($M = .15$) over answers ($M = .04$), whereas third graders showed no preference (hints $M = .07$ vs. answers $M = .07$).

Simple effects tests were performed on the motivation group × self-assessment × help type interaction. As predicted, the motivation group × help type interaction was not significant for responses perceived to be correct, $p < .20$; it was, however, significant for responses perceived to be wrong, $p < .02$. This significant motivation group × help type interaction for perceived wrong responses is presented in Figure 1. As can be seen in Figure 1, the proportion of hints sought did not differ from the proportion of answers sought by either of the two groups of low IM children. In contrast, the high IM groups tended to request help more often in the form of hints than in the form of answers when they perceived their responses to be incorrect. Planned comparisons of the effects of motivational orientation on the preference for hints over answers indicated that the observed difference in requests for hints versus answers was significant for both high IM groups only (p's $< .005$).

DISCUSSION

The aims of this study were twofold: to examine the relation between children's assessment of their need for help and the tendency to seek task-related help in achievement settings, and to explore age- and motivation-related patterns in black children's use of help seeking as a problem-solving strategy. The results of the present study confirm the significance of obtaining self-assessments of need in understanding children's use of help seeking as an alternative means of

goal accomplishment. The findings also document the existence of important age-related differences and individual differences in the help-seeking behavior of average achieving black children.

As predicted, self-assessment of performance was an important determinant of children's decision to seek help, accounting for nearly one-half of the variance in rates of help seeking, in comparison to the much smaller amount (one-quarter) of variance accounted for by objective correctness of performance. Children tended not to seek help when they perceived their responses to be correct. Yet, when children perceived their responses to be incorrect (i.e., when they perceived the need to arise), they were more likely than not to seek help. In the present study, children were responsible for monitoring their own performance on an item-by-item basis. The use of cognitive strategies such as performance monitoring may increase the rate of help seeking because the individual is thereby more likely to identify the need for help. This interpretation is supported by findings of studies (e.g., Karabenick, 1987) reporting that adult learners who use cognitive learning strategies (i.e., elaboration, planning, monitoring, self-regulation, and allocation of attention and study time) in response to perceived need are also more likely to seek help when required, whereas learners who do not tend to employ such cognitive learning strategies are also less likely to seek the help they need. In sum, these results clearly support the utility of taking the help seeker's assessment of need into account when making judgments about the necessity of help seeking.

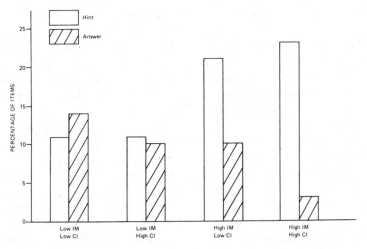

FIGURE 1   Mean percentage of items perceived to be wrong for which hints or answers were sought as a function of motivation group.

The results of greatest interest from the present study are those documenting important individual differences in motivational orientation among this sample of average achieving black children. As hypothesized, children characterized by high intrinsic orientation toward mastery and learning in academic achievement settings showed a clear preference for help that allowed them to figure out solutions for themselves as opposed to help that directly supplied a ready-made solution. In contrast, children characterized by low intrinsic orientation toward mastery showed no clear preference for one type of help over the other. That these differential preferences for type of help are manifestations of individual differences in motivation becomes more evident when considering the nature of the situational performance incentives. In the present study, a response-contingent reward system was implemented to encourage children to confine their requests to help to those instances in which they perceived it necessary to make a correct final response to an item. This payoff system might have affected children's overall rate of help seeking. However, because there was no differential payoff for correct solutions achieved with hints versus those achieved with direct answers, variations in the type of help requested cannot be attributed directly to this immediate situational influence. It is important to note that motivational orientation had no effect on the type of help sought when children requested help with items they perceive themselves to have answered correctly. It appears to be the adoption of learning and mastery goals in the face of failure that underlies the tendency to prefer hints to direct answers as help. Thus, it is more likely that differential preferences for the forms of help available in this study can be better explained by individual differences in achievement orientations and achievement goals that children brought to the task setting.

Consistent with other research findings on children's use of help seeking as a problem-solving strategy (Nelson-Le Gall, 1987; Nelson-Le Gall & Glor-Scheib, 1985), the results of the present study indicate that with increasing age children come to employ help seeking as an alternative means of goal accomplishment. As expected, older children perceived the need for help more often and sought help accordingly. Also, older children clearly preferred to overcome difficulties in performing the task by seeking indirect help in the form of hints rather than by seeking direct help in the form of ready-made answers. In contrast, the younger children's help-seeking behavior did not evidence a clear preference for either form of help. Nevertheless, children overall sought indirect help more often than they did direct help and hence demonstrated an active, coping style by assuming responsibility for arriving at the solution to the problems they perceived. The responses made by these children under conditions of perceived failure do not lend themselves to the general characterization of black children as lacking in confidence and interest in achievement settings, but suggest instead the need to further explore the range of individual differences among black children and the range of problem-solving settings and tasks that engender and support black children's active, confident, and goal-directed functioning (see Holliday, 1985; Rotheram & Phinney, 1987).

In conclusion, the present study has been fruitful in expanding the normative descriptions and understanding of black children qua black children. It furthers the appreciation of the heterogeneity within the black population. This research raises some intriguing questions about the patterns of individual differences among average-achieving black children and the relations among these individual differences and their academic learning and achievement. For example, what are the interrelations between individual differences in intrinsic orientation to mastery and learning, help seeking, and school achievement (as measured both by classroom teachers and by standardized tests)? Because of the narrow range of achievement levels of children in this sample, the current study does not provide adequate data to explore these relationships. Also, it is interesting that the preference for hints over direct answers appeared to be more strongly associated with scores on the Independent Mastery subscale than with scores on the Curiosity/Interest scale. This pattern of findings may be a function of the specific problem-solving situation and/or task employed in the present study; hence, caution is advised in drawing generalizations in the absence of confirmatory evidence from additional empirical studies. Larger samples of children with mixed motivational subscale profiles should be included in future studies to permit further assessment of the significance of these subscale differences for children's help-seeking behaviors. Additional studies in this area should broaden the age/grade levels examined to track the pattern of changes in the nature of these interrelations associated with increasing age and school experience. Longitudinal studies of black children from different SES groups and in a variety of classroom environments are also warranted. Finally, aspects of the self-system, such as perceptions of academic and social competence, and of general self-esteem deserve attention in future studies in order to determine their influence on black children's instrumental use of help seeking in academic achievement settings.

References

Ames, R. (1983). Help-seeking and achievement orientation: Perspectives from attribution theory. In B. DePaulo, A. Nadler, & J. Fisher (Eds.), *New directions in helping. Vol. 2: Help* seeking (pp. 165-188). New York: Academic Press.

Anderson, S., & Messick, S. (1974). Social competency in young children. *Developmental Psychology, 10,* 282–293.

Banks, W. C., McQuarter, G., & Hubbard, J. (1979). Toward a reconceptualization of the social-cognitive bases of achievement orientation in blacks. In A. W. Boykin, A. J. Franklin, & J. F. Yates (Eds.), *Research directions of black psychologists* (pp. 294–311). New York: Russell Sage.

Brown, A. (1978). Knowing when, where, and how to remember: A problem of metacognition. In R. Glaser (Ed.), *Advances in instructional psychology* (Vol. 1, pp. 77–165). Hillsdale, NJ: Erlbaum.

Brown, A., Bransford, J., Ferrara, R., & Campione, J. (1983). Learning, remembering, and understanding. In J. Flavell & E. Markman (Eds.), P. H. Mussen (Series Ed.), *Handbook of child psychology: Vol. 3. Cognitive development* (pp. 77–166). New York: Wiley.

Dweck, C., & Elliott, E. (1983). Achievement motivation. In E. M. Hetherington (Ed.), P. H. Mussen (Series Ed.), *Handbook of child psychology: Vol. 4. Socialization, personality and social development* (pp. 643–692). New York: Wiley.

Fischer, P., & Torney, J. (1976). Influence of children's stories on dependency, a sex-typed behavior. *Developmental Psychology, 12,* 489–490.

Harter, S. (1981). A new self-report scale of intrinsic versus extrinsic orientation in the classroom: Motivational and informational components. *Developmental Psychology, 17,* 300–312.

Holliday, B. (1985). Developmental imperatives of social ecologies: Lesson learned from black children. In H. McAdoo & J. McAdoo (Eds.), *Black children* (pp. 53–69). Beverly Hills, CA: Sage.

Karabenick, S. (1987, August). Cognitive learning strategies: Their relation to perceived need and help-seeking behavior.

In W. J. McKeachie (Chair), *The integration of motivation and cognition in different instructional settings.* Symposium conducted at the meeting of the American Psychological Association, New York.

Murphy, L. (1962). *The widening world of childhood.* New York: Basic.

Nelson-Le Gall, S. (1981). Help-seeking: An understudied problem-solving skill in children. *Developmental Review, 1,* 224–246.

Nelson-Le Gall, S. (1985). Help-seeking in learning. In E. Gordon (Ed.), *Review of research in education* (Vol. 12, pp. 55–90). Washington, DC: American Educational Research Association.

Nelson-Le Gall, S. (1987). Necessary and unnecessary help-seeking in children. *Journal of Genetic Psychology, 148,* 53–63.

Nelson-Le Gall, S., & Glor-Scheib, S. (1985). Help-seeking in elementary classrooms: An observational study. *Contemporary Educational Psychology, 10,* 58–71.

Rotheram, M., & Phinney, J. (1987). Ethnic behavior patterns as an aspect of identity. In J. Phinney & M. Rotheram (Eds.), *Children's ethnic socialization* (pp. 201–218). Beverly Hills, CA: Sage.

Sears, R., Maccoby, E., & Levin, H. (1957). *Patterns of child rearing.* Evanston, IL: Row & Peterson.

Swanson, H. L. (1985). Children's lack-of-knowledge inference about memory. *Child Study Journal, 15,* 71–82.

Washington, V. (1982). Racial differences in teacher perceptions of first and fourth grade pupils on selected characteristics. *Journal of Negro Education, 51,* 60–72.

Winterbottom, M. (1958). The relation of need for achievement to learning experiences in independence and mastery. In J. Atkinson (Ed.), *Motives in fantasy, action, and society* (pp. 453–478). Princeton, NJ: Van Nostrand.

Yando, R., Seitz, V., & Zigler, E. (1979). *Intellectual and personality characteristics of children.* Hillsdale, NJ: Erlbaum.

26

The Effect of Peer and Adult-Child Transactive Discussions on Moral Reasoning

---

ANN CALE KRUGER

Social interaction plays an important role in the development of morality. Discussions with peers and adults about moral issues create opportunities for children to consider moral views that are different from their own and thereby help them to develop their moral reasoning abilities. One question psychologists have raised about the process of moral development concerns the relative importance of moral discussions with peers versus those with adults. Whereas, as Piaget contends, peers may provide arguments that are closely matched to those of the child and therefore may be more accessible to understanding and analysis, others argue that adults may provide more mature models of morality and thereby facilitate growth. In the following paper, Ann Cale Kruger describes her research examining this question. Her results support Piaget's contention that peer discourse may be more beneficial for enhancing moral reasoning in children than adult-child discourse and extend this view by suggesting exactly what type of discourse within peer exchanges may be most beneficial for moral development.

Reprinted with permission from *Merrill-Palmer Quarterly*, *38*, 1992, 191–211. Copyright 1992 by Wayne State University Press.

   A brief. version of this paper was presented at the meeting of the Society for Research in Child Development, Kansas City, MO, April 1989. The author thanks the mothers and children who made this research possible. The assistance of Sara Mannie and Steven Cole in data preparation is acknowledged with appreciation. The author is grateful to Michael Tomasello for his helpful comments on the manuscript. Correspondence may be sent to Ann Cale Kruger, Department of Psychology, Oglethorpe University, 4484 Peachtree Rd., Atlanta, GA 30319.

Piaget (1932) hypothesized that children's interactions with peers during middle childhood are essential to their moral reasoning development. To test this hypothesis, 48 female focal subjects (M age = 8.6 years) were paired with either a female agemate or their mother. All focal subjects were pretested and posttested for moral reasoning abilities. In the intervention, the adult-child and peer dyads engaged in consensus-seeking discussions of two moral dilemmas. Focal subjects' moral reasoning at pretest and posttest and their use of reasoning (transacts) in the intervention discussions were measured. As predicted, focal subjects paired with peers showed significantly more sophisticated moral reasoning subsequent to their discussions than did focals paired with adults. In addition, focals paired with peers used more active transacts in their discussions than did focals paired with adults. Styles of dyadic discussion that featured active transacts by focal subjects were positively correlated with the focals' moral reasoning at posttest, whether the focal subject was paired with a peer or an adult. The more sophisticated posttest reasoning by focals paired with peers was attributed to the greater use of active discussion styles in peer dyads.

Piaget (1932) hypothesized that peers are uniquely important in children's moral development because, during middle childhood, children's interactions with peers are egalitarian, marked by a symmetry of competence and influence. When peer interaction results in the conflict of egocentric, but equally valid points of view, the child is prompted to take another perspective into account and to use reasoning to integrate the perspectives. Piaget asserted that this process of conflict and resolution is crucial to development (1970), and he contended that opportunities to resolve sociomoral differences are a more frequent and more typical feature of peer interaction (1932).

Interactions with adults during this time are not as likely to foster this type of developmental process. Adults' greater authority and interpersonal power contribute to their social dominance in interactions with children. Piaget observed that when children and adults experience conflict, the children, acknowledging the asymmetry of the relationship, yield to the adult solution, which removes the child's motivation to use reasoning and to abstract new sociomoral rules. Thus, for Piaget (1932), it is the independent negotiation that children conduct with peers that is vital to moral development.

This hypothesis is untested, although one part of Piaget's idea has been supported by training studies, most involving adult subjects. These studies suggest that interpersonal conflict resolved by consensus-seeking discussions results in change in moral reasoning. Neither personal consideration of moral dilemmas nor open-ended group discussion of them is as successful in promoting the developmental change in moral reasoning as is group discussion with the goal of resolution and consensus (Maitland & Goldman, 1974). Dyads who actively debate moral dilemmas to consensus change more than do those who passively listen to moral arguments (Arbuthnot, 1975), and the more conflict that dyads experience in their discussions, the more likely they are to change as a result (Berkowitz, Gibbs, & Broughton, 1980).

A fine-grained analysis of this developmental process of conflict and resolution was conducted by Berkowitz and Gibbs (1983). They compared moral discussions by adult dyads who showed subsequent developmental change to discussions by dyads who showed no change. Their results indicated that changing dyads, as opposed to unchanging dyads, are distinguished by the presence of transaction in their discussions. Berkowitz and Gibbs defined *transaction* as reasoning about reasoning: one individual uses reasoning that operates on the reasoning of the partner or that significantly clarifies his or her own ideas. Damon and Killen (1982) conducted a similar investigation of triads that were composed of children age 5 to 9 years. Like Berkowitz and Gibbs, they found that the children who advanced as a result of a moral discussion were those who both directed transforming (transacting) statements to their partners and received transactive statements from their partners.

Kruger and Tomasello (1986) applied this process analysis to investigate differences in the dialogues that children have with adults and with peers. To reflect the developmental level of the subjects and the process differences in adult-child and peer dialogues, they examined two aspects of transacts: the activity required for production (spontaneous transactive statements and questions vs. passive transactive responses) and the personal orientation of the transaction (reasoning about the listener's ideas vs. reasoning about the speaker's ideas). They showed that children who were paired with peers used transactive reasoning more often than did children paired with adults. Furthermore, the transacts between peers were more likely to be critiques of the listener's ideas, rather than clarifications of the speaker's ideas, and were produced more spontaneously. Children who were paired with adults were more passive and self-oriented in their use of reasoning because adult partners dominated the discussions by asking many questions.

It has been demonstrated, thus, that sociomoral conflict and its resolution lead to developmental change and that a key element in this process is transactive reasoning. It also has been demonstrated that discussions between peers feature more and qualitatively different transacts than do discussions between adults and children. However, the crucial assertions in Piaget's hypothesis remain untested. It is not known if indeed peer discussions produce greater changes in moral reasoning than do adult-child discussions. Nor is it known if the different use of reasoning in the process of adult-child and peer discussions is responsible for such changes. The purpose of the present study, therefore, was to test these hypotheses by comparing the moral reasoning of children before and after their moral discussions with either a peer or an adult. It was hypothesized that: (a) At posttest, focal subjects in peer dyads show greater moral reasoning as a result of their discussions than do focal subjects in adult-child dyads. (b) In their discussions, focal subjects in peer dyads, as compared to focals in adult-child dyads, use more transacts, use them more spontaneously, and focus their transacts on their partner's ideas, rather than their own. And (c) the use of spontaneous transacts in discussions, no matter the partner, is positively related to moral reasoning level at posttest.

METHOD

Subjects

Focal subjects were 48 middle-class females (45 white, 3 black) recruited from Girl Scout troops in metropolitan Atlanta. The mean age of the subjects was 8.6 years (range = 7.3 to 10.2 years). The sample was restricted to a single sex because of the preference for same-sex dyads and because of the greater availability of female adults as participants. All subjects were selected from a small set of comparable neighborhoods.

Subjects were recruited by mail. For a subject to be considered for participation, it was required that she receive parental permission and that her mother volunteer to participate in the study. It was further required that the subject nominate a friend (same-sex agemate) to participate with her. The parents of the nominated friends were contacted by mail and requested to allow their children to participate. From this pool of focal subjects, each with two potential

partners (a parent volunteer and a peer volunteer), focal subjects were randomly assigned to participate with either their parent or their peer as a partner; the other partner was dropped from the study. This procedure yielded 24 adult-child dyads and 24 peer dyads.

Procedure

Each dyad met on one occasion in the focal child's home. This choice of setting has ecological validity because children's personal dilemmas are likely to be discussed with important others in comfortable environments. The outline of the procedure was: The pretest consisted of two private interviews, one between the experimenter and the focal subject and one between the experimenter and the partner subject (counterbalanced for order across conditions). This interview was followed by dyadic discussion (intervention) of two dilemmas between focal subject and partner. The procedure ended with a posttest interview between the experimenter and the focal subject.

PRETEST The subjects were interviewed privately by the experimenter, a white adult female, using Damon's standard positive justice interview (1975, 1977, 1980). The interviews and all other components of the experiment were tape-recorded. In this pretest interview, the subjects were presented with a dilemma about fairness, sharing, and distributive justice. The dilemma was presented, illustrative drawings were provided, and a set of probing questions followed. The questions were designed to learn the subjects' solution to the problem and, more importantly, the reasoning process used to arrive at the solution. These were nondirective interviews. Although all subjects, including adult partners, were given the pretest, only the focal subjects' pretests were transcribed and scored.

A total of four positive justice dilemmas was used in the present study. All four addressed similar issues and were similar in structure. Dilemma 1 and Dilemma 4 were used as the pretest and posttest. Previous research has shown that the scores derived from interviews using Dilemma 1 and interviews using Dilemma 4 are highly correlated ($r = 86$; Damon, 1980). The order of the pretest interviews (focal subject or partner going first) and the dilemma used (1 or 4) were fully crossed and counterbalanced across conditions.

INTERVENTION Following the pretest, the focal girl and partner subjects were reunited, and two dilemmas were presented. Dilemmas 2 and 3 were used in the intervention, always in the same order (2 followed by 3). The dilemmas were illustrated with line drawings. The experimenter read Dilemma 2 and the probe questions, but did not allow immediate discussion. Instead, the subjects were instructed to discuss competing solutions to the dilemma until they agreed on the best one. The possibility of a disagreement and the meaning of consensus were discussed. Subjects were encouraged to take their time and to consider all solutions to avoid a superficial discussion. The experimenter left the room immediately after providing instructions and was not present during the discussion. Following the discussion of Dilemma 2, Dilemma 3 was read and the same procedure was followed.

POSTTEST Following the intervention, the subjects were instructed that there was time left for one more story and that, for this final interview, the focal girl's name had been selected in advance by drawing straws. This mild deception appeared to satisfy the children's sense of fairness. The procedure for the posttest was identical to that of the pretest.

Scoring Procedure: Pretest and Posttest

Transcripts of the focals' pretests and posttests were scored according to Gerson and Damon's criteria (1975). The scoring procedure focused on the reasoning process used by the subjects, specifically, the nature of the considerations articulated by the subjects in arriving at solutions and how the considerations related to one another.

Damon's (1980) index of moral reasoning is an ordered, six-step sequence that has been validated for several populations of North America, Europe, Asia, and the Middle East in both longitudinal and cross-sectional studies. In scoring the interviews, each subject's responses were divided into "chunks" of reasoning. A *chunk* was a sentence, statement, or group of statements that corresponded to a characteristic of one of Damon's stages. For example, when asked, "Why do you share with Sally?" one child may respond, "Because she's a girl. I'm a girl, and I share with girls." This response corresponds to one characteristic of stage 0-B: an assertion of size, sex, or other physical characteristic as justification for a choice. Each chunk was scored as corresponding to a stage level.

All posttest interviews were scored prior to the scoring of the pretest interviews. A random sample of 20% of the pretests and posttests was independently rescored to assess scorer reliability. The random selec-

tion was constrained so that a representative number of focal pretests and focal posttests were rescored. The obtained agreement was excellent, Cohen's kappa = .84.

For purposes of statistical analysis, subjects were assigned a weighted mean reasoning score for each interview. Assigned weights were: 10 points to each chunk scored as 0-B, 20 points to each chunk scored as 1-A, 30 for 1-B, 40 for 2-A, and 50 for 2-B. The assigned values were summed and averaged. Thus, the subject's score reflected the mean level of reasoning expressed in each interview. Similar weighting schemes have been used in previous training studies (Berkowitz et al., 1980).

Coding Procedure: Intervention Discussions

The 48 tape recordings of the intervention discussions were transcribed for coding. The unit of analysis was the conversational turn. Each time a subject spoke (uninterrupted) was considered one conversational turn. Turns ranged in length from one word to several sentences. Conversational turns were identified as either *nontransactive* (no code) or *transactive*, as defined by Berkowitz and Gibbs (1983) and adapted for younger subjects by Kruger and Tomasello (1986). Three specific types of transacts were coded, each with two orientations: transactive statements (self-oriented and other-oriented), transactive questions (self-oriented and other-oriented), and transactive responses (self-oriented and other-oriented).

Transactive statements were defined as spontaneously produced critiques, refinements, extensions, or significant paraphrases of ideas. Operations on the partner's ideas were labeled as *other-oriented*. (Example: "Your idea might get the little girl in trouble.") Spontaneously produced clarifications of one's own ideas were coded as *self-oriented*. (Example: "No, you see, my solution is only about the teacher.")

Transactive questions were defined as spontaneously produced requests for clarification, justification, or elaboration. Requests for such elaboration of the partner's ideas were coded as *other-oriented*. (Example: "Why do you think the class should use your solution?") Requests for evaluative feedback regarding one's own ideas were coded as *self-oriented*. (Example: "Do you think my idea is fair or unfair?")

Transactive responses were defined as clarifications, justifications, or elaborations of ideas given in answer to a transactive question. Responses that elaborated on the partner's ideas were coded as *other-oriented*, whereas those that elaborated on one's own ideas were coded as *self-oriented*. Response transacts were given only in response to and immediately following transactive questions. It should be noted that transactive statements and transactive questions were defined as actively self-generated by the subject. However, transactive responses were passive replies to requests and were not spontaneously produced.

A random sample of 20% of the transcripts, equally distributed between the groups, was independently recoded to assess coder reliability. Coders scored copies of the same unmarked transcripts, and the obtained agreement was excellent, Cohen's kappa = .87.

For purposes of statistical analysis, scores were assigned to subjects as follows: Each conversational turn in the intervention discussions was assessed independently. If a turn contained no transactive content, it received no code. If a turn was transactive, it was coded with one of the six mutually exclusive and exhaustive transact codes described earlier. Each turn received only one code. In no transcripts did a subject generate two or more of the six transacts in one turn.

Discussions varied in length, that is, in their total frequency of conversational turns (for the 48 dyads, $M = 47.25$, range = 15 to 94 turns). Consequently, the frequency of total transacts varied (for the 48 dyads, $M = 10.06$, range = 0 to 18 transacts). Because discussions varied, subjects' transactive reasoning in the intervention session was quantified as proportions. Each subject received a score for each of the six codes, computed as that code's frequency divided by that subject's total frequency of conversational turns. In addition to these six measures, each subject also received four summary scores: total transactive statements (self-orientation and other-orientation combined), total transactive questions (self-orientation and other-orientation combined), total transactive responses (self-orientation and other-orientation combined), and total transacts (all transacts combined). Each summary score was calculated as a proportion, using total frequency of conversational turns as the divisor.

By definition, transacts reflect the context of the discussion. Coding transacts requires taking into consideration the content of the preceding turns. However, for statistical purposes, the transacts by the focal subjects and the transacts by the partner subjects were summarized separately. Therefore, for each dyad the coding procedure yielded 20 proportions, 10 proportional transacts (six individual measures and four summary measures) for each member of the dyad (focal subject and partner).

RESULTS

Group Differences in Reasoning at Posttest

Focals who were paired with peers and focals who were paired with adults were equal in their level of pretest reasoning, with means of 32.77 (focals with peers) and 31.97 (focals with adults), t = n.s. As predicted, focals who were paired with peers produced significantly higher levels of reasoning at posttest ($M = 35.34$, $SD = 4.44$) than did focals paired with adults ($M = 32.46$, $SD = 5.32$), $t(46) = 2.03$, $p = .025$ (one-tailed).[1]

Group Differences in Transacts

A 2 (Group: adult, peer) × 3 (Transact Type: statements, questions, responses) × 2 (Transact Orientation: self-orientation, other-orientation) mixed model analysis of variance (ANOVA) for repeated measures was calculated. This first analysis was based on data generated by focal subjects only. No significant main effect for group was found, $F(1, 46) = 2.94$, $p = .09$. There was no group difference in the proportions of focal girls' conversational turns that were coded as transactive across types and orientations (for focals with peers, $M = 0.214$, $SD = 0.122$; for focals with adults, $M = 0.158$, $SD = 0.103$). As expected, group differences in the type and orientation of the transacts generated by focal girls were found.

As predicted, a significant three-way interaction was found (Group × Transact Type × Transact Orientation), $F(2, 92) = 5.40$, $p = .01$. Analyses of the six simple, simple main effects contained in this interaction (that is, analyses of the variability due to group

---

[1]Given the absence of pretest differences and the random assignment of subjects to experimental groups, posttest scores are the preferred outcome variable for the measurement of change in the present study (Achenbach, 1978; Cronbach & Furby, 1970; Linn & Slinde, 1977). Change scores as outcome variables are highly problematic, one of the often-noted problems being the regression to the mean. A negative correlation between pretest scores and change scores indicates that there has been such an effect (Borg & Gall, 1983). In the present study, the correlation between pretest and change was negative and significant, $r = -.373$, $p < .01$. Thus, change scores are unreliable and posttest scores are the preferred measure of change.

alone for the six transacts) revealed that, as predicted, focal girls who were paired with adults produced proportionally more self-oriented responses ($M = 0.073$, $SD = 0.062$) than did focal girls who were paired with peers ($M = 0.018$, $SD = 0.037$), $F(1, 92) = 20.00$, $p < .001$. Also consistent with predictions, focals paired with peers produced proportionally more other-oriented statements ($M = 0.124$, $SD = 0.081$) than did focals paired with adults ($M = 0.030$, $SD = 0.045$), $F(1, 92) = 70.96$, $p < .001$. None of the remaining simple, simple main effects reached significance.

Thus, focals in the two groups generated the same proportional number of transacts, but those generated by focals with peers were more spontaneous (i.e., statements) and other-oriented, and those generated by focals with adults were more passive (i.e., responses) and self-oriented. Figure 1 is a graphic representation of the differences between the groups in the types and orientations of transacts generated by the focals.[2]

Also of interest were the transacts generated by the adult and peer partner subjects. A second ANOVA was calculated, based on the transact data generated by the partner subjects only. A 2 (Group) × 3 (Transact Type) × 2 (Transact Orientation) mixed model ANOVA for repeated measures was calculated. No significant main effect for group was found, $F(1, 46) = 0.96$, $p = .33$, indicating no difference between peer and adult partners in the proportions of their conversational turns that were identified as transactive across types and orientations (for peer partners, $M = 0.225$, $SD = 0.113$; for adult partners, $M = 0.257$, $SD = 0.115$). As predicted, a significant three-way interaction effect was found (Group × Transact Type × Transact Orientation), $F(2, 92) = 8.98$, $p < .0001$. Analyses of the six simple, simple main effects contained in this interaction indicated that, as predicted, adult partners produced proportionally more other-oriented questions ($M = 0.117$, $SD = 0.089$) than did peer partners ($M = 0.025$, $SD = 0.039$), $F(1, 92) = 62.71$, $p < .0001$. Also consistent

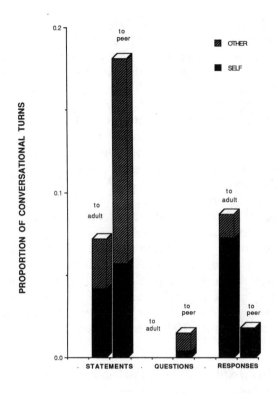

TRANSACTS BY FOCAL SUBJECTS

FIGURE 1   Group differences in focals' types and orientations of transacts.

with predictions, peer partners produced proportionally more other-oriented statements ($M = 0.146$, $SD = 0.072$) than did adult partners ($M = 0.109$, $SD = 0.068$), $F(1, 92) = 9.87$, $p < .01$. In addition, peer partners generated proportionally more self-oriented statements ($M = 0.043$, $SD = 0.050$) than did adult partners ($M = 0.017$, $SD = 0.032$), $F(1, 92) = 5.02$, $p < .05$. None of the remaining simple, simple main effects reached significance. Figure 2 is a graphic representation of group differences in the type of transacts produced by the partners.[3]

---

[2]Other results from this analysis, not directly addressed by the present hypotheses, were: no main effect for transact orientation was found, $F(1, 46) = 0.32$, $p = .57$. A significant main effect for transact type was found, $F(2, 92) = 35.79$, $p < .001$. A significant Group × Transact Type interaction effect occurred, $F(2, 92) = 19.58$, $p < .001$. A significant Group × Transact Orientation interaction effect was found, $F(1, 46) = 22.06$, $p < .001$. A significant Transact Type × Transact Orientation interaction effect was found, $F(2, 92) = 17.01$, $p < .001$.

[3]Other significant effects from this analysis, not directly addressed by the present hypotheses, occurred: a main effect for transact type, $F(2, 92) = 57.74$, $p < .001$; a main effect for transact orientation, $F(1, 46) = 100.57$, $p < .001$; a Group × Transact Type interaction effect, $F(2, 92) = 17.21$, $p < .001$; a Group × Transact Orientation interaction effect, $F(1, 46) = 5.65$, $p < .05$; a Transact Type × Transact Orientation interaction effect, $F(2, 92) = 38.89$, $p < .001$.

To summarize the foregoing analyses of the intervention discussions: All subjects, focals and partners, children and adults, generated the same proportional numbers of transacts in their conversations. However, consistent with predictions, group differences appeared in the nature of the transacts generated, that is, in the types and orientations used. Focals paired with peers produced more other-oriented statements than did focals paired with adults, and peer partners produced more other-oriented statements than did adult partners. Thus, peer dyads were characterized by their mutual use of other-oriented transactive statements. In contrast, focals paired with adults produced more self-oriented responses than did focals paired with peers. Adult partners produced more other-oriented questions than did peer partners. Therefore, adult-child dyads were characterized by a pattern of adult questions and child responses. These patterns are consistent with expectations and with previous findings (Kruger & Tomasello, 1986).

Relationships among Partner, Transacts, and Reasoning at Posttest

The differential use of transacts by subjects in the two conditions was predicted to be related to the differential posttest reasoning by those subjects. To assess this possibility, multiple regression analyses were made after a complete correlation matrix had been constructed. This correlation matrix (presented in Table 1) served as the basis for the selection of variables to be included in the multiple regressions, and it described the relationships between 20 transact measures (10 proportional scores for the 48 focal subjects and 10 proportional scores for the 48 partner subjects, both children and adults, as previously described) and focal posttest scores. Thus, for both the correlations and the multiple regressions, the focal posttest score was the outcome variable.[4]

Analysis of styles. The correlation matrix was calculated for the two experiment groups separately and for the total sample, and the results showed that specific types and orientations of transacts by focals in the intervention discussions correlated with reasoning at posttest. However, in addition to the focals' use of transacts, specific patterns in the partners' trans-

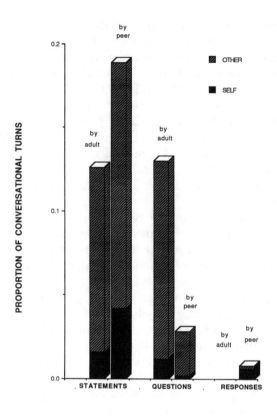

TRANSACTS BY PARTNER SUBJECTS

FIGURE 2   Group differences in partners' types and orientations of transacts.

acts influenced focals' reasoning as well. These results suggested an influence of dyadic style on focal reasoning at posttest. A dyadic influence on reasoning is logical, given the interactional nature of the transact measures. Furthermore, dyadic style differences were found in the analyses of transacts previously reported and were suggested by patterns in the correlations. Therefore, four types of dyadic discussion style were described post hoc. The styles, conceptualized by combining the focal and partner transact measures that independently predicted focal posttest, represent four distinct interactional patterns observed and reflect transaction at the level of the dyad. However, for the purpose of hypothesis-testing, the four dyadic

---

[4]Due to the lack of reliability of change scores, their use can attenuate correlations between predictors and outcome, particularly when the correlation between pretest and posttest is high (Linn & Slinde, 1977). In the present study, the correlation between pretest and posttest is positive and highly significant, $r = .545$, $p < .001$. In this experiment, the null hypothesis states that the two treatments have the same effect; therefore, the crucial question is whether the posttest scores vary between the groups. Thus, the posttest score is the preferred criterion variable (Achenbach, 1978).

Pearson Product Moment Correlations: Transacts and Posttest Scores

	Adult-Child	Peer	Total sample
Focals			
Self-oriented statements	.230	.006	.144
Other-oriented statements	.445*a	−.050	.279*
Total statements	.436*	−.032	.281*
Self-oriented questions	.000	.322†	.253*
Other-oriented questions	.000	.298†	.268*
Total questions	.000	.346*	.293*
Self-oriented responses	−.070	.043	−.163
Other-oriented responses	−.028	.000	−.094
Total responses	−.064	.043	−.163
Total transacts	.263	.072	.244†
Partners			
Self-oriented statements	.167	−.537**	−.114
Other-oriented statements	.459*	−.181	.219†
Total statements	.561	−.382*	.118
Self-oriented questions	−.022	.223	−.029
Other-oriented questions	.085	.177	−.078
Total questions	.065	.243	−.076
Self-oriented responses	.000	.270	.233†
Other-oriented responses	.000	.223	.178
Total responses	.000	.297†	.250*
Total transacts	.378*	−.211	.067
Dyadic styles			
Egocentric	.268	−.306†	.045
Socratic	.023	.116	−.177
Egalitarian	.597***	−.139	.307*
Leadership	—	.337*	.284*

a All probability values are one-tailed. *$p < .05$. **$p < .01$. ***$p < .001$. †$p < .10$.

styles may be ranked hierarchically to reflect four degrees of transactive engagement with the partner from the focal subject's point of view.

Egocentric style is defined as the combination of self-oriented statements by the focal subject and self-oriented statements by the partner. It represents an absence of engagement with the partner and a focus on the self. Egocentric style was suggested by a pattern of negative correlations in the peer group.

Socratic style is defined as other-oriented questions by the partner combined with self-oriented responses by the focal subject. It represents the focal's passive engagement in the transactive dialogue and features the focal's compliance with the partner's requests for transacts. Socratic style was suggested by the question-and-response pattern typical of discussions by adult-child dyads reported earlier.

Egalitarian style, defined as the combination of other-oriented statements by the focal subject and other-oriented statements by the partner, represents the focal's active and spontaneous collaboration with the partner in the transactive dialogue. It features the focal's and partner's equal status, and was suggested by the pattern of transacts typical of discussions by peer dyads previously reported and by a pattern of significant positive correlations in the adult-child group.

Leadership style is defined as the total questions by the focal subject combined with total responses by the partner. It represents the focal's most active level of engagement in the transactive dialogue. Leadership style features the focal's spontaneous control of the interaction by way of questioning and passive compliance by the partner, and was suggested by a pattern of significant positive correlations in the peer group.

For these four specific discussion styles, scores were assigned to dyads by simply adding the individual proportional transact scores involved. Each dyad, then, received four style scores, one score for each of the four discussion styles. Thus, the dyads were not characterized as using one style as opposed to the other three. Instead, the proportional use of the four styles in each dyad's discussions was measured. There was no difference between the groups in the use of egocentric style (for the adult-child group, $M = 0.06$, $SD = 0.06$; for the peer group, $M = 0.10$, $SD = 0.09$; t = n.s.). However, as suggested by the previously reported results, adult-child dyads featured more socratic style interaction ($M = 0.19$, $SD = 0.14$) than did peer dyads ($M = 0.04$, $SD = 0.07$), $t(46) = 4.44$, $p < .001$. Peer dyads featured more egalitarian style interaction ($M = 0.27$, $SD = 0.12$) than did adult-child dyads ($M = 0.14$, $SD = 0.09$), $t(46) = 4.27$, $p < .001$. In addition, peer dyads featured more leadership style interaction ($M = 0.02$, $SD = 0.05$) than adult-child dyads ($M = 0.00$, $SD = 0.00$), $p = .02$ (Fisher's Exact Test). A Fisher's Exact Test was employed to compare the groups' use of leadership style due to a lack of variability in the adult-child group. The four discussion styles were correlated with focal posttest scores for the two groups separately and for the total sample (see Table 1), with one exception. The absence of variability in the use of leadership style in the adult-child group (zero evidence of its use) made a correlation coefficient inappropriate for that group. These correlations between the dyadic

styles and focal posttest scores also served the selection of variables for the multiple regressions.

MULTIPLE REGRESSIONS All measures significantly correlated with posttest reasoning were selected to enter the multiple regression equations with one exception: When two correlating measures were not mutually exclusive, such as other-oriented statements and total statements, the measure with the highest correlation coefficient was selected to enter the equation. This was done to eliminate the collinearity of the two predictors, protecting that assumption of multiple regression analysis.

For the total sample, the adult-child group, and the peer group, equations were calculated two ways, utilizing as predictors (a) the individual transact measures and (b) the discussion style transact measures. All variables competed to enter the equations. Results of the multiple regression analyses are presented in Table 2.

Two equations were written to describe the total sample. For the first equation, the following predictors were entered: focals' total statements, focals' total questions, partners' other-oriented statements, and partners' total responses. The equation created by the four individual transact variables was not successful in describing the entire sample, $F(4, 43) = 1.88$, $p = .13$, multiple $r^2 = .15$. The variables did not independently make significant contributions to the model.

In the second equation, egalitarian style and leadership style were selected for entry by the aforementioned criteria. The equation created by the two discussion styles accounted for 15% of the variance and the contribution was significant, $F(2, 45) = 4.05$, $p = .02$. The two variables contributed to the model at a marginally significant level (.06 and .09 for egalitarian and leadership, respectively), which was superior to the level of contribution of individual transact measures and suggests that the discussion style variables may be more powerful predictors than individual transact measures.

Two equations were written to describe the adult-child group. The first equation utilized individual transact measures. Focals' other-oriented statements and partners' total statements were entered. The equation successfully described the adult-child group, $F(2, 21) = 5.55$, $p = .01$, multiple $r^2 = .35$. Focals' other-oriented statements did not contribute significantly to the model ($p = .33$), but partners' total statements did ($p = .04$). The second equation utilized egalitarian style as a predictor and was highly successful, $F(1, 22) = 12.15$, $p = .002$, multiple $r^2 = .36$. Egalitarian style contributed significantly to the model ($p < .0001$).

TABLE 2
Multiple Regression Analyses

Model				Predictors	Predictors' contributions	
F	df	p	R^2	Predictors	t	p
				Total Sample		
1.88	4, 43	.13	.15	Partner—other-oriented statements	0.90	.37
				Focal—total statements	1.05	.30
				Focal—total questions	1.07	.29
				Partner—total responses	−0.30	.77
4.05	2, 45	.02	.15	Egalitarian	1.95	.06
				Leadership	1.76	.09
				Adult-Child Group		
5.55	2, 21	.01	.35	Focal—other-oriented statements	−1.00	.33
				Partner—total statements	2.18	.04
12.15	1, 22	.002	.36	Egalitarian	3.49	.00
				Peer Group		
3.91	3, 20	.02	.37	Focal—total questions	0.62	.54
				Partner—self-oriented statements	−2.82	.01
				Partner—total responses	0.20	.85
3.71	2, 21	.04	.26	Egocentric	−2.05	.05
				Leadership	2.18	.04

Two equations were written to describe the peer group. The first equation utilized individual transact measures: focals' total questions, partners' self-oriented statements, and partners' total responses. This equation successfully described the peer group, $F(3, 20) = 3.91$, $p = .02$, multiple $r^2 = .37$. However, only one variable, partners' self-oriented statements, contributed significantly to the model ($p = .01$), having a negative relationship with reasoning.

The second equation utilized discussion style variables, egocentric style and leadership style. This equation was significant, $F(2, 21) = 3.71$, $p = .04$, multiple $r^2 = .26$. Both variables contributed significantly to the model. Egocentric style made a significant contribution ($p = .01$), with a negative relationship with reasoning; leadership style contributed significantly ($p = .04$) with a positive relationship with reasoning.

The discussion styles that predicted outcome varied between the groups: Egalitarian style was predictive in the adult-child group; leadership style was positively predictive in the peer group; and egocentric style was negatively predictive in the peer group. This difference in predictors was tested for significance: First, the correlation between egalitarian style and focal posttest scores was calculated for the adult-child group and for the peer group (as reported in Table 1). The correlations for the two groups are significantly different, $z = 2.68$, $p < .01$. Second, the correlation between egocentric style and focal posttest scores was calculated for the two groups (Table 1); the correlations are significantly different, $z = 2.00$, $p < .05$. Third, the correlation between leadership style and focal posttest scores was calculated for the peer group (Table 1). It was inappropriate to calculate a correlation in the adult-child group because of zero evidence of leadership style use. Therefore, it was impossible to compare correlations between the adult-child and peer groups. However, given the absence of leadership style in the adult-child group, and given the significant correlation between leadership style and posttest scores in the peer group, it appears that the two groups varied meaningfully in the presence of a relationship between leadership style and outcome.[5]

To summarize the multiple regressions: For the sample as a whole, leadership style and egalitarian style were the best positive predictors of posttest reasoning. That is, those dyadic styles consisting of greater spontaneity and activity by focal subjects were most predictive of growth. For adult-child dyads considered alone, egalitarian style was predictive, and for peers considered alone, leadership style predicted reasoning.

DISCUSSION

These results support Piaget's hypothesis (1932) that interaction with peers during middle childhood is important to the development of moral reasoning. The findings of the present study indicated that children paired with peers for a discussion of sociomoral dilemmas produced more sophisticated moral reasoning, subsequent to the discussion, than did children paired with adults.

Other results of the present study confirmed another part of Piaget's hypothesis. As Piaget predicted, children who were paired with peers used reasoning (transacts) in their intervention discussions in a qualitatively different way then did children who were paired with adults. A pattern of activity in peer transaction and passivity in adult-child transaction was found in Kruger and Tomasello (1986) and here as well. Although Kruger and Tomasello also found quantitative differences in transacts, this finding was not replicated here in that form. In the present study, focal girls with adults generated as many transacts as did focal girls with peers overall, but they were of a different nature in the two situations. The transacts generated by focals paired with adults were passive, elicited by the adults and not spontaneously produced. The transacts produced by focals paired with peers were active in nature, spontaneously generated without prompting by the partner. The present finding of differences in the quality of transaction is of more crucial theoretical significance. The active quality of transaction, rather than the amount of transaction, is hypothesized to be related to reasoning development.

A third set of results here supported Piaget's contention of a causal link between the use of reasoning in discussions with peers and the greater reasoning level subsequent to peer interaction. In the present study, the use of spontaneous, self-generated transacts by focal girls was predictive of their subsequent reasoning. Dyadic styles that featured such activity by the focal girl, egalitarian and leadership, were predictive of posttest reasoning for the total sample. Whether a child was paired with a peer or an adult, active reasoning in dyadic discussions led to a more sophisticated reasoning at posttest.

Thus, this third set of results, when viewed in light of group differences in dyadic style, is critical to the Piagetian hypothesis. The differential level of reasoning subsequent to discussions with peers and adults may be attributed to the differential use of reasoning by the groups. Children who were paired with peers engaged in egalitarian- and leadership-style discussions more often than did children who were paired with adults. These two types of discussions were predictive of focal moral reasoning at posttest for the total sample. The interpretation of these findings is that the type, rather than the amount, of transactive discussion generated was important to subsequent reasoning and that the partner in the discussion, whether peer or adult, constrained the type of transacts produced. Peer symmetry of power allowed greater activity of reasoning, from egalitarian co-construction to leadership, and this activity was critical to development.

In both groups, the type of focal transacts that were predictive of reasoning represented control and responsibility. Children paired with adults who engaged in active critiquing subsequently showed greater reasoning skills. Instead of a consistent pattern of compliance, they showed the ability to share control of the conversation and were willing to criticize the adult's thinking, to treat the adult as a peer. Children who were paired with peers generally engaged in shared control of the interaction and showed greater posttest scores than children who were paired with adults. Those focals in peer dyads who assumed an even greater share of responsibility were particularly likely to show improvement. That is, when children paired with peers acted as adults, assumed more control, and questioned the other, they developed in their reasoning.

---

[5]Because there were trivial differences in pretest scores, partial correlations also were performed, measuring the relationship between discussion styles and posttest scores, controlling for pretest scores. The pattern of results was unchanged, but the degree of some relationships was affected. Egalitarian style: adult-child group, $r = .442$, $p < .05$; peer group, $r = -.187$, n.s.; $z = 2.14$, $p < .05$. Egocentric style: adult-child group, $r = .225$, n.s.; peer group, $r = -.305$, $p < .10$; $z = 1.75$, $p < .10$. Leadership style: adult-child group, not measured (as before); peer group, $r = .290$, $p < .10$.

Two considerations may limit the generality of the current findings. First, these data represent the effect of a single, brief experience by the subjects. Although the present intervention was brief, however, it was designed to enhance thinking in a specific content area, distributive justice, and this is what was measured at pre- and posttest. Furthermore, other training studies with brief interventions (e.g., Nelson & Aboud, 1985) have been effective and have recorded effects beyond the time of the experiment (e.g., Damon & Killen, 1982). Although it remains an empirical question, long-term interventions may promote the effectiveness of Socratic dialogue. At present, the importance of such adult-child interaction is undefined, but it has been demonstrated that, in general, moral discussions between children and adults can be related to changes in reasoning (Azrak, 1978; Grimes, 1974; Hoffman, 1970, 1980; Holstein, 1972; Parikh, 1980; Stanley, 1976). Second, observation may have affected adults and children differentially, but such differences in response to "performance pressure" may reflect similar differences between adults and children in their approaches to interaction in general. Often adults may feel motivated to regulate and guide children (Kaye & Charney, 1981; Martinez, 1987; Rogoff & Wertsch, 1984; Vygotsky, 1978), particularly in discussions of moral dilemmas (Youniss, 1980). Children, by contrast, may view such interactions less seriously, creating a looser, more playful experience.

The present study has demonstrated the importance of peer interaction in the development of the sociocognitive skill of moral reasoning. Other researchers have compared the effect of peer and adult-child interaction on cognitive tasks, such as planning, and have produced results that differ sharply from those presented here. It has been demonstrated that peer dyads and adult-child dyads differ in their problem solving style when engaged in a planning task (Gauvain & Rogoff, 1989), and adult-child interaction is more effective than peer interaction in fostering the development of planning skills (Radziszewska & Rogoff, 1988). Whether these different findings are attributable to different methodologies or whether, in fact, the beneficial social process in problem solving is dependent on the domain of the task involved remains an important empirical question.

It has been demonstrated previously that transacts are important to change in moral reasoning in training studies with adults (Berkowitz & Gibbs, 1983) and with children (Damon & Killen, 1982). It also has been established that children use transacts in qualitatively different ways with peers and adults (Kruger & Tomasello, 1986). In the present study, evidence is presented for the first time that peer discussions of moral dilemmas result in greater improvement in moral reasoning than do discussions between children and adults. In addition, these data indicate that a spontaneous, active use of reasoning is conducive to moral reasoning development.

Mutual engagement in transactive dialogue was predictive of posttest scores when it occurred between children and adults as well as when it occurred between peers. However, here, children in peer dyads had the freedom to use this important, active reasoning more often than did children paired with adults. The peers' equal status allowed a critical reciprocity that was infrequent in adult-child dyads. Thus, Piaget's contention (1932) that symmetry of power leads to greater moral reasoning development is supported, and the current study indicates that active reasoning is the essential element in the process.

References

ACHENBACH, T. M. (1978). *Research in developmental psychology: Concepts, strategies, and methods.* New York: The Free Press.

ARBUTHNOT, J. (1975). Modification of moral development through role playing. *Developmental Psychology, 11,* 319–324.

AZRAK, R. (1978). Parental discipline and early adolescent moral development. *Dissertation Abstracts International, 39,* 2747A–2748A.

BERKOWITZ, M., & GIBBS, J. (1983). Measuring the developmental features of moral discussion. *Merrill-Palmer Quarterly, 29,* 399–410.

BERKOWITZ, M., GIBBS, J., & BROUGHTON, J. (1980). The relation of moral judgment stage disparity to developmental effects of peer dialogues. *Merrill-Palmer Quarterly, 26,* 341–357.

BORG, W. R., & GALL, M. D. (1983). *Educational research: An introduction* (4th ed.). New York: Longman.

CRONBACH, L. J., & FURBY, L. (1970). How we should measure "change"—or should we? *Psychological Bulletin, 74,* 68–80.

DAMON, W. (1975). Early conceptions of positive justice as related to the development of operational reasoning. *Child Development, 46,* 301–312.

DAMON, W. (1977). *The social world of the child.* San Francisco: Jossey-Bass.

DAMON, W. (1980). Patterns of change in children's social reasoning: A two-year longitudinal study. *Child Development, 51,* 1010–1017.

DAMON, W., & KILLEN, M. (1982). Peer interaction and the process of change in children's moral reasoning. *Merrill-Palmer Quarterly, 28,* 347–367.

GAUVAIN, M., & ROGOFF, B. (1989). Collaborative problem solving and children's planning skills. *Developmental Psychology, 25,* 139–151.

GERSON, R., & DAMON, W. (1975). *Scoring manual for positive justice.* Unpublished manuscript, Clark University, Worcester, MA.

GRIMES, P. (1974). Teaching moral reasoning to eleven year olds and their mothers: A means of promoting moral development. *Dissertation Abstracts International, 35,* 1498A–1499A.

HOFFMAN, M. L. (1970). Conscience, personality, and socialization techniques. Human *Development, 13,* 90–126.

HOFFMAN, M. L. (1980). Moral development in adolescence. In J. Adelson (Ed.), *Handbook of adolescent psychology.* New York: Wiley.

HOLSTEIN, C. B. (1972). The relation of children's moral judgement level to that of their parents and to communication patterns in the family. In R. C. Smart & M. S. Smart (Eds.), *Readings in child development and relationships.* New York: Macmillan.

KAYE, K., & CHARNEY, R. (1981). Conversational asymmetry between mothers and children. *Journal of Child Language, 8,* 35–49.

KRUGER, A. C. & TOMASELLO, M. (1986). Transactive discussions with peer and adults. *Developmental Psychology, 22,* 681–685.

LINN, R. L., & SLINDE, J. A. (1977). The determination of the significance of change between pre- and posttesting periods. *Review of Educational Research, 47,* 121–150.

MAITLAND, K., & GOLDMAN, J. (1974). Moral judgment as a function of peer group interaction. *Journal of Personality and Social Psychology, 30,* 699–704.

MARTINEZ, M. A. (1987). Dialogues among children and between children and their mothers. *Child Development, 58,* 1035–1043.

NELSON, J., & ABOUD, F. E. (1985). The resolution of social conflict between friends. *Child Development, 56,* 1009–1017.

PARIKH, B. (1980). Development of moral judgment and its relation to family environmental factors in Indian and American families. *Child Development, 51,* 1030–1039.

PIAGET, J. (1932). *The moral judgment of the child.* London: Kegan Paul.

PIAGET, J. (1970). Piaget's theory. In P. Mussen (Ed.), *Carmichael's manual of child psychology* (Vol. 1). New York: Wiley.

RADZISZEWSKA, B., & ROGOFF, B. (1988). Influence of adult and peer collaborators on children's planning skills. *Developmental Psychology, 24,* 840–848.

ROGOFF, B., & WERTSCH, J. V. (Eds.). (1984). *Children's learning in the "zone of proximal development."* San Francisco: Jossey-Bass.

STANLEY, S. (1976). A curriculum to affect the moral atmosphere of the family and the moral development of adolescents. *Dissertation Abstracts International, 36,* 7221A–7222A.

VYGOTSKY, L. S. (1978). *Mind in society.* Cambridge, MA: Harvard University Press.

YOUNISS, J. *(1980). Parents and peers in social development: A Sullivan-Piaget perspective.* Chicago: University of Chicago Press.

27

Determinants of Complexity in Mexican-American and Anglo-American Mothers' Conceptions of Child Development

JEANNIE GUTIERREZ AND ARNOLD SAMEROFF

The following article investigates variations in mothers' views of child development in relation to their ethnic background and extent of acculturation within the larger U. S. society. By comparing middle-class Mexican-American mothers who differ in their degree of acculturation with Euro-American mothers who are also from the middle class, Jeannie Gutierrez and Arnold Sameroff provide insight into the relationship between acculturation and traditional cultural values and its effect on how mothers think about how to raise their children.

Complexity of parental reasoning about child development was studied in mothers who varied in ethnic background and biculturalism. Middle-class mothers from Mexican-American and Anglo-American backgrounds were compared on their level of concepts of development on a scale from categorical to perspectivistic reasoning. Categorical mothers interpreted child development as being caused by single constitutional or environmental factors. Perspectivistic mothers interpreted development as the result of the dynamic interplay between constitution and environment over time and ac-

Reprinted with permission from *Child Development*, 61, 1990, 384–394. Copyright 1990 by The Society for Research in Child Development.

This research was completed in partial fulfillment of the requirements for the degree of Doctor of Philosophy at the University of Illinois at Chicago by the first author.

cepted that the same developmental outcome could have multiple determinants. In a comparison among moderately acculturated Mexican-Americans, highly acculturated Mexican-Americans, and Anglo-Americans, the highly acculturated Mexican-American group scored as more perspectivistic than the other two groups, despite the fact that the Anglo-Americans were the most acculturated. When the 2 Mexican-American groups were subdivided into monocultural (Mexican or American) and bicultural subgroups and compared with the Anglo-American group, the bicultural subgroup of the highly acculturated Mexican-American mothers was the most perspectivistic. These results suggest a complex picture of diversity in Mexican-American mothers who retain values and beliefs from their own culture, as well as taking on values and beliefs of the American culture. Maternal intelligence and adherence to traditional cultural values were not found to correlate significantly with level of developmental reasoning.

Child development is regulated by patterns of child rearing. These patterns are influenced by parental beliefs and values (Goodnow, 1988), which vary from one culture to another and from one social status to another within cultures (Kohn, 1969). Although many find it easy to agree that culture influences social and perhaps emotional development, there is far less accord about social influences on cognitive processes. Wertsch, Minick, and Arns (1984) contrast individualistic theories of cognitive development as represented by Piaget (1950) with social theories as represented by Vygotsky (1978). Wertsch et al. (1984) suggest that in Vygotsky's view cognitive development is explained by sociocultural mediation and modes of activity. The intellectual outcome for any individual is the product of a dialectic between the constructivistic aspects of cognition and social patterns of activity.

The typical arena for studying such issues in cognitive development is in the classroom using concept-formation tasks. However, the social influence on the nature of thought may also be studied in the broader area of cognitions about human growth and development. Analogies to the parents' structuring of tasks for the child may be found in cultural structuring of how parents raise children. More specifically, this study is an investigation of cultural influences on how parents conceptualize child development.

The social context in which development occurs influences both parenting cognitions and how parents relate these cognitions to the characteristics of the child. Modern American culture is characterized by a great diversity of child-rearing practices, many of them rooted in the ethnic traditions of the family. Immigrants from more agrarian, less industrialized countries bring with them many child-rearing beliefs and practices that diverge from families that have been fully acculturated (Werner, 1979). The acculturation process has often been described as accommodation to the host culture in terms of giving up traditional forms of behavior and adopting modal behaviors of the host country (Garcia & Lega, 1979; Szapocznik, Scopetta, Kurtines, & Aranalde, 1978). An amplification of this view is that modern cultures permit and promote more diversity than traditional cultures, and thus acculturation would involve not just changing from one pattern of behavior to another but changing the way one thinks about behavior, changing one's concepts of development.

The concepts of development that parents hold will influence the way they understand the behavior of their children. Sameroff and Feil (1985) proposed a hierarchy of developmental concepts moving from a categorical belief that single causes were associated with single outcomes, to a compensating belief that outcomes could have multiple causes, to a perspectivistic belief that these multiple causes could interact and be transformed over time to produce alternative outcomes. To the extent that these concepts are flexible or perspectivistic, parents will be able to adapt to a variety of outcomes for their children. To the extent that these beliefs are rigid or categorical, parents will have difficulty adapting their rearing for children who differ from parent expectations in either appearance or behavior, especially if the children are handicapped. In a study of intellectual functioning in preschool children, it was found that the higher the level of the mother's concepts of development, the higher the IQ of the children at 4 years of age (Sameroff, Seifer, Barocas, Zax, & Greenspan, 1987). Furthermore, these concepts of development have great stability over many years. A high correlation ($r = .65$) was found between parents' scores on a concepts-of-development questionnaire given when their children were 4 and again when their children were 13 (Sameroff & Seifer, 1989).

Diversity in parenting cognitions both within and between ethnic groups must be interpreted within the socioeconomic and cultural context in which they exist. For Mexican-American families the cultural context includes socializing their children as part of a larger host culture. Exposure to a different cultural context can induce dramatic, often conflictual, changes within families. Part of what influences change in parenting values is the immigrants belief system at the time of immigration, as well as the parenting values endorsed by the host culture. The immigrant may have come from a society or community with either a traditional, transitional, or contemporary value orientation (Karrer, 1986). Recently, acculturation has been viewed as a transactional process involving change in both the immigrant group and the host culture (Karrer, 1986; Padilla, 1980; Szapocznik & Kurtines, 1980). In many ways the acculturation process is an accommodation between the two groups that unfolds as a function of their reactions to each other and the cultural context of the society. The cultural context must include the process of acculturation, as well as the level of cultural evolution of the ethnic group at the time of immigration (Karrer, 1986).

In regard to beliefs about children, Gutierrez, Sameroff, and Karrer (1988) proposed that acculturation would move parents to more flexible concepts of development in which more possibilities for parent and child behavior would be entertained. By comparing mothers in different states of acculturation, they examined the relation between adaptation to a modern industrial culture and concepts of development. Gutierrez et al. (1988) compared higher- and lower-SES groups of Mexican-American and Anglo-American mothers. The Mexican-American mothers were selected to be at low, moderate, or high levels of acculturation ranging from recent immigrants who planned to return to Mexico to second- and third-generation parents who had less involvement in Mexican culture or language. SES was found to be a major correlate of the concepts of development score, with both Mexican-American and Anglo American low-SES mothers scoring as more categorical than high-SES mothers. The predicted acculturation effect was found only among the high-SES mothers, with the more acculturated Mexican-American mothers scoring as more perspectivistic than the less acculturated ones. A surprise, however, was that the highly acculturated Mexican-American mothers were even more perspectivistic than the SES matched Anglo-American mothers. In order to explain these results, Gutierrez et al. hypothesized that perspectivism was enhanced by the need for highly acculturated Mexican-Americans to operate in two cultures, as compared with Anglo-Americans or less acculturated Mexican-Americans who functioned predominantly in one culture, either American or Mexican. However, this hypothesis could not be tested because there was no individual assessment of the degree to which each mother was involved in one or two cultures, that is, the degree to which she was monocultural or bicultural.

Szapocznik and Kurtines (1980) have suggested that the concept of biculturalism be incorporated in acculturation models. According to this model, acculturation is a complex process of accommodation to a total cultural context that may be unidirectional or bidirectional depending upon the type of cultural context involved. Given that Mexican-Americans tend to function in both Mexican and American communities, they need to be able to participate in both cultural contexts. In this respect, it may be important for individuals both to take on values of the dominant culture and to retain values and characteristics of the culture of origin. Bicultural individuals who live in a bicultural context may be more likely to have additional flexibility for coping with their social environment.

The present study was designed to test this hypothesis by examining the relation of both acculturation level and biculturalism to mothers' levels of concepts of development. Specifically, we predicted that mothers who were bicultural—who lived comfortably in both Mexican and American cultural contexts—would be more perspectivistic in their beliefs about child development than mothers who were monocultural. Further, we predicted that biculturalism would be a more important influence on parental concepts of development than level of acculturation into the dominant culture.

METHOD

Subjects

The subjects were 60 middle-class, professional Mexican-American and Anglo-American mothers, divided into three groups; a group of 20 moderately acculturated Mexican-American mothers, a group of 20 highly acculturated Mexican-American mothers, and a group of 20 Anglo-American mothers. The three groups were matched for age and socioeconomic status (SES). Socioeconomic status was established using a modification of the Hollingshead (1957) Two-Factor Index of Social Position (ISP), which combines head of household's occupational and educational levels; the modification was that mothers' and fathers' educational levels were averaged before computing the ISP (Sameroff & Seifer, 1983). Only mothers' education and occupation were used in father-absent families. Only families in SES categories 1 and 2 (primarily professional employment and advanced educational status) were included in the study. Subjects were recruited into the three groups (moderately acculturated Mexican-American, highly acculturated Mexican-American, and Anglo-American) to maximize educational and occupational equivalence for the groups. This stringent condition made subject recruitment difficult due to the higher likelihood of finding Mexican-American mothers with less education and lower occupational status in the lower acculturation group. However, less acculturated, professional, educated Mexican-American mothers were successfully sought out who had equivalent occupational and educational experience to the more acculturated Mexican-American mothers. Table 1 presents demographic data on maternal occupation, education, age, number of children, and generation in the United States for the Mexican-American and Anglo-American mothers, subdivided into monocultural and bicultural subgroups (moderately acculturated monocultural Mexican-American, moderately acculturated bicultural Mexican-American, highly acculturated monocultural Mexican-American, highly acculturated bicultural Mexican-American, and monocultural Anglo-American). The categories for education and occupation are those used by Hollingshead. For example, the mothers' occupational categories were major professional (lawyer, accountant), lesser professional (teacher, social worker), and

minor professional (physical therapist). Only third-generation Anglo-American mothers who were not involved in any ethnic group and neither they nor their parents spoke another language were included in the study.

Measures

All interviews were conducted in the subjects' homes and in their preferred language. The measures were translated into Spanish using a back-translation technique (English into Spanish and Spanish back into English) until they were easily understandable to monolingual Spanish-speaking subjects.

CONCEPTS OF DEVELOPMENT   The Concepts of Development Vignettes (CODV) were used to assess the level of complexity at which mothers understood development (Sameroff & Feil, 1985). The instrument consists of six vignettes that depict developmental problems common to all cultures. The mothers

TABLE 1

Maternal Demographic Data for Monocultural and Bicultural Subgroups of Mothers

| | Mexican-American | | | | |
| | Moderately acculturated | | Highly acculturated | | |
	Mono	Bi	Mono	Bi	ANGLO (Mono)
n	10	10	8	12	20
Maternal age	36.4	41.2	34.0	34.5	35.3
Number of children (*M*)	1.9	2.4	2.0	1.9	2.2
Maternal occupation:					
Major professional	4	3	4	3	7
Lesser professional	6	7	4	9	12
Minor professional	0	0	0	0	1
Maternal education:					
Less than BA	1	2	0	3	2
College graduate	5	5	4	6	11
Postgraduate	4	3	4	3	7
Generation in United States:					
First	7	6	1	1	0
Second	3	4	5	8	0
Third	0	0	2	3	20

were told the vignettes and asked to explain why the child or parent acted as described. Responses were scored according to the detailed codebook given in Sameroff and Feil (1985) into six levels of complexity: transition to categorical (1.5), categorical (2.0), transition to compensating (2.5), compensating (3.0), transition to perspectivistic (3.5), and perspectivistic (4.0). Examples of responses coded at different levels of complexity to one of the vignettes are shown in Table 2 (for more examples see Gutierrez et al., 1988; Sameroff & Feil, 1985). Thirty vignettes were scored

by two raters to determine reliability; there was perfect agreement on 80% and agreement within a half point on the remaining 20%.

ACCULTURATION The Acculturation Rating Scale for Mexican Americans (ARSMA), developed by Cuellar, Harris, and Jasso (1980), was used to measure level of acculturation. The ARSMA consists of 20 items designed to assess acculturation such as language familiarity, usage, and reference; ethnic identity and generation; reading, writing, and cultural ex-

TABLE 2

Sample of Responses to Concepts of Development Vignettes:
Vignette 5

Mr. and Mrs. Raymond have two children: Billy, who is 5, and Mary, who is 3. Billy was a very demanding baby and still asks for a lot of attention from his parents. Billy would get very angry if he didn't get what he wanted from his parents. Lately, Mr. and Mrs. Raymond have had a lot of money problems because Mr. Raymond was laid off from his job. One evening at bedtime Mrs. Raymond heard Billy and Mary fighting over a toy. She stormed into the bedroom and began spanking Billy very hard and she wouldn't stop. Mr. Raymond had to pull her away from the boy and had a hard time calming her down.

How would you explain Mrs. Raymond's behavior?

2.0 *Categorical*. "It seems like Mrs. Raymond is having a lot of trouble dealing with the financial problems due to husband losing his job. Maybe they can't meet their bills and they might not have money saved to cover their current expenses. It seems that the problem doesn't have a whole lot to do with Billy. Instead of finding out who had the toy last she let out her emotions on him. It was the straw that broke the camel's back—the kids fighting over a menial toy. She just seems to be getting her anger out, it was the mounting pressure of not having enough money for the family." *Scoring criteria: (a)* environment is the singular causal agent.

3.0 *Compensating*. "I think her behavior is from built-up tension from lack of money due to husband being laid off and the 5-year-old who has always been demanding. Yes, she's releasing her pent-up anxiety over money problems on her son. Since he's very demanding and gets angry when he doesn't get what he wants from his parents, he probably magnifies or exacerbates their lack of money. She's probably dealt with incident over incident with the boy, so from this tension and the lack of money comes her frustration and then her hitting. Normally

when kids fight over a toy you would take toy away from both; here she focuses on him due to stress and his personality. He is headstrong; sometimes these kinds of kids don't change, they are just born like this. He seems to have the kind of personality that gets on people's nerves. Maybe Mrs. Raymond doesn't see other qualities he might have, like he might be good at playing games alone. Maybe if she saw his good points he wouldn't get on her nerves so much." *Scoring criteria: (a)* environmental and constitutional causal agents, and (*b*) parental perception of child can compensate for negative qualities.

4.0 *Perspectivistic*. "This is a complicated one; it seems like her behavior is coming from a position of anger, she's not so mad about the kids fighting, but other things she is unable to deal with, maybe that are coming from her. To begin with she has always had to give Billy a lot of attention; he may have been born with colic. Now she may resent him and even feel closer to him. You usually strike out at those you feel closer to. She may also feel angry toward husband for being laid off. They may not be talking about this very stressful situation, or they may not be reaching out to others. Mrs. Raymond may be feeling that she is not getting what she needs from her husband. I see a parallel in son as he felt he had to take everything himself and maybe felt he wouldn't get what he needed. There seems to be a pattern in this family of reacting with their feelings to stress. Billy might have trouble as he gets older, because this kind of behavior will not be tolerated by his teachers. This family may need counseling or need to reach out to others." Scoring *criteria: (a)* environmental, constitutional, and psychological influences interact to determine outcome; (*b*) psychological process fully differentiated; (*c*) developmental consequences described; and (*d*) remediation suggested.

posure; and ethnic interaction. Each item is scored on a 5-point Likert-type scale, and the cross-items average is used to categorize subjects into acculturation groups, from very "Mexicanized" to very "Anglicized."

The mothers fell into two acculturation groups utilizing Cuellar's established cut-off points: (1) 20 mothers were assigned to a moderately acculturated (MA) Mexican-American group that included subjects with a score of 2.00-3.20 (M = 2.6), and (2) 20 mothers were assigned to a highly acculturated (HA) Mexican-American group that included subjects with a score of 3.21–3.90 (M = 3.5). Mothers were not included in the study if they scored lower than 2.00 (low acculturation). In addition, as in the previous study (Gutierrez et al., 1988), no Mexican-American mothers scored as extremely acculturated (ARSMA score above 4.00).

BICULTURALISM The Bicultural Involvement Questionnaire (Szapocznik, Kurtines, & Fernandez, 1980) was used to assess biculturalism. The Bicultural Involvement Questionnaire (BIQ) measures the degree to which a person feels comfortable and involved in Hispanic and Anglo-American cultures independently of each other. Symmetrical items for each culture are rated on a 5-point Likert scale. The questionnaire measures a dimension of biculturalism that ranges from monoculturalism to biculturalism. An Americanism score is derived by summing all of the items reflecting involvement with American culture, while a Hispanicism score is obtained by summing all the items reflecting involvement with Hispanic culture. Scores on the biculturalism scale are derived by subtracting the Americanism score from the Hispanicism score. Scores close to zero indicate biculturalism and scores deviating from zero indicate monoculturalism. A positive-difference score reveals monoculturalism in the Hispanic direction, whereas a negative-difference score suggests monoculturalism in the Anglo direction.

INTELLIGENCE Maternal intelligence was estimated by administering the vocabulary subtest of the Wechsler Adult Intelligence Scale-Revised (WAIS-R) or the equivalent form in Spanish, the Escala de Inteligencia Wechsler Para Adultos (EIWA), which was normed on a Spanish-speaking population (Wechsler, 1968). The vocabulary subtest of the WAIS-R correlates (.82–.85) highly with the full-scale score of the WAIS-R, as does the vocabulary subtest of the EIWA (.86) with the full-scale score of the EIWA, and these were considered satisfactory estimates of maternal intelligence.

The WAIS-R and EIWA vocabulary subtests were administered and scored as recommended in the WAIS-R and EIWA manuals. The subjects were presented with the word list, and the experimenter pointed to each word and asked its meaning. This process was discontinued after five consecutive failures. Each subject's full-scale IQ was estimated by converting the subject's raw vocabulary subtest score to a scale score and then multiplying by 11 to obtain an estimate of the sum-of-scales score. The subject's sum-of-scales score was then used to estimate the full-scale IQ. The scores ranged from 79 to 150 (M = 103.32 and SD = 16.19), with only one subject choosing administration of the vocabulary subtest in Spanish.

TRADITIONALISM The Traditional Family Ideology Scale (TFIS) was used to assess endorsement of traditional values (Levinson & Huffman, 1955). The scale is composed of 12 six-point Likert-type items. A score of 1 indicated strong agreement with traditional values, and a score of 6 indicated strong disagreement with traditional values. The 12 items were averaged to obtain the subject's nonendorsement of traditional values. For example, a mother who agreed with the following type of items was judged to be more traditional, while a mother who disagreed with these items was judged to be less traditional: "some equality in marriage is a good thing, but by and large the husband ought to have the main say-so in family matters," and "a child should never be allowed to talk back to his parents, or else he will lose respect for them."

RESULTS

Acculturation Analyses

To determine if the two main findings of the Gutierrez et al. (1988) study could be replicated, several analyses were done. To see if Mexican-American mothers at higher levels of acculturation would score higher on concepts of development, a one-way analysis of variance comparing the effects of acculturation to mothers' conceptions of development was performed. Three groups of SES-matched mothers were examined: (1) moderately acculturated (MA) Mexican-American mothers, (2) highly acculturated (HA) Mexican-American mothers, and (3) Anglo-American mothers. The one-way analysis of variance produced a significant main effect for groups, $F(2,57)$ = 8.91, $p < .01$. The mean CODV scores for the groups are presented in Table 3.

To determine if more acculturated Mexican-American mothers scored higher on concepts of

TABLE 3

Mean CODV Scores for the MA and HA Mexican-American Mothers and the Anglo-American Mothers and Correlations Between CODV and Intelligence and Traditionalism

	Mexican-American		
	MA	**HA**	**ANGLO (AA)**
n	20	20	20
Concepts of development	2.62	3.04	2.77
Correlations between CODV and intelligence	.05	−.36	.41
Correlations between CODV and traditionalism	.35	−.23	.14

development than Anglo-American mothers, a mean comparison was done between the two groups. The HA Mexican-American mothers scored significantly higher on the CODV than did the Anglo-American

mothers, $t(57) = 2.68$, $p < .01$. These data replicate the previous finding that HA Mexican-American mothers were more perspectivistic than their Anglo-American counterparts (Gutierrez et al., 1988).

Mean comparisons were also made between the MA Mexican-American and HA Mexican-American groups and between the MA Mexican-American and the Anglo-American groups. The HA Mexican-American group scored significantly higher than the MA Mexican-American group, $t(57) = 4.16$, $p < .001$. The MA Mexican-American and Anglo-American groups did not differ significantly from each other in terms of concepts of development.

Biculturalism Analyses

To test the prediction that bicultural mothers would be more perspectivistic in their concepts of development than mothers who were monocultural (either Mexican or American), the two Mexican-American groups were further subdivided into monocultural and bicultural subgroups and compared with the monocultural Anglo-American group. The subgroups were: (1) an MA monocultural group, (2) an MA bicultural group, (3) an HA monocultural group, (4) an HA bicultural group, and (5) a monocultural Anglo-American group.

TABLE 4

Means and Standard Deviations on Concepts of Development, Biculturalism, Traditionalism, and Intelligence for the Mexican-American and Anglo-American Monocultural and Bicultural Subgroups

	Mexican-American				
	Moderately acculturated		Highly acculturated		
	Mono	**Bi**	**Mono**	**Bi**	**ANGLO(Mono)**
Concepts of development	2.44	2.77	2.61	3.33	2.77
	(.16)	(.19)	(.14)	(.10)	(.32)
Biculturalism	68.77	79.45	64.00	80.16	50.70
	(4.40)	(5.10)	(4.56)	(2.88)	(4.14)
Traditionalism	4.21	4.35	5.03	4.73	5.08
	(.79)	(.96)	(.57)	(.45)	(.61)
Intelligence estimate	97.35	94.36	122.00	108.33	104.07
	(14.18)	(11.60)	(22.16)	(12.73)	(14.15)

Note: Standard deviations are in parentheses.

COMPARISON OF THE MEXICAN-AMERICAN SUBGROUPS   A 2 × 2 analysis of variance comparing the effects of acculturation (MA. vs. HA) and biculturalism (monocultural vs. bicultural) to mothers' conceptions of development revealed significant main effects for acculturation, $F(1,39) = 52.91$, $p < .001$, and biculturalism, $F(1,39) = 120.73$, $p < .001$, and an acculturation × biculturalism interaction effect, $F(1,39) = 16.14$, $p < .001$. As can be seen in Table 4, CODV scores did not vary along an acculturation dimension for the monocultural Mexican-American mothers; both monocultural Mexican-American groups tended to give lower CODV level responses. Concepts of development did vary with level of acculturation for the bicultural Mexican-American mothers. The HA bicultural Mexican-American mothers gave the highest CODV responses, followed by the MA bicultural mothers and then the HA and MA monocultural mothers.

COMPARISON OF THE HA MEXICAN-AMERICAN AND ANGLO-AMERICAN SUBGROUPS   Mean comparisons were made between the HA bicultural Mexican-American group, the HA monocultural Mexican-American group, and the monocultural Anglo-American group. As expected, all Anglo-American mothers scored as monocultural. The HA bicultural Mexican-American group scored significantly higher on concepts of development than did the HA monocultural Mexican-American and the monocultural Anglo-American groups. A significant difference was not found between the HA monocultural Mexican-American and monocultural Anglo-American groups.

Regression Analyses

We predicted that biculturalism would account for variance in concepts of development that was independent of the effects of accumulation and ethnicity. Specifically, within the Mexican-American mothers, biculturalism would be a more important influence on concepts of development than level of acculturation. In addition, when comparing Mexican-American and Anglo-American mothers, biculturalism would be a more important influence on concepts of development than the effects of ethnicity (membership in the Mexican or Anglo group).

To test these hypotheses, two hierarchical regressions were performed. The first hierarchical regression analysis was performed among the Mexican-American subjects. The predictor variables were entered in the following order: (1) years of maternal education, (2) maternal occupation, (3) traditionalism, (4) intelligence, (5) acculturation, and (6) biculturalism. The first four categories of variables were entered first to control for the possible confounding effects of maternal background and attitudinal variables. Biculturalism was entered after acculturation to test the unique variance accounted for by this variable after the effects of acculturation were removed. The multicollinearity found between the two important predictor variables, acculturation and biculturalism, was minimal ($r = -.15$). This low and nonsignificant correlation suggests an empirically sound basis for utilizing a regression analysis to test the hypothesis. Table 5 presents the results expressed as cumulative R^2 and changes in R^2 as each variable is entered into the analysis.

Although the subjects were of equivalent SES backgrounds, some research has suggested that the component SES variables of maternal education and maternal occupation can affect maternal values differently (Kohn, 1969; Laosa, 1980). Maternal education and occupation each accounted for nonsignificant percentage of the variance. Traditionalism and intelligence were entered next, and each accounted for a nonsignificant percentage of the variance.

It was expected that acculturation would account for a significant portion of variance in concepts of development. This prediction was confirmed. The acculturation variable accounted for 11% of unique variance. The prediction that biculturalism would account for a larger portion of variance than acculturation was strongly confirmed. Biculturalism ac-

TABLE 5

Percent Variance Accounted for by Maternal Education, Occupation, Intelligence, Traditionalism, Acculturation, and Biculturalism as Predictors of Concepts of Development for Subjects of Mexican Descent

Predictor variable	R^2	R^2 Change
Maternal education	.0020	.0020
Maternal occupation	.0023	.0003
Traditionalism	.0702	.0679
Intelligence	.0703	.0001
Acculturation	.1849	.1147*
Biculturalism	.6592	.4742***
Total R^2	.6592**	

* $p < .05$.
** $p < .01$.
*** $p < .001$.

counted for an additional 47% of unique variance in parental concepts of development. These results powerfully support the hypothesis that biculturalism would increase parental concepts of development for Mexican-American mothers.

The second hierarchical regression analysis was performed among the HA Mexican-American and Anglo-American subjects. The predictor variables were entered in the order as the previous hierarchical regression. Table 6 presents the results. Again, maternal education, occupation, traditionalism, and intelligence were not significant contributors to concepts of development.

It was expected that ethnicity would account for a significant amount of variance in parental reasoning. This prediction was confirmed, with ethnicity accounting for 12% of unique variance. The prediction that biculturalism would account for a larger portion of the variance than ethnicity was also confirmed. Biculturalism accounted for an additional 39% of unique variance in parental concepts of development. These results support the hypothesis that biculturalism would increase parental concepts of development.

IQ and Traditionalism Analyses

Several analyses were done to examine determinants of parental reasoning about development other than acculturation and biculturalism. One factor that might influence parental cognitions is intellectual capacity. For the entire sample, the correlation, $r(59) = .15$, between the WAIS-R estimated full-scale IQ and CODV was not significant, indicating that for this sample of middle-class professional mothers general intellectual capacity did not account for level of complexity in concepts of development.

The relation between general intelligence and concepts of development for each of the three groups was also examined. The correlation coefficients were $r(19) = .05$ for the moderately acculturated Mexican-American group, and $r(19) = .41$ for the Anglo-American group (see Table 3). General intelligence was not related significantly to parental reasoning about development for any of the three groups.

Another question was whether parental reasoning about development was related to endorsement of traditional values. For the entire sample, the correlation, $r(59) = .19$, between the TFIS and CODV was not significant, suggesting that a mother's ability to think in complex ways about development was not related to level of traditionalism. Traditionalism was not related to concepts of development for any of the three groups: the correlation for the moderately acculturated Mexican-American group was $r(19) = .35$, the correlation for the highly acculturated Mexican-American group was $r(19) = -.23$, and the correlation for the Anglo-American group was $r(19) = .14$ (see Table 3).

TABLE 6

Percent Variance Accounted for by Maternal Education, Occupation, Intelligence, Traditionalism, Ethnicity, and Biculturalism as Predictors of Concepts of Development for HA Mexican-American and Anglo-American Mothers

Predictor Variable	R^2	R^2 Change
Maternal education	.0027	.0027
Maternal occupation	.0037	.0010
Traditionalism	.0158	.0121
Intelligence	.0251	.0093
Ethnicity	.1538	.1267*
Biculturalism	.5429	.3891***
Total R^2	.5429***	

* $p < .05$.
** $p < .01$.
*** $p < .001$.

DISCUSSION

The Gutierrez et al. (1988) finding that complex developmental explanations are given by more acculturated rather than less acculturated Mexican-American mothers was replicated in the present study. The more acculturated Mexican-American mothers, like their counterparts in the previous study, were more perspectivistic than the Anglo-American mothers. Although acculturation is an important contributor to concepts of development, it alone cannot explain parental complexity (Gutierrez et al., 1988). Acculturation has typically referred to an individual's ability to function within the host culture value orientation. Karrer (1986) and Szapocznik and Kurtines (1980) have both emphasized bidirectional rather than unidirectional models of acculturation, that is, the ability of an individual to function both in the culture of origin and in the host culture. It has been suggested by Carringer (1974) that flexibility or complexity in thinking is related to biculturalism. For these reasons, parents at different levels of acculturation and biculturalism are likely to differ in their interpretation of the developmental process.

Biculturalism was found to be a correlate of complexity in Mexican-American mothers' concepts of development. The relative effects of acculturation and biculturalism were examined in a comparison of Mexican-American mothers who varied on both dimensions. There were separate effects of both factors, with more acculturated and more bicultural mothers scoring at higher levels of concepts of development. But when the two factors were combined, there was a synergistic interaction effect such that the Mexican-American mothers who were high on both acculturation and biculturalism had even higher scores than would be expected from the addition of the two factors. These mothers also scored significantly higher than the well acculturated third-generation Anglo-American mothers. The Anglo-American mothers' scores were the same as those of Mexican-American mothers who were high on acculturation and monocultural or low on acculturation and bicultural. In addition, biculturalism accounted for the largest amount of variance compared to acculturation or ethnicity. Intellectual capacity, level of traditionalism, and maternal occupation or education did not contribute significantly to maternal reasoning about development for any of these middle-class groups.

The concepts-of-development measure was designed to assess the level of complexity at which parents understood development. Parents who are environmentalists can score at the same level as parents who are constitutionalists. If they see environment or constitution as a singular causal agent for a specific child outcome, they would score at a low categorical level. If they see environmental or constitutional factors interacting, among themselves or with each other, they would score as more perspectivistic. The bicultural, highly acculturated Mexican-American mothers were the only group in which the average concepts-of-development score was above 3.0, that is, between the compensating and perspectivistic level. Their modal response was that at least two explanations were possible for every vignette. Every other group's modal response was between categorical and compensating levels where singular causes were the frequent explanation of developmental outcomes. More perspectivistic parents are seen as being more flexible in their interpretation of and reaction to variations in child behavior.

How can we explain the connection between biculturalism and perspectivism? Our findings are in accord with other studies that have shown a relation between cognitive flexibility and biculturalism (Ben-Zev, 1977; Peal & Lambert 1962). The connection is not simply acculturation into a more complex society or the greater number of alterative behavioral styles

found in modern societies. We found no significant correlation between concepts of development and traditionalism in any of the groups in the study. Mothers with categorical and perspectivistic reasoning endorsed both traditional and nontraditional values.

The connection to higher-level concepts of development is not through the higher intelligence that would be expected in more acculturated groups. We did find that the more acculturated Mexican-American mothers had higher IQs than less acculturated ones who were matched for both education and occupational level. However, the bicultural subgroups of mothers who scored higher on the concepts of development had lower IQ scores, emphasizing the lack of correlation found between concept-of-development scores and IQ.

The explanation we would propose is in the spirit of Vygotsky's belief in the social regulation of thought. Within any traditional culture there is a modal pattern of acceptable behavior and explanations and rationalizations for that behavior. It is in the necessity of integrating two cultures that an individual must transcend these rationalizations to appreciate that each culture has a different form of acceptable behavior. Such integrations require a perspectivism that appreciates the relativism of belief systems in each specific culture. Such perspectivism has been described by Bertalanffy (1968) as typifying the development of our understanding of history. For Bertalanffy, each historical epoch has a modal correct belief system that supplants the previous incorrect belief system. He sees a new perspectivistic philosophy now emerging in which belief systems are understood as contextually dependent, which means that there will always be new belief systems if contexts change.

It must be understood, however, that higher levels of concepts of development need not be better than lower levels when context is taken into account. Kohn (1969) identified a dimension of parental values in which conforming values were associated with lower-SES life and self-directing values were associated with higher-SES conditions. In his analysis, he did not argue that one orientation was better than another, but that each represented an appropriate adaptation to a subcultural context. Similarly, a parent's level of concepts of development reflects an adaptation to the cultural context. What we found is that bicultural contexts are related to more perspectivistic concepts of development because bicultural life requires an appreciation that each culture may differ in values and behavior.

In a society where a group is a minority in a larger majority culture, the worldview of the larger society either supports or acts to suppress certain values of the minority culture. The worldview of the immigrant group is also important in effecting the acculturation process. A group immigrating from a society with a traditional value orientation will have a different experience than a group immigrating from a society with a modern value orientation. It is important to be aware of the cultural and socioeconomic contexts in which an ethnic group functions to obtain a clearer picture of that group. In previous studies (Gutierrez et al., 1988; Sameroff & Feil, 1985) we found strong relations between social class and concepts of development. In this study, complexity in Mexican-American mothers' concepts of development was strongly related to where the mother was in terms of both acculturation and biculturalism.

The melting pot image of American society has given way in recent decades to the encouragement of cultural diversity within a common society. A variety of values have been attributed to the maintenance of ethnic roots within families. This study has identified another consequence of maintaining a biculturalism identification, that is, enhanced perspectivism and flexibility of thought about human development. The correlates of this flexibility are that parents may be more accepting of a variety of outcomes for their children and more flexible in their ability to react to such diversity, perhaps in the direction of encouraging and supporting adaptive functioning.

References

Ben-Zev, S. (1977). The influence of bilingualism on cognitive development. *Child Development*, 48, 1009–1018.

Bertalanffy, L. von. (1968). *Organismic psychology and systems theory.* Barre, MA: Clark University Press.

Carringer, D. A. (1974). Creative thinking abilities of Mexican youth. *Journal of Cross Cultural Psychology*, 5, 492–504.

Cuellar, I., Harris, L. C., & Jasso, R. (1980). An acculturation scale for Mexican-American normal and clinical populations. *Hispanic Journal of Behavioral Sciences*, 2, 199–217.

Garcia, M., & Lega, L. I. (1979). Development of a Cuban ethnic identity questionnaire. *Hispanic Journal of Behavioral Sciences*, 1, 247–261.

Goodnow, J. J. (1988). Parents' ideas, actions, and feelings: Models and methods from developmental and social psychology. *Child Development*, 59, 286–330.

Gutierrez, J., Sameroff, A. J., & Karrer, B. M. (1988). Acculturation and SES effects on Mexican-American parents' concepts of development. *Child Development*, 59, 250–255.

Hollingshead, A. B. (1957). *Two-Factor Index of Social Position.* Unpublished manuscript.

Karrer, B. M. (1986). Families of Mexican descent: A contextual approach. In R. B. Birrer (Ed.), *Urban family medicine* (pp. 228–232). New York: Springer Verlag.

Kohn, M. L. (1969). *Class and conformity.* Chicago: London: University of Chicago Press.

Laosa, L. (1980). Maternal teaching strategies and cognitive styles in Chicano families. *Journal of Educational Psychology*, 72, 45–54.

Levinson, D., & Huffman, P. (1955). Traditional family ideology and its relation to personality. *Journal of Personality*, 23, 251–273.

Padilla, A. M. (1980). The role of cultural awareness and ethnic loyalty in acculturation. In A. M. Padilla (Ed.), *Acculturation: Theory, models, and some new findings* (pp. 47–84). Boulder, CO: Westview.

Peal, E., & Lambert W. E. (1962). The relation of bilingualism to intelligence. *Psychological Monographs*, 76, 1–23.

Piaget, J. (1950). *The psychology of intelligence.* New York: International Universities Press.

Sameroff, A. J., & Feil, L. A. (1985). Parental conceptions of development. In I. E. Sigel (Ed.), *Parental belief systems: The psychological consequences for children* (pp. 83–105). Hillsdale, NJ: Erlbaum.

Sameroff, A. J., & Seifer, R. (1983). Familial risk and child competence. *Child Development*, 54, 1254–1268.

Sameroff, A. J., & Seifer, R. (1989). *Social regulation of developmental continuities.* Paper presented at the annual meeting of the American Association for the Advancement of Science, San Francisco.

Sameroff, A. J., Seifer, R., Barocas, B., Zax, M., & Greenspan, S. (1987). IQ scores of 4-year-old children: Social-environmental risk factors. *Pediatrics*, 79, 343–350.

Szapocznik, J., & Kurtines, W. (1980). Acculturation, biculturalism and adjustment among Cuban Americans. In A. M. Padilla (Ed.), *Acculturation: Theory, models and some new findings* (pp. 139–159). Boulder, CO: Westview.

Szapocznik, J., Kurtines, W., & Fernandez, T. (1980). Bicultural involvement and adjustment in Hispanic-American youths. *International Journal of Intercultural Relations*, 4, 353–365.

Szapocznik, J., Scopetta, M., Kurtines, W., & Aranalde, M. A. (1978). Theory and measurement of acculturation. *International Journal of Psychology*, 12, 113–130.

Vygotsky, L. S. (1978). *Mind in society: The development of higher psychological processes.* Cambridge, MA: Harvard University Press.

Werner, E. E. (1979). *Cross-cultural child development: A view from the planet Earth*. Monterey, CA: Brooks/Cole.

Wertsch, J. V., Minick, N., & Arns, F. J. (1984). The creations of context in joint problem solving. In B. Rogoff & J. Lave (Eds.), *Everyday cognition: Its development in social context* (pp. 151–171). Cambridge, MA: Harvard University Press.

Wechsler, D. (1968). *Escala de Intelligencia Wechsler Para Adultos*. Copyright by the Psychological Corporation, San Antonio, TX.

28

Mechanisms in the Cycle of Violence

KENNETH A. DODGE, JOHN E. BATES, AND GREGORY S. PETTIT

One of the most disheartening aspects of modern life is that many children live in fear and pain as a result of an abusive family situation. Psychologists are concerned both about the immediate effects of family violence on the young child and about possible long-term effects that may persist into adulthood and affect the next generation. Kenneth A. Dodge, John E. Bates, and Gregory S. Pettit explore the psychological risks for children who have been abused. In particular they examine whether and how exposure to violence as a child may lead to aggressive patterns, either as an abuser or a victim, when abused children reach adulthood.

Two questions concerning the effect of physical abuse in early childhood on the child's development of aggressive behavior are the focus of this article. The first is whether abuse per se has deleterious effects. In earlier studies, in which samples were non-representative and family ecological factors (such as poverty, marital violence, and family instability) and child biological variables (such as early health problems and temperament) were ignored, findings have been ambiguous. Results from a prospective study of a representative sample of 309 children indicated that physical abuse is indeed a risk factor for later aggressive behavior even when the other ecological and biological factors are known. The second question concerns the processes by which antisocial development occurs in abused children. Abused children tended to acquire deviant patterns of processing social information, and these may mediate the development of aggressive behavior.

In spite of the fact that child maltreatment has occurred since the beginning of civilization (1), it was only several generations ago that modern society finally began to recognize the enormity of this problem (2). Testimony before the U.S. Congress indicates that in the United States alone, billions of dollars are spent every year in the medical, psychosocial, and social service treatment of physically abused children (3). Little is known empirically, however, of the long-term consequences of early abuse or of the mechanisms by which abuse might have an impact on behavioral development.

It is now becoming established that being the object of physical harm by an adult is a risk marker for the development of violent behavior toward others later in life (4). Early retrospective and clinical case studies are being supplanted by prospective, controlled studies to demonstrate this risk (5, 6). For example, Widom (7) reported that individuals who had been identified by juvenile courts as abused or neglected during childhood were 42% more likely than controls to perpetuate this cycle of violence by obtaining a criminal record of violence as adults. Methodological problems aside, this literature has yet to resolve two major questions regarding this cycle of violence. These questions are considered in this article, and empirical findings are reported that shed light on this topic.

WHAT IS THE RISK FACTOR IN CHILD ABUSE?

The first question concerns possible related factors that might account for the increased risk that is associated with early physical harm. Almost all prospective studies in this area have followed children who have been brought to the attention of juvenile courts or human service agencies (5, 7). These studies confound the experience of abuse with subsequent actions by these agencies, which usually involve separation of the child from her or his parents, foster home placement, labeling of the child and family, or other drastic measures that might account for the reported increased risk in this population. Also, by relying on agency reports, such studies include only a small, biased portion of all children who are physically harmed in early life. Interviews with national probability family samples reveal that a full 18% of children have been the object of a "severe violent act" (more serious than spanking or slapping) (8) by parents at some time in their lives, with 11% experiencing an event in the past year (9). What is needed is a prospective study of children who have been severely physically harmed in early life but who have not necessarily been identified by public agencies. The study reported here has those characteristics.

It is also known that abuse is likely to occur in an ecological context of other risk variables (10). By this context, it is meant that abuse is more common among lower socioeconomic classes (11), among single-parent families (12), within stressful environments (13), and among families in which there is marital conflict or interspousal physical violence (14). To date, no study has assessed the impact of child abuse on later violence while taking into account these variables (15); thus, it is not clear that the experience of physical harm per se is responsible for later antisocial development. In fact, most studies have confounded the experience of physical abuse with child neglect, a more general problem of inadequate parental care. We focus on physical abuse and distinguish abuse from other risk variables.

Yet another possibility is that certain biologically based characteristics of the child lead adults to engage in physical harm toward that child, and it is those characteristics that are also responsible for the child's later violence. According to an extreme "child effects" (16) model, physical abuse is a marker of risk but does not contribute to the risk. There is clinical evidence that child temperament (fussiness, unadaptability, and resistance to control) is associated with physical abuse (17) and that children with health problems at birth (such as prematurity or low birth weight) are at risk for abuse (18). No study has controlled these factors while examining the possible aggression-inducing effects of abuse on children.

THROUGH WHAT INTRAPERSONAL MECHANISMS DOES ABUSE HAVE ITS EFFECT?

If it is established that physical harm does lead to later aggression, a separate goal must be to understand how this effect occurs. Widom has argued that "the goal should be further knowledge of the processes involved. . . . Research should be directed at understanding how these early experiences relate to later violent behavior" (7, p. 165). Theory and empirical findings point toward social-information-processing factors as mechanisms of child aggressive behavior. According to several models (19, 20), individuals ordinarily respond to environmental stimuli by first encoding relevant cues, interpreting those cues, accessing possible behavioral responses from long-term memory stores, evaluating the consequences of possible behaviors, and finally selecting and enacting a behavior. Aggressive children, relative to average children, have been found to display chronic biases and deficits in the processing of provocation stimuli. These children display deficits in attending to and encoding relevant social cues (19, 21) and biases and errors in over-attributing hostile intent to others (22).

They access many aggressive responses and few competent responses from repertoires stored in memory *(23, 24)*, and they tend to evaluate the outcomes of aggression as interpersonally and instrumentally positive *(25)*. These processing patterns build on each other such that a comprehensive assessment of all these patterns yields a stronger prediction about the likelihood of aggressive behavior *(19, 24)*.

It is hypothesized that abusive socializing experiences will lead to chronic aggressive behavior by having an impact on the development of social-information-processing patterns. The two major intrapersonal theories of the effects of child abuse, attachment theory *(26, 27)* and social learning theory *(28)*, both posit that physical abuse could have such effects. According to attachment theory, insecure attachments associated with abuse may lead a child to develop internal working models of the world as a threatening place. In social-information-processing terms, these children may fail to develop appropriate attention to interpersonal interactions (that is, they fail to encode relevant social cues) *(29)* and may become hypervigilant toward hostile cues. Crittendon and Ainsworth noted that "such vigilance resulting from internal models of conflict and dominance could easily lead the abused child to misinterpret the behavior of others and to respond with aggression himself" *(27)*. Social learning theory posits that the experience of physical abuse will lead to later aggression to the extent that it makes aggressive responses salient in one's response repertoire and leads one to evaluate aggressive responses as efficacious in leading to positive outcomes *(30)*.

These theories suggest a model of the development of violence in which the experience of severe physical harm is associated with later chronic aggressive behavior, but the mechanism through which this association operates is the acquisition of a set of biased and deficient patterns of processing social provocation information. Four hypotheses are posited in this model: (i) The experience of severe physical harm will increase a child's risk of later chronic aggressive behavior, above and beyond the risk that accrues from related environmental and temperamental characteristics. (ii) The experience of severe physical harm in early life will predict the later development of biased and deficient patterns in the processing of social information. (iii) Biased and deficient processing patterns will predict the occurrence of chronic aggressive behavior toward others. (iv) Social-information-processing patterns will mediate the relation between early physical harm and later aggression; that is, this relation will become nonsignificant once patterns of social information processing are taken into account.

THE MULTI-SITE CHILD DEVELOPMENT PROJECT

To test these hypotheses, a descriptive longitudinal study was conducted in which a representative sample of 309 four-year-old children was identified at the time of kindergarten preregistration and then followed over time. Three kinds of information were collected on each subject: child physical harm and related family experiences (in early life); child social-information-processing patterns (at age five); and child aggressive behavior (in school 6 months after collection of processing pattern data).

Children were selected for participation from three geographical regions: Nashville, Tennessee (*n* = 103; midsize, urban community, with one-fourth of the selected sample living in federally subsidized housing); Knoxville, Tennessee (*n* = 100; Appalachian rural and small urban, mixed socioeconomic status); and Bloomington, Indiana (*n* = 106; small city and semi-rural, with much of the sample from working class backgrounds). At the time of kindergarten preregistration in April 1987, parents of matriculating children were solicited (in person at the child's school or by mail) at random to become involved in a longitudinal study of child development. About 70% agreed. Interested parents were then visited at home by research staff, who explained the project in detail and obtained written permission for all phases of data collection. Families were paid $20 each for participation.

The sample was demographically diverse and representative of the geographic regions (53% male, 47% female; 83% white, 16% African-American, 1% other). The parents of 18% of the sample were not married at the time of the child's birth, and 29% of the children lived in single-parent households at age four (three children lived in foster care). The mother's mean age at the time of the child's birth was 27 years (SD = 5.0; range, 17 to 39), and the father's mean age was 29 years (SD = 5.6; range, 18 to 50). The mother's median education level was 12 years (SD = 2.4; range, 5 to 20), and the father's was 13 years (SD = 2.9; range, 6 to 20). The Hollingshead four-factor index of social status (based on job status and education) ranged from 14 to 66 (possible range is 8 to 66), with a median of 38.5 (SD = 14.1). Eight percent of subjects came from the lowest socioeconomic class, with 16%, 28%, 30%, and 18% from the other classes, in ascending order.

ASSESSMENT OF PHYSICAL HARM AND RELATED VARIABLES Mothers were interviewed privately in their homes in a 90-minute session *(31)*. Following a "comfort-inducing" preliminary period, mothers were asked to recall the era between the child's birth and 12 months ago (*32*). They were asked questions about child misbehavior and discipline practices and then were asked whether the child had ever been physically harmed by an adult. Immediately following a detailed discussion, the interviewer rated the probability that the child had been physically abused, using a criterion of visible bruises or medical attention. Next, the mother was asked to consider the past 12 months and was asked the same questions. The interviewer then completed a rating for this era (*33*). Children were categorized as physically harmed if the interviewer had rated the likelihood of physical harm as probable or higher in at least one era. Forty-six children (15%) were so classified (*34–35*).

During the same standardized interview, additional questions were asked to assess factors that have been hypothesized to co-occur with abuse, including early family ecological and child biological variables. To assess the former, each mother was asked to describe her relationships with spouses and boyfriends during the child's life, particularly any physical conflicts to which the child might have been exposed. The interviewer then rated on five-point scales the degree to which the child had been exposed to adult physical conflict in each of the two life eras, and these ratings were averaged (*36*). Assessments of family marital status and socioeconomic status at the time of the child's birth and later were also made from standardized questions. To assess biological variables, the mother was asked to recall her pregnancy, particularly any health problems experienced by the child and herself during birth and delivery. Mothers reported that 6% of children had major health difficulties at birth, with an additional 21% having minor health difficulties at that time. Mothers experienced major health problems during delivery in 7% of cases, with an additional 20% experiencing minor health problems during delivery. Responses were scored on two three-point scales (0 if no problems, 1 if minor problems, and 2 if major problems). Each mother also completed a retrospective version of the Infant Characteristics Questionnaire (*37*), rating child temperament in infancy. Three reliable scale scores were derived from this instrument: fussiness, unadaptability, and resistance to control.

ASSESSMENT OF CHILD SOCIAL INFORMATION PROCESSING Using videorecorded and cartoon stimuli, a trained adult (blind to the child's status as abused and to all knowledge of the child's behavior) assessed the child's characteristic patterns of processing social information during a home visit. Each of 24 vignettes was presented on a portable television monitor to each child, who then answered questions about

each story. The child was asked to imagine being the protagonist in each vignette, which depicted a negative event for the child (either a direct provocation such as having one's building blocks knocked over by a peer or rebuff from an attempt to initiate play with one or more peers). The intention of the peer provocateur in each vignette systematically varied as hostile, benign, or ambiguous.

To assess the child's ability to attend to appropriate and relevant social cues, the child was asked to recall what had happened in the story. Responses were scored as 0 (not at all relevant), 1 (partially relevant), or 2 (fully relevant), and were averaged across the 24 vignettes.

As an assessment of the child's tendencies to attribute hostile intent to others, each of eight hypothetical ambiguous provocation stimuli were presented in cartoon-format. The child was asked how and why the peer might have acted the way that he or she did. Responses were scored as 0 (benign intent) or 1 (hostile intent), and were averaged across the eight stories.

To assess the child's response accessing tendencies, after each of the 24 video vignettes was presented, the child was asked how he or she would respond if the provocation had actually occurred. Responses were scored as aggressive, withdrawn or inept, or assertive and competent, and the proportions of each type across the 24 vignettes were computed. Because the score for withdrawal responses was redundant with the other two, it was dropped from analysis. To assess the child's ability to generate numerous behavioral responses to social problems, each of eight hypothetical social problems was also presented. The child was asked to generate as many behavioral solutions as possible (up to 10). The mean number generated per problem was computed.

To assess the child's response evaluation tendencies, after each video vignette was presented, each of three possible behavioral responses (aggressive, non-aggressive-inept, and competent) was also presented, in random order. The child was asked to evaluate the probable outcomes of each response on a four-point scale (1, very bad; 2, bad; 3, good 4, very good). Relative endorsement scores for aggressive and competent responses were computed as the score for each type of response divided by the total score (*38*).

ASSESSMENT OF CHILD AGGRESSIVE BEHAVIOR Six months (±2 months) following the maternal and child interview, the child's aggressive behavior in the school peer environment was assessed by teacher ratings, peer nominations, and direct observation. The teacher completed the widely used teacher's report form of the Child Behavior Checklist (CBCL) (*39*). The aggression scale score was computed. Peer nominations were also collected because of their utility in predicting current and later violent behavior *(40)*. In individual interviews, every peer in the child's classroom for whom parental permission was obtained *(41)* was asked to nominate up to three children as fitting each of three behavioral descriptions of highly aggressive behavior (starting fights, getting angry, and being mean toward others). Scores were tallied for all children in the classroom as the standardized (by z-score) number of nominations received for each item, and then averaged across items, yielding one peer-rated aggression score for each child *(42)*.

Direct observations of aggression were conducted by trained observers using a focal-child, event-based system on the playground and in the classroom. Each child was observed for 12 5-min periods, broken down into 10-s intervals, in which the observer noted each occurrence of aggression by the child. Scores were computed as the rate of aggressive acts per hour *(43)*. The three aggression scores were positively correlated ($r = 0.61$, 0.19, and 0.20; each $P < 0.001$).

FINDINGS

EFFECTS OF ABUSE ON AGGRESSIVE BEHAVIOR

The first hypothesis was tested by multivariate analysis of variance, in which early physical harm and sex were factors and the three aggression scores were dependent variables *(44)*. A statistically significant main effect of abuse [$F(3, 298) = 4.01$, $P < 0.008$] indicated that children who had been physically harmed in early life became more aggressive toward peers than did those who had not been harmed. Univariate analyses revealed statistically significant effects of harm for the teacher rating [$F(1,300) = 11.90$, $P < 0.001$] and for the peer rating [$F(1,300) = 4.77$, $P < 0.03$]. As shown in Figure 1, the teacher-rated aggression scores of harmed children were, on average, 93% higher than those of non-harmed children. The peer-rated scores averaged one-fourth of a standard deviation higher (meaning that about twice as many peers nominated harmed children as aggressive as they did non-harmed children), and the observed aggression rates averaged 30% higher. These findings were similar for girls and boys.

To test the hypothesis that these differences would hold even when family ecological variables and child biological variables are taken into account, multivariate analysis of covariance was conducted, with physical harm and child's sex as factors and nine variables as covariates. Four of these were family ecological variables: the Hollingshead socioeconomic status score, family status at the child's birth (parents

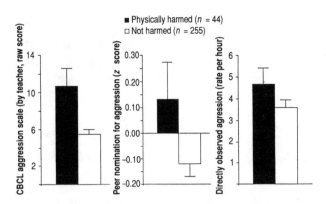

FIGURE 1 Teacher-rated, peer-rated, and directly observed aggressive behavior in groups of physically harmed and not harmed children. Bar represents the group mean with the standard error.

married or living together = 1, and mother alone = 2), family status since birth (parents married = 1, and parents ever divorced = 2), and marital (or mother-boyfriend) physical conflict and violence (interviewer rating noted above). Five covariates were child biologically related variables: mother's health problems in pregnancy or at birth (scale noted above), child's health problems at birth (scale noted above), and the three scales of maternal recollections of child temperament in first year of life (fussiness, unadaptability, and resistance to control). These variables did correlate overall with the occurrence of physical harm to the child [$F(9,292) = 2.94$, $P < 0.002$], with all four family ecological variables predicting harm to the child (Table 1). None of the five child biologically related variables predicted harm to the child.

Even when all nine of these variables plus child's sex were controlled statistically, the multivariate main effect of physical harm on the child's aggressive behavior was still statistically significant [$F(3,289) = 3.18$, $P < 0.024$], indicating that physical harm is predictive of later child aggressive behavior, above and beyond any correlated contribution that family ecology and child biologically related characteristics might make.

EFFECTS OF ABUSE ON CHILD SOCIAL INFORMATION PROCESSING

The second hypothesis was tested with harm and child's sex as factors and the seven processing variables as dependent variables. As hypothesized, physically harmed children developed different processing styles than non-harmed children [$F(7,294) = 2.10$, $P < 0.043$]. Harmed children (relative to non-harmed children) came to be significantly less attentive to relevant social cues, more biased toward attributing hostile intent, and less likely to

TABLE 1

Family Demographic Variable Mean Scores of
Physically Harmed and Not Harmed Children

| | Subject group | | | |
	Harmed ($n = 46$)	Not harmed ($n = 258$)	$F(1,300)$	P
Hollingshead socioeconomic status score (range, 14–66)	33.9 (2.2)*	41.4 (0.9)	10.36	0.001
Family status at child's birth (% with mother living alone)	30	16	4.84	0.028
Family status since birth (% ever divorced)	47	26	7.72	0.006
Marital violence rating (range = 1–5)	2.54 (0.21)	2.05 (0.05)	15.02	0.001

*Numbers in parentheses represent standard errors.

generate competent solutions to interpersonal problems (Table 2). These findings were similar for girls and boys.

RELATION BETWEEN EARLY CHILD SOCIAL INFORMATION PROCESSING AND LATER AGGRESSION

Multiple regression analyses revealed that the seven processing variables significantly predicted later aggression (the third hypothesis), as assessed in all three ways: as rated by teachers [$R = 0.24$, $F(7,294) = 2.51$, $P < 0.017$], as rated by peers [$R = 0.25$, $F(7,294) = 2.70$, $P < 0.01$], and as directly observed ($R = 0.29$, $F(7,294) = 3.86$, $P < 0.001$) (45). Bivariate correlations indicated that teacher-rated aggression was predicted by poor encoding of cues ($r = 0.16$, $P < 0.006$), accessing of aggressive responses ($r = 0.16$, $P < 0.007$), and a failure to access competent responses ($r = -0.17$, $P < 0.003$). Peer-rated aggression was predicted by poor encoding of cues ($r = 0.13$, $P < 0.027$) and accessing of aggressive responses ($r = 0.19$, $P < 0.001$). Directly observed aggression was predicted by hostile attributional biases ($r = 0.14$, $P < $

TABLE 2

Social Information Processing Mean Scores of Physically
Harmed and Not Harmed Children

| | Subject group | | | |
	Harmed ($n = 46$)	Not harmed ($n = 258$)	$F(1,300)$	P
Encoding of relevant cues (z-score)	0.19 (0.13)*	−0.04 (0.04)	5.07	0.025
Hostile attributional bias (% hostile attributions)	0.47 (0.06)	0.25 (0.04)	6.00	0.015
Number of responses generated to each social problem	4.16 (0.32)	4.48 (0.14)	<1	NS†
Proportion of aggressive responses	0.49 (0.05)	0.40 (0.02)	2.84	NS
Proportion of competent responses	0.10 (0.02)	0.16 (0.01)	4.33	0.038
Positive evaluation of the outcomes of aggressing (z-score)	0.26 (0.15)	−0.06 (0.07)	3.28	NS
Positive evaluation of the outcomes of acting competently (z-score)	−0.18 (0.19)	0.02 (0.08)	1.03	NS

*Numbers in parenthesis represent standard errors.
†Not significant (NS).

0.018), generating few solutions to interpersonal problems ($r = -0.21$, $P < 0.001$), and evaluating aggression as leading to positive outcomes $r = 0.16$, $P < 0.005$). Thus, a child's patterns of processing social information at age five appear to predict that child's aggressive behavior patterns at a later date.

SOCIAL INFORMATION PROCESSING AS A MECHANISM IN THE EFFECT OF EARLY HARM ON AGGRESSIVE BEHAVIORAL DEVELOPMENT To test the fourth hypothesis, physical harm and child sex were factors, the three child aggression scores were dependent variables, and the seven child social-information-processing variables were covariates. As hypothesized, when child processing was covaried, early physical harm no longer had a statistically significant effect on later child aggression [$F(3,290) = 2.16$]. On the other hand, when stepwise regression analyses were conducted and physical harm was covaried (by first entry), the seven processing variables continued to predict later aggression: for teacher-rated aggression, $F(7,294) = 2.11$, $P < 0.043$; for peer-rated aggression, $F(7,294) = 2.20$, $P < 0.035$; and for directly observed aggression, $F(7,294) = 3.76$, $P < 0.001$. The findings are consistent with the hypothesis that early physical harm has its effect on a child's aggressive behavioral development largely by altering the child's patterns of processing social information.

CONCLUSIONS

Our findings offer evidence that the experience of physical abuse in early childhood is a risk marker for the development of chronic aggressive behavior patterns. A full 36% of the children defined as "harmed" received teacher-rated aggression scores in the deviant range (defined as >1 SD above the mean), in contrast with just 13% of other children. This almost threefold increase in risk held even when the nine demographic and child biological variables were first considered. Even though nonexperimental data such as these can never be used to prove a causal relation, the current evidence indicates that the risk is not due to co-occurring family ecological factors (low socioeconomic status, single parenthood, marital dissolution, and marital violence) or child health problems and temperament. Because the cases of harm had generally not involved interventions, the risk is not likely to be due to treatment by social service agencies. Thus, this prospective study provides stronger evidence than ever before to support the hypothesis that physical abuse leads to a cycle of violence.

Analyses indicate that child abuse is relatively likely to occur in a context of poverty, deprivation, and marital conflict, even though instances of abuse were reported in all family contexts. But it appears that the experience of physical abuse raises one's risk for developing chronic aggressive behavior problems beyond the risk afforded by these other factors (46). It is still possible, however, that the risk afforded by child abuse is due to some other co-occurring family or environmental factor that was not assessed.

In contrast, child health problems and perceived temperament were not correlated with physical abuse at all. The child's contribution to her or his own physical abuse is a matter of controversy (13, 47). Although child "difficultness" has been shown to have short-term effects on parental reactions (48) and has been speculated, on the basis of case studies, to raise the chances of abuse, the current findings indicate that child factors do not account for the occurrence of child abuse. There is no evidence in our data for blaming the victim of abuse.

Our findings also offer initial support for a theory of how physical harm has its effect on child development. We found that harmed children are likely to develop biased and deficient patterns of processing social information, including a failure to attend to relevant cues, a bias to attribute hostile intentions to others, and a lack of competent behavioral strategies to solve interpersonal problems. These patterns, in turn, were found to predict the development of aggressive behavior. Moreover, the path between early physical harm and later child aggression appeared to go through these processing patterns. The findings are consistent with the hypothesis that the experience of physical harm leads a child to conceptualize the world in deviant ways that later perpetuate the cycle of violence.

Several caveats must be expressed about these findings. Our measure of abuse is maternal report, which is subject to inaccurate recall, lack of knowledge, and lying. Alternate measures, such as official records, are equally subject to inaccuracies and biases, however, and may also be associated with subsequent confounding variables such as stigma, intervention, and self-fulfilling prophecies (7). Our logic for relying on maternal report is that we doubt that mothers would over-report abuse (thus, our "abused" group is probably accurately labeled), and underreporting of abuse (false negatives in our control group) would serve only to weaken any correlation that we could find between abuse and later outcomes. Also, any bias in reporting by mothers is probably equally represented in mothers' reports about marital violence and child temperament. Abuse was found to predict later child aggression even when these variables (and, therefore, maternal reporting bias) was controlled. Thus, to the extent that our measure of abuse is invalid, our estimates of the magnitude of the effects of abuse may actually be underestimates.

Another limitation is our use of child behavior in kindergarten as the outcome. Numerous studies have indicated remarkable stability of aggressive behavior across time, with estimates as high as the stability of the intelligence quotient *(40, 49);* however, we did not assess aggressive behavior in adolescence or adulthood. One cannot conclude from this study that physical abuse has effects on child behavior that persist over many years. This question awaits further longitudinal follow-ups.

A third limitation is that we do not mean to suggest that the mediating variables that we have studied are the only possible mechanisms in the abuse-aggression cycle. It is also possible, for example, that early physical abuse has an effect on the child's physiological reactivity (either by emotional trauma or by direct physical impact to the brain), and this acquired overreactivity mediates later aggressive tendencies. We are intrigued by such a theory, but it does not contradict the current perspective. In fact, physiological explanations require cognitive counterparts and vice-versa.

Finally, one must not conclude that the effects of abuse are limited to behavioral outcomes of aggression. Even though our study focused on aggression,

our findings indicate that abused children, particularly girls, are also at risk for the development of internalizing problems, such as withdrawal and isolation, that have been hypothesized to be precursors of depression. Teacher-reported internalizing problems (measured by the CBCL internalizing scale score) were 19% higher in harmed boys (mean ± standard error, 4.85 ± 1.37) than non-harmed boys (4.05 ± 0.39) and 87% higher in harmed girls (6.46 ± 1.17) than non-harmed girls (3.46 ± 0.38), a statistically significant effect of harm [$F(1,294) = 6.67$, $P < 0.01$]. It is interesting that our hypothesized mediators of aggressive outcomes, namely processing patterns of hostile attributional biases and aggressive problem solving, did not mediate internalizing outcomes. The main effect of physical harm on the CBCL internalizing score remained statistically significant after controlling for the seven social-information-processing variables [$F(1,286) = 6.27$, $P < 0.013$]. We would not expect the mediators to be the same for both types of outcomes; in fact, we suspect that internalizing outcomes of early physical abuse may be mediated by the development of a different set of processing patterns (including attributions of self-blame and expectations that aggression would not succeed in creating negative outcomes). Why some children follow a path of hostile attributions and aggression and other children a path of self-blame and depression awaits further inquiry.

References and Notes

1. C. Ross, in *Child Abuse: An Agenda for Actions*, G. Gerbner, C. Ross, E. Zigler, Eds. (Oxford Univ. Press, New York, 1980), pp. 63–81.

2. B. Nelson, *Making an Issue of Child Abuse* (Univ. of Chicago Press, Chicago, 1984).

3. H. Dubowitz, "Child maltreatment in the United States: Etiology, impact, and prevention," background paper prepared for the Congress of the United States by the Office of Technology Assessment (1986).

4. Even though the relative risk is greater for these persons than for the general population, most abused children do not grow up to be abusing adults [J. Kaufman and E. Zigler, *Am. J. Orthopsychiatr.* 57, 186 (1987)].

5. J. D. Alfaro, "Report on the relationship between child abuse and neglect and later socially deviant behavior" (New York State Assembly, Albany, 1981).

6. W. Altemeier, S. O'Connor, P. Vietze, H. Sandler, K. Sherrod, *Child Abuse and Neglect* 12, 393 (1984); D. O. Lewis, S. S. Shanok, J. H. Pinkus, G. H. Glaser, *J. Am. Acad. Child Psychiatr.* 18, 307 (1979); M. Rosenbaum and B. Ben-

nett, *Am. J. Psychiatr.* 143, 367 (1986); M. Rutter and H. Geller, *Juvenile Delinquency: Trends and Perspectives* (Guilford, New York, 1983).

7. C. P. Widom, *Science* 244, 160 (1989).

8. M. A. Straus and R. J. Gelles [in *Family Abuse and its Consequences: New Directions in Research*, J. T. Kirkpatrick and M. A. Strauss, Eds. (Sage, Newbury Park, CA, 1988), pp. 14–36] report that almost all children in the United States are spanked at some time in childhood; thus, "abuse" is defined by societal norms as more severe. "Severe violence," which Straus and Gelles equate with child physical abuse, includes the following acts: kicked, bit, punched, beat up, burned or scalded, and threatened with or used a gun or knife.

9. G. T. Hotaling, M. A. Straus, A. J. Lincoln, in *Family Violence*, L. Ohlin and M. Tonry, Eds. (Univ. of Chicago Press, Chicago, 1989), pp. 18-40; M. Straus and R. Gelles, *J. Marriage Family* 48, 465 (1986).

10. See integrative, ecological models by J. Belsky, *Am. Psychol.* 35, 320 (1980); D. Ciccheti and R. Rizley, *New*

Direct. Child Dev. 11, 31 (1980); J. Garbarino, J. *Marriage Family* 39, 721 (1977).

11. Abuse occurs in all socioeconomic classes but disproportionately so in the lower classes (W. Tonge, D. James, S. Hillman, *Br. J. Psychiat. Spec. Ed. 11* (1975).

12. B. Horowitz and I. Wolcock, in *The Social Context of Child Abuse and Neglect,* L. Pelton, Ed. (Human Sciences Press, New York, 1981).

13. R. Pianta, B. Egeland, M. F. Erickson, in *Child Maltreatment,* D. Cicchetti and V. Carlson, Eds. (Cambridge Univ. Press, New York, 1989), pp. 203–253; B. Wauchope and M. A. Straus, in *Physical Violence in American Families,* M. A. Straus and R. J. Gelles, Eds. (Transaction Books, New Brunswick, NJ, 1990), pp. 133–150; D. A. Wolfe, *Psychol. Bull.* 97, 462 (1985).

14. M. Straus, R. Gelles, S. Steinmitz, *Behind Closed Doors* (Doubleday, New York, 1980).

15. The study by Widom, (7) controlled only for sex, race, age, and the hospital of the child's birth (or general neighborhood).

16. R. Bell, *Psychol. Rev.* 75, 81 (1968).

17. D. G. Gil, *Violence Against Children: Physical Abuse in the United States* (Harvard Univ. Press, Cambridge, MA, 1970); R. Gelles, *Am. J. Orthopsychiatr.* 43, 611 (1973); R. D. Parke and C. W. Collmer, in *Review of Child Development Research,* F. D. Horowitz, Ed. (Univ. of Chicago Press, Chicago, 1975), pp. 509–590.

18. M. Klein and L. Stern, *Am. J. Dis. Child.* 122,15 (1971); V. McCabe, *Child Dev.* 55, 267 (1984).

19. K. A. Dodge, G. S. Pettit, C. L. McClaskey, M. Brown, *Society for Research in Child Development Monogr. 51* (1986).

20. R. M. McFall, *Behav. Assess.* 4, 1 (1982); K. H. Rubin and L. R. Krasnor, in *Minnesota Symposium on Child Psychology,* M. Perlmutter, Ed. (Erlbaum, Hillsdale, NJ, 1986), vol. 18, pp. 1–68.

21. K. A. Dodge and A. Tomlin, *Soc. Cogn.* 5, 280 (1987).

22. K. A. Dodge, *Child Dev. 51,* 162 (1980); M. F. M. Sancilio, J. M. Plumert, W. W. Hartup, *Dev. Psychol.* 25, 812 (1989).

23. J. R. Asarnow and J. W. Callan, *J. Con. Clin. Psychol. 53,* 500 (1985).

24. R. G. Slaby and N. G. Guerra, *Dev. Psychol.* 24, 580 (1989).

25. D. G. Perry, L. C. Perry, P. R. Rasmussen, *Child Dev. 56,* 700 (1986).

26. L. A. Sroufe, *ibid., p. 1.*

27. P. M. Crittendon and M. D. S. Ainsworth, in *Child Maltreatment,* D. Cicchetti, Ed. (Cambridge Univ. Press, New York, 1989), pp. 432–463.

28. W. Mischel, *Psychol. Rev.* 80, 252 (1973); A. Bandura, *Social Foundations of Thought and Action: A Social Cognitive Theory* (Prentice-Hall, Englewood Cliffs, NJ, 1986).

29. D. Stem, *The Interpersonal World of the Infant* (Basic, New York, 1985).

30. A. Bandura, *Aggression: A Social Learning Analysis* (Prentice-Hall, Englewood Cliffs, NJ, 1973).

31. Parents were informed of the range of questions to be asked and were told of the legal and ethical obligation by staff to report any suspicion of physical danger to the child. This statement was made in the context of wanting to help the family.

32. The child's life was originally segmented into the periods birth to age 1, age 1 to 12 months ago, and the past 12 months in order to help the mother recall specific events and because of staff fears that mothers would be less revealing about current physical harm than about past behavior. The first two eras were combined, yielding two eras. In this way, mothers could reveal past abuse without fear of being reported to authorities, as long as the danger was not current. (This is consistent with local reporting laws.) In spite of this procedure, three mothers reported current abuse (by the father or a boyfriend).

33. Ratings from the two periods were positively correlated ($r = 0.56$, $P < .001$), and the rating averaged across the two periods was reliable, with the coefficient $\alpha = 0.72$, $P < .001$.

34. This proportion is similar to that found in national probability samples by Straus and Gelles *(8)*.

35. As a check on this classification, mothers also completed the conflict tactics scale, the most widely used written instrument to assess physical abuse (8). Parent-to-child aggression scale scores for each of the two age periods were significantly greater for mothers of physically harmed children than for those of non-harmed children (each $P < 0.001$). Interview ratings, rather than CTS scores, were used to classify children because the interviewer's probes offered an opportunity to clarify actual harm and severity, thus limiting the number of abuse cases.

36. The reliability of this score was computed as the coefficient α of the two constituent scores and was found to be high (0.85, $P < .001$). As a check on these ratings, mothers completed the conflict tactics scale for spousal relationships. Aggression scale scores for husband-to-wife and wife-to-husband aggression correlated significantly with interviewer ratings ($r = 0.47$ and 0.41, respectively, each $P < 0.001$).

37. J. E. Bates and K. Bayles, *Merrill-Palmer* Q. 30, 111 (1984). The ICQ is a reliable measure of maternal perception of child temperament.

38. Reliabilities (internal consistencies) were calculated by coefficient α. All were significant (each $P < 0.001$): relevance of attention 0.79; hostile attributional bias, 0.72; the number of problem solutions generated, 0.92; the tendency to access aggressive responses, 0.95; the tendency to access competent responses, 0.92; the evaluation of aggressive responses, 0.87; and the evaluation of competent responses, 0.84.

39. T. M. Achenbach and C. Edelbrock, *Manual for the Teacher's Report Form and Teacher Version of the Child Behavior Profile* (University of Vermont, Department of Psychiatry, Burlington, VT 1986). The behavior problem and aggression scores are reliable, as indicated by a 1-week test-retest correlation of 0.90, a 15-day stability correlation of 0.84, a 2-month stability correlation of 0.74, a 4-month stability correlation of 0.68, and an inter-rater (teacher and

aide) correlation of 0.57 (0.63 for the aggression scale) (all $P < 0.001$).

40. J. Parker and S. Asher, *Psychol. Bull.* 102, 357 (1987).

41. At least 70% of peers responded in each classroom. Peers were not told of the interest in the target child but only of a general interest in peer play.

42. The reliability of this score was significant, 0.87 ($P < 0.001$) by coefficient α.

43. Interobserver agreement on this score was evaluated by having a second observer code the child's behavior at the same time, for 130 observation sessions. Agreement on occurrence [no. agreements(no. agreements + no. disagreements)) was 96%, and the K was 0.63 ($P < 0.001$).

44. For all analyses, the problem of missing data was resolved by substituting the population mean score. This is a common resolution that is conservative because between-group differences will be reduced. This strategy was taken because, even though missing data were rare (fewer than 3% of cases), casewide elimination of a subject with any missing data would have reduced the n significantly. Also, all analyses were replicated with a single child aggression score that was the mean of the three standardized aggression scores. All reported findings held up with this alternate score.

45. The incremental prediction from processing variables at time 1 (t_1) to aggression at time 2 can best be assessed by holding the child's level of aggression at t_1 constant. Because the child was not yet in school at t_1, our only measure of aggression at that time was the mothers report (assessed by the aggression scale of the CBC). When this score was covaried (by first entry in hierarchical regression analyses), the seven processing variables still tended to predict later aggression, as rated by teachers [$F(7,280) = 1.96$, $P < 0.06$], peers [$F(7,279) = 1.90$, $P < 0.07$], and directly observed [$F(7,275) = 3.50$, $P < 0.002$].

46. These findings are consistent with those collected in a retrospective study by J. A. Seltzer and D. Kalmuss, *Soc. Forces,* 67, 473 (1988).

47. A. J. Sameroff and M. J. Chandler, in *Review of Child Development Research,* F. D. Horowitz, Ed. (Univ. of Chicago Press, Chicago, 1975).

48. J. E. Bates, in *Temperament in Childhood,* G. A. Kohnstamm, J. E. Bates, M. K. Rothbart, Eds. (Wiley, Chichester, England, 1989), pp. 321–355.

49. D. Olweus, *Psychol. Bull.* 86, 852 (1979).

50. Support provided by NIMH grant 42498, an NICHD Research Career Development Award to K.A.D., and a CASBS fellowship from the John D. and Catherine T. McArthur Foundation to K.A.D. We are grateful for the statistical consultation of M. Appelbaum and the contributions of A. Bakshi, K. Bayles, D. Bennett, J. Brown, J. Deer, A. Harrist, T. Kelly, E. Lemerise, D. Marvinney, J. Orrell, M. Raab, B. Ridge, D. Schwartz, J. Shroff, Z. Strassberg, and B. Weiss. We appreciate the support of the Metropolitan Nashville (Tennessee) Public Schools, the Bloomington (Indiana) Public Schools, and the Knox County (Tennessee) Public Schools.

29

Longitudinal Studies of Effects of Divorce on Children in Great Britain and the United States

---

ANDREW J. CHERLIN, FRANK F. FURSTENBERG, JR., P. LINDSAY CHASE-LANSDALE,
KATHLEEN E. KIERNAN, PHILIP K. ROBINS, DONNA RUANE MORRISON,
AND JULIEN O. TEITLER

An increasingly common circumstance of children's lives is the divorce of their parents. For many years, research on the impact of divorce on children's later developments used cross-sectional designs which compared the later development of children whose parents had, or had not, divorced when they were at a particular age.

In recent years, researchers interested in the developmental impact of divorce have come to recognize that the changes in relationships among family members that result in divorce typically begin long before the legal termination of the parents' marriage. As a means of assessing the relative impact of family interaction patterns that occur before a divorce versus the changes brought about when the mother and father no longer live together, researchers have begun to use longitudinal studies that follow the fate of children and their parents over extended periods of time. This article by Andrew Cherlin and his colleagues summarizes the new insights gained by the application of longitudinal methods to this important issue in lives of children and their parents.

National, longitudinal surveys from Great Britain and the United States were used to investigate the effects of divorce on children. In both studies, a subsample of children who were in two-parent families *during the initial interview (at age 7 in the British data and at ages 7 to 11 in the U.S. data) were followed through the next interview (at age 11 and ages 11 to 16, respectively). At both time points in*

Reprinted with permission from the authors and *Science, 252,* 1991, 1386–1389. Copyright 1991 by the American Association for the Advancement of Science.

the British data, parents and teachers independently rated the children's behavior problems, and the children were given reading and mathematics achievement tests. At both time points in the U.S. data, parents rated the children's behavior problems. Children whose parents divorced or separated between the two time points were compared to children whose families remained intact. For boys, the apparent effect of separation or divorce on behavior problems and achievement at the later time point was sharply reduced by considering behavior problems, achievement levels, and family difficulties that were present at the earlier time point, before any of the families had broken up. For girls, the reduction in the apparent effect of divorce occurred to a lesser but still noticeable extent once preexisting conditions were considered.

At current rates, about 40% of U.S. children will witness the breakup of their parents' marriages before they reach 18 (*1*). The research literature leaves no doubt that, on average, children of divorced parents experience more emotional and behavioral problems and do less well in school than children who live with both biological parents (*2*). But much less is known about why children whose parents divorce do less well. Most observers assume that their troubles stem mainly from the difficult adjustment children must make after their parents separate. Studies emphasize how difficult it can be for a recently separated mother or father to function effectively as a parent. "Put simply," wrote Wallerstein and Kelly, "the central hazard which divorce poses to the psychological health and development of children and adolescents is in the diminished or disrupted parenting which so often follows in the wake of the rupture and which can become consolidated within the post-divorce family" (*3*). Largely because of the widespread perception that marital disruption makes children more vulnerable to problems, a series of social policies and legal reforms were enacted in the 1970s and 1980s to increase and enforce child support payments and to encourage new custody practices that promote contact and cooperation between divorced parents (*4*).

We agree that events occurring after the separation can be critical for children's adjustment and that adequate child support payments and workable custody arrangements are indispensable. However, we present evidence that, at least for boys, tempers the conclusion that the aftermath of divorce is the major factor in children's adjustment. Our evidence, which comes from statistical analyses of national, longitudinal studies of children in both Great Britain and the United States, indicates that a substantial portion of

what is usually considered the effect of divorce on children is visible before the parents separate. For boys, the apparent effect of divorce on behavior problems and school achievement falls by about half to levels that are not significantly different from zero, once preexisting behavior problems, achievement test scores, and family difficulties evident before the separation are taken into account. For girls, the same preexisting conditions reduce the effects of divorce to a lesser but still noticeable degree.

The observed differences between children from families in which the parents have separated or divorced and children from two-parent families may be traced to three distinct sources. The first source is the effect of growing up in a dysfunctional family—a home where serious problems of the parents or the children make normal development difficult. Parents with psychological impairments are reportedly more prone to divorce and their children are more likely to experience developmental difficulties (*5*). A second source, often accompanying the first, is severe and protracted marital conflict, which is known to harm children's development and often leads to divorce (*6*). The third source is the difficult transition that occurs only after couples separate—the emotional upset, fall in income, diminished parenting, continued conflict, and so forth. Although some researchers acknowledge the potentially adverse contribution of each source (*7*), nearly all empirical studies have focused exclusively on the third—the period after the separation—and have collected information only after the separation occurred (*8*).

Moreover, the current understanding of the effects of divorce on children is largely based on intensive, observational studies of a relatively small number of families (*9*). These studies are invaluable because of the detailed observations of family interaction and child development they provide, but they typically are based on nonrandom samples of the population. In some influential clinical studies, there has not been a comparison group of intact families (*3*).

THE BRITISH NATIONAL CHILD DEVELOPMENT STUDY

We describe two prospective studies that began with large samples of intact families. The British data come from the National Child Development Study (NCDS). Originally a study of perinatal mortality, the NCDS began as a survey of the mothers of all children born in England, Scotland, and Wales during the week of 3 to 9 March 1958 (*10*). Interviews were completed with 17,414 mothers, representing 98% of all women giving birth (*11*). In 1965, when the children were 7, the parents (usually the mothers) of 14,746 children were successfully reinterviewed. Local authority health visitors (trained nurses who normally saw every family before and after the birth of a child and frequently conducted follow-up visits, especially to families with difficulties) asked the mothers the majority of questions from the Rutter Home Behaviour Scale, which measured the children's behavior problems (*12*), and reported on the family's difficulties and use of social welfare services.

Our factor analyses of the Rutter items identified the two clusters of behavior problems typical of assessments such as these: "externalizing disorders" (aggression, disobedience) and "internalizing disorders" (depression, anxiety). However, the reliability of the internalizing subscale was considerably lower than that of the externalizing subscale. Consequently, we constructed a single, 18-item summated scale (α reliability = 0.72). The items were: temper tantrums, reluctance to go to school, bad dreams, difficulty sleeping, food fads, poor appetite, difficulty concentrating, bullied by other children, destructive, miserable or tearful, squirmy or fidgety, continually worried, irritable, upset by new situations, twitches or other mannerisms, fights with other children, disobedient at home, and sleepwalking.

In addition, the children's teachers filled out a detailed behavioral assessment at age 7, the Bristol Social Adjustment Guide (BSAG) (*13*). Again, our factor analyses showed the externalizing versus internalizing distinction, but the internalizing subscale was weaker. So again we constructed a single scale (α = 0.68). The children also were given reading and mathematics tests (*14*) and physical examinations at age 7. Then in 1969, when the children were 11, another round of interviews and testing was undertaken. Parents again were asked questions on children's behavior problems, and teachers once again filled out the BSAG (*15*). The reading and mathematics tests that had been given earlier were not appropriate for 11-year-olds; instead, the study used reading and mathematics achievement tests constructed specifically for this round of the NCDS, and standardized against normal populations, by the National Foundation for Educational Research in England and Wales (*16*).

DIVORCE AND CHILDREN'S ADJUSTMENT

We use parent-rated and teacher-rated behavior problems and reading and mathematics achievement, all measured at age 11, as the four outcome measures of

children's adjustment in our analyses. In order to evaluate the relative contributions of pre- and post-separation sources of children's adjustment at age 11, we restricted our analyses to children whose parents were in an intact first marriage in 1965, when the children were 7—the first time we have detailed information about the children's behavior and achievement. Then we followed these children as they split into two groups by age 11: those whose parents had divorced or separated and those who parents had remained together (*17*). (Henceforth by "divorce" we mean divorce or marital separation; we do not distinguish between them.)

The number of children living with both parents at age 7 and for whom outcome variables were observed at age 11 ranged from 11,658 to 11,837 for the four outcome variables. Among these, there were 239 instances of a divorce occurring between ages 7 and 11. A remarriage before age 11 occurred in only 47 of these instances, so we have not analyzed separately data on non-remarried and remarried cases but rather have combined them. One limitation of the NCDS is that it did not obtain the exact date at which a marital disruption occurred. We can determine whether or not a divorce occurred between the age 7 and age 11 interviews, but we cannot determine the exact timing of the divorce. We conducted all analyses separately by the child's gender because of evidence in the literature that the effect of divorce is different for boys than for girls (*2*).

As expected, we found that boys and girls whose parents had divorced between the age 7 and age 11 interviews showed more behavior problems at age 11, as rated by parents and by teachers, and scored lower than other children on reading and mathematics achievement tests at age 11, even after controlling for predictors such as social class and race (*18*) (model 1 in Figure 1). On average, the magnitude of the differences was modest, although significantly different from zero. For example, boys whose parents divorced showed 19% [standard error (SE) = 8%] more behavior problems at age 11, according to ratings by their parents, than did boys whose parents were together, controlling for social class and race (Figure 1A).

Unlike nearly all previous studies, we were able to introduce information on the children and parents before any of the families broke up. The measures we introduce may be proxies for family, dysfunction and marital conflict. We first added the comparable 7-year-old behavior problems scale or achievement test score of the child (model 2 in Figure 1). This step essentially adjusted the estimated effect of divorce for preexisting differences in behavior or achievement between children whose families would later divorce

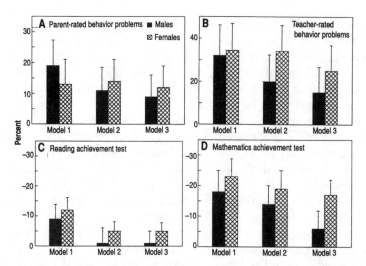

FIGURE 1   Effects of a parental divorce or separation between ages 7 and 11 on four outcome measures for children age 11 in 1969 from the National Child Development Study, Great Britain (estimates restricted to children living with two married parents in 1965). (**A**) Behavior problems scale score as reported by parents. (**B**) Behavior problems scale score as reported by teachers. (**C**) Reading achievement test score. (**D**) Mathematics achievement test score. The height of the boxes shows the percentage by which the score of children whose parents divorced or separated between ages 7 and 11 was greater or less than the score of children whose parents remained married. In each of the four diagrams, three estimates of the effects of divorce are shown. Model 1 controls only for the social class and race of the child; model 2 controls additionally for the child's score on the same outcome measure at age 7, before anyone's parents were divorced; and model 3 adds further controls for characteristics of the child and family when he or she was 7. These included scales of family problems and difficulties from the Health Visitor's report and physician's reporting of physical handicap, mental retardation, or emotional maladjustment. Error bars represent one standard error.

and children whose families would remain intact. For boys, the apparent effects of divorce dropped for all four outcome measures; for girls there was a drop in reading and mathematics achievement test scores. Finally, we controlled for other age 7 characteristics of the child and his or her family, such as the physician's rating of the child's mental and physical health and the Health Visitor's rating of the family's difficulties and use of social services (*19*) (model 3 in Figure 1). After all the preseparation characteristics were taken into account, the apparent effect of divorce for boys fell by about half to levels that no longer were significantly different from zero for all four outcomes. For example, boys whose parents divorced now showed just 9% (SE = 7%) more behavior problems, according to parent ratings. For girls, the decline was smaller, and the remaining effect was significantly different from zero for two of the four outcomes (*20*).

THE U.S. NATIONAL SURVEY OF CHILDREN

In order to determine whether these findings were generalizable beyond Great Britain in the 1960s, we estimated a similar set of models from U.S. data from the National Survey of Children (NSC), which began in 1976 with a random-sample survey of 2279 children aged 7 to 11 from 1747 families (*21*). In 1981, when the children were ages 11 through 16, additional interviews were conducted with parents and children in all families in which there already had been a separation or a divorce by 1976 or in which there was substantial marital conflict in 1976, and in a randomly selected subsample of intact, low-conflict families in 1976.

In both waves of the survey, a parent, usually the mother, was asked a series of questions about behavior problems similar in content to the Rutter Home Behaviour Scale in the NCDS (*12*) and to items in the Achenbach Child Behavior Checklist (*22*). In parallel with the procedure for the NCDS, we constructed single-factor scales from nine items in the 1976 data (α = 0.69) and 24 items in the 1981 data (α = 0.90). The items in the 1976 scale are fights too much, cannot concentrate, often tells lies, easily confused, breaks things, acts too young, very timid, has strong temper, and steals things. The items in the 1981 scale are changes in mood, feels no one loves him or her, high strung, tells lies, too fearful, argues too much, difficulty concentrating, easily confused, cruel to others, disobedient at home, disobedient at school, impulsive, feels inferior, not liked by other children, has obsessions, restless, stubborn or irritable, has strong temper, sad or depressed, withdrawn, feels others are out to get him or her, hangs around with kids who get into trouble, secretive, and worries too much.

Married parents in 1976 also were asked questions about conflict with their spouses covering nine areas, as follows: "Most married couples have some arguments. Do you ever have arguments about (i) chores and responsibilities, (ii) your children, (iii) money, (iv) sex, (v) religion, (vi) leisure time, (vii) drinking, (viii) other women or men, or (ix) in-laws?" We constructed a scale of marital conflict, which was the number of affirmative responses; scores ranged from 0 to 8 with a mean of 2.26 (α = 0.63).

As with the British data, we restricted our analyses to children who were living with both of their parents at the first interview in 1976. As in the British study, these children were followed as their families split into divorced and nondivorced groups by 1981. Parent-rated behavior problems was the only outcome that could be compared adequately with the British findings (Figure 2). The results for U.S. boys are similar to the results for British boys. Controlling for social class, race, and whether the mother was employed outside the home in 1976, boys whose parents had divorced between 1976 and 1981 showed 12% (SE = 4%) more behavior problems, on average (model 1). But when a control was added for behavior problems in 1976, before any of the parents divorced, the effect of divorce fell (model 2). And after a second control was introduced for the amount of marital conflict that was present in the home in 1976, the effect of divorce had fallen by approximately half, as in the British data, to 6% (SE = 4%), and it was no longer significantly different from zero.

For girls, however, the results are different from the British study. Controlling for class and race (model 1), there is little difference between girls from divorced families and girls from intact families. But

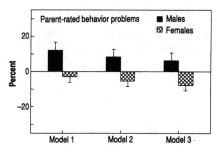

FIGURE 2 Effects of a parental divorce between 1976 and 1981 on the behavior problems of children in 1981, when the children were ages 11 to 16, based on a behavior problems scale score as reported by parents on the U.S. National Survey of Children (estimates are restricted to children living with two married parents in 1976). The height of the boxes shows the percentage by which the score of children whose parents divorced between 1976 and 1981 was greater (or less) than the score of children whose parents remains married. Three estimates of the effects of divorce are shown: model 1 controls only for social class, race, and whether the mother was employed outside the home in 1976; model 2 controls additionally for the child's score on the behavior problems scale in 1976, as reported by parents, before anyone's parents were divorced; and model 3 adds further controls for the parents' score on a nine-item marital conflict scale in 1976. Error bars represent one standard error.

with controls for 1976 behavior problems (model 2) and 1976 marital conflict (model 3), girls whose parents had divorced were showing somewhat fewer behavior problems than girls from intact families. In view of the inconsistency with the British data, we think it is prudent to be skeptical of this finding until it can be confirmed.

CONCLUSION

Overall, the evidence suggests that much of the effect of divorce on children can be predicted by conditions that existed well before the separation occurred. These predivorce effects were stronger for boys than for girls. Just when children begin to experience the process that precedes a divorce we cannot say. Our survey-based studies do not allow us to differentiate between a generally dysfunctional family and a family that has functioned adequately until the time that marital conflict becomes acute and the divorce process begins. It is also possible that the effects of divorce may differ for children older or younger than the ones in our studies or that divorce may have long-term effects on adult behavior. Nevertheless, the British and U.S. longitudinal studies suggest that those concerned with the effects of divorce on children should consider reorienting their thinking. At least as much attention needs to be paid to the processes that occur in troubled, intact families as to the trauma that children suffer after their parents separate.

References and Notes

1. L. L. Bumpass, *Demography* 21, 71 (1984).

2. R. E. Emery, Marriage, *Divorce, and Children's Adjustment* (Sage, Beverly Hills, CA, 1988); P. L. Chase-Lansdale and E. M. Hetherington, in *Life-Span Development and Behavior*, P. B. Baltes, D. L. Featherman, R. M. Lerner, Eds. (Erlbaum, Hillsdale, NJ, 1990), vol. 10, pp. 105-150; S. S. McLanahan, *Am. J. Sociol.* 94, 130 (1988).

3. J. S. Wallerstein and J. B. Kelly, *Surviving the Breakup: How Children and Parents Cope with Divorce* (Basic Books, New York 1980), p. 316.

4. See for example, L. J. Weitzman, *The Divorce Revolution: The Unexpected Consequences for Women and Children* (Free Press, New York, 1985); M. A. Glendon, *Abortion and Divorce in Western Law* (Harvard Univ. Press, Cambridge, MA, 1987); I. Garfinkel and S. S. McLanahan, *Single Mothers and Their Children: A New American Dilemma* (The Urban Institute Press, Washington DC, 1986).

5. K. E. Kiernan, *Popul. Stud.* 40, 1 (1986).

6. R. E. Emery, *Psychol. Bull.* 92, 310 (1982).

7. E. M. Hetherington, M. Cox, R. Cox, in *Mother-Child, Father-Child Relations,* J. H. Stevens and M. Matthews, Eds. (National Association for the Education of Young Children Press, Washington, DC, 1978); E. M. Hetherington and K. Camara, in *Review of Child Development Research*, R. D. Parke, Ed. (Univ. of Chicago Press, Chicago, 1984), vol. 7.

8. But see J. H. Block, J. Block, P. F. Gjerde, *Child Dev.* 57, 827 (1986); N. Baydar, *J. Marriage Family 50,* 967 (1988).

9. The leading set of studies of this type have been conducted by E. M. Hetherington, M. Cox, and R. Cox [in *Nontraditional Families, Parenting, and Child Development*, M. E. Lamb, Ed. (Erlbaum, Hillsdale, NJ, 1982); *J. Am. Acad. Child Psychiatr.* 24, 518 (1985)] and E. M. Hetherington [in *Remarriage and Stepparenting Today*, K. Pasley and M. Ihinger-Tallman, Eds. (Guilford Press, New York, 1987)].

10. The NCDS is described in a paper by P. M. Shepherd, "The National Child Development Study: An introduction to the background to the study and the methods of data collection" (Social Statistics Research Unit, City University, London, October 1985).

11. Information in medical records at birth also was recorded. Between 1958 and 1965, a supplementary sample was added consisting of 1142 children from recent immigrant families who had 3 to 9 March 1958 birth dates. We include this sample in our analyses.

12. M. Rutter, J. Tizard, K. Whitmore, Eds., *Education, Health, and Behaviour* (Longman, London, 1970).

13. D. H. Stott, *The Social Adjustment of Children* (Univ. of London Press, London, 1969).

14. V. Southgate, *Southgate Group Reading Tests: Manual of Instructions* (Univ. of London Press, London, 1962); M. L. K. Pringle, in *The Sixth Mental Measurements Yearbook*, O. K. Buros, Ed. (Gryphon Press, Highland Park, NJ, 1965). The mathematics test was developed for the NCDS by M. L. K. Pringle, N. Butler, and R. Davie [*11,000 Seven Year Olds* (Longman, London, 1966)].

15. Ten of the 11 items in the parent-rated scale ($\alpha = 0.68$) were identical to the items in the age 7 parent-rated scale *(12)*. For the BSAG scale at age 11, $\alpha = 0.71$.

16. K. Fogelman, *Br. J. Educ. Psychol.* 48, 148 (1978).

17. There are two sources of nonrandomness that could have arisen with respect to the sample of families analyzed in 1969, when the children were 11: (i) the restriction that when the child was 7 the family was intact, was successfully found and reinterviewed, and had valid data on behavior and achievement; and (ii) the restriction that when the child was 11 the family was successfully reinterviewed and had valid data on behavior and achievement. To determine whether these sources of nonrandomness could possibly have biased our results, we specified and estimated several selection models. [G. S. Maddala, *Limited Dependent and Qualitative Variables in Econometrics* (Cambridge Univ. Press, Cambridge, 1983).] The coefficients for the effect of divorce were nearly identical in the selection models and the ordinary least squares (OLS) models we present here.

18. Among boys, the coefficient for the effect of divorce on three of the four outcomes was positive and at least twice its standard error in model 1 of Fig. 1 (for the reading test, the coefficient was 1.8 times its standard error). Among girls, all the coefficients for the effect of divorce, except on parent-rated behavior problems, were more than twice their standard errors in model 1. As in any nonexperimental study, it is possible that the variables we "control" for are actually markers for other, unmeasured variables. However, we have relied on a large literature in sociology and developmental psychology to guide our choice of variables. In the OLS regressions (17) for the NCDS, which form the basis for Fig. 1, we used the natural logarithms of the outcomes as dependent variables because the logarithmic transformation resulted in a more normally shaped distribution of the scale scores. The key independent variable was a dummy variable that indicated whether or not a divorce occurred during the time between the age 7 and age 11 interviews. Let β be the coefficient for the divorce dummy variable. Then, for the logarithmically transformed outcomes, the percentage change in the scale score produced

by the occurrence of a divorce is $(e^\beta - 1) \cdot 100$. In model 1, the only additional independent variable in the equation (all measured at age 7) were father's social class (six-category classification), housing tenure (whether renting from a public agency, renting in the private market, or owning one's home), number of persons per room, and race (white, Asian, black, mixed). In our regression models, mean values were imputed for missing information on independent variables.

19. From the health visitor's report at age 7 we constructed five scales: use of children's services (five items, $\alpha = 0.56$), family conflict (two items, $\alpha = 0.44$), family problems (two items, $\alpha = 0.64$), and use of mental health services (three items, $\alpha = 0.60$). For models in which behavior problems at age 11 were the dependent variables, the age 7 reading test score was entered at this stage; and for models in which age 11 achievement tests were the dependent variables, age 7 teacher-rated behavior problems were added at this stage.

20. For boys, none of the model 3 estimates in Fig. 1 was twice its standard error; for girls, two of four were twice their standard errors. The death of a parent between the ages of 7 and 11 had no significant effects for girls on any of the four outcome measures and no significant effect on behavior problems for boys, even before controls for age 7 characteristics. The death of a parent did have a negative effect on reading and mathematics achievement at 11 for boys; this effect was reduced by age 7 controls but remained statistically significant.

21. See F. F. Furstenberg, Jr., C. W. Nord, J. L. Peterson, N. Zill, *Am. Sociol. Rev.* 48, 656 (1983). We restricted the sample to include only families that were intact in 1976, in which the biological mother of the child or children was the parent respondent at both times and was living with the target child or children, and in which the father was not reported to have died between 1976 and 1981. Among this subsample of 822 children, there were 65 cases of a divorce or separation occurring between the 1976 and 1981 interviews.

22. T. M. Achenbach and C. S. Edelbrock, *Monogr. Soc. Res. Child Dev.* 33 (no. 166) (1981).

23. Supported primarily by NICHHD grant HD25936, with additional support from NSF grant SES-8908503. We thank M. Trieb for computer programming assistance. Complete sets of the estimated coefficients and other detailed documentation are available from A.J.C.

PART V

Adolescence

30

Is Adolescence a Phenomenon of Modern Times?

VIVIAN C. FOX

Is adolescence a universal stage of human development? If it is a stage, has it historically always been so? Vivian C. Fox raises these issues in the following essay and by so doing provides an historical context for understanding adolescent development. She argues that particular historical circumstances have helped shape our current views of the existence and shape of adolescence as a unique period of development.

Most of the recent discussions concerning the historical dimensions of adolescence place its conceptual origins in modern times—somewhere from the beginning to the close of the 19th century.[1] Thus, Phillipe Aries believes the first youth to portray the qualities of the modern adolescent was in the 19th century with Wagner's *Siefried*[2], while Tamara Hareven suggests the invention of adolescence evolved during the first half of the 19th century.[3] In an article entitled, "Adolescence in Historical Perspective," John and Virginia Demos maintain "the concept of adolescence, as generally understood and applied, did not exist before the last two decades of the nineteenth century" and point to G. Stanley Hall as the formulator of this modern concept.[4] John R. Gillis in *Youth and History,* places the emergence of adolescence in the period of 1870–1900.[5] Although it is clear that leading authorities such as these differ among themselves as to exactly when adolescence arose, they do adopt a common position that prior to modern times one cannot find what we know and identify as adolescence.

What seems to be central to their recognition of *when* adolescence occurs is that it is primarily to be recognized as a form of psychology and behavior exhibited by pre-adults and that it results from the peculiar social conditions which arose in the last century.

Reprinted with permission from *Journal of Psychohistory*, 5, 1977, 271–290. Copyright 1977 by Atcom, Inc.

Among the personality traits most associated
with adolescence by historians, social scientists, psychologists and psychoanalysts are an inner-turmoil,
experienced during a time of "storm and stress", of
uncertainty but of conformity with peers. It is a stage
of life when the individual is seeking self-identity and
in this process becomes inwardly absorbed, perhaps
egoistic, sometimes cruel. However, it is also a most
spontaneous, energetic and promising phase, one devoted to ideals and romanticizing, and is as concerned with the demonstration of physical and sexual
prowess as it is characterized by laziness, unsteadi-
ness, preoccupation with sex and possibly criminal
acts. Adolescence, finally, is a phase of life when
youth is most "pliable, plastic and formative."[6]

For Demos, as well as for Hareven, Gillis and
Aries, the social phenomena for the necessary emergence of adolescence occurred during the 19th century, the time of modernization. What do they see as
the characteristics of this period—the social conditions—which made it so uniquely capable of producing adolescence? For one, the expansion and
extension of education led to a greater economic dependence on parental financial support as well as to a
clearer separation of children from adults than had
ever previously existed. The point is made over and
over again that in preindustrial society children and
youth were miniature adults: treated, dressed and
identified with adults.[7] It is apparently central to their
thesis that during the 19th century this changed, as
seen, for example, in the segregation of youth by age
groups in the school room which created a *de facto*
distinction between adults and children. With the further introduction of school age-grading there grew
even finer distinctions among the children themselves.[8] Nineteenth century education, therefore, is
said to be a major force in bringing about a sharp
preadult youth status, increased cohort segregation
and a longer dependence on parents: in short a unique
"adolescent experience."[9]

At about the same time, the 19th century's increased industrialization and urbanization also
played an important role in the development of adolescence. These social processes brought more and
more people, including youth, to the city to look for
work. As a consequence, it is noted by historians
that youth came to engage in a form of behavior
which historical authorities identified as the "mark"
of adolescence. Namely, they were attracted to join
cohort groups, some of which appeared as gangs
which became major social problems as a result of
their criminal activity. Scholars have drawn our attention to the concern of authorities who questioned
why so many young people seemed inclined to cause
trouble.[10] Then, as now, there was the prevailing no-

tion that previous generations of youths had not been
as "bad" or dangerous.[11] Historians also note that
concerned middle-class parents were alarmed by what
they viewed as the increase in delinquent violence.
Both parents and officials were also apprehensive
about the sexual changes that occurred during puberty. In the attempt to shield their offspring from these
dangers of the adolescent period, parents and reform
groups suggested school activities to help channel
youthful energy feared to be sexual in nature.[12]

Another highly relevant characteristic of the 19th
century was the new burgeoning middle class family
which was having fewer children as a result of its
increasing use of contraception. With fewer children,
they were able to focus greater and greater attention
on them. Indeed, according to Aries, parental concentration on children generated greater control,
hence loss of "freedom" previously experienced when
they were more neglected.[13]

School status, parental control, extended dependence on parents, creation of cohort groups or gangs,
all conveyed, it is suggested, similar meaning to the
youth: that they were pre-adults and not yet in control of their destiny. Confronted by this extended
period of control, whether at school or with parents,
facing an increasingly industrial complex and changing world, youth became bewildered and confused
about the process of becoming an adult and thereby
was spawned what historians identify as the unique
psychological features of adolescence. A pillar of this
psychology is the confrontation with one's identity
and the accompanying commitment to ideals. Skolnick sums up the picture, "Thus, economic, familial,
and cultural changes transformed the experience of
growing up; adolescence became an important stage
of the individual's biography. The opening of a gap
between physical maturation and the attainment of
social adulthood led to the psychological characteristics that have become known as the adolescent
experience—the urge to be independent from the
family: the discovery of the unique and private world
of the self: the search for an identity: and the questioning of adult values and assumptions which may
take the form of idealism, or cynicism, or both at the
same time."[14]

These are the explanations for the recent emergence of adolescence. There is, however, reason to
believe that adolescence is a far older phenomenon
than is thus generally acknowledged, and this paper
undertakes to re-examine the historic basis for assert-
ing adolescence to be a product of modern times. It is
not, however, the purpose of this paper to relocate the
rise of adolescence to a different time in history. The
more limited aim is simply to point out that we cannot rest satisfied with some historians' view that

adolescence emerged in modern times. The re-examination reveals that:

1. Adolescent personality traits were identified and described in a manner similar to modern characterizations of adolescence well before the modern era;

2. The adolescent years were seen as a period of transition to adulthood well before the modern era;

3. What is accepted today as social behavior that is typically adolescent was ascribed to youth well before the modern era; and

4. Well before the modern era, conceptions of a human developmental life cycle made explicit provision for a stage of adolescence.

Before outlining the evidence to support these propositions, the modern conception of adolescence may usefully be compared with the following:

> The young are in character prone to desire and ready to carry any desire they may have formed into action. Of bodily desires it is the sexual to which they are most disposed to give away, and in regard to sexual desire they exercise no self-restraint. They are changeful too and fickle in their desires, which are as transitory as they are vehement: for their wishes are keen without being permanent . . . They are passionate, irascible, and apt to be carried away by their impulses. They are slaves, too, of their passion as their ambition prevents their ever brooking a slight and renders them indignant at the mere idea of enduring an injury . . . They are charitable rather than the reverse, they are sanguine too, for the young are heated by Nature as drunken men by wine, not to say that they have not yet experienced frequent failures. Their lives are lived principally in hope, as hope is of the future and memory of the past; and while the future of youth is long, its past is short . . . They are inclined to be valorous, for they are full of passion, which excludes fear, and of hope, which inspires confidence . . . They are bashful, too, having as yet no independent standard of honor and having lived entirely in the school of conventional law . . . Youth is the age when people are most devoted to their friends or relations . . . if the young commit a fault, it is always on the side of excess and exaggeration . . . They regard themselves as omniscient and are positive in their assertions . . .[15]

This description of youth should sound familiar to us today even though it was written over 2,000 years ago by Aristotle. Aristotle was able to capture the emotional swings of this age, when he wrote youth was bashful, yet assertive, fickle yet devoted to their friends. In the 19th century G. Stanley Hall, claimed by some to be the modern formulator of adolescence, appears more to echo Aristotle's observation of the emotional swings of the adolescent stage than to present views unheard before:

> Often those most tender and considerate, most prone to take pains, to prefer other's enjoyment to their own, and to renounce . . . and conquer the strongest natural desires . . . were those most liable occasionally to fall lowest in gloating self-gratification at the expense of others. [16]

In light of this one might well be ready to question whether the stage of adolescence was unknown or only vaguely known prior to the 19th century. The historical evidence appears to place a substantial appreciation of that stage well before that time.[17]

SEXUAL DEVELOPMENT AS A PROBLEM OF ADOLESCENCE

Inner-turmoil, the "storm and stress" are taken as signs that the adolescent stage is being experienced. Some of the stress has been seen to be a result of pubescent changes which spark sexual desire, but which, however, conflict with social values of sexual repression. Long before Freud recognized the struggles between the demands of civilization and the urges of the Id, St. Augustine in his *Confessions* described this new flood of feelings which caused him inner anguish throughout his adolescent period:

> I will now call to mind my past foulness, and the carnal corruptions of my soul . . . in which I was torn to pieces, while, turned away from Thee the One, I lost myself among many vanities . . . But what was it that I delighted in save to love and to be loved? But I held it not in moderation, mind to mind, the bright path of friendship, but out of the dark concupiscence of the flesh and the effervescence of youth exhalations came forth which obscured and overcast my heart, so that I was unable to discern pure affection from unholy desire. Both boiled confusedly within me.[18]

Other autobiographical material from 17th century England also confirms that there were acknowledgements of feelings of an inner turmoil generated by the onset of puberty and in sharp opposition to Christian morality. A youth leaving home for school, for example reported:

> then did youthful lust and corruption begin to prevail over me, stronger in me than the grace of God.[19]

So, too, with a 17th century apprentice in London, burdened with recognition that "the corruption of my heart showed itself abundantly in lust." When he left his apprenticeship his anguish intensified. He recorded that on a journey to Rome,

> I began to be troubled with that nightly disease which we call the mare, which afterwards increased upon me very grievously that I was scarce any night free from it, and seldom it left me without nocturnal pollutions and visions. Oft-times I verily thought that I descended into Hell and there felt the pains of the damned, with many hideous things. Usually in my dreams me thought I saw my father always grievously angry with me.[20]

Youth in the past suffered from conflict and experienced guilt because sexual maturity affected their actions, which were in opposition to the values they identified with the adult world.

Most writers about adolescence accept the fact that puberty ushers in biological changes. But the psychological manifestations of these changes have not been acknowledged as more or less similar over time. Aristotle reported that Greek youth were primarily preoccupied with sexual gratification, and this has been similarly attested to by St. Augustine as well as by youth of the 17th century. The autobiographical material, however, provides additional psychological insight into inner conflict which the Aristotlian observation does not address. Perhaps this was because Aristotle's comment was about youth not from them. From his point of view, however, the stage of youth was inherently extreme, passionate, lacking moderation, a value cherished by the Greeks.

ADOLESCENCE AS A CONFLICT WITH ADULT VALUES: RELIGION AND EDUCATION

As the last section indicated, there is evidence that control of sexual urges has long been recognized by youth itself as a developmental hurdle to be surmounted during adolescent years. Similar recognition

of the need to restrain certain aspects of adolescent development, among which sexuality was but one characteristic, can be found in the exhortations of pre-modern authorities. Paramount among this group were religious and educational leaders, since much of what they identified as primary features of youth were in sharp conflict with the values they deemed significant.

Many of the writers during the early modern period were acutely aware of special personality traits associated with the adolescent stage of life. As Stephen Smith has pointed out in this *Journal,* in 17th-century London, religious and moral books can be found which painted youth as fickle, full of strength and vigor, as sinful, exuberant, immature, lustful, sensual, proud, vain, over-talkative, hasty, susceptible to peer pressure and so on.[21]

One can observe in the religious literature, for example, a pre-modern recognition of adolescence. The struggles to suppress and otherwise deal with these characteristics is strikingly close to the task described by modern psychologists such as G. Stanley Hall:

> The most critical revolution in life, to successfully accomplish which is to make catharses of our lower nature and to attain full ethical maturity without arrest of perversion; this is the very meaning of adolescence.[22]

At the same time, other authors thought youth to be a most unique and promising stage of life. In *Apples of Gold,* for example, Brooks wrote, "it is no small honor to you, who are in the spring and morning of your days, that the Lord hath left upon record several instances of his love and delight in young men."[23] Special lectures and sermons were directed especially to youth because of their promise, and also because of the concern for their particular adolescent vulnerabilities. In such a sermon given to youthful scholars at Eton, Thomas Horn urged that religious education should begin at an early age because,

> 1— it is the great foundation of wisdom; 2— it makes a person less liable to error in later life; 3— it is a preventative of sin and the best means of enabling a person to overcome temptation; 4— it makes a man more obedient and socially useful. [24]

The sermons, the books, the lectures were designed to help guide youth through their critical, stressful transition period, when the heat of man according to *The Anglia Notitia,* a 17th-century English encyclopedia, was at its height.[25]

New England Puritan religious leaders in the early 18th century shared similar anxieties concerning their youth. About this, N. Ray Hiner, also in this *Journal*, concludes:

> Scarcely a year passed that did not bring forth a large number of sermons and essays concerning youth, their behavior, their social and psychological characteristics, and their spiritual needs.[26]

The response of the religious community to the particular problems of youth resulted from the increased secularization of their society, from problems in recruiting youthful conversions, as well as from the extended period of youthful dependence. Sensuality and pride were the epithets characterizing youth, and the ones the religious community wanted to be redirected through conversion. Thus they called upon youth to follow the religious instruction of their elders, and not be influenced by the wanton ways of their peers. Yet, as their English religious colleagues had recognized a century before, American Puritan ministers described youth as a promising time, when their capabilities were most flourishing,[27] and beckoned them to resist temptation and maximize their spiritual and productive capabilities. Puritan ministers used techniques not different from those "developmental tasks of adolescence as described by modern psychologists."

> 1— self-control (sublimation and neutralization of libidinal and aggressive drives); 2— independence (detachment from infantile and object ties); and 3— identity (consolidation and integration of personality, and the organization of behavior into available social roles.)[28]

Thus it appears religious and moral leaders in 17th century England and in early 18th century America acknowledged youth as a recognizable group whom they must protect, while at the same time conceding that this group might itself pose special dangers to society if not subjected to appropriate controls. They became "youth watchers" because they were the guardians of morality of their society; and in the process were sensitized to this stage of life. They were, however, not the only ones in this surveillance role.

There existed another group of "youth watchers". These were pedagogues, educational theorists, humanists and teachers of youth, who believed that at each educational stage, an indelible imprint was left on the individual psyche.[29] Therefore, the nature of the education became a most important consideration, an obligation society should not ignore. It was with such considerations in mind that the humanist Thomas More wrote his *Utopia,* which was in effect a treatise on education. That More was so incensed at the false values and improper training accorded most youth clearly implies an awareness of the social significance of the adolescent stage:

> When you allow your youth to be badly brought up and their characteristics, even from early years, to become more and more corrupt, to be punished, when as grown-up men, they commit the crimes which from boyhood they have shown every prospect of committing, what else, I ask, do you do but first create thieves and then become the very agents of their punishments.[30]

Thomas More was but one among many humanist educators of his day who regarded the human growth process along a developmental, accumulative and irreversible path and as a result of this thinking he considered investment in youth a value society could not overlook.[31]

One group of educators, during the 16th century, was especially preoccupied with reaching humans at their "impressionable age" during their childhood and youth.[32] Each of these categories of pre-adulthood was viewed differently. German Protestant reformers, anxious to draw and keep a large group of citizens in their churches, made the conscious decision to achieve this goal by concentrating on the education of the young through the establishment of elementary and secondary schools, which were separate from one another. In order to determine the best curriculum to influence youth in the secondary schools, they drew upon a literary tradition which "supplied a ready made and coherent set of assumptions about the nature of children and young people." The literary tradition predicted the behavior and illustrated the possible responses of the adolescent period.[33] The reformers were, furthermore, aware of the ancient terms, *infantia, pueritia and adolescentia* which differentiated childhood from youthful development. Indeed, Jacob Wimpheling entitled his educational book, *Adolescentia.*[34] Among these reformers, consonant with the tradition which they read and absorbed, the ages 14–16 appeared to them to be the most vulnerable to corruption.

> Unrestrained by experience of consequence and with no care about the future, adolescents, in the first flush of their physical powers, are driven to "natural" vices: lying, blasphemy, violence, and cruelty. Theft, disobedience of parents and disrespect towards their elders, idle-

ness, gambling, recklessness and lack of shame, and "to come to the point-voluptuous desires which consume the body and mind" namely masturbation and sexual advances.[35]

One of the methods these reformers proposed to "redirect" some of the natural proclivities of youth was to remove any kind of sexual stimulus until the flush of passion was reduced by education and/or age. Reformers such as Jean Gerson appealed to both secular and religious authorities to assist in restraining youth from the dangers which they recognized to be inherent at the adolescent stage.[36]

ADOLESCENT YOUTH AS A PERIOD OF TRANSITION IN PRE-MODERN TIMES

One of the commonly accepted indices of modern adolescence is its transitional nature. Both adult and youthful characteristics appear to coexist.

In early modern times youth was viewed as a transition between children's roles and responsibilities of adults while they were being trained for some adult roles, mostly occupational, they were at the same time restricted from a premature assumption of other adult social roles.[37]

By the 17th century the period of apprenticeship had more or less begun to coincide with the period of adolescence. There is evidence that apprenticeship commonly terminated from between the ages of 21–24. As Smith argues, the fact that apprenticeship was a seven year period strongly suggests that adolescence was the transitional period when training for adult occupation was undertaken.[38] Yet it was also clear that during the transitional training time some adult roles were prohibited. Thus, during the year 1603 "three London apprentices were sent to jail for refusing to cut their hair and renounce the sartorial splendor that was causing distress among both their masters and local authorities."[39] Moreover, it was the duty of masters to watch that their charges did not prematurely enter adulthood by indulging in drink, gambling or sex. Nor were these pre-adults permitted the sort of mobility generally associated with adulthood. Curfew hours were established to keep servants and youth at home during the night hours.[40]

Apprenticeship was not the only occasion for the training of youth for some adult roles and the simultaneous denial of others. English youths attending schools, universities, the inns of court and those who worked as servants were subject to similar kinds of regulations.

Transition can be observed in another dimension as well, namely that of responsibility. If young children can be seen as having virtually no responsibility for controlling their behavior and adults as being fully responsible, there is much historical evidence to suggest that youth belongs to a middle area between childhood and adulthood. This middle area can best be illustrated by participation in a scheme of collective responsibility. Examples of this abound in premodern times. Whenever youths joined clubs or "fraternal orders" they were subject to strict rules and regulations of the group, such as, for example the rule of continence. In order to bind them to these rules each novice was subject to initiation rites.[41] In Germany, for example, during the 16th century, new students who were called *adolescens,* were hazed up until about a year, or at least until strenuous "moral and social" tests were passed.[42]

The principal theme underlying most of these controls centered around sexual regulations of youth during their years of pre-adulthood. The youth groups themselves had direct responsibility in controlling their members. Throughout preindustrial Europe most male and possibly female youths from about the age of 14 till marriage belonged to organizations which regulated sexual behavior of its participants. These "fraternal orders" often controlled access to the eligible females of the community, and at times acted as a collective morality to the community in which they lived. Thus, courting practices were composed and enforced by the youth themselves. Intruders into a community, and older men were often cruelly deprived of the eligible females, and sometimes promiscuous girls found "their doorways decorated with the obscene symbol of the gorse bush."[42] The groups were called Abbeys of Misrule or in Germany and parts of Switzerland, *Bruderschaften.*[43] They all shared similar characteristics: they organized youth from puberty to marriage into a subculture and prohibited premarital sex among their members.

By assuming leadership of their community's as well as their own morality, this sub-culture of youth was preparing itself to enter the adult world. Simultaneously, during this transition period they learned a trade or trained for a profession. Most of these youths were attached to households as servants or apprentices and their masters shared in the responsibility for adhering to the rules. This stage of youth, as previously indicated, may have lasted until the mid-twenties, when apprenticeship ended and they became economically independent, or when they married and could then achieve full membership in their community.[44] It would thus appear that an extended preadult status is not an exclusive feature of modern life.[45]

ADOLESCENT SOCIAL BEHAVIOR OF PRE-INDUSTRIAL YOUTH

The kinds of tensions and energies generally ascribed to modern adolescence were also exhibited by preindustrial youth. For example, youthful frolic helped to release their energies, but was not always appreciated by the older generation. During the early modern era in England, for example, the hiring season was a time of frivolty allowing the youth in concert to behave like adolescents. Philip Stubbs describes one such event on Pack Rag Day at the end of the 16th century.

> All the wildheads of the parish, conventing together, choose them a grand captain (of all mischief) whom they enoble with the title of "my lord of Misrule", and him they crown with great solemnity, and adopt for their king . . . Then march these heathen company towards the church and churchyard, their pipers piping, their drummers thundering, their stump dancing, their bells jingling . . . They have also certain papers, wherein is painted some bablery or other of imagery worked, and these they call "my Lord of Misrule's badges." These they give to everyone that will give money for them to maintain them in their heathenry, devilry, whoredome, drunkenness, pride or what not.[46]

Compare the report of Philip Stubbs with the comments of a reformer in the 19th century:

> It must be confessed that an irreverent unruly spirit has come to be prevalent, an outrageous evil among young people.[47]

The equivalent of modern adolescent tensions between adolescents and adults was also found between masters and their apprentices. Despite society's efforts to look upon the master's household as a surrogate family and despite apprentices being told to be as obedient to their masters as to their fathers, apprentices were mistreated and complained. According to Steven Smith, "the records of the Middlesex Sessions of the Peace and of other Mayor's Court contain numerous cases of apprentices suing their masters as a result of mistreatment." The converse was also true. The literature of the times complained about "dishonest and rowdy apprentices."[48] The ideal relationship of obedient apprentices nurtured, watched over and trained by a stern but kindly master was just that, an ideal. Apprentices rebelled and misbehaved, and were not always treated with generative kindness.

A central feature of modern adolescence is its adherence to a set of ideals or values. Aspects of reform movements of the past demonstrate that youth often channeled their energy to an ideology and through it attempted to gain an identity. Herbert Moller's article,[49] "Youth as a Force in History" illustrated the extent to which youth from early modern times joined new ideologically motivated groups with which they could find identity. During the Reformation, for example, students were attracted to the religious ideas initiated by Luther. These youth rejected the older generation's religion, finding the new ideological outlook of Lutheran Protestantism more consonant with their "ideological mind", as Erikson phrased it, as well as a means to release their energy. The appeal that ideology had for youth is further evidenced by their involvement in the religious revolts of the 16th century:

> In several towns in Provence-Marseille, Toulon and elsewhere—Catholic Youths stoned Protestants to death and burned them. The reputation of the adolescents in Sens and Provens was so frightening that a member of a well-known Huguenot family was afraid to walk through the streets . . . In Toulouse, Catholic students had the university in an uproar, whistling and banging in lectures when the canon law or the "old religion" was mentioned. In Poitiers in 1559 and again in 1562, Protestant youngsters and students take the initiative in smashing statues and overturning altars. Indeed, youths are mentioned as a part of almost all the great iconoclastic disturbances—in the Netherland, in Rouen and elsewhere.[50]

In sum, there appears to be a plethora of evidence indicating that both the psychology and behavior of the 19th century adolescent are clearly observable in premodern youth. In the past, youth joined peer groups, frolicking, behaving irreverently and causing general disturbances. They identified with new ideological movements and, in the name of ideology, with their cohorts became violent and destructive, making people fear to walk in the streets. How representative was this of all youth in the past? It is difficult to tell. But on the other hand, it is far from clear that the descriptions of modern adolescents are truly representative either.[51]

More important, however, in an evaluation of the significance of the evidence which has been presented, is the role of the long-held beliefs about human growth and development.

ADOLESCENCE AS PART OF THE LIFE CYCLE

A concept of adolescence, as has been previously stated, was known as early as Greek times. It was an integral part of their perspective of the human life cycle which they believed to be developmental, because change and development were considered to be intrinsic to the nature *(physis)* of all living things. In order to comprehend the *physis* of man it was necessary to understand his successive stages of development, an understanding which encompassed man's origins and his ultimate purpose of "final cause" as Aristotle conceived it.[52] According to Aristotle, "a plant", or human being had "a development which consist[ed] of the determinable sequence of changes proceeding from its very structure and" was as 'necessary' to its being as any other intrinsic attribute."[53]

Skolnick's characterization of modern developmental psychology seems to suggest a similar philosophic perspective which appears to include all of the essential Greek developmental elements. "Although each [developmental psychological] theory selects a different aspect of the child as the key to understanding the process of development, they all agree on several things:

1. Development is self-propelled and teleological—that is, the "push" to change comes from within the organism, and the endpoint of development is implicit at the beginning. [Aristotle's idea of the structure or intrinsic attribute.]

2. The adult is categorically, or qualitatively different from the child. The different stages of childhood are also qualitatively different from each other. [The Greek idea of the successive stages of development.]

3. Developmental theories are organized around specific concepts of adult competence. For Freud, the endpoint of development is the genital, heterosexual adult, parent to children, with a place in the occupational world. For Piaget, the endpoint of development is the stage of formal operational thinking—the ability to think hypothetically and abstractly." [Aristotle's Final Form or Cause.][54]

With the Greek idea of a developmental life cycle moving from stage to stage, it is not surprising, as we observed with Aristotle, that they were able to perceive what they considered to be both the inherent and universal nature of youth. Each stage of the life cycle moved on to the next because it contained dialectically its own specific characteristic while bear-ing the "seed" or internal attribute for the change into the next stage. Within childhood were the mechanisms for change into adolescence, specifically triggered by puberty.

The laws of Plato, for example, illustrate an educational appropriateness for different ages of the young and imply a reliance on a developmental sequential concept. His educational program began while the baby was still inside its mother;[55] for the years 0-3 nurses were told to try to distinguish between the cries of the babies, while not overindulging them; from 3-6, informal co-education began with spontaneous play under the careful supervision of nurses. At six, the sexes were to be separated but educated similarly if the female so desired. The purpose of their education was twofold: "training of the body and cultural education to perfect personality."[56] Thus, for example, from 10-13, literature should be studied, while at 13, the lyre was to be learned. Educational training, beginning in the womb, was to "re-direct . . . natural development along the right line."[57]

This paradigm of the life cycle, with its inherent developmental modes, has influenced Western thought ever since its inception. Strauss notes that:

> Augustine distinguishes between the nursing and the learning-to-speak phases of infancy, and between the *puer loquens,* who has just emerged from childhood helplessness, and a later condition of *puerita,* just preceding puberty, when reason begins to be active . . . There was no doubt about the significance of one . . . stage, adolescence coming at fourteen. It would be difficult to improve upon the picture of the inner storms and pressures, the restless longing and seeking for something not clearly perceived which is conveyed by Augustine in his *Confessions.*[58]

CONCLUSION

Basic to the question of adolescent's vintage is the matter of whether the conditions of any century or historical period can be identified as the cause for the emergence of adolescent psychology and behavior. An affirmative response to this query represents an extreme form of environmentalism, a position which the historians under discussion appear to have adopted. The implicit denial of the historically important role of inherent characteristics is not warranted. Certainly social conditions have varied greatly over time, but the evidence of adolescent behavior and psychology which has occurred so frequently in Western history must be explained, at least in part, by the influence of human biological development. For example, there are wide differences between the religious ideological commitment of youth in 16th-century France and Germany and the ideologically oriented uprisings in Western universities in the 1960's, but both may well be expressions of the same human developmental qualities of adolescence which has persisted through time.[59]

In light of this it seems paradoxical that many of the historians who contend adolescence to be a 19th-century phenomena also accept the developmental life cycle model. The terms they use in identifying adolescent behavior and the framework they apply to the life process comes from developmental psychology whose central assumption is that it is timeless.[60]

Adolescence thus appears not to be a product of modern times. In its most recognizable behavioral features it has been acknowledged and in its psychological manifestations it has been recorded at least since Greek times.

References

1. Some social scientists place the emergence of adolescence earlier. Arlene Skolnick suggests the 18th century and identifies Rousseau as the possible initiator of this conception. See "The Limits of Childhood Conceptions of Child Development and Social Context" in *Law and Contemporary Problems* (Summer, 1975), p. 61, on the other hand, in the same volume see F. Raymond Marks, "Detours on the Road to Maturity: A View of the Legal Conception of Growing Up and Letting Go" places adolescence in the 20th century. "Adolescence—in a social sense—is largely a twentieth century creation.", p. 78.

2. Philip Aries, *Centuries of Childhood* (New York, 1962), p. 30. Aries considers the 20th century "The Century of Adolescence."

3. Tamara K. Hareven, "Historical Adulthood and Old Age" *Daedalus*, No. 4 (Fall, 1976), p. 17. Hareven is included among the historians who locate adolescence in the 19th century, but her focus in this article is not on adolescence.

4. John and Virginia Demos, "Adolescence in Historical Perspective" in *The American Family in Social-Historical Perspective* edited by Michael Gordon (New York, 1973), p. 210.

5. John R. Gillis, *Youth and History* (New York, 1974), pp. 98–99.

6. This compilation of adolescent qualities can be observed in the following literature. See for example, Demos and Demos, pp. 211–218; Gillis, Chapters 3 and 4; Peter Blos, *On Adolescence: A Psychoanalytic Interpretation* (New York, 1962); Erick H. Erikson, "Youth: Fidelity and Diversity," *Daedalus* (Winter, 1962); G. Stanley Hall, *Adolescence* (New York, 1904), Vol. 2.

7. One wonders even if children and youth were treated as "miniature adults" if they felt like adults. See Ross W. Beales, Jr., "In Search of the Historical Child: Miniature Adulthood and Youth in Colonial New England" in *American Quarterly* 27 (1975) which presents a re-examination of this entire question of Miniature Adulthood. Beales looks at the law and the attitude of religious reformers and comes to the conclusion that children and youth were perceived and treated differently from adults.

8. For an account of the expansion of education see among others, Gillis, pp. 98–105 and Aries especially, Chapter IV and pp. 412–413; Skolnick, pp. 69–70.

9. See Skolnick, p. 63.

10. For an excellent discussion on the fears of reformers during the 19th century see Sanford J. Fox, "Juvenile Justice Reform: An Historical Perspective" in the *Stanford Law Review*, Vol. XXII (June 1970).

11. See for example, Demos and Demos, p. 211, and Gillis especially p. 134.

12. Demos and Demos suggest concern for sexual maturity and its effects on youthful behavior were muted because of Victorian sentiment, but discussions became more open after 1870; see p. 213. In England, however, the subject of "puberty" and its consequences was more open. See Gillis, pp. 112–115.

13. Aries, pp. 413–415.

14. Skolnick, p. 63.

15. Aristotle, quoted in Norman Keil, *The Universal Experience of Adolescence* (New York, 1964), pp. 18–19.

16. See G. Stanley Hall, Vol 2, pp. 75–90, quoted in D. Ross, G. Stanley Hall, *The Psychologist as Prophet* (The University of Chicago Press, 1972), p. 327.

17. Although the term adolescence was known and used from Greek times, for approximately the same years as youth, prior to the modern era youth was the word generally applied to pre-adults after the childhood stage. Even Demos and Demos acknowledge that the 19th century used the word youth rather than adolescence. But they add, "Lest it be imagined that Americans of the 19th century had no special concern whatsoever for the period which we now call adolescence (and which in their day was simply termed "youth"). p. 212. Then they go on to demonstrate that adolescent behavior existed in the 19th century. Thus, they implicitly acknowledge that the semantic usage of the word youth in the 19th century means adolescence. Yet, John Demos, in *A Little Commonwealth: Family Life in Plymouth Colony* (N.Y. 1970) seems to conflict with his view. Claiming that the widespread use of the word adolescence is only about seventy-five years and that in earlier

times the word youth was used vaguely, he then goes on to say, "These semantic details point to a very substantial area of contrast in the developmental process then and now." p. 145. The semantic distinctions, however, are still unclear even seventy-five years after the word adolescence has gained widespread currency. In some of the modern literature on adolescence both words are used while the conceptual differences are not yet obvious. See for example, *Adolescence in the Life Cycle,* edited by Glenn H. Elder, Jr. (New York, 1975). On page 3 Elder states, with unusual clarity, "In this volume, adolescence and youth are employed interchangeably in reference to the years between 7th grade and (relatively) complete independence from the family of origin. " This paper also uses the words adolescence and youth interchangeably. Puberty marks the beginning of this stage, while relatively complete economic independence or marriage is taken as the terminal point of adolescence and youth.

18. *The Confessions of St. Augustine,* translated by J. G. Pilkington, (New York, 1943), pp. 27–28.

19. Walter Pringle, "The Memoir of Walter Pringle," in *Selected Biographies* edited by W. K. Tweedie (Edinburgh, 1845) 1, p. 423, quoted in Steven R. Smith, "Youth in 17th Century England" in *History of Childhood Quarterly,* 2 (1975), p. 506.

20. Richard Norwood, *The Journal of Richard Norwood, Surveyor of Bermuda,* (New York, 1945), p. 26 in Smith, "Youth," pp. 507–508.

21. See for example, Smith, "Youth," pp. 498–501. Also, Steven Smith "The London Apprentices as Seventeenth Century Adolescents" in *Past and Present,* No. 61 (November, 1973), pp. 153–155.

22. Hall (2:337) in Ross, p. 331.

23. Thomas Brooks, *Apples of Gold in Young Men and Women and a Crown of Glory from Old Men and Women* (London, 1667), in Smith "Youth" p. 497.

24. Smith, "Youth," pp. 502–503.

25. E. Chamberlayne, *Anglia Notitia* (London, 1669) 15th edition ed. 1700. See Chapter V 'Of Women, Children and Servants'. In this edition, the age 25 is considered a time when the "Heat of Youth is Somewhat Abayed." Thus it is not an unwarranted inference that youth was considered the time when the heat of man is at its height.

26. N. Ray Hiner, "Adolescence in Eighteenth Century America" *History of Childhood Quarterly* (1975), p. 254.

27. Hiner, p. 267.

28. Hiner, p. 272.

29. See Gerald Strauss, "The State of Pedagogical Theory c 1530: What Protestant Reformers Knew About Education" in Lawrence Stone, *ed., Schooling and Society, Studies in the History of Education* (The John Hopkins University Press, 1976), p. 75.

30. Thomas More, *Utopia* in the *Yale Edition of the Complete Works of St. Thomas More,* edited by Edward Surz and J. H. Hexter, (1967), p. 71.

31. See Strauss, pp. 77–89 who suggests these ideas are as old as the Greeks; see footnotes 29–32.

32. Strauss, p. 70.

33. Strauss, p. 70.

34. Strauss, p. 71, see also Aries, p. 21. The 17th century book, *The Office of Christian Parents* divided life into six stages, of which youth was 14 to 28 years, [n.a.] as quoted in Smith, "Youth," p. 495. See also forthcoming book by Vivian C. Fox and Martin H. Quitt, eds. *The Anglo-American Family Cycle 1500-1800* (Psychohistory Press) which delineates the stages of childhood: into infancy, childhood and youth.

35. Strauss, p. 76.

36. Strauss, p. 76.

37. Marks notes this as a characteristic of modern adolescence, "Although able to work, engage in mature sexual relations and make moral choices, he is denied full adult status", p. 78.

38. Smith, "Apprentices" p. 157.

39. Gillis, p. 22.

40. See for example, Smith, "Apprentices" p. 157; Ivy Pinchbeck and Margaret Hewitt, *Children in English Society, From Tudor Times to the Eighteenth Century,* (London 1969) Vol. I Chap. IX. Also Alan Macfarlene, *The Family Life of Ralph Josselin, a Seventeenth Century Clergyman: An Essay on Historical Anthropology* (Cambridge, 1970), especially pp. 205–210; Gillis, pp. 22–3.

41. Gillis, p. 23.

42. Gillis, p. 24.

43. Gillis, pp. 29–30; see also Natalie Z. David, "The Reasons of Misrule: Youth Groups and *Charvaris* in Sixteenth Century France," *Past and Present,* No. 50 (February, 1971) also Natalie Z. Davis, "The Rites of Violence, Religious Riot in Sixteenth Century France," *Past and Present,* No. 59 (May, 1973).

44. See for example, Smith, "Apprentices," p. 157, also Peter Laslett, *The World We Have Lost, 2nd edition,* (London, 1971), p. 94.

45. The idea that adolescence is prolonged is in current vogue. See Kenneth Keniston in *The Uncommitted: Alienated Youth in American Society* (1965), pp. 196–200.

46. Philip Stubbs, *The Anatomie of Abuses* (1583) quoted in Gillis, p. 27.

47. Warren Burton, *Helps to Education* (Boston, 1863), pp. 38–39, quoted in Demos and Demos, p. 211.

48. Smith, "Apprentices," pp. 152–153.

49. Herbert Moller, "Youth as a Force in History," *Comparative Studies in Social History* 10 (1968), p. 238. Moller reports in 1519, when Luther Cardstadt and Melancthon set out for Leipzing debate—nearly 2,000 students and other supporters joined.

50. Davis, "The Rites of Violence," p. 87.

51. See for example, Daniel Offer, *The Psychological World of the Teen-ager; A Study of Normal Adolescent Boys* (New York, 1969) and Frank Musgrove, "The Problem of

Youth and the Structure of Society in England," in *Youth and Society,* Vol I (Sept. 1969). Musgrove states in the 1960's "An English empirical study . . . shows clearly that average 15 year old English boys and girls identify closely with their parents, rather than their peers," p. 41. Compare this with his book, *Youth and the Social Order* (Indiana University Press, 1964).

52. See for example, Robert A. Nisbet, *Social Change and History: Aspects of the Western Theory of Development* (Oxford University Press, 1969), especially Chapter 1, pp. 24–25. Also Arthur O. Lovejoy, *The Great Chain of Being: A Study of the History of An Idea* (Harper, 1936), Chapter 2. Also Werner Jaeger, *Paideia, The Ideals of Greek Culture,* Vol. I translated by Gilbert Highet (New York, 1944).

53. Nisbet, p. 39.

54. Skolnick, pp. 50–51. For an interpretation which claims that the Greek idea of development was not truly developmental; see, Louis Breger, *From Instinct to Identity: The Development of Personality* (Englewood Cliffs, N.J., 1974) Chapter 1. I am grateful to my colleague, Martin H. Quitt, for drawing my attention to this book.

55. Plato, *The Laws,* Penguin (1970), p. 227.

56. Plato, p. 281.

57. Plato, p. 298.

58. Strauss, p. 75; see also Aries, p. 21; also, Smith, "Youth," p. 495. Robert Nisbet's book traces the Greek idea of Life Cycle and Developmentalism up to the present day.

59. See S. N. Eisenstadt, "Archetypal Patterns of Youth" in *Youth: Change and Challenge,* ed. by Erik H. Erikson. (N.Y. 1963). Eisenstadt examines the "subtle dialectics" between the biological aspects of adolescence and cultural variations which help define the expression of the adolescent period.

60. See Skolnick, pp. 49–52, especially, p. 51, in which she says, " Developmental theories claim to be universal."

31

Content, Context, and Process in Reasoning During Adolescence: Selecting a Model

_____

MARCIA C. LINN

Adolescents are often capable of far more complex reasoning than younger children, and as a result they show increasing interest in problems involving multiple variables and abstract ideas. One clear finding that has emerged from cognitive developmental research with young children in recent years is that the content and context of a cognitive problem affects performance. Does this dependence of the quality of thinking on content and context hold true for adolescents even though they are said to be increasingly capable of abstract or decontextualized under-standing? Marcia C. Linn explores this question, and provides a persuasive argu-ment for examining adolescent thinking as a process directly tied to both the content and context of cognitive activity.

Reprinted with permission from _Journal of Early Adolescence_, 3, 1983, 63–82. Copyright 1983 by Sage Publications, Inc.

This material is based upon research supported by the National Science Foundation under grant numbers 81-12631 and 79-19494. Any opinions, findings and conclusions, or recommendations expressed in this publication are those of the author and do not necessarily reflect the views of the National Science Foundation.

Philosophers Harvey Siegel and Nick Burbules provided opportunities for discussion of how models from philosophy of science might inform psychological researchers; their encouragement and contributions have been invaluable. In addition, this paper draws on experiments conducted by the Adolescent Reasoning Project; helpful discussions with staff members including Kevin Delucchi, Tina de Benedictis, and Steven Pulos are gratefully acknowledged.

Models of how reasoning occurs and develops shape thinking and research about adolescent cognition. Four models of historical, current, or potential interest are considered in this paper. For each model, the role of content, context, and process information is delineated. In a subsequent section, some research results concerned with content and context influences are summarized. The usefulness of these models for interpreting the research results forms the focus of the final section.

This paper emphasizes cognitive models and cognitive research results. Models primarily emphasizing social, personality, or physiological factors, for example, are not represented. Cognitive models can have implications for these factors, however. For example, Damon and Hart (1982) demonstrate the role of cognitive models of self concept in interpreting the development of self esteem.

Inhelder and Piaget's (1958) book initiated serious interest in the period of adolescence and described a model of reasoning which has had profound influence on research. What is referred to as the Piagetian model in Table 1 emphasizes the role of process knowledge in adolescent reasoning. Process knowledge is knowledge of logical strategies such as the combinatorial strategy or the proportionality strategy. Inhelder and Piaget (1958) emphasized the structure of logical reasoning and the difficulty of altering the speed or course of the development of reasoning. They hypothesized that certain strategies, which underlie reasoning, develop during adolescence and lead to qualitative changes in reasoning performance. Unfortunately, the period of adolescence was of less interest to Piaget than Piaget has been to researchers of adolescent reasoning.

In contrast to the Piagetian model, the mental ability model of reasoning focuses on the gradual acquisition of a broad range of knowledge. Charac-

terized by the work of Cattell (1971) this approach focuses on individual differences. Work on aptitude treatment interactions reflect this perspective (e.g., Cronbach & Snow, 1977). Constructs such as fluid and crystallized ability as well as cognitive style and ego control have been measured. Adolescence has received limited attention as a special period from those following the mental ability model.

Recently, those following the mental ability model have extended their interests to include information processing analysis of mental ability tasks (e.g., Snow, Federico, & Montague, 1980; Sternberg, 1977). This approach offers considerable promise for characterizing the nature of intelligence. Snow and his co-workers for example, (e.g., Kyllonen, Woltz, & Lohman, 1982; Kyllonen, Lohman, & Snow, 1982) suggest that "flexibility" in strategy selection characterizes expert performance on mental ability tests.

There are several reasons why adolescence has not been studied separately by those following the mental ability model. First, life span research (e.g., Baltes, 1963) has been fraught with methodological problems. Second, researchers have found it difficult to measure the same abilities at different ages. For example, in a meta-analysis of gender differences in spatial ability, Linn and Peterson (Note 1) found that measures, such as paper folding, used in adolescence had no clear counterpart in tests for younger children. Thus, most researchers have focused on college age individuals when building models of mental ability.

Recently, models of reasoning performance have emerged from a field called cognitive science (Larkin, McDermott, Simon & Simon, 1980; Simon, 1980). Cognitive science represents a collaboration of cognitive psychology and computer science. A common methodology in this field is to build a computer simulation of performance and then modify the simu-

TABLE 1

Models of Reasoning Performance During Adolescence and Adulthood

Model	Focus	Emphasis	Methodology
Piagetian	Processes or strategies which govern reasoning	Underlying logical structure	Clinical interviews using apparatus
Mental ability	Acquisition of a variety of abilities	General ability	Mental testing
Cognitive science	Acquisition and structuring of knowledge	Knowledge organization	Simulations of skilled and unskilled performance
Philosophy of science	Change in scientific ideas over time	Factors influencing change	Case studies

lation based on input from the performance of individuals being simulated. These researchers have focused primarily on content or subject matter knowledge and on how that knowledge is stored and retrieved from memory. A popular approach has been to contrast skilled and unskilled performance on complex tasks, such as physics problem solving, to clarify reasoning processes (e.g., Heller and Reif, Note 2).

A fourth category of models of reasoning performance comes from philosophy of science. Although models from philosophy of science have, as yet, received little attention, they have tremendous potential (Carey & Block, 1982; Linn and Siegel, in press). This potential lies in the focus of philosophers of science on persistence and *change* in reasoning performance. Very little theoretical or empirical work has addressed how reasoning changes, yet understanding change in reasoning is essential for fostering effective reasoning. Models from philosophy of science can also aid understanding because they often emphasize context influences on reasoning which are minimized in other models. The societal context, for example the context of religious beliefs can have tremendous impact on the reasoning of groups of scientist. Similarly, context has impact on the reasoning of individuals (e.g., Mishler, 1979). Philosophy of science offers models for change in scientists' collective ideas which may have implications for changes in individuals' ideas.

These four models are characteristic of those used by cognitive researchers to investigate reasoning during adolescence. The labels chosen are somewhat arbitrary, others might choose them differently. For example Keating (this volume) refers to the psychometric model which closely parallels the mental ability model and the information processing model of which the cognitive science model is a part. The important point is that models place different emphasis on content or subject matter knowledge, on context or beliefs, and on processes or strategies. The emphasis determines how researchers choose problems to study. Thus, those following Piaget have tended to focus on the emergence of logical strategies while those from cognitive science have tended to contrast the character of subject matter knowledge for subjects who are skilled in a narrow subject matter domain with those who are unskilled.

Recent research on adolescent reasoning has examined the assumptions of the Piagetian model and suggested the potential of the other models by showing the importance of content and context in reasoning. The next section describes some of the research findings emphasizing content and context influences on adolescent reasoning. These studies suggest why researchers are turning to new models of reasoning performance.

RESEARCH RESULTS

Research suggesting that investigators place greater emphasis on content and context influences on adolescent reasoning has recently emerged. Three examples illustrate the sort of findings models of reasoning during adolescence might need to explain.

Effects of Subject Matter Knowledge on Reasoning: The Wason Selection Task

Wason first described the selection task in the literature in 1966. As described below, subsequent researchers have found that this difficult logical task is facilitated when translated to certain types of familiar subject matter (e.g., Griggs & Cox, 1982; Johnson-Laird, Legrenzi & Legrenzi, 1972). This task illustrates the complex nature of subject matter knowledge influences on reasoning.

The selection task, which has also been referred to as the four card problem, typically features four cards lying on a table. The participant is told that each has a letter on one side, and a number on the other; the visible symbols are "A," "B," "2" and "3." The participant is then asked to test the truth of the following rule: "If there is an A on one side of the card then there is a 2 on the other side of the card."

The participant must decide which card or cards need necessarily be turned over, in order to discover whether the rule is true or false. The correct answer is the "A" and the "3" since only a card with an A on one side and a number that is *not* 2 on the other could disprove the rule. Typically, subjects choose either the "A" alone or the "A" and the "2."

This response was originally explained as a motivation to verify, rather than falsify, the rule (see Wason & Johnson-Laird, 1972). Subsequently, manipulations of the rule statement revealed that these responses may simply reflect a tendency to match responses to the card named in the rule. That is, if the rule is stated with a negative consequent, e.g., "If there is an A on one side of the card then there is *not* a 2 on the other side of the card," the matching choices (A and 2) are chosen more frequently (and are also logically correct). Far more subjects give the correct solution on the rule with the negative consequent than on the same rule with an affirmative consequent. This finding, however, does not explain why close to 95% of the respondents get the affirmative version of the task wrong.

A long series of studies evaluated what was referred to as the "thematic materials effect" in the selection task. These studies employed rules using subject matter which might facilitate performance such as transportation to towns (e.g., if I went to Dover I went by train) and values for postage stamps (e.g., if the envelope is unsealed the letter has a 12 pence stamp). As Griggs (in press) summarizes, some of these versions facilitated performance while others did not. For example, those familiar with the postal regulation in England concerning unsealed envelopes performed better on that version of the selection task than they did on the abstract version.

Recently, researchers have identified a class of problems with subject matter which facilitates reasoning performance (Cox & Griggs, in press; D'Andrade, Note 3; Griggs & Cox, 1982). An example from Griggs and Cox (1982) involves the legal drinking age in Florida. The rule subjects investigated was: "If a person is drinking beer, then the person must be over 19." The subjects were told to imagine that they were police officers responsible for ensuring that the regulation was followed. Four cards, representing information about four possible people sitting at a table, were presented. They were labeled "DRINKING BEER," "DRINKING COKE," "16 YEARS OF AGE," and "22 YEARS OF AGE." The task was to select those people (cards) that definitely needed to be turned over to determine whether or not they were violating the rule. Seventy-four percent of Griggs and Cox's respondents made the correct selection for this problem, while not one did so for the abstract problem using letters and numbers.

Griggs and Cox (1982) used a memory cuing explanation to interpret these results (see also Manktelow & Evans, 1979). Griggs and Cox argued that performance is facilitated by content which permits the respondent to recall past experience with the content of the task, with the relationship (rule) in the problem, and with a counterexample to the rule. Further research is underway to clarify the role of subject matter knowledge in performance on the selection task.

Thus, some forms of subject matter knowledge must be represented in our models of reasoning performance. From these studies of the selection task, one might hypothesize that a representation of the structure of knowledge of alcoholic beverage consumption for the drinking age problem would be sufficient to understand reasoning performance on that problem. Our other research findings broaden this view.

THE ROLE OF SUBJECT MATTER KNOWLEDGE IN REASONING: PREDICTING DISPLACED VOLUME

Another example of how subject matter knowledge influences complex problem solving involves a task called predicting displaced volume. In this task, il-

lustrated in Figure 1, subjects are told that there are two metal blocks, both of which sink when immersed in water. They are asked to predict which of the two blocks will displace the most liquid when immersed in water. A typical student (referred to as John) responded as illustrated in Figure 1. What alternative conception is John using to predict which of the two metal blocks will make the water go up higher?

John's responses indicate that his alternative conception is "The greater the weight of the solid immersed in water, the more liquid it will displace." Thus, John uses what we refer to as the weight conception for predicting how much water will be displaced. For a more detailed discussion of this task, and the alternative conceptions used by subjects, see Linn and Pulos (1983).

1. Blocks A and B are the same size. Block B weighs more than block A.

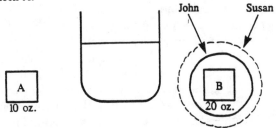

Which block will make the water go up higher?

　Block A

　Block B

　Both the same

2. Block D is larger than block C. Block C weighs more than block D.

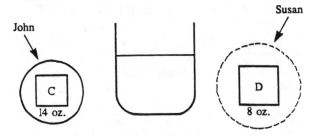

Which block will make the water go up higher?

　Block C

　Block D

　Both the same

FIGURE 1　John and Susan's response to the water glass puzzle.

Another typical student, referred to as Susan, responded as shown in Figure 1. Susan's conception is more complex than John's. Essentially, Susan's conception is: "If the blocks differ in size, then the bigger one makes the water go up higher, and if the size of the blocks is the same, then the heavier one makes the water go up higher. " Linn and Pulos (1983) frequently found this response among twelve- to sixteen-year-old adolescents; in fact, less than one-third of the 778 twelve- to sixteen-year-olds studied, used the correct volume-only rule.

These examples illustrate that learners generate alternative conceptions for reasoning problems rather than simply giving wrong answers. John's and Susan's responses to the predicting displaced volume task, tell us how they used subject matter knowledge to solve the problem.

Generally, students are consistent in their responses. The responses of Susan and John represent consistent alternative conceptions for predicting displaced volume (alternatives to the correct answer that the volume of the block is the only factor which influences how much liquid is displaced) which Linn and Pulos (1983) find occur regularly.

Why do learners have alternative conceptions for predicting displaced volume? In general, their knowledge about weight contributes to their performance: they expect weight to be influential when it is not. Weight is often a variable in other domains. Individuals solving predicting displaced volume may use an improper analogy and expect that weight is important in predicting displaced volume because it is also important in how far an object moves when hit by another object or how much one's toe hurts when something is dropped on it. Thus, individuals may have knowledge about the role of weight which they consider relevant to this situation.

Is it easy to alter the students' ideas concerning the role of weight in predicting displaced volume? If teachers demonstrate that weight is not a variable in this situation, do most students accept this pronouncement and move on to the next task? Evidently not. Predicting displaced volume is a topic in most science curricula in 7th and 8th grade, yet over 50 percent of 12th grade respondents to this task use an incorrect alternative conception which involves weight in some respect (Linn & Pulos, 1983).

Furthermore, when we investigated the role of instruction, we found that many participants failed to learn the volume rule when taught. We demonstrated how much water was displaced by solids of varying size and weight during about ten minutes of instruction for subjects who initially used a weight based alternative conception for solving predicting displaced volume (Pulos, de Benedictis, Linn, Sullivan,

& Clement, 1982). In general, subjects made only slight gains in performance following this instruction.

One subject, when confronted with a contradiction to the weight conception responded: "Humm, the water went up the same in both the containers even though one of those cubes weighs more than the other. You must have *magic* water." This subject felt that the experimenter was being tricky and using water that did not have the usual properties. The subject believed that weight was an important factor and was willing to suggest that the experimenter was using magic water in order to defend the role of weight in predicting displaced volume.

Clearly subject matter knowledge influences performance and is somewhat resistant to change. It should be noted that tenacious defense of erroneous ideas has proven valuable in the history of science (Lakatos, 1972), so tenacious defense of ideas concerning a scientific phenomena may not be totally inappropriate. However, in predicting displaced volume, weight does not determine displacement. His view needs to be remediated, perhaps after the subject tenaciously and creatively defends it.

This study illustrates that subject matter knowledge influences reasoning. Many researchers have identified alternative conceptions which govern scientific reasoning (e.g., McClosky, Carramazza, & Green, 1980; Viennot, 1979). Models of reasoning performance which incorporate both prevalent alternative conceptions and the propensity of alternative conceptions to resist change, will foster understanding of adolescent reasoning.

The Role of Context in Reasoning: An Example from Reasoning about Advertisements

A summary of results reported by Linn, de Benedictis, and Delucchi (1982) of how adolescents reason about advertisements, illustrates how the reasoning context might influence performance. We studied adolescent reasoning about advertising because we wished to investigate a prevalent reasoning problem. Since adolescents view over 20,000 advertisements annually we felt this was an area where adolescent reasoning was frequently required.

We investigated how reasoners respond to advertisements displaying product tests. The reasoning context may influence performance. For example, reasoners may accept the message in the ad because too much effort is required to refute it or to generate alternatives (e.g., Shugan, 1980; Wright, 1975). Simon (1969) suggested that individuals "satisfice" rather than "optimize" in this sort of complex context. That is, reasoners may accept their less than optimal reasoning as satisfactory, given the circumstances. For example, Shor (1980, p. 61) remarks, "Still another means of prescientific irrationalism in daily life is known as 'brand name' loyalty. People become totemistically allied to a commercial product. . . ." Reasoners' ideas about how advertisements are generated, about their ability to avoid persuasion combined with their limited information contradicting the message, may create a context of uncritical acceptance of commercial messages.

One characteristic of the reasoning context concerns how adolescents view advertisements. In a study of adolescent reasoning about advertising, Linn, et al., (1982) found that adolescents were extremely skeptical of advertisers and of the methods advertisers use to substantiate ad claims (see Figure 2). Almost two-thirds (62%) expect that advertisers often or always lie or cheat.

Another aspect of the reasoning context concerns beliefs about produce tests. Adolescents generally believe that tests reported by advertisers are unfair. Responses to "How do advertisers get the results they want?" fell into four categories. About 27 percent said advertisers lie by not doing a test at all or by testing but fabricating the results (e.g., "they switch labels on products"), about 61 percent said advertisers do unfair testing, and about 19 percent said advertisers do many tests and pick supporting results. Thus, over three-quarters (88%) of adolescents think advertisers lie or do unfair tests.

Adolescents' views of advertisements are consistent with surveys of adolescent attitudes toward advertisers (e.g., Moschis & Churchill, 1979), and with Elkind's (1967, 1968) observations that adolescents are skeptical of social and political systems. They also reflect Lewis' (1981) findings that between 7th and 12th grade adolescents increase in awareness of "vested interests" in social and political groups and in cautious treatment of information reflecting vested interests.

How do adolescents reason about advertisements, given the context in which their reasoning takes place? In spite of their skepticism, adolescents tend to believe the claims in ads they view (See Figure 4). When Linn *et al.* (1982) asked adolescents whether they believed the claims in three ads over half the subjects said they did. Furthermore 43% of the subjects said they believed the ad because it said the product was effective. In contrast, only 9 percent expressed the general skepticism reported above, while 33 percent named a specific flaw in the ad. Thus close to half of adolescents interviewed believe ads, basing their belief on the results in the ads, which is consistent with other evidence that adolescents focus on results rather than procedures (Tschirgi, 1980; Linn, 1978). This finding is consistent with the notion that reasoners accept the message in the advertising context because too much effort is required to refute it. Adolescents appear to give up on trying to find the possible misleading aspects of ads, possibly because they consider the task too difficult.

To test the strength of this acceptance, Linn *et al.* (1982) pointed out possible procedural flaws in the ads. When presented with this information, an average of 86 percent of adolescents agreed that the procedures used by the advertisers could be unfair or misleading. Thus, adolescents recognize misleading procedures when probed, but they do not mention them spontaneously when asked whether they believe a product claim.

After the procedural flaws had been pointed out, Linn *et al.* (1982) asked whether the participants believed the ads in light of these potential problems. A surprisingly high percentage (41%) said they still believed the ads and an average of 37 percent said they would buy the advertised product, in spite of these potential flaws in the procedures used to test the product (Figure 3).

Adolescents, when reasoning about advertisements seem to respond to the elements of the reasoning context by accepting the messages of advertisers. Adolescents' extreme skepticism of advertisers (e.g., "advertisers always lie and cheat"), may accompany suspension of critical thought due to the difficulty of detecting lies. Adolescents seem to expect advertisers to be devious, but not to expect that they can recog-

How often do you think advertisers lie or cheat?

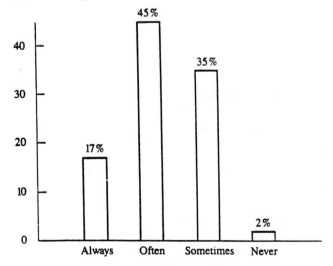

Percentage of 7th and 8th graders responding in each category

FIGURE 2 Skepticism of advertisers.

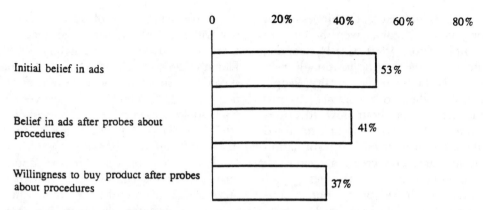

FIGURE 3   Percentage of adolescents who believe the results of tests reported in ads.

nize this deviousness. Thus, the context of adolescent reasoning about advertisements includes extreme skepticism which may interfere with logical analysis of the advertisers' message.

Adolescents may fail to act on their criticism of ads because they lack an alterative to advertising as a source of brand information, or because they have no information to *contradict* that presented in the ad. Ads may fill an "information void" for adolescents who lack experience with many brands. Adolescents appear to have the ability to criticize ads, but, when viewing an ad, they tend to accept it These findings suggest the importance of the reasoning context when interpreting reasoning performance.

Linn *et al.* (1982) contrasted the scientific context with the advertising context by asking adolescents to design experiments about Bending Rods and about Shampoo effectiveness. They used the standard procedure for Bending Rods based on Inhelder and Piaget

(1958) and a similar procedure for Shampoo reported in Linn *et al.* (1982).

Two main results emerged. First, there was little relationship between performance on Shampoo and performance on Bending Rods, suggesting the influence of reasoning context. Second, the tests designed for Shampoo reflected a lack of rigor in three ways: (a) participants did not use all the opportunities to test the shampoo, (b) although they were instructed to design tests relevant to their own hair characteristics, only one third of the tests designed by participants were unconfounded and relevant; (c) although participants were able to choose as many subjects for their tests as they wished without penalty, most indicated they would use fewer than 25 subjects per test (See Figure 4).

These results suggest that adolescents do not fully comprehend the value of repeated experimentation. In general, they do not take advantage of the oppor-

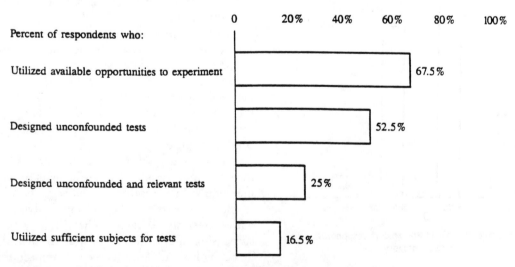

FIGURE 4   Quality of experiments designed by 7th and 8th graders to test shampoo.

tunity to design many tests or use large numbers of subjects. Tversky and Kahneman (1974) report similar results for adults.

These results also suggest that adolescents when confronted with an advertisement, have difficulty designing tests relevant to their own interests. Consistent with Linn (1977) many choose to design tests that make a big difference in the outcome. Consistent with Tschirgi (1980) some prefer to replicate the positive outcome reported in an advertisement. Adolescents seem to lose track of the purpose of their tests, choosing to make sure the test shows a big difference or to test the advertiser's claim rather than gathering information relevant to their own decision (Linn, Delucchi, & de Benedictis, 1982).

The reasoning context seems to influence reasoning performance. Adolescents' skepticism seems to be so extreme that they fail even to consider information they could refute. Adolescents' concepts of evidence, when reasoning about advertisements, differ substantially from those described for formal reasoning. In general, adolescents appear to make decisions based on limited information and to seek only a limited amount of information when given the opportunity to gather evidence for a decision. Adolescents' reasoning about advertisements appears expedient rather than thoughtful consistent with Simon's notion of "satificing" (e.g., Simon, 1969) and may result in acceptance of misleading claims. Such expediency may stem from the belief that advertisers are too devious to understand.

INTERPRETING RESEARCH RESULTS USING MODELS OF REASONING PERFORMANCE

How do the four models of reasoning deal with the content and context effects described above? Since research is generally governed by a particular model, results from studies reflecting one model may not be interpretable from another perspective. A useful educational model, however, should shed light on findings which are educationally relevant, such as those described above.

As noted above, the Piagetian model pays limited attention to content and context effects. Piagetian theory focuses on strategy acquisition. Acquisition is insufficient to explain the inconsistencies in performance on tasks such as Shampoo and Bending Rods which require the same strategy. Given that most reasoners appear to use the formal reasoning strategies on some problems, one could argue that the strategies are acquired but not used in all situations (e.g., Linn, Clement, & Pulos, in press; Flavell & Wohlwill,

1969). In contrast, Wason (in press) has argued that the strategies cannot be separated from content and treated as separate entities, as Piaget has hypothesized. Suppose that the formal strategies are acquired but not used in all situations, then what explains performance?

As Siegel (in press) has argued, advances in reasoning, once the logical strategies of formal reasoning have been acquired, cannot result from enhanced logic. Formal operations is the zenith of logical stages. The strategies characterizing formal reasoning also characterize the reasoning of scientists. The formal reasoning stage is as thoroughly logical as a stage can be. Thus, researchers must focus on other factors to explain the performance of reasoners who have achieved formal reasoning.

Turning to the mental abilities model, it is clear that this model, before the influence of information processing approaches, says more about who reasons at a given level than about how individuals reason. The mental abilities model does emphasize subject matter knowledge in crystallized ability tests. Whereas analysis of the aptitude characteristics of reasoners displaying particular types of reasoning could prove useful, thus far payoff has been limited (e.g., Cloutier & Goldsmith, 1976; Linn, Pulos & Gans, 1981; Linn & Swiney, 1981). As Hill (this volume) notes, this has also been a problem in social psychological investigations. Ford (1982) in an exhaustive investigation of social competence illustrates the shortcomings of the mental ability model. There appears to be a level of analysis problem in that the precision of the aptitude measures is insufficient to differentiate among responses on tasks such as controlling variables or social competence. In addition, this approach makes it difficult to identify precise explanations for observed relationships. A high correlation indicates that two measures require the same process but does not clearly indicate what that process is. Thus, Linn and Kyllonen (1981) identified an aspect of cognitive style which they called familiar field, and showed that it contributed variance to measures of scientific reasoning such as predicting displaced volume (Linn & Pulos, 1983), but this information was not sufficient to clarify what familiar field actually measured.

In contrast, the information processing approach reflected in the work of Sternberg (1977, 1981), Snow and his coworkers (e.g., Kyllonen, Lohman & Snow, 1982), and Keating (this volume) offers promise for understanding the processes involved in performance on mental ability tests. This direction offers possibilities for understanding the nature of intelligence. In particular, flexible switching from one distinct solution procedure to another in solving a series of mental ability items appears to characterize performance (e.g., Kyllonen, et al., 1982). These findings tell us what processes underlie performance on mental test items and can be combined with research on broader facets of performance (such as subject matter knowledge), to enhance our understanding of the development of reasoning.

In contrast to the Piagetian model and the mental ability model, the cognitive science model focuses specifically on subject matter knowledge, how it is represented and how it is retrieved. Researchers using the cognitive science model, by emphasizing subject matter knowledge, have gained insight into performance on the selection task. As Griggs and Cox (1982) and D'Andrade (1982) illustrate, examination of how subject matter knowledge about the selection task is represented and recalled, reveals why some versions are more difficult than others. Research on predicting displaced volume also suggests the usefulness of the cognitive science approach of focusing on subject matter knowledge. This approach provides methodology for researchers to state precise hypotheses about reasoning (using models) and to examine these hypotheses.

The cognitive science model focuses on content and offers approaches for understanding how subject matter knowledge representation influences reasoning. The models employed by cognitive scientists have tended to represent knowledge at a given point in time, rather than to represent how knowledge changes. Researchers have contrasted skilled and novice performance more than they have modeled change from novice to skilled performance. This approach depends dramatically on how knowledge is represented. Advances in methods for modeling knowledge are helping us understand how content or subject matter knowledge influences reasoning.

Two types of findings in the research studies described above suggest ways that models from philosophy of science might be incorporated into models from cognitive science. One finding concerns the role of context in reasoning performance, for example the role of context in reasoning about advertising. Another finding concerns persistence and change in ideas. As research on predicting displaced volume illustrates, reasoners persist with ideas in spite of contradiction and, when they do change, may change from one conception like the weight rule to a totally different conception, like the volume rule.

Philosophers of science have focused on the role of societal context in reasoning. The societal context profoundly influences the development and acceptance of scientific ideas. Consider ideas about motion that emerged during the Renaissance. At this time, Aristotle's ideas were challenged by Galileo. This challenge reached the very core of current societal values. Aristotle believed that everything moved to its specific fulfillment. (Note, however, that Aristotle did *not* impute will to objects, only a destiny; Artistotle's view of causality was largely teleological.) Objects, according to Aristotle, are simultaneously pushed and pulled to their destinations. In contrast, Galileo expressed what has been called a "clockwork" notion, suggesting that once the world was set in motion, it operated according to its own autonomous laws. Galileo set out to uncover the laws governing movements. Galileo's notion that the universe operated according to autonomous laws was considered heretical within the societal context. Galileo's ideas about motion were challenged largely because of their relationship to current societal values.

Philosophers of science such as Kuhn (1972), Hanson (1961) and Lakatos (1972) have proposed models to explain how societal context influences the collective reasoning of scientists. These models might also help researchers understand how societal context influences the reasoning of individuals.

Both persistence with erroneous ideas and sudden change to new ideas characterize the history of science and therefore interest philosophers of science. Philosopher of science Lakatos (1972) offers some especially thought provoking ideas relevant to these issues.

Lakatos refers to ideas about a particular phenomenon or concept as a research program. A research program is a series of theories. Two characteristics of research programs as described by Lakatos seem useful. One is the distinction between the "protective belt" of ideas and the "hard core" of ideas. The other is the distinction between a "progressing" and a "degenerating" research program. The hard core consists of unquestioned assumptions which are not challengeable by data. The protective belt is differentiated from the hard core in that it consists of ideas which change as often as necessary, responding to data. A scientific research program is a series of theories with the same hard core of ideas and differing protective belts. A *progressing* research program is a series of theories that predicts novel facts. A *degenerating* research program does not predict new facts.

Persistence is clearly useful for advancing knowledge. If reasoners changed all their ideas after each contradiction, they would gain little insight into a problem. Persistence, even with wrong ideas, leads to refinements of ideas which ultimately prove useful. Lakatos' distinction between the "hard core" of ideas and the "protective belt" of ideas clarifies how persistence fosters understanding. Scientists, when confronted with data that contradict their viewpoint, change the protective belt so that the hard core can remain unchanged. Thus, Lakatos differentiates the ideas in the hard core, which are immune to data, from ideas in the protective belt, which are responsive to data.

In the research on predicting displaced volume, the subject who mentioned the magic water could be seen as protecting a hard core idea. For this subject, the weight rule appeared to be a hard core idea. This subject, when confronted with a contradiction to the rule, sought to alter the protective belt to protect the hard core. In this case protective belt ideas concerning the nature of water, and the nature of experimenters, were altered to protect the idea about how weight influences displacement.

An example of a hard core idea in the history of science would be Kepler's idea that the orbit of Mars must be circular. Kepler accepted Aristotle's pronouncement that planets exhibit "perfect motion" which was circular motion. Kepler developed a procedure called the method of area for verifying an orbit. Using this method, Kepler found that his calculations did not conform to observations of the position of Mars. Rather than question the shape of the orbit of Mars, since that was part of his hard core of ideas, Kepler came to doubt his method of area. In this example, the hard core of ideas influenced how new information was incorporated into a conceptualization. Further, Kepler refined his method of area because it made erroneous predictions. By pursuing his hard core idea of perfect motion, Kepler refined his notions about measuring planetary motion. Thus pursuing a hard core idea may advance knowledge even though that hard core idea is later changed because the research program is degenerating.

Creative and tenacious protection of the hard core results in development of more powerful ideas. If reasoners can be perceived as having research programs, the development of their reasoning can be evaluated by examining the development of their research programs. One can assess how reasoners protect their hard core. One can document the tenacity with which the hard core is defended and the creativity with which the hard core is protected. Such protection occurs, it appears, when reasoners confronted with anomalies—experimental results incompatible with their theories—creatively alter the protective belt such that the anomaly becomes positive evidence for the hard core.

Eventually even creative persistence in defending the hard core fails to predict novel facts. Lakatos characterizes change in the hard core as cataclysmic change. Degenerating research programs have inadequate hard cores and fail to predict novel facts. They are completely replaced by new research programs, which are new series of theories attached to new hard cores. Similarly, reasoners in the predicting displaced volume research, when they do change their views, often change from a weight rule to a volume rule, dropping weight altogether. Thus, Lakatos provides a perspective on both persistence and change in scientific ideas which is congruent with research on persistence and change in ideas held by adolescents.

CONCLUSIONS

Content and context effects influence reasoning in dramatic ways. Their influence needs to be represented in models of reasoning performance. Process knowledge as described by Inhelder and Piaget (1958) may be necessary for sophisticated reasoning but not sufficient. Models from information processing, cognitive science, and philosophy of science offer promising perspectives on reasoning performance.

Although the process influences on reasoning described by Piaget cannot be ignored, they may need to be reconceptualized to include a role for content and context influences. One view is that many or most adolescents have acquired the process knowledge inherent in formal reasoning. Another view is that the process knowledge of formal reasoning does not exist independent of content; process knowledge therefore is a type of subject matter knowledge associated with a particular problem. Using either perspective, researchers might incorporate process knowledge into a knowledge representation for a particular problem.

Perhaps the most pressing problem in research on reasoning concerns how it changes. As the myriad of unsuccessful training studies attest (e.g., Linn, 1980), teaching formal reasoning as a generalized process is difficult. In addition, presenting contradictions as was done in the predicting displaced volume training does not have complete success. Reasoners' ideas do persist. Following Lakatos, we may surmise that reasoners alter their protective belts as in the "magic water" example, while protecting their hard core ideas. We need a deeper understanding of the process of change which philosophy of science, with its concern with persistence, may bring us.

One reason that ideas persist is that they are alternative conceptions of phenomena rather than random ideas. Reasoners such as mature scientists may still hold "alternative conceptualizations" for certain phenomena. Di Sessa (1981), for example, provides evidence that sophisticated scientists often apply what he calls "naive physics" to everyday non-textbook problems. Physicists often have difficulty explaining the forces on a yo-yo, when the yo-yo is laid on the table and the string is pulled horizontally. Similarly, physicists and other mature reasoners frequently display "naive physics" when asked to indicate what happens to the motor of a vacuum cleaner when its air intake valve is blocked. Thus, many reasoners may have alternative conceptualizations of problems from physics and other problems.

From Lakatos' perspective, these alternative conceptions form a persistent hard core. Efforts to teach individuals to change to a new hard core will not succeed immediately. Reasoners will protect their hard core. One implication of Lakatos' view is that educators could benefit from recognizing that reasoners may need many contradictions to their ideas before they change their hard core. Further, such lengthy processes may lead to better understood and more generalizable ideas in the long run. Thus, rather than becoming frustrated when learners fail to accept new ideas, educators could examine how learners adjust to new ideas.

If we view learners as having hard core ideas, it becomes apparent that educators would benefit from knowing alternative conceptions likely to be hard core ideas in their particular subject matter area. For example, curriculum people could design effective contradictions to these conceptions for teachers and explain to teachers that learners will be slow to give up their conceptions. Curricula might even reassure teachers by explaining that the slow process of changing conceptions, although seemingly frustrating to the instructor has advantages for the learner and ultimately, for the instructor. Thus, one direction for new research is to identify alternative conceptions in important subject matter areas, areas such as smoking, alcoholism, or obesity seem especially timely, and to characterize how reasoners will respond to these contradictions.

Thus content, context, and process influences on reasoning need to be incorporated into models of adolescent reasoning performance. Both models from cognitive science and models from philosophy of science offer promise. Simon (1980) referred to cognitive science as a revolution in thinking about reasoning performance. Combining recent advances in philosophy of science with models from cognitive science promises to enhance the revolutionary forces.

Reference Notes

1. Linn, M. C. & Petersen, A. C. *The emergence of gender differences in spatial ability: A metaanalysis.* Paper presented at the AERA Special Interest Group on Research on Women in Education, Mid-Year Conference, November, 1982.

2. Heller, J. I. & Reif, F. *Cognitive mechanisms: Facilitating human problem solving in physics: Empirical validation of a prescriptive model.* Paper presented at the annual meeting of the American Educational Research Association, New York, March, 1982.

3. D'Andrade, R. *Reason versus logic.* Talk for Symposium on the Ecology of Cognition: Biological, Cultural, and Historical Perspectives, Greensboro, North Carolina, April, 1982.

References

Baltes, P. B. Longitudinal and cross-sectional sequences in study of age and generation effects. *Human Development, 1968, 11,* 145–171.

Carey, S. & Block, N. *NSE-NIE project,* Massachusetts Institute of Technology, 1982.

Cattell, R. B. *Abilities: Their structure, growth, and action.* Boston: Houghton Mifflin, 1971.

Cloutier, R., & Goldschmid, M. Individual differences in the development of formal reasoning. *Child Development, 1976, 47,* 1097–1102.

Cox, J. R., & Griggs, R. A. The effects of experience on performance in Wason's selection task. *Mem. Cog.,* in press.

Cronbach, L. J., & Snow, R. E. *Aptitude Treatment Interactions.* New York: Irvington, 1977.

Damon, W., & Hart, D. The development of self-understanding from infancy through adolescence. *Child Development, 1982, 53,* 841–864.

Elkind, D. Cognitive development in adolescence. In J. F. Adams (Ed.), *Understanding adolescence.* Boston: Allyn & Bacon, 1968.

Elkind, D. Egocentrism in adolescence. *Child Development, 1967, 38,* 1025–1034.

Flavell, J. H., & Wohlwill, J. F. Formal and functional aspects of cognitive development. In D. Elkind & J. Flavell (Eds.),

Studies in Cognitive Development: Essays in Honor of Jean Piaget. New York: Oxford University Press, 1969.

Ford, M. E. Social cognition and social competence in adolescence. *Developmental Psychology,* 1982,18, 323–340.

Griggs, R. A. The role of problem content in the selection task and THOG problem. In J. St. B. T. Evans (Ed.), *Thinking and Reasoning: Psychological Approaches. London.* Routledge & Kegan Paul, in press.

Griggs, R. A., & Cox, J. R. The elusive thematic-materials effect in Wason's selection task. *British Journal of Psychology,* 1982, 73, 407–420.

Hanson, N. R. *Patterns of Discovery. An Inquiry Into the Conceptual Foundations of Science.* Cambridge, England: University Press, 1961.

Inhelder, B., & Piaget, J. *The Growth of Logical Thinking from Childhood to Adolescence.* New York: Basic Books, 1958.

Johnson-Laird, P. N., Legrenzi, P., & Legrenzi, M. Reasoning and a sense of reality. *British Journal of Psychology,* 1972, 63, 395–400.

Kuhn, T. S. *The Structure of Scientific Revolutions,* (2nd Edition, enlarged). Chicago: University of Chicago Press, 1972.

Kyllonen, P. C., Lohman, P. F., & Snow, R. E. *Effects of aptitudes, strategy training and task facets on spatial task performance,* School of Education, Stanford University, 1982.

Kyllonen, P. C., Woltz, D. J., & Lohman, D. F. *Models of strategy and strategy-shifting in spatial visualization performance.* Tech. Report 17, Aptitude Research Project, School of Education, Stanford University, 1982.

Lakatos, I. Falsification and the methodology of scientific research programmes. In I. Lakatos & A. Musgrave (Eds.), *Criticism and the Growth of Knowledge.* Cambridge, England: Cambridge University Press, 1972.

Larkin, J., McDermott, J., Simon, D. P., & Simon, H. A. Expert and novice performance in solving physics problems. *Science,* 1980, 208, 1335–1342.

Lewis, C. How adolescents approach decisions: Changes over grades seven to twelve and policy implications. *Child Development,* 1981, 52, 538–544.

Linn, M. C. Cognitive style, training, and formal thought. *Child Development,* 1978, 49, 874–877.

Linn, M. C. Scientific reasoning: Influences on task performance and response categorization. *Science Education,* 1977, 61, 357–369.

Linn, M. C. Teaching children to control variables; Some investigations using free choice experiences. In S. Modgil and C. Modgil (Eds.), *Toward a theory of psychological development within the Piagetian framework,* London: National Foundation for Educational Research, 1980.

Linn, M. C., Clement, C., & Pulos, S. M. Is it formal if it's not physics? The influence of laboratory and naturalistic content on formal reasoning. *Journal of Research in Science Teaching,* in press.

Linn, M. C., de Benedictis, T., & Delucchi, K. Adolescent reasoning about advertisements: Preliminary investigations. *Child Development,* 1982, 53, 1599–1613.

Linn, M. C., Delucchi, K., & de Benedictis, T. *Adolescent reasoning about advertisements: Relevance of product claims.* Adolescent Reasoning Project Report, ARP-A-8, 1982. Lawrence Hall of Science, Berkeley, CA.

Linn, M. C., & Kyllonen, P. The field dependence-independence construct: Some one, or none. *Journal of Educational Psychology,* 1981, 73, 261–273.

Linn, M. C., & Pulos, S. Male-female differences in predicting displaced volume: Strategy usage, aptitude relationships and experience influences. *Journal of Educational Psychology,* 1983, 75, 86–96.

Linn, M. C., Pulos, S., & Gans, A. Correlates of formal reasoning: Content and problem effects. *Journal of Research in Science Teaching,* 1981, 18, 435–447.

Linn, M. C., & Siegel, H. Post-formal reasoning: A progressing research program. In M. Commons (Ed.), *Models of Post Formal Reasoning,* Praeger Publishers, in press.

Linn, M. C. & Swiney, J. Individual differences in formal thought: Role of expectations and aptitudes. *Journal of Educational Psychology,* 1981, 73, 274–286.

Manktelow, K. I., and Evans, J.St.B.T. Facilitation of reasoning by realism: Effect or non-effect? *British Journal of Psychology,* 1979, 70, 477–88.

McCloskey, M., Carramazza, A., & Green, B. Curvilinear motion in the absence of external forces: Naive beliefs about the motion of objects. *Science,* 1980, 210, 1139–1141.

Mishler. E. G. Meaning in context: Is there any other kind? *Harvard Educational Review,* 1979, 49 (1), 1–19.

Moschis, G. P., & Churchill, G. A. An analysis of the adolescent consumer. *Journal of Marketing,* 1979, 43, 40–48.

Pulos, S., de Benedictis, T., Linn, M. C., Sullivan, P., & Clement, C. Predicting displaced volume: A training study. *Journal of Early Adolescents,* 1982, 2, 61–74.

Shor, I. *Critical Teaching and Everyday Life.* Boston, MA: South End Press, 1980. Shugan, S. M. The cost of thinking. *Journal of Consumer Research,* 1980, 7, 99–111.

Siegel, H. On the parallel between Piagetian cognitive development and the history of Science. *Philosophy of the Society Sciences,* 1982, in press.

Simon, H. A. The behavioral and social sciences. *Science,* 1980, 209, 72–78.

Simon, H. A. *The Sciences of the Artificial.* Cambridge, MA: M.I.T. Press, 1969.

Snow, R. E., Federico, P. A., & Montague, W. (Eds.). *Aptitude, learning and instruction: Cognitive process analysis (Vol.* 1). Hillsdale, N.J.: Erlbaum, 1980.

Sternberg, R. J. Intelligence and nonentrenchment. *Journal of Educational Psychology,* 1981, 73, 1–16.

Sternberg, R. J. *Intelligence, information processing, and analogical reasoning: The componential analysis of human abilities.* Hillsdale, N.J.: Lawrence Erlbaum Associates, 1977.

Tschirgi, J. E. Sensible reasoning; A hypothesis about hypotheses. *Child Development,* 1980, 51, 1–10,

Tversky, A., & Kahneman, D. Judgment under uncertainty: Heuristics and biases. *Science,* 1974, *185,* 1124–1131.

Viennot, L. Spontaneous reasoning in elementary dynamics. *European Journal of Science Education,* 1979, *1,* 205–221.

Wason, P. C. Realism and rationality in the selection task. In J. St. B.T. Evans (Ed.). *Thinking and reasoning.* London: Routledge and Kegan Paul, in press.

Wason, P. C., & Johnson-Laird, P. N. *Psychology of Reasoning: Structure and Content,* Cambridge, MA: Harvard University Press, 1972.

Wright, P. Consumer choice strategies: Simplifying vs. optimizing. *Journal of Marketing Research,* 1975, *12,* 60–68.

32

Prosocial Development in Adolescence: A Longitudinal Study

NANCY EISENBERG, PAUL A. MILLER, RITA SHELL, SANDRA MCNALLEY, AND CINDY SHEA

An important aspect of developing morality is the development of prosocial behaviors, that is behaviors that benefit others. Nancy Eisenberg and colleagues have studied the development of prosocial moral reasoning during early to mid-adolescence. In the study reported here, they examine the relationship between prosocial reasoning, empathy, perspective taking, and prosocial behavior over the teen years, and by so doing help to clarify how children become mature, responsible, moral beings.

Change in prosocial moral reasoning over an 11-year period, gender differences in prosocial reasoning in adolescence, and the interrelations of moral reasoning, prosocial behavior, and empathy-related emotional responses were examined with longitudinal data and data from adolescents interviewed for the first time. Hedonistic reasoning declined in use until adolescence and then increased somewhat (primarily for boys). Needs-oriented reasoning, direct reciprocity reasoning, and approval and stereotypic reasoning increased until mid-childhood or early adolescence and then declined. Several modes of higher level reasoning emerged in late childhood or adolescence. Girls' overall reasoning was higher than boys'. Consistent with expectations, there was some evidence of high level prosocial reasoning being associated with prosocial behavior and empathy and of a relation between sympathy or empathy and prosocial behavior.

Reprinted with permission from the authors and *Developmental Psychology, 27,* 1991, 849–857. Copyright 1991 by the American Psychological Association.

This research was supported by National Science Foundation Grant BNS8807784 and National Institute of Child Health and Development Career Development Award K04 HDO0717 to Nancy Eisenberg. We thank the mothers and students in our longitudinal samples and the principals, students, and teachers at Connolly Junior High School and Tempe High School for their participation.

The roles of cognition and affect in morality have been a topic of discussion for centuries (e.g., Hume, 1777/1966; Kant, 1797/1964). In recent years, psychologists such as Kohlberg (1981) have argued that cognition is the foundation of morality, whereas others such as Batson (1990) or Hoffman (1987) have emphasized the role of sympathy and empathy in moral behavior, particularly in altruism. In recent research and writings, the role of each has been acknowledged (e.g., Hoffman, 1987; Underwood & Moore, 1982).

The cognitive process most closely linked with morality, including prosocial behavior, is moral reasoning. Cognitive developmentalists have argued that developmental advances in the sociocognitive skill of perspective taking underlie age-related changes in moral reasoning and that the quality of individuals' thinking about moral issues affects the maturity of their moral functioning. In support of this view, higher level moral reasoning or self-attributions have been associated with frequency of prosocial behavior and with higher quality (e.g., more altruistic) behavior (Bar-Tal, 1982; Eisenberg, 1986; Underwood & Moore, 1982).

Although most researchers studying moral judgment have focused on reasoning about moral dilemmas in which rules, laws, authorities' dictates, and formal obligations are central (Kohlberg, 1981; Rest, 1983), some investigators have studied issues related to positive morality (e.g., Damon, 1977; Eisenberg, 1986; Gilligan & Attanucci, 1988). One type of reasoning that investigators have explored is prosocial moral reasoning, that is, reasoning about moral dilemmas in which one person's needs or desires conflict with those of another (or others) in a context in which the role of prohibitions, authorities' dictates, and formal obligations is minimal.

In cross-sectional research on the prosocial moral reasoning of children and adolescents in industrialized cultures, age-related changes in prosocial moral judgment have been delineated. These changes are, in general, consistent with Kohlberg's (1969, 1981) view that the capability for complex perspective taking and for understanding abstract concepts is associated with advances in moral reasoning. However, levels of prosocial moral reasoning are not viewed as hierarchical, integrated structures (with the result that individuals' reasoning is primarily at one stage) or as being invariant in sequence and universal (Eisenberg, 1986). Specifically, young children tend to use primarily hedonistic reasoning or needs-oriented (primitive empathic) reasoning. In elementary school, children's reasoning begins to reflect concern with approval and enhancing interpersonal relationships as well as the desire to behave in stereotypically good

ways, although such reasoning also appears to decrease in use from the elementary to high school years. Contrary to initial expectations, direct reciprocity reasoning, which reflects an orientation to self-gain, has been found to increase in the elementary school years, perhaps because of the cognitive sophistication involved in thinking about reciprocity over time. In late elementary school and beyond, children begin to express reasoning reflecting abstract principles, internalized affective reactions (e.g., guilt or positive affect about the consequences of one's behavior for others or living up to internalized principles), and self-reflective sympathy and perspective taking. Nonetheless, even in adolescence people frequently verbalize other, less mature modes of reasoning, although hedonistic reasoning decreases with age (Eisenberg-Berg, 1979a; see Eisenberg, 1986).

In the limited longitudinal research on prosocial reasoning, change in moral reasoning has been examined from age 4–5 years to 11–12 years (Eisenberg, Lennon, & Roth, 1983; Eisenberg et al., 1987). A longitudinal study of prosocial moral reasoning was initiated because intraindividual change can be examined only with longitudinal data and because longitudinal procedures overcome the confound between developmental change and cohort inherent in cross-sectional research. In this research, we have for the most part replicated the aforementioned findings in the cross-sectional research for preschool and elementary school children. However, consistent with Gilligan's (Gilligan & Attanucci, 1988) argument that females use more care-oriented reasoning than do males, we found that the initial increase in self-reflective other-oriented modes of reasoning in late elementary school was primarily for girls. Because no longitudinal study has included participants older than age 12, the declines in some modes of reasoning (e.g., stereotypic, approval oriented) noted during adolescence in cross-sectional research have not been replicated with a longitudinal design; nor has the developmental course of direct reciprocity reasoning (primitive other-oriented reasoning, which increases during elementary school) or needs-oriented reasoning (which has been found to increase into the mid-elementary school years and then to level off in usage) been adequately delineated. Furthermore, some of the higher level modes of reasoning that seem to emerge in adolescence have not been examined longitudinally, even though sociocognitive changes during this age period are substantial (Colby, Kohlberg, Gibbs, & Lieberman, 1983; Hoffman, 1987; Selman, 1980).

Thus, the primary purpose of this study was to examine change in prosocial moral reasoning during early and midadolescence (i.e., at ages 13–14 and 15–

16). The subjects in this study have been followed since age 4–5 years for 11 years. Because of the changes in early and midadolescence in logical reasoning, perspective-taking skills (Selman, 1980), and Kohlbergian moral reasoning (Colby et al., 1983), it seemed reasonable to expect the development of more abstract and morally sophisticated modes of reasoning during this period of development. Moreover, changes in the complexity of the child's social environment as he or she moves into adolescence might be expected to stimulate perspective taking and, consequently, moral reasoning (see Kohlberg, 1981). In addition, given the debate over the possible existence of a gender difference in moral reasoning in adolescence and adulthood (Gilligan & Attanucci, 1988; Walker, 1984), we were also interested in determining whether the sex difference in the emergence of other-oriented modes of reasoning found at age 11–12 persisted into adolescence.

The second purpose of this study was to examine the relations among prosocial moral reasoning, prosocial behavior, and empathy-related emotional reactions in adolescence. Few investigators have examined prosocial reasoning or empathy in adolescence, and even studies of adolescents' prosocial behavior are relatively few in number (Eisenberg, 1990). Indeed, the prosocial side of morality in adolescence has been neglected by researchers.

Theorists such as Kohlberg (1981) and Rest (1983) have argued that moral reasoning influences individuals' moral decisions and behavior. Consistent with this view, moral reasoning, including prosocial moral judgment, does seem to be correlated with the performance of prosocial behaviors, although the empirical associations generally are modest (Eisenberg, 1986; Underwood & Moore, 1982). Specifically, elementary school children's prosocial behavior generally has been positively related to needs-oriented reasoning and negatively related to hedonistic reasoning (Eisenberg, 1986; Eisenberg et al., 1987). In one of the only studies on this topic involving adolescents, Eisenberg-Berg (1979b) found that the level of moral judgment was positively correlated with helping behavior, but only for males. In this study, we sought to further examine the relation of prosocial moral reasoning to prosocial behavior in early and midadolescence. Investigators have hypothesized that the relation between reasoning and behavior increases with age because higher level reasoning is associated with the "progressive stripping away of bases for justifying behavior that are extrinsic to principle" (Rholes & Bailey, 1983, p. 104), resulting in a stronger motive to maintain consistency between attitudes and behaviors at higher stages of development. Thus, we hypothesized that helping behavior in

adolescence would be positively correlated with other-oriented modes of reasoning, as well as with overall level of reasoning, and negatively related to hedonistic reasoning.

The relation of empathy to prosocial moral reasoning has been studied very infrequently, although some modes of moral reasoning explicitly reflect cognitive role taking, empathy, and sympathy. Indeed, investigators have suggested that sympathy (concern for others based on the apprehension of another's state) and empathy (an emotional reaction elicited by and congruent with another's state) stimulate the development of internalized moral principles reflecting concern for others' welfare (Hoffman, 1987) and prime the use of preexisting moral cognitions reflecting concern for others (Eisenberg, 1986).

The very limited empirical data are consistent with the argument that there is an association between empathy and prosocial moral reasoning. In the last two follow-ups of our longitudinal research, we found that scores on Bryant's (1982) empathy scale were positively related to needs-oriented and higher level moral reasoning and negatively related to hedonistic reasoning. However, the associations generally were stronger at age 9–10 years than at age 11–12 years. Thus, it was unclear whether the association would continue into adolescence, although level of prosocial reasoning was associated with global empathy in one study of high school students (Eisenberg-Berg & Mussen, 1978).

In addition, in previous research on the relation of prosocial reasoning to vicarious emotional responding, only the association of empathy to moral reasoning has been examined. However, researchers have found that it is important to differentiate among various emotionally based reactions that often stem from empathy, including sympathy and personal distress (i.e., a self-oriented aversive response to another's state; Batson, 1987). Sympathy, which is viewed as stemming from perspective taking (e.g., Batson, 1987; Hoffman, 1987) and as leading to other-oriented, altruistic motivations (Batson, 1987), has been positively related to altruistic behavior (e.g., Batson, 1987, 1990). In contrast, personal distress appears to be associated with egoistic motives and behavior (Batson, 1987; Eisenberg & Fabes, 1991), particularly with the motive to alleviate one's own negative emotional state. Thus, at the most recent follow-up, we examined the relations of sympathy and personal distress, as well as perspective taking, to prosocial moral reasoning.

The positive relation between empathy and prosocial behavior has been documented more frequently than has the relation between empathy and moral reasoning (see Barnett, 1987; Eisenberg & Miller,

1987). Indeed, empathy and sympathy are viewed by many theorists as important motivators of altruism (Batson, 1990; Hoffman, 1987; Staub, 1978). Consistent with this view and with the finding of weaker relations in childhood than during adulthood (Eisenberg & Miller, 1987), in our longitudinal research empathy was associated with prosocial behavior at age 11–12 years but not 10–11 years. In other studies, there does seem to be some positive relation between empathy and prosocial behavior in adolescence (Eisenberg & Miller, 1987; Underwood & Moore, 1982); however, the research on this association in adolescence is quite limited, and no one, to our knowledge, has published research concerning the relations of sympathy and personal distress to adolescents' prosocial behavior. Thus, another goal of this study was to examine the aforementioned relations at two ages during adolescence.

Finally, in any study in which moral development is assessed with self-report data one must be concerned with the possibility that responses are contaminated by self-presentational concerns. Thus, in this study we examined the relation of social desirability to our other moral indexes.

In summary, the purposes of this study were to examine change in prosocial moral reasoning in adolescence and the interrelations among moral reasoning, prosocial behavior, and empathy-related responses at that stage of life. To do so, we conducted two longitudinal follow-ups of children studied since the age of 4–5 years, one at age 13–14 years and one at age 15–16 years, and also tested additional students at each age.

METHOD

Subjects

Three groups of middle-class children participated in this study. The primarily longitudinal cohort (C1) consisted of 16 girls and 16 boys (all White except 2) who had been interviewed five times previously, at ages 4–5, 5½–6½, 7–8, 9–10, and 11–12 (at 108, 90, 72, 48, and 24 months before the first assessment in this study); the seven testing sessions henceforth are referred to as T1 through T7. The mean ages of the children at T6 and T7 were 163 months (range = 154–171 months; approximately 13–14 years of age) and 187 months (approximately 15–16 years of age). No children have been lost since T3 (in 8 years); 1 was lost in the past 9.5 years and 5 have been lost over the 11-year period (3 boys and 2 girls; the original sample was 37 children).

The second sample (C2) consisted of 39 eighth graders from a middle-class, predominantly White

neighborhood (20 girls and 19 boys; mean age = 164 months, range = 154–176 months). These children attended a school in the suburban city in which the longitudinal subjects lived at the beginning of the study. They were interviewed for the first and only time at T6. A similar group (C3) of 34 tenth graders (17 of each sex) was interviewed for the first and only time at T7 (mean age 189 months, range = 180–199 months).

Instruments

Children's prosocial moral reasoning was assessed with the same four moral reasoning stories used in prior follow-ups (see Eisenberg et al., 1983, 1987), although a few words were changed to make the stories sound less childlike (e.g., "birthday party" was changed to "birthday celebration"). However, an additional story previously used with school-aged children and adolescents in another study (concerning going into the hospital to donate a rare type of blood at a cost to the self; Eisenberg-Berg, 1979a) was also used in these two follow-up sessions. This story was added because the costs of helping in some of the other stories appeared to be rather low for adolescents (e.g., missing a birthday celebration), whereas the costs of helping in the giving-blood story would likely be substantial for adolescents (losing time at work and school).

As at T4 and T5, subjects at T6 in C1 and C2 were also administered Bryant's (1982) 22-item Empathy scale (αs =.78 and .69) and Crandall's 47-item Social Desirability (SD) Scale for children (αs = .92 and .87, respectively; Crandall, Crandall, & Katkovsky, 1965). To assess social desirability at T7, children in C1 and C3 completed 25 items from the Marlowe-Crowne Social Desirability Scale (αs = .86 and .74, respectively; Crowne & Marlowe, 1964), which appeared to be more age-appropriate for adolescents than the Crandall et al. index. To assess capabilities related to empathy, students in C1 and C3 at T7 were also administered three subscales of Davis's Interpersonal Reactivity Scale: Sympathy (α = .83), Perspective Taking (73), and Personal Distress (.74). In addition, at both T6 and T7, children filled out a 23-item adapted version of Rushton, Chrisjohn, and Fekken's (1981) self-report Altruism scale (αs = .86 and .90 at T6 and T7, respectively). Children indicated on a 5-point scale (ranging from *never* to *very often*) how frequently they engaged in 23 behaviors such as giving money to charity or volunteer work. Finally, children at T6 and T7 were given an opportunity to assist the experimenter by filling out some additional questionnaires and returning them in a stamped, addressed envelope.

Mothers of children in C1 also filled out the modified Rushton et al. Altruism scale; however, they filled it out in regard to their child rather than themselves. Because they were given the additional option of "don't know," alphas could not be computed for these scales (due to the fact that items with this response were considered missing, resulting in few mothers with all items completed).

For all of the aforementioned questionnaires, scores for the various items were summed (after reversing their direction, if necessary). For mothers' reports of children's prosocial behavior, this sum was divided by the number of items the mothers answered. Two indexes of helping behavior were computed: whether the students returned the questionnaires and whether all parts of the questionnaires were completed.

Procedures

C1 Interviews for C1 took place in the home or at the university. In either case, mother and child were interviewed in different rooms, the mother by a woman and the child by a man (at T6) or a woman (at T7) who had not been involved in any previous follow-ups. For the children, the prosocial dilemmas were presented first in random order; they were read to the children while the children read along (responses were taped). Children repeated dilemmas to check for comprehension, and a standard sequence of questioning was followed (Eisenberg et al., 1983). The moral reasoning task was always administered first because it was considered most important and we did not want to influence the children's responses by having it follow other procedures.

Subsequent to the moral interview, the children completed the measures of empathy, social desirability, and self-reported prosocial behavior (presented in random order). The students were told that their responses were confidential. Next, after the children were paid for their participation ($5 at T6 and $10 at T7), the experimenter told the students that he or she would appreciate their filling out a few more forms at home, but that they need not do so if they did not want to. If the student agreed to take the questionnaires (all did), they were given the forms and a stamped envelope.

C2 AND C3 C2 and C3 students were individually administered the procedures at their schools. Their mothers were not present. Tapes for moral interviews of 4 C2 students were lost due to mechanical difficulties.

Scoring

PROSOCIAL REASONING STORIES Scoring of prosocial reasoning was done in two ways. First, the children's judgments were coded into the categories of reasoning outlined by Eisenberg et al. (1983, 1987; Eisenberg-Berg, 1979a). Those used by children with any frequency were as follows:

HEDONISTIC REASONING (a) *hedonistic gain to the self* (orientation to gain for oneself), (b) *direct reciprocity* (orientation to personal gain because of direct reciprocity or lack of reciprocity from the recipient of an act), and (c) *affectional relationship* (orientation to the individual's identification or relationship with another or liking for the other);

PRAGMATIC (orientation to practical concerns that are unrelated to selfish considerations);

NEEDS-ORIENTED (orientation to the physical, material, or psychological needs of the other person; e.g., "He needs blood," or "He's sad");

STEREOTYPES OF A GOOD OR BAD PERSON (orientation to stereotyped images of a good or bad person);

APPROVAL AND INTERPERSONAL ORIENTATION (orientation to others' approval and acceptance in deciding what is the correct behavior;

SELF-REFLECTIVE EMPATHIC ORIENTATION (a) sympathetic orientation (expression of sympathetic concern and caring for others), (b) role taking (the individual explicitly takes the perspective of the other or has the story protagonist do so), (c) internalized positive affect related to consequences (orientation to internal positive affect as a result of a particular course of action because of the consequences of one's act for the other person), and (d) internalized negative affect related to consequences (the same as [c] but for negative affect);

INTERNALIZED AFFECT BECAUSE OF LOSS OF SELF-RESPECT AND NOT LIVING UP TO ONE'S VALUE (a) positive (orientation to feeling good, often about oneself, as a consequence of living up to internalized values), (b) negative (concern with feeling bad as a consequence of not living up to internalized values);

INTERNALIZED LAW, NORM, AND VALUE ORIENTATION (orientation to an internalized responsibility, duty, or need to uphold the laws and accepted norms or values);

OTHER ABSTRACT OR INTERNALIZED TYPES OF REASONING (a) generalized reciprocity (orientation to indirect reciprocity in a society, that is, exchange that is not one-to-one but eventually benefits all or a larger group), (b) *concern with the condition of society* (orientation to improving the society or community as a whole), (c) *concern with individual rights and justice* (orientation to protecting individual rights and preventing injustices that violate another's rights), and (d) *equality of people* (orientation to the principle of the equal value of all people).

Children were assigned scores indicating the frequency with which they used each of the various types of reasoning when discussing both the pros and cons of helping the needy other in the story dilemma (1 = no use of category; 2 = vague, questionable use; 3 = clear use of a mode of reasoning; and 4 = a major type of reasoning used). Next, the scores for each category were summed across the stories. At each time period, two coders scored either half or all the data; interrater reliabilities for T1, T2, T3, T4, and T5 have been presented in previous articles (Eisenberg et al., 1983, 1987; Eisenberg-Berg & Roth, 1980). For all time periods, the primary coder was the same person, whereas five persons have served as reliability coders over the 7 time periods. To prevent bias in scoring, the coders were blind to the identity of the children. The primary coder was also blind to any information regarding the subjects' scores on other measures (e.g., prosocial behavior and empathy); this was usually the case for the reliability coder. Interrater reliabilities (Pearson product-moment correlations) computed for each reasoning category at T6 and T7 (using data for all subjects at T6 and for half the subjects at T7) ranged from .81 (for positive affect-self at T6) to 1.00, with most being above .85. (These reliabilities are for four stories; those for five stories were very similar.)

As was just noted, the primary coder for the moral reasoning protocols was the same person who scored the data at all previous follow-ups. This procedure was used to prevent differences across different coders at different times being interpreted as age-related changes in reasoning. To determine if there was any change in the primary coder's scoring over the years (and to prevent the primary coder from knowing the age of subjects being coded), five protocols from each of the previous follow-ups were mixed together with the various protocols from T6 and T7 and were rescored by the primary coder to determine if there was any change in her scoring over the years (the coder was blind to which protocol was from which follow-up). Scoring of the data from earlier sessions was highly similar to the original scores for the same data (agreement on codings within one point

was 75% or higher on all categories; correlations were .89 and higher).

The categories of reasoning are viewed as representing components of developmental levels of prosocial moral reasoning; these levels were derived from the results of cross-sectional research (Eisenberg-Berg, 1979a; see Eisenberg, 1986). Briefly, the levels are as follows: Level 1, hedonistic, self-focused orientation; Level 2, needs of others orientation; Level 3, approval and interpersonal orientation and stereotyped orientation; Level 4, self-reflective, empathic orientation; and Level 5, strongly internalized orientation. On the basis of these levels, a score representing level of moral judgment was computed for each child. The level score was constructed in a manner similar to that used to score Kohlbergian reasoning; that is, subjects were assigned composite scores by weighing the proportion of the child's reasoning at each level (see Eisenberg et al., 1983, for more detail). Because it is debatable whether Level 5 is more moral than Level 4 and because Levels 4 and 5 were weighted equally in previous follow-ups, they were weighted equally in the analyses presented in this article (although the data changed little if Level 5 was weighted higher).

RESULTS

Age Changes in Moral Judgment

To examine age changes in moral reasoning for C1 over the 11 years, multivariate analyses of variance (MANOVAs) and univariate trend analyses of variance (ANOVAs) were computed with one within-subjects factor (time, adjusted for unequal time gaps when appropriate) and one between-subjects factor (sex). On the basis of prior research and theoretical formulations in which types of reasoning involving more complex perspective taking and abstract concepts are expected to increase with age (Eisenberg, 1986; Kohlberg, 1981), we expected the self-reflective and internalized-abstract modes of reasoning to increase with age into adolescence. In contrast, direct reciprocity, approval, and stereotypic modes of reasoning, which increased in childhood, were expected to decrease in usage in adolescence, whereas levels of needs-oriented and hedonistic reasoning were not expected to change much in adolescence (although the latter modes of reasoning do exhibit dramatic change in childhood).

Different MANOVAs had to be computed for groups of reasoning that emerged at different ages because of the linear dependencies in the data that occur if a particular mode of reasoning is not used at more than one time period (and because quadratic trends could occur if a type of reasoning was not used much in childhood and then emerged in adolescence). Only categories of reasoning used with some frequency during at least one time period were included in the analyses. Because types of reasoning that were used infrequently tended to be positively skewed, a logarithmic transformation was performed on the data (although the means presented in Table 1 and in the text are nontransformed means). Linear, quadratic, and cubic trends were examined when possible because from early childhood to adolescence some categories of reasoning were expected to show both increases and decreases in usage, sometimes with a period of relative stability in use (which could result in a cubic trend analysis, for example, when a period of little use of a type of reasoning was followed by an increase in use during midchildhood and then a

decline in its use in adolescence). In the first analysis, the categories of reasoning were those that had been used with some frequency (by at least one sex) at six or more time periods (i.e., hedonistic, needs-oriented, pragmatic, direct reciprocity, approval-oriented, and stereotypic; see Eisenberg et al., 1987). Scores were computed from the four stories used at all seven follow-ups. The multivariate Fs for the linear, quadratic, and cubic effects of time were highly significant, $Fs(7, 24) = 40.86, 9.60$, and $4.58, ps < .001, .001$, and $.002$, respectively. For hedonistic reasoning, the univariate Fs for the linear and quadratic trends were highly significant, $Fs(1, 30) = 116.72$ and $53.58, ps < .001$, respectively. Hedonistic reasoning decreased sharply with age until 11–12 years and then increased slightly in adolescence (see Table 1). Interestingly, perusal of the means indicated that the scores in hedonistic reasoning for girls changed little in adolescence ($Ms =$

TABLE 1

Moral Reasoning Categories: Means for Cohort 1

Reasoning category	1	2	3	4	5	6	7
Hedonistic	12.12	8.66	6.31	5.88	4.69	4.75	5.28
Direct reciprocity	4.00	4.09	4.09	4.31	5.38	5.91	4.88
Affectional relationship	4.03	4.38	4.00	4.25	4.19	4.09	4.53
Pragmatic	4.12	4.47	4.28	5.03	5.25	5.81	6.28
Needs-oriented	8.53	11.59	13.62	13.12	13.59	12.25	12.00
Stereotypic	4.50	4.31	4.68	5.12	5.62	6.72	6.47
Approval-interpersonal	4.00	4.06	4.22	4.44	4.88	5.34	4.97
Sympathetic	4.00	4.03	4.00	4.19	4.38	4.06	4.19
Role taking	4.00	4.00	4.06	4.59	4.62	5.12	5.81
Positive affect—simple or related to consequences	4.00	4.00	4.09	4.56	4.78	5.09	5.53
Negative affect—simple or related to consequences	4.00	4.00	4.00	4.16	4.28	4.22	4.44
Positive affect regarding self-respect	4.00	4.00	4.09	4.03	4.00	4.19	4.28
Negative affect regarding self-respect	4.00	4.00	4.00	4.06	4.00	4.09	4.06
Internalized law, norm, or value orientation	4.00	4.00	4.03	4.00	4.00	4.16	4.47
Generalized reciprocity	4.00	4.00	4.00	4.00	4.00	4.03	4.38
Condition of society	4.00	4.00	4.00	4.00	4.00	4.03	4.16
Individual rights	4.00	4.00	4.00	4.00	4.12	4.16	4.03
Equality of individuals	4.00	4.00	4.00	4.00	4.03	4.00	4.25

Note: Means are based on the nontransformed data.

4.56, 4.56, and 4.62 for T5, T6, and T7, respectively), whereas such reasoning clearly increased during adolescence for boys (Ms = 4.81, 4.94, and 5.28 for T5, T6, and T7, respectively). For needs-oriented reasoning, there was a highly significant quadratic trend and weaker (but highly significant) linear and cubic trends, $Fs(l, 30) = 47.04, 11.89,$ and 10.02, $ps < .001, .002,$ and $.004$, respectively; needs-oriented reasoning increased with age until 7–8 years, was relatively stable from 7–8 to 11–12 years (with a small decrease at age 9–10 followed by a small increase at age 11–12, and declined somewhat through early to midadolescence; see Table 1). According to a highly significant linear trend and weaker quadratic and cubic trends, $Fs(l, 30) = 49.02, 4.13,$ and 20.93, $ps < .001, .051,$ and $.001$, respectively, direct reciprocity reasoning was used with little frequency until age 9–10, increased in use until early adolescence (13–14 years), and then started to decline. Similarly, stereotypic and approval-oriented judgments exhibited strong linear trends, $Fs(l, 30) = 42.24$ and $25.20, ps < .001$, respectively, and weaker cubic trends, $Fs(l, 30) = 4.52$ and $4.29, ps < .042$ and $.047$, respectively; these types of reasoning were used infrequently until mid to late elementary school, increased in use until age 13–14, and then decreased slightly in use in midadolescence. Finally, pragmatic reasoning increased in a linear fashion with age, $F(1, 30) = 34.20, p < .001$, whereas affectional relationship reasoning fluctuated in amount of use in elementary school (but was never used much) and then increased somewhat at T7, cubic $F(1, 30) = 8.73, p < .006$.

A second 2 (sex) × 5 (time) trend analysis was computed for those higher level categories of reasoning used with any frequency at T3 or T4 (sympathetic, role taking, internalized positive affect about consequences, internalized negative affect about consequences, internalized positive affect about values, internalized negative affect about values, and internalized law, norm, or value orientation reasoning). The multivariate F for the linear effect of time was significant, $F(7, 24) = 5.28$, $p < .001$. Role taking, positive affect/consequences, and internalized norm, rule, and law reasoning increased in usage with age, $Fs(1, 30) = 13.37, 31.77,$ and $6.46, ps < .001, .001,$ and $.016$, respectively.

Although the multivariate Fs for sex and for Sex × Time ($ps < .12$ and $.92$, respectively) were not sig-

nificant, it is important to look at the univariate Fs because of the gender differences in trends noted in some of these types of reasoning at T5. None of the Sex × Time interactions were significant, although across all time periods, girls used more role-taking and positive affect/values reasoning than did boys, $Fs(l, 30) = 4.41$ and $4.21, ps < .044$ and $.049$, respectively.

In a third 2 (sex) × 3 (time) analysis, we examined age changes in the use of categories of reasoning that emerged only in adolescence (generalized reciprocity, concern with society, rights and justice, and equality of people reasoning). These categories of reasoning were used quite infrequently (see Table 1); nonetheless, the multivariate F for time was marginally significant, $F(7, 24) = 2.40, p < .075$, and there was a linear increase with age in generalized reciprocity reasoning, $F(1, 30) = 4.97, p < .033$.

In a summary analysis, we examined change in C1 students' moral reasoning composite scores from the follow-up preceding the two reported in this article, that is, T5 to T6 and T7. According to a 2 (sex) × 3 (time) trend analysis, there were main effects of both sex and the linear trend, $F(1, 30) = 12.00$ and $11.29, ps < .002$, respectively. Girls scored higher than boys on the composite scores, and scores increased with age (Ms = 227, 241, and 254 for T5, T6, and T7, respectively).[1]

It is also of interest to examine intraindividual patterns of change. However, given that children frequently used a variety of types of moral reasoning (reflecting different levels of moral judgment) and higher levels of reasoning were weighted more heavily, a composite score at a given level did not necessarily indicate the predominance of a given mode of reasoning. For example, a score of 200 was obtained when subjects verbalized all needs-oriented reasoning or when they used half hedonistic reasoning and half stereotypic reasoning.

Nonetheless, we examined whether individuals' composite scores dropped considerably at any point in development (in comparison to any prior point). A drop of 50 points is roughly equivalent to a change of half a stage (because all hedonistic reasoning equals a score of 100, all needs-oriented reasoning equals a score of 200, etc). Nine children exhibited a drop of 50 points or more (3 dropped about 100 points) at

---

[1]For the entire sample of longitudinal and cross-sectional subjects, there was not a significant sex difference in the moral reasoning composite scores at T6 (although girls were somewhat higher), whereas at T7 girls scored higher than boys on the composite scores composed of both four and five stories, $ps < .008$ and $.006$. For the entire sample at T7, girls scored higher than boys on stereotypic and positive affect/self-reasoning, $ps < .047$ and $.024$, respectively, whereas boys scored higher on hedonistic reasoning, $p < .03$ (ps are for five stories; those for four stories are similar).

one point in their development. Thus, although reasoning generally increased in sophistication with age, there were sizable declines in some children's reasoning at various points in their development.

According to additional analyses using the five (instead of four) moral reasoning stories at T6 and T7 (with the scores multiplied by .8 to adjust for the number of stories), the findings were generally the same or stronger. Moreover, the age trends in the children's reasoning did not seem to be the result of repeated testing. If they were, one would not expect the reasoning for C1 to be similar to that of children of the same age interviewed for the first time at T6 or T7 (C2 or C3). However, at T6, the only difference in reasoning between C1 and C2 was that C1 used more direct reciprocity reasoning, $t(65) = -2.32$, $p < .032$. At T7, the only differences were that C1 used more affectional relationship and role-taking reasoning, $t(64) = -2.25$ and -2.11, $ps < .028$ and .039, respectively, whereas C3 used more rights/justice reasoning, $t(64) = 2.28$, $p < .026$. Affectional relationship and rights/justice reasoning were used infrequently by both groups, and there were clear age trends for these types of reasoning. Thus, it seems unlikely that the repeated testing significantly affected the results of the analyses.[2]

Consistency of Indexes from T6 to T7

Most of the measures for C1 were fairly consistent from T6 to T7. The Bryant empathy scale from T6 ($M = 33.28$) was positively related to Davis' measures of sympathy ($M = 27.39$) and perspective taking at T7 ($M = 23.74$), but not to personal distress ($M = 18.38$), $rs(30) = .48$ and .45, $ps < .006$ and .01, respectively.[3] Social desirability, although measured with different scales at the two time periods ($Ms = 60.63$ and 34.35 at T6 and T7, respectively), was also consistent over time, $r(30) = .37$, $p < .037$, as were the

children's ($Ms = 62.28$ and 71.75 at T6 and T7, respectively) and mothers' reports ($Ms = 2.71$ and 3.00 at T6 and T7, respectively) of prosocial behavior (on the modified Rushton et al., 1981, scale), $rs(30)$ and $(29) = .59$ and .51, $ps < .001$ and .003, respectively. Similarly, whether subjects helped was positively correlated from T6 to T7 (percentage of subjects helping at T6 and T7 were 46% and 53%, respectively), $r(30) = .41$, as was the composite index of helping, $r(30) = .37$, $p < .038$ (see next section); whether subjects completed all questions was nonsignificantly positively related ($r = .23$; 33% and 48% of subjects at T6 and T7, respectively, completed all parts). The only correlations that dropped substantially when sex was partialed out were those between the Bryant scale at T6 and the Sympathy and Perspective-Taking scales at T7; nonetheless, these correlations were still marginally significant, partial $rs(29) = .32$ and .34, $ps < .083$ and .059, for sympathy and perspective taking, respectively.

Interrelations of Prosocial Indexes

The two indexes of helping—whether subjects returned the questionnaires and whether all parts were completed (those who did not return anything were coded as not completing the questionnaires)—were highly intercorrelated at both T6 and T7 (using C1 and either C2 or C3), rs (69) and (64) = .58 and .91, $ps < .001$, respectively. Thus, the two indexes of helping were standardized and combined at both T6 and T7; these composite scores were then used in subsequent analyses.

At T6, the composite index of helping was significantly related to mothers' reports of children's prosocial behavior, $r(29) = .51$, $p < .003$, but not with children's reports on the modified Rushton self-report scale. Mothers' and children's reports of prosocial behavior were significantly, positively related, but only for boys, $r(13) = .53$, $p < .041$. At T7, the composite

---

[2] On the basis of a small replication sample of 10 children interviewed six times between 4–5 and 13–14 years of age (a younger sample than C1; four girls, six boys; M age = 139 months at T5 and 163 months at T6), hedonistic reasoning decreased with age, $F(1, 8) = 20.40$, $p < .024$, whereas needs-oriented and approval-oriented reasoning increased with age, $F(1, 8) = 8.11$ and 16.42, $ps < .022$ and .004, respectively. Stereotypic reasoning increased with age until 13–14 years and then dropped in use at age 15–16; linear and quadratic trends were $F(1, 8)$ 12.76 and 10.24, $p < .007$ and .013, respectively. Finally, according to Linear and Sex × Time quadratic trends for direct reciprocity reasoning, $F(1, 8) = 7.16$ and 10.24, $ps < .028$ and .015, respectively; direct reciprocity reasoning increased steadily with age for boys but increased for girls until age 13–14 ($M = 5.00$) and dropped off in use at age 15–16 ($M = 4,00$).

[3] Nineteen C1 subjects also returned the Davis perspective-taking, sympathy, and personal distress scales as part of the helping task at T6. For them, sympathy, perspective-taking, and personal distress were highly correlated from T6 to T7, $rs(17) = .72$, .48, and .63, $ps < .001$. .039, and .004, respectively.

index of helping was not significantly correlated with either mothers' or children's reports of helpfulness; nor were mothers' and children's reports of prosocial behavior significantly related.

Relation of Sex to Prosocial Behavior, Empathy and Related Constructs, and Social Desirability

T tests were performed to determine whether there were sex differences in scores for the indexes of prosocial behavior, empathy, and social desirability at either T6 or T7. In these and all subsequent analyses, data from C2 and C3, as well as C1, were used when possible. At T6, girls scored higher than boys on the empathy scale and the composite index of helping, $ts(69) = 6.89$ and 2.17, $ps < .001$ and $.037$, respectively. At T7, girls also scored higher on the empathy-related scales, that is, on sympathy, perspective taking, and personal distress, $ts(64) = 5.11, 2.27$, and 2.52. $ps < .001, .027$, and $.014$, respectively, as well as on students' and mothers' reports of prosocial behavior, $t(64) = 2.56$ and $t(30) = 2.38$, $ps < .013$ and $.024$, respectively. This pattern of findings is, of course, consistent with sex role stereotypes.

Relation of Social Desirability to Moral Judgment, Moral Behavior, and Empathy

In these and subsequent analyses involving moral judgment, results for the composite scores based on all five stories are reported because composite scores based on more stories are generally assumed to be more reliable (Rushton, Brainerd, & Pressley, 1983) and the new story was considered to be more age-appropriate than some of the other four stories. However, the findings based on these composite scores generally were very similar to those based on data from the four stories.

At T6 and T7, the Social Desirability scale was not significantly related to the moral judgment composite scores. In addition, social desirability was not significantly correlated with any moral reasoning category used with some frequency at T6 (ie., those categories in the first 2 MANOVAs conducted for C1 in *the Age Changes in Moral Judgment* section; only these categories of reasoning were used in any correlational analyses). At T7, the Social Desirability scale was negatively related to sympathy reasoning, $r(64) = -.29$, $p < .017$.

Children's social desirability was unrelated to helping at either T6 or T7, although their self-reported prosocial behavior was positively related to social desirability at T7, $r(64) = .37$, $p < .002$. In addition, social desirability was significantly, posi-

tively related to most of the various indexes of empathy-related reactions. At T6, the Empathy scale was positively correlated with social desirability, $r(69) = .29$, $p < .015$, although this relation was due solely to the correlation for boys, $r(33) = .42$, $p < .012$; $r(34) = -.01$ for girls. At T7, social desirability was positively related to the Sympathy and Perspective-Taking scales, $rs(64) = .38$ and $.51$, $ps < .002$ and $.001$, respectively, and these correlations were substantial for both sexes. Because of the aforementioned relations between social desirability or sex and some of our measures (particularly empathy-related indexes and the modified Rushton helping scale), partial correlations controlling for social desirability and sex were computed in addition to zero-order correlations in subsequent analyses. In addition, we note when the pattern of findings was markedly different for boys and girls.

Relation of Moral Reasoning to Prosocial Behavior

At T6, the helping composite index was not significantly related to the moral reasoning composite scores. However, consistent with findings in prior follow-ups, helping was negatively related to hedonistic reasoning, $r(67) = -.28$, $p < .023$; partial $r(63) = -.25$, $p < .048$, controlling for sex and social desirability. Children's self-reported prosocial behavior was unrelated to moral reasoning; mothers' reports of children's prosocial behavior were positively related to children's pragmatic moral reasoning, $r(29) = .45$, $p < .001$; partial $r(27) = .52$, $p < .004$.

At T7, the helping behavior was positively related to higher scores on the moral reasoning composite score, $r(64) = .30$, $p < .015$; partial $r(62) = .25$, $p < .049$. Mothers' and children's reports of the children's prosocial behavior were not significantly related to the moral judgment composite score, although children's reports of prosocial tendencies were negatively related to hedonistic reasoning, $r(64) = -.38$, $p < .002$; partial $r(62) = -.30$, $p < .017$, particularly for boys, $r(31) = -.45$, $p < .009$; $r(31) = -.11$ for girls.

Relations of Moral Reasoning to Empathy and Related Constructs

At T6, the Bryant empathy index was not significantly related to the moral judgment composite scores, although it was negatively related to hedonistic moral reasoning, $r(65) = -.43$, $p < .001$; partial $r(63) = -.41$, $p < .001$, controlling sex and social desirability. At T7 there were more relations between empathy-related indexes and moral judgment, although the relations were nearly always due to the boys' data. Scores for perspective taking were positively related to the composite judgment scores, $r(64) = .28$, $p < .022$; partial $r(62) = .27$. The correlation between perspective taking and the composite reasoning score was due primarily to the data for boys, $r(30) = .44$, $p < .01$. In addition, sympathy and perspective taking were negatively related to hedonistic reasoning, $rs(64) = -.40$ and $-.35$, $ps < .001$ and $.004$, respectively, whereas sympathy was positively related to needs-oriented reasoning, $r(64) = .32$, $p < .008$, and these correlations remained significant when sex and social desirability were partialed, partial $rs(62) = -.29, -.28,$ and $.35$, $ps < .019, .027,$ and $.005$, respectively. Again, however, these relations were due to the boys' data: $rs(31) = -.46, -.43,$ and $.44$, $ps < .008, .012,$ and $.011$, respectively, and partialing social desirability had virtually no effect on these correlations ($rs = -.06, -.17,$ and $.17$ for girls). Moreover, when sex and social desirability were partialed, scores on perspective taking tended to be positively correlated with sympathetic moral reasoning, partial $r(62) = .28$, $p < .027$; partial $r(30) = .49$, $p < .004$, for boys; $r = .08$ for girls. None of the relations for personal distress were significant when social desirability was partialed from the correlations.

Relation of Prosocial Behavior to Empathy and Related Constructs

At T6, helping was positively correlated with Bryant empathy scores, $r(71) = .33$, $p < .006$, although this correlation dropped somewhat when the effects of sex and social desirability were partialed, partial $r(67) = .22$, $p < .068$. Similarly, children's self-reported prosocial behavior was positively related to Bryant empathy scores, $r(69) = .27$, $p < .023$; partial $r(67) = .24$, $p < .043$. At T7, the empathy-related indexes were unrelated to helping behavior. However, children's reported prosocial behaviors (but not maternal reports) were positively related to both sympathy and perspective taking, $rs(64) = .52$ and $.57$, $ps < .001$, respectively; partial $rs(62) = .34$ and $.43$, $ps < .006$ and $.001$.

DISCUSSION

Several important findings were obtained in this study. First, we clarified the pattern of some modes of prosocial moral reasoning that previously were unclear. For example, we obtained the first longitudinal data indicating that approval and stereotypic prosocial moral reasoning start to decline in use in mid-adolescence. With this finding, we can reconcile the potentially discrepant findings that such reasoning increases in the elementary school years (Eisenberg et al., 1987) but that it has been found to decrease in use in a cross-sectional study of elementary and high school students (Eisenberg-Berg, 1979a). Moreover, the pattern obtained in this study for approval and stereotypic reasoning is consistent with that for Kohlbergian moral reasoning (Colby et al., 1983). However, given the relatively weak cubic trends obtained for approval and stereotypic reasoning (due to either periods of no change or minor fluctuations, followed by an increase and then a drop in usage), it is important to examine the further development of these modes of reasoning in late adolescence.

In addition, the developmental course of direct reciprocity reasoning has been clarified somewhat. Direct reciprocity reasoning, which is scored as a low level of prosocial moral judgment, increased significantly with age in elementary school and then decreased in use in adolescence. The initial increase with age in this mode of reasoning may be because it involves cognitive concepts of exchange and coordination between people and consequently is more sophisticated cognitively than merely a focus on what the self desires (e.g., hedonistic reasoning). Thus, direct reciprocity reasoning seems to be a relatively sophisticated mode of self-oriented reasoning, but one that decreases in use in mid-adolescence.

Moreover, in these follow-ups, we were able to observe the emergence of some of the higher level modes of reasoning (e.g., internalized norm, rule, and law reasoning and generalized reciprocity) during adolescence. An additional finding of interest was that although role taking and sympathetic reasoning emerged earlier for girls than for boys (i.e., at age 11–12; Eisenberg et al., 1987), the developmental curves for these modes of reasoning were very similar in adolescence. Girls did use somewhat higher levels of reasoning overall; however, there was little evidence of girls using more of the other-oriented modes of reasoning after age 11–12. Thus, it appears that girls used other-oriented, self-reflective modes of reasoning earlier than did boys, but boys caught up in their use of these modes of reasoning within 2 years.

The fact that girls exhibited a higher level of reasoning overall was probably due in part to the modest increase in boys' hedonistic reasoning in adolescence (which had decreased in use until adolescence), as well as to the tendency for girls to use somewhat more of some higher level modes of reasoning. Consistent with our data, Ford, Wentzel, Wood, Stevens, and Siesfeld (1989) found that high school boys made fewer socially responsible choices on a questionnaire index than did girls and their choices were more a function of self-interested emotions. As Ford et al. concluded, perhaps issues concerning responsibility for others are more problematic for adolescent boys than girls.

Another important finding is that we obtained some evidence of relations between moral reasoning and adolescents' prosocial behavior. At T6, helping was negatively related to hedonistic reasoning; at T7, helping was positively related to overall level of moral reasoning. Thus, as at younger ages, children's level of prosocial moral judgment seemed to be reflected in actual behavior (although the direction of causality is unclear). These relations are impressive given that the index of helping was fairly weak (i.e., did not involve much cost to the helper).

Adolescents' moral reasoning also was related to their empathy (at T6) and sympathy and perspective taking (at T7), although the relations at T7 held primarily for boys. The reason for the sex difference in the patterns of relations at T7 is unclear; global empathy was positively related to level of moral reasoning for both sexes in a previous study conducted with adolescents (Eisenberg-Berg & Mussen, 1978). The lack of a relation for girls' sympathy at T7 could be due to the restricted range of their responses (mean for sympathy was 30.30 out of a range of 7–35; for boys, $M = 24.48$); recall that girls scored higher on both sympathy and perspective taking. However, a ceiling effect was not evident for perspective-taking scores (means for girls and boys were 25.15 and 22.33) and the standard deviations for boys' and girls' sympathy and perspective taking were not markedly different. Although social desirability was significantly, positively related to both boys' and girls' sympathy ($rs = .38$ and $.47$, $ps < .029$ and $.005$, respectively) and perspective taking ($rs = .41$ and $.60$,

$ps < .017$ and $.001$, respectively), these relations were somewhat stronger for girls—a finding that suggests that the indexes of sympathy and perspective taking were slightly more valid for boys. Whatever the reason, the data for T6 and for boys at T7 are consistent with the view that other-oriented concerns and perspective-taking tendencies are intimately involved in moral reasoning (Eisenberg, 1986; Hoffman, 1987).

The findings in regard to the relations between empathy-related responses and prosocial behavior were mixed, albeit all findings were in the predicted direction. Empathy-related reactions were significantly, positively related to helping behavior only at T6. At T7, children's reports of sympathy and perspective taking were positively related to their reported helping behavior; however, the validity of the students' self-reported prosocial behavior is questionable because of the relation of these indexes to social desirability and the lack of their relation to actual helping behavior. Given the relations of indexes of empathy-related reactions with social desirability, it would be useful in the future to replicate the positive relations between adolescents' prosocial actions and empathy-related responses by means of non-self-report indexes. Moreover, given the relatively small number of subjects in this study, replication of these findings with larger samples would be useful.

In summary, in this study we obtained longitudinal data confirming, for the most part, the predicted pattern of development for prosocial moral reasoning in adolescence. In addition, prosocial moral reasoning, prosocial behavior, and empathy/sympathy and perspective taking were interrelated in theoretically meaningful ways, although sex differences in the relations of sympathy and perspective taking to moral reasoning merit further attention.

References

Bar-Tal, D. (1982). Sequential development of helping behavior: A cognitive-learning approach. *Developmental Review, 2,* 101–124.

Barnett, M. A. (1987). Empathy and related responses in children. In N. Eisenberg & J. Straver (Eds), *Empathy and its development* (pp. 146–162). Cambridge, England: Cambridge University Press.

Batson, C. D. (1987). Prosocial motivation: Is it ever truly altruistic? In L. Berkowitz (Ed.), *Advances in experimental social psychology* (Vol. 20, pp. 65–122). New York: Academic Press.

Batson, C. D. (1990). How social an animal? The human capacity for caring. *American Psychologist, 45,* 336-346.

Bryant, B. K. (1982). An index of empathy for children and adolescents. *Child Development, 53,* 413-425.

Colby, A.. Kohlberg. L., Gibbs, J., & Lieberman, M. (1983). A longitudinal study of moral judgment. *Monographs of the Society for Research in Child Development, 48(1–2,* Serial No. 200).

Crandall, V. C., Crandall. V. J., & Katkovsky, W (1965). A child's social desirability questionnaire. *Journal of Consulting Psychology, 29,* 27–36.

Crowne, D. P.. & Marlowe, D. (1964.). *The approval motive.* New York: Wiley.

Damon, W. (1977). *The social world of the child.* San Francisco: Jossey-Bass.

Eisenberg, N. (1986). *Altruistic emotion, cognition and behavior.* Hillsdale, NJ: Erlbaum.

Eisenberg, N. (1990). Prosocial development in early and mid adolescence. In R. Montemayor, G. R. Adams, & T. P. Gullotta (Eds.), *From childhood to adolescence: A transitional period? Advances in adolescence* (Vol. 2. pp. 240–269). Newbury Park, CA: Sage.

Eisenberg, N., & Fabes. R. A. (1991). Prosocial behavior and empathy: A multimethod, developmental perspective. In P. Clark (Ed.). *Review of personality and social psychology* (pp. 34–61). Newbury Park, CA: Sage.

Eisenberg, N., Lennon, R., & Roth, K. (1983). Prosocial development: A longitudinal study. *Developmental Psychology, 19,* 846–855.

Eisenberg, N., & Miller, P A. (1987). The relation of empathy to prosocial and related behavior. *Psychological Bulletin, 101,* 91–119.

Eisenberg, N., Shell, R., Pasternack, J., Lennon, R., Beller, R., & Mathy, R. M. (1987). Prosocial development in middle childhood: A longitudinal study. *Developmental Psychology, 23,* 712–718.

Eisenberg-Berg, N. (1979a). Development of children's prosocial moral judgment. *Developmental Psychology, 15,* 128–137.

Eisenberg-Berg, N. (1979b). The relationship of prosocial moral reasoning to altruism, political liberalism, and intelligence. *Developmental Psychology, 15,* 87–89,

Eisenberg-Berg, N., & Mussen, P. (1978). Empathy and moral development in adolescence. *Developmental Psychology, 14,* 185–186.

Eisenberg-Berg, N., & Roth, K. (1980). The development of children's prosocial moral judgment: A longitudinal follow-up. *Developmental Psychology, 16,* 375–376.

Ford, M. E., Wentzel, K. R., Wood, D., Stevens, E., & Siesfeld, G. A. (1989). Processes associated with integrative social competence: Emotional and contextual influences on adolescent social responsibility. *Journal of Adolescent Research, 4,* 405–425.

Gilligan, C., & Attanucci, J. (1988). Two moral orientations: Gender differences and similarities. *Merrill-Palmer Quarterly 34,* 223–238.

Hoffman, M. L. (1987). The contribution of empathy to justice and moral judgment. In N. Eisenberg & J. Strayer (Eds), *Empathy and its development* (pp. 47–80). Cambridge, England: Cambridge University Press.

Hume, D. (1966). *Enquiries concerning the human understanding and concerning the principles of morals* (2nd ed.). Oxford, England: Clarendon Press. (Original work published 1777).

Kant, I. (1964). *The doctrine of virtue.* New York: Harper & Row. (Original work published 1797).

Kohlberg, L. (1969). Stage and sequence: The cognitive-developmental approach to socialization. In D. A. Goslin (Ed), *Handbook of socialization theory and research* (pp. 325–480). Chicago: Rand McNally.

Kohlberg, L. (1981). *The philosophy of moral development: Moral stages and the idea of justice.* San Francisco: Harper & Row.

Rest, J. R. (1983). Morality. In P Mussen (Ed.), *Handbook of child psychology. Vol. 3. Cognitive development* (pp. 556–629). New York: Wiley.

Rholes, W. S., & Bailey, S. (1983). The effects of level of moral reasoning in consistency between moral attitudes and related behaviors. *Social Cognition, 2,* 32–48.

Rushton, J. P., Brainerd, C. J., & Pressley, M. (1983). Behavioral development and construct validity: The principle of aggregation. *Psychological Bulletin, 94,* 18–38.

Rushton, J. P., Chrisjohn, R. D., & Fekken, G. C. (1981). The altruistic personality and the self-report altruism scale. *Personality and Individual Differences, 2,* 1–11.

Selman, R. L. (1980). *The growth of interpersonal understanding.* San Diego, CA: Academic Press.

Staub, E. (1978). *Positive social behavior and morality: Social and personal influences (Vol. 1).* New York: Academic Press.

Underwood, B. & Moore, B. (1982). Perspective-taking and altruism. *Psychological Bulletin, 91,* 143–173.

Walker, L. (1984). Sex differences in the development of moral reasoning: A critical review. *Child Development, 55,* 677–691.

33

A Developmental Perspective on Antisocial Behavior

GERALD R. PATTERSON, BARBARA DEBARYSHE, AND ELIZABETH RAMSEY

Violence toward other people and willful destruction of property are disturbing crimes that shatter our trust in one another, regardless of the age of the perpetrators. However, when such acts are committed by youth, they strike an especially deep chord. What are the explanations for and origins of these behaviors? Developmental psychologists have examined these questions from many perspectives, including the role of peer relations, academic experience, and poverty. But by far the largest portion of research on this topic has focused on the role of family relations, especially parent-child interaction, as a determining factor in the development of conduct disorders. The research by Gerald R. Patterson and colleagues that is described in the following article offers a rich framework for understanding how parent-child interaction may influence the organization and development of delinquency.

A developmental model of antisocial behavior is outlined. Recent findings are reviewed that concern the etiology and course of antisocial behavior from early childhood through adolescence. Evidence is presented in support of the hypothesis that the route to chronic delinquency is marked by a reliable developmental sequence of experiences. As a first step, ineffective parenting practices are viewed as determinants for childhood conduct disorders. The general model also takes into account the contextual variables that influence the family interaction process. As a second step, the conduct-disordered behaviors lead to academic failure and peer rejection. These dual failures lead, in turn, to increased risk for depressed mood and involvement in a deviant peer group. This third step usually occurs during

Reprinted with permission from the authors and *American Psychologist*, 44, 1989, 329–335. Copyright 1989 by the American Psychological Association.

We gratefully acknowledge the support of National Institute of Mental Health Grants 2 RO1 MH 37940 and 5 T32 MH 17126 in the preparation of this article.

later childhood and early adolescence. It is assumed that children following this developmental sequence are at high risk for engaging in chronic delinquent behavior. Finally, implications for prevention and intervention are discussed.

In 1986, more than 1.4 million juveniles were arrested for nonindex crimes (e.g., vandalism, drug abuse, or running away) and almost 900,000 for index crimes (e.g., larceny-theft, robbery, or forcible rape; Federal Bureau of Investigation, 1987). The United States spends more than $1 billion per year to maintain our juvenile justice system. The yearly cost of school vandalism alone is estimated to be one-half billion dollars (Feldman, Caplinger, & Wodarski, 1981). These statistics are based on official records and may represent only a fraction of the true offense rate. Data on self-reported delinquent acts indicate that police records account for as little as 2% of the actual juvenile law violations (Dunford & Elliott, 1982).

Of course, not all costs can be counted in dollars and cents. Antisocial children are likely to experience major adjustment problems in the areas of academic achievement and peer social relations (Kazdin, 1987; Walker, Shinn, O'Neill, & Ramsey, 1987; Wilson & Herrnstein, 1985). Follow-up studies of antisocial children show that as adults they ultimately contribute disproportionately to the incidence of alcoholism, accidents, chronic unemployment, divorce, physical and psychiatric illness, and the demand on welfare services (Caspi, Elder, & Bem, 1987; Farrington, 1983; Robins, 1966; Robins & Ratcliff, 1979).

Antisocial behavior appears to be a developmental trait that begins early in life and often continues into adolescence and adulthood. For many children, stable manifestations of antisocial behavior begin as early as the elementary school grades (see Farrington, Ohlin, & Wilson, 1986; Loeber, 1982; and Olweus, 1979, for reviews). As Olweus noted, stability coefficients for childhood aggression rival the figures derived for the stability of IQ. Findings that early behaviors such as temper tantrums and grade school troublesomeness significantly predict adolescent and adult offenses suggest the existence of a single underlying continuum. If early forms of antisocial behavior are indeed the forerunners of later antisocial acts, then the task for developmental psychologists is to determine which mechanisms explain the stability of antisocial behavior and which control changes over time.

From a policy standpoint, a serious social problem that is predictable and understandable is a viable target for prevention. The purpose of this article is to present an ontogenic perspective on the etiology and developmental course of antisocial behavior from early childhood through adolescence. Evidence is presented in support of the notion that the path to chronic delinquency unfolds in a series of predictable steps. This model is presented in detail by Patterson, Reid, and Dishion (in press). In this model, child behaviors at one stage lead to predictable reactions from the child's social environment in the following step. This leads to yet further reactions from the child and further changes in the reactions from the social environment. Each step in this action-reaction sequence puts the antisocial child more at risk for long-term social maladjustment and criminal behavior.

A DEVELOPMENTAL PROGRESSION FOR ANTISOCIAL BEHAVIOR

Basic Training in the Home

There is a long history of empirical studies that have identified family variables as consistent covariates for early forms of antisocial behavior and for later delinquency. Families of antisocial children are characterized by harsh and inconsistent discipline, little positive parental involvement with the child, and poor monitoring and supervision of the child's activities (Loeber & Dishion, 1983; McCord, McCord, & Howard, 1963).

Two general interpretations have been imposed on these findings. Control theory, widely accepted in sociology (Hirschi, 1969), views harsh discipline and lack of supervision as evidence for disrupted parent–child bonding. Poor bonding implies a failure to identify with parental and societal values regarding conformity and work. These omissions leave the child lacking in internal control. Several large-scale surveys provide correlational data consistent with this hypothesis. The correlations show that youths who have negative attitudes toward school, work, and authority tend to be more antisocial (Elliott, Huizinga, & Ageton, 1985; Hirschi, 1969). The magnitude of these correlations tends to be very small. Because the dependent and independent variables are often provided by the same agent, it is difficult to untangle the contribution of method variance to these relations.

In contrast, the social–interactional perspective takes the view that family members directly train the child to perform antisocial behaviors (Forehand, King, Peed, & Yoder, 1975; Patterson, 1982; Snyder, 1977; Wahler & Dumas, 1984). The parents tend to be noncontingent in their use of both positive reinforcers for prosocial and effective punishment for deviant behaviors. The effect of the inept parenting practices is to permit dozens of daily interactions with family members in which coercive child behaviors are reinforced. The coercive behaviors are directly reinforced by family members (Patterson, 1982; Snyder, 1977; Snyder & Patterson, 1986). While some of the reinforcement is positive (attend, laugh, or approve), the most important set of contingencies for coercive behavior consists of escape-conditioning contingencies. In the latter, the child uses aversive behaviors to terminate aversive intrusions by other family members. In these families, coercive behaviors are functional. They make it possible to survive in a highly aversive social system.

As the training continues, the child and other family members gradually escalate the intensity of their coercive behaviors, often leading to high-amplitude behaviors such as hitting and physical attacks. In this training, the child eventually learns to control other family members through coercive means. The training for deviant behaviors is paralleled by a lack of training for many prosocial skills. Observations in the homes of distressed families suggest that children's prosocial acts are often ignored or responded to inappropriately (Patterson, 1982; Patterson, Reid, & Dishion, in press; Snyder, 1977). It seems that some families produce children characterized by not one, but two problems. They have antisocial symptoms and they are socially unskilled.

A series of structural equation modeling studies by Patterson and his colleagues support the theory that disrupted parent practices are causally related to child antisocial behavior. They used multiple indicators to define parental discipline and monitoring practices, child coercive behavior in the home, and a cross-situational measure of the child antisocial trait. In four different samples, involving several hundred grade school boys, the parenting practices and family interaction constructs accounted for 30-40% of the variance in general antisocial behavior (Baldwin & Skinner, 1988; Patterson, 1986; Patterson, Dishion, & Bank, 1984; Patterson et al., in press). Forgatch (1988) used a quasi-experimental design based on data from families referred for treatment of antisocial boys. She showed that changes in parental discipline and monitoring were accompanied by significant reductions in child antisocial behavior. There were no changes in antisocial child behavior for those families who showed no changes in these parenting skills.

Social Rejection and School Failure

It is hypothesized that coercive child behaviors are likely to produce two sets of reactions from the social environment. One outcome is rejection by members of the normal peer group, and the other is academic failure.

It is consistently found that antisocial children show poor academic achievement (Hawkins & Lishner, 1987; Wilson & Herrnstein, 1985). One explanation for this is that the child's noncompliant and undercontrolled behavior directly impedes learning. Classroom observations of antisocial children show they spend less time on task than their nondeviant peers (Shinn, Ramsey, Walker, O'Neill, & Steiber, 1987; Walker et al., 1987). Earlier classroom observation studies showed that they were also deficient in academic survival skills (e.g., attending, remaining in seat, answering questions) necessary for effective learning (Cobb, 1972; Cobb & Hops, 1973; Hops & Cobb, 1974). Two studies showed a significant covariation between antisocial behavior and failure to complete homework assignments (Dishion, Loeber, Stouthamer-Loeber, & Patterson, 1983; Fehrmann, Keith, & Reimers, 1987).

The association between antisocial behavior and rejection by the normal peer group is well documented (Cantrell & Prinz, 1985; Dodge, Coie, & Brakke, 1982; Roff & Wirt, 1984). Experimental studies of group formation show that aggressive behavior leads to rejection, not the reverse (Coie & Kupersmidt, 1983; Dodge, 1983). Rejected children are also deficient in a number of social-cognitive skills, including peer group entry, perception of peer group norms, response to provocation, and interpretation of prosocial interactions (Asarnow & Calan, 1985; Dodge, 1986; Putallaz, 1983).

It is often suggested that academic failure and peer rejection are causes rather than consequences of antisocial behavior. However, a stronger case may be made that antisocial behavior contributes to these negative outcomes. For example, some investigators have predicted that successful academic remediation will lead to a reduction in antisocial behavior (e.g., Cohen & Filipczak, 1971). However, it has been repeatedly demonstrated that programs improving the academic skills of antisocial youths have not achieved reductions in other antisocial symptoms (Wilson & Herrnstein, 1985); similar findings have been obtained for social skills training (Kazdin, 1987).

Deviant Peer Group Membership

Antisocial behavior and peer group rejection are important preludes to deviant peer group membership (Dishion, Patterson, & Skinner, 1988; Snyder, Dishion, & Patterson, 1986). These analyses also suggest that lax parental supervision also accounts for unique variance to the prediction of deviant peer affiliation.

A large number of studies point to the peer group as the major training ground for delinquent acts and substance use (Elliott et al., 1985; Hirschi, 1969; Huba & Bentler, 1983; Kandel, 1973). Peers are thought to supply the adolescent with the attitudes, motivations, and rationalizations to support antisocial behavior as well as providing opportunities to engage in specific delinquent acts. There are, however, only a small number of studies designed to investigate the hypothesized training process. One study in an institutional setting showed that delinquent peers provided considerable positive reinforcement for deviant behavior and punishment for socially conforming acts (Buehler, Patterson, & Furniss, 1966).

It seems, then, that the disrupted family processes producing antisocial behavior may indirectly contribute to later involvement with a deviant peer group. This particular product may function as an additional determinant for future antisocial behavior. In effect, the deviant peer group variable may be thought of as a positive feedback variable that contributes significantly to maintenance in the process. Common adult outcomes for highly antisocial youths include school dropout, uneven employment histories, substance abuse, marital difficulties, multiple offenses, incarceration, and institutionalization (Caspi et al., 1987; Huesmann, Eron, Lefkowitz, & Walder, 1984; Robins & Ratcliff, 1979).

Figure 1 depicts the relation among the concepts discussed up to this point.

SOME IMPLICATIONS OF THE DEVELOPMENT PERSPECTIVE

Early Versus Late Starters

Boys starting their criminal career in late childhood or early adolescence are at the greatest risk of becoming chronic offenders (Farrington, 1983; Loeber, 1982). Studies of prison populations have shown that recidivists are generally first arrested by age 14 or 15, whereas one-time offenders are first arrested at a later age (Gendreau, Madden, & Leipciger, 1979). Farrington found that boys first arrested between 10 and 12 years of age average twice as many convictions as later starters (Farrington, Gallagher, Morley, St. Ledger, & West, 1986); this comparison holds into early adulthood.

One implication of the aforementioned developmental perspective is that early forms of age-prototypic antisocial behavior may be linked to the early onset of official juvenile offenses. Following this logic, the child who receives antisocial training from the family during the preschool and elementary school years is likely to be denied access to positive socialization forces in the peer group and school.

On the other hand, the late starter would be someone committing his or her first offense in middle to late adolescence. This individual lacks the early training for antisocial behaviors. This implies that he or she has not experienced the dual failure of rejection by normal peers and academic failure.

Only about half the antisocial children become adolescent delinquents, and roughly half to three quarters of the adolescent delinquents become adult offenders (Blumstein, Cohen, & Farrington, 1988; Farrington, 1987; Robins & Ratcliff, 1979). At some point in late adolescence, the incidence of delinquent acts as a function of age group begins to drop; the drop continues into the late 20s. One interpretation of these data is that many of the delinquent offenders drop out of the process. We assume that many of these dropouts are late starters, but more research is clearly needed to specify what factors determine the probability of an individual's dropping out of the

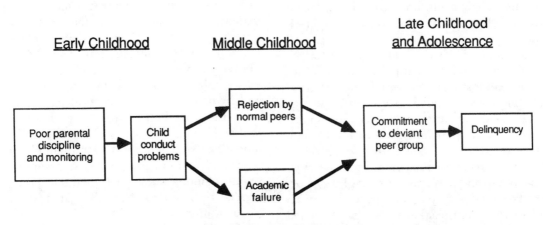

FIGURE 1 A developmental progression for antisocial behavior.

antisocial training process. A proper developmental theory of antisocial behavior must delineate not only the variables that lead a child into the process but those that cause some of them to drop out of it.

CONTEXTUAL VARIABLES FOR FAMILY DISRUPTION

Because parent–child interaction is a central variable in the etiology of antisocial behavior, it is important to determine why a minority of parents engage in highly maladaptive family management practices. A number of variables, which shall be referred to as disruptors, have negative effects on parenting skill. These variables also correlate with the probability of children's antisocial behavior. Thus, the effect of disruptors on children's adjustment is indirect, being mediated through perturbations in parenting. Potential disruptors include a history of antisocial behavior in other family members, demographic variables representing disadvantaged socioeconomic status, and stressors—such as marital conflict and divorce—that hamper family functioning.

Antisocial Parents and Grandparents

There is a high degree of intergenerational similarity for antisocial behavior (Farrington, 1987; Robins & Ratcliff, 1979). As a predictor of adult antisocial personality, having an antisocial parent places the child at significant risk for antisocial behavior; having two antisocial parents puts the child at even higher risk (Robins & Earls, 1985). Concordance across three generations has also been documented (Elder, Caspi, & Downy, 1983; Huesmann et al., 1984; Robins, West, & Herjanic, 1975).

There is considerable evidence that parental discipline practices may be an important mediating mechanism in this transmission. Our set of findings shows that antisocial parents are at significant risk for ineffective discipline practices. Ineffective discipline is significantly related to risk of having an antisocial child. For example, Elder et al. (1983) found a significant relation between retrospective accounts of grandparental explosive discipline and paternal irritability. Irritable fathers tended to use explosive discipline practices with their own children who tended to exhibit antisocial behavior. Patterson and Dishion (1988) also found a significant correlation between retrospective reports of grandparental explosive reactions in the home and parental antisocial traits. Furthermore, the effect of the parents' antisocial trait on the grandchildren's antisocial behavior was mediated by parental discipline practices.

Family Demographics

Demographic variables such as race, neighborhood, parental education, income, and occupation are related to the incidence of antisocial behavior, particularly in its more severe forms (Elliott et al., 1985; Rutter & Giller, 1983; Wilson & Herrnstein, 1985). We presume that the effect of social class on child adjustment is mediated by family management practices.

The empirical findings linking social class to parenting practices are not consistent. But, in general, middle-class parents seem more likely to use reasoning and psychological methods of discipline, allow their children more freedom of choice and self-direction, show egalitarian parenting styles, express positive affect toward their children, verbalize, and support cognitive and academic growth (Gecas, 1979; Hess, 1970). Lower class parents are more likely to use physical discipline, be controlling of their child's behavior, exhibit authoritarian parenting styles, and engage in less frequent verbal and cognitive stimulation.

The findings from the at-risk sample at the Oregon Social Learning Center are in keeping with the trends in the literature (Patterson et al., in press). Uneducated parents working in unskilled occupations were found to be significantly less effective in discipline, monitoring, problem solving, positive reinforcement, and involvement.

Family Stressors

Stressors impinging on the family such as unemployment, family violence, marital discord, and divorce are associated with both delinquency (Farrington, 1987) and child adjustment problems in general (Garmezy & Rutter, 1983; Hetherington, Cox, & Cox, 1982; Rutter, 1979). Although stressors may well have direct and independent effects on child behavior, we assume that the major impact of stress on child adjustment is mediated by family management practices. If the stressors disrupt parenting practices, then the child is placed at risk for adjustment problems. For example, in the case of divorce, postseparation behavior problems occur with diminished parental responsiveness, affection, and involvement, and increased parental punitiveness and irritability (Hetherington et al., 1982; Wallerstein & Kelley, 1981). Structural equation modeling using data from a large sample of recently separated families provided strong support for the relation among stress, disrupted discipline, and antisocial behavior for boys (Forgatch, Patterson, & Skinner, in press).

We assume that antisocial parents and parents

with marginal child-rearing skills are perhaps most susceptible to the disrupting effects of stressors and socioeconomic disadvantage. Elder, Caspi, and Nguyen (in press) described this interaction as an *amplifying effect*. External events are most disabling to those individuals who already exhibit negative personality traits or weak personal resources because stressors amplify such problems in adjustment. The interaction between the aforementioned disruptors and parental susceptibility is presented in Figure 2.

When antisocial parents or parents with minimal family management skills are faced with acute or prolonged stress, nontrivial disruptions in family management practices are likely to occur. It is these disruptions that are thought to place the child at risk for adjustment problems. A recent study by Snyder (1988) provided strong support for the mediational hypothesis. Roughly 20 hours of observation collected in the homes of three mother–child dyads showed significant covariation across days between stress and both disrupted maternal discipline and maternal irritability. Days characterized by high stress prior to the observation showed higher rates of disrupted behavior for the mother and increased child problem behaviors. A similar covariation was shown in the study by Wahler and Dumas (1984).

Is Prevention a Possibility?

Reviews of the literature summarizing efforts to intervene with antisocial adolescents invariably lead to negative conclusions (Kazdin, 1987; Wilson & Herrnstein, 1985). At best, such interventions produce short-term effects that are lost within a year or two of treatment termination. For example, efforts to apply behavior modification procedures in a half-way house setting (Achievement Place) showed no treatment effects after youths returned to their homes and communities (Jones, Weinrott, & Howard, 1981). Similarly, systematic parent training for families of delinquent adolescents produced reductions in offenses, but this effect did not persist over time (Marlowe, Reid, Patterson, Weinrott, & Bank, 1988).

Successful intervention appears to be possible for preadolescents, with parent-training interventions showing the most favorable outcomes (Kazdin, 1987). Parent training refers to procedures in which parents are given specific instructions in ways to improve family management practices (e.g., Forehand, Wells, & Griest, 1980; Patterson, Reid, Jones, & Conger, 1975). As shown in the review by Kazdin (1987), the parent-training programs have been evaluated in a number of random assignment evalua-

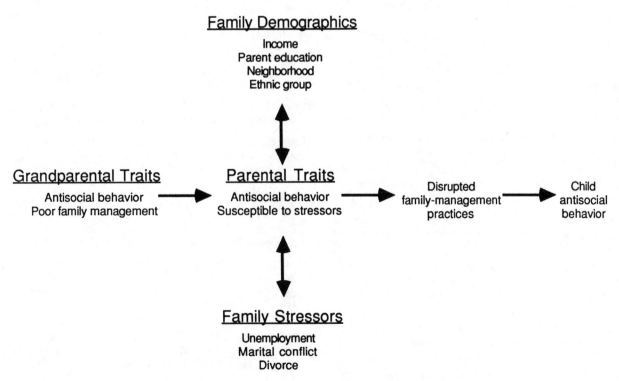

FIGURE 2   Disruptors of effective parenting.

tion studies including follow-up designs (six-month to four-year intervals). In general, the findings support the hypothesis that parent training is effective when applied to younger antisocial children. That several major studies failed to show a treatment effect led most investigators to conclude that parent training techniques *and* soft clinical skills are necessary for effective treatment. Current intervention studies have expanded their scope to include teaching academic and social-relational skills in addition to parent train-

ing. In order to alter both the problem child's lack of social skills and his or her antisocial symptoms, it seems necessary to design these more complex interventions.

We believe that prevention studies are now feasible. It seems reasonable to identify children in the elementary grades who are both antisocial and unskilled. Successful programs would probably include three components: parent training, child social-skills training, and academic remediation.

References

Asarnow, J. R., & Calan, J. R. (1985). Boys with peer adjustment problems: Social cognitive processes. *Journal of Consulting and Clinical Psychology, 53,* 80–87.

Baldwin, D. V., & Skinner, M. L. (1988). *A structural model for antisocial behavior: Generalization to single-mother families.* Manuscript submitted for publication.

Blumstein, A., Cohen, J., & Farrington, D. P. (1988). Criminal career research: Its value for criminology. *Criminology, 26,* 1–35.

Buehler, R. E., Patterson, G. R., & Furniss, J. M. (1966). The reinforcement of behavior in institutional settings. *Behavior Research and Therapy, 4,* 157–167.

Cantrell, V. L., & Prinz, R. J. (1985). Multiple predictors of rejected, neglected, and accepted children: Relation between sociometric status and behavioral characteristics. *Journal of Consulting and Clinical Psychology, 53,* 884–889.

Caspi, A., Elder, G. H., & Bem, D. J. (1987). Moving against the world: Life course patterns of explosive children. *Developmental Psychology, 23,* 308–313.

Cobb, J. A. (1972). The relationship of discrete classroom behavior to fourth grade academic achievement. *Journal of Educational Psychology, 63,* 74–80.

Cobb, J. A., & Hops, H. (1973). Effects of academic skill training on low achieving first graders. *Journal of Educational Research, 63,* 74–80.

Cohen, H. L., & Filipczak, J. (1971). *A new learning environment.* San Francisco: Jossey Bass.

Coie, J. D., & Kupersmidt, J. B. (1983). A behavioral analysis of emerging social status in boys' groups. *Child Development, 54,* 1400–1416.

Dishion, T J., Loeber, R., Stouthamer-Loeber, M., & Patterson, G. R. (1983). Social skills deficits and male adolescent delinquency. Journal *of Abnormal Child Psychology, 12,* 37–54.

Dishion, T J., Patterson, G. R., & Skinner, M. L. (1988). *Peer group selection processes from middle childhood to early adolescence.* Manuscript in preparation.

Dodge, K. A. (1983). Behavioral antecedents of peer social status. Child *Development, 54,* 1386–1399.

Dodge, K. A. (1986). A social information processing model of social competence in children. In M. Perlmutter (Ed.), *Minnesota symposium on child psychology* (Vol. 18, pp. 77–125). Hillsdale, NJ: Erlbaum.

Dodge, K. A., Coie, J. D., & Brakke, N. P. (1982). Behavior patterns of socially rejected and neglected preadolescents: The roles of social approach and aggression. *Journal of Abnormal Child Psychology, 10,* 389–410.

Dunford, F. W., & Elliott, D. S. (1982). *Identifying career offenders with self-reported data* (Grant No. MH27552). Washington, DC: National Institute of Mental Health.

Elder, G. H., Jr., Caspi, A., & Downey, G. (1983). Problem behavior in family relationships: A multigenerational analysis. In A. Sorensen, F. Weinert, & L. Sherrod (Eds.), *Human development: Interdisciplinary perspective* (pp. 93–118). Hillsdale, NJ: Erlbaum.

Elder, G. H., Jr., Caspi, A., & Nguyen, T. V. (in press). Resourceful and vulnerable children: Family influences in stressful times. In R. K. Silbereisen & K. Eyferth (Eds.), *Development in context: Integrative perspectives on youth development.* New York: Springer.

Elliott, D. S., Huizinga, D., & Ageton, S. S. (1985). *Explaining delinquency and drug use.* Beverly Hills, CA: Sage.

Farrington, D. P. (1983). Offending from 10 to 25 years of age. In K. T. Van Dusen & S. A. Mednick (Eds.), *Prospective studies of crime and delinquency* (pp. 17–37). Boston: Kluwer-Nijhoff.

Farrington, D. P. (1987). Early precursors of frequent offending. In J. Q. Wilson & G. C. Loury (Eds.), *From children to citizens: Vol. III. Families, schools, and delinquency prevention* (pp. 27–51). New York: Springer-Verlag.

Farrington, D. P., Gallagher, B., Morley, L., St. Ledger, R. J., & West, D. J. (1986). *Cambridge study in delinquent development: Long term follow-up.* Unpublished annual report, Cambridge University Institute of Criminology, Cambridge, England.

Farrington, D. P., Ohlin, L. E., & Wilson, J. Q. (1986). *Understanding and controlling crime: Toward a new research strategy.* New York: Springer-Verlag.

Federal Bureau of Investigation. (1987). *Crime in the United*

States: Uniform crime reports, 1986, Washington, DC: Government Printing Office.

Fehrmann, P. G., Keith, T. Z., & Reimers, T. M. (1987). Home influences on school learning: Direct and indirect effects of parental involvement in high school grades. *Journal of Educational Research, 80,* 330–337.

Feldman, R. A., Caplinger, T. E., & Wodarski, S. S. (1981). *The St. Louis conundrum: Presocial and antisocial boys together.* Unpublished manuscript.

Forehand, R., King, H. E., Peed, S., & Yoder, P. (1975). Mother-child interactions: Comparison of a non-compliant clinic group and a nonclinic group. *Behaviour Research and Therapy, 13,* 79–85.

Forehand, R., Wells, K., & Griest, D. (1980). An examination of the social validity of a parent training program. *Behavior Therapy, 11,* 488–502.

Forgatch, M. S. (1988, June). *The relation between child behaviors, client resistance, and parenting practices.* Paper presented at the Earlscourt Symposium on Childhood Aggression, Toronto.

Forgatch, M. S., Patterson, G. R., & Skinner, M. (in press). A mediational model for the effect of divorce on antisocial behavior in boys. In E. M. Hetherington (Ed.), *The impact of divorce and step-parenting on children.* Hillsdale, NJ: Lawrence Erlbaum Assoc.

Garmezy, N., & Rutter, M. (Eds,). (1983). *Stress, coping, and development in children.* New York: McGraw Hill.

Gecas, V. (1979). The influence of social class on socialization. In W. R. Burr, R. Hill, F. I. Nye, & I. L. Reiss (Eds.), *Contemporary theories about the family* (Vol. 1, pp. 365–404). New York: Free Press.

Gendreau, P., Madden, P., & Leipeiger, M. (1979). Norms and recidivism rates for social history and institutional experience for first incarcerates: Implications for programming. *Canadian Journal of Criminology, 21,* 1–26.

Hawkins, J. D., & Lishner, D. M. (1987). Schooling and delinquency. In E. H. Johnson(Ed.), *Handbook on crime and delinquency prevention* (pp. 179–221). New York: Greenwood Press.

Hetherington, E. M., Cox, M., & Cox, R. (1982). Effects of divorce on parents and children. In M. Lamb (Ed.), *Nontraditional families* (pp. 233–288). Hillsdale, NJ: Erlbaum.

Hess, R. D. (1970). Social class and ethnic influences on socialization. In P. H. Mussen (Ed.), *Charmichael's manual of child psychology* (Vol. 2, pp. 457–558). New York: Wiley.

Hirschi, T. (1969) *Causes of delinquency.* Berkeley, CA: University of California Press.

Hops, H., & Cobb, J. A. (1974). Initial investigations into academic survival-skill training, direct instruction, and first-grade achievement. *Journal of Educational Psychology, 66,* 548–553.

Huba, G. J., & Bentler, P. M. (1983). Causal models of the development of law abidance and its relationship to psychosocial factors and drug use. In W. S. Laufer & J. M. Day (Eds.), *Personality theory, moral development and criminal behavior* (pp. 165–215). Lexington, MA: Lexington Books.

Huesmann, L. R., Eron, L. D., Lefkowitz, M. M., & Walder, L. O.(1984). Stability of aggression over time and generations. *Developmental Psychology, 20,* 1120–1134.

Jones, R. R., Weinrott, M. R., & Howard, J. R. (1981). *The national evaluation of the Teaching Family Model.* Unpublished manuscript, Evaluation Research Group, Eugene, OR.

Kandel, D. B. (1973). Adolescent marijuana use: Role of parents and peers. *Science, 181,* 1067–1081.

Kazdin, A. E. (1987). Treatment of antisocial behavior in children: Current status and future directions. *Psychological Bulletin, 102,* 187–203.

Loeber, R. (1982). The stability of antisocial and delinquent child behavior: A review. *Child Development, 53,* 1431–1446.

Loeber, R., & Dishion, T. J. (1983). Early predictors of male delinquency: A review. *Psychological Bulletin, 94,* 68–99.

Marlowe, H. J., Reid, J. B., Patterson, G. R., Weinrott, M. R., & Bank, L.(1988). *Treating adolescent multiple offenders: A comparison and follow up of parent training for families of chronic delinquents. Manu*script submitted for publication.

McCord, W., McCord, J., & Howard, A. (1963). Familial correlates of aggression in nondelinquent male children. *Journal of Abnormal and Social Psychology, 62,* 79–93.

Olweus, D. (1979). Stability of aggressive reaction patterns in males: A review. *Psychological Bulletin, 86,* 852–875.

Patterson, G. R. (1982). *A social learning approach: 3. Coercive family process.* Eugene, OR: Castalia.

Patterson, G. R. (1986). Performance models for antisocial boys. *American Psychologist, 41,* 432–444.

Patterson, G. R., & Dishion, T J. (1988). Multilevel family process models: Traits, interactions, and relationships. In R. Hinde & J. Stevenson-Hinde (Eds.), *Relationships within families: Mutual influences* (pp. 283–310). Oxford: Clarendon Press.

Patterson, G. R., Dishion, T J., & Bank, L. (1984). Family interaction: A process model of deviancy training. *Aggressive Behavior, 10,* 253–267.

Patterson, G. R., Reid, J. B., & Dishion, T. J. (in press). *Antisocial boys.* Eugene, OR: Castalia.

Patterson, G. R., Reid, J. B., Jones, R. R., & Conger, R. E. (1975). *A social learning approach to family intervention: Vol 1. Families with aggressive children.* Eugene, OR: Castalia.

Putallaz, M. (1983). Predicting children's sociometric status from their behavior. *Child Development, 54,* 1417–1426.

Robins, L. N. (1966). *Deviant children grown up: A sociological and psychiatric study of sociopathic personality.* Baltimore: Williams & Wilkins.

Robins, L. N., & Earls F. (1985). A program for preventing antisocial behavior for high-risk infants and preschoolers: A research prospectus. In R. L. Hough, P. A. Gongla, V. B. Brown, & S. E. Goldston (Eds.), *Psychiatric epidemiology and prevention: The possibilities* (pp. 73–84). Los Angeles: Neuropsychiatric Institute.

Robins, L. N., & Ratcliff, K. S. (1979). Risk factors in the continuation of childhood antisocial behavior into adulthood. *International Journal of Mental Health, 7(3–4),* 96–116.

Robins, L. N., West, P. A., & Herjanic, B. L. (1975). Arrests and delinquency in two generations: A study of black urban families and their children. *Journal of Child Psychology and Psychiatry, 16,* 125–140.

Roff, J. D., & Wirt, R. D. (1984). Childhood aggression and social adjustment as antecedents of delinquency. *Journal of Abnormal Child Psychology, 12,* 111–116.

Rutter, M. (1979). Protective factors in children's responses to stress and disadvantage. In M. W. Kent & J. E. Rolfe (Eds.), *Primary prevention of psychopathology: 3. Social competence in children.* Hanover, NH: University Press of New England.

Rutter, M., & Giller, H. (1983). *Juvenile delinquency: Trends and perspectives.* New York: Penguin Books.

Shinn, M. R., Ramsey, E., Walker, H. M., O'Neill, R. E., & Steiber, S. (1987). Antisocial behavior in school settings: Initial differences in an at-risk and normal population. *Journal of Special Education, 21,* 69–84.

Snyder, J. J. (1977). Reinforcement analysis of interaction in problem and nonproblem families. *Journal of Abnormal Psychology, 86,* 528–535.

Snyder, J. J. (1988). *An intradyad analysis of the effects of daily variations in maternal stress on maternal discipline and irritability: Its effects on child deviant behaviors.* Manuscript in preparation.

Snyder, J. J., Dishion, T. J., & Patterson, G. R. (1986). Determinants and consequences of associating with deviant peers during preadolescence and adolescence. *Journal of Early Adolescence, 6(1),* 20–43.

Snyder, J. J., & Patterson, G. R. (1986). The effects of consequences on patterns of social interaction: A quasi-experimental approach to reinforcement in natural interaction. *Child Development, 57,* 1257–1268.

Wahler, R. G., & Dumas, J. E. (1984). Family factors in childhood psychopathology: Toward a coercion neglect model. In T. Jacob (Ed.), *Family interaction and psychopathology.* New York: Plenum Press.

Walker, H. M., Shinn, M. R., O'Neill, R. E., & Ramsey, E. (1987). Longitudinal assessment and long-term follow-up of antisocial behavior in fourth-grade boys: Rationale, methodology, measures, and results. *Remedial and Special Education, 8,* 7–16.

Wallerstein, J. S., & Kelley, J. B. (1981). *Surviving the breakup: How children and parents cope with divorce.* New York: Basic Books.

Wilson, J. Q., & Herrnstein, R. J. (1985). *Crime and human nature.* New York: Simon & Schuster.

34

Adolescent Sexual Behavior

JEANNE BROOKS-GUNN AND FRANK F. FURSTENBERG, JR.

Few developmental topics receive more attention in the popular press than teenage sexuality. Although biological changes initiate development of sexual interest, social and cognitive factors are critical in determining behavioral practices and decision making associated with adolescent sexual activity. In the following article, Jeanne Brooks-Gunn and Frank F. Furstenberg, Jr. review historical patterns in this area of development and discuss social and cognitive changes that directly influence adolescent sexual behavior. Certainly, no discussion of adolescent sexuality can conclude without some attention to applied concerns such as contraceptive use and issues related to sexually transmitted diseases. How these issues are addressed, both publicly and privately, is critical for securing and maintaining adolescent health and vitality in the world today.

What is known about adolescent sexual behavior is reviewed. First, the onset of sexual behavior in the teenage years is considered as a function of cohort, gender, and ethnic differences. Omissions in the research on sexual behavior other than intercourse are highlighted. Possible biological, social, and social cognitive processes underlying teenage sexual behavior are then considered. Next, demographic trends in the use of contraceptives and antecedents of regular birth control use are reviewed. Finally, some of the successful program initiatives directed toward altering sexual and contraceptive practice are discussed, keeping in mind the importance and relative lack of well-designed and carefully evaluated programs.

Reprinted with permission from the authors and *American Psychologist, 44,* 1989, 249–257. Copyright 1989 by the American Psychological Association.

The current support of the Robert Wood Johnson Foundation, the Ford Foundation, and the Office of Adolescent Pregnancy Programs (Department of Health and Human Services) is greatly appreciated. The Russell Sage Foundation, where we are visiting scholars, also is thanked for their assistance. Roberta Paikoff, Laurie Zabin, Lindsay Chase-Lansdale, and Brent Miller deserve special thanks for their critical reading of this article. We are grateful for help in manuscript preparation from R. Deibler and F. Kelly.

The tension between sexuality as pleasure and sexuality as reproduction is probably a universal human condition. All societies attempt to manage sexuality in order to regulate fertility. This task is both necessary and difficult because sexual desire guarantees species perpetuation. Typically, efforts to control fertility and arousal emerge during puberty, as the child is transformed into a reproductively mature adult. Chaperonage, seclusion, bride-price, and residence with the bridegroom's family prepubertally are mechanisms in traditional societies for managing fertility prior to marriage. These practices have been linked to the economic value of the female reproductive potential in societies where high birth rates were necessary given agricultural work and childhood mortality (Paige, 1983). Today's concern over teenage sexuality also is often couched in political and economic terms, as evidenced by discussions of the societal and individual cost of teenage parenthood (the proportion of Aid to Families with Dependent Children payments going to families of young childbearers and the reduced prospects of employment and education for teenage mothers). As sexuality, marriage, and childbearing have become less closely linked during the last quarter century, societal strategies for regulating sexuality have been revised accordingly, which is the focus of this article. First, we take a brief historical tour of teenage sexual behavior as studied by social scientists, in order to highlight the sometimes glaring research omissions. Then we turn to what is known about fertility management, keeping in mind that other aspects of sexual behavior have been woefully understudied. The onset of sexual behavior is considered in light of historical, gender, and ethnic changes that have occurred in the last 20 years. Possible biological, social, and social cognitive processes underlying teenage sexual behavior are examined in an effort to go beyond a mere listing of known antecedents. This is followed by a look at patterns of contraceptive use and their antecedents, since fertility may be controlled by delaying the onset of intercourse or by practicing birth control. Finally, within the small universe of well-designed and carefully evaluated programs, successful initiatives directed toward altering sexual or contraceptive practices are examined.

SOCIAL SCIENCE AND THE STUDY OF TEENAGE SEXUAL BEHAVIOR

Perhaps the best known and most influential work on sexual behavior was conducted by Kinsey and his colleagues in the 1940s and 1950s (Kinsey, Pomeroy, & Martin, 1948; Kinsey, Pomeroy, Martin, & Gebhard, 1953). Documenting increases in premarital intercourse since World War I led to speculation on the role of sex in mate selection. In the 1950s and 1960s, as Gagnon (1987) suggested, most studies were quite delicate in their handling of such topics, focusing on attitudes and, when behavior was the emphasis, on the age of first intercourse. A few exemplary studies (Gagnon & Simon, 1973; Jessor & Jessor, 1975, 1977; Reiss, 1960) in the late 1960s embedded sexuality in the adolescent experience, collecting data on other adolescent behavior.

However, subsequent research did not provide broader perspectives for the study of sexuality; nor did it provide theoretical models to explain sexual desires and behavior. One source of this limited vision can be traced to the rising concern about teenage fertility in the late 1960s and early 1970s. Given the increase in out-of-wedlock births and the decrease in age of intercourse, research focused almost solely on fertility control (sexual onset and contraceptive use). What sexuality means to adolescents, how it relates to other aspects of teenage life, and what strategies teens use to manage or incorporate it into their lives have not been studied in any detail. Particular specific research omissions (in both the adolescent and adult literature) include the following: (a) frequency of behaviors other than intercourse and variations in type and frequencies of sexual behavior by gender, ethnicity, age, social class, and sex of partner; (b) pubertal education aimed at boys on topics such as ejaculation and condom use (many young men today still learn about ejaculation from magazines, locker room jokes, or their first nocturnal emission; Gaddis & Brooks-Gunn, 1985); (c) same-sex preferences and behavior; (d) the relation of sexual behavior to other adolescent behavior and life events (as an exception, see Jessor & Jessor, 1977); (e) the meaning of eroticism in adolescents' sex lives; (f) the influence of social contexts (school and community environments) on the regulation and expression of social behaviors; (g) differences between younger and older adolescents in all of the above; and (h) comparisons of fertility regulation and onset of sexual activity in other cultures.

TRANSITION TO SEXUAL BEHAVIOR

Historical Trends

Perhaps reflective of our society's ambivalence about teenage sexuality, national survey data on age of intercourse were not collected until 1971. Earlier estimates were based on selective samples, such as that of Kinsey. Dramatic increases in the number of teenage girls having intercourse have taken place in the last 50 years. In 1938 to 1950, approximately 7% of White females had intercourse by age 16 (Kinsey et al., 1948). By 1971, one third of never-married White girls 16 years of age had had intercourse, with the figure rising to 44% by 1982 (Hofferth & Hayes, 1987; Zelnik & Kantner, 1980). Trends have been carefully documented in the 1970s and 1980s. The proportion of all never-married girls ages 15 to 19 who have had intercourse is illustrated in Figure 1 by race and by time (1971 to 1982). Large increases occurred between 1971 and 1979, after which time the percentage of sexually active girls remained stable or perhaps even declined. Black girls had significantly higher rates of intercourse than White girls at all time points, although the difference had dropped to only 13% by 1982.

Historically, boys were much more likely to make their sexual debut as teenagers than girls. Estimates of selected samples from the 1940s to 1960s are that one third to two thirds of male teenagers were sexually active (Hofferth & Hayes, 1987). Data comparable to that just reported for teenage girls in the 1970s and 1980s do not exist for boys, perhaps reflective of the fact that fertility regulation is considered a female, not a male, issue. The rises in teenage sexual behavior are probably not as pronounced for boys as for girls, since many more of the former engaged in intercourse in previous decades. What has happened is that the gap between male and female teenagers narrowed as more and more girls became sexually active. Cumulative percentages using the National Longitudinal Survey of Youth by age of initiation, sex, and race in

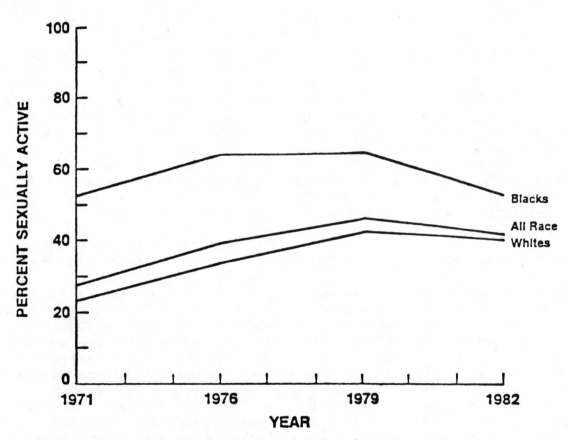

FIGURE 1   Sexual activity of adolescent girls ages 15 through 19, from 1971 to 1982. Note: Data are from "Sexual Activity, Contraceptive Use and Pregnancy Among Metropolitan Area Teenagers: 1971–1979" by M. Zelnik and J. F. Kantner, 1980. *Family Planning Perspectives, 12(5),* pp. 230–237, Copyright 1980 by Alan Guttmacher Institute, NY; "The Use of Family Planning Services by Sexually Active Teenagers" by W. F. Pratt and G. E. Hendershot, 1984, *Population Index,* 50(3), pp. 412–413. Copyright 1984 by Office of Population Research, Princeton University, Princeton. NJ; and *Risking the Future: Adolescent Sexuality, Pregnancy, and Childbearing* (Vol. 1, p.41), edited by C. D. Hayes, 1987, Washington, DC: National Academy Press. Reprinted by permission.

1983 tell the story (Hofferth & Hayes, 1987). Sixty percent of White male teens had intercourse by age 18, and 60% of White girls just a year later, by age 19. Greater gender disparities are evident for Black teenagers: 60% of Black male teens had intercourse by age 16, and 60% of Black girls two years later, by age 18. Racial differences for boys are greatest at early adolescence. Indeed, in 1983, 42% of Black boys had had intercourse by age 15 or earlier; in some male subgroups, prepubertal initiation is common.

We have much less information on aspects of sexual behavior other than intercourse: Information on percentages of teenage girls who have had intercourse only once, frequency of intercourse, number of partners, and relationship with first partner is sparse. The little available information on the patterns of sexual activity suggests that many youth have intercourse only very occasionally when they initiate coitus. It is not uncommon for a teen to have first intercourse at age 14 or 15 and then not to have sexual relations again for a year or two. Age at intercourse may be a relatively poor proxy for risk of pregnancy under these circumstances.

Antecedents of Sexual Behavior

Most teens do not consciously plan to become sexually active, and they often do not foresee their first sexual experience. As such, it frequently is not experienced as a decision but rather as something that "happened" (Chilman, 1983). Studies on the antecedents of sexual activity in adolescence show that some but not all of the factors associated differ for Blacks and Whites and for boys and girls (see Hofferth & Hayes, 1987).

BIOLOGICAL PERSPECTIVES   Of the biological changes associated with puberty, hormonal factors are thought to account in some part for the onset of sexual activity, either by effects occurring prenatally or activation effects that change hormonal levels at puberty. Hormonal activation may influence behavior directly by increasing arousal or indirectly by the social stimulus associated with physical changes. The fact that levels of testosterone are associated with sexual activities in boys, independent of secondary sexual development, is evidence for a direct effect (Udry, Billy, Morris, Groff, & Raj, 1985). In girls, sexual interests, but not behavior, are associated with testosterone levels, suggesting that social factors may play a greater role in their coital behavior (Udry, Talbert, & Morris, 1986). However, whether engagement in sexual intercourse increases androgen level or vice versa is not known.

In addition, contextual effects, if entered into the equation, might account for more of the variation in sexual activity than hormonal levels. Initiation of sexual behavior is highly associated with what is perceived as normative in one's peer group (Furstenberg, Moore, & Peterson, 1986), so it is likely that while very early sexual initiations may be in part hormonally mediated, by the time that behavior is normative, social factors may account for sexual initiation (see Gargiulo, Attie, Brooks-Gunn, & Warren, 1987, for a similar argument about dating behavior). Thus, even when hormonal effects are demonstrated, they must be evaluated relative to social factors before assuming direct or large hormonal-sexual behavior associations (Brooks-Gunn & Warren, 1989). Race differences in the initiation of intercourse prior to puberty also speak to the importance of social and contextual factors on sexual behavior.

The developing body acts as a stimulus for behavior change regardless of hormonal status. (No one-to-one correspondence exists between hormonal levels and secondary sexual characteristics.) For example, more physically mature girls seem to elicit more freedom from parents, perhaps making it more likely that they engage in dating and ultimately early sexual behavior. At the same time, pubertal children expect to be granted more autonomy in terms of friends and curfews than prepubertal children. Early-maturing girls are more likely to have older friends, which is associated with intercourse, smoking, and drinking (Brooks-Gunn, 1988; Magnusson, Strattin, & Allen, 1985). Such facts may in part explain associations between early maturation and intercourse beyond the potential influence of hormonal factors.

PARENTAL INFLUENCES   Parental influences on sexual behavior are believed to be strong, although research is surprisingly sparse (Ooms, 1981). Teens who rate perceived communication with their parents as poor are more likely to initiate sex early; they also are likely to begin smoking and drinking early (Jessor & Jessor, 1977). Close relationships with parents as well as feelings of connectedness and supportiveness seem to be associated with later onset of intercourse (Inazu & Fox, 1980; Jessor & Jessor, 1977). However, as Hofferth and Hayes (1987) suggest, familial communication prior to first intercourse is usually not measured; nor are different aspects of communication, the age at which discussions occur, or the context in which it is embedded. Parents are often uncomfortable discussing sexual topics associated with reproduction with their postpubertal children, as are their children (the exception being mothers and daughters about menarche; Brooks-Gunn & Ruble, 1982). The cultural acceptance of sexuality in boys but not girls also may influence the nature of communication; for example, in one study, mother–daughter communication was associated with later intercourse, as was mother–son communication. However, sons' discussions with the father and earlier sexual activity were linked (Kahn, Smith, & Roberts, 1984). Fathers may condone sexual activity in their sons, given the sexual script of male potency. Parental supervision also is associated with later onset of intercourse. These associations are in part mediated by neighborhood influences as well as residence in single-parent households (Hogan & Kitagawa, 1985; Newcomer & Udry, 1987).

More process-oriented research directed at how parents may influence their teens' sexual behavior is sorely needed. Several approaches may be profitable. Certain styles of family interactions enhance social cognitive abilities, such as role taking, decision making, and moral judgments (Cooper, Grotevant, & Condon, 1983). Ego development and autonomy also are associated with interaction styles characterized as enabling, authoritative, and legitimating (Brooks-Gunn & Zahaykevich, in press; Grotevant & Cooper, 1986; Hauser et al., 1984). More autonomous adolescents who are able to consider situations from several perspectives and make well-informed decisions may be more likely to delay the onset of sexual behavior or to use contraceptives more effectively. At the same time, the parental styles just mentioned may promote greater feelings of self-efficacy, which in turn could influence sexual behavior (Bandura, 1982; Strecher, McEvoy, Becker, & Rosenstock, 1986). Such premises await further testing.

PEER INFLUENCES As pointed out by Hofferth and Hayes (1987), beliefs about the importance of peers in the initiation of sexual behavior are much stronger than the actual research evidence. Perceptions about what one's peers are doing or what is normative in one's peer group are more strongly associated with sexual behavior than actual behavior, which is not frequently measured (Cvetkovich & Grote, 1980). Friendship choices may be predicated in part by sexual activity, at least for some subgroups. In addition, age may also mediate peer effects; it is thought that younger adolescents are more susceptible to peer pressure, although little research exists on this point.

Not surprisingly, early dating and early intercourse are associated. Of more interest are differences in sexual norms associated with precoital sexual activity, often seen in the context of dating. For example, White teenagers are more likely to engage in a predictable series of behaviors prior to first intercourse than are Black teenagers. Black girls, who are more likely to move from necking to intercourse without intermediate steps, may be less likely to be pre-

pared for intercourse, in the sense that there is little time to think about and obtain contraceptives (Smith & Udry, 1985).

ACADEMIC PERSPECTIVES Teenagers who are not doing well in school and have lower educational aspirations are more likely to have sex during adolescence than those faring better in school (Hofferth & Hayes, 1987). School functioning itself is mediated by education, job, and welfare status of the mother (Furstenberg, Brooks-Gunn, & Morgan, 1987). It is no surprise, then, that children in poverty are clearly at risk for school failure and early sexuality.

It is important to place the association between academic failure and early sexuality into the context of the school experience, especially for young adolescents. Entrance into middle school is considered one of the most difficult educational transitions and often results in drops in academic performance (Hamburg, 1986). Providing support for the transition to middle school, especially for vulnerable children, seems essential, both to avoid increases in school failure experiences and to promote health behaviors.

SOCIAL COGNITIVE PERSPECTIVES Social cognitive abilities often associated with sexual decision making provide yet another and largely unexplored perspective for understanding sexual transitions among adolescents. We know that the abilities to integrate domain-specific knowledge into a coherent system, to understand the nature of social relationships, to consider the future, and to anticipate consequences of decisions all increase during adolescence (Damon & Hart, 1982; Harter, 1983). The sparse literature on social cognitive abilities and sexual behavior is illustrative. Using a Piagetian approach to study the understanding of "where babies come from," concrete operational responses give way to more formal operational ones during childhood and early adolescence: Formal operations are characteristic of the majority of 11- to 12-year-olds, whereas they are rare in younger children (Bernstein & Cowan, 1975). In a cross-sectional study, North American adolescents were slower in attaining formal abilities related to "where babies come from" than their peers in England, Sweden, and Australia (Goldman & Goldman, 1982). These authors suggest that the North Americans are lagging because of the cultural context (teenage sexual activity being less acceptable in the United States than other Western countries) and education (sex education being later, less complete, and less accepted in the United States). Recently, four stages of reasoning about sexual behavior have been proposed, following other cognitive developmental stage models. These stages are related to age and ego to age and ego development during adolescence and young adulthood but not in later adulthood (Gfellner, 1986). Whether such reasoning is associated with sexual behavior has not been studied.

Other social cognitive processes might be applied to the study of teenage sexual behavior including self-definitions, self-efficacy, and social comparisons (Bandura, 1982; Higgins, Ruble, & Hartup, 1983). For example, at the time of menarche, girls construct a self-definition of what it means to be a mature, reproductive woman based on actual experiences, information seeking, and interactions with others (Brooks-Gunn, 1987).

CONTRACEPTIVE USE

Rates of sexual activity among teens in the United States are not notably higher than the rates in several countries in Western Europe. Yet, the incidence of adolescent pregnancy and childbearing in the United States, especially among younger teens, exceeds the level of most other industrialized nations (Jones et al., 1985; Westoff, Calot & Foster, 1983). This is partly due to poor contraceptive use among American teenagers. Case studies by the Alan Guttmacher Institute suggest that American youth are exposed to mixed messages about contraception and that birth control services are not effectively delivered to the teenage population (Jones et al., 1985). When considering the difficulties adolescents have in using contraceptives, it is important to recognize that many American adults are poor contraceptive users as well. Indeed, the most widely used method of contraception among married adults in their 30s is sterilization (Bachrach, 1984; Jones et al., 1988). Presumably, mature adults resort to sterilization because they have many of the same apprehensions and problems with contraception that teenagers do.

Initiating the Use of Contraceptives

About one half of all teenagers do not use contraceptives the first time they have sexual relations (Zelnik & Shah, 1983). Younger adolescents are much less likely to use contraceptives than are older adolescents. In addition, more Whites than Blacks have used birth control methods during the first intercourse, although these racial differences largely disappear after controlling for age of initiation (Zelnik, Kantner, & Ford, 1981). Little comparable data on use of contraceptives by gender exist. In one study, more than half of the White teenage boys and almost three quarters of the Black teenage boys had not used a method of birth control during first intercourse: This

compared to a little less than half of the White teenage girls and a little more than half of the Black teenage girls not having used contraception during the first intercourse (Zelnik & Shah, 1983).

Of those who use a method, male methods seem to be the overwhelming choice, as reported by both boys and girls, Blacks and Whites. For example, two thirds to three quarters of all White teenagers and Black teenage boys reported using a male method; in contrast, approximately 45% of Black girls reported using a male method, in that they were much more likely to use a female prescription method than the other three groups. In addition, among both boys and girls, those who planned first intercourse were much more likely to have used contraception than those who did not plan the first intercourse. Reasons for not having used a method at first intercourse were provided in this same survey. The reasons, in descending order of their being mentioned, were as follows: Intercourse was not planned, they did not know about intercourse, they did not want to use contraceptives, they did not think about using contraceptives, contraceptives were not available, and pregnancy was thought to be impossible. White teenagers were more likely than Black teenagers to state that contraception was not available, and more Black than White teenagers said that they did not know about contraception (Zelnik & Shah, 1983).

Contraceptive Use After Sexual Initiation

Failure to use contraception the first time intercourse occurs is unfortunately not a one-time event. The percentage of teenagers who use birth control only occasionally or not at all is substantial. These delays have serious consequences. One half of all first pregnancies occur in the first six months following intercourse, and one fifth in the first month (Zabin, Kantner, & Zelnik, 1979). In a study of 1,200 teenagers attending a family planning clinic for the first time, one third came to the clinic because of a possible pregnancy, and 14% came prior to the initiation of intercourse (Zabin & Clark, 1981). Of the remaining young women, only 8% found their way to the clinic within three months of sexual initiation (Zabin & Clark, 1981). However, three quarters of those coming to the clinic had used some form of contraception previously. Most conspicuous among the many reasons for not coming to a family planning clinic earlier were procrastination and ambivalence as well as fear that parents would find out. Many teens believed, incorrectly, that parental consent or notification was necessary for clinic attendance. Clearly, this finding has important implications for altering perceptions about clinics among sexually active teenagers. It also underscores the lack of communication between parents and children about matters associated with sexuality.

Antecedents of Girls' Contraceptive Use

Antecedents of contraceptive use have been studied extensively. The following is a brief summary of these findings (Chilman, 1986; Morrison, 1985). In general, the characteristics of early sexual initiation are similar to those for irregular contraceptive use. Irregular contraceptive use is associated with lower social class, nonattendance of college, and fundamentalist Protestant affiliation. Situational determinants include not having a steady partner, having never had been pregnant, infrequent intercourse, and no access to free confidential family planning. Familial correlates include little communication with parents, perceived troubled relationship with parents, and lack of knowledge of parents' contraceptive experience. Peer influences include having friends who become parents. Academically, low educational achievement and aspirations are associated with irregular contraceptive use. From a personality perspective, high levels of anxiety, low self-esteem, and feelings of fatalism, powerlessness, and alienation are associated with poor contraceptive use.

Lack of knowledge about the safe time of the month also contributes to poor contraceptive use. However, we have little information about sexual knowledge and its relation to sexual behavior more generally. A few relevant surveys suggest that knowledge of contraception and abortion increases during adolescence, which is often attributed to education. However, taking a sex education course does not guarantee adequate knowledge (only one third of 15- to 19-year-olds were able to identify the cycle phase in which risk of pregnancy was the greatest; Zelnik & Kantner, 1977). It appears that knowledge is a necessary but insufficient determinant of effective contraceptive use.

The social cognitive perspective so relevant to understanding the onset of sexual behavior could be applied equally well to contraceptive use and unplanned pregnancy. Almost all girls report being surprised at finding themselves pregnant (Shah, Zelnik, & Kantner, 1975). What accounts for their surprise? Reasons include (a) the belief that they could not become pregnant because of cycle phase (although the majority of adolescents are unable to identify the time at which ovulation occurs); (b) the misperception that they did not have sex often enough, had used withdrawal, had not had an orgasm, or were too young; (c) even while knowing the risk, believing they would not get "caught"; and (d) procrastination or forgetting to use birth control, perhaps indicating a

denial of personal responsibility for their behavior. Unfortunately, most of these studies surveyed only pregnant girls or girls obtaining a pregnancy test, so it is unclear whether these reasons constitute post hoc explanations or rationalizations. Furthermore, although contraceptive use has been attributed to self-insight and future orientation, this assumption has not been directly examined. Theoretical models for contraceptive use should include social cognitive and motivational processes (Morrison, 1985).

Male Contraceptive Use

We know very little about boys' attitudes about contraceptive use or distinguishing characteristics of regular and irregular contraceptive users. Approximately 40% of girls rely on male methods and therefore depend on the "vigilance" of their male partner. Like girls, boys know very little about reproduction, even the time during the menstrual cycle when conception is likeliest to occur. Boys also may be less knowledgeable about specific contraceptives and may have even more reservations about contraceptive use than girls.

Sexual Activity and Other Adolescent Behaviors

Teenage sexual activity and contraceptive use must be considered in light of other adolescent experiences. For example, teenage sexual behavior is generally associated with alcohol and drug use as well as declines in school achievement and interest. Adolescents may engage in such behaviors for many different reasons, including (a) efforts to achieve what seem to be unavailable goals, (b) a way of coping with personal frustrations and anticipated failure, (c) an expression of opposition to conventional society, and (d) membership in peers' subcultures (Hamburg, 1986; Jessor & Jessor, 1977). Just describing demographic trends in sexual behavior and antecedent factors does not offer much insight into why adolescents engage in sexual activity or other behaviors. Intervention efforts have been hampered by the lack of research on the context in which sexuality occurs, the possible personal correlates of certain behavior patterns, and the interaction of the two.

It is important to consider differences between older and younger adolescents' goals and motivations. For example, sexual behavior is more likely to be termed problem behavior for younger than older adolescents. Whether the motivations of young adolescents are different from those of older adolescents has not been studied. From a developmental perspective, it is not known whether early engagement in sexual behavior and other risk-taking behaviors truncates the process of adolescent development, making it less likely that these teens achieve autonomy and a healthy sense of self. However, it is clear that the young adolescents' life course trajectory might be more likely to be negatively affected by early engagement in sexual behavior, as reflected in school problems, early pregnancy, and poor job prospects, than the adolescent who has already completed high school. (For more discussion of these issues, see our companion article on pregnancy and childbearing in this issue.)

SEXUALLY TRANSMITTED DISEASES

Adolescents are at high risk for sexually transmitted diseases (STDs). Excluding homosexual men and prostitutes, female teenagers have the highest rates of gonorrhea, cytomegalovirus, chlamydia cervicitis, and pelvic inflammatory diseases of any age group (Cates & Rauh, 1985; Mosher, 1985). Risk factors for STDs include early age of intercourse and no or irregular contraceptive use.

Of pressing concern is the incidence of the acquired immune deficiency syndrome (AIDS). Although few adolescents have been reported to have AIDS, the numbers have been doubling in recent years. In addition, one fifth of all cases have occurred in 20- to 29-year-olds, and the virus has a long incubation period, suggesting that many of these cases may have originated in the late adolescent years (Curran et al., 1988). If the proportion of reported cases increases in the heterosexual population, as many expect it will, adolescents may be at relatively high risk for infection, given their current rates of other STDs and their contraceptive histories (Brooks-Gunn, Boyer, & Hein, 1988). Educational programs about STDs generally and AIDS in particular are becoming more commonplace in school sex educational programs. In a recent national survey by Harris, virtually all parents wanted AIDS education in the schools (Meade, 1988). Many of the preventative strategies discussed in the next section could be tailored to include behavioral interventions aimed at reducing the incidence of STDs and AIDS by increasing the use of condoms, advocating the practice of less risky sexual behaviors, reducing the use of intravenous drugs, and minimizing the sharing of needles among intravenous drug users. These are behavior changes advocated for adults as well as for adolescents (Koop, 1988; see review of adolescent AIDS by Brooks-Gunn et al., 1988).

PREVENTION STRATEGIES

Several preventative strategies have been proposed and implemented: offering access to contraception, providing knowledge about sexuality and contraception, influencing sexual attitudes, and enhancing life options (Dryfoos, 1984). The majority of programs offer services (family planning) or knowledge (sex education); fewer attempt to change motivational constructs such as strengthening competing goals (school achievement), providing alternative means of achieving goals (intimacy without sexual behavior or with regular contraceptive use), or altering peer group norms (making early sexual activity less desirable; Hamburg, 1986). What follows is a very brief review of some of the preventative strategies currently being used. (See Hofferth & Hayes, 1987, for a more complete discussion, especially of interventions that have not been systematically evaluated or are currently being evaluated, such as programs to delay first intercourse or abstain from sexual activity.) Family life and sex education, media programs, family planning services, and school-based clinic programs are reviewed. Other approaches using more specific social psychological principles include decision making, peer counseling, peer resistance training, behavioral skills training, and decreases in risk-taking behavior generally (Botvin, 1986; Perry, 1984). Systematic application of such approaches to sexual behavior is rare. Most prevention strategies focus on females.

Family Life and Sex Education

The primary purpose of family life and sex education is to provide information about human reproduction and, increasingly, about contraceptive use. Once believed to be exclusively in the province of the family, responsibility for sex education has shifted in part to the school. A vast majority of parents, other adults, and adolescents support sex education in the schools (Norman & Harris, 198 1). In the early 1980s, three quarters of all school districts provided some sex education and three quarters of adolescents in national surveys reported having had some sex education (Zelnik & Kim, 1982). Only one state currently prohibits instruction on reproductive topics. However, the timing, extensiveness, and intensiveness of sex education programs are widely divergent. Almost all school districts include decision making about sexual behavior as a goal of their sex education programs. Three quarters include reproductive knowledge, and a scant one quarter include reduction of sexual activity and teenage childbearing as goals. Most programs are short (10 hr or less), and perhaps less than 10% of all students have taken comprehensive programs (40 hr or more; Kirby, 1984). Elementary school programs seem to be rare, although pubertal education is provided in many fifth and sixth grades (no systematic review of these programs exists). Junior high school programs focus on puberty, reproduction, and dating, but typically not on contraception. High school coverage is more inclusive: Three quarters of all programs include family planning, contraceptive methods, and abortion, and one half include masturbation and homosexuality as topics (Hofferth & Hayes, 1987; Orr, 1982).

Several tests of the efficacy of sex education have been performed in recent years. Generally, knowledge about reproduction increases after such programs, especially in younger adolescents. Of more interest is whether such programs alter behavior. The fear that sex education would promote early sexuality is largely unfounded (Furstenberg et al., 1986; Zelnik & Kim, 1982). Such programs may promote contraceptive use among sexually active teens, but evidence is mixed (Kirby, 1984). Because sex education is part of the adolescent experience in the United States today, it is clear that more evaluation is needed as well as design of new approaches. Peer counseling and parent-adolescent communication programs have been developed, although little is known about their effectiveness.

SCHOOL-BASED CLINICS Such clinics are perhaps the most major programmatic effort, and the most hotly debated one, to be initiated in the 1970s and 1980s. In the most well-known program in St. Paul, Minnesota, fertility rates dropped from 79 per thousand to 26 per thousand from 1973 to 1984; continuation rate for contraceptive use was high (more than 80% over a two-year period); dropout rates for girls with babies dropped from 45% to 10% from 1973 to 1976-1977 (Edwards, Steinman, Arnold, & Hakanson, 1980). Another innovative program has recently been evaluated in Baltimore, where a health clinic was opened adjacent to a junior high and a high school. Using a pre-post, comparison-treatment design, first intercourse was delayed by seven months for girls who were exposed to the program for three years, clinic attendance increased for girls prior to first intercourse, and many boys attended. Most impressive, conceptions dropped in the program schools during the three-year period while increasing in the comparison schools (Zabin, Hirsch, Smith, Strett, & Hardy, 1986). However, not all program evaluations have yielded such positive results.

Media

Information provided in the media is a way to reach almost all teens and their families. However, tele-

vision executives have been hesitant to address issues related to sexual behavior and contraceptive use in regular programming and in advertisements. Public health messages and advertisements about sexuality and contraception also do not make their way into the major networks with any frequency. In 1985, the three major networks refused to place public service announcements on teenage pregnancy, although they have done so subsequently with no negative public response. In 1987, all three networks rejected a public education message about oral contraceptive use as too controversial. In 1988, even though public health service messages on condom use to prevent AIDS were aired, network executives state that they would turn down identical advertisements by condom manufacturers; public service announcements on contraceptives not linked to disease prevention are still not being aired by the three major networks (although a few local stations do so).

Family Planning Services

Family planning services play a major role in teenagers' fertility regulation, especially since three quarters of teenage girls using contraception use prescription methods (primarily oral contraceptives). One half of all teenage girls obtaining services use family planning clinics and one half use private physicians. A disproportionate number of clinic users are young, Black, and poor (Pratt & Hendershot, 1984). About two thirds of family planning clinics' funds are provided through federal grants (Title X, Maternal and Child Health Grants, Medicare Funds, and State Block Grants). Issues under study include how to encourage regular scheduled visits, how to decrease the time between first intercourse and first clinic visits, and how effective family planning clinics have been in reducing unwanted pregnancies. Little effort is directed toward bringing male teenagers into the system; for example, less than 1% of all patients served by family planning clinics are male.

CONCLUSION

In 1987, the National Academy of Sciences Panel on Early Childbearing recommended that the rate and incidence of unintended pregnancy among adolescents be reduced. Recommended programs included ones to enhance life options (school performance, role models, and employment opportunities), delay sexual initiation, and encourage contraception after the sexual debut. The panel urged that sex education include sections on contraceptive use, decision making, and assertiveness training; that medical and community services work together to provide integrative, continuous services; that the media be discouraged from glorifying sex; that the media be encouraged to promote contraceptive advertising; and that more school-bill clinics be designed and evaluated (Hayes, 1987). Many of these policy initiatives have been suggested before or are being attempted in select communities, but no large-scale efforts have been undertaken yet.

Perhaps ironically, directing research to girls' fertility, although arising from what is clearly an important policy issue, may have made it difficult to design effective interventions; that is, in the absence of data on the meaning and frequency of different sexual behaviors, program development occurs in what seems to be a social science vacuum. Often untested assumptions have driven program initiatives, some of which have turned out to be good bets and others unfortunate guesses. Our lack of knowledge is all the more distressing given the haunting specter of AIDS and the rapid rise of STDs in adolescents. How do we alter

sexual practices among homosexual teenagers or in intravenous drug users (the two groups at greatest risk for AIDs) if we do not know how many there are, where they are located, or what their current sexual practices are? How might teens be encouraged to use condoms (the most effective protection against human immunodeficiency virus infection known today) when almost no information exists as to how teens initiate sexual activity, how they view and use the condom, what they know about proper use of the condom, how they discuss condom use with a partner, and so on? Clearly, we are limited in what may be said about every aspect of sexuality except fertility control, specifically age of intercourse onset and (girls') contraceptive use. Although a critical concern, in that teenage parenthood extracts a cost to the young mother, the young father, and their children (see our companion piece in this issue, Furstenberg, Brooks-Gunn, & Chase-Lansdale, pp. 313-320), other concerns are not addressed by social scientists generally or psychologists in particular.

References

Bachrach, C. A. (1984). Contraceptive practice among American women, 1973-1982. *Family Planning Perspectives, 16,* 253–259.

Bandura, A. (1982). Self-efficacy mechanism in human agency. *American Psychologist, 37,* 122–147.

Bernstein, A. C., & Cowan, P. A. (1975). Children's concepts of how people get babies. *Child Development, 46,* 77–91.

Botvin, G. J. (1986). Substance abuse prevention research: Recent developments and future directions. *Journal of School Health, 56(9),* 369–374.

Brooks-Gunn, J. (1987). Pubertal processes and girls' psychological adaptation. In R. Lemer & T. T. Foch (Eds.), *Biological-psychosocial interactions in early adolescence: A life-span perspective* (pp. 123–153). Hillsdale, NJ: Lawrence Erlbaum Associates.

Brooks-Gunn, J. (1988). Antecedents and consequences of variations in girls' maturational timing. *Journal of Adolescent Health Care, 9(5),* 1–9.

Brooks-Gunn, J., Boyer, C. B., & Hein, K. (1988). Preventing HIV infection and AIDS in children and adolescents: Behavioral research and intervention strategies. *American Psychologist, 43,* 958–964.

Brooks-Gunn, J., & Ruble, D. N. (1982). The development of menstrual-related beliefs and behaviors during early adolescence. *Child Development, 53,* 1567–1577.

Brooks-Gunn, J., & Warren, M. P. (in press). Biological contributions to affective expression in young adolescent girls. *Child Development.*

Brooks-Gunn, J., & Zahaykevich, M. (in press). Parent–daughter relationships in early adolescence: A developmental perspective. In K. Kreppner & R. Lerner (Eds.), *Family systems and life-span development.* Hillsdale, NJ: Erlbaum.

Cates, W., Jr., & Rauh, J. L. (I 985). Adolescents and sexually transmitted diseases: An expanding problem. *Journal of Adolescent Health Care, 6,* 1–5.

Chilman, C. S. (1983). *Adolescent sexuality in a changing American society: Social and psychological perspectives for the human services professions* (2nd ed.). New York: Wiley.

Chilman, C. S. (1986). Some psychosocial aspect of adolescent sexual and contraceptive behaviors in a changing American society. In J. B. Lancaster & B. A. Hamburg (Eds.), *School-age pregnancy and parenthood: Biosocial dimensions* (pp. 191–217). New York: Aldine De Gruyter.

Cooper, C., Grotevant, H., & Condon, S. (1983). Individuality and connectedness in the family as a context for adolescent identity formation and role-taking skill. *New Directions for Child Development, 22,* 43–60.

Curran, J. W., Jaffe, H. W., Hardy, A. M., Morgan, W. M., Selik, R. M., & Dondero, T. J. (1988). Epidemiology of HIV infection and AIDS in the United States. *Science, 239,* 610–616.

Cvetkovich, G., & Grote, B. (1980). Psychological development and the social problem of teenage illegitimacy. In C. Chilman (Ed.), *Adolescent pregnancy and childbearing: Findings from research* (pp. 15–41). Washington, DC: U.S. Department of Health and Human Services.

Damon, W., & Hart, D. (1982). The development of self-understanding from infancy through adolescence. *Child Development, 53,* 841–864.

Dryfoos, J. G. (1984). A new strategy for preventing unintended teenage childbearing. *Family Planning Perspectives, 16,* 193–195.

Edwards, L., Steinman, M., Arnold, K., & Hakanson, E. (1980). Adolescent pregnancy prevention services in high school clinics. *Family Planning Perspectives, 12,* 6-14.

Furstenberg, F., Jr., Brooks-Gunn, J., & Chase-Lansdale, L. (1989). Teenaged pregnancy and childbearing. *American Psychologist. 44,* 313–320.

Furstenberg, F. F. Jr., Brooks-Gunn, J., & Morgan, S. P. (1987). *Adolescent mothers in later life.* New York: Cambridge University Press.

Furstenberg, F. F., Jr., Moore, K. A., & Peterson, J. L. (1986). Sex education and sexual experience among adolescents. *American Journal of Public Health, 75,* 1221–1222.

Gaddis, A., & Brooks-Gunn, J. (1985). The male experience of pubertal change. *Journal of Youth and Adolescence, 14(1),* 61-69.

Gagnon, J. H. (1987). *Some notes on aspects of sexual conduct relevant to the AIDS epidemic.* Unpublished manuscript.

Gagnon, J., & Simon, W. (I 973). *Sexual conduct: The social sources of human sexuality.* New York: Aldine de Gruyter.

Gargiulo, J., Attie, I., Brooks-Gunn, J., & Warren, M. P. (1987). Dating in middle school girls: Effects of social context, maturation, and grade. *Developmental Psychology, 23(5),* 730–737.

Gfellner, B. M. (1986). Concepts of sexual behavior: Construction and validation of a developmental model. *Journal Of Adolescent Research,* 1(3), 327–347.

Goldman, R. J., & Goldman, J. D. G. (1982). How children perceive the origin of babies and the roles of mothers and fathers in procreation: A cross-national study. *Child Development, 53,* 491–504.

Grotevant, H. D., & Cooper, C. R. (1986). Individuation in family relationships. *Human Development, 29,* 82–100.

Hamburg, B. A. (1986). Subsets of adolescent mothers: Developmental, biomedical, and psychosocial issues. In J. B. Lancaster & B. A. Hamburg (Eds.), *School-age pregnancy and parenthood: Biosocial dimensions* (pp. 115–145). New York: Aldine De Gruyter.

Harter, S. (1983). Developmental perspectives on the self-system. In E. M. Hetherington (Ed.), *Socialization, personality, and social development: Vol. 4. Handbook of child psychology* (4th ed.). New York: Wiley.

Hauser, S., Powers, S. I., Noam, G. G., Jacobson, A. M., Weiss, B., & Follansbee, D. J. (1984). Familial contexts of adolescent ego development. *Child Development, 55,* 195–213.

Hayes, C. D. (Ed.). (1987). *Risking the future: Adolescent sexuality, pregnancy, and childbearing* (Vol. 1). Washington, DC: National Academy Press.

Higgins, E. T, Ruble, D. N., & Hartup, W. W. (1983). *Social cognition and social development: A sociocultural perspective.* New York: Cambridge University Press.

Hofferth, S. L., & Hayes, C. D. (Eds.). (1987). *Risking the future: Adolescent sexuality, pregnancy, and childbearing: Vol. 2. Working papers and statistical reports.* Washington, DC: National Academy Press.

Hogan, D. P., & Kitagawa, E. M. (1985). The impact of social status, family structure, and neighborhood on the fertility of Black adolescents. *American Journal of Sociology, 90,* 825–855.

Inazu, J. K., & Fox, G. L. (1980). Maternal influence on the sexual behavior of teenage daughters. *Journal of Family Issues, 1,* 81–102.

Jessor, R., & Jessor, S. L. (1977). *Problem behavior and psychosocial development.* New York: Academic Press.

Jessor, S. L., & Jessor, R. (1975). Transition from virginity to nonvirginity among youth: A social-psychological study over time. *Developmental Psychology, 11(4),* 473–484.

Jones, E., Forrest, J. D., Goldman, N., Henshaw, S., Lincoln, R., Rosoff, J., Westoff, C., & Wulf, D. (1985). Teenage pregnancy in developed countries: Determinants and policy implications. *Family Planning Perspectives, 17(2),* 53–63.

Jones, E., Forrest, J. D., Henshaw, S. K., Silverman, J., & Torres, A. (1988). Unintended pregnancy, contraceptive practice and family planning services in developed countries. *Family Planning Perspectives, 20(2),* 53–67.

Kahn, J., Smith, K., & Roberts, E. (1984). *Familial communication and adolescent sexual behavior* (Final report to the office of adolescent Pregnancy Programs). Cambridge, MA: American Institutes for Research.

Kinsey, A. C., Pomeroy, W. B., & Martin, C. E. (1948). *Sexual behavior in the human male.* Philadelphia: W. B. Saunders.

Kinsey, A. C., Pomeroy, W. B., Martin, C. E., & Gebhard, P. H. (1953). *Sexual behavior in the human female.* Philadelphia: W. B. Saunders.

Kirby, D. (1984). *Sexuality education: An evaluation of programs and their effects.* Santa Cruz, CA: Network Publications.

Koop, C. E. (1988). *Understanding AIDS.* Rockville, MD: The Surgeon General and the Centers for Disease Control, U.S. Public Health Service.

Magnusson, D., Strattin, H., & Allen, V. L. (1985). Biological maturation and social development: A longitudinal study of some adjustment processes from mid-adolescence to adulthood. *Journal of Youth and Adolescence, 14(4),* 267–283.

Meade, J. (1988). What parents should know when AIDS comes to school. *Children Magazine,* pp. 59–65.

Morrison, D. M. (1985). Adolescent contraceptive behavior: A review. *Psychological Bulletin, 98(3),* 538–568.

Mosher, W. D. (1985). Reproductive impairments in the United States, 1965–1982. *Demography, 22,* 415–430.

Newcomer, S., & Udry, J. R. (1987). Parental marital status

effects on adolescent sexual behavior. *Journal of Marriage and the Family, 49,* 235–240.

Norman, J., & Harris, M. (1981). *The private life of the American teenager.* New York: Rawson Wade.

Ooms, T. (Ed.). (1981). *Teenage pregnancy in a family context: Implications for policy.* Philadelphia: Temple University Press.

Orr, M. (1982). Sex education and contraceptive education in U.S. public high schools. *Family Planning Perspectives, 14,* 304–313.

Paige, K. E. (1983). A bargaining theory of menarcheal responses in preindustrial cultures. In J. Brooks-Gunn & A. C. Petersen (Eds.), *Girls at puberty: Biological and psychosocial perspectives* (pp. 301–322). New York: Plenum Press.

Perry, C. L. (1984). Health promotion at school: Expanding the potential for prevention. *School Psychology Review, 13(2),* 141–149.

Pratt, W. F., & Hendershot, G. E. (1984). The use of family planning services by sexually active teenagers. *Population Index, 50(3),* 412–413.

Reiss, R. L. (1960). *Premarital sexual standards in America.* New York: Free Press.

Shah, F., Zelnik, M., & Kantner, J. (1975). Unprotected intercourse among unwed teenagers. *Family Planning Perspectives. 7,* 39–44.

Smith, E. A., & Udry, J. R. (1985). Coital and non-coital sexual behaviors of white and black adolescents. *American Journal of Public Health, 75,* 1200–1203.

Strecher, V. J., McEvoy, B., Becker, M. H., & Rosenstock, I. M. (1986). The role of self-efficacy in achieving health behavior change. *Health Education Quarterly, 13(1),* 73–91.

Udry, J. R., Billy, J. O. G., Morris, N. M., Groff, T R., & Raj, M. H. (1985). Serum androgenic hormones motivate sexual behavior in boys. *Fertility and Sterility, 43(1),* 90–94.

Udry, J. R., Talbert, L., & Morris, N. M. (1986). Biosocial foundations for adolescent female sexuality. *Demography, 23(2),* 217–230.

Westoff, C. F., Calot, G., & Foster, A. D. (1983). Teenage fertility in developed nations: 1971–1980. *Family Planning Perspectives, 15(3),* 105–110.

Zabin, L. S., & Clark, S. D., Jr. (1981). Why they delay: A study of teenage family planning clinic patients. *Family Planning Perspectives, 13(5),* 205–217.

Zabin, L. S., Hirsch, M. B., Smith, E. A., Strett, R., & Hardy, J. B. (1986). Evaluation of a pregnancy prevention program for urban teenagers. *Family Planning Perspectives, 18,* 119–126.

Zabin, L. S., Kantner, J. F., & Zelnik, M. (1979). The risk of adolescent pregnancy in the first months of intercourse. *Family Planning Perspectives, 11(4),* 215–222.

Zelnik, M., & Kantner, J. F. (1977). Sexual and contraceptive experience of young unmarried women in the United States, 1976 and 1971. *Family Planning Perspectives, 9,* 55–71.

Zelnik, M., & Kantner, J. F. (1980). Sexual activity, contraceptive use and pregnancy among metropolitan area teenagers: 1971–1979. *Family Planning Perspectives, 12(5),* 230.

Zelnik, M., Kantner, J. E., & Ford, K. (1981). *Sex and pregnancy in adolescence* (Sage Library of Social Research, Vol. 133). Beverly Hills: Sage.

Zelnik, M., & Kim, Y. J. (1982). Sex education and its association with teenage sexual activity, pregnancy and contraceptive use. *Family Planning Perspectives, 14(3),* 117–126.

Zelnik, M., & Shah, R. K. (1983). First intercourse among young Americans. *Family Planning Perspectives, 15(2),* 64–70.

35

Dropping Out of High School: An Inside Look

_____

MICHELLE FINE

Despite great concern among educators, the high school drop out rate in the United States is increasing. Of particular concern, poor youth, especially those from African American and Hispanic American communities, are more likely than other adolescents to drop out, thus exacerbating their already bleak situation. In order to combat this personal and social tragedy we need better understanding of why youth drop out of school in the first place. To explore this issue, Michelle Fine conducted an ethnographic study of the New York City schools, asking youths themselves why they dropped out.

In September, 1984, I began an ethnography of student life in and out of a New York City public high school to figure out why urban students drop out of high school at such extraordinary rates. By December, why urban students stay in high school through graduation struck me as an equally compelling question.

Funded by the W. T. Grant Foundation in New York City, I spent the fall four days a week in one school: in the deans' offices, the guidance office, attendance room, and in classes.

In spring of 1985, 30 students who had been discharged over the past four months and another 15 who left this school four years ago were interviewed, primarily in their homes. A survey was also mailed to 350 graduates, transfers, and dropouts from the 1978–1979 cohort. I visited a number of GED programs, a "pregnancy school," and some private business "academies," attended the school's Parents' Association executive and general meetings, and met with representatives of a number of community-based organizations and dropout prevention programs.

Everyone was fully informed of my research interest and my role as observer in residence. Every teacher, administrator, paraprofessional, school aide, and guard, with few exceptions, was warm, welcoming, and allowed me to invade territories that many would have been more exclusive about. I was reminded repeatedly that university professors know little about what "really" goes on in schools, and I now know that to be true.

This school, like others, is a complex institution filled with contradictions. In many ways, as leftist scholars of education have argued before,[1] it reproduces the very class, gender, and race-based stratifications that prevail in the larger society: the very inequities schools portend to undo. Infused with meritocratic ideologies, competitive grading, tracking, and a pervasive, demoralized attitude that "students from *that* community don't have much of a chance," the school perpetuates, for the most part, the social inequities that constrain the material opportunities and psychological visions of these teens.

But, at the same time, this school generates from its Black and Hispanic student body, from its largely white administration and teachers, and predominantly Black and Hispanic paraprofessional and aide staff some carefully crafted moments of and possibilities for liberatory education, critical thinking, and even empowerment. One teacher drills students on grammar with exercises including "Women in Puerto Rico (is) (are) oppressed." A biology teacher has students write creative essays on "my life as child of an alcoholic" and then "my life as an alcoholic" despite her chairman's disapproval of the exercise. An English teacher organized her initially passive Regents Competency Test preparation class into a writing support group and soon generated a quite animated and energized collective. These teachers located the learning relationship inside the life experiences of students and created moments of critical, if atypical, education.

These lower-income and working-class students, as Willis and Everhart have described,[2] were by no means totally accepting in the face of teacher-generated culture. Clearly, some were just passive, many compliant, and others just disruptive. But, many teachers actively embraced and transformed their classrooms. Some altered classroom practice, alone and together, and generated questions rather than answers, opened rather than closed conversations, and introduced complexity in place of simplicity.

For example, in early June, a teacher structured an in-class debate on Bernard Goetz—New York City's "subway vigilante." She invited "those students who agree with Goetz to sit on one side of the room, and those who think he was wrong to sit on the other side." To the large residual group who remained mid-room the teacher remarked. "Don't be lazy. You have to make a decision. Like at work you can't be passive." A few wandered over to the "pro-Goetz" side.

About six remained in the center. Somewhat angry, the teacher continued: "OK, first we'll hear the pro-Goetz side and then the anti-Goetz side. Those of you who have no opinions, who haven't even thought about the issue, you won't get to talk unless we have time."

Deidre, a Black senior, bright and always quick to raise contradictions otherwise obscured, advocated the legitimacy of the middle group. "It's not that I have no opinions. I don't like Goetz shootin' up people who look like my brother, but I don't like feelin' unsafe in the projects or in my neighborhood either. I got lots of opinions. I ain't bein' quiet cause I can't decide if he's right or wrong. I'm talkin'."

Deidre's comment legitimized for herself and others the right to hold complex, perhaps even contradictory positions on a complex situation. Such legitimacy was rarely granted by staff—with obvious exceptions of those who imported politics from other spheres of their lives, including the Marxist historian, the feminist English teacher, the paraprofessionals who lived in central Harlem with the kids and understood and respected much about their lives.

This article draws on life inside and outside of this school filled with contradictory tensions and possibilities, as a case for examining the dynamics of the now popular "dropout problem." Social and economic stresses experienced by these students, school-based factors including pedagogy, policies, and practices, as well as the collective and individual psychologies of students together contribute to the high rate of students who leave high school without a degree. The analysis relies upon life in this school as a way of examining how the act of dropping out, even if intended as an act of social resistance, ultimately reproduces and exacerbates social inequities.

CALCULATING THE FIGURES

In 1983 it was determined that 73.9 percent of ninth graders in the United States would complete high school.[3] Blacks and Hispanics are less likely to graduate than are whites, and males and females graduate at approximately equal rates. Students in urban areas graduate at rates approximating 50 percent, and social class remains the best predictor of dropping out.

The New York State graduation rate is approximately 66.7 percent, and in 1984 the New York City Board of Education estimated that 42 percent of its ninth graders would drop out of high school prior to graduation.[4] Aspira challenged the Board's figures and calculated that 68 percent of all high school students, 72 percent of Black students, and 80 percent of

Hispanic students drop out of New York City schools.[5]

To calculate this school's dropout and survival rates, a cohort analysis of 1,221 ninth graders from 1978–1979 was followed through their school records. The analysis showed that 19.66 percent of the cohort graduated from this school by June, 1985, and almost all of these students applied to college. Of the 1,221, 44 percent have been discharged, and 'no records have been sent since to another educational institution. Another 17.69 percent of these students have transferred to another educational facility to which records were sent (of these 29 moved to Puerto Rico, the Dominican Republic, or Nicaragua, and 31 moved out of state within mainland United States). Seven percent were considered "not found." Six percent entered GED programs and the remaining 5.65 percent left with records sent to the military or a private business school. Very few students received a terminal high school degree. These adolescents, for the most part, either dropped out or enrolled in college.

To determine a dropout rate the "discharged no records sent" group was combined with the "not founds," adding a generous estimate of 50 percent of the transfers, military/business, and GEDs who might graduate. A 66 percent dropout rate results from these calculations: a figure that is extremely high for the country and the state, and relatively high for the city. That the rate is high represents a number of factors, including the fact that this school is quite honest in its record keeping. The administration does not maintain "ghost students" on the register to increase revenues, and the school efficiently discharges students who have been truant for 20 consecutive days—following all legal guidelines.

This 66 percent figure is particularly striking in contrast to the principal's oft' heard claim that "80 percent of our graduates go on to college." It is this claim that sits at the central contradiction of the school. This school does nurture, intellectually and emotionally, those 20 percent who ultimately graduate. One mother praised this school for getting her daughter into college: "That's more than I can say for the elite public high schools my other children go to." The problem is that the 20 percent who "make it" do so, in part, at the expense of the 66 percent who don't.

Two questions therefore arise: What is the nature of the semi-autonomous institutional life—limited resources, routine scheduling into remedial and low-track classes, atypical honors classes that "encourage me a lot, but I know my brother in one of them general classes and he just sleeps in his class and gets sent to the dean"—that operates so that approximate-ly 20 percent "make it" while the remaining students appear to "drop out" due to individual inabilities?

And second, doesn't the collective act of dropping out—even by students like Leo who scored 1200 on the SATs prior to his discharge and remarked, "This school doesn't help me think, just learn what teachers think is right"—eventually reproduce precisely the kinds of class, race, and gender stratifications schools promise to transcend?

THE CONTEXT FOR DROPPING OUT

When one begins a discussion of why students drop out of school it is necessary to place in context schooling in the larger sphere of economic and social arrangements. Dropping out of high school can be considered a problem only if one assumes that schooling actually contributes to the educational or social well being of students, and/or that schooling and graduation credentials facilitate social mobility.

Many of these lower-income and working-class students, however, see little promise of a good job resulting from a high school degree. Given the Community Service Society analysis that dropouts from the wealthiest regions of New York City experience a 42 percent employment to population ratio compared to high school graduates from the poorest sections who experience a 31 percent employment to population ratio,[6] these adolescents have good reason to be suspect.

Daily they witness life in a city ravaged by the effects of advanced capitalism marked by racism and sexism. Even if they don't make the connection, and most don't, their lives are filled with bombed-out buildings in their neighborhoods, high infant mortality rates, the presence of police and arrests, age peers who drop out routinely, deal in dope, and have children, hear that an "improved economic picture" means more white collar and upgraded service jobs, fewer manufacturing positions, and a depleted housing market.

They live in a city in which 32 percent of children subsist in poverty, and 55 percent of children living in female-headed households subsist in poverty. A city in which the appeal of the streets, of quick money from "scramblin'—you know, selling dope," is often more tempting and perhaps more available than legitimate work for comparable income, and where daily life is filled with health, housing, and economic hassles.

But at the same time as they voice cynicism, these adolescents also believe deeply in the need for a high school degree, for the few jobs that are available, and to prove "that I can do something, not just be a failure." And again they are right. Those without a high school degree who live in the poorest sections of the city suffer a 15 percent employment to population ratio. The question is: would the employment to population ratio in these neighborhoods actually improve if all these adolescents stayed in school through graduation?

These adolescents drop out of high school not only because of the ravages of societal inequities, but because systematic features of school structures, policies, and practices contribute significantly to the high dropout rate. While "fixing" these policies and procedures will not alter the oppressive arrangements that structure the society and may not even dent the dropout rate, public schools can not abandon their obligation to enable and empower the percent who, by coercion or choice, are purged from schools.

THE SCHOOL STRUCTURE

As a comprehensive zoned high school surrounded by "theme" schools that can set their own entry criteria, this school enrolls a disproportionate number of low-skill students. The mean reading level of the entering students is 7.0, with math at 6.8, lower than any other high school in Manhattan.[7] The principal's policy of accepting "any child who comes through the doors" reflects a sincere commitment to city kids, especially monolingual and bilingual Spanish speakers who are served by few public schools. This policy, while generous relative to other city schools, promotes severe overcrowding. On register were 3500 students. Teachers' lunch periods span from 9:45 a.m. until 2:00 p.m. The school day consists of 10 periods. One estimate holds that the school operates at 144 percent capacity.[8]

Fiscal constraints further compound the effects of overcrowding. The 1985 Educational Priorities Panel analysis indicates that comprehensive zoned high schools have higher than average student/teacher ratios, lower than average skills levels, and receive less fiscal allocations than vocational schools. Vocational high schools have class size capped at 28 instead of 34, and 13 of the 17 best funded high schools in the city are vocational.[9] Public high schools are reimbursed as a function of the Curriculum Index, that is, the average number of courses taken per student and not per capita. As a consequence, schools with low-skill students and high truancy rates have no fiscal incentive to reduce class size or bring back long-term absentees or truants. Schools with high dropout rates are financially punished rather than assisted in their efforts to retrieve students.

This school also faces a profound sense of disempowerment by teachers, paraprofessionals, school aides, students, and parents. In chorus, although not in harmony, they complain that "nobody's listening to me." One mother echoed others: "Those white people don't respect me. If I go in there and raise hell about my daughter, they're only gonna get her worse." Parents are alienated, frightened, and uninformed of their rights.

Not only do students and parents experience a sense of disempowerment, but teachers frequently disparage the hierarchical and "encrusted" structure of their school. Researchers from Teachers College surveyed the faculty of this school and found that "approximately two out of three teachers felt that there was little interest shown in their classroom work either by staff or administrators."[10] What is the impact of teacher disempowerment on education and on students? In another study, 170 teachers and counselors were surveyed about their perceived institutional power and their views of students.[11] A significant relationship was found between educators who felt disempowered: "No one around here listens to me" and "school policy doesn't reflect what I think"; and those who disparaged students: "These students are bad kids" and "these students can't be helped." The "causal" direction of this relationship remains unclear, and is probably bi-directional. But this finding, in concert with the growing literature on worker collectives, participatory management, and social/psychological outcomes,[12] suggests that empowered teachers may be more likely to view students holistically, optimistically, and compassionately, whereas disempowered teachers may be more likely to disparage, discredit, and further disempower their students.

Teachers who feel they don't have a voice in a school and are not involved in decision making, planning, and policy setting may also be more likely to enforce high control, heavy lecture, teacher-dependent, and passive student classes. From classroom observations it is obvious that, while there are many exceptions, the "typical" student spends much of a day recording notes (or not recording notes) written on blackboards, listening (or not) to teachers' versions of truth, copying Instructional Objectives that often have little to do with classroom practice, and in silence. The silent student, often a girl who says nothing for eight hours a day, is rarely identified as a problem. Working in an overcrowded, undersupported, and understaffed classroom may promote a situation in which the adolescent who never speaks is merely seen as one less problem.

Another condition facing this school, although not unique to it, is the obvious lack of Black faculty: six or seven out of over 120 teachers in this school. This situation contrasts poorly with cities such as

Philadelphia, which recently mandated that high schools have a minimum of 21.3 percent and a maximum of 35.5 percent Black teachers.[13]

The absence of Black teachers not only limits role models for Black teens, it reinforces students' and adults' beliefs in race-stratified organizations, and reproduces prevailing social and economic inequalities. The lack of Black teachers also inhibits those much needed classroom conversations about social inequities. A belief prevails, predominantly among white teachers, that *not* having a conversation with students about racism can be empowering. Black and Hispanic students are assumed to be unaware of the experience and effects of racism, sexism, and classism on their lives, and they are assumed better off for their ignorance.

Certainly not all Black teachers believe that a critique of class, race, and gender arrangements belongs in the classroom. But while a white teacher explained, "I won't talk about racism or unemployment because it demoralizes the students," Black teachers and paraprofessionals routinely mentioned the racism felt on their jobs—obvious in curricular topics selected and rejected, and overhead in lunchroom conversations about "those students and their families."

THE STUDENTS' RESPONSES

Students leave high school before graduation for myriad reasons. According to the national survey of graduates and dropouts conducted by the National Center for Educational Statistics, the primary reason was "school was not for me" (34.8 percent of males and 31.1 percent of females, selected from among nonexclusive categories). "Poor grades" was a close second (35.9 percent for males, 29.7 percent for females). Males said they were offered a job or chose to work (26.9 percent), didn't get along with teachers (20.6 percent), or were expelled/suspended (13.0 percent).[14] In New York State, 23.9 percent of all students are Black, while 36.1 percent of expelled students and 34.2 percent of suspended students are Black.

Females in large numbers claimed they were getting married (30.7 percent) or were pregnant (23.4 percent). National estimates indicate that almost half of females drop out because of pregnancy, 85 percent of teen mothers vs. 8 percent of childless girls drop out, and self-identified adolescent fathers under the age of 18 are 40 percent more likely than their nonparenting counterparts to drop out.[15] A Yale study of high school students and dropouts indicates that 67 percent of teens who got pregnant and then married were pregnant again within 26 months, and

fared worse educationally and economically than teens who got pregnant and didn't marry (who had a 39 percent second pregnancy rate).[16]

Through interviews with dropouts at this school, their claims for leaving high school appear comparable to the national data. More frequently mentioned by the New York City group are situations in which students leave school in order to assist their families. These students come from lower-income and working-class households. Many exist on public assistance that dwindled from 91 percent of the poverty threshold in 1974 to 67 percent in 1981.[17]

Many of these adolescents have to work full time, sometimes as the sole or primary bread winner in their household. Others leave school because they and/or a family member is ill or needs nurturing, linguistic, or social service attention. The "good daughter" (or son, if he is an only child or grandchild) may leave school because of overwhelming family pressures. Staying in high school would have been "selfish," one girl reminded me. "My mother passed and I was 16 with my brothers and sisters. I couldn't stay."

While health, social, and economic concerns are severe, compelling, and deserve policy attention, adolescents also report pedagogical and school-based factors as reasons for leaving high school. The ways in which the curriculum is structured, knowledge is valued, and classroom practice is implemented affect students' commitment to schools. The dropouts, in interviews, express a strong commitment to education but voice an equally powerful critique of schooling as practiced. For one, their lives and experiences are basically exempt from the mainstream curriculum and excluded from what is considered valued classroom knowledge.

Adolescents respond to and reflect on this hegemonic curriculum in varied ways. Some are critical. Cheray remarked on the knowledge delivered and the attitudes conveyed: "We learned Columbus Avenue stuff and I got to translate it into Harlem. They think livin' up here is unsafe and our lives are so bad." Tony questioned the modes of teaching as he provocatively explained. "I never got math when I was in school. Then I started sellin' dope and runnin' numbers and I picked it up right away. They should teach the way it matters."

Alicia was less critical and more accepting of school knowledge as standard and distinct from what she knows: "I'm wise, not smart. I knows what people are thinkin' and what's going'down, but not what he be talkin' about in history." Others internalize a personal inability to grasp school-based knowledge. After two months out of school, Monique admits, somewhat embarrassed, "I'm scared to go out lookin' for a job. They be usin' words in the interview that I don't know, I can't be askin' them for a dictionary. It's like in school. You ask and you feel like a dummy."

Dropouts describe classrooms as many observers would. Classrooms are more often than not organized around control. "Nathaniel, take off your hat," than around conversation; more often around the authority of the teacher than the autonomy and creativity of the students. As John Goodlad found in his comprehensive analysis of classroom practice, 70 percent of class-based time was spent on teacher to student talk, 5 percent to create response, and less than 1 percent to generate an open student response.[18]

Classrooms are also designed around student competition rather than collaboration. It has been interesting to observe that while teachers usually try to structure a competitive or individualistic context, students more often organize themselves cooperatively or position themselves as a group against the teacher. In class students would support each other, offer each other answers, and share homework. They would sometimes spontaneously applaud—if somewhat sarcastically—for the student who correctly answered a teacher's question. They would conspire in activities of resistance and general classroom participation. Teachers usually read student cooperation of any sort as cheating. Clearly there was cheating, but students talking to each other in the back of the room were routinely questioned. "What are you two doing, cheating?" The lower the presumed skill level the more frequent were accusations of cheating and struggles around control, and teachers' authority predominated. And the higher the dropout rate.

THE DISCHARGE PROCESS

Beyond the structure of this school, its pedagogy, and classroom teaching, another school practice most directly contributes to the high dropout rate. Students in New York City, when they reach age 17, can be discharged from school and are, in large numbers. Some are *actively* discharged because of a history of "chronic cutting," mouthing off, wearing a coat in class one time too many, or being in the wrong place at the wrong time. Most are *passively* discharged. Absent for over 20 days, students over age 17 receive a letter indicating that they will be discharged unless they and a parent/guardian come to the building. Students who don't show up are then discharged. Some who come in are re-enrolled. Many are encouraged to consider alternatives to public day school.

There persists a pervasive commitment to ridding the school of "difficult students," as soon as they can be released legally. Data provided by the New York City Board of Education confirm that this school has higher than average rates of discharging students at age 17, when a student can be discharged as "over-age." In 1982–1983, 48 percent of the students discharged from this school left at age 17 compared to 32 percent citywide: 30 percent of the females and 34 percent of the males were discharged from this school during their ninth year as compared to 19 percent and 18 percent, respectively, for the city.[19] The same pattern holds for 1983–1984. Citywide, 70 percent of discharges from day high schools were catalogued as "over 17," whereas for this school this figure reached 85 percent.

But even the discharge process is rife with the contradiction between trying to cleanse the school and trying to assist the now-exiled adolescent to consider her/his alternatives. The emotional labor of the school splits between discipline and purging versus care and supporting. Discipline is the dominant ethos, enacted largely by men in their role as administrators, guards, and deans. Care is primarily the preserve of a small group of women. And the "we are a family" metaphor pervades public discourse, especially when parents are being addressed.

Confused by this seeming contradiction, I met with a group of 15 deans, administrators, and guidance counselors, the principal and his assistants, to share my observations of the discharge process. The administrator for attendance agreed with my observation that students are routinely discharged, after 20 days of consecutive absence, required letters, and phone calls to their homes. "That's what the Board requires us to do." The fact that a school *can* discharge a student at 17 has turned into a *should*. Another administrator explained angrily and with some frustration, "We can only *save* a few with the resources we have. Is it worth spending a lot of time, energy, and money on one kid who is out on the streets, who we can't even find, instead of the kids who are here?" Finally one of the guidance counselors, the only Black woman in the room, said softly, "Michelle's right. We do throw these kids out and I'm worried about it." As another guidance counselor rose to support the first, three men's arms went up, all deans. They justified why the school needs to get rid of these kids, why these kids need a different environment and questioned the validity of the counselor's perceptions.

The administrator in charge of guidance then mediated. She offered a most provocative analysis. "Years ago, when I worked in the attendance office, our job was to get rid of those kids who were on the register but not in school. We cleared the register. Then I moved to the dean's office and my job was to get kids who were troublesome out of the school. Now I'm in charge of guidance and we're supposed to be helping these same students. I think we're working at cross purposes within the school." Her perspective captures well the schizophrenic division of emotional labor that produces large numbers of "dropouts" with no one adult appearing responsible for the purge, only responsible to the security of the school.

One way for these administrators, teachers, and counselors to "help" was to suggest "alternatives" to a high school degree, including the military, private business schools, and/or GED programs. Routinely recommended to these working-class and low-income students,. it is hard to imagine these same programs being suggested to a middle-class adolescent. Commonly accepted assumptions about the limited life chances of this group enabled "these alternatives" to be offered unself-consciously.

Race and class biases notwithstanding, each of these presumed alternatives poses serious problems for these youths. For example, nearly 50 percent of high school dropouts who entered the military in 1981 were not expected to complete their first tour of duty, according to Army projections. "Among those without high school diplomas, 46 percent of the men and 63 percent of the women will be discharged early."[20]

Also the private business schools in New York were recently investigated by the New York State Education Department that found unethical practices such as the fact that more than 70 percent of the Tuition Assistance Program recipients fail to complete their programs of study, inappropriate recruitment and entrance procedures, and unfulfilled promises of jobs at the conclusion of the training period. These business schools generate more revenue when students fail to pursue their program than when they complete them.[21]

Lastly, students are often counseled into GED programs but never informed that New York State has the lowest GED pass rate in the country at 48.5 percent. [22]

When a student who is 17 and in the ninth grade shows up in the guidance or attendance office, it *is* hard to know what fair and good advice would look like. Especially because the student has, in all likelihood, been held back because of extensive truancy and/or cutting. The administrator responsible for what to do next often feels trapped. But even alternative high schools with demonstrated success are rarely recommended.[23] Instead, the military, business school, or GED routes are suggested routinely, uncritically, often with some enthusiasm. Never have I heard a student informed of her or his right to a public school education through the age of 21, a right protected by New York State Education Law.

Within this context, coercive discharges are all but unnecessary. Many of these adolescents see little economic promise in a high school degree, most do not enjoy the experience of a participatory and expansive education, many have had their sense of entitlement to a better life and their sense of curiosity and vision long suffocated.

STEMMING THE TIDE OF DROPOUTS

Witnessing the policies and practices of public education in this school, it is easy to conclude that neither the state nor many within the education system want to do anything but perpetuate existing class, race, and gender arrangements. Denying these youths their due education and appropriate credentials virtually condemns them to lives of poverty, unemployment, crime, and multiple pregnancies. It is no coincidence that the students who most desperately need the skills of critical thinking, the experience of intellectual and social empowerment, and the credentials of educational completion are the very students being denied access.

With city unemployment rates as high as they are, combined with the rapid loss of jobs in manufacturing and recent influx of immigrants, the corporate sector of New York City has no obvious self-interest in keeping these high-risk students in school. With educational monies allocated on the basis of the number of courses students take, schools have no obvious investment in retaining or bringing back students who have had some difficulty in academic ability or commitment to education as currently practiced in schools. And with the federal government and national reform movements pushing for "excellence," recent recommendations are likely to swell not diminish the ranks of adolescents who leave high school without a diploma.

If a concerted effort were mobilized to decrease the number of potential dropouts and bring back dropouts, educational practitioners, theorists, and advocates would know what to do. But before these possibilities are considered, it is important to heed the lessons of history as recalled by Michael Katz: "we should at long last stop relying on the schools for social reform. Crime, poverty, inequality, alienation, and other social problems are rooted in social and economic structure. They will be solved, if solved at all, through an attack on their origins, which will mean a redistribution of power and resources. They will not be eliminated, or seriously alleviated, in the schools, which cannot be expected to do more than reflect the social structure in which they exist."[24]

Black and Hispanic low-income and working-class students in New York City are not likely to stay in school if they see no "payoffs": "a very large fraction of the city's Black and Hispanic teenage population has withdrawn from the labor market. There are undoubtedly many reasons for this, among them the perception that halfway suitable employment opportunities are simply not available in sufficient numbers to make it worth one's while to make the effort, even though the alternative options of scratching by on a combination of welfare, illegal, and off-the-books activities are bleaker still."[25]

School reforms designed to reduce dropout rates must, therefore, be developed and implemented in tandem with efforts to improve the overall life conditions of working-class and low-income people in a community. School reforms must be developed along with policies for jobs programs, housing improvements, provision of child care, social and health services, as well as a commitment to affirmative action policies and enforcement of antidiscrimination laws.

In such a context, school-based reforms are not only essential, but effective ones are possible. The health and social needs of students must be addressed, and this is beginning to happen in a number of sites. Case management of students' "personal" problems is being introduced in many schools. More educationally and socially meaningful strategies could be developed so that students work collaboratively as peer case managers to provide support, investigate available resources in their communities, and agitate for improvements and expansion of existing resources.

Another educational innovation rapidly gaining popularity is the school-based health clinic.[26] These clinics are being established to serve the physical and mental well-being of students, as well as offer contraception and abortion services to teens. The success of a school-based health clinic in St. Paul has been most encouraging. Across seven years, this clinic, located inside a public school, helped to reduce teen pregnancy rates by 50 percent.

Concurrent to the provision of contraception and abortion information/services is the need for school-based child care for teen mothers and fathers. Growing research indicates, that the provision of child care along with educational and jobs programs can reduce the likelihood of a second pregnancy for teenagers.[27]

Services for students are necessary but not sufficient to enhance attendance and retention rates. There must be a reason for coming to school. The organizational structures of schools, the pedagogical practices, and the school's policies vis a vis discharging students should be re-examined. Drawing on the literature from worker collectives, strategies for enhancing teachers', paraprofessionals', aides', parents', students' input into school policies and practices can reduce the sense of isolation and estrangement and facilitate an environment that nurtures intellectual curiosity, initiative, and creativity. Teachers, parents and students need opportunities to create and to critique.

Modified pedagogies that value creativity, innovation, and collective work have been demonstrated effective in both the transfer of knowledge and in promoting social relations across race, gender, and class lines.[28] Curricula rooted in the experiences of students can generate energy rather than resistance. Classroom discussions that examine social arrangements critically can be empowering and further education's role as a source of social commentary and critical thinking.[29]

Alternative schools appear to be relatively successful with hard to reach students, in particular because they are small.[30] According to the Public Education Association report, alternative schools retain even high-risk students if they feel they belong, have access to a curriculum grounded in their lives, receive personal counseling, are encouraged to participate in class discussions, involved in school administration and evaluations, and feel like a member of a community.

Students can be a part of minischools within larger schools so that they don't feel anonymous; so that hiding in a sea of faces in the lunchroom would mean missing something and being missed. Teachers and other staff need to be compensated for time to assist with homework, counseling, even conduct independent studies, not just reimbursed on the basis of five courses per day.

CONCLUSION

I began studying high school dropouts while working on an evaluation research project in the South Bronx. By the post-test, 30 percent of the students had dropped out. Using the pretest data, those who had dropped out were compared with those who were still in school.

Compared to the students still in school, dropouts were *less* depressed as measured by Beck's Depression Inventory, *more* likely to say their problems are about racism, poverty, and their personality. Dropouts were also more likely to say: "If a teacher gave me a B and I deserved an A, I would do something about it,' 'talk to her,' 'demand the A'"; students still in school were more likely to say: "I would do nothing" or "teachers are always right."[31]

That was in 1982. This year strong voices of critique, resistance, and pride were documented in my study. Adolescents don't like to be treated as though they are stupid, incompetent, not worth listening to. Some resent it, some ignore it, and others believe it. The wave of students who drop out, I would still maintain, needs to be considered a symptom of social resistance. But dropouts themselves do not necessarily articulate or even conceptualize a sophisticated critique of schooling and labor-market arrangements. While for some the motivation to leave is autonomy and critique, for others it is merely a sense of helplessness and rejection.

Either way the consequences of leaving high school without a diploma are usually devastating and result in the worst of social reproduction: exacerbated class, race, and gender stratification, which then appears to be the outcome of a personal "choice" to leave high school early. It is true that some adolescents, upon leaving high school without a degree, get their lives in order—taking and passing the GED, going to college, entering the police academy, or getting another job. But most don't. Dropouts are more likely to be in prison, to have multiple pregnancies and children, to be on welfare, unemployed, or in dead-end jobs than high school graduates. This is par-

ticularly true for girls: a diploma means the difference between being a domestic and being a clerical worker.

With few jobs available and with fewer job-training programs, Black and Hispanic adolescents in and out of school will continue to question the value of a high school diploma. Without an engaging pedagogy, one which liberates as it coaches, informs as it incites, students will continue to feel bored and uninterested in attending an institution in which they don't feel very good about themselves. And without knowledge of their legal rights, students and parents will continue to feel alienated from the one institution that promises to offer a way out of poverty but which more often than not insures lives of impoverishment.

And so, a contradiction lingers in the minds of many of these youths, students and dropouts alike. The contradiction is best captured by Ronald who at age 18 is in 10th grade, himself a likely candidate for dropping out. He turned to me, during his remedial reading class, and explained: "You know why I stay in school? Cause every morning I see this guy, the same drunk in the subway station. And I think 'not me. I'm staying in school.' But then I think 'I bet he has a high school degree.'"

Notes

[1]Henry Giroux, *Theory and Resistance: A Pedagogy for the Opposition* (South Hadley, Mass: Bergin & Garvey Publications, 1983). See also Martin Carnoy and Henry Levin, *Schooling and Work in the Democratic State* (Palo Alto: Stanford University Press, 1985).

[2]Paul Willis, *Learning to Labour* (Westmead, Farnborough Hants, England: Saxon House, 1977): Richard Everhart, *Reading, Writing and Resistance* (Boston: Routledge and Kegan Paul, 1983).

[3]*High School and Beyond* (Washington, D.C.: National Center for Education Statistics, 1982).

[4]New York City Board of Education, Dropouts *from New York City Public Schools, 1982-83* Educational Management Information Unit, OSIS, New York; New York City Board of Education, *The 1983–1984 Dropout Report,* OEA Data Analysis Section, Office of Educational Assessment (May, 1985).

[5]Aspira, *Racial and Ethnic High Dropout Rates in New York City. A Sum Report, 1983.*

[6]Emanuel Tobier, *The Changing Face of Poverty: Trends in New York City's Population in Poverty, 1960–1980* (New York Community Service Society, 1984).

[7]Office of the Superintendent of Manhattan High schools, *PSEN Results of Academic Zoned High schools, 1985.*

[8]*Personal communication, 1985.*

[9]*Educational Priorities Panel Education Budget Options Fiscal Year 1985.*

[10]Teachers College survey, Pearl Kane, Principal Investigator, 1985.

[11]Michelle Fine, "Perspectives on Inequity: Voices from Urban Schools," in L. Bichman (ed.), *Applied Social Psychology Annual, IV* (Beverly Hills: Sage Publications, 1983).

[12]Virginia Vanderslice, *A Critical Analysis of Leadership and Followership: A Look at Worker Collectives.* Unpublished manuscript (1985).

[13]School District of Philadelphia, Office Personnel Operations. *Faculty Integration Calculations* (May 2, 1985).

[14]National Center for Educational Statistics, op. cit.

[15]*Preventing Children, Having Children* (Washington, D.C.: Children's Defense Fund, 1985). See also K. Dillard and L. Pol "The Individual Economic Costs of Teenage Childbearing," *Family Relations* (April, 1982) pp. 249–259; Lorraine Klerman and J. F. Jekel, *School Age Mothers: Problems, Programs, and Policies* (Hamden, Conn.: Linnett Books, 1973).

[16]Children's Defense Fund, op. cit.

[17]Emanuel Tobier, op. cit.

[18]John Goodlad, *A Place Called School* (New York: McGraw-Hill, 1984).

[19]New York City Board of Education statistics from the office of Ray Domanico, 1984.

[20]*Militarism Resource Project Newsletter* (Spring, 1985).

[21]New York State Education Department, Staff Report to the Interagency Task Force: on Student Financial Aid Programs, *Issue Relating to Financial Aid for Students at Registered Business Schools* (March, 1985).

[22]New York State Education Department statistics sent to author (1984).

[23]Eileen Foley and Peggy Crull, *Educating the At-Risk Adolescent : More Lessons from Alternative High Schools* (New York City Public Education Association, 1984).

[24]Michael Katz, "The Origins of Public Education: A Reassessment." *History of Education Quarterly* (Winter, 1976), pp. 381–407.

[25]Tobier, op. cit., pp. 93–94.

[26]Joy Dryfoos, *A Review of Interventions the Field of Prevention of Adolescent Pregnancy.* (New York: Rockefeller Foundation, 1983).

[27]Joy Dryfoos, "School-Based Health Clinics: A New Approach to Preventing Adolescent Pregnancy?, *Family Planning Perspective* (Mar/Apr., 1985).

[28]See for example, N. Blaney, C. Stephan, D. Rosenfieid, E. Aronson and J. Sike, "Interdependence in the Classroom: A Field Study," *Journal of Educational Psychology* (1977), pp. 121–128.

[29]Paolo Freire, *Education for Critical Consciousness* (New York: Seabury Press, 1978).

[30]Eileen Foley and Peggy Crull, op cit.

[31]Michelle Fine and Pearl Rosenberg, "Dropping out of High School: Ideologies of Work and School," *Journal of Education* (June, 1983).